SIR WILLIAM LAIRD CLOWES was born in 1865 and made his reputation as naval correspondent of *The Times* between 1890 and 1895. He was a member of the Navy League and involved in the agitation for greater naval resources, and his anonymous articles which appeared in the *Daily Graphic* in 1893 undoubtedly influenced the naval Estimates.

He wrote and compiled this seven-volume history of the Royal Navy between 1897 and 1903, involving a number of distinguished contemporary writers to assist him. From America he employed Captain Mahan, author of *The Influence of Sea Power upon History*, and Theodore Roosevelt who covered the history of the war with the United States. Sir Clements Markham, President of the Royal Geographical Society, dealt with the history of voyages and discoveries, and H W Wilson, author of *Battleships in Action*, described many of the minor naval operations.

D0916657

SAM·PEPYS·CAR·ET·IAC·ANGL·REGIB·A·SECRETIS·ADMIRALIÆ·

G. Kneller pinx.   R. White sculp.

Mens cujusque is est   Quisque

Lemerciergravure.   Printed in Paris

Samuel Pepys
Clerk of the Acts, Secretary of the Admiralty, Captain, R.N.
from R. White's engraving, after the picture by Sir G. Kneller.

The Royal Navy

A History

From the Earliest Times to the Present

By

Wm. Laird Clowes

Fellow of King's College, London; Gold Medallist U.S. Naval Institute;
Hon. Member of the R.U.S. Institution

Assisted by

Sir Clements Markham, K.C.B., P.R.G.S.
Captain A. T. Mahan, U.S.N.
Mr. H. W. Wilson
Mr. Theodore Roosevelt, Assist. Sec. U.S. Navy
Mr. L. Carr Laughton
etc.

Vol. II.

Chatham Publishing

LONDON

PUBLISHER'S NOTE
In the original edition the nineteen photogravure plates
and the full-page illustrations faced the text pages as
listed on page XI. In this edition these illustrations are
collected at the back of the book after page 548, in the
order in which they appeared in the first edition.

Published in 1996 by
Chatham Publishing,
1 & 2 Faulkner's Alley, Cowcross Street,
London EC1M 6DD

Chatham Publishing is an imprint of
Gerald Duckworth and Co Ltd

First published in 1898 by
Sampson Low, Marston and Company

ISBN 1 86176 011 6

A catalogue record for this book is available from the British Library

Printed and bound in Great Britain by Biddles Ltd, Guildford, Surrey

INTRODUCTION TO VOLUME II.

THE present volume appears at a date three months later than that at which it was originally hoped to produce it. It appears also with a slight change in the names which were originally intended to figure on its title-page. For the delay I am, I fear, myself mainly responsible. Continuous ill-health, which has rendered it impossible for me to live, except for brief periods at a time, anywhere save in high altitudes, has made it particularly hard for me to work with steady regularity upon the book, and has of course, complicated in an extreme degree the difficulty of preparing a history which is largely based upon the study of original documents. The delay is, however, in some measure due also to the same cause which has necessitated the substitution on the title-page of the name of Mr. L. Carr Laughton for that of Mr. E. Fraser. Mr. Edward Fraser, in the early part of 1896 undertook to contribute to this volume the chapters dealing with the operations of the Navy in the period 1603–1660. Not until long after the expiration of the limit at first assigned to him for the completion of those chapters did I reluctantly realise that I could afford to grant him no further concession of time. He assures me that he regrets that he has been unable to keep faith with me, and through me, with the publishers and with my readers; and I need scarcely add that I regret it also. Yet I believe that in a son of Professor Laughton, the veteran writer on naval history, I have found no inefficient substitute. Mr. Laughton describes the active work of the Navy under James I., Charles I., and the Commonwealth. For the remainder of this volume Sir Clements Markham and myself are responsible.

Mr. Laughton has succeeded in throwing some fresh light upon the history of the operations of the fleets of the early Stuarts, and upon the events of the First Dutch War. I have spent a large amount of time in researches among the voluminous Dutch records relating to the Second and Third Dutch Wars; and I trust that I have thus obtained many hitherto unpublished facts concerning them. I have also been granted by the French Ministry of Marine opportunities of consulting the departmental archives which illustrate the Second Dutch War and the Wars of the League of Augsburg and of the Spanish Succession. But I have been happy in being able to draw upon yet other sources of original information. A few years ago I chanced to acquire—strangely enough, from a German bookseller—a large mass of papers relating to the Royal Navy under William and Mary and their immediate successor. I suspect that some at least of these papers must at one time have belonged to the Admiralty, seeing that the collection includes numerous orders, etc., bearing the autograph signatures of Thomas, Earl of Pembroke, Edward Russell, Prince George of Denmark, Sir John Leake, Josiah Burchett, and other leading Admiralty officials. Whether they were improperly removed, or were, long ago, sold as rubbish by persons who were ignorant of their value, I have no means of determining. I regard myself, however, as unusually fortunate in having been able to utilise some of the information contained in them.

The indexing of Vol. I. left, I am aware, somewhat to be desired. I took all possible pains with it, but full materials for the preparation of a thoroughly satisfactory index were lacking. Owing to defective records, it was often impossible to decide, for example, whether a given Captain Smith, who was mentioned on one page, was or was not identical with a Captain Smith, who was mentioned on another page. The records of the period which is dealt with in the present volume are naturally more perfect, and those of the latter part of the period are, indeed, much more so. I have therefore been able to prepare what is, I hope, a proportionately more thorough and serviceable index. I have not, in this index, thought it necessary to attempt to distinguish between successive British ships bearing the same name; but I have endeavoured to distinguish between homonymous persons, and especially between homonymous naval officers. In cases where there were serving at the same, or nearly at the same time, two officers of one name, I have been careful, wherever possible, to indicate in the index the seniority of each by means of the figures (1), (2), etc.; and I think that it will be found that should there arise in the mind of the reader any doubt as to the identity of two or more homonymous officers who are mentioned in the text, that doubt can be quickly set at rest by reference to the index. I would also point out that all naval officers, from 1660 onwards, are here indexed according to the highest rank to which each had attained at the conclusion of his career in the service. Thus, Captain Arthur Herbert must be looked for, not under "Herbert," but under "Torrington"; Captain Edward Russell under "Orford," and so on. Again, a student who may wish to turn to the services of Clowdisley Shovell as a lieutenant will find them indexed under "Shovell, Admiral of the Fleet, Sir Clowdisley." But I have, of course, introduced such cross references as will prevent even the most uninstructed reader from becoming confused.

It has long been a favourite project of mine to prepare some record which should be available for enabling officers and others who may be now or henceforth serving in Her Majesty's ships to readily discover the history and services of previous ships bearing the same name. It cannot but be a healthy and inspiring thing for the ships' companies of our present *Royal Sovereign*, *Swiftsure*, *Resolution*, *Grafton* and *Swallow* to know what perils and what glories have been associated with those fine ship-names in the past. I have often, where requested, compiled historical records for certain ships, such, for example, as the *Britannia*, the *Vernon*, the *Dreadnought*, the *Edgar* and the *Indus*; and copies of these are, I believe, exhibited in the existing vessels for the information and encouragement of those who take an interest in the Navy's work in bygone days. The manner in which these volumes are being indexed will, I hope, not only assist the project to which I allude, but also enable any one who cares to devote an hour or two to the subject to compile for himself a tolerably full record of the history of any given ship-name. Many a Queen's ship nowadays has the great exploits of her wooden ancestors emblazoned about her decks, on the break of her poop, on her wheel, or in other suitable positions. It is to be hoped that the practice may become general. In the French Navy it is, I am informed, encouraged by the Ministry of Marine.

I have seized the opportunity here and there throughout this volume to acknowledge my indebtedness to various officers and gentlemen who have in various ways specially assisted me, either by the loan of documents, etc., or by granting permission for the reproduction of portraits. But it is fitting that I should acknowledge here the great and kindly help which I have received at the hands of H.S.H. Captain Prince Louis of Battenberg, R.N., G.C.B., who, besides taking a lively interest in the progress of the work, has placed at my disposal for reproduction the finest specimens from his unrivalled collection of naval medals. Some of these are shown in this volume ; many more will be shown in the volumes which are still to come.

To have brought down the history of the Royal Navy to the year 1762 would have involved the expansion of this instalment to almost unmanageable dimensions. On the other hand, to have begun the history of the period 1714–1762, and not to have completed it in the same volume, would have been unsatisfactory and disappointing. It has been thought well, therefore, to take the death of Queen Anne and the accession of the House of Brunswick as a convenient halting place. Volume III., in the preparation of which I have the assistance of Sir Clements Markham, Captain A. T. Mahan, Mr. H. W. Wilson, and Mr. L. Carr Laughton, will, I hope, carry the story as far as the outbreak of the War of the French Revolution ; and it is already so far advanced that I trust I am not too sanguine in promising it for publication in the early spring.

W. L. C.

DAVOS-AM-PLATZ, SWITZERLAND.
Dec. 1897.

CONTENTS.

VOLUME II.

————•◦•————

CHAPTER XXIV.

CHAPTER XXV.

PUBLISHER'S NOTE
The photogravure plates and full-page illustrations listed below appear in this
edition at the back of the book, after page 548.

LIST OF ILLUSTRATIONS.

VOLUME II.

PHOTOGRAVURE PLATES.

FULL-PAGE ILLUSTRATIONS.

ILLUSTRATIONS IN THE TEXT.

[The Illustrations marked thus (¹) *are taken from 'A Naval Expositor,' by Thomas Riley Blanckley;
with engravings by Paul Fourdrinier. London, 1750.]*

NAVAL HISTORY.

CHAPTER XVII.

CIVIL HISTORY OF THE ROYAL NAVY, 1603–1649.

James I. and the Navy—Shipbuilding—Sheathing—Girdling—The *Royal Prince*—The *Sovereign of the Seas*—The ships of James I.—Fate of Elizabethan vessels—Additions to the fleet under Charles I.—Guns—Restrictions on trade in ordnance—Shot—Extravagant salutes—Pay—Lieutenants—Inefficiency of the Service—Neglect of the seamen—Increase of pay in 1647—Contributions to the Chest—Changes in the Administration—Corruption—The Commissions of 1608 and 1618—Malversation—Pluralist officers—Pursers' profits—The Dockyards—The Chatham chain—Punishments—Bounties for hired ships—Pirates in the home seas—Duty on sea-borne coal—Rations—Prize-money—Flags—Signalling—Ship-money—The origin of the Dutch troubles—Improvements in navigation—Colonial shipping.

ELIZABETH had brought the Navy to a point of force and efficiency to which it had never before attained. She had made England respected abroad, and she had preserved peace and order in the Narrow Seas. On March 24th, 1603, James VI. of Scotland became also King of England, and received the glorious legacy of the fleet which, under his predecessor, had created for itself a world-wide reputation.

There is no evidence that James took less interest than Elizabeth in the Navy; indeed, in some respects, he may be said to have taken more; and, undoubtedly, he spent more money on it. Yet, owing to his weakness of character, his usually unfortunate choice and employment of officials, and perhaps also the growing softness and corruption of the times, the Navy, during the greater part of his reign, went steadily downwards; and, but for

Buckingham's exertions in 1618, would have become absolutely contemptible ere Charles I. succeeded to the throne in 1625. Buckingham was a meritorious re-organiser, and Buckingham was, of course, James's selected favourite.   Save, however, in the appointment of Buckingham to share in the management of naval affairs, James, in spite of his excellent intentions, did considerably more harm than good to the service.   The numerical decrease of the fleet during the two and twenty years, was not particularly striking, though there was a decrease.   What was significant was that whereas Elizabeth left a Navy fit to go anywhere and do anything,

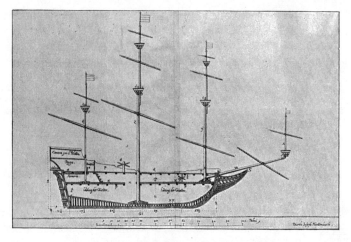

A SHIP OF WAR OF THE SEVENTEENTH CENTURY.
Sectional elevation.
(*From the 'Architectura Navalis' of J. Fürttenbach (Ulm,* 1695.))

James left one largely composed of vessels unfit for any duty whatsoever.

The art of the shipbuilder[1] does not seem to have greatly advanced during the reign.   Among the ships built under James, one, the *Royal Prince*, was a larger man-of-war than had up to that time been constructed in England; but there is no evidence that she was a more seaworthy or less leewardly craft, or that she carried her guns better than the best of her Elizabethan predecessors.   Speaking generally, indeed, the ships of the period gave dissatisfaction to those who had to handle them and to all who

---

[1] The Shipwrights' Company, however, was incorporated in 1605; and this may be taken as evidence that the subject was receiving attention.

were best qualified to criticise them. Ralegh,[1] after enumerating the most desirable qualities in a man-of-war, *i.e.*, strong build, speed, stout scantling, ability to fight the guns in all weathers, ability to lie to easily in a gale, and ability to stay well, declared that in none of these requirements were the King's ships satisfactory. And Captain George Waymouth,[2] a professional expert, and a contemporary authority on the theory of shipbuilding, lamented that he " could never see two ships builded of the like proportion by the best and most skilful shipwrights, though they have many times undertaken the same . . . because they trust

A SHIP OF WAR OF THE SEVENTEENTH CENTURY.

Spars, rigging and sails.

(From the 'Architectura Navalis' of J. Fürttenbach (Ulm, 1695.))

rather to their judgment than their art, and to their eye than their scale and compass." Mr. Oppenheim[3] cites, as an illustration of the loose methods of calculation in vogue, that when the *Royal Prince* was built, Phineas Pett and William Bright, her constructors, estimated that 775 loads of timber would be required, whereas 1627 loads were actually used, with a consequent increase of £5908 in the cost.

Lead sheathing, which had been employed in the Spanish Navy

---

[1] 'Observations on the Navy.'

[2] Add. MSS. 19,889 : 'The Jewell of Artes,' 135, etc.

[3] 'Admin. of Royal Navy,' 186, quoting Add. MSS. 9294, Nov. 1610.

since 1514,[1] and which had been applied to English merchant ships since 1553, was still untried in the Navy, possibly because it had been found to set up galvanic action with the iron of the rudder pintles, etc.   Nor was Hawkyns's sheathing of double planks, with tar and hair between them, as generally adopted as it should have been, though it remained in some favour until late in the seventeenth century.   Much more care, in fact, was devoted to making ships look well than to making them really serviceable; and the result often was that after her completion a vessel was found to be so crank that it was doomed necessary to "fur" or "girdle" her with a partial, or even an entire external planking beyond her original skin.[2]

As the *Royal Prince* [3] was the greatest constructive effort of the reign of James I., some account must be here given of her.   Her keel was laid at Woolwich on October 20th, 1608, her chief constructor being Phineas Pett.   Her nominal tonnage was 1200, but, measured according to the rules in force in 1632, it was 1035 nett, and 1330 gross.   After the work had been some time in progress, and had met with much adverse criticism from rival shipwrights, a commission, consisting of Captain George Waymouth, Matthew Baker (who had been a principal constructor for more than half a century), William Bright, Edward Stevens, and others, was ordered to report on what was being done.   Pett hated Waymouth, and Baker despised the Pett family, while Bright was particularly jealous of Phineas.   But Pett had powerful protectors in the Lord High Admiral and Sir Robert Mansell; and after there had been not only inquiry and further inquiry, but also a special scrutiny by the King and Prince Henry, Phineas Pett emerged triumphant. An attempt to launch the ship was made on September 24th, 1610, but it failed, owing to the dockhead being too narrow to allow her to pass.   She was, however, successfully launched a little later.[4]

Pett, on this occasion, owed more to his protectors than to the merits of his work, for the *Royal Prince*, though a striking object in the water, was both ill-designed and ill-built.   As early as 1621, it was reported to Buckingham [5] that although she had cost

[1] Duro's 'Armada Española,' 121.

[2] Harl. MSS. 2301: 'Nomenclator Navalis' (Manwayring's 'Dictionary').

[3] Often called *Prince Royal*, or simply *Prince*.

[4] Oppenheim, 'Admin. of Royal Navy,' 204.

[5] Coke MSS. i. 114.

£20,000, a further £6000 would be needed to make her fit for service, she being built of decaying timbêr and of green unseasoned stuff. At that time she had, nevertheless, been tried by no hard work.[1]

The *Royal Prince* has often been described as the first three-decker of the Royal Navy; but, in the modern sense, she was not a three, but a two-decker. She had, that is to say, two complete covered batteries, and an armed upper deck. Stow says of her: "This year the King builded a most goodly ship for warre, the keel whereof was 114 feet in length, and the crossbeam was 44 feet in length; she will carry 64[2] pieces of ordnance, and is of the burthen of 1400 tons. This royal ship is double built, and is most sumptuously adorned, within and without, with all manner of curious carving, painting, and rich gilding." Writing in 1801, Charnock[3] says, with some degree of truth: "The vessel in question as most worthy of remark, as it may be considered the parent of the identical class of shipping which, excepting the removal of such defects or trivial absurdities as long use and experience have pointed out, continue in practice even to the present moment. Were the absurd profusion of ornament with which the *Royal Prince* is decorated removed, its contour, or general appearance, would not so materially differ from the modern vessel of the same size as to render it an uncommon sight, or a ship in which mariners would hesitate at proceeding to sea in, on account of any glaring defect in its form, that, in their opinion, might render it unsafe to undertake a common voyage in it."

Stow's expression, "double built," means double planked. All the bulkheads were also double bolted with iron.[4] Both these features were innovations. Yet by far the greatest amount of attention was given to the decorations. The carvings, including fourteen lions' heads for the round ports, cost £441,[5] and to Robert Peake and Paul Isaackson was paid at one time a sum of £868 for painting and gilding.

The *Royal Prince* remained the show ship of the service until 1637, when the *Sovereign of the Seas* was launched. She was the first of the real three-deckers; and it is curious and significant that,

---

[1] She was rebuilt in 1641, and was renamed *Resolution* under the Commonwealth.

[2] She eventually mounted fifty-five, but had vacant ports to which some of these could be shifted in case of need.

[3] 'Mar. Architecture,' ii. 199.

[4] Add. MSS. 9294.

[5] Pipe Off. Accts. 2249.

although the authorities of Trinity House, as late as 1634, declared that "the art or wit of man cannot build a ship fit for service, with three tier of ordnance,"[1] the very vessel which they stigmatised as impossible was afloat three years later.

In January, 1635, an estimate for a ship of 1500 tons was called for; and in the following March, Phineas Pett was ordered to prepare a model of the projected craft, and was informed that he was fixed upon to superintend the building of her.[2] In April, Pett met, and consulted as to the dimensions, with Sir John Penington, Sir Robert Mansell, and John Wells, storekeeper at Deptford; and it was determined that the tonnage should be 1466 by depth, 1661 by draught, and 1836 by beam.[3] The estimated cost was only £13,680; but the sum finally expended on the vessel was, excluding the cost of her guns, no less than £40,833 8s. 1½d.[4]

In his journal, under the date May 14th, 1635, Pett writes :—

"I took leave of his Majesty at Greenwich, with his command to hasten into the north, and prepare the frame, timber, plank, and tressels for the new ship to be built at Woolwich. . . . I left my sons to see the moulds and other necessaries shipped in a Newcastle ship, hired on purpose to transport our provisions and workmen to Newcastle. Attended the Bishop of Durham with my commissions and instructions, whom I found wonderfully ready to assist us with other knights, gentlemen, and justices of the county, who took care to order present carriage; so that in a short time there was enough of the frame ready to lade a large collier, which was landed at Woolwich: and as fast as provisions could be got ready, they were shipped off from Chapley[5] Wood, at Newcastle, and that at Barnspeth[6] Park, from Sutherland. . . . The 21st of December we laid the ship's keel in the dock. Most part of her frame, coming safe, was landed at Woolwich. . . . The 16th of January, his Majesty with divers lords came to Woolwich to see part of the frame and floor laid, and that time he gave orders to myself and my son to build two small pinnaces out of the great ship's waste. The 28th[7] his Majesty came again to Woolwich with the Palsgrave his brother, Duke Robert,[8] and divers other lords, to see the pinnaces launched, which were named the *Greyhound* and *Roebuck*."

The great ship herself was launched in October, 1637.

The dimensions, etc., of the *Royal Prince* of 1610, and of the

---

[1] Oppenheim, 'Admin. of Royal Navy,' 204, n., 260; S. P. Dom. cclxxiii. 25.

[2] S. P. Dom. cclxiv. 67a, 87a.

[3] *Ib.* cclxxxvi. 44; but it is not apparent how the various computations were made, nor what they mean.

[4] *Ib.* cclxxxvii. 73; Aud. Off. Dec. Accts. 1703–77, cited by Oppenheim.

[5] Chopwell.

[6] Brancepeth.

[7] Month missing; obviously not January, 1636.

[8] Better known in English naval history as Prince Rupert. The "Palsgrave" was the Elector Friedrich V. of the Palatinate, who married Elizabeth, sister of Charles I.

Sovereign of the Seas of 1637 respectively, were, according to statistics which appear to possess official authority, as follows :—

.	Length of keel.	Length over all.	Beam.	Depth.	Tons gross.	Guns.	Men.
	Feet.	Ft. in.	Ft. in.	Ft. in.			
Royal Prince . .	115	. .	43 0	18 0	1187	55	500
Sovereign of the Seas [1] .	127	167 9	48 4	19 4	1683	100	600

During the interregnum, the *Sovereign of the Seas* was, on account of her crankness, cut down in 1652 to a 100-gun two-decker. There was a disposition to rename her the *Commonwealth*, but eventually she became known as the *Sovereign* simply. After the Restoration she became *Royal Sovereign*. She saw much service throughout the Dutch and French wars, and existed until January 27th, 1696, when, being laid up at Chatham in order to be rebuilt, she was accidentally burnt, owing to a candle having been carelessly left alight in the cook's cabin.

Thomas Heywood, who is supposed to have designed the very elaborate decorations of the *Sovereign*, published a long account of the ship,[2] with a picture of her. His facts, so far as they relate to the ornaments, are probably correct enough; but the remaining details, and the picture, seem to be quite untrustworthy. The figure-head, or beakhead, represented King Edgar on horseback, trampling upon seven kings; upon the stern-head was a cupid bestriding a lion; upon the forward bulkhead were six emblematic statues; and the stern was a mass of useless carving and gilding.

In the last year but one of the reign of James I., the Royal Navy consisted of the following effective vessels.[3] (See pp. 8 and 9.)

Of Elizabethan ships which existed during part of the reign of James, the *Foresight*, of 1570, had been condemned in 1604; the *St. Andrew* and *St. Matthew*, prizes of 1596, had been given to Sir John Leigh in 1604; the *Mercury*, of 1592, had been sold in 1611;

---

[1] From a list in the Dept. of the Cont. of the Navy. The number of guns is nominal. She really carried one hundred and two, all brass, which cost £24,753 8s. 8d. S. P. Dom. ccclxxiv. 30, and ccclxxxvii. 87. Pett's original design was for ninety guns only.

[2] 'A True Description,' etc., 1637.

[3] S. P. Dom. clxi. 68 (1624), supplemented, as to details, from numerous sources too numerous to specify.

	Built, or *Rebuilt.	Tons.	Length of keel.	Beam.	Depth.	Guns.	
			Feet.	Ft. In.	Ft. In.		
First rates :—							
1. *Prince* . .	161)	1187	115	43	18	55	
2. *Bear* . . .	*1599	915	110	37	18	40	Sold in 1629.
3. *Merhonour* .	*1611–14	800	104	38	17	44	Sold in 1650.
4. *Anne Royal* ,	*1608	800	103	37	16	44	The *Ark Royal*, of 1587, rebuilt and renamed. She was bilged on her anchor in 1636, raised at great cost, and then broken up.
Second rates :—							
5. *Repulse* . .	*1610	700	97	37	15	40	Broken up about 1645.
6. *Warspite* . .	1596	648	90	36	16	29	Cut down to a lighter for harbour service, 1635.
7. *Victory* . .	1620	875	108	35 9	17	42	
8. *Assurance*. .	*1603–5	600	95	33	14 6	38	The *Hope*, of 1559, rebuilt and renamed. Broken up about 1645.
9. *Nonsuch* . .	*1603–5	636	88	34	15	38	The *Nonpareil*, of 1584, rebuilt and renamed. Sold under Charles I.
10. *Defiance* . .	*1611–14	700	97	37	15	40	Sold in 1650.
11. *Lion* . . .	*1609	650	91	35 2	16	38	Or *Red Lion*, the *Golden Lion*, of 1582, rebuilt and renamed.
12. *Vanguard* .	*1615	650	102	35	14	40	
13. *Rainbow* . .	*1618	650	102	35	14	40	
14. *Constant Re-formation* .	1619	752	106	35 6	15	42	Named to celebrate Buckingham's accession to office. Carried off, 1648, to the Prince of Wales.
15. *Swiftsure* . .	1621	887	106	36 10	16 8	42	
16. *St. George* .	1622	895	110	37	16 6	42	Renamed *George* under the Commonwealth.
17. *St. Andrew* .	1622	895	110	37	16 6	42	Renamed *Andrew* under the Commonwealth.
18. *Triumph* . .	1623	922	110	37	17	42	
Third rates :—							
19. *Dreadnought* .	*1611–14	450	84	31	13	32	Broken up about 1645.
20. *Antelope* . .	*1618	450	92	32	12 6	34	Carried off to the Prince of Wales, 1648.

* In several cases there is much doubt as to how far the ships were rebuilt. Some of those thus marked may have merely undergone extensive repairs.

	Built, or *Rebuilt.	Tons.	Length of keel.	Beam.	Depth.	Guns.	
			Feet.	Ft. In.	Ft. In.		
21. *Speedwell* . .	*1607	400	..	..	..	..	Lost, Nov. 1624, near Flushing. She was the *Swiftsure*, of 1592, rebuilt and renamed.
22. *Adventure* .	1594	343	88	26	12	26	Broken up about 1645.
23. *Convertine* .	1616	500	..	..	..	34	ex *Destiny*, of Ralegh's last voyage. Carried off to the Prince of Wales, 1648.
24. *Happy En-trance* . .	1619	582	96	32 6	14	32	Named to celebrate Buckingham's accession to office. Burnt at Chatham, 1658.
25. *Bonaventure* .	1621	675	98	33	15 8	34	Taken by the Dutch, 1652.
26. *Garland* . .	1620	683	93	33	16	34	Taken by the Dutch, 1652.
27. *Mary Rose* .	1623	394	83	27	13	26	Wrecked off Flanders, 1650.
Fourth rates :—							
28. *Phœnix* . .	1612	250	70	24	11	20	Sold under Charles I.
29. *Seven Stars* .	1615	140	60	20	9	14	
30. *Charles* . .	..	80	63	16	7	16	
31. *Desire* . . .	1616	80	66	16	6	6	
With four galleys and several hoys.							

* In several cases there is much doubt as to how far the ships were rebuilt. Some of those thus marked may have merely undergone extensive repairs.

the *Garland*, of 1590, and *Mary Rose*, of 1589, had been used in the construction of a wharf at Chatham; and the *Nuestra Señora del Rosario*, the prize of 1588, after having been placed in support of her ancient antagonists in the dockyard, had been finally broken up in 1622. Most of the remaining ships had been broken up or disposed of.[1] James also rebuilt two vessels which were disposed of or broken up ere his reign ended. These were the *Lion's Whelp*, purchased in 1601 and rebuilt in 1608, and the *Primrose*, purchased in 1560 and rebuilt in 1612. He also seems to have ordered the purchase in 1622[2] of the *Mercury* and *Spy*, built by Phineas Pett for

[1] The *Answer* and *Crane*, of 1590, and the *Moon* and *Merlin*, however, survived into the reign of Charles I., though they were then ineffective.

[2] The order is dated August 31st.

his own purposes in 1620, and sent out to Algier, under Captains
Phineas Pett and Edward Giles, to Mansell, whom they joined on
February 26th, 1621; but there is no evidence that these vessels
were ever added to the Navy.

The additions under Charles I. were as follows :—

—	Built. *Rebuilt. †Prize. ‡Bought.	Tons.	Length of keel.	Beam.	Depth.	Guns.	—
			Ft. In.	Ft. In.	Ft. In.		
1. *St. Claude* . . .	†1625	300	..	..	..	..	
2. *St. Denis*	†1625	528	104	32 5	11 9	38	
3. *St. Mary* . . .	†1626	100	..	..	..	..	⎰Given to Sir John Chud-
4. *St. Anne*	†1626	350	..	..	..	..	⎱ leigh, 1629.
5. *Espérance*. . .	†1626	250	..	..	..	..	
6. *Henrietta* . . .	1626	68	52	15	6 6	6	⎰Sold under the Common-
7. *Maria*. . . .	1626	68	52	15	6 6	6	⎱ wealth.
8. *Spy*	1626	20	..	..	..	..	
9–18. *Lion's Whelps* (10)[1]	1627	185	62	25	9	12	⎧One only survived to the days of the Common- wealth.
19. *Fortune* . . .	†1627	200	..	..	..	..	
20. *St. Esprit* . .	†1627	800	105	35	..	42	⎧Built in Holland for France. Taken in the Texel.
21. *Vanguard* . .	*1630	750	112	36 4	13 10	40	
22. *Charles* . . .	1632	810	105	33 7	16 3	44	⎧Renamed *Liberty* under the Commonwealth. Wrecked off Harwich, 1650.
23. *Henrietta Maria*	1632	793	106	35 9	15 8	42	⎧Renamed *Paragon* under the Commonwealth. Accidentally burnt, 1655, in the West Indies.
24. *James* . . .	1633	875	110	37 6	16 2	48	
25. *Unicorn* . . .	1634	823	107	36 4	15 1	46	
26. *Leopard* . . .	1634	515	95	33	12 4	34	Taken by the Dutch.
27. *Swallow* . . .	1634	478	96	32 2	11 7	34	⎰Carried off, 1648, to the Prince of Wales.

[1] Two of the *Whelps* differed slightly in size from the rest. All were square rigged
with three masts, and were fitted for using sweeps. The original armament of each
was four culverins, four demi-culverins, and two brass sakers; but to these two demi-
cannon were added. Two were lost, returning from La Rochelle, while quite new; one
blew up in action with a Dunquerquer; No. 6 had disappeared by 1631 and seems to
be the one which was given by the King to Buckingham, on August 11th, 1625, for an
attempt at the North-West Passage; No. 4 was lost on August 14th, 1636; another
was expended for experimental purposes; No. 5 sank off the Dutch coast in 1637.
No. 10, the last survivor, remained in commission till 1654. The *Whelps* were built
by contract at £3 5s. a ton. S. P. Dom. lviii. 25; ccclxiii. 29, etc.

—	Built. *Rebuilt. †Prize. ‡Bought.	Tons.	Length of keel.	Beam.		Depth.		Guns.	—
			Ft. In.	Ft.	In.	Ft.	In.		
28. *Swan* . . .	†1636	..	..	..		..		..	Taken from the Dunquerquers. Lost off Guernsey, Oct. 1638.
29. *Nicodemus* . .	†1636	105	63	19		9	6	6	Taken from the Dunquerquers. Sold under the Commonwealth.
30. *Roebuck* . . .	1636	90	57	18	1	6	8	10	Carried off, 1648, to the Prince of Wales.
31. *Greyhound* . .	1636	126	60	20	3	7	8	12	Blown up in action, 1656, by her captain, Geo. Wager.
32. *Expedition* . .	1637	301	90	26		9	8	30	
33. *Providence* . .	1637	304	90	26		9	9	30	
34. *Sovereign of the Seas* . . .	1637	1683	127	48	4	19	4	100	
35. *Lion*	*1640	717	108	35	4	15	6	52	
36. *Prince* . . .	*1641	1187	115	43		18		64	Renamed *Resolution* under the Commonwealth. Renamed *Prince*, 1660.
37. *Crescent* . . .	‡1642	150	..	..		..		14	Carried off, 1648, to the Prince of Wales.
38. *Lily*	‡1642	80	..	..		..		8	
39. *Satisfaction* . .	1646	220	..	..		..		26	Carried off, 1648, to the Prince of Wales.
40. *Adventure* . .	1646	385	94	27		9	11	38	
41. *Nonsuch* . . .	1646	389	98	28	4	14	2	34	
42. *Assurance* . .	1646	341	89	26	10	11		32	
43. *Constant Warwick*	1646	379	90	28		12		30	Built as a privateer. Bought by Parliament Jan. 20th, 1649.
44. *Phœnix* . . .	1647	414	96	28	6	14	3	38	Taken by the Dutch, Sept. 7th, 1652. Retaken, Nov. 1652.
45. *Dragon* . . .	1647	414	96	30		12		38	
46. *Tiger*	1647	447	99	29	4	12		38	
47. *Elizabeth* . .	1647	471	101 6	29	8	14	10	38	
48. *Old Warwick* .	†1646	..	..	..		..		22	
49. *Falcon* . . .	†	..	..	..		..		..	Merchantman taken from the Cromwellians.
50. *Hart*	†	..	..	..		..		10	Do. do.
51. *Dove*	†	..	..	..		..		6	Do. do.
52. *Truelove* . . .	†	259	..	..		..		20	Do. do.
53. *Concord* . . .	†	..	..	..		..		..	Do. do.
54. *Dolphin* . . .	†	100	..	..		..		..	Do. do.
55. *Fellowship* . .	†	300	..	..		..		28	Do. do.
56. *Globe* . . .	‡	300	..	..		..		24	Purchased merchantman.
57. *Hector* . . .	‡	300	.	..		..		20	Do. do.

Although the *Sovereign of the Seas* was nominally a 100-gun ship, 102 brass guns were thus classed and distributed in her:—

				Length.	Weight.
				Ft.	Cwt.
Lower deck:					
Broadside guns .	. .	20	cannon drakes [1]	9·0	45
Stern chasers	. . .	4	demi-cannon drakes . . .	12·5	53
Bow chasers	. . .	2	,, ,, ...	11·5	48
Luffs .	. . . .	2	,, ,, ...	10·0	44
Middle deck:					
Broadside guns .	. .	24	culverin drakes	8·5	28
Stern chasers	. . .	4	culverins	11·5	48
Bow chasers	. . .	2	,, ...	11·5	48
Main deck:					
Broadside guns .	. .	24	demi-culverin drakes . . .	8·5	18
Stern chasers	. .	2	demi-culverins	10·0	30
Bow chasers	. . .	2	,, ...	10·0	30
Upper deck:					
Forecastle .	. . .	8	demi-culverin drakes . . .	9·0	20
Half-deck .	. . .	6	,, ,, . . .	9·0	20
Quarter-deck	. . .	2	,, ,, . . .	5·5	8
Forecastle, pointing aft		2	culverin drakes	5·5	11

Throughout the reign of James I. and Charles I., ships were systematically over-gunned, and, in consequence, when at sea, captains often dismounted some of their pieces and stowed them in the ballast in the hold. The price of guns varied from £12 to £15 a ton, and the manufacture of them was practically the monopoly of a few, chief among whom was John Browne, King's Gunfounder, who in 1626 gained a reward of £200 for casting lighter pieces than had been previously made, yet pieces capable, nevertheless, of standing double proof. The place of proof for all guns was Ratcliff Fields. Their export without licence was forbidden; they might be bought and sold only at East Smithfield, and shipped and landed only at Tower Wharf. Yet in spite of these restrictions, many went abroad, and of these not a few had been stolen from royal forts, and probably from ships as well.

Stone shot continued to be carried in certain small proportions until about 1625, after which they seem to have been wholly discontinued. It was not until James I. had been for several years on the throne that the extravagant practice of firing shotted charges

[1] The affix "drake" signified that the gun was suited for heavy charges of powder, whereas "perier," after it had ceased to mean a gun throwing a stone shot, meant one suited for low charges.

as salutes ceased, and up to the time of the Revolution the
expenditure of powder in salutes was enormous, although repeated
orders were issued in order to check waste. On joyous occasions
the number of rounds, as is still the rule, was generally odd; on
occasions of death, etc., it was even, but the exact number of rounds
was not prescribed, and all sorts of excuses were invented for firing
them. In 1628, the fleet at Plymouth "shot away £100 of powder
in one day in drinking healths,"[1] and Mr. Oppenheim, who cites the
above, says elsewhere:[2] "In one gunner's accounts we find: 'One
faucon when the master's wife went ashore . . . One minion the
master commanded to be shot off to a ship his father was in.'"
The evil was not materially abated until the close of the seventeenth
century.

During the reign of James I., the lunar monthly pay of a seaman
was 10s. On the occasion of the attack upon Cadiz, in 1625, it
was temporarily raised to 14s., and it was raised permanently, in
1626, to 15s., subject to deductions of 6d. for the Chatham Chest,
4d. for the chaplain, and 2d. for the surgeon; and so the scale
remained until the Civil War.

The Caroline Navy was the first to be divided into six rates.
The rates of ships were not always determined by the size and
importance of the vessels, as was the case in later periods. Indeed,
the rating only gradually assumed a systematic plan. But upon the
rating of a ship always depended the rate of pay of the officers
serving in her. The maximum (first-rate), and minimum (sixth-
rate) scales, up to the time of the Revolution, per month of twenty-
eight days were: captains, £14 to £4 14s. 4d.; lieutenants (allowed
only in the first three rates), £3 10s. to £3; masters, £3 13s. 9d. to
£2 6s. 8d.; pilots, £2 5s. to £1 10s.; masters' mates, £2 5s. to £1 10s.;
boatswains, £2 5s. to £1 3s. 4d.; boatswains' mates, £1 6s. 3d. to
£1 0s. 8d.; pursers, £2 to £1 3s. 4d.; surgeons, £1 10s.; surgeons'
mates, £1; quartermasters, £1 10s. to £1; quartermasters' mates,
£1 5s. to 17s. 6d.; yeomen of sheets, jeers, tacks, or halliards, £1 5s.
to £1 1s.; carpenters, £1 17s. 6d. to £1 1s.; carpenters' mates, £1 5s.
to 18s. 8d.; corporals,[3] £1 10s. 4d. to 18s. 8d.; gunners, £2 to
£1 3s. 4d.; gunners' mates, £1 2s. 6d. to 18s. 8d.; cooks, £1 5s. to
£1; master trumpeters, £1 8s. to £1 5s.; other trumpeters, £1 3s. 4d.;

---

[1] Yonge's 'Diary': Camden Soc.
[2] 'Admin. of Royal Navy,' 290.
[3] Then newly allowed. The corporal drilled the men in small-arms.

drummers,[1] £1; fifers,[1] £1; armourers, £1 1*s*.; gunmakers, £1 1*s*. The pay of gromets was 11*s*. 3*d*., and that of boys, 7*s*. 6*d*.[2]

The rank of lieutenant had, as has been seen, existed in the Navy at the time of the Armada. It had subsequently disappeared, to be revived under Charles I. Mr. Oppenheim[3] cites the Egerton MSS. (2541, f. 13), as declaring that the appointment of lieutenants was—

"to breed young gentlemen for the sea-service. . . . The reason why there are not now so many able sea-captains as there is use of is because there hath not been formerly allowance for lieutenants, whereby gentlemen of worth and quality might be encouraged to go to sea. And, if peace had held a little longer, the old sea-captains would have been worn out, as that the State must have relied wholly on mechanick men that have been bred up from swabbers, and . . . . to make many of them would cause sea service in time to be despised by gentlemen of worth, who will refuse to serve at sea under such captains."

The efficiency of the Navy, which had steadily deteriorated under James I., continued to decrease during the early years of his son and successor, although Charles took a much more intelligent interest in the fleet than James had ever been capable of taking. In the opinion of Mr. Oppenheim, the Cadiz expedition of 1625 probably indicated the low water mark of English seamanship. "There have," he says, "been many previous and subsequent occasions when fleets were sent to sea equally ill-found and ill-provided, but never before or since have we such accounts of utter incapacity in the mere everyday work of a sailor's duties. The shameful picture of that confused mass of ships crowded together helplessly, without order or plan, colliding with each other, chasing or deserting at their own will, the officers losing spars and sails from ignorance of the elementary principles of their art, is the indictment against the government of James I., which had allowed the seamanship of Elizabeth to die out in this generation."[4]

The worst feature in the situation—and it was a feature which grew darker as the years of Charles's reign went on—was that the seamen, being ill-fed, ill-clothed, and irregularly paid, were terribly discontented. Wages, as has been seen, were raised, but for many years the increment was practically a paper one only. The men got neither the old scale nor the new, except at uncertain intervals.

---

[1] In the first four rates only.
[2] S. P. Dom. xxxv. 19: Add. MSS. 9339, 24.
[3] 'Admin. of Royal Navy,' 226.
[4] *Ib.* 220.

They mutinied, they rioted, they turned marauders in order to
supply their empty stomachs; they even threatened to besiege the
Court at Whitehall,[1] and they actually seized the Guildhall at
Plymouth.[2] In 1629, Sir Henry Mervyn, commanding in the
Narrow Seas, officially set forth the sad state of the men, and
prophetically concluded: " His Majesty will lose the honour of his
seas, the love and loyalty of his sailors, and his Royal Navy will
droop."[3] In course of time wages were paid more regularly, but
there was no other improvement. The provisions were bad and
scanty; the ships were floating pest-houses; the sick were turned
ashore starving. And so it is hardly astonishing that soon after the
beginning of the Civil War large bodies of sailors offered their
services to the Parliament, and that when King and Parliament
appointed rival commanders in the persons of Penington and
Warwick, there was a general adhesion to the latter, in spite of the
fact that Penington, the Royalist, was personally popular in the
Navy. The opinion among the seamen seems to have been that
things were so bad that any change must be a change for the better.
If so, it was justified by the event. Wages were raised to 19s. a
month, and were regularly paid; the food improved in quality, and
the sick were taken care of. The pay of officers was not raised by
Parliament until 1647, when it became as follows: Captains, £21 to
£7; lieutenants, £4 4s. to £3 10s.; masters, £7 to £3 18s. 8d.;
masters' mates, £3 5s. 4d. to £2 2s.; pilots, £3 5s. 4d. to £2 2s.;
carpenters, £3 3s. to £1 15s.; boatswains, £3 10s. to £1 17s. 4d., and
gunners, £3 3s. to £1 15s.

The prescribed contributions to the Chatham Chest were still
invariably deducted, but the fund itself was mismanaged, and often
misapplied. Sums, for example, were taken from it to pay wages.
A Commission appointed in December, 1635, to inquire into the
administration of the Chest, reported in April, 1637, and as a result
some reforms were effected.[4]

At the accession of James I., Charles Howard, Earl of Nottingham, was still Lord High Admiral. Before dealing more particularly
with the changes and reforms effected in the Administration, it may
be convenient here to set down in a succinct form the successive

[1] S. P. Dom. liii. 9, 10; xxxv. 44; xli. 56; lxiv. 76; lxxxv. 61, etc.
[2] *Ib.* xcviii. 26.
[3] *Ib.* cxlix. 92.
[4] *Ib.* ccclii. 78; Add. MSS. 9301, f. 156.

alterations in the high *personnel* of the Admiralty during the period
now under review.   These were :—

LORD HIGH ADMIRAL.

July 8, 1585—
  Charles Howard, Earl of Nottingham.
Jan. 28, 1619—
  George Villiers, Duke of Buckingham.
Sept. 20, 1628—
  Richard, Lord Weston.
  Robert, Earl of Lindsey.
  William, Earl of Pembroke.
  Edward, Earl of Dorset.
  Dudley, Viscount Dorchester.
  Sir John Coke.
Nov. 20, 1632—
  Richard, Lord Weston.
  Robert, Earl of Lindsey.
  Edward, Earl of Dorset.
  Sir John Coke.
  Francis, Lord Cottington.
  Sir Francis Windebank.
  Sir Henry Vane, senior.
March 16, 1636—
  William Juxon, Bishop of London.
  Francis, Lord Cottington.
  Robert, Earl of Lindsey.
  Edward, Earl of Dorset.
  Sir John Coke.
  Sir Francis Windebank.
  Sir Henry Vane, senior.
March 18, 1638—
  Prince James, Duke of York.
April 13, 1638—
  Algernon Percy, Earl of Northumber-
  land (*acting* substitute).

In commission, with Edward Nicholas as Secretary.

———

"PRINCIPAL OFFICERS."

TREASURER OF THE NAVY.

Dec. 22, 1598. Fulke Grevill, Lord Brooke.
      1604. Sir Robert Mansell.

May 10, 1618. Sir William Russell.
April 5, 1627. Sir Sackville Crowe.
      1629. Sir William Russell.
Jan. 12, 1639. Sir William Russell. ⎫
            Sir Henry Vane, junior.⎭
      1642. Sir William Russell.
Aug.   1642. Sir Henry Vane, junior.

SURVEYOR OF THE NAVY.

Dec. 20, 1598. Sir John Trevor.
      1611. Sir Richard Bingley.

CONTROLLER OF THE NAVY.

Dec. 20, 1598. Sir Henry Palmer.
      1611. Sir Guildford Slingsby.
  [In 1618, the Surveyor and Controller
  were "sequestered from their posts," and
  their duties were entrusted to a Board of
  Navy Commissioners.]

NAVY COMMISSIONERS.

Feb. 12, 1619.[1] Sir Lionel Cranfield.[2]
            Sir Thomas Weston.
            Sir John Wolstenholme.
            Sir Thomas Smith.
            Nicholas Fortescue.
            John Osborne.
            Francis Gofton.
            Richard Sutton.
            William Pitt.
            John Coke.[3]
            Thomas Norreys.
            William Burrell.[4]

SURVEYOR OF THE NAVY (re-appointed 1628).

      1628. Sir Thomas Aylesbury.
Dec. 19, 1632. Kenrick Edisbury (*alias*
            Wilkinson).
Sept. 26, 1638. William Batten.

---

[1] Date of Letters Patent. These, with few changes, held office until 1628. Pepys
('Diary,' March 14, 1669) calls this the Grand Commission. It was renewed, with
alterations, in 1625.

[2] Created a baron in 1621, and later Earl of Middlesex. He was impeached and
imprisoned in 1624, and died in 1645.

[3] Knighted 1624.

[4] Burrell had been Master Shipwright to the East India Company, and was one of
the chief shipwrights in the reign of James I. He was succeeded as Master Shipwright
by Peter Pett in 1629, and died in 1630.

CONTROLLER OF THE NAVY (re-appointed
1628).

Feb.　　1628. Sir Guildford Slingsby.
　　　　1632. Sir Henry Palmer.

CLERK OF THE NAVY (later "of the
Acts").

1600. Peter (later Sir Peter)
Buck.
Denis Fleming.
Feb. 16, 1639. Thomas Barlow.

EXTRA PRINCIPAL OFFICERS.

1629. William Burrell (assist.).
Phineas Pett (assist.).

Oct.　　1630. Sir Kenelm Digby.
Jan.　　1631. Phineas Pett.

SURVEYORS OF VICTUALLING.

1595. Marmaduke Darell.
Aug. 16, 1603. Sir Marmaduke Darell.⎫
Sir Thomas Bludder. ⎭
Dec. 31, 1612. Sir Marmaduke Darell.[1]⎫
Sir Allen Apsley.[2] ⎭
Jan.　8, 1623. Sir Allen Apsley. ⎫
Sir Sampson Darell.⎭
1630. Sir Sampson Darell.
Nov. 20, 1635. John Crane.

After the commencement of the Civil War the greater part of the civil staff of the Admiralty went over to the service of the Parliament, which assumed control through the mediumship of committees.

Nottingham was already fifty-two at the time of the defeat of the Spanish Armada. At the accession of James I., he was sixty-seven. Yet he remained Lord Admiral until he was eighty-two. He was, undoubtedly, an honest man; but in his old age he left far too much to his subordinates, some of whom, especially Sir Robert Mansell, the Treasurer, were not honest, and, in consequence, the administration of the Navy became most corrupt and inefficient. As early as 1608, the numerous scandals compelled the formation of a commission of inquiry, which consisted of the Earls of Nottingham and Northampton, Lord Zouche, Sir Edward Wotton, Sir Julius Cæsar, Sir Robert Cotton, and others; and this sat from May, 1608, to June, 1609. But the only experienced seaman on the commission was the Earl of Nottingham, who never attended the meetings. A report[3] was drawn up, and the King himself lectured the parties who were found to have been guilty of malpractices; but no effective steps were taken for securing reforms.

The evils, in consequence, continued and increased. In 1613, Cotton attempted to obtain another inquiry, but failed. In 1618, however, when, as Gardiner says, "the household was one mass of peculation and extravagance," the efforts of the party of reform met

---

[1] Darell died in 1622.
[2] Later Apsley became Lieutenant of the Tower. He died in 1630.
[3] S. P. Dom. Jac. I. xli. The depositions are in Cott. MSS. Julius, F. iii.

with more success, mainly, perhaps, because Buckingham, who was in the height of his power, desired to have the post of Lord Admiral for himself. Nottingham was superseded and pensioned. Mansell was got rid of ; Bingley, the surveyor, and Slingsby, the controller, were " sequestered " ; Navy Commissioners inquired, reported, and were given charge of the surveyorship and controllership ; and various radical changes were effected.

The report [1] issued by the Commissioners upon their assumption of office was a very long and searching one. It showed, among other things, to quote Mr. Oppenheim,[2] that—

" All the frauds of 1608 were still flourishing, with some new ones due to the lapse of time. Places were still sold, and at such high prices that the buyers ' profess openly that they cannot live unless they may steal '; the cost of the Navy had of late been some £53,000 a year, ' that could not keep it from decay.' For building a new ship in place of the *Bonaventure* £5700 had been allowed, but, although £1700 had been paid on account of it, no new vessel had been commenced ; and, though this same ship ' was broken up above seven years past, yet the King hath paid £63 yearly for keeping her.' Further, ' the *Advantage* was burnt about five years since, and yet keepeth at the charge of £104 9s. 5d. ; the *Charles* was disposed of in Scotland two years since, and costeth £60 16s. 10d. for keeping.' For repairing the *Merhonour, Defiance, Vanguard,* and *Dreadnought*, £23,500 had been paid, ' for which eight new ships might have been built as the accounts of the East India Company do prove; yet all this while the King's ships decayed : and if the *Merhonour* were repaired, she was left so imperfect that before her finishing she begins again to decay.' In nine years £108,000 had been charged for cordage : and the Commissioners express their intention of reducing the expenditure on this item by two-thirds."

The Commissioners made very great reforms in many directions, and, at the close of their first five years of office, delivered a report [3] of the work done by them. They had, they said, found in 1618, twenty-three serviceable and ten unserviceable ships, of together 15,670 tons, with four decayed galleys and four hoys, costing £53,000 a year ; and they had, in 1624, thirty-five serviceable ships of 19,339 tons, besides the galleys and hoys, though the expense was little more than £30,000 a year, inclusive of the charges for building ten new vessels.[4] But even the Commissioners themselves were not beyond suspicion. Coke suspected some of his colleagues of bribery in connection with the Algier Expedition, and kept them under espionage.[5] And several gross abuses, such, for example,

[1] S. P. Dom. c. and ci. 3.

[2] ' Admin. of Royal Navy,' 195.

[3] S. P. Dom. clvi. 12.

[4] But the Pipe Office Accounts show the total naval expenditure in 1623 (inclusive of that for the fleet sent to Spain for Prince Charles) to have been £62,000.

[5] S. P. Dom. cli. 35.

as the employment as captains of influential landsmen, were not corrected, nor even seriously attacked, until a much later period.[1]

And, in course of time, direction by Commissioners was found to be slow and cumbersome. Charles I. complained of it to Buckingham in 1627.[2] After Buckingham's assassination, it was deemed more convenient to put the office of Lord High Admiral into commission, and to allow the Principal Officers of the Navy to resume their full duties. The Treasurer's office had by that time become almost entirely financial. In 1630 his emoluments were increased by the grant of a house at Deptford, and of a poundage of threepence on all payments, including wages, made to him. In 1634, his fixed salary was raised from £270 13s. 4d. to £645 13s. 4d.[3]

The other Principal Officers flourished correspondingly, by foul means as well as by fair. Palmer once excused himself for selling government cordage and pocketing the proceeds, by saying that " his predecessors had done the like." Digby, who had no defined duties on the Board, proposed at one time to purchase from Sir Henry Mervyn the latter's command in the Channel; but Mervyn seems to have asked too much, viz., his arrears of pay to the amount of £5000, and the £3000 which he himself had given for his position. In 1628, the Principal Officers met in St. Martin's Lane ; but in 1630 rooms for them were taken in Mincing Lane at a rent of £30 a year. They cost £150 to furnish; twelve months' beer for the officers and their staff cost £13 8s. at a time when beer was but £1 10s. a tun ; and, upon the whole, it is clear that so long as comfort and perquisites were obtainable, the efficiency of the service was a secondary consideration. In 1634, Palmer, Pett, and Fleming, Clerk of the Acts, were suspended for malversation of stores. They were no worse than their inferiors. The dockyard officials robbed wholesale ; the captains turned their ships into cargo boats for their own profit, and conspired with the pursers to forge and sell seamen's tickets ; carpenters, gunners, boatswains, and pursers, cheated and swindled ; imaginary men were borne in nearly all ships, and their wages were shared among the officers ; and government storehouses were converted into surreptitious

---

[1] A Special Commission appointed in 1626 to inquire into the State of the Navy produced no results.

[2] 'Royal Letters' (Halliwell), ii. 277.

[3] Add. MSS. 9301, f. 110.

residences for government servants and their families.[1]   There were also sinecurists and pluralists.   In 1626, a Rochester man, to sell it again, offered £100 for the pursership of the *Anne Royal*, which he could not himself hold.   Another man was simultaneously purser of the *George* and cook of the *Bear*, and filled both offices by deputy. And the pursers made ever increasing profit on the sale of slop-clothes, the issue of which had begun in 1623 ;[2] and derived illegitimate fees from the contractors who delivered them on board. As a result, the seamen bought hardly any slops, and preferred to go ragged.

The Earl of Northumberland, as acting Lord High Admiral, reduced and regulated the pursers' profits on slop clothes by orders issued in 1641 ;[3] and, at about the same time, public opinion within the Navy apparently began to improve, and, if not actually to condemn, at least to look askance on, peculation, fraud, and the sale of places.   But there was no noticeable cessation of the evil practices until the establishment of the Commonwealth ; and they flourished again with full vigour for many years after the Restoration.

In the reign of James I., Deptford was still the principal dock-yard, but Chatham was beginning to rival it.   In the reign of Charles I., Portsmouth drew a little to the front, and Woolwich, temporarily discarded, was leased in 1633 to the East India Company for £100 a year.[4]   Under James, the dry dock at Deptford was enlarged, and the yard was surrounded by a paling; and a ropehouse was established at Woolwich.   In 1619, the paling at Deptford gave place to a brick wall.   Four years later, the dry dock at Portsmouth, the earliest of the kind built in England, was filled up, apparently because that part of the yard was threatened by incursions of the sea.[5]   Chatham obtained two mast docks in 1619 and 1620, and much additional ground, on part of which a dock, a ropehouse, and various brick and lime kilns were erected.[6]   Another dock was under construction in 1623.   The chief officers of the yard had up to about that time lodged at Winchester House ; they appear to have then removed to a house on Chatham Hill, leased from the Dean and Chapter of Rochester.   Portsmouth largely owed to

---

[1] For an exposure of these and other evils, see John Hollond's 'Discourse of the Navy' (Add. MSS. 9335), printed by the Navy Records Society, 1896.

[2] "To avoyde nastie beastlyness by continuall wearinge of one suite of clothes, and therebie boddilie diseases and unwholesome ill smells in every ship."

[3] S. P. Dom. ccccxxix. 33.   [4] Add. MSS. 9302, f. 42.

[5] Pipe Off. Accts. 2261.   [6] *Ib.* 2260.

Buckingham its growth in importance, and from his time some vessels were always stationed there; but not till 1638 was a master shipwright ordered into permanent residence at the yard ; and a new dry dock was not begun there until 1656. As a naval centre, indeed, Portsmouth was still far behind Chatham.

The chain, drawn by Hawkyns across the Medway at Upnor, was repaired in 1606, and, in 1623, gave place to a boom composed of masts, iron, cordage, and the hulls of two ships and two pinnaces. A new boom or a new chain was probably placed in position about 1635.[1]

Naval punishments were, as in previous periods, of a barbarous type, ducking, keel-hauling, tongue-scraping, and tying up with weights about the neck being common. The ancient custom of lashing to the bowsprit a seaman who had four times slept upon his watch, and of letting him drown or starve there, also survived. But some of these punishments were not strictly legal ; and in the days of Charles many officers, and especially Penington and Mervyn, leant in the direction of a less ferocious *régime*. Yet the regulations were still strict.

"Prayer," says Mr. Oppenheim,[2] " was said twice daily—before dinner, and after the psalm sung at setting the evening watch ; and anyone absent was liable to twenty-four hours in irons. Swearing was punished by three knocks on the forehead with a boatswain's whistle, and smoking anywhere but on the upper deck, 'and that sparingly,' by the bilboes. The thief was tied up to the capstan, 'and every man in the ship shall give him five lashes with a three-stringed whip on his bare back.' This is, I think, the first mention of any form of cat. The habitual thief was, after flogging, dragged ashore astern of a boat and ignominiously dismissed with the loss of his wages. For brawling and fighting the offender was ducked three times from the yardarm, and similarly towed ashore and discharged ; while for striking an officer he was to be tried for his life by twelve men, but whether shipmates or civilians is not said. If a man slept on watch, three buckets of water were to be poured upon his head and into his sleeves ; and anyone, except 'gentlemen or officers,' playing cards or dice incurred four hours of manacles. It is suggestive to read that 'no man presume to strike in the ship but such officers as are authorised.' "

Neither the public sense nor the law, however, seems to have been outraged when the letter of legality was overstepped by captains, either in the Navy or in the merchant service. The master of a Virginia trader hung up an insubordinate boy by the wrists, and tied two hundredweights to his feet. The boy laid a complaint before the Admiralty Court, but the judge, Sir H.

---

[1] S. P. Dom. cccii. 27.
[2] 'Admin. of Royal Navy,' 239, citing S. P. Dom. lvi. 101 (1627), and ccccvii. 32.

Martin, refused redress, on the ground that the maintenance of sea discipline was necessary.[1]

During the whole of this period it was usual, when extra vessels were needed for naval purposes, to hire ships from the merchants, and to arm them. But Penington, like other commanders, had but a low opinion of such craft, considering fifteen of them not a match for two regular men-of-war, their guns being defective, and their ammunition small in quantity.[2] Their discipline also was bad. " In 1625, they had to be forced under fire at Cadiz by threats ; in 1628, at Rochelle, they fired vigorously, but well out of any useful or hazardous range. In this year, the captain of one of them killed, injured, and maltreated his men, while he and five gentlemen volunteers consumed sixteen men's allowance of food every day ; and in January, 1627, when some of them, lying in Stokes Bay, were ordered westward, they mutinied, and would only sail for the Downs." [3] The rate of hire under James I. and his successor was two shillings per month per ton ; but this was often not paid for several years.[4] Up to 1624, and again from 1626 onwards, a bounty of five shillings a ton was offered to induce the building of merchant vessels suitable for adaptation to the purposes of war. After 1642, the Parliament, instead of paying so much per ton per month, offered £3 15s. 6d. per man per month, the owner supplying his vessel completely armed, manned, and equipped for sea, and the State being responsible in case of her loss.

The police of the home seas was disgracefully mismanaged under both James I. and Charles I. Dunquerque privateers infested the Channel, and rovers from the Mediterranean hovered about the coasts ; while the people of Ireland and the western counties were many of them either pirates themselves or in league with such freebooters.[5] It was sought to cope with the evil by granting warrants to the merchants to cruise against the pirates, and to retain three-fourths of any goods seized from them.[6] In the middle of James's reign, a Sallee rover was taken in the Thames, and a fleet of thirty Mussulman corsairs cruised in the Atlantic. Between 1609 and 1616, no fewer than four hundred and sixty-six British vessels were captured by the Algerines, and their crews enslaved. Mansell's expedition of 1621 checked the evil only for the moment.

[1] S. P. Dom. cclxxi. 12.
[2] *Ib.* xlii. 100.
[3] 'Admin. of Royal Navy,' 229.
[4] Add. MSS. 9302, f. 24.
[5] Cott. MSS. Otho E, viii. f. 316,
[6] S. P. Dom. lxxxvi. 101.

The Newfoundland Company complained that since 1612 it had received damage from the pirates to the value of £40,000 ; Swanage was in terror of the Turks, and petitioned for a blockhouse; and Trinity House objected to the Lizard Light on the ground that it would be of assistance to the marauders. Under Charles I., the nuisance grew even graver. Such men-of-war as cruised to protect trade in home waters were not good enough sailers to come up with the fast Dunquerquers and lateen-rigged Turks. Within only ten days in 1625, according to the Mayor of Plymouth, the pirates took twenty-seven vessels and two hundred men.[1] Nor was this all. On the night of June 30th, 1631, a body of Algerines landed at Baltimore in Munster, sacked the town, and carried off two hundred and thirty-seven British subjects into slavery.

The Government was too much in fear of the adoption of retaliatory measures to be very severe upon such Algerines as were caught from time to time.[2] They were not executed, because there were in Sallee two thousand English people in peril of their lives. These freebooters had much their own way on the west and south. On the east the Dunquerquers enforced something almost akin to a blockade; so that at one time, at Ipswich alone, fifty-eight vessels were laid up, and, at another, Lynn was plundered and partially burnt.[3] Tunnage and poundage was supposed to provide for the protection of the coasts ; but in 1628, in addition, duties were levied on sea-borne coal from Sunderland and Newcastle to pay for it; yet without any perceptible abatement of the scourge. Even when the ship-money fleets were at sea, coasters and Dover packets'were overhauled and pillaged almost in sight of his Majesty's ships, and the Channel was full of Algerines.[4] Rainborow's expedition to Sallee, like Mansell's to Algier, gave but temporary relief ; for in 1640 there were sixty sail of Algerines off the south coast, and the unbelievers executed a successful raid near Penzance.[5]

The comparative impunity with which the Mediterranean corsairs carried out their operations was due perhaps almost as much to the disunion of the Christian Powers as to the weakness of Britain. Yet it is strange that while Britain in her own seas was at the mercy of these pirates, she still jealously maintained the right of her flag as against civilised states. Monson enforced it in the Downs in

---

[1] S. P. Dom. v. 6, 24, 36.
[2] *Ib.* xxx. 17; xliii. 46.
[3] *Ib.* xxxiv. 85; lvi. 66.

[4] 'Admin. of Royal Navy,' 276.
[5] S. P. Dom. cccclix. 8, 60.

1604, when a Dutch squadron lay there ; Mansell enforced it in 1620 against a French squadron on the coast of Spain; Selden, in 1634, wrote his ' Mare Clausum ' in defence of it, Charles ordering a copy of the book to be kept for ever as a piece of evidence in the Court of Admiralty.   Lindsey was sent to sea in 1635 especially to vindicate the honour claimed by Great Britain, and in 1636 Northumberland received the mark of deference both from the Dutch and from the Spaniards.[1]

The rations of the seamen were nominally, and when they were served out in full, the same as in the age of Elizabeth, viz., one pound of biscuit and one gallon of beer daily, with, on four days of the week, two pounds of salt beef (or alternatively on two of those days one pound of bacon or pork, and one pint of peas), and on the other three days fish, dried or fresh, two ounces of butter, and a quarter of a pound of cheese.   The allowance paid to the contractors for these victuals in 1622 was, per head, $7\frac{1}{2}d$. per day in harbour, and $8d$. at sea ; but in Elizabeth's time the allowance had been but $4\frac{1}{2}d$. and $5d$.   In 1635 the allowance rose further, the rates being $7\frac{1}{2}d$. and $8\frac{1}{2}d$., but owing to the advance in prices, the contractor, even on those terms, declared that he lost money, and in 1638 he gave notice to terminate the arrangement.   At that time beef was about $2\frac{3}{4}d$. and pork about $1\frac{1}{2}d$. a pound, stockfish about £4 5s. a cwt., biscuit about 15s. a cwt., and beer about £1 16s. a tun.

Previous to the Civil War, the crew of one of H.M. ships received no regular and fixed proportion of the proceeds of their captures, though, under an Order in Council of October, 1626, they were to be given "a competent reward."   But in October, 1642, Parliament assigned to the officers and men of a ship, in addition to their pay, one-third of the value of the prizes taken by them.   For many years, however, it was the practice to make unjustifiable deductions on various pretexts, and owing to this, and to delays in making payment, there was much naval discontent until the Commonwealth became firmly established.

Soon after the union of England and Scotland in 1603, all British vessels for a time flew the Union Flag of the crosses

---

[1] These examples might be largely added to.   In July, 1626, for instance, the captain of Deal Castle fired at a Dutchman which came into the roads with her colours flying, and made her master pay ten shillings, the cost of the shot.   And in 1632 the captain of a man-of-war, sent to Calais to fetch the body of Sir Isaac Wake, forced the French to lower their flag to him.   ' Admin. of Royal Navy,' 291.

of St. George and St. Andrew,[1] but on May 5th, 1634, it was ordered by proclamation[2] that men-of-war only were to fly it in future, and that merchantmen, according to their nationality, were to wear the St. George's or the St. Andrew's Flag merely. This rule endured until February, 1649, when Parliament directed men-of-war to wear as an ensign the St. George's Cross on a white field.

Little progress was made in the art of signalling at sea. At

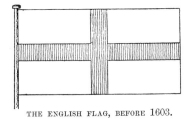

THE ENGLISH FLAG, BEFORE 1603.

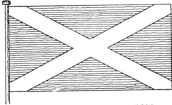

THE SCOTS FLAG, BEFORE 1603.

night two lights from the flagship, to be answered by one light from each private ship, signified " shorten sail "; three lights arranged vertically astern signified " make sail "; waving a light

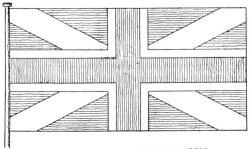

THE UNION FLAG, AS ORDERED IN 1606.

from the poop signified " lie to," etc. Day signalling by means of flags was still in its infancy. In fleets the van flew the blue at the

---

[1] It was carried, under an order of April 13th, 1606, in the main-top, English and Scotch vessels also carrying their national colours in the fore-top. The first Union Flag is heraldically described as : " Azure a saltire Argent, surmounted of a cross Gules fimbriated of the second." The fimbriation was made one-third of the width of the red cross, and the red cross was made one-fifth of the width of the flag. Contemporary pictures seem to show that ensigns of red, white, or blue, bearing St. George's Cross on a white canton next the staff, were also commonly carried until the time of the Commonwealth.

[2] ' Fœdera,' xix. 549.

main, and the Union at the fore; the rear flew the white at the main, and the Union at the mizen; and the centre flew the Union at the main, for distinction of squadrons.

Repeated mention has been made in these pages of the ancient practice of creating fleets by the process of summoning vessels from the port towns and coast counties. Part of the fleet for the Cadiz Expedition of 1625 was collected in the old manner. But in 1634, the position of foreign affairs suggested to Charles I. the advisability of raising a fleet of better fighting value in order to maintain the sovereignty of the seas, prevent the French from taking Dunquerque, assert his right to the North Sea fisheries, and induce the co-operation of Spain in certain projects. Noy, the Attorney-General, suggested that the requisite money for equipment of vessels should be levied from the coast towns, a somewhat similar measure having been occasionally adopted in previous ages, though without parliamentary warrant.[1] A ship-money writ was accordingly issued in October, 1634, and after some remonstrance was submitted to. In 1635 a second writ required the inland towns and counties to contribute also. There was much opposition, but in December the King obtained from ten judges an opinion that the levy of ship-money upon all was lawful. A third writ was issued in October, 1636, and in spite of a further favourable opinion from the judges, provoked increasing hostility. A fourth writ was issued in the autumn of 1637, a fifth in January, 1639, and a sixth in 1640.

By the writ of 1635, a ship of 450 tons, manned and equipped for six months, or in default a sum of £4500, was demanded from the county of Buckingham. The constitutional struggle arose out of this fact, John Hampden, of Great Hampden, refusing to pay his share, and standing his trial in respect of 20*s.* claimed from him for lands in the parish of Stoke Mandeville. Judgment was given in June, 1638, seven out of twelve judges deciding for the Crown,

---

[1] In 1619, soon after Buckingham's appointment as Lord High Admiral, King James, apprehensive of a rupture with Spain, ordered that six ships of the Royal Navy should be prepared for immediate service. Fourteen other ships were to be equipped by the merchants; and directions were given to the City Companies to pay £40,000 which had been assessed upon them. It was also decided that the old tax of ship-money should be levied at the other ports; and the magistrates were accordingly required to make up the sum of £8550 amongst them. The sums assessed were as follows:— Bristol, £2500; Exeter, £1000; Plymouth, £1000; Dartmouth, £1000; Barnstaple, £500; Hull, £500; Weymouth, £450; Southampton, £300; Newcastle, £300; the Cinque Ports, £200; Yarmouth, £200; Ipswich, £150; Colchester, £150; Poole, £100; Chester, £100; Lyme, £100.

three for Hampden on all grounds, and two for him on technical grounds only. Charles I. was at one time willing to allow the judgment to go before the House of .Lords upon a writ of error, and be reversed, but various considerations prevented the carrying out of that plan. When the Long Parliament met, the Commons on December 7th, 1640, and the Lords on January 20th, 1641, agreed to resolutions declaring the levying of ship-money to be illegal, and a bill to the same effect, being brought in by Selden, received the royal assent on August 7th, 1641.[1]

The fleets raised by ship-money were ill-found and ill-organised, but of imposing proportions, and Mr. Oppenheim, who nowhere conceals his contempt for the methods of those who raised them, and, indeed, for the Stuarts in general, is forced to admit that but for the forces which the writs enabled King Charles to send to sea, " the strife with France and Holland might have been precipitated by nearly half a century. That they had some such intimidating influence was shown by the care taken by the French fleets, also cruising, to avoid meeting them, and the efforts of the French Court to evade the question of the dominion of the Narrow Seas." [2]

Just as the ship-money question had an important bearing upon the internal history of the country, so an episode of 1623 had an important bearing upon the history of the country's foreign relations. This episode was known as the Amboyna affair. Amboyna, one of the Moluccas, had been taken by the Dutch from the Portuguese in 1607. The English, after having been expelled from the place, obtained in 1619 the right to trade there ; but the treaty was ill-kept on both sides, and in February, 1623, the Dutch tortured to death several English factors, upon pretence that they had intrigued with the natives.[3] This massacre was one of the main causes of the bad feeling between England and Holland in the middle of the seventeenth century, and although Holland, after the war of 1651-54, submitted to pay £300,000 to the descendants of the victims, the massacre was not forgotten in England, and its memory, for many years afterwards, often provoked ill-blood.

The properties of the geometrical series which constitute the foundation of the doctrine of logarithms seem to have been known

---

[1] Hallam, 'Const. Hist.'; Gardiner, 'Hist. of England'; Clarendon, 'Hist. of the Rebellion'; Nugent, 'Memorials of Hampden.' Hampden was mortally wounded at Chalgrove Field on June 18th, 1643.

[2] 'Admin. of Royal Navy,' 218.

[3] For an account of the details of this affair, see Chap. XVIII.

as long ago as the days of Archimedes ; they are also touched upon
in the writings of sixteenth century German mathematicians. But
these properties and their advantageous utilisation were not properly
understood until the publication by John, Lord Napier of Merchis-
toun, in 1614, of his work, '*Mirifici Logarithmorum Canonis
Descriptio.*' The discovery was further improved by Henry Briggs,
who at the time of Napier's publication was Professor of Geometry
at Gresham College, and who later became Savilian Professor at
Oxford.   The work of Napier and Briggs, and of their contemporaries Adrian Valcq of Gouda, and Henry Gellibrand of
Gresham College, in connection with this subject, had a most-
valuable influence upon the development of the practice of navigation, as well as of other branches of mathematics, and deserves
commemoration here.

While England was drifting towards the great constitutional
struggle which more than any other laid the foundations of her
freedom, her small transatlantic colonies, though still in their
feeblest infancy, were also doing something towards the making of
the prosperity and greatness to which, under independent government, they have since attained.   A small ship was built at or near
Boston, Massachusetts, as early as 1633, and in 1639 laws for the
encouragement of the American fisheries were passed.   These
exempted fishermen during the season, and shipwrights at all
seasons, from military duty, and no doubt had much effect in
turning the attention of the colonists to the advantages of sea life.
Two years later a ship of 300 tons was constructed at Salem, and
in 1646 a vessel of 150 tons was built in Rhode Island.[1]   Such were
the small beginnings of a mercantile marine which, two hundred
years afterwards, seemed about to challenge, at least for a time,
Great Britain's supremacy as the ocean carrier of the goods of
the world.

[1] J. F. Cooper, 'History of the Navy of the U.S.A.' (1840), i. 18, 19.

CHAPTER XVIII.

MILITARY HISTORY OF THE ROYAL NAVY, 1603–1649.

L. CARR LAUGHTON.

James I. and the succession—The Honour of the Flag—The East India Company— James Lancaster—Sir Henry Middleton—Thomas Best—Nicholas Downton—A great Portuguese carrack—Capture of Ormuz—Buckingham and the Company— The Dutch in the East Indies—Relations with the Dutch—The Banda Islands— Nathaniel Courthope—Sir Thomas Dale—The Amboyna Massacre—Anglo-Dutch combination—Fight off Gombroon—Heavy Portuguese loss—Fight off Damaun— Loss of the *Lion*—Peace with Spain—Growth of piracy—Sir William Monson— The Barbary pirates—Expedition to Algier—Rainborow at Sallee—Relations with Holland and Spain—Rich's piracy—Argall in Virginia—Dunquerquers in Scottish ports—Spanish vessels in the Downs—Penington's ships used against La Rochelle —The Cadiz Expedition—War with France—The *St. Peter* of Le Hâvre—Lord Willoughby's Expedition—Buckingham's fleet—The Expedition to Rhé—Its failure —Capture of the *St. Esprit*—Denbigh's failure—Buckingham's unpopularity— His assassination—Lindsey sails to La Rochelle—Surrender of La Rochelle— Recrudescence of piracy—The Dutch herring busses—The Ship-Money fleets— Oquendo in the Downs—Attitude of the English—Scheme of the King—Tromp's victory—The Irish Rebellion—The Civil War—The allegiance of the Navy—The dual appointment—Rainborow set ashore—The Royalist fleet.

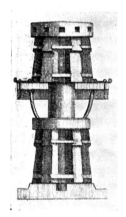

THE death of Elizabeth entirely changed the course of naval affairs. James cared little for the old Elizabethan sentiment that looked on the Spaniard as a natural enemy; nor was the fact that the war could be made to pay its own expenses inducement enough to make him forego the delights of peace. Elizabeth had had in preparation two squadrons destined to cruise against Philip; "for the Queen held it both secure, and a profitable course, to keep a continual force upon the Spanish coasts."[1] Of these squadrons, the first, which should have sailed in February, was to have been commanded by Sir Richard Leveson; and the latter, intended to recruit the former in June, was to have

---

[1] Monson, 'Tracts,' p. 206, in Churchill's Voyages, vol. iii.

gone out under Sir William Monson. The first squadron was ready
for sea, but in view of the Queen's illness and the possibility of a
disputed succession, did not sail. As, in preparation for the peace
signed in August, 1604, James began by forbidding the capture of
Spanish prizes, these ships never proceeded to their destination.
From them, however, was composed a fleet of eight sail which,
under Leveson, with Monson as second-in-command, cruised on the
coasts of France and Flanders, ready to take action should any
attempt be made from abroad to interfere with the succession.[1] But
Henry IV., whether overawed or not by this fleet, which kept well
in with the French coast, made no demonstration. At the end of
the summer the ships were recalled to Chatham ; and, from that
moment until the end of the reign, the Royal Navy had but scant
opportunities of seeing active service.

The Dutch had been in the habit of attacking Spanish vessels
wherever they met them, and, so long as we were ourselves at war
with Spain, no opposition had been offered to their so doing, even
in English waters.   Now, however, pending the signing of the
peace, James determined to assert his rights : Monson was appointed
Admiral of the Narrow Seas, and sailed early in 1605 to uphold the
honour of the flag.   Incidentally it is worth noticing how this zeal
was made to forward the scheme which the King had most at heart.
This action on the part of the English helped to augment the ill-
feeling which was already growing up in Holland against us, and to
pave the way for the many petty quarrels which resulted in the first
Dutch War. On May 10th, 1605, Monson, coming into the Downs,
found there six Dutch ships. Having learnt that their presence was
due to a Dunquerquer which was then lying in Sandwich Harbour,
he ordered them to stay two tides after she had sailed, and
threatened to sink them if the Dunquerquer were molested.[2] In the
same year the Dutch drove under the guns of Dover a squadron of
eight Spanish ships carrying one thousand soldiers to Flanders.
Again the Dutch could not reach their enemy, but many months
passed before the Spaniards could find a chance of eluding the
blockade and putting over to Dunquerque.

Yet notwithstanding the odium which we were incurring on their

---

[1] Whether by accident or design the flagship *Repulse* was less powerful than
Monson's ship the *Merhonour*. Monson himself said that the reason for this was that
the Council was not sure of Leveson, but did not like to supersede him. 'Tr.' p. 510.

[2] 'Tracts,' p. 242.

behalf, "notwithstanding the peace with Spain was concluded, the Spaniards continued their depredations on our merchants, and began to lead King James by the nose." [1] But James "shunned hostilities with a caution that was proof against the insults of his neighbours," [2] and, on one side only, the old maxim, that no peace held good "south of the line," was fully maintained.

Yet though the King's ships lay idle for many years, the armed vessels of the newly-founded [3] East India Company were busy laying for us the foundations of an empire in the Far East. In them the Company's servants followed the Portuguese and the Dutch into eastern waters, much as the *Jesus* and the *Golden Hind* had followed the Spaniards into the Far West; and, though less is generally known of the exploits of Best and Downton than of those of John Hawkyns and Francis Drake, this would seem to be due, in great measure, to the want of romance in their setting out, as compared with the glamour of chivalry which surrounded the semi-religious [4] undertakings of the Elizabethan worthies.

First in the field in the East Indies were the Portuguese; [5] after them came the Dutch, and last of all, three years after the Dutch, came the English. The East India Company was founded in 1600, while England was still at war with Spain, and while Portugal was still a province of Spain. This alone was reason enough to account for the fighting that ensued. That hostilities did not cease in the Far East when peace was made in Europe was but in accordance with the spirit of the age; a war of reprisals went on, and when to this was added trade jealousy, and the Portuguese belief in the Papal Bull, [6] which conferred on them sole rights in those seas, it will be easily understood that the struggle became intensely bitter.

The ships of the Company were built at least as much for war as for trade; [7] most of them were of 500 tons and upwards and carried from twenty to thirty guns of moderate calibre, with crews of two hundred men. They were just such ships, in fact, as swelled the fleets that fought in European waters in the sixteenth and seventeenth centuries.

---

[1] Lediard, ' Nav. Hist.' p. 403.
[2] Macaulay, ' Hist.' i. 35.
[3] Cal. S. P. E. Ind. 1513–1616..265, 281, 440, 1069.
[4] Spanish Armada, N. R. S. vol. i. pp. xx, etc.
[5] 1513. Cal. S. P. E. Ind.
[6] Cal. S. P. E. Ind. 1513–1616..2.
[7] Cal. S. P. E. Ind. May 15th and 19th, Aug. 21st, 1607 ; July 5th, 1609, etc.

The expedition of James Lancaster,[1] the first that was sent out
by the new Company, gave a foretaste of what was to come. It has
been described in Chap. XVI.

Sir Henry Middleton was a worthy successor to Lancaster, and
commanded in two of the Company's voyages. In the first, which
sailed from Gravesend, March 25th, 1604, he was so much weakened
by famine and fever at sea, and by the scattering of his squadron,
that he was capable of little interference when he found that the
Dutch had seized Amboyna, and were struggling with the Portuguese
for tho possession of Ternate and Tidore in the Moluccas.[2]

In 1610 Middleton sailed in command of the Company's sixth
voyage; his flagship being the *Trade's Increase* of 1000[3] tons. With
him were two men who, a few years later, did notable service :
these were Nicholas Downton, in command of the *Peppercorn* of
250 tons, and Nathaniel Courthope, in the little *Darling* of 90 tons.
Reaching Aden, Middleton left the *Peppercorn* there while he
himself and the *Darling* went on to Mocha. There the *Trade's
Increase* went aground, and it became necessary to lighten her in
order to get her off. As the Aga was profuse in his protestations
of friendship, Middleton set to work to land cargo and stores. The
work was rudely interrupted by a treacherous attack made on a
large landing party, of whom eight were killed, and fifty, including
Middleton, were taken prisoners.[4] An attack made on the *Darling*
was easily beaten off. Middleton was allowed to communicate with
the ships, and was therefore able to restrain Downton, who arrived
at this juncture from Aden, from making reprisals. Middleton did
this, fearing lest hostile action on his part might involve the Company in an unprofitable quarrel. Middleton was also allowed to send
to the ships for provisions, and of this permission he availed himself
to make his escape. He ordered a quantity of wine and spirits to
be landed, and plied his keepers with them, "so that at noone they
went home to rest their laden braines."[5] He got on board the
Darling, and, with the *Peppercorn*, blockaded Mocha until the
prisoners, the stores that had been landed, and his ship were given
up. He then went east and acted much as Lancaster had done.

[1] Cal. S. P. E. Ind. 27 Oct. 1600.
[2] Cal. S. P. E. Ind. 244, 350.
[3] Stow, 'Annals,' calls the *Trade's Increase* a ship of 1200 tons.
[4] Cal. S. P. 1513–1616. .570.
[5] Purchas, 'Pilgrims,' i. 583.

Off Surat [1] he skirmished with eighteen Portuguese "frigates," [2] and for a time was enabled to trade with the town, where as yet we had established no factory. When, in fear of the Portuguese, the governor closed the town to him, he returned to the Straits of Bab el Mandeb and tried to make his profit by seizing Indian ships and holding them to ransom. He did make money by these means, and he also obtained compensation from the Turks for the treatment he had experienced at Mocha ; but the method does not seem to have been so satisfactory as to encourage others to adopt it. In the Red Sea he met John Saris, then on his way to open up our first trade with Japan,[3] but a quarrel soon arose which separated the squadrons. Middleton then went on to Bantam, where the *Trade's Increase* was careened for repairs to her hull. By some accident the ship fell over on her side, and the Javanese burnt her as she lay, Middleton[4] and many of the crew perishing with her.

The Portuguese now began to pay more heed to the equipment of such of their ships as were likely to meet the Company's squadrons. The English usually sailed with a force sufficient to save them from serious molestation ; and the Portuguese, discovering that their trading vessels were no match for these powerful armaments, came at last to fit out regularly-appointed war squadrons from their local factories. Surat was the first port of call for vessels from England, and there they could be found with their cargoes still on board, and with hulls and men still the worse for the long voyage out.

The first of the actions which this policy entailed was fought in October, 1612.[5] Hearing that Lancaster's old ship, the *Dragon*,[6] Captain Thomas Best, had just arrived from England with but one small craft, the *Osiander*, Captain Christian, in company, the enemy hastened to send up from Goa a squadron of four galleons and a flotilla of the so-called "frigates." Surat lies on the left bank, and at the mouth, of the Tapti River. Parallel with the coast and

---

[1] Cal. S. P. E. Ind. Oct. 12th, 1611.

[2] These "frigates" were large open boats, crowded with men, who were for the most part native sailors, but they mounted no guns. In light winds or calms they proved very dangerous neighbours.

[3] Lediard, p. 428.

[4] Cal. S. P. E. Ind. 8th June, 1614.

[5] Cal. S. P. Ind. 1612..638.

[6] Or *Red Dragon*, formerly the *Scourge of Malice*.

close in with it runs a shoal.   Inside this is the anchorage in the
Sutherland Channel, or, as it was then called, the Swally.   There
the English ships were lying on October 29th when the Portuguese
hove in sight.   Not to be taken by surprise, Best, in the *Dragon*,
weighed and stood out to sea.   The *Osiander* was unable to get
out, but the *Dragon*, passing between the enemy's admiral and
vice-admiral, gave each a broadside, and so handled them that
they were glad to sheer off for that day.   Next day, the *Osiander*
made her way out of the channel, " and bravely redeemed the
time she lost the day before.   The fiery *Dragon* (bestirring herself)
in about three hours' hot fight drove three of the galleons on
the sands, and then the *Osiander*, drawing little water, danced
the hay about them, and so paid them that they dare not show
a man upon their decks, killing and spoiling their men and battering
their ships exceedingly." [1]   On the third day little was done.   The
Portuguese, having the wind, contented themselves with sending
down a " frigate " as an impromptu fireship, and this Best sank.
When, shortly afterwards, Best resumed his voyage, the enemy
declined to meddle further with him.   On their own admission
the Portuguese had lost one hundred and sixty men killed,[2] while
Best reported [3] but one man killed in his ships.

The immediate result of this action was an enormous increase
of English prestige with the natives.   The Great Mogul ceased to
regard Englishmen as interlopers, and granted permission to establish factories at Surat and elsewhere on the coast.[4]   To protect
these factories the Company provided itself with a few " grabs " or
" galivats," native boats mounting no more than four or five guns,
yet often wrongly spoken of as " galleys."   These boats are interesting as marking the origin of what grew to be first the Bombay
Marine, and then the Indian Navy.[5]

Best, following up this voyage, reached Acheen, where he was
hospitably entertained [6] by the King.   His trade was satisfactory, and

---

[1] Journal of Nicholas Witherington, factor in the voyage.   In Lediard, p. 433.

[2] This great loss was probably sustained chiefly in the open boats.   Lediard makes
it even heavier, suggesting that three hundred were killed.

[3] Cal. S. P. E. Ind. 1612..638.

[4] *Ib.* 1614, June 22.

[5] Low, ' Hist. Ind. Navy,' vol. i. ch. ii.

[6] Among other entertainments the King gave a river " feast," at which the company
sat in the water and were served by boys swimming.   Five hundred dishes are
mentioned as having been served, with corresponding hot drinks.   Best was allowed to

for this he was thanked by the Company; but dissatisfaction was expressed[1] at his "great private trade," with the result that he did not go out again.

In October, 1614, Nicholas Downton reached Surat with a squadron of four ships. These were,[2] his own, the *New Year's Gift*, a new vessel of 550 tons ; the *Hector*, 500 tons, vice-admiral ; the *Merchant's Hope*, of 300 tons; and the *Solomon* of 200. The Portuguese viceroy at Goa, hearing of Downton's presence, saw an opportunity of avenging Best's victory. He collected a force of six large galleons and three smaller ships, two galleys—probably "grabs"—mounting in all 134 guns—and 60 "frigates." Some of the guns were 42-pounders, and the ships were manned by 8600 men, of whom 2600 were Europeans. Against this armada Downton could show but four ships, two of them small, and three or four grabs, mounting in all 80 guns of small calibre, and manned by 600 men, many of whom were sick. Seeing the great disparity of force, the Nawab of Surat was anxious to make his peace ; but the viceroy rejected his overtures, and the battle began.[3]

The English were anchored in line ahead in the Swally and close to the shoal; Downton's ship was the northernmost, and the *Merchant's Hope* was the last ship in the line. We are not told how the wind was, but it seems that Downton had satisfied himself that the enemy would pass round by the north channel. This, however, they did not dare to do. The galleons anchored abreast of the English ships, but outside the shoal. From that position they maintained a comparatively harmless long-range fire, while the smaller vessels swarmed across the sands and tried to carry Downton's ships by boarding. The *Merchant's Hope* was most easily approached, and she bore the brunt of the attack, repelling the boarders time after time. This was practically the whole of the battle, but the *Hope* was for some time in a critical position. The enemy, finding that their open boats gave them no protection alongside a high-charged ship, hastily set fire to many of their "frigates" and jumped overboard. The *Hope* with difficulty cleared

---

rise an hour before the rest of the guests, but "the Captayne of the Dutch house took his bane, either with hote drinkes, or cold sitting so long in the water, and soon after dyed."—Purchas, 'Pilgrims,' i. 613.

[1] Cal. S. P. E. Ind. 26th July, 1614.
[2] Lediard, p. 436.
[3] Cal. S. P. E. Ind. 1513–1616..1072, 1127.

herself from the blazing boats; but before she had done so her mainmast was on fire. While the boats were burning out on the shoal, it went over the side. So ended the fight as far as that day, January 20th,[1] was concerned. The Portuguese lost many "frigates," and three small ships taken by the *Hope*, but afterwards burnt; and in men, burnt, killed, or drowned, about 500. The English loss was slight—only four killed and one wounded; but as this last man had an arm shot off, it would appear that a wound was not counted as such unless it was very severe. The next night, and for some nights afterwards, the Portuguese sent fire-ships across the sands, fortunately without doing any harm. On February 13th they withdrew. The English position had proved too strong for them. The Nawab came in state to congratulate Downton, and presented to him his sword "with hilt of massie gold"; and, says Downton, in a Homeric spirit, "in lieu thereof, I returned him my sute, being sword, dagger, girdle, and hangers . . . which made a great deal better show, though of less value.'[2]

On March 3rd the English weighed to go to Bantam, but no sooner were they outside than they sighted the Portuguese. The two fleets stayed in presence of one another for some days, when, as the enemy showed no intention of attacking either him or Surat, Downton resumed his course. Two years previously he had visited Bantam, and on that occasion had written in his journal: "He that escapes without disease from that stinking stew of the Chinese part of Bantam must be of strong constitution." This visit proved the correctness of his opinion; he died at Bantam on August 6th, 1615.

A year after Downton's death there was fought an action highly creditable to the vanquished. A great Portuguese carrack was met near the Comoro Islands by four outward-bound ships under Captain Benjamin Joseph in the *Charles*.[3] This time the advantage lay clearly with us, for, though the carrack was of 1500 tons—a ship far greater than any we then had—yet the *Charles* was of 1000 tons, as was also the *James*. The attack began with a broadside from the big ship, and thereafter the fight was kept up with great spirit for half an hour, when darkness fell. Captain Joseph had been killed at the outset. The carrack made no attempt to escape, but held her course till midnight, with lights burning. Then she anchored, the four ships anchoring near her. She did not weigh till the following night, when she was again pursued. by the Company's ships. At daybreak the fight was renewed, the four ships keeping up a fire which entirely dismasted the carrack, and, according to Mr. Edward Terry, chaplain of the *Charles*,[1] "had made such breaches in her thick sides, that her case seemed so desperate as that she must either yield or perish." But, rather than yield, her crew, after a most stubborn defence, ran her ashore and set fire to her.

The next action of importance in Eastern waters took place in the beginning of 1622. In January Captains Blythe and John Weddell appeared in the Persian Gulf with orders for reprisals against the Portuguese. They purposed to take Ormuz, a small island in the mouth of the gulf. Desert in itself, its importance lay in its having become a great trade centre. The Arabs had used it as an emporium from the beginning of the fourteenth century, and, early in the sixteenth, it was of such surprising opulence as to attract the attention of the Portuguese, who, under d'Albuquerque took possession of it. Its wealth may have waned somewhat under its new masters, but it still had the reputation of being enormously wealthy. The Persians were jealous of its prosperity, and readily agreed to act with the English. From the 20th to the 30th of January the ships besieged the fort of Kishm, in which d'Andrade, the Portuguese admiral, commanded in person. On its fall an advance was made to Ormuz, which in turn surrendered on April 23rd. When it came to looting the town, the English stood little chance with the Persians either in point of numbers or in mere thieving power. They did, however, contrive to load one of the ships, the *Whale*, with booty to the value of £100,000. Unfortunately, the ship, with all the treasure, was lost on the bar outside Surat. So far as concerned the Company, the expedition resulted in a loss; for on the return of the ships to England, Buckingham, then Lord High Admiral, preferred a claim to a tenth part of the booty. The argument that the whole of the £100,000 had been lost was of no avail; so the Company claimed that it had acted by right of its charter, and not in virtue of letters of marque from the Lord High Admiral. "Then," said Buckingham, "you have acted as pirates, and the whole is forfeit to the Crown." The matter ended in the Company's paying to Buckingham his tenth, and to the King £10,000 as a fine for having no letters of marque.[2]

---

[1] Low, 'Hist. Ind. Navy,' vol. i. ch. i.   [2] Frankland, 'Annals,' p. 155.

But the Portuguese were by no means the only rivals we were called upon to face in the East Indies. Though we were at peace with the Dutch, they, like the Portuguese, persisted in regarding us as interlopers. Thus, although for a considerable time there was no serious rupture, there were heard in England continual complaints of unfriendly dealings on the part of the Dutch. This was notably the case on the return of William Keeling's expedition of 1607, and of the expedition taken out by David Middleton, brother to Sir Henry, in 1609.

The fault did not lie with the Dutch commanders, though no excess of peacefulness was to be looked for in men who commanded vessels equipped at least as much for war as for commerce. The real difficulty of the position "lay in the success of the English merchants in establishing a treaty right to share in the commerce of islands which were under the territorial sovereignty of another nation."[1] The Dutch, on their first coming into Eastern waters, had decided that their most profitable course would be to get the Moluccas[2] and the Banda Islands into their own possession, for from these islands alone in all the known world could spices be obtained. That they had found the Portuguese in possession and had driven them from Amboyna, Ternate, and Tidore, mattered little to the Company. What concerned the Company more immediately was the resistance offered by the Dutch to all attempts made by the English to establish themselves in the Banda Islands.

Arriving there in 1613, Sir Henry Middleton found that the Dutch had four years before built a fort on the Great Banda, and that, in May, 1610, the English had been forced to transfer their factory to Bantam. From Banda the Dutch hoped to make sure of the rest of the group of islands. In 1616 they took Pulo Way.[3] But late in that same year Nathaniel Courthope was sent from Bantam to hold the neighbouring island of Pulo Ron. His difficulties were many. A meditated Dutch attack was only stayed by the erection of batteries on shore. Of his two ships one was captured, the other was surrendered by her mutinous crew.

But Courthope still held out. In March, 1618, two vessels sailing to his relief were taken by the Dutch after a seven-hours' fight in sight of the island. The agreements arrived at by the

---

[1] Gardiner, iii. 179.   [2] Burchett, 'Transactions,' Bk. iii. 292.

[3] Gardiner, iii. 169, *sqq.*

Commissioners sitting in London were not known to him. Late in 1618, Sir Thomas Dale [1] was sent out in command of a force of six ships. With these he met and defeated a Dutch squadron off Jacatra; [2] but when he might have used his victory to relieve Courthope and ensure our possession of Pulo Ron, he preferred to land a force to besiege the Dutch fort at Jacatra, [3] and to disperse his ships for trade. Nor did the open war declared by Dale bring profit to England. The Dutch had a vast preponderance of force ; and during 1619 they used it in capturing many of the Company's ships   Courthope himself fell a victim. Met at Lantore by two Dutch ships, while he had but a native boat, he was slain by a musket bullet. Directly afterwards the Dutch took both Lantore and Pulo Ron, and our hopes in the Banda Islands were gone. [4] The news of the signature of the treaty in England did not reach the East Indies till March, 1620. The greatest loss had been sustained in the year that passed between the date of the signature and the day on which news of it reached Bantam.

For a while after the receipt of this news relations became more friendly. But bit by bit the old jealousies re-arose, and in 1623 was perpetrated what has been considered in England as a very terrible crime. On pretence of having discovered a plot by which the English in Amboyna, with the help of the natives, intended to possess themselves of the island, the Dutch seized the English residents, [5] 18 or 20 in number, including Gabriel Towerson the agent, as well as some Japanese suspects, and subjected them to torture. Judging the evidence thus obtained to be conclusive, they executed ten of the English, including Towerson, and drove the remainder away to other islands. They afterwards took Ceram.

This was on February 27th, 1623. When the news became known in England a great outcry [6] was raised by the Company ; and the memory of Amboyna lived to become one of the many causes of the first Dutch War. We know now the value of evidence taken under torture ; but in estimating the Dutch position it must be remembered that such evidence was then generally held to be good.

[1] Formerly Governor of Virginia.   [2] Colliber, ' Col. Rostr.' 83.
[3] Dale died at Jacatra of swamp fever.   [4] Purchas, i. 664-679.
[5] Lediard, p. 470.
[6] The populace was then too busy with the Spanish marriage to be ready to pay much heed to the Dutch. Amboyna was more spoken of in England years after the receipt of the news than it was at the time. Gardiner, v. 242.

Yet Towerson and his men died protesting their innocence ; and in their innocence their countrymen firmly believed.[1]

As a result of this "massacre" the Dutch were left in possession of the whole of the Banda group ; but elsewhere a semi-piratical war of reprisals continued to be waged. In face of the relations between the representatives of the two countries, it seems strange at first sight that we should find an Anglo-Dutch fleet combined against the Portuguese. The reason for the combination appears to have been merely the dislike, common to both English and Dutch, of being looked down upon with contempt as interlopers. Both Companies had shown themselves so little inclined to respect the treaty of 1619, that this joint action cannot be spoken of as the result of that treaty. It was enough for English and Dutch that their interests coincided for the time being.

After having been in company with a Dutch squadron of four ships at the end of November, 1624, John Weddell parted from them on the 19th and 21st with the intention of going to Surat. As he had information of a large Portuguese force at Goa equipping against Ormuz, he gave the Dutch a rendezvous at Gombroon, where, after being joined by the *Eagle* at Surat, he joined them on 17th December. The joint force then amounted to eight ships ; viz : the *Royal James*, Weddell's ship, with the *Jonas*, *Star* and *Eagle*, belonging to the English Company, and the *South Holland*, with Albert Becker in command, the *Bantam*, *Maud of Dort* and *Weasope*,[2] belonging to the Dutch.[3] On January 31st the Portuguese were sighted, their force being made out to consist of eight galleons and sixteen "frigates."[4] That night it fell calm and the English, with an assurance from the Dutch that "they would stick to them like their shirts to their backs," waited for dawn to open the fight. The Dutch, weighing before daybreak, went first into action,[5] being closely followed by the English. The dying away of the wind about noon gave the enemy an advantage, for they

[1] After all the question was not really "Was Towerson guilty?" It was rather, "Supposing that he was guilty, by what right did the Dutch act?" The treaty of 1619 ordained that international disputes should be referred to a mixed council of the two nations.

[2] The names of these Dutch vessels are given as they appear in the English records. I can find no trace of the action in De Jonge.—W. L. C.

[3] Lediard, p. 477.

[4] Cal. S. P. 1513–1616..122.

[5] Accounts of the fight; Weddell to E. I. Co. 25th April, 1625; and the narrative of one present, seemingly in the *James*, given in Lediard, 478.

could make use of their "frigates" to tow them into position, "which help we wanted." However, the *James*, with the help of her barge, got her broadside to bear and continued the fight. In the afternoon a breeze sprang up in favour of the Portuguese. The admiral and vice-admiral, being near the *James*, bore down on her, intending to board one on each side. When the *James* felt the wind she bore away with the wind on the quarter in order to separate the two ships somewhat. The Portuguese vice-admiral then altered course parallel with the *James*, but Weddell, as he drew up, hauled to the wind and weathered him. The admiral, seeing that the *James* would weather him too if he held his course,

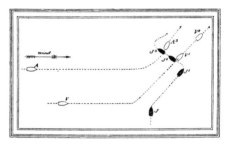

J. The *Royal James*.
A. The Portuguese admiral.
V. The Portuguese vice-admiral.
A V J. Position when the wind sprang up.
J¹ V¹. *Royal James* tacking to weather the Portuguese vice-admiral.

J³ A³. Portuguese admiral hove to, hoping that the *Royal James* would tall on board him. *Royal James*, passing under his stern, rakes him, and then puts helm up, and follows him.

PLAN OF WEDDELL AND BECKER'S ACTION WITH THE PORTUGUESE,
FEBRUARY 1ST, 1625.

hove to in hopes that the *James* would run aboard him; but Weddell, passing close under his stern, raked him fore and aft, and then stood after him.[1]

When the squadrons anchored, two leagues apart, the *James* had lost eight men killed, and in the *South Holland* Becker was dead. The 2nd was spent in refitting, and on the 3rd the English and Dutch, having the wind, ran down in line, the *Royal James* leading, with the *South Holland* next astern of her. As the *James* drew within range, the Portuguese opened fire, but she did not answer

---

[1] The account quoted by Lediard is not quite clear. The Portuguese admiral "put to stay" should mean that he went about; but this does not agree with the rest of the manœuvring, so that it seems necessary to take it to mean that he "put his mainsail (or foresail) a backstays."

till, passing between the leading ship and the admiral, she gave each a broadside and separated the leader from the rest of the fleet. The *Eagle*, Captain John Johnson, and the *Weasope* now came up and engaged this ship, thus preventing her from rejoining the squadron. The *Royal James* pressed on and engaged many ships in succession, but found that they would not stay by her. The other vessels, English and Dutch, made their way into the fight, and in the afternoon the *Eagle*, probably with the *Weasope*, returned from chasing the ship that had been separated from the enemy's squadron in the morning, and which, it is most likely, they had succeeded in dismasting. Soon after this the *James* backed her foresail within biscuit-throw of an enemy. Weddell called upon Johnson, who was coming up astern, to board on the enemy side, and although the *Eagle* failed him, Weddell remained alongside the Portuguese ship till she was a wreck.

When night fell neither side had given way. The Dutch had lost their admiral and the *Royal James* was much shattered, but the joint squadron had lost few spars and was quite ready to renew the engagement. In the enemy's fleet, on the contrary, but three ships had any topmasts left standing; and both their admiral and their vice-admiral had fallen.[1]

Weddell had meant to send a fireship against the Portuguese admiral, but, when the time came, she was not in her place. She had been chased by the "frigates," which forced Darby, her master, to fire her at a distance from the fleets. That night, whether brought by the tide or towed by the enemy's boats, she came burning among the English and Dutch, who slipped their cables and escaped without damage. On the 4th the enemy was chased into shallow water. It was judged unwise, however, to pursue too far, both for fear of running aground, and because the enemy might have batteries on the island of Lowrack. And, as they were "implacable, malicious and politick," in fact very good enemies, it was feared that they might chain three or four fireships together and send them out on the ebb.

Failing in their purpose, the allies resolved to look after their trade in Gombroon, and at the same time to refit. They did not sail again till the 13th, when the Portuguese, being once more in fighting trim, weighed to meet them, and by sunset were within saker shot.[2] That night it blew hard. A Portuguese ship carried

---

[1] Johnson to E. I. Co. 27th April, 1625.   [2] *I.e.* about half a mile.

away her mainmast. Till noon of the 14th, the allies found themselves encumbered with some merchantmen that had sailed from Gombroon with them, but the battle was raging again by two o'clock. Weddell now altered his tactics. On the second day he had fought against a succession of antagonists; but on this, the last day of the fight, he preferred to throw an accumulation of force upon one ship of the enemy. In pursuance of this plan, the *James* and the *Jonas* for a time poured a succession of broadsides into the Portuguese admiral; but after a while the fight became a duel between the flagships, and this continued till another galleon came to the relief of the Portuguese ship, and, pushing between her and the *James*, took Weddell's fire. This ship seems to have been the *San Sebastian*, wearing the rear-admiral's flag.

The action continued general till dusk. At nightfall the Portuguese were edging in with the Arabian coast, and the joint fleets were chasing them. After dark the pursuit was abandoned, both because ammunition was running short, and because English as well as Dutch were anxious to land their cargoes at Surat and get off the Malabar coast before the south-west monsoon.

Lediard[1] gives the following list of the Portuguese force and losses. It is said to have been drawn up by Peter Hillion, a Frenchman present on board Batellia's flagship.

Ship.	Guns.	Men.	Killed.	Commander.
1. *S. Francisco*, admiral . . .	48	350	38	Don Aliud Batellia.
2. *S. Francisco*, vice-admiral .	32	250	31	Francisco Burge.
3. *S. Sebastian*, rear-admiral .	40	400	20	Antonio Tela.
4. *S. Salvador*	24	250	41	Francisco de Suar.
5. *S. Jago*	22	200	83	Simon de Kintall.
6. *Trinidad*	22	250	243	Alva Botelia.
7. *S. Antonio*	22	200	22	Antonio Burallia.
8. *Miserere Cordium* . . .	22	200	3	Samuel Rodriguez Chava.

1. Had the admiral and two other officers killed.
2 and 4. Lost their captains.
5 and 7. Were unseaworthy and were lost soon after.
6. Was quite dismasted and was towed off by the rear-admiral.
Besides all which losses, every vessel is returned as having been more or less dismasted.

The English losses, as given in an official report[2] to the Company, were twenty-nine men killed, thirteen of whom were in the *James*, eleven in the *Jonas*, four in the *Star* and one in the *Eagle*.

[1] p. 482.   [2] Cal. S. P. E. Ind. 1513–1616..122.

The Dutch lost about the same number of men, but among them was Becker. The report also says that the *James* received 450 shot, some of them 27¼ inches in circumference,[1] and that the Portuguese lost 800 men, including, it was thought, their commander. Weddell, in reporting to the Company,[2] said that the enemy had sixteen[3] "frigates." It is not stated that these tried to board; it is indeed implied that they did not; but while they were engaged in towing, on February 1st, heavy loss must have fallen on them.

In this way it is just possible that the enemy lost 800 men. That this 800 includes wounded, or is a random guess, is far more likely. That the *Trinidad* was left with only seven men alive is absurd on the face of it. Yet, if she was the ship which the *Eagle* and *Weasope* engaged, and also if she was the ship mentioned as having been towed off, it is likely that she had suffered very heavily.

Before the English were firmly established in India there were many further fights; but of these the last one of any importance took place in this same year, 1625.

Early in October, 1625, there were two English and three Dutch ships[4] lying in the Swally, when a Portuguese squadron appeared off Surat. These ships did not put to sea to meet the enemy. In a letter written shortly afterwards to one of the East India Company[5] it was said, "There were four great galleons came from Lisbon and challenged the English and Dutch ships in Swally Road, but they refused." But while the Portuguese were still off the port, in company with a detachment of "frigates" from Goa, the *Palsgrave*, *Dolphin* and *Lion* arrived from England. Seeing the galleons, and thinking the ships in the Swally to be also Portuguese, the fresh English stood out to sea with a northerly wind. Their commanders, Blyth and Richard Swanley, decided on this course that the enemy might gain no addition of strength; that the "frigates" might be shaken off; and that, if the English ships sailed the better, they might go to Ormuz, which Rufrero's "frigate" squadron was blockading. But the English ships, foul from the long passage out and hampered by their cargo, were soon overtaken. At four o'clock the Portuguese admiral and vice-admiral came up with the *Lion* off Damaun. The wind, however, fell light and the enemy could not reach the *Palsgrave* and *Dolphin*. Expecting help from his con-

---

[1] *I.e.* 60-prs. *Vide* vol. I., 410, *supra*.   [3] Lediard says 32.
[2] April 27th, 1625.   [4] Cal. S. P. E. Ind. 1625–1629, p. xviii.
[5] Thos. Friday to Bell; Cal. S. P. E. Ind. 358.

sorts, Swanley, in spite of his lower deck guns being in the hold, shortened sail and stayed within musket shot of the enemy. But the other two ships held on their course. The *Lion* had already suffered severely, and at nightfall found herself boarded on both sides as well by the ships as by some "frigates" which the calm had allowed to creep up. By eleven that night Richard Swanley was dead and had been succeeded in the command by Henry Crosbey.

As the *Lion* could not keep her decks clear nor free herself from the ships alongside, she dropped anchor and let the tide take the enemy away. The ship, however, was not abandoned by the Portuguese, for fifty or sixty of them had been left on her poop and could not be dislodged. These had to be got rid of. Some barrels of gunpowder were placed in the round house and the enemy, together with the stern of the ship, were blown into the sea. Thinking that the *Lion* would be destroyed by fire, the Portuguese admiral passed on to engage the two other vessels. These had been already overtaken by the Portuguese ships which had not been delayed by the *Lion*. The fight lasted for more than twenty-four hours, and then at length the *Palsgrave* and *Dolphin* managed to disable and shake off their enemies.[1] Meanwhile the *Lion* refitted to the best of her power, and, being unable to reach her consorts or to help them in any way, shaped her course for Ormuz in accordance with the plan proposed on October 7th by Captain Blyth.

Arrived at Gombroon, she lay for some days landing cargo, refitting, watering, and mounting her heavy guns. On November 8th, Rufrero with eighteen or "twenty" frigates came down upon her from Ormuz. It was quite calm and the ship could not manœuvre; but, though the "frigates" avoided her broadside, she managed to sink four of them. So brisk a small-arm fire was kept up that she was forced to close her ports, upon which the enemy had no difficulty in setting fire to her. Her upper deck fell in and killed many of the crew. Of the rest twenty-seven, who had jumped overboard, were picked up, but the remnant, about forty in number, ended a most stubborn defence by blowing up the ship. Rufrero saved one of the men whom he had taken, and sent him to carry the news to the Company. The rest he beheaded.

For some time anxiety prevailed regarding the *Palsgrave* and *Dolphin*; but they returned to Surat[2] early in the following year.

[1] Cal. S. P. E. Ind. 328.   [2] *Ib.* 1625-1629..378.

In November the President at Surat spoke of the *Palsgrave* as likely to postpone her trading if she saw a chance of annoying the Portuguese.[1] There is no record that she did anything to atone for her bad conduct of October 7th, 1625.

Such in brief were the services that gave us foothold in India proper, to the ruin of the hopes of Portugal; such the Anglo-Dutch relations which sowed the seed of that ill-feeling that was destined to yield so bloody a harvest.

Whether the conclusion of the treaty with Spain was bought by Spanish gold scattered freely in the English court,[2] or whether James would have braved the opposition of his advisers for the sake of his desire for peace are questions that have no place here. The effect of the peace is certain. It gave to Spain breathing space in which to recover her strength, and thus robbed the Navy of the well-deserved right of bringing the quarrel to an honourable close. It also opened the door to that gross mismanagement which allowed our seas to become infested with pirates of all nations.

A great deal of trouble was given all round our coasts by purely native pirates; from Scotland and from Ireland numerous complaints were made, but, of all towns, Bristol seems to have suffered the most severely.[3] The reason of this is not far to seek. Not only was Bristol second to no city but London in wealth and trade, but also, lying far west, she was away from the protection, such as it was, afforded by the King's ships, and was nearer to the wilder parts of the kingdom where the pirates gathered.

Between 1604 and 1616 Sir William Monson was constantly employed as Admiral of the Narrow Seas, and during that period not the least important of his duties was the restraint of privateering and piracy.

In May, 1603, Captain George Baynard brought into Torbay a Portuguese prize, taken by him in virtue of his letters of marque, where he left her; but no sooner was he at sea again than a Dunquerque squadron under Derickson carried her off. Strong representations were made[4] for her restitution.

The orders which Monson received show that the King was aware of the growing evil; that he under-estimated the danger

---

[1] Kerridge to the Company, 29th November, 1626.

[2] Osborne, 'Traditional Memoirs,' pp. 3, 4; Lediard, p. 400.

[3] Cal. S. P. Dom. 1605, throughout.

[4] Cal. S. P. Dom., James I. xvii. 100.

appears from the frequency of pardons granted to pirates taken in
the Narrow Seas.[1] As soon as they realised that the Navy was to
be starved, many men who had so far cruised lawfully enough
against the Spaniard seem to have decided that there was no need
to let the peace drive them from their occupation. The King's
clemency confirmed them in this opinion ; and so bold did they
become that, in 1610, we find one of their number openly using
Lundy as his headquarters, and styling himself king of that
island.[2]

Monson appears to have done little to keep these men in check ;

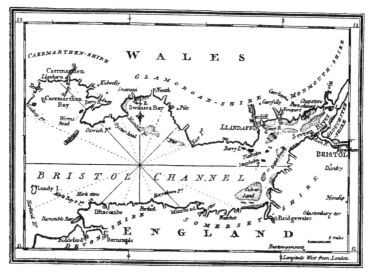

THE BRISTOL CHANNEL.

(From a chart published by Joyce Gold, 1816.)

but when we consider that he was at sea for a comparatively short
space each year, that much of his time was occupied in ferrying
ambassadors to and from the continent,[3] and the rest of it in more
or less fruitless attempts to convince the Dutch that James was
sovereign of the seas ; when we consider, in addition, that the King's

---

[1] Cal. S. P. Dom. April 20th, November 13th, December 20th, 1604, February 9th,
1605, etc.

[2] Cal. S. P. Dom. 17th April, 1610.

[3] Monson claimed that he was £1500 out of pocket, first and last, by this service
and that he could never recover any part of that sum. 'Tracts,' p. 250.

ships sailed notoriously badly, it will no longer seem strange that of all trades piracy was the most prosperous.

In 1614 however it was recognised that something must be done. Monson, in the *Lion*, with Sir Francis Howard in company, sailed from Margate for Leith on May 14th.[1] At Leith they had news of pirates to the north, so northward they went, and put themselves in communication with the Earl of Caithness, who told them of two pirates using those coasts. Of these, one gave himself up to Monson, saying that he wished to return to honest courses; the other, Clarke, was not to be found at Orkney, at Shetland, nor among the Hebrides.[2] Monson gave up the chase, and, using the knowledge of the pirate he had with him, steered for Broad Haven in Mayo. This place was the earthly paradise of the pirates. The whole population, men and women, found its profit in courting them, and it was but rarely that the law reached so far west. The English were advised to allow themselves to be mistaken for pirates, and to enjoy the hospitality of the local gentry. This they did, and after a few days spent in collecting evidence, declared themselves. Monson however was lenient; he profited by the consternation of the people to bind them to his interests; and with such good results that they helped him to ensnare a pirate ship which appeared on the coast a few days afterwards.

After hanging the officers of this ship, and ascertaining that there were no more pirates then on the coast, Monson pursued his voyage, and on August 10th reached the Downs without further capture. He himself claimed that the result of this cruise was the termination of piracy in home waters. That the respite was more than momentary is doubtful, for, only eighteen months later, James was petitioned to send two small ships to protect the northern fisheries.[3] The King's refusal was based on the ground of expense.

But, serious as were the ravages of these native pirates, the harm done to our trade by rovers from the Barbary ports was infinitely greater. While the Scots and Irishmen of the west coasts were for the most part "mean paltry rogues" that preyed on fishing

---

[1] 'Tracts,' p. 246. [2] *Ib.* 247.

[3] Cal. S. P. Dom., James I. lxxxvi. 58, 61. A little later still one of the charges in Buckingham's impeachment was that he had allowed the seas to be infested. Frankland, p. 153.

boats and small craft, the pirates from Tunis and Algier, from
Tangier and Sallee blockaded the trade routes in force and inflicted
enormous damage within the Straits and without.   In 1617 a
Turkish pirate was taken in the Thames.   For villages in England
and Wales, as well as on the Irish coast, to be raided, and their
inhabitants carried away to slavery, was no uncommon thing.[1]
In England all these rovers were called Turks ; that Sallee and
Tangier were not even nominally under the sway of the Sultan
was of no importance.

The pirate vessels were specially adapted for the work.   Prizes
taken from European nations, they had their half-decks and all
possible weight cut away.   To give the ships elasticity, many of
the knees were knocked out, and a high degree of speed was
attained, " like a man that is tight trussed and hath his doublet
buttoned, that by loos'ning it he is able to run the faster." [2]   The
weakening of the ships did not matter to the pirates, for they never
lacked prizes out of which to make more cruisers.   As it was their
practice to board, they did not carry many guns.   When pursued by
men-of-war they sought safety in flight.   Neither was there any
difficulty in raising a crew ; at Algier a ship could be manned in a
few minutes.

Ships thus equipped and manned sailed, with permission of
their Bey or governor, either singly or in squadrons.   In July, 1611,
Sir Ferdinando Gorges wrote that a Barbary fleet of forty ships,
manned by two thousand men, was at sea ;[3] and, in March, 1613,
Nottingham granted to the mayor of Exeter a commission to
cruise against them and keep what he could catch.   Other similar
commissions were granted.[4]

The consequence was that vessels trading to any distance were
heavily armed.   In fact, they sailed practically in the condition in
which they were hired out to the King when need arose.   Such a ship,
the *Dolphin* of London, Edward Nichols, master, mounting nineteen
heavy guns besides smaller pieces, fell in with a Turkish squadron
of five ships off Sardinia on 22nd January, 1617.[5]   The pirates
were all big ships, and their admiral was an English adventurer

[1] When one of our cruisers, unless she chanced to be a King's ship, did capture a
pirate, she too made her profit by selling her captives for slaves.

[2] Monson, 'Tracts,' p. 301.

[3] S. P. Dom., James I. lxv. 16.

[4] *Ib.* ; Cal. lxxii. 93, and lxxxvi. 101.

[5] Lediard, p. 440, quoting an account published by Nichols.

who sailed under the name of Walsyngham,[1] which presumably was not his own. Of the other captains also two were Englishmen. The admiral's ship was the first into action, and boarded, after a heavy cannonade. Beaten off, she drew out of the fight to stop her leaks. Two more ships closed, exchanged broadsides and boarded. A pirate going aloft to strike the *Dolphin's* flag was shot by the steward, the decks were cleared and these ships also drew off. Of the two last ships, one could not get to close quarters before she was crippled by the *Dolphin's* guns, but the other boarded. Again the English retired into their close fights[2] and cleared their decks with murderers;[3] but the pirates fired the ship. No further attempt was made, and the *Dolphin*, after getting the fire under, put into the Sardinian shore to bury her dead and refit. Of a total crew of thirty-eight men and boys, she had seven killed and ten wounded, of whom four afterwards died. The ship herself was sound enough to ride out a heavy gale on the 25th, and it is satisfactory to know that she reached the Thames in safety.

In October of the same year news reached England that the homeward bound Newfoundland fishing fleet had been met by thirty Turkish "frigates," and had lost seven of its number.[4] It was for a time supposed that Sir Richard Hawkyns[5] was among those lost, but this proved to be a false report.

So serious was the evil that the king agreed that something must be done. An estimate of the cost of fitting out four ships, to be supplemented by eight more from the merchants, was formed.[6] The expedition was to be aided by Holland, and would, it was thought, prove sufficient "if well commanded." But news reached England that Spain was fitting out a vast armament, and fresh considerations arose.

It was believed in England that Philip might attack Ireland.

---

[1] There were many of these renegades, the most notorious being Ward, Sir Francis Verney, and the Dutchman Dansker, Gard. iii. 65. Though they were held in special detestation, this man Walsyngham seems to have returned to England and made his peace. He commanded a fireship in the Algier Expedition of 1620, and two years later was sent to the Tower for conspiring to seize the *Dreadnought* and return to piracy. S. P. Dom. 17th April, 1622.

[2] Barricaded and loopholed strongholds under the poop and forecastle.—W. L. C.

[3] Light guns, often charged with langridge.—W. L. C.

[4] Cal. S. P. Dom., James I. xc. October 17th.

[5] The son of John Hawkyns, and the same man who had commanded the *Swallow* against the Armada.

[6] Cal. S. P. Dom., James I. civ. 145.

In Venice the folk made sure that the fleet, with its 40,000 troops, was to be used against them. But avowedly the destination of the force was Algier, and it is not impossible that it was so in reality.[1] In 1617, Monson had written his views on the suppression of piracy, and had suggested the co-operation of England with Spain and Holland.[2] It is possible that his opinions may have had some influence on the turn of affairs.

James immediately offered to co-operate against the pirates, and hinted that the Dutch also would help. Meanwhile the estimate for the English expedition was largely increased and ship-money was levied on the principal ports to pay the cost.[3] Thus James would be ready in any event; either to deal with the Spaniards if their nominal object were a pretence, or to take in hand seriously the repression of piracy. For once his policy was successful. The Dutch refused to agree to his proposal, but the Spanish preparations were discontinued. And it was no small advantage to him that he had successfully revived an old method of levying money.

Meanwhile the Duke of Buckingham became Lord High Admiral. Under his guidance no high-sounding project was likely to be abandoned. The fleet was to be strong enough to do the work without co-operation, and the objective was to be Algier. Monson had written that 9000 tons of shipping and three thousand six hundred seamen would be enough to destroy the whole of the pirate resources.[4] That with over 6000 tons and two thousand five hundred men he failed to destroy one town out of four is little to the credit of Sir Robert Mansell.

Mansell's commission was dated June 6th, 1620 ;[5] his Vice-Admiral was Sir Richard Hawkyns, the Vice-Admiral of Devon ; his Rear-Admiral, Sir Thomas Button. There was some friction about these appointments. Button had hoped to be second in command,[6] but Mansell pointed out that the post had been offered to Hawkyns

---

[1] 'Cabala,' i. 206, 207 ; Gardiner, iii. 287.

[2] 'Tracts,' p. 250.

[3] Gardiner, iii. 288. The sums assessed in a total of £48,500 included—

London	. . .	£40,000.	Hull	. . . .	£500.
Bristol	. . .	2,500.	Weymouth	. .	450.
Exeter	. . . ⎫		Southampton	. . ⎫	
Plymouth	. . ⎬	1,000 each.	Newcastle	. . ⎬	300 each.
Dartmouth	. . ⎭		Cinque Ports	. .	200.
Barnstaple	. .	500.		and other small sums.	

[4] 'Tracts,' p. 250.   [5] 'Fœdera,' vii. iii. 165.   [6] 'Cabala,' i. 140 (2).

in the belief that Button would not be able to leave the command on the west coast of Ireland to which he had succeeded on Monson's removal in January, 1616. The fleet was very late in starting. It was October 22nd before it left Plymouth.[1]

With Mansell in this expedition there were [2]—

HIS MAJESTY'S SHIPS (6).

Ships.	Tons.	Guns.	Men.	Commanders.
1. *Lion*, Admiral	600	40	250	Sir Robert Mansell.
2. *Vanguard*, Vice-Admiral .	660	40	250	Sir Richard Hawkyns.
3. *Rainbow*, Rear-Admiral .	660	40	250	Sir Thomas Button.
4. *Constant Reformation* . .	660	40	250	Arthur Mainwaring.
5. *Antelope*	400	34	160	Sir Henry Palmer.
6. *Convertine*	500	36	220	Thomas Love.

MERCHANT SHIPS (12).

7. *Golden Phœnix*	300	24	120	Samuel Argall.
8. *Samuel*	300	22	120	Christopher Harris.
9. *Marygold*	260	21	100	Sir John Fearn.
10. *Zouche Phœnix*	280	26	120	John Penington.
11. *Barbary*	200	18	80	Thomas Porter.
12. *Centurion*.	200	22	100	Sir Francis Tanfield.
13. *Primrose*	180	18	80	Sir John Hamden.
14. *Hercules*	300	24	120	Eusaby Cave.
15. *Neptune*	280	21	120	Robert Haughton.
16. *Bonaventure*	260	23	110	John Chidley.
17. *Restore*	130	12	50	George Raymond.
18. *Marmaduke*	100	12	50	Thomas Harbert.

Passing down the Spanish coast, the fleet saluted the various towns, for even then it was hoped that some help might be forthcoming from Spain ;[3] but they heard no news of any. The Admiral divided his fleet into its three squadrons; he himself held on about six leagues from the shore, the Vice-Admiral was three leagues outside him on his bow, and the Rear-Admiral three leagues inside him and on his quarter. They made no prize however, and on December 7th anchored at Algier.

In view of the fact that Mansell subsequently accounted for his failure by pointing out that his commission made him uncertain whether to adopt peaceful or warlike methods,[4] it is well to

---

[1] A pamphlet published 1621 and preserved, with MS. notes by Coke, in S. P. Dom., James I. cxxii. 106.

[2] S. P. Dom., James I. cxxii. 106.   [3] 'Tracts,' p. 257.   [4] *Ib.*

notice that he tried both and failed in both. He began by negotiating for the release of prisoners. The Dey was polite, offered
refreshments, admitted that he had forty captives, whom he gave
up, but could not be persuaded to treat seriously. In the
meantime the pirates continued to bring in prizes before Mansell's
very eyes. On 13th December six Spanish ships arrived in pursuit
of some pirates, and exchanged a few shots with the town; but
they did not join the English, who sailed on the 17th. Until
they went back to Algier the English passed most of their time
in port, at Malaga, Majorca or Alicant. Occasionally Turkish
vessels were pursued, more for the sake of appearance than with
any hope of success. On the night of January 4th, eight or nine
pirate ships fell amongst the English fleet; but, even so, none
were taken. On the 6th, the Rear-Admiral's squadron pursued two
ships, but returned unsuccessful on the 8th to Alicant, where the
fleet was lying. On February 7th, the fleet fell in with the Admiral
of Zeeland with seven men-of-war. He told Mansell that his
entire fleet was twenty-two strong, but he would not co-operate.
Soon afterwards the English Admiral decided to fit out fireships
in readiness and then go to Algier to burn the ships within the
mole. Accordingly he returned to Alicant with his whole fleet,
which had been augmented on February 26th by the *Spy*, 18,
Captain Edward Giles, and the *Mercury*, 20, Captain Phineas Pett.
There he bought three brigantines rowing nine oars a side, and hired
a polacca of 120 tons. The former he converted into fireships; and
he did the same with some spare boats and two small Turkish
vessels which he had managed to secure.

On the last day of May the fleet was drawn up off Algier, closing
the entrance.[1] The Dey seems to have decided that his enemies
would not attack the port. They had tried to negotiate on their
former visit; negotiation, he probably believed, was their aim now.
Such being his attitude, a surprise seemed easy. Twice the attempt
was foiled by a calm. The final attack was made on June 3rd. The
boats had nearly reached the mole when the wind fell and the
moon shone out brightly. It was too late to draw off. They were
seen, but pulled in as fast as they could. Most of the pirate crews
were on shore, so that the English were able to fire the ships in
many places. A musketry fire was opened on them, but they got off
with little loss. That the shipping was not destroyed was due, said

---

[1] Coke's note here is: " Why was not this done the first time ? "

Mansell, to the calm, to an unfortunate shower, and to a sally of
"the cowardly Turks."[1] Probably an undue eagerness to be gone
on the part of the boats had as much to do with it. A few ships
put out from the mole. One was forced ashore, and another was
sunk by the *Hercules* and *Bonaventure*. The only prize was a "fly-
boat" taken in the bay.[2]

A council of war decided that nothing more could be done; and
the fleet sailed next day. A few days later a merchant vessel, with
warlike stores for Algier, was taken. This was the only capture
of any importance, though it was learnt afterwards that, by sailing
when they did, the English missed a squadron of pirates and prizes
that put in to Algier the night after they had left it. On the 9th
the fleet returned to Algier; but a boom had been made and boats
were continually rowing guard. If they had failed when there were
none of these obstacles, argued the council, they could not succeed
in the face of them. Again the fleet left Algier. Four ships were
detached to return home, and at the last minute four more were
added as being unserviceable. There is no need to follow the fortunes
of the remaining twelve; they did nothing, and sailed for England
soon after the others.

The whole affair was carried out in a half-hearted manner.
There was no striving to overcome difficulties; there was not even
any bombardment. What most struck Monson was that the ships
"besides their coming and going, spent not forty days at sea, but
retired into harbour, where the pirates could find them; but not
they the pirates."[3] As no English ship could catch a pirate at sea,
it is not clear where the point of his argument lay. The lamentable
fact was that nothing had been done to check the ravages on our
trade. During the following year about thirty-five English and
Scots ships were taken.[4]

The only further action taken by James in the matter was to
proclaim against the export of arms to Tunis and Algier.[5] Charles
consequently found matters as bad as ever, Sallee rovers being in
the Channel in 1625.[6] He had work enough for his fleet, and could
only send out Captain John Harrison in the *Rainbow* to negotiate
an exchange of prisoners[7] with the Barbary States. Two years

[1] 'Cabala,' i. 140; Mansell to the Duke.
[2] *Ib.*
[3] 'Tracts,' p. 257.
[4] Burchett, 368; Lediard, 466.
[5] Rushworth, VII. iv. 59.
[6] Gardiner, v. 364, 424.
[7] 'Fœdera,' VIII. ii. 123.

later, a proclamation was issued to restrain loyal subjects from acting in any way against Algier, Tunis, Sallee, or Tetuan,[1] but it was followed in the next year by a warrant of contrary effect.[2] This put the matter on its old footing, and the cruising continued with as much, or as little, result as before.

All of importance that was done was pacific. William Rainborow, in 1637, was sent to Sallee with six ships. He blockaded the port and demanded that captives should be given up to him. The King of Marocco found it inconvenient to resist at that time, for he was engaged in a civil war. He therefore agreed to buy Rainborow's neutrality by the delivery of two hundred and seventy-one English captives.[3] This successful mission was followed in December, 1638, by the appointment of William Woodhouse to be consul at Tunis.[4]

In spite of our peculiar relations with the Dutch in the East Indies, there was no serious threat of a rupture in Europe. Friction constantly arose in matters of piracy and Dunquerque privateering, but the defensive league of 1608 between England and the States,[5] and the Truce of Antwerp, so far restrained the Dunquerquers, that for some years English ships in the Narrow Seas saw little service.

In June, 1611, Lady Arabella Stuart tried to escape to France. She had left Dover twenty-four hours before Monson received orders to follow; but, having met with baffling winds, she was overtaken within four miles of Calais.

In 1612 there seemed to be for a time a threat of a war with Spain. We had driven the Spaniards from the whale fisheries and had claimed exclusive rights. The Spaniards made ready to attack Virginia, but, inspired by a due appreciation of their own weakness and a hope that the colony would die out, they abandoned the project.[6] From that time friction increased with Spain in proportion as matters ran more smoothly with Holland. Such Dutch pirates as were brought in were given up to Holland,[7] whereas in 1616 Rich accepted a commission from the Duke of Savoy to cruise against the Spaniards. Rich's proceedings, both in that year and in 1618, were in no whit better than those of the Elizabethan seamen whose methods had been so detestable to James;[8]

---

[1] 'Fœdera,' VIII. iii. 4.
[2] *Ib.* 64, 141, 144.
[3] Gardiner, viii. 270.
[4] Thurloe, S. P. I. 2.

[5] 'Fœdera,' VII. ii. 160.
[6] Gardiner, ii. 164.
[7] Cal. S. P. Dom., James I. lxxiv. 18.
[8] 'Fœdera,' VII. iii. 64.

and not the least disgraceful page in the King's history is that Rich passed unpunished while Ralegh, who, in spite of his desire to waylay the Mexico fleet,[1] was guilty of no aggression, was hurried to the block.

In 1618 one of the Dutch ships which had acted against Courthope in the Bandas was in the Channel. Application was made for leave to take her by way of reprisals, but before anything could be done she was safe in port. In that same year, Argall, Governor of Virginia, heard news of a French settlement to the north of New England. Arrived there, he found a ship lying in front of a fort, and took both.[2] Possibly this breach of the peace was one of the reasons for his recall in 1619.

In December, 1621, the commission on East India differences was at high words, and Oxford, then Admiral of the Narrow Seas,[3] was ordered to chase homeward-bound East Indiamen. The Dutch were brought to their senses, but demanded Oxford's recall,[4] which James was weak enough to grant.

Meanwhile the Truce of Antwerp ended and the Dutch began to suffer again from the Dunquerquers. In September, 1622, they blockaded two of these ships in Leith and Aberdeen, and in April, 1623, two ships had to be sent to prevent a Dutch attack on the fugitives while lying in the King's waters. As Denbigh[5] had gone with ten ships to bring home Prince Charles from Spain, the senior officer in the Downs, and the man on whom this duty fell, was Captain Best.[6] For a time it seemed that his mission would be successful. But the ship at Leith tried to escape at night and ran aground. The Dutch shot her to pieces where she lay, and, in spite of protests, burnt the wreck.

Worse followed. The ship in Aberdeen was to be escorted back to Dunquerque by Best and the Dutch. An order from the States-General was to cause the blockading squadron off Dunquerque to let her pass unharmed. This plan miscarried through the folly of the Dunquerque captain, who crowded sail for a while as if to escape, and then hove to to wait for the convoy. The Dutch came up first

---

[1] Gardiner, iii. 48. Rohan had offered to help him with ships if he would guarantee an attack on this fleet. Cal. S. P. Dom., James I. ciii. 16.

[2] Lediard, p. 455.　　　　　　　　　　　　　[3] 'Fœdera,' VII. iii. 221.

[4] Gardiner, iv. 274.

[5] William Fielding, first Earl of Denbigh.

[6] Gardiner, v. 81. Best was the man who had defeated the Portuguese off Surat in 1612. In 1623 he was captain of the *Garland*.

and opened a heavy fire, and when Best in turn arrived he fired on the Dutch, who drew out of range. The *Garland* and her charge anchored in the Downs, the Dutch off the South Foreland. Choosing a dark night, Best dropped down among the latter and drove them out. For this work Best was treated as Oxford had been treated before him. He was superseded by Sir Richard Bingley, who carried the ship in dispute to Flanders.

But the Pacific reign of James was nearly at end, and the time was drawing on when Buckingham's adventurous projects would be allowed free scope. In March, 1624, Kensington wrote to the Duke that France was ready to enter into an alliance against Philip,[1] and in the following month an attack on the Spaniards in the Gulf of Mexico was proposed to Buckingham.[2]

In May orders were given to equip twelve ships and thirty merchant vessels. Spain too was arming. In June a squadron of four Spanish ships, bound to Spain from Dunquerque, was blockaded in the Downs by a Dutch fleet, and James refused to interfere. He stood well with the Dutch at that time, and was hoping for help from them in the coming quarrel with Spain. The four Spaniards chose heavy weather for their escape; but while three got clear, the fourth blew up together with her opponent.[3] Before, however, the war with Spain broke out, there was interposed an incident which was in no small degree responsible for the disastrous war against France.

Shortly before his death, James entered into an agreement[4] by which the *Vanguard*, Captain John Penington, of the Royal Navy, together with the *Great Neptune*, Captain Sir Ferdinando Gorges, and six other armed merchant ships were to be put at the disposal of the King of France, to use against any enemy, save only England and Scotland. The history of this agreement is somewhat obscure;[5] but as in 1617 Ralegh had put forward a scheme for the joint action of an English fleet and a French army against Genoa, a state bound by the closest ties to Spain; and, as a Franco-Savoyard army was now preparing to attack Genoa and needed the co-operation of ships, which both England and Holland had agreed to supply, there can be no doubt that the original intention

---

[1] 'Cabala,' i. 282.   [2] *Ib.* 343.   [3] Gardiner, v. 245.

[4] That the ships were specified appears from S. P. Dom., James, clxxxv. 99, a letter from Conway directing the Clerk of the Signet to draw up a warrant for the delivery to France of the ships named.

[5] Gardiner, v. 301.

was to reduce Genoa. It was, doubtless, hoped that in the following year the French would help Buckingham in an attack on the Spanish coast; that the Plate fleet would be captured, and that Spain would cease to be a power in Europe.

But these fond hopes were shattered when Soubise sailed into the harbour of Blavet in December, 1624, and, by capturing six of Louis's ships, lighted once more the torch of civil war in France.

ADMIRAL SIR JOHN PENINGTON, KT.

[From an anonymous print. The face bears a striking resemblance to that in a well authenticated contemporary portrait belonging to Mrs. W. Willes.]

Louis had few ships, but James had been prepared to lend him eight. The bargain might still stand, and Louis, instead of employing them against Genoa, might use the ships against his unruly subjects. Buckingham offered no objection to this. Shortly afterwards James died, though not before he had approved, verbally,[1]

[1] Gardiner, v. 306.

the altered scheme. Charles, his successor, was forced to stay the preparations against Spain for want of money.

With regard to Penington's ships, there was great difficulty in persuading their captains to admit the French.[1] They were afraid that they should lose the ships, and pointed out that they had no guarantee for their value.[2] The duplicity was on the part of Buckingham. The French intended to put on board as many soldiers as the ships would carry, and to keep in the vessels only as many English as would serve to navigate them. All this the Duke could not allow to be known while the ships were still in England. Had the design leaked out, the captains would never have sailed. As it was, Penington did not reach Dieppe[3] until June 13th, although the ships had been ready since April, the captains, notably Gorges, having hung back. Arrived at Dieppe, the English refused to admit the great numbers of soldiers the French proposed to embark. They must, said they, be masters in their own ships. Penington wrote to the Duke[4] to represent this objection, and added that the English would not be content unless it was guaranteed that on service they should remain in one squadron under his—Penington's—command. Shortly afterwards, alleging that the weather was too stormy to allow him to lie longer in an open road, he put back to the English coast. Meanwhile Richelieu assured Buckingham that a show of force at La Rochelle would be all that was needed; and Buckingham, always ready to believe the truth of what he wished to be true, seems to have been convinced. Penington received orders to go to Dieppe and there surrender the ships. He asked to be superseded, but was privately informed that the government did not really wish the ships to be given up. Accordingly he proceeded to Dieppe, prepared to allow his crews to mutiny,·if need be, to prevent the delivery of the ships.[5] Charles was, it was pretended, not eager for the delivery, and it was suggested that the device of a mutiny would serve, in case the French should fail to make such a mistake as would justify the King in breaking off the matter. The mutiny followed, and the sailors brought the ships home about July 28th. But Penington at length received a definite warrant for the delivery.

---

[1] The delivery of the ships was made one of the charges against Buckingham, and on that charge being delivered the whole story appeared. Frankland, 'Annals,' 161–166; Granville Penn, i. 30, *sqq.*

[2] The French removed this difficulty by giving ample security.

[3] Gardiner, v. 380, *sqq.*   [4] 'Cabala,' i. 150.   [5] Gardiner, v. 383.

The King was said to have satisfied himself that, after all, the ships would be used against the King of Spain or his allies,[1] and Penington was to hand over the *Vanguard*, and to force the others to obey, " even unto sinking." He returned to Dieppe on August 3rd, and surrendered, but not until he had found it necessary to fire on the merchant ships, whose masters obeyed at last, all save Gorges, who carried his ship back to England. The conduct of Gorges was more to English taste than Penington's. Gorges was not punished for his disobedience, but Penington's obedience invested him with the character of being over deeply attached to the King's schemes ; and this was not to his advantage in after years. Of the English crews, but one man served with the French against La Rochelle ; the rest returned to England with Penington. The ships were used in the autumn against La Rochelle. On September 5th, Soubise was defeated off the town and driven for refuge to an English port: " as for the *Vanguard*, she mowed them down like grass." The indignation in England was allayed by the return of the ships in the following summer.

Meanwhile Buckingham's ambition drove him to advance £30,000 to complete the equipment of the Spanish armament. The fleet seems to have been thus composed :—

The Admiral's Squadron.

1. *Anne Royal* . . Viscount Wimbledon . . . . . Capt. Sir Thomas Love.
2. *St. Andrew* . . Lord Denbigh, Vice-Admiral . . . „ Watts.
3. *Convertine* . . Sir W. St. Leger, Rear-Admiral . . „ (Thomas) Porter.

With four groups of transports mounting each ten or twelve guns, and carrying in all four regiments of one thousand men. Also one victualler. In all, thirty ships.

The Vice-Admiral's Squadron.

1. *Swiftsure* . . . Earl of Essex, Admiral . . . . Capt. Sir S. Argall.
2. *St. George* . . Lord Valentia, Vice-Admiral . . . „ Gilbert.
3. *Constant Refor-*} Lord de la Warr, Rear-Admiral . . „ Greeves.
mation . . .

With four similar groups of transports, of which, however, one carried no troops. In all, twenty-nine ships.

The Rear-Admiral's Squadron.

1. *Lion* . . . . Sir Francis Steward, Admiral . . Capt. (Mitchell).
2. *Rainbow* . . . Lord Cromwell, Vice-Admiral . . „ (John) Chidley.
3. *Bonaventure* . . Sir Henry Palmer, Rear-Admiral . „ (Collins).

With four groups similar to those of the vice-admiral's squadron. In all, thirty ships.

---

[1] S. P. Dom., Charles I. iv. 136, 137.

There went in addition to these the *Assurance, Dreadnought, Mary Rose*, and the "pinnace" *Mercury*. The *Prince Royal* is entered at the end of the latest lists, but in none which are official. It may be concluded that it was intended that she should sail, but that she could not be made ready for sea in time.[1]

The Dutch also agreed to send twenty ships,[2] so that the total of the fleet rose to well over a hundred sail. As a soldier, Wimbledon was a man of some note, but he had never held any high command, and was moreover quite ignorant of sea warfare. The appointment was made by Buckingham, who had received a commission[3] empowering him to set forth the whole of the enterprise.

By the terms of his commission Wimbledon's main object was to be the destruction of Spanish shipping. The taking of a town was not directly contemplated, save so far as it might conduce to the first-named purpose, or might serve to make the expedition pay for itself. Whether the Plate fleet was to be dealt with or not was to be at Wimbledon's discretion.

Mismanagement appeared from the first. The troops were raw levies, and of a nominal two thousand brought from the Low Countries, five hundred never appeared. The fleet was as bad. The bulk of it was composed of merchant ships of ten or twelve guns, commanded by their own captains,[4] men who made it their chief study how to avoid danger. In short, the force was worthy of no confidence, and its leader had none in it.

A Dunquerque squadron was known to be on the Spanish coast. Buckingham gave orders for it to be sought and taken.[5] But when they fell in with an enemy, the English ships did not attack.

After the fleet had sailed, it was found that it had not all its ammunition on board,[6] and that many of the Dutch ships had not joined. The blame was Buckingham's; but not less fatal was the utter incapacity of Wimbledon. Though he sailed with no proclaimed destination, Wimbledon called no council of war till Finisterre had been rounded; and thus such ships as parted company in the Bay knew not where to rejoin; and four did not reach Cadiz until the expedition was leaving it.

It had been half intended to go to San Lucar, but off the Spanish

---

[1] S. P. Dom., Charles I. vii. 47–53.

[2] Sixteen ships were actually sent, under Lieut.-Admiral Willem de Zoete, better known as Haultain, who was later joined by other craft.—W. L. C.

[3] 'Fœdera,' VIII. i. 129.   [5] *Ib.* vi. 17.

[4] Cal. S. P. Dom., Charles I. ii. 106.   [6] *Ib.* vii. 10.

coast the captains remembered, as they might have done in England, that the bar would be impassable. Gibraltar was suggested, but Wimbledon was afraid of being shut up in the Straits, and of not being able to get out in time to intercept the Plate fleet. Finally, Argall suggested St. Mary Port,[1] where the landing was easy, and from which St. Lucar might be reached. The fleet accordingly entered Cadiz Bay, the *Swiftsure* leading. Seeing a crowd of ships

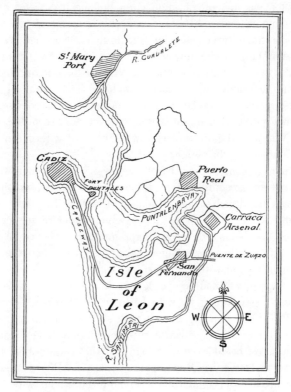

CHART OF CADIZ HARBOUR.

and galleys under the walls of Cadiz, Essex pushed forward to the attack. Not realising that he was unsupported, the Spanish ships fled into the inner harbour, and Essex was recalled.

The fleet anchored off St. Mary Port, and a few Dutch ships and merchantmen were told off to bombard Fort Puntal, which protected the inner harbour. Wimbledon went to bed. In the morning

[1] Gardiner, vi. 15.

he found that the merchantmen had kept out of danger, and that the Dutch had lost two ships. When such conduct passed unpunished, it was easy to foresee what support could be counted on. Wimbledon gave further orders; the troops landed; Sir John Burgh summoned the fort, and, fortunately, it surrendered :—fortunately, because, as afterwards appeared, the troops had not even brought scaling-ladders ashore.

No attempt had been made to pursue the ships up the harbour. Wimbledon had been told that there was not enough water, and had asked no further. He did not consider that Drake had sailed into the harbour before him, and that he might have passed up, as Drake had passed, with the lead going on both sides. Throughout he ignored his commission. Instead of burning the Spanish ships, fifty-nine sail in all,[1] as he had been ordered, he landed troops and marched towards Zuazo bridge.[2] Arrived there he found that his troops had no food — none had been landed — and he stupidly marched them into the village where was stored the wine for the West India fleets. The whole army at once drank itself into a state of madness, and all that Wimbledon could do was to decide that the bridge was not worth holding, or even destroying, and to march his troops back again. Yet this bridge Essex, in 1596, had decided must be held by any one who would hold the town,[3] for it was the only means of access from the mainland to Leon Island, on which Cadiz lies. All that Wimbledon did was, to take Fort Puntal and evacuate it, to take the bridge and abandon it, and to capture a few boats from St. Mary Port to replace the long boats which had been lost on the rough passage out.

It was now decided to look for the Plate fleet, and, on November 4th, Wimbledon's squadrons took up their positions in a long line stretching south from Cape St. Vincent. They might have saved themselves the trouble had they known that the fleet had taken the southern route and, creeping up in shore, had reached Cadiz two days after the English had left it.

Wimbledon had intended to cruise till the 20th, but on the 16th he was persuaded to bear up for England. His ships were foul and leaking, the crews were dying fast. Burchett[4] tells a story that,

[1] 'Tracts,' p. 273.
[2] Called the bridge of Suaco, in vol. I. 514, 515.
[3] 'Tracts,' p. 273.
[4] Bk. III. Chap. xviii.

when he found a plague breaking out on board some of the ships, Wimbledon caused the sick to be scattered through the fleet, two to each ship, presumably to prevent any of the ships from being short-handed. It is almost incredible that this was done, nor is the tale corroborated. What is certain is that the ships were too weak to make England. The *Anne Royal* put into Kingsale, and landed one hundred and sixty sick. She had already buried one hundred and thirty men,[1] and many other ships had suffered in a like proportion.

Recriminations followed, of course.[2] A series of charges against Wimbledon was laid upon the council table. But it was to Buckingham's interest that no serious investigation should take place, and so the matter was hushed up.

On October 13th, while the fleet was still away, a gale had scattered the Dutch blockading squadron, and twenty-two Dunquerquers had slipped out. The blow fell on the Dutch fishing-fleets, and Buckingham hastened to improve the opportunity by suggesting an Anglo-Dutch attack on Dunquerque; but he found the Prince of Orange less ready than himself to begin a siege in November.

Many causes combined to bring on the war with France, but the two chief were the affair of Penington's ships, and a cruise made by Argall in September, 1625. Argall had been sent out against the pirates, but had returned with a string of French prizes[3] which he charged with carrying contraband of war to the Spanish Nether-lands. It so happened that the King needed money badly. These prizes were, therefore, sold before they had been legally condemned. Among them was the *St. Peter*, of Le Hâvre, a ship that was eventually added to the English Navy. There was an immediate outcry in France; reprisals were made, and Charles was obliged to see the wisdom of restoring the *St. Peter*. But Soubise[4] was in an English port, and his presence reminded Charles of the help which he had given against La Rochelle. To repair the hurt, he determined to relieve the town, and to demand the immediate restoration of the ships. As a first step, the *St. Peter*[5] was re-seized

---

[1] Out of a crew of three hundred and fifty or four hundred.

[2] 'Cabala,' i. 135.

[3] Gardiner, vi. 40.

[4] Soubise had lately been cruising against Spain with letters of marque from Buckingham.

[5] She, and another prize made in 1625, figure as the *St. Claude* and *St. Denis* in the list on p. 10.

before she had left England. A quarrel would, no doubt, have followed, had not a pacification between Louis and La Rochelle been agreed upon. For long the negotiations went on, but it was Charles who stood in the way of peace. His nature would admit of no compromise ; concession must always come from his opponent.

Meanwhile a fleet of thirty-nine sail was preparing for Lord Willoughby, who was to remedy the failure of the year before on the Spanish coast.[1] It was with the utmost difficulty that money could be found to equip the fleet for sea. When it did sail, in October, it was driven back by a storm and did not put to sea again. The only success won against Spain was when Warwick[2] with three ships scattered a fleet of transports bound for Dunquerque with troops. That year, too, Lord Denbigh brought in some valuable French seizures, and so gave occasion for the arrest of the whole of the English wine fleet in France.

Penington was at the time Admiral in the Narrow Seas ; and, the French king being said to have ships in Le Hâvre, Penington was ordered to destroy them. A cruise was undertaken with fifteen ships, assessed on the merchants of London. "Very mean things," Penington thought them; but Le Hâvre proved to be empty. When ordered to sea again the crews grew mutinous,[3] but a few fortunate prizes gave money to pay the men for a short time and the outlook improved.

Charles had deliberately forced the war upon Louis ; and now another armament was made ready. It consisted of the following King's ships :—[4]

Triumph	Admiral the Duke of Buckingham .	Capt. Sir John Watts.
Repulse	Vice-Admiral Lord Lindsey . . .	„ Thomas Best.
Vanguard . . .	..	„ Sir John Burgh.[5]
Victory	Rear-Admiral Lord Harvey . . .	„ Thomas Kettleby.
Rainbow	..	„ John Weddell.
Warspite . . .	..	„ Thomas Porter.
Nonsuch	..	„ Sir Allen Apsley.
Esperance . . .	..	„ Shipworth.
Lion	..	„ John Penington.
and six small craft.		

---

[1] 'Fœdera,' VIII. ii. 83.

[2] 'Col. Rostr.' p. 82.

[3] They had shipped for three months. This period, they claimed, had expired ; and they refused to sail save for the Downs.

[4] S. P. Dom. lvi. 87, 88.   [5] Commanding the troops.

The fifty merchant ships that went as transports included the *St. Peter*, of Le Hâvre, and three other French prizes. In addition, a squadron of ten Dutch ships sailed with the fleet.

On June 27th, 1627, the fleet left Stokes Bay with a fresh east wind. As it began by chasing Dunquerquers, it was carried far to leeward of the French coast, and, as a result, reached Rhé in two detachments, the earlier of which was not strong enough to attack without the other, but served very well to put the French on their guard.[1] Moreover, there had sailed from Plymouth at the same time as the English fleet, a Dutchman. This ship reached Rhé some days in advance of Buckingham, and warned the French of the sailing of the English fleet, and was able to give particulars.

A consideration of the map will show the mistakes made in this miserable campaign. To begin with, Soubise had advised the English to land in Oleron, which was unfortified.[2] It would have served their purpose as well as Rhé, and by taking it they would have had a base to work from. But Buckingham's commission,[3] of course, had made him absolute, and he seems to have understood that he was above the advice, as well as the orders, of his associates. Second under Buckingham was the commander of the troops, Sir John Burgh.

On the night of the arrival,[4] the *Convertine* and the *Abraham*, threw a few shot into the small fort of La Prée. On the next day the landing of the troops began at the easternmost end of the island. St. Martin's was not ready to resist an attack, but no attempt was made upon it till it had had time to get in such stores and provisions as were to be had.

Meanwhile it had been ascertained that the Rochellers would not co-operate with the English until the latter should have made themselves masters of the island.

As our troops landed, a charge of French threw them into confusion, and many men were drowned. However, the troops rallied and drove off the enemy. The ships had been ordered to cover the landing with their guns, but it does not appear that their fire had any great effect.

On the 15th, the troops began their march along the island. Instead of attempting the little fort of La Prée, they took a

---

[1] 'Tracts,' pp. 276, 277.   [2] Burchett.   [3] 'Fœdera,' VIII. ii. 175.
[4] Account of the operations at Rhé in Lord Lansdowne's works, ii. 316, *sqq.*, and Gardiner, vol. v. ch. lx.

circuitous route inland. This blunder was most serious; for the fort then could not have been held; but the enemy immediately strengthened it. It was left to them without dispute, and from it they commanded the road running east from St. Martin's to the place where the troops had landed.

On the following day the English marched into St. Martin's. The town was taken possession of without difficulty; but the citadel

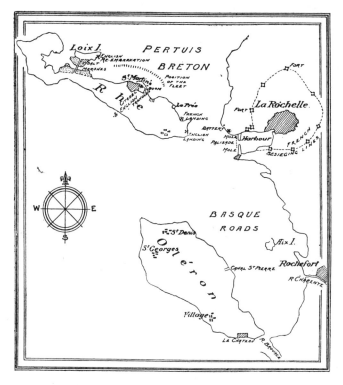

CHART OF LA ROCHELLE.

on the east side of it remained in the hands of the French. Toiras, commanding the enemy, did what he could to gain time in which to provision the citadel. On the 18th, an exchange of fire was maintained between the fort and a few guns which Buckingham had landed. Little was done, but Sir John Burgh decided that the place was too strong to assault. He advised that the troops should lay waste the island and then go to Oleron.

Already difficulties were growing, and Sir William Beecher was sent home to hasten the Irish regiments and the supplies which had been promised. There was also a report abroad[1] that a fleet of forty Spanish warships and twenty Dunquerquers would soon arrive to help the French in holding the island.[2]

For two days Buckingham busied himself in landing guns, but in his determination to reduce St. Martin's, he failed to see that trenches would be needed. It was not until August that these were made. In the interval, provisions began to reach the fort. The ships could not keep out the small boats used for this service. No small craft had been provided with the expedition, and even of the ships' boats many had been lost. An attack on some of the ships was beaten off on the 23rd, and was not repeated. The boats of the fleet rowed guard to keep provisions out of the fort, but with indifferent success. The siege began to seem tedious to Buckingham, and, against advice, an assault was delivered.

When this was repulsed, he decided that the siege must be laid in form, and, on August 20th, he began a boom which should keep provisions from the citadel. A storm destroyed this before it was complete : it was therefore replaced by hawsers stretched from ship to ship.

Meanwhile, on 2nd September, some reinforcements, two thousand five hundred strong, arrived under Sir Ralph Bingley. Holland was still expected with eight thousand. In his great need of men, Buckingham had landed five hundred sailors under Captain Weddell, but they proved of little use. Bingley's Irish troops were ordered to assault La Prée. A few guns were landed at La Flotte, but, when the preparations were well advanced, the order was foolishly cancelled.

Provisions were running short. They had been ordered in England,[3] but bad weather had delayed their departure. When Sir John Burgh was killed, even Buckingham began to despair of success. Though the Rochellers had joined us there was little help to be had from them. Even such provisions as could be procured from them were only bought at an exorbitant rate.[4] But at the end of September, Sir Henry Palmer arrived from England with the

---

[1] 'Harl. Misc.' v. 111.

[2] The treaty between France and Spain had been signed on religious grounds. Politically, there could be no union between the countries.

[3] Cal. S. P. Dom. lxx. 45, and *cf.* ' Fœdera,' VIII. ii. 207.

[4] 'Harl. Misc.' v. 3.

long-expected provisions, and Buckingham plucked up courage so much that, when the citadel demanded a parley, he refused to treat, save for its surrender.

Though boats had continually run the blockade, the fort was in such straits that it was agreed to surrender on September 28th, if no relief should come meanwhile. But on the night of the 27th, the carelessness of the ships let a flotilla of small craft pass, and provisions for two months were landed at St. Martin's in spite of Buckingham's efforts to destroy the boats as they lay under the castle.

It was now Buckingham's turn to despond. On October 9th he shipped his sick, for the army was now rotten and the " men died apace." The guns had already been re-embarked, save only those in the one floating battery that commanded the face of the citadel. Holland had been detained by bad weather and was despaired of. The whole of the colonels advised a retreat, the more so as the French had brought down 4000 foot and 200 horse and were preparing to land them in the island.

But Buckingham would not give up without one last effort. Against all hope, orders were given to storm the fort. Heavy rain postponed the attack for some days, during which the English left their trenches to face the landing of French troops near La Prée, and had to recover them on their return.

Though the walls of the citadel were intact, the attempt to storm it was persisted in. The attack was delivered on October 27th, and four hundred dead were left under the walls. On the following day the army was in full retreat.

The French had thrown two thousand men into La Flotte during the month, and thus Buckingham's neglect was bitterly repaid. There was no hope of embarking save at the west end of the island. The direction of the retreat was left to the senior colonel, Sir William Courtney, whose share in the campaign was more disastrous even than the Duke's. The troops were marched towards Loix Island. There was no other place at which they could embark. The French, with two thousand foot and some horse, hung on the rear of the column, but could not be drawn to an attack.

But when the English reached the causeway and bridge that led over the salt marshes to the island, the French cavalry swooped down. The English rear was soon a mob, and was cut to pieces.

The only stand was made by Sir Pierce Crosby and Sir Thomas Fryer,[1] who with a few hundred pikes held the causeway till the survivors had crossed.

On November 11th, the remnant of the expedition reached England. By famine, pestilence and the sword Buckingham had lost 4000 men : but it may be remembered in his favour that he had not spared himself, and that he did not throw the blame on his subordinates. The reason of the failure, said the King, lay in the non-arrival of help from England ; and in this, if he set aside the Duke's incompetence, the King spoke the truth.

While these events were in progress, Sir Sackville Trevor. had been cruising with the *Assurance, Adventure,* and five prizes or small craft on the Dutch coast.[2] The French were building ships in Holland, and his mission was to add these to the English Navy. Charles was determined " to crush the crocodile in the shell." At the beginning of October, Trevor heard of a great ship completed for sea in the Texel, and lying there half manned. He bribed a pilot to take him in at once, and in spite of the presence of eighteen Dutch men-of-war, poured in a broadside. Two or three of the other ships did the like, and she hauled down her flag. The prize, which proved to be the *St. Esprit,* of 800 tons, was brought to England without protest from the Dutch.

Charles still intended to relieve La Rochelle. Denbigh was appointed to command the sixty-six vessels which were to carry the provisions to the starving town. But want of men and money as usual delayed the start. Although the date determined on for sailing was March 1st, 1628, it was just two months later when Denbigh appeared off La Rochelle. The French had not been idle ; the defence towards the harbour had been strengthened with moles and palisades so that not a boat could pass, and the blockade by sea was as close as by land. Denbigh saw nothing to do save to make an attempt with fireships, but as the wind came off the land before he was ready, he determined to return to England to avoid being himself set on fire. Charles was very angry at the return, and ordered Denbigh to go back to La Rochelle ;[3] but plague, discontent, leaky vessels and the raiding of Dunquerquers on the storeships so weakened the squadron that movement was impossible.

---

[1] Buckingham was wounded while conversing with Fryer.
[2] 'Harl. Misc.' v. 108.
[3] Gardiner, vi. 291.

Yet Buckingham had not done with the problem. Another great fleet was fitting out, and again the preparations were attended by the difficulties of want of money and want of men. As a desperate means of raising supplies, Charles suggested a general levy of ship-money; but the time was not ripe, and he had to draw back. The men were pressed as usual, but were more than usually mutinous. A spirit of disaffection was abroad to which even Buckingham was disposed to make concessions.

Nothing would, it was true, be gained by the relief of La Rochelle, for the French king was prepared to tolerate his Protestant subjects, though he insisted upon being absolute. But to Buckingham this went for nothing. He had pledged his word to help the town, and the fleet was preparing.

So slowly, however, were things advanced at Portsmouth, that even Buckingham grew almost hopeless. On August 22nd, a mutiny broke out, and it was thought that the Duke's life was in danger. It was so, indeed, but from another direction.

On August 23rd, 1628, as he left breakfast Buckingham was stabbed to the heart. His assailant was John Felton, who had held a lieutenancy in the Rhé expedition,[1] and who thought his action to be but one of public justice.

At length, nevertheless, the fleet was nearly ready to sail. Lindsey was appointed to command it[2] on September 2nd, and on 7th it left port. On the 18th it anchored off St. Martin's; and though on the 23rd and 24th a show was made of attempting the relief, there was no real fighting. A fleet of French vessels was anchored in front of the moles, and with these a harmless long range fire was maintained. There was no attempt to board, though Lindsey held it to be quite feasible. While Charles at home was exhorting the force to persevere, the struggle was abruptly ended by the surrender of the town on 18th October.

The most remarkable action at sea this year was the capture of the Silver Fleet by the Dutch admiral, Piet Hein, near Havana. In 1627, Rich had cruised in hopes of waylaying it, but, happily perhaps, had met with no success.

Sir Kenelm Digby, cruising in the Mediterranean with six small ships against the French, found a squadron lying near Scanderoon.[3] Though four Venetian vessels elected to take the part of the French,

---

[1] S. P. Dom., Charles I. lxviii. 77.   [2] 'Fœdera,' VIII. ii. 275.
[3] Lediard, p. 514.

Digby won a complete victory. He compelled the Venetians to draw off, and of the French took three ships and sank one.

The next few years may be passed over rapidly. They do but illustrate the contempt into which Buckingham's failures had brought the English Navy. Disdaining their enemies, and aided by a proclamation of Charles restraining his subjects from attacking them,[1] the Turkish pirates grew more troublesome than ever. In our own waters they kept Button, in command of the Irish squadron, busy, and occupied Penington who was Admiral of the Narrow Seas.

Articles of peace were agreed on between France and England,[2] and the treaty was signed in April, 1630. It was not till December that Charles could proclaim the conclusion of a peace with Spain.[3]

In 1632, Charles had in view a plan which was to give him Dunquerque if he would join Spain against France;[4] but Philip could not be brought to pay the price. Indeed, Charles's value as an ally was considerably depreciated. As time went on and the course of the war seemed likely to deprive Spain of all other ways into the Netherlands,[5] the value of Dunquerque rose, and the town remained in Spanish hands till it was taken by the French in October, 1646.

Ere that time, Charles began to contemplate an assertion of his sovereignty of the seas,[6] and certainly there was work to be done. The northern herring fisheries were almost exclusively in the hands of the Dutch, who kept nearly 3000 busses at sea,[7] and whose trade in herrings, taken on our coasts without licence from the King, amounted to about £1,000,000 annually. Against these Dutch fishers, and against the pirates, strenuous action was very necessary; but the main interest of the fleets sent forth for the purpose lay in the manner in which they were paid for. The difficulty of equipping a force " to protect commerce from the pirates," was solved by the levying of ship-money.

But before the ship-money fleet sailed, other fleets had put to sea. The French and Dutch were in alliance, and in 1635 the war

---

[1] 'Fœdera,' VIII. iii. 4.   [2] *Ib.* 52.

[3] *Ib.* 136, 141, 144.   [4] Gardiner, vii. 214.   [5] *Ib.* p. 348.

[6] Sir John Borough's book, ' The Sovereignty of the Seas,' appeared at the end of 1633 (old style) and had a great effect on Charles.

[7] 'England's Way to Win Wealth,' by Tobias Gentleman, 1614, is a description of the Dutch fisheries, and a recommendation that England should cease to allow all this wealth to be drawn from her by foreigners.

between France and Spain broke out anew. A strong Franco-Dutch fleet left port and was known to be off Portland in June.

Lindsey had joined his command on May 26th, 1635; Monson was his Vice-Admiral; Penington,[1] his Rear-Admiral. The fleet was very strong; it consisted of nineteen ships of the Royal Navy, and twenty-six merchant vessels.[2] For fighting purposes it would have proved vastly superior to any armament previously sent out during this period. But it was not destined to meet with an enemy. Lindsey's instructions were to defend the King's honour, but to make no nation his foe. But as the King's honour was threatened by the strong Franco-Dutch fleet, it seemed as though the intention was not so pacific as was pretended. Charles, indeed, was disappointed that the fleet returned without fighting. The credit of avoiding hostilities belongs to Richelieu, who kept the French flag-officers out of Lindsey's sight.[3] Towards the end of its commission the fleet seized a Dutch man-of-war which had attacked Dunquerquers in English waters. It was its only hostile act.

Lindsey's instructions to his officers[4] included the following article: "If you find foreigners in His Majesty's ports under false colours, you are to arrest them; their wearing the false colours is a decoy to help them in their piracy." He had also settled his plan of action in case of a hostile encounter. He himself would attack the Admiral: his Vice- and Rear-Admirals would similarly single out opponents of equivalent rank; and the rest of the ships were to match themselves to the best of their power.

For the equipment of the fleet of 1636,[5] there was sent out on August 4th the first general issue of ship-money writs.[6] There was no great opposition to the levy. It is important to remember that ship-money in case of national danger might be levied without raising an outcry, and that the tax only became unpopular when Charles let it become a regular means of raising supplies.[7]

The fleet was considerably stronger than that of 1635, and it would have been even stronger than it was, but for the lubberly conduct of the master of the *Anne Royal*. In bringing the ship

---

[1] Knighted the year before on board the *Unicorn*.
[2] 'Tracts,' p. 290 ; and ' Fœdera,' IX. i. 27.
[3] Coke to Conway, S. P. Dom. ccxci. 59.
[4] 'Tracts,' 333, *sqq.*
[5] See note (⁵) on next page.
[6] ' Fœdera,' IX. ii. 41. *See also antea*, pp. 26, 27.
[7] *Ib.* 113 ; and *Ib.* iii. 26.

out of the Medway, this man, Peter White, quarrelled with the pilot. The pilot went ashore, leaving the ship at anchor, and as the tide fell the ship touched. Her crew then manned the capstan, thinking that she was touching a bank, but hove her on to her anchor. When the ship was bilged and half full of water, White made sail on her and overset her. Many were drowned. It was blowing hard at the time, and the ship was known to be tender-sided. Though raised afterwards, she was found to be useless and was broken up.[1]

Tho *James,* coming from Portsmouth to the Downs with two hundred and sixty men on board, had not ten, besides officers, able to take a turn at the helm.[2]

[5] THE SHIP-MONEY FLEET OF 1636.

(S. P. Dom., Charles I. cccxvi. 69, I.)

1. *Triumph* . .	Admiral the Earl of Northumberland. . . . . Wm. Rainborow, Captain . .	Mr. Noise, Lieut.
2. *Anne Royal*[1] .	Vice-Admiral Sir John Penington	,, Foxe, Lieut.
3. *James* . . .	Rear-Admiral Sir Henry Mervyn	,, Andrew Mennes, Lieut.
4. *Repulse.* . .	Capt. Montague	,, Francis Smith, Lieut.
5. *Victory.* . .	,, Stewart	Capt. Bardsey, Lieut.
6. *Unicorn* . .	,, Sir Henry Mainwaring .	,, Owen, Lieut.
7. *Defiance* . .	,, Murray	Mr. Philip Hills, Lieut.
8. *Charles* . .	,, Thomas Kettleby . . .	,, Wynd, Lieut.
9. *Henrietta Maria*	,, Porter	,, Edwd. Popham, Lieut.
10. *Nonsuch* . .	,, Povey	,, Lidcott, Lieut.
11. *Convertine.* .	,, John Mennes	,, Bargrave, Lieut.
12. *Assurance* . .	,, Lewis Kirke	Capt. Love, Lieut.
13. *Garland* . .	,, Fogge	Mr. Moyle, Lieut.
14. *Bonaventure* .	,, Henry Stradling . . .	,, Button, Lieut.[2]
15. *Happy Entrance*	,, George Carteret . . .	Capt. Browne, Lieut.
16. *Adventure* . .	,, Paramour.	. .
17. *Mary Rose* . .	,, Jeremy Brett.	. .
18. *Black George* .	,, William Smith.	. .
19. *Second Whelp* .	,, Price.	. .
20. *Fourth Whelp* .	,, Penruddock.	. .
21. *Fifth Whelp* .	,, Lindsey.	. .
22. *Tenth Whelp* .	,, Johnson.	. .
23. *Great Pinnace.*	,, Turner.	. .
24. *Lesser Pinnace*	,, Slingsby.	. .
25. *Jonas* . . .	,, Fielding	Mr. Appleton, Lieut.
26. *Great Neptune.*	,, Thomas Kirke	,, Edwd. Powell, Lieut.
27. *Third Whelp* .	,, Fletcher.	

[1] The *Anne Royal* was wrecked in Tilbury Hope while sailing from Chatham to join the fleet, 9–19 April. The *St. Andrew* was substituted for her.
[2] Possibly a son of Sir Thomas Button who had died in 1634.

[1] Cal. S. P. Dom. vol cccxviii. 61, 78, vol. cccxix. 4, 13–15, 24, 36, etc.
[2] Mervyn, ' Relation Concerning Prestmasters,' Dec. 1636.

From the Downs the fleet sailed west. It was known that there was a large French fleet in La Rochelle, and Northumberland was to watch it, since its destination might be Dunquerque. But though England was at peace, no fleet would sight the English Admiral. Eight Dutch men-of-war fled from him off Portland; the French he could not find. Off Ushant, in June, he discovered that they had left port. Believing the word of the first Irishman he sighted, he sailed east in pursuit of them. But, arrived in the Downs, he found that they had not been heard of in that direction. A south-westerly wind blew. While waiting in the Downs for it to change, Northumberland received orders to go north to the herring fisheries. He sailed, and tried to issue licences to the Dutch busses. Some accepted and paid for licences [1] which should carry a protection from Dunquerquers. Others refused. Northumberland fired on the fleet, sunk several craft, and dispersed the rest.[2] Actively this great fleet had done very little; indirectly it had had the effect of keeping the French out of the Channel.

In August, 1636, the *Fourth Whelp* was lost. Her pilot ran her on a rock off Jersey in daylight, when she was before the wind with a smooth sea. In 1637 the *Fifth Whelp* went down off the Dutch coast. She was rotten, and her bottom seems to have fallen out. It was blowing no more than a fresh breeze at the time, and Captain Edward Popham and most of the crew managed to save themselves in the boats; but seventeen were drowned. The survivors joined an English ship in Hellevoetsluis.

Northumberland, with his great fleet, was at sea again in 1637; but there was even less for him to do than before. Again he went north to offer licences to the busses; but, hearing of the presence of twenty-three Dutch men-of-war, and not wishing to have trouble, he sent a merchant ship on ahead. This vessel was not allowed even to speak the busses, and the great fleet was reduced to pretending that the offer had been, not of licences to fish, but of protection for the homeward journey.[3]

In 1638 James, Duke of York, became Lord High Admiral. Northumberland acted as his deputy. Penington commanded in the Downs, as he did again in the year following.

---

[1] Frankland, 'Annals,' 477, says that after being fired on, the Dutch agreed to pay a yearly tribute of £30,000 for the right. It was paid that year and the busses finished the season; next year it was refused.

[2] Lediard, p. 516.   [3] Gardiner, viii. 220.

In 1639 Tromp [1] found some Spanish soldiers for Dunquerque on board English ships, and seized the men ; but did not harm the English.   To Northumberland and Penington his action seemed perfectly natural; not so to Charles, whose animus against the Dutch was thereby greatly increased.

During the summer, Tromp's vice-admiral fell in with a great Spanish fleet bound up Channel. With this fleet were eight English transports which, at sight of the Dutch, took refuge in an English port.   The Dutch were only seventeen strong, Oquendo's fleet about sixty ; but a running fight was maintained.   When the fleets reached Dungeness, Tromp, who at Dunquerque had heard the firing, joined his vice-admiral. A battle was fought in the Strait, and the Spaniards were forced, with heavy loss, into the Downs. The Dutch followed and anchored to the south.   That night Oquendo got twelve transports safely round the North Sand Head and into Dunquerque.

Penington was in the Downs,[2] but his squadron, nineteen strong, was not enough to control the Dutch, who had added to their fleet and kept Oquendo fairly shut in.   Penington gave out that he would attack the side that fired the first shot ; though the Dutch professed that they would be content if he remained neutral.   Tromp tempted Oquendo to fire on him on October 18th, and at once joined battle.[3] A Dutch squadron was told off to watch Penington.

Penington did not move.   On the one hand his crews would, in all probability, have refused to fight for Spain ; on the other the King was expecting £150,000 from Spain as the price of his help against the Dutch.[4] So the battle took its course, and Penington merely protected such Spanish ships as had been run ashore.   But if the money had arrived, Charles would have taken part with Spain. That such was his intention appeared from the fact that he had already placed an embargo on the shipping in the river.   The King wished to have ships ready to his hand.

Penington had desired to induce the Dutch to give the Spaniards two tides' law ; but, though the custom was common enough, Northumberland held that it did not apply to such large fleets, and therefore declined to back his subordinate.   His interpretation

---

[1] Marten Harpertszoon Tromp, then forty-two years old.

[2] Cal. S. P. Dom., Charles I. ccccxxxi. 3, 4.

[3] Tromp knew that Oquendo had just received a supply of powder and had not yet got it on board. Gardiner, ix. 65.

[4] Gardiner, ix. 61.

was due, doubtless, to the fact that he saw little chance of being obeyed.

In October, 1641, there broke out the Irish rebellion. The King was satisfied that this was no "rash insurrection," but one that would have to be suppressed by a "sharp war."[1] The squadron in the Irish Sea was therefore strengthened and put under the command of Captain Richard Swanley.

In the following year, before the King raised his standard at Nottingham, there arose the question of the ownership of the fleet. In June, 1642, the Parliament had appointed the Earl of Warwick to command in chief, Northumberland being too ill to serve. The King, on the other hand, nominated Penington. But Parliament thought Penington far too staunch a Royalist, and applied to Northumberland, in whose power the appointment lay, to nominate Warwick. This he did; but his doing so angered the King who, while persisting in thrusting Penington forward, dismissed Northumberland from his office of Lord High Admiral.[2]

The attitude of the seamen was at first Royalist to all appearance. In January they swore "to acknowledge Charles king; to stand for the privileges of Parliament."[3] But this should perhaps be taken as meaning that they were convinced that Charles ought to govern with a Parliament, and that they did not foresee the strife that was to follow.

When, in view of the dual appointment, Warwick made the best of his way on board, he was welcomed readily enough. There was but a faint show from four or five captains in favour of Penington,[4] who was in Kent, wasting time in waiting for orders. Warwick, meanwhile, appointed Sir William Batten to be his Vice-Admiral. The fleet in home waters consisted of sixteen ships of the Navy and sixteen merchantmen. In Ireland there were ten ships, of which only two belonged to the Navy.

In France, Richelieu was dead, and Charles saw a hope of gaining naval support from that quarter.[5] Mazarin allowed freer communication between Henrietta Maria and her brother than Richelieu had permitted, but he was not in the least disposed to go to war for the sake of a renewal of Charles's misgovernment.

At the beginning of the new year the King and Parliament

[1] G. Penn, i. 12.
[2] *Ib.* 55.
[3] *Ib.* 19.
[4] Rushworth, iv. 752.
[5] Gardiner, 'Civ. War,' i. 42.

opened negotiations; but as the very first of the King's " proposi-
tions " included a demand for the fleet, there could be no hope of
peace.

In February the Queen sailed from Holland with four ships laden
with treasure and stores for the King. A landing was made, after
a long, rough passage, at Bridlington Quay. A little later Batten,
with a squadron, came upon the scene, and immediately opened
fire on the ships. Ignorant of where the Queen lay, he could
not know that her house chanced to be right in the line of fire, and
that many of his shot were striking it. But so it was ; and on the
supposition that this conduct was intentional, Royalist writers have
served out scant justice to Batten.[1] The fall of the tide and possibly
the presence of Tromp, who had escorted the Queen across, caused
Batten to desist.

Northumberland would not accept a renewal of his commission
from Parliament, though he continued on good terms with that
party. Warwick accordingly was named Lord High Admiral.
The instructions issued to him bade him require foreigners to salute
the flag,[2] as though the fleet still represented the King. This caused
difficulties with the Dutch, who, on occasion, insisted that the
salute of former days was a mark of respect to the King's majesty,
and therefore could not be claimed by Parliament.[3]

The fleet of 1643 was very strong. There were in the Narrow
Seas twenty-eight vessels great and small, besides merchant ships,
and the Irish squadron had been raised from two vessels of the
Navy to eight.[4] Yet it was complained that there were not
enough small craft for the work on the Irish coast. The larger
ships, also, were constantly employed. In August, 1642, Warwick
had helped to take Portsmouth ; in August following he failed to
relieve Exeter. Three of his ships went aground with the ebb, and
of them two were taken and the other burnt.[5] In May, 1644, he
relieved Lyme ;[6] while another good, if unscrupulous, service, was
done for the Parliamentary cause by Swanley, who sank off
Pembrokeshire a vessel bringing Irish soldiers to Charles's help,
and drowned all on board.

---

[1] With Clarendon, ii. 143,; cp. Rushworth, 'Hist.' vi. 156 ; both quoted at length
in Granville Penn, i. 72, *sqq.*

[2] G. Penn, i. 65.

[3] In May, 1647, Batten brought into Portsmouth fifteen Swedish vessels that refused
to salute his flag. G. Penn, i. 243.

[4] G. Penn, i. 68.   [5] Lediard, 530.   [6] Rushworth, v. 680.

Ere the civil contest had gone far, the King discovered that the Parliament was using against him letters of marque which had been granted by himself, and at the end of December he withdrew, by proclamation, all which had been issued previous to July, 1642.[1]

In the spring of 1645, Penington died, and was succeeded in the style of king's Vice-Admiral by Sir John Mennes.[2] In Ireland, Swanley was superseded by Sir Robert Moulton as parliamentary Vice-Admiral.

The war ended without any interference from foreigners. The Navy had done its work well. In addition to the power of gaining help from abroad, the King had lost much of the consideration of "his allies, the neighbour princes, who saw the sovereignty of the seas now in other hands."[3] But it must be borne in mind that the Navy served the Parliament in an honest hope and belief that it was helping to effect a reconciliation which would secure the rights of all parties.[4] When such a reconciliation began to appear each day farther off, there arose doubts as to their loyalty in the minds of many of those who commanded on behalf of the Parliament.

Foremost among these was Sir William Batten. The Committee was aware of a growing spirit of discontent, and in writing to Batten, in June, 1647,[5] was at pains to point out how hard this seemed to the Parliament, which had maintained seamen's wages at a higher rate than ever before. What the Committee apparently did not realise, was that its party was daily becoming more divided, and that the pre-eminence was going to the Independents—the army faction. After commanding the fleet of 1647, with Rear-Admiral Richard Owen as his second in command, Batten, actuated by some such thought as this, went before the Committee, in September, and resigned his command, not, he declared, from discontent. On the contrary, he would be ready to resume the command if called upon.

But a week afterwards, on October 5th, Colonel Thomas Rainborow was appointed to succeed Batten, and ordered to take command of the winter guard.[6] This appointment was, in itself, unpopular, as evidencing a triumph of the Independents. And Rainborow was not a man to conciliate favour. Five months later, when he tried to go on board his flagship, the *Constant Reforma-*

[1] 'Fœdera,' IX. iii. 107.   [4] G. Penn, i. 96.
[2] G. Penn, i. 76.   [5] *Ib.* 247, 248.
[3] Clarendon, i. 679.   [6] *Ib.* 251.

tion, to take command of the fleet for 1648, his sailors refused to receive him.

It has been alleged that Rainborow was unwelcome mainly as being no seaman. In this there may be some truth; but as his father, William Rainborow, had served afloat all his life, and had been flag-captain to Northumberland, in the *Triumph*, in 1636, it seems likely that the son had been brought up to the sea. That he had deserted the sea for the land service was more probably the secret of his naval unpopularity.[1]

Parliament, on receiving the news, and a letter from Rainborow complaining of the attitude both of the fleet and of the county of Kent, reappointed Batten.

Batten was welcomed on board, for he was popular with the fleet, and not the less so because he seemed to have been the martyr of the faction which the sailors disliked. While the fleet was in this temper, and petitioning for a personal treaty with the King, Batten withdrew from the river with eleven ships,[2] and joined the Royalists in Holland.[3] The accessions of this time brought the Prince's squadron up to seventeen sail. But Batten, a Presbyterian, was not a welcome commander to the Royalists. The fleet clamoured that James, the Duke of York, should be its admiral. The Prince of Wales returned from France to Holland at this juncture, and he himself assumed the command.

When the ships revolted from Parliament, the three castles in the Downs—Walmer, Deal, and Sandown—did likewise. There seemed some danger of the movement spreading, but the squadron of eight ships at Portsmouth remained staunch, and three vessels at the mouth of the Colne prevented any relief of Colchester from the sea.

[1] G. Penn, i. 255, *sqq.*

[2] Ships carried off to the Prince of Wales in June, 1648, by Sir William Batten:— *Swallow, Constant Reformation, Convertine, Antelope, Satisfaction, Constant Warwick, Blackmoor Lady, Hind, Crescent, Roebuck, Pelican.* The *Satisfaction* and *Hind*, with the *Truelove*, returned to their allegiance to the Parliament in November. The *Truelove* was then under Captain John Sherwin. The *Constant Warwick* reverted to the Parliament at once. The *Blackmoor Lady* joined, or was taken by, Charles in the Downs in July.

[3] S. P. Dom., Interreguum, 9 E., pp. 154, 155. This action brought the Parliament's fleet to Holland in the autumn and put the States in a false position. They could not allow the Prince to be attacked; neither did they wish to offend the party which held power in England. Accordingly they massed as many of their ships as they could collect to keep the peace between the rival squadrons. This end was attained, yet there arose the further difficulty that Warwick refused to give Rupert two tides' law; but, Warwick sailing first, and Rupert slipping out of port without being met, this stumblingblock also was avoided.—Basnage, 'Annales,' i. 139.

On 22nd July, the Prince of Wales arrived off Yarmouth with his fleet. He decided not to attempt any operation at Colchester, but came into the mouth of the Thames, calling on the ships there to join him. Meeting with no response, he went to the Downs. So distressed was he for money, that he was forced to hazard his cause by seizing English ships. His men refused to return to Holland, and insisted on sailing up the river. Near the Nore, Warwick's fleet was sighted. Neither commander was sure enough of his men to be willing to risk an engagement, but any chance of a meeting was removed by a calm, which kept the fleets apart, and which was followed by a breeze that blew the Royalists over to Holland.

Walmer and Deal had fallen to Nathaniel Rich ; Warwick joined with the Portsmouth squadron, and reduced Sandown—the King's last hope in Kent. Warwick then went over to Holland, and blockaded the Royalist fleet in Hellevoetsluis. While there he found that the enthusiasm for the Prince was waning, and four of the ships rejoined him. The Prince himself had left the fleet, and the second in command, Willoughby, was superseded by Prince Rupert.

Under the command of Rupert and his brother Maurice, the squadron sailed from Hellevoetsluis, with the expressed intention of upholding the Royalist cause in Ireland. The subsequent history of Rupert's squadron will appear when Blake's first command under the Commonwealth is described.

CHAPTER XIX.

VOYAGES AND DISCOVERIES, 1603–1649.

SIR CLEMENTS MARKHAM, K.C.B., F.R.S.

Prince Henry supports discovery—The early ventures of the East India Company—Saris to Japan—Attempts at the North-West Passage—George Waymouth—John Knight—The Muscovy Company and the North-East Passage—Henry Hudson's three voyages and death—Prince Henry and Ralegh—Thomas Button—The merchants discoverers of the North-West Passage—Death of Prince Henry—Captain Gibbons—Captain Bylot—William Baffin—Captain Hawkridge—Captain John Smith in Virginia—Annexation of Bermuda—Ralegh's last voyage and execution—Death of Hakluyt—Captain Luke Fox—Captain James.

 THE impetus given to maritime enterprise by the encouragement of the government of Queen Elizabeth did not lose its force at her death, but continued in full vigour for at least twenty years afterwards. This was due partly to that love of adventure which had been so thoroughly aroused, and to the patriotic zeal which had been instilled into the minds of the merchants and seamen of England, but also to the warm and active support which the great Queen's policy received from her young godson, Prince Henry.

The first voyage despatched by the East India Company was followed by annual ventures. In 1604 Sir Henry Middleton led the second expedition, visiting Ternate and Tidore, and in the third voyage Captain William Hawkyns reached Surat and Agra, obtaining a footing for the Company on the mainland of India. But these East Indian ventures[1] now pass away from the province of discovery and exploration, with the exception, perhaps, of the voyage of Captain Saris, which brought the distant empire of Japan within the knowledge of English seamen. A letter from William Adams of Gillingham, who had been shipwrecked in a Dutch vessel on the coast of Japan, dated October, 1611, induced

---

[1] Such of these voyages as involved serious fighting have been described in Chap. XVIII.

the East India Company to send Captain John Saris in a ship called the *Clove,* accompanied by the *Thomas* and the *Hector,* to attempt to open commercial relations with the Japanese. In June, 1612, the *Clove* anchored in the haven of Firando, where the Dutch had already established a factory. Saris, with the help of William Adams, obtained ample privileges for trade. He sailed from Japan in December, 1613, leaving eight Englishmen to form a factory at Firando, but it was abandoned in 1624, and the establishment of friendly relations between England and Japan, so auspiciously commenced by Elizabethan seamen, was postponed for more than two centuries.

The East India Company, constantly kept alive to the importance of geographical discovery by their first governor, Sir Thomas Smith, also made some efforts to discover a route by the north-west. In 1602 an expedition consisting of two vessels of forty and fifty tons, named the *Discovery* and *Godspeed,* had been sent out under the command of an experienced seaman named George Waymouth. He sailed from the Thames in May, but was obliged to return, after reaching the Labrador coast, owing to a mutiny, fomented by the chaplain, one John Cartwright. It was intended to employ Waymouth again, but the project fell through. The Company, however, did not abandon the attempt to discover a passage, for we find a captain named John Knight, who had previously served in a Danish expedition to Greenland, employed to discover the north-west passage in 1606. He sailed from Gravesend in April, on board the *Hopewell,* of forty tons, and steered across the Atlantic until the coast of Labrador was sighted. But his journal ceases abruptly on the 26th of June. On that day he landed, leaving two men in the boat, and walked over a hill with three companions. They were never seen or heard of again. The ship returned to Dartmouth in September, and Sir Thomas Smith had much difficulty in maintaining the zeal of his brother directors for discovery. When Captain Waymouth had returned unsuccessful, it had sunk very low, and some of them had proposed that the attempt " should be utterly left off." The disappearance of Captain Knight still further disheartened them ; but fortunately Sir Thomas Smith had greater influence with the Muscovy Company. That body of merchant adventurers agreed to despatch an expedition to discover a route to Cathay by the north-east.

Henry Hudson, whom we now hear of for the first time, was

selected to lead this daring enterprise. He fitted out a little vessel
of eighty tons, and weighed anchor at Greenwich on May 1st, 1607.
He had with him only ten men, and his own little son John.
Hudson first sighted the east coast of Greenland in 73° N. on
the 22nd of June, and then examined the edge of the ice until he
sighted the N.W. cape of Spitzbergen, and named it Hakluyt
Headland. He made a careful examination of the western coast
of Spitzbergen, and on his way home discovered the island since
called Jan Mayen, which he named " Hudson's Tutches."

In 1608 Hudson fitted out a second expedition to explore the
sea between Spitzbergen and Novaya Zemlya. He coasted along
the edge of the ice, making more than one resolute effort to penetrate into it, until he sighted Novaya Zemlya on the 25th of June.
The practical consequence of these ably conducted exploring voyages
was the establishment of a rich and prosperous Spitzbergen fishery,
which continued to flourish for two centuries. In the four succeeding
years, the Muscovy Company sent Captain Jonas Poole on voyages
to kill morses and whales, and he was succeeded by Fotherby and
Baffin, whose work in the Spitzbergen seas extended over the years
from 1613–1615. Subsequently Captain Edge was the leading spirit
in these voyages, and between the years 1607 and 1622 English
seamen completed the delineation of the Spitzbergen group, while
enriching their employers with full cargoes procured by facing
dangers and hardships of a kind of which they had had no previous
experience. The fleets in the northern seas and on the Newfoundland banks formed admirable nurseries for our Navy.

Hudson's last voyage was undertaken to search for a passage
by the north-west, by a strait which is marked on the globe of
Molyneux as the " Furious Overfall," and of which Hudson had also
heard from Captain Waymouth. The funds were supplied by Sir
Thomas Smith, Sir Dudley Digges, and Sir John Wolstenholme,
merchant princes, whose patriotic munificence is deserving of all
praise. The *Discovery*, of 55 tons, was equipped, and Henry
Hudson sailed from the Thames on April 22nd, 1610, with his young
son John and a crew of doubtful character, though including some
good men and true. Passing the " Furious Overfall," as placed by
Davis on the globe of Molyneux, and down the ice-encumbered
strait, Hudson entered the great inland sea which was, from thenceforward, to bear his name. He named the island on the south side
of the entrance to Hudson's Bay, where he observed that myriads

of birds were breeding, Cape Digges, and here his own journal comes to an end, on the 3rd of August. The story is continued by one of the crew named Habakkuk Prickett, whose narrative is confused and unsatisfactory. Húdson examined the eastern shore of the great inland sea, and was eventually obliged to winter in a bay at its southern extremity.

During the long winter nights a spirit of mutiny began to manifest itself, caused by the hardships and misery of the crew, and fostered by two or three designing villains. As soon as Hudson got his vessel out of winter quarters in the following spring, he shaped a course towards the strait on the 18th of June, 1611. The mutineers feared that the provisions would not last out, and they resolved to diminish the number of mouths by turning the sick and weak adrift. As they knew that their captain would never consent to this crime, he and his son were also to be abandoned. After the ship had been three days at sea, the diabolical act was perpetrated. Four sick men, three who were loyal, Captain Hudson and his son Jack, who had accompanied him in all his voyages and who was then eighteen, were forced into the shallop, and she was cast adrift. They were given a fowling-piece, a little ammunition, an iron pot, and some meal. Hudson and his doomed companions were never heard of more. Eleven men remained on board. Only five survived to reach England, including old Bylot the mate, and Prickett, a servant of Sir Dudley Digges, who wrote the narrative. No one was punished, yet there was a feeling that search should be made for the great navigator. He had found a grave in the midst of his discoveries, and his name is immortalised by the strait and the inland sea which bear his name.

At that period the natural leaders of maritime enterprise were more or less disabled. Sir Walter Ralegh, the accomplished navigator and fervent patriot, was in prison, having been condemned on a false charge. Prince Henry, on whom the mantle of his godmother had fallen, was but a boy, full of zeal and ardour, but inexperienced. The friendship between the illustrious prisoner and the young Prince is a very touching episode in our history. Queen Anne first took her son to see Ralegh in 1606, when the boy was only twelve years old; but their most intimate friendship was from 1610 to the Prince's untimely death in 1612. Prince Henry constantly consulted Ralegh, and was much guided by his advice. He learned the rudiments of shipbuilding from Phineas

Pett, and of navigation from Edward Wright; but it was Ralegh who gave life to his studies, who taught him the principles of seamanship, and filled his young mind with some of his own enthusiasm. The boy longed to sail in the Narrow Seas, and aspired to the command of a British fleet in the West Indies if there should again be war with Spain.

The news of Hudson's abandonment aroused young Henry to action. Under his auspices an expedition was fitted out to follow up the discoveries of Hudson, and Thomas Button, an experienced officer, was entrusted with the command. His instructions were drawn up by Prince Henry, doubtless with the aid of Ralegh, whose guiding hand is visible throughout. They are dated April 5th, 1612. Button's orders were to make the best of his way to Digges Island, and thence, without loitering, to steer direct for the opposite mainland, and to spend no time in the search for anything but the passage. Button was on board the *Resolution*. He was accompanied by two friends named Gibbons and Hawkridge, and by Prickett and Bylot, who had been with Hudson. The second vessel was Hudson's old ship, the *Discovery*, commanded by Captain Ingram. The expedition sailed in April, 1612, reached Digges Island, and, in obedience to Prince Henry's instructions, shaped a course westward across Hudson's Bay. The western shore was sighted at a point named by Button "Hopes Checked," and Port Nelson was reached on August 15th. There the *Resolution* was lost, and the expedition wintered. In the spring Button, in the *Discovery*, continued his search for a passage to the north-west, exploring the whole western shore of Hudson's Bay until he reached the strait in 65° N., known as "Sir Thomas Roe's Welcome." Thence he proceeded homewards, arriving in the autumn of 1612.

Soon after the departure of Button's expedition a charter was granted to a "Company of Merchants Discoverers of the North-West Passage," including Sir Thomas Smith, Sir Dudley Digges, Wolstenholme, Jones, Lancaster, Mansell, Freeman, Stone, Wyche, Bell—whose names all survive on bays and headlands of Spitz-bergen or round Baffin's Bay. Prince Henry was the official protector of the Company. The charter was dated July 26th, 1612, and the common seal had the Prince of Wales's feathers and his motto: "*Juvat ire per altum.*"

But a terrible calamity followed soon after the return of Button's expedition. Queen Elizabeth's godson, the hope of England, was attacked by a fatal illness. His mother suspected poison. A cordial prepared by Sir Walter Ralegh did him good and soothed his last hours; but on November 6th, 1612, Prince Henry died in his nineteenth year. His father had promised the Prince to release Sir Walter Ralegh on the following Christmas. The son being dead, James broke his word. " No king but my father would keep such a bird in a cage," young Henry had indignantly exclaimed.

The Company of Merchants Discoverers of the North-West Passage continued its efforts; and in December, 1614, the Directors of the East India Company voted £300 a year, for three years, to further the same object. In 1612 the *Discovery* was again despatched, under the command of Sir Thomas Button's companion, Captain Gibbons, with Bylot as his mate. Gibbons failed to enter Hudson's Strait, and was driven by the ice into a bay in 58° 30′ N., where he was beset for ten weeks. It was called by the crew "Gibbons his Hole." When he was released he returned home. In 1615 an expedition was fitted out at the expense of Sir Thomas Smith, Sir Dudley Digges, and Alderman Jones. Again the old *Discovery* of 55 tons was used, and the command was given to Robert Bylot, who had served with Hudson, Button, and Gibbons. The pilot, who wrote the narrative of the voyage, was William Baffin, and the crew consisted of sixteen men and two boys. They had some difficulty with the ice at the entrance of Hudson's Strait, but eventually sailed along the northern shore, until the ships were beset off some land which Baffin named "Broken Point." There Baffin took a complete lunar observation, the second recorded to have been ever taken at sea, the first having been that observed by Pedro de Sarmiento on March 31st, 1580. Baffin's lunar was observed on June 21st, 1615. On the 27th the ice opened out, and the *Discovery* proceeded on her voyage as far as the north-west coast of Southampton Island, where the closeness of the pack stopped further progress. Bylot returned in September, 1615.

Another voyage was undertaken in the following year by the same merchant adventurers, and Bylot again took command of the *Discovery*, with Baffin as his pilot. This time they were to explore the sea to the northward of the farthest point of Davis, called "Sanderson's Hope." Sailing from Gravesend in March, 1616, they sighted the coast of Greenland, and passed Sanderson's Hope on the 30th of May. Baffin crossed Melville Bay with little or no obstruction from the ice, reaching the "north water" on the 1st of

July. He named a headland Cape Dudley Digges, and a deep bay,
twelve leagues farther north, was called Wolstenholme Sound. To
another bay he gave the name of Whale Sound, and an island was
called after Richard Hakluyt. In 78° N. an opening received the
name of Smith Sound—"the greatest and largest in all this sea,"
says Baffin. A group of islands was named after the ship's husband,
Alwyn Cary. Standing to the westward in an open sea, with a stiff
gale, it suddenly fell calm, and Jones and Lancaster Sounds were
discovered on the western coast. Baffin returned along the western
side of Davis Strait, crossed to Cockin Sound, on the Greenland
coast, where scurvy grass was collected for the sick, and arrived off
Dover on the 30th of August, 1616. Baffin's conclusion was that
there was no strait and no passage to the north of Davis Strait. He
was wrong. His sounds named after Smith, Jones, and Lancaster
were all straits. But he had discovered Baffin's Bay, and had thus
crowned his Arctic career by an important achievement. He was a
diligent observer and a scientific seaman. The death of this great
navigator took place at Kishm Island, in the Persian Gulf, when he
was in the service of the East India Company, on the 23rd of
January, 1622. His was the last Arctic voyage deriving its impulse
from Elizabethan days.

The futile voyage, set forth in 1619, can scarcely be counted.
Captain Hawkridge, who was a friend of Sir Thomas Button, and
had served in his expedition, received command of a vessel in that
year to discover the passage. The chief promoter was Sir John
Wolstenholme, and the East India Company subscribed £200.
Hawkridge entered Hudson's Strait. He seems to have made
regular observations, but he cruised about in an aimless manner,
and the abstract of his journal, preserved by Luke Fox, proves him
to have been an incapable commander. He appears to have been
off Mansell Island in Hudson's Bay, and to have returned home in
September.

While Sir Walter Ralegh was in prison his great enterprise
of establishing a permanent colony in Virginia was completed by
others; but, owing to the representations of himself and of his
friend and admirer, Richard Hakluyt, a company of adventurers
received a charter on April 10th, 1606, and three ships left England
in January, 1607. The *Susan Content*, of 100 tons, was commanded
by Captain Christopher Newport, the *Godspeed*, of 40 tons, was
entrusted to Bartholomew Gosnold, who had already made a voyage

to America, when he reached the New England coast and gave the name to Cape Cod. John Ratcliffe had charge of the *Discovery*, of 20 tons. The three vessels carried one hundred and five colonists; and among them was Captain John Smith.

This remarkable man was born at Willoughby, in Lincolnshire, in 1579, and he had passed through many and most extraordinary adventures in the wars of the Low Countries and Hungary before he embarked in the Virginian expedition. On the 13th of May, 1607, the colonists landed and formed their first settlement of Jamestown, on the northern shore of the James River in Virginia. At first they suffered from famine and disease, and before September fifty emigrants, including Captain Gosnold, were dead. Captain Smith's high character and great abilities pointed to him as the ruling spirit, and the chief management of affairs devolved upon him. But in one of his numerous exploring excursions up the Virginian rivers he was taken prisoner by the natives and placed in the power of King Powhatan, whose residence was on the north side of the York River. It is stated, in his ' True Relation of Virginia,' that he was sentenced to death, but, when the weapon was raised to strike, the king's daughter Pocahontas, a child of twelve, rushed forward and clasped his head in her arms, determined to save his life or share his fate. Her conduct touched her father's heart and Smith's life was spared.[1] He was allowed to return to Jamestown. In June, 1608, Captain Smith explored the Chesapeake and discovered the courses of the rivers Potomac and Rappahannock, returning to Jamestown in July. He was elected President of the colony, and on May 23rd, 1609, a new charter was granted to the Virginia Company. But this able administrator was to be super-seded, Lord De la Warr being appointed Captain-General of the colony, with Sir Thomas Gates as Lieutenant-General, and Sir George Somers as Admiral. Lord De la Warr was to be preceded by Gates and Somers. Sailing in May, 1609, they were ship-wrecked at Bermuda. The other ships, forming the squadron of Sir George Somers, arrived safely at Jamestown, and in the autumn of 1609 Captain John Smith returned home. He left behind him a colony consisting of four hundred and ninety souls, with pro-visions, arms and ammunition, stores of clothing, boots, and domestic animals. The English looked upon him as the saviour

---

[1] But Mr. Charles Deane gives reasons for discrediting this story, in a note at p. 28 of his edition of the ' True Relation.'

of the colony; the respect of the natives for him hardly stopped short of idolatry, and as an explorer he takes a high place among English geographers. He discovered Chesapeake Bay and the principal Virginian rivers. His 'True Relation,' published in 1608, is a most interesting narrative of events from the first landing of the colonists, and in 1612 his important map of Virginia was engraved at Oxford.

Meanwhile the *Sea Venture*, with Sir George Somers, Sir Thomas Gates, and Captain Newport on board, had been cast ashore on the Bermudas. Out of the wreck, and with the cedars on the island, two vessels were built called the *Patience* and the *Deliverance*. By this means the company of one hundred and forty men and women was safely conveyed from Bermuda to Jamestown in May, 1609. Sir George Somers afterwards returned to Bermuda with the object of forming a plantation. He died there before his intentions could be fulfilled, but the colony at Bermuda was established and has since had a continuous history.[1]

John Smith did not remain idle after his return to England. In March, 1614, he sailed with two vessels belonging to some London merchants, which were commanded by himself and Captain Hunt. Reaching the coast of Maine they were occupied in fishing during the months of July and August; while Captain John Smith himself, in a small boat, examined and surveyed the whole coast from Penobscot to Cape Cod. This enabled him afterwards to construct a map of the country, to which he gave the name of New England. The name of Cape Cod, as already noted, had been given by Captain Gosnold in 1602. On his return Captain Smith entered the service of a Plymouth company, and two vessels were again equipped. They sailed in March, 1615, but Smith was captured by a French squadron, in open defiance of the laws of nations, and taken to La Rochelle. He reached Plymouth towards the end of the year and wrote the narrative of his voyage to New England, which was published in 1616 with a map.

Captain Smith was indefatigable in striving to awaken an interest in the subject of settling America, and personally distributed many copies of his work. He passed the remainder of his days in England, publishing his 'General History of Virginia, New England, and the Summer[2] Isles' in 1626, the 'Sea Grammar and

---

[1] The Bermudas are still alternatively known as the Somers Islands.—W. L. C.
[2] Thus spelt in the title.

Accidence for Young Seamen' in 1627, and the narrative of his extraordinary early adventures in 1630. With the exceptions of Ralegh and Hakluyt, no one man did so much towards colonising the coast of North America as Captain John Smith ; and the stirring and romantic narrative of his life and adventures will ever secure a living interest in this noble Englishman, who, amidst many trials and temptations, maintained his honour spotless and his name untarnished. Two books which were used by Captain John Smith when he was young were Macchiavelli's 'Art of War' and the 'Thoughts' of the Emperor Marcus Aurelius. These works supplied the education of a great man. John Smith " was great," says Mr. Long, " in his heroic mind and his deeds of arms, but greater still in the nobleness of his character." He died in London in 1631, in his fifty-second year.

The sad story of the betrayal and death of Sir Walter Ralegh must needs have a place in the narrative of English exploration and discovery. He had strongly represented the existence of rich gold mines in Guiana, and declared himself ready to discover and work them for the enrichment of his country. He was not granted a full pardon, but he received a commission giving him the power of life and death, which was an equivalent. He was allowed to undertake this enterprise on the impossible condition that no complication with the Spanish Government should result. He was released from the Tower, after an unjust detention of fifteen years, in January, 1616.

Robert Harcourt of Stanton Harcourt, in 1609, had sailed with his brother Michael to the Guiana coast, and, leaving a few colonists, had returned to England. He published a very interesting account of his voyage in 1613, but was unable, from want of funds, to continue his efforts for establishing a colony. Besides this Harcourt enterprise, nothing had been done by the English since the death of the Queen.

Sir Walter Ralegh contributed the remains of his fortune, and received £15,000 from his friends, with which he equipped a few vessels. But one was detained by creditors, another sank in a gale off Scilly, another was driven up the Bristol Channel, and a fourth deserted at Lanzarote. His own ship was the *Destiny*, with his young son Walter, aged twenty-four, as captain, and his life-long friend, Captain Keymis. Another vessel, the *Thunder*, was commanded by William St. Leger. Sailing from Cork in August, 1617, the one bright spot in the melancholy story is the short stay at the

island of Gomera, the point of departure of Columbus, where Sir
Walter Ralegh was most kindly received by the governor and his
English wife. There was terrible mortality in crossing the Atlantic.
Mr. Fowler, the chief gold refiner, and John Talbot, who had been
Ralegh's secretary in the Tower for eleven years, died. Finally, Sir
Walter himself was struck down with fever. He was prematurely
old, and enfeebled by long confinement. At length the *Destiny*
anchored in the Cayenne River, and for a fortnight they found rest
and refreshment during the last half of November.

In December the ship was off the island of Trinidad, but Ralegh
was too ill himself to undertake the boat voyage up the Orinoco in
search of the gold mine. He sent the boats in command of Captain
Keymis, accompanied by his own son Walter and his nephew,
George Ralegh. They attacked and captured the Spanish settlement
of San Tomas. Young Walter was killed in the assault. Keymis
returned with the news of hopeless failure. The unfortunate
leader saw that this fatal mistake would be used for his destruction.
In the heat of the moment he upbraided Keymis. The faithful
fellow said that there was but one thing left for him to do. He
went into his cabin and shot himself. The crew became mutinous
and insisted upon returning home. From St. Kitt's Sir Walter
Ralegh wrote a full explanation to Sir Ralph Winwood, the
Secretary of State, one of his few loyal friends. But, alas!
Winwood was already dead. The *Destiny* reached Plymouth on
the 21st of June, 1618, and Ralegh was joined by his devoted
wife. On November 29th the crime was perpetrated, and with
that great Englishman's life ended the glorious roll of Elizabethan
navigators. Queen Anne died in the same year. She was a steadfast
friend, she had taught her son to admire and sympathise with true
greatness, and, if Prince Henry had lived, England would have
been saved from the infamy of Sir Walter Ralegh's execution.
Richard Hakluyt had died two years earlier, in November, 1616,
when Ralegh was preparing for his last expedition.

There was a long period which is almost blank as regards
maritime enterprise. But in 1631 two voyages were planned for
continuing discoveries in the direction of Hudson's Bay. One, the
Maria, was fitted out at Bristol, and sailed on May 3rd, 1631,
under the command of Captain James, who reached Cape Digges
on the 15th of the following July. The other was equipped
in the Thames by Captain Luke Fox, of Hull, a clear-headed,

intelligent seaman, full of enthusiasm to advance the cause of Arctic discovery.

It is to Fox that we owe all our knowledge of the expedition of Sir Thomas Button, and of other voyages which would otherwise have been lost to us. For besides being a thorough seaman, he was a quaint and very entertaining writer. He sailed in the *Charles*, of 80 tons, with a crew of twenty men and boys, his equipment having been superintended by those steady friends to Arctic discovery, Sir Thomas Roe and Sir John Wolstenholme. Fox was perfectly satisfied with himself, his crew, his ship, and everything on board. On the 15th of July he entered Hudson's Bay, and gave names to several islands, proceeding to Port Nelson, where Button had wintered. Not finding any opening, he retraced his steps, meeting the *Maria*, in command of Captain James, on the 1st of August. Fox then steered northwards, along the western side of the coastline which trends northwards from the western entrance to Hudson's Strait. All this was new discovery as far as a point in 66° 47' N., which he named "Fox his Furthest." In after years, Sir Edward Parry gave the name of Fox's Channel to the opening which leads to Fox's farthest point. There the bold Yorkshireman decided upon returning home, and he arrived at the Downs with all his crew sound and well.

The cruise of the *Maria* was not so fortunate. Captain James determined to take shelter in a bay near the southern extremity of Hudson's inland sea. The crew wintered in a house on shore. Several men died of scurvy, but the vessel was got afloat in the spring, and arrived safely at Bristol in September, 1632. James was the last of the pioneers in Hudson's Bay. These gallant seamen, commencing from Hudson, increased geographical knowledge, and prepared the way for more complete modern research; and their discoveries led to the formation of a great company which carried on a lucrative trade, by way of Hudson's Strait and Bay, for two centuries.

CHAPTER XX.

CIVIL HISTORY OF THE NAVY, 1649–1660.

Parliamentary management of the Navy—Commissioners of the Navy and Customs—
The Naval Committee of the Council of State—Commissioners of the Admiralty
and Navy—The Navy Commissioners—Dockyard Commissioners—Admiralty
buildings—The Treasurership—Rapacity of Hutchinson—The Admirals and
Generals at Sea—The Commonwealth Captains—The spirit of the Service—Wages
—Midshipmen—Treatment of seamen—Sick and wounded—Medical comforts—
The Chatham Chest—Pay of officers—Pensions—Punishments—Prize-money—
Medals—Naval law—Soldiers afloat—Slop clothes—Victuals—The grievances of
the lower deck—The police of the seas—Privateering—Dockyards—Naval expenditure—Ships of the Commonwealth—Improvements in shipbuilding—Painting
of ships—Boats—Private yards—Rating of ships—The Navigation Laws—Flags
and ensigns—The Right of the Flag.

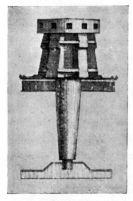

WHEN the Civil War had fairly begun,
and the control of the major part of
the Navy had passed out of the hands of the
King, the Parliament managed the service
by means of committees, the members of
which were constantly changed. There
was a Parliamentary Naval Committee,
with, subordinate to it, a body of Commissioners of the Navy and Customs ; and
the duties previously undertaken by the
Principal Officers were, with the exception
of those attached to the office of Treasurer,
given over to a board of Commissioners of the Navy.[1]

A Lord High Admiral, in the person of Robert, Earl of
Warwick,[2] was appointed in July, 1642, in place of Algernon, Earl

[1] The members of this board were, at first, Captains Richard Cranley, John Norris,
Roger Tweedy, William Batten, and Phineas Pett. Batten went to sea in 1645, and, in
1646, Peter Pett and Thomas Smith were added to the board. John Hollond also seems
to have been a member of it in 1644, and until 1646.

[2] Robert Rich, Earl of Warwick. Born, 1587. Appointed by Northumberland
Vice-Admiral to command the fleet, 1642. Retained command in opposition to the
will of Charles I., and established the ascendancy of the Parliament with the Navy.
Died, 1658.

of Northumberland ;[1] but he resigned in April, 1645, being, however, re-appointed on May 29th, 1648. This second appointment was cancelled on February 23rd, 1649. The Commissioners of the Navy and Customs had very little to do with administrative matters, and the body was dissolved in 1654. The Parliamentary Naval Committee also by degrees lost its authority after the conclusion of the Civil War. After Warwick's final retirement, a Committee of the Council of State succeeded to his responsibilities, until, on December 3rd, 1653, Commissioners of the Admiralty and Navy were appointed by Act of Parliament.[2] These met originally at Whitehall, but from January, 1655, occupied Derby House. With several changes the board existed until May 21st, 1659, when another body of commissioners, with little real power, was appointed, and Parliament itself assumed the chief responsibilities of Admiralty government.

After the fall of Charles I. a new body of Navy Commissioners was appointed on February 16th, 1649. It consisted of John Hollond (with the duties of Surveyor), Thomas Smith, Peter Pett, Robert Thompson, and Colonel William Willoughby. Willoughby died in 1651, and his successor, Sir Robert Moulton, in 1652. In 1653, Colonel Francis Willoughby, Edward Hopkins, and Major Nehemiah Bourne were added to the board. In 1654, George Payler superseded Hollond, and in 1657 Nathan Wright superseded Hopkins.[3] Hollond, as Surveyor, received £300, and the others each £250 a year, with, in 1653, an additional £150, on account of the unusual stress of that year. Never, probably, did men do better work for such remuneration. They were laborious, prompt, and it would seem, conscientious and honest ; and they had enormous responsibilities, for, on and after May 22nd, 1649, admirals and captains addressed them direct on all administrative details ; and it is abundantly evident that in course of time the Navy Commissioners supplanted in importance the Admiralty Committee.

[1] Algernon Percy, Earl of Northumberland. Born, 1602. Admiral, Custos Maris, Captain-General, and Governor of the Fleet (Lord High Admiral) 1638–1642. Died, 1668.

[2] The first Commissioners of the Admiralty and Navy were Generals Robert Blake, George Monck, John Disbrowe, and William Penn ; Colonels Philip Jones, John Clerk, and Thomas Kilsey ; Major William Burton ; and Messrs. John Stone, Edward Horseman, and Vincent Gookin. They also controlled the Ordnance Department.

[3] Attached to the Commissioners, as Admiralty Agents, were Captain Henry Hatsell, at Plymouth; Thomas White, at Dover ; Major Richard Elton, at Hull ; and Major William Burton, at Great Yarmouth.

From June 2nd, 1649, the Navy Commissioners occupied rooms in the Victualling Office on Tower Hill. During the Dutch War, a Commissioner took charge at each of the dockyards, Willoughby going to Portsmouth, and Pett to Chatham. Bourne also went to Harwich, which owing to its position with regard to Holland, became of great temporary value. In 1654, Sir John Wolstenholme's house in Seething Lane was purchased for the Commissioners at a cost of £2400, and it remained the Navy Office until the establishment was transferred, in the last quarter of the eighteenth century, to Somerset House. The Treasurer's Office, however, was distinct, and occupied a house in Leadenhall Street. The Commissioners had no secretary, and, until the autumn of 1653, but one clerk apiece. Each was then allowed two clerks, and two purveyors were appointed, to assist in the purchase of stores.

Sir Henry Vane, junior, was Treasurer of the Navy until the end of 1650, when he retired with a pension.[1] He was succeeded on January 1st, 1651, by Richard Hutchinson, who was given a salary of £1000 in lieu of all former fees and perquisites attaching to the office. But Hutchinson, unlike the Navy Commissioners, was by no means a disinterested patriot. In 1653 he procured for himself an extra allowance of £1000 ; in 1654 he obtained £2500 besides £1000 on every £100,000 disbursed in excess of £1,300,000; and from January, 1655, he received £1500, with £100 on every £100,000 disbursed in excess of £700,000.[2]

After the cancelling of Warwick's second appointment as Lord High Admiral, the duties of commander-in-chief afloat were put into commission, and entrusted to Edward Popham, Richard Deane,[3] and Robert Blake[4] as joint Generals-at-Sea.[5] To these were added, as Generals, George Monck, in 1652, and, after the death of Deane

---

[1] He was granted an estate worth £1200 a year.

[2] Oppenheim : ' Admin. of Roy. Navy,' 351, 352.

[3] Richard Deane. Born, 1610. Served in the Parliamentary Army. Appointed one of the Generals-at-Sea, 1649. Commanded jointly with Blake and Monck against the Dutch, and fell in the action of June 3rd, 1653.

[4] Robert Blake. Born, 1599, at Bridgewater. Educated at Wadham Coll., Oxford. Engaged in commercial pursuits. Served in the Parliamentary Army. Appointed one of the Generals-at-Sea, 1649. Burnt Prince Rupert's ships at Cartagena, 1650. Reduced the Scilly Isles and Jersey, 1651. Commanded against the Dutch, 1652–54. Badly wounded in the action off Portland, 1653. Reduced the pirates of Tunis and Algier, 1655. Destroyed shipping at Santa Cruz, 1657. Died, August 7th, 1657. Buried in Westminster Abbey. After the Restoration his body was dug up and thrown into a common grave in St. Margaret's churchyard.

[5] Appointed February 27th, 1649.—Cal. of S. P. Dom., 1649–50, 23.

in the action of June 3rd, 1653, William Penn[1] and Edward Montagu,[2] in 1654. Of these officers two only were seamen by bringing-up. Popham had been in command of the *Fifth Whelp* when, on June 28th, 1637, she foundered in the North Sea. Penn had commanded a ship when he was but three-and-twenty ; but Deane, Blake, Monck, and Montagu were military men, who had little or no naval experience until they were suddenly thrust into positions of the highest responsibility. Deane and Montagu perished gloriously, while still in their prime. Monck became a distinguished admiral. Blake, although he was never at sea until he was fifty, developed into one of the two or three greatest sea-captains that Britain has ever known. It is a significant fact that when, under the Commonwealth, Great Britain entered upon a more ambitious and difficult naval policy than she had previously dared to essay, the chiefs who best served her at sea were, by training, land officers, and consequently men of wider attainments and more general education and experience than belonged to the regular sea officers of the time.

And, indeed, it would appear that the Commonwealth possessed comparatively few captains who deserved elevation to more responsible positions. They were, for the most part, "tarpaulins," with little learning, no manners, and scant honesty. "Among officers," says Mr. Oppenheim,[3] "captains were the class who gave most trouble throughout these years, the number tried for or accused of various delinquencies yielding a much higher percentage of the total employed than that afforded by the men, or by officers of any other rank. This was perhaps largely due to the rapid promotion necessitated by the sudden increase of the Navy, commanders being chosen mainly for professional capacity ; and if they were considered politically safe, few questions were asked about their religious or

---

[1] William Penn. Born, 1621. Commanded the *Fellowship*, 1644. Rear-Admiral of the Irish Squadron, 1648. Vice-Admiral, 1650. Served in the first Dutch war, and at the capture of Jamaica in 1655, when he was one of the Admirals and Generals-at-Sea. "Great Captain Commander" under the Duke of York, 1665. Died, 1670. Disbrowe was nominated at about the same time as Penn; but he never actually served as a General-at-Sea.

[2] Edward Montagu, or Mountagu, Earl of Sandwich. Born, 1625. Served in the army during the Civil War. A General-at-Sea, 1654. Served in conjunction with Blake, 1656–57. Commanded the fleet which brought back Charles II. Created Earl of Sandwich. Admiral (B.) in the action of June 3rd, 1665. Admiral (B.) at Solebay, and there perished, May 28th, 1672.

[3] 'Admin. of Roy. Navy,' 352. The naval captains of the time were often spoken of as "colonels."

moral qualifications. Many, again, had risen from the forecastle, and possibly brought with them reminiscences of the habits existing in the Caroline Navy; others had been privateer captains, an occupation which did not tend to make their moral sense more delicate. Professional honour was not yet a living force, and in some orders issued by Monck to the captains of a detached squadron, the threat of loss of wages as a punishment for disobedience came after, and was obviously intended as a more impressive deterrent than, the disgrace of being cashiered." The chief offences were embezzlement, theft, drunkenness, and cruelty. Drunkenness was shamefully common throughout the service. The rule of the ex-military officers seems to have been instrumental in gradually ameliorating the tone of the Navy, and in creating a feeling of professional pride which, though only incipient in the seventeenth, grew rapidly in the eighteenth century, and produced its finest results early in the nineteenth.

But there were other reasons for the improvement of the spirit of the service. The Navy was becoming a life's career instead of a mere episodal avocation, and the status both of men and of officers was being rapidly bettered. During the Civil War, the Parliament paid its seamen 19s. a month. While Prince Rupert was at sea, the men in the squadrons sent against him were paid 25s. From January 1st, 1653, the regular wages were: for able seamen, 24s.; for ordinary seamen, 19s.; for gromets, 14s. 3d.; and for boys, 9s. 6d. It was ordered that every man's rating or ability should be marked upon his wages' ticket at his paying off, and thus he obtained a kind of certificate of efficiency, which, if satisfactory, was doubtless of great value to him. For the further encouragement of the men it was directed, on January 29th, 1653, that a certain proportion[1] of them were to be rated midshipmen, with pay varying from £1 10s. to £2 5s. a month, according to the ship in which they served; and it was stipulated that from December 14th, 1655, no one was to be so rated unless able in case of need to undertake officer's duties. This opened up a systematic way of promotion from the forecastle to the quarterdeck. There had been midshipmen during the time of Charles I., but it does not appear that any special standard of competency had been exacted from them, or that the rating was regarded as one likely to lead to rank and professional honour.

---

[1] *I.e.,* in first-rates, 20; in second-rates, 16; in third-rates, 12; in fourth-rates, 8; in fifth-rates, 6; and in sixth-rates, 4.—'Admin. of Roy. Navy,' 314.

Mr. Oppenheim notes that the earliest mention of midshipmen known to him occurs in the letter of a Mr. Cook, dated February 7th, 1643, in which the writer declares that he will not undervalue himself by allowing his son to accept a midshipman's place. But from 1655 the rating became one of the recognised introductions to officer's rank.

It must not be supposed that the Commonwealth always paid its seamen regularly. The rule lay rather in the other direction, and at the Restoration, wages to the amount of above £300,000 were owing, and some ships' companies had received nothing for four years. Yet the Commonwealth did make serious efforts to treat its men better than James and Charles had treated theirs. There was, for example, no deliberate neglect of the sick and wounded. During the Dutch War the London hospitals were ordered to accommodate some, and various coast towns to provide for others. Ships, too, were regularly allowed "medical comforts" to the value of £5 per one hundred men per six months, and men invalided to the shore were retained in pay until their recovery or their death. It would seem, indeed, that, bearing in mind the then condition of the surgical, medical, and sanitary sciences, the sick and wounded fared remarkably well, and were in many respects better off than the able-bodied. For the better care of them, a board of four Commissioners of Sick and Wounded was established on September 29th, 1653, with offices in Little Britain. These Commissioners undertook the surgical and medical direction of the Navy, and were invested with power to grant gratuities up to £10, and pensions up to £6 13s. 4d. Incidentally, they had charge of prisoners of war. The Chatham Chest, on the other hand, was mismanaged and in debt. Pensions were paid from it to the widows of officers, but not to those of men, and many men's pensions were in arrears. An inquiry, instituted after the Restoration, into the conduct of the Chest, revealed the fact that extravagance and carelessness, if not actual corruption, hindered the efficiency of this admirable benevolent fund under the Commonwealth.

The pay of officers was raised in 1649, and again in 1653, from which period it stood as follows (see next page).

Pensions to the widows of officers seem to have been always small, but they were in some instances augmented by gifts or gratuities of considerable value. Thus, for instance, in 1653, seven captains' widows received gifts of from £400 to £1000.

THE PAY OF OFFICERS.

	1st-rate.			2nd-rate.			3rd-rate.			4th-rate.			5th-rate.			6th-rate.		
	£	s.	d.	£	s.	d.	£	s.	d.	£	s.	d.	£	s.	d.	£	s.	d.
Captain	21	0	0	16	16	0	14	0	0	10	0	0	8	8	0	7	0	0
Lieutenant . . .	4	4	0	4	4	0	3	10	0	3	10	0						
Master	7	0	0	6	6	0	4	13	8	4	6	2	3	7	6			
Master's Mate . } Pilot . . . . }	3	6	0	3	0	0	2	16	2	2	7	10	2	2	0	2	2	0
Midshipman . .	2	5	0	2	0	0	1	17	6	1	13	9	1	10	0	1	10	0
Boatswain . . .	4	0	0	3	10	0	3	0	0	2	10	0	2	5	0	2	0	0
Boatswain's Mate .	1	15	0	1	15	0	1	12	0	1	10	0	1	8	0	1	6	0
Quartermaster . .	1	15	0	1	15	0	1	12	0	1	10	0	1	8	0	1	6	0
Quartermaster's Mate	1	10	0	1	10	0	1	8	0	1	8	0	1	6	0	1	5	0
Carpenter . . .	4	0	0	3	10	0	3	0	0	2	10	0	2	5	0	2	0	0
Carpenter's Mate .	2	0	0	2	0	0	1	16	0	1	14	0	1	12	0	1	10	0
Gunner	4	0	0	3	10	0	3	0	0	2	10	0	2	5	0	2	0	0
Gunner's Mate . .	1	15	0	1	15	0	1	12	0	1	10	0	1	8	0	1	6	0
Surgeon. . . .	2	10	0	2	10	0	2	10	0	2	10	0	2	10	0	2	10	0
Corporal. . . .	1	15	0	1	12	0	1	10	0	1	10	0	1	8	0	1	5	0
Purser	4	0	0	3	10	0	3	0	0	2	10	0	2	5	0	(2	0	0¹)
Master Trumpeter .	1	10	0	1	8	0	1	5	0	1	5	0	1	5	0	1	4	0
Cook	1	5	0	1	5	0	1	5	0	1	5	0	1	5	0	1	4	0

PER LUNAR MONTH OF TWENTY-EIGHT DAYS.

¹ The captain of a 6th-rate usually did purser's duties.

From 1649, the pay of officers having charge of stores was increased, and from 1652 such officers had to furnish sureties for the honest performance of their duties. These measures no doubt tended to check forgery, falsification of accounts, malversation, and peculation on the part of pursers, boatswains, gunners and others. Reform was also aided by the making of regulations that pursers should go to sea as clerks of the check, with limited powers, and that all their papers should be countersigned by their captains; but it was not found necessary to prolong the arrangement as to pursers being clerks of the check after 1655; and these officers then resumed their old position.

The system of punishments and rewards also had its effect in bettering the moral tone of the service, and especially of the officers. The death penalty, though prescribed for a great number of offences, was seldom enforced. Other punishments were, however, very severe. A carpenter who had stolen stores, but returned them before his arrest, was taken from ship to ship in the Downs with a paper recording his offences pinned to his breast. This paper was read alongside each ship, and he was then thrice ducked from the yard-arm, and cashiered. William Haycock, carpenter's mate of the *Hound*, for drunkenness, swearing, and uncleanness, was sentenced to receive ten lashes alongside each flagship, a punishment which Mr. Oppenheim detects as the origin of the later practice of flogging round the fleet.[1]

In the matter of rewards, the Commonwealth was much more liberal than preceding governments had been. An Act of 1649 gave the seamen, in addition to their wages, one-half of the value of men-of-war taken, the other half going to a fund for the relief of sick, wounded, widows and orphans.[2] Men-of-war destroyed were paid for by the State at the rate of from £12 to £20 a gun. The proceeds of merchant prizes taken by men-of-war went, one-third to the officers and men, one-third to the sick and wounded fund, and one-third to the State; and the proceeds of merchant prizes taken by hired vessels went, two-sixths to the officers and men, two-sixths to the sick and wounded fund, one-sixth to the owners, and one-sixth to the State. The " tenths," paid at an earlier date to the Lord Admiral, went towards the provision of special rewards and of medals. In 1653 a new scheme was introduced, and under it officers and men became entitled to 10s. per ton of every prize taken, besides £6 13s. 4d. for each gun carried by her, and to £10 per gun for every man-of-war destroyed, while the old " tenths " were given to the sick, wounded, and widows' fund. It is true that the sums due were often not paid for years, but there is no reason to doubt the good intentions of the government. The immense difficulties under which it laboured may be pleaded in some extenuation of its shortcomings.

The giving of medals, sometimes with chains attached, to distinguished officers was no new thing in England. Charles I., for example, had given a medal to Rainborow for his conduct of the Sallee Expedition in 1637. Parliament continued the practice, if practice it can be called, giving medals to both captains and flag-officers for the victory over the Dutch in 1653; but it also gave medals to seamen. Mr. Oppenheim cites as a somewhat doubtful reference an order of the House, of November 15th, 1649, for medals to be conferred on " several mariners " who had done good service in the previous year, but who may possibly have been officers. There is, however, no room for doubting that after Captain Robert Wyard, of the *Adventure*, hired merchantman, fought his action off Harwich in 1650 with a greatly superior force, he and his officers

---

[1] 'Admin. of Roy. Navy,' 357, 358.

[2] This Act amplified a somewhat less generous Parliamentary resolution of 1642.

and men were given medals of different values, ranging from £50 down to 5*s*., and that each medal had, as was directed, "the service against six ships engraved on one side and the arms of the Commonwealth on the other."[1] Nevertheless, the number of medals given to seamen was certainly not large, for the entire number of medals granted, to officers included, for the Dutch War was only one hundred and sixty-nine, the cost of them being £2069. This sum seems to have also covered the cost of the gold chains conferred on Blake, Monck, and Penn. Yet that medals were obtainable by them, even though rarely, cannot but have encouraged the seamen.

GOLD MEDAL FOR THE ACTION WITH THE DUTCH FLEET, 1653.

(*The original by T. Simon, was presented by the English Government, with a large additional border, to the Flag Officers, and, as above, to the Captains engaged.*)

Naval law may be said to have received its first codification under the Commonwealth. More than once in these pages mention has been made of disciplinary instructions issued to their fleets by particular commanders upon particular occasions. These instructions, however, lapsed with the various occasions which called them into being. Rules of the kind for the government of the Earl of Warwick's fleet were passed by the Commons in March, 1649; and

---

[1] 'Admin. of Roy. Navy,' 328, citing S. P. Dom., August 16th, 1650. Some of these medals were shown at the Royal Naval Exhibition of 1891, by Mr. J. G. Murdoch, who showed also the very rare medal " for eminent service in saving the *Triumph*," in July, 1653, together with " Naval Rewards " of 1650 and 1653.

on December 25th, 1652, a modification of these rules was enacted
for the government of the whole Navy. These were the first regular
Articles of War; [1] and to Mr. Oppenheim belongs the credit of being
the first to point out that interesting fact. Until he did so it had
been generally supposed that the consecutive history of the Articles
of War began in 1661; but, as Mr. Oppenheim justly says, "these
latter were only based upon those previously existing, which are the
groundwork of all subsequent modifications and additions experience
has shown to be necessary down to the present day." [2] There were
thirty-nine of them, thirteen prescribing death, and twelve more
prescribing either death or a lighter punishment alternatively,
according to the view taken by the Court of War trying the
offender. But though the code was then, on paper, extremely
severe, it was enforced with mercy and discretion; and up to the
time of the Restoration there is no known instance of a death
sentence pronounced under it having been carried out. Even the
fomenters of mutiny escaped. Three men of the *Portland*, convicted of that most serious offence, or of having incited to it, in
1653, when the country was at war, were let off with the comparatively light though very cruel penalty of having to stand for
one hour with their right hands nailed to the mainmast of the
flagship and with halters about their necks. Three of their fellows
received only thirty lashes apiece.

No force akin to the modern Royal Marines was afloat in British
ships until after the Restoration; but the urgency of the situation
during the Dutch War led to the embarkation of considerable bodies
of soldiers, who assisted in the work of the vessels, and, in fact, did
marines' duties. They behaved extremely well, although they went
on board under none of their own officers above the rank of sergeant;
and, no doubt, it was the recollection of their excellent service that
suggested the formation, in the days of Charles II., of a regular
force of sea soldiers.

There was still no uniform for naval officers, and seamen dressed
as they chose. The practice, prevalent in the early part of the reign

---

[1] The rules of 1652 and 1661, however, must not be regarded as the sole source
from which the present Articles of War have been evolved. Additional sources
continued to be supplied, by means of successive Admirals' instructions, until the
commencement of the eighteenth century; and only then did it cease to be the practice
for Commanders-in-Chief to issue, as it were, special laws of their own. For a further
discussion of this subject, see Chap. XXVI.

[2] 'Admin. of Roy. Navy,' 311.—Thomason Pamphlets $\frac{681}{9}$.

of Henry VIII., of supplying the men with some sort of regulation
coats or jackets had long since died out. But, as in the time of
Charles I., slop-clothes were for sale on board every ship, and these,
which were supplied at a specified price, seem also to have been of a
prescribed pattern. Purchase of them was not, however, obligatory,
and, if a seaman had enough clothes to give him a moderately decent
appearance, no one cavilled at their cut or colour. In 1655 it was
ordered that for the future no clothiers should send clothes for sale
on board ship without the licence of the Navy Commissioners ;
and early in 1656 the prices of slops were thus fixed :[1] Canvas
jackets, 1s. 10d. ; canvas drawers, 1s. 8d. ; cotton waistcoats, 2s. 2d. ;
cotton drawers, 2s. ; shirts, 2s. 9d. ; shoes, per pair, 2s. 4d. ; linen
stockings, per pair, 10d. ; cotton stockings, per pair, 10d. The
Commissioners declined responsibility for the quality of the clothes ;
but, if a man lost his kit while on service, they usually granted him
a small sum wherewith to buy another : so that it may be said that
under the Commonwealth the seaman's dress became for the first
time since the days of Henry VIII. a question which seriously
occupied the attention of the Government.

At least equal attention was paid to the seaman's victuals. In
1650 Colonel Pride and five others took a contract to supply the
fleet at 8d. per head at sea, and 7d. per head in harbour. The
contractors did not give complete satisfaction, and after 1652 a
system of inspection of victuals was established. In that year also
new buildings for the Victualling Department were erected or acquired at various ports. In 1653 the sea-rate for victualling was
advanced from 8d. to 9d. a head ; but in 1654 the victualling contractors gave notice of their intention to terminate an arrangement
which, even at that price, did not pay them : and the result was the
formation of a Victualling Office, with Captain Thomas Alderne at
its head. Alderne, until his death in 1657, was paid £500 a year, and
did his work under the superintendence of the Navy Commissioners.
He was succeeded by three of the Commissioners—Robert Thompson, Bourne, and Francis Willoughby, who were thenceforward
called Commissioners of the Navy and Victualling, and who were
paid £250 a year each for the extra service.[2] The Commissioners
seem to have done their business as well as was possible in view of
the straitened financial situation of the Government, which, towards

---

[1] S. P. Dom. cxvii. 64 ; cxxxiv. 64.
[2] ' Admin. of Roy. Navy,' 324–326.

the end of the Commonwealth, was in debt to every one in England who had been willing to give it credit. But after the death of Oliver Cromwell all the affairs of the Navy became involved in hopeless confusion. In the summer of 1659 a sum of £371,930[1] was owing for wages alone. It is scarcely astonishing that the prospect of the return of Charles II. and of a change in the management of the Navy failed to arouse any noteworthy republican demonstrations in the fleet.

One very remarkable feature of the period is the deference paid by the governing powers to the common seamen. There were, of course, political causes for this; but the improved education of all classes, and their greater reasonableness, must also, to some extent, have been responsible. Thus, when in 1654 the seamen petitioned Cromwell for a redress of certain alleged grievances, the petition, instead of being shelved, was referred to a Council of War composed of two flag and twenty-three other officers, who decided that the men had a legal right to petition, and that the alleged grievances, with a single exception, were real ones.

In spite of the disadvantages under which they suffered, the men generally did their duty. The administration, too, though over-burdened and impoverished, never omitted to vindicate the honour of the country. Piracy, which had been so prevalent in the Narrow Seas under Charles I., became almost unheard of. The French, Dutch, and Spanish privateers still cruised, but, except for a short time after the Dutch War, they effected little, and numbers of them were taken. As soon, moreover, as the Ostenders and the Dunquerquers became really troublesome, Cromwell instituted a blockade of their ports. As for British subjects found serving in foreign privateers, they were summarily deported to the Plantations. The Commonwealth, indeed, did not look very kindly on priva-teering, even when it was practised in the interests of Great Britain. In 1652 all privateers were put under the direct control of the admirals afloat; soon afterwards the issue of letters of marque was severely restricted, it being found that the lax discipline and freer life of the irregular cruisers had a prejudicial effect upon the regular naval service; and, from 1655 onwards, privateering was no longer allowed at all, apparently because it had too often tended to degenerate into piracy, or something very like it.

Little progress was made in the development of the Government

[1] S. P. Dom. ccxii. 109.

Dockyards. "In 1653," says Mr. Oppenheim,[1] "there was a double dry-dock at Chatham, Woolwich, and Deptford respectively, and one at Blackwall, probably in the East India Company's yard: these were the only docks directly belonging to, or available by, the State. No addition appears to have been made to Chatham Yard, except the purchase of a wharf and storehouse adjoining the old dock in 1656. In October, 1653, a contractor from Chatham was either repairing an old, or constructing a new, dock at Deptford; and in 1657 some wharves were built there alongside the waterside. A new dry-dock was ordered for Woolwich in 1653, and completed the next year: storehouses were built in 1656, and two years later a lease was taken from John Rymill, butcher, of London, of one acre of land, known as Chimney Marsh, on the east side of Ham Creek, 'next to the State's Yard,' for ten years, at £4 a year. The sizes of the yards may, perhaps, be inferred from the number of watch-men attached to each: Chatham, thirty-two; Deptford, eighteen; Woolwich, sixteen; and Portsmouth, thirteen." A dry-dock at Portsmouth was built in 1656–57 at an estimated cost of £2100. The yard there began to be again used for building purposes, and to acquire a reputation for economical construction. Dover and Harwich, as subsidiary naval stations and bases, were much used during the Dutch War.

The naval expenditure, during almost the whole of the Common-wealth period, was, relatively speaking, enormous. In 1656–57, out to of a total revenue of £1,050,000, a sum of £809,000 was devoted the Navy; in 1657–58, £624,000 out of £951,000; and in 1658–59, £848,000 out of £1,517,000. In 1652–53 the naval expenditure had been, in round figures, £1,400,000, out of a total expenditure of £2,600,000.[2] In comparison with these disbursements the naval estimates of modern times are, indeed, ridiculously small in propor-tion. Under the Commonwealth Britain spent more than half her income upon the sea service: under Queen Victoria she has never spent one-fourth of it on the same object. Yet who can say that the necessity is less in the nineteenth century than it was in the seventeenth? Cromwell and his advisers may not have understood as we understand it the influence of sea power upon history; but they certainly did not underrate the importance to this country of

---

[1] 'Admin. of Roy. Navy,' 364, citing S. P. Dom., lviii. 108; lx. 12; lxxxi. 194; cxxxv. 17; clxxx. 170: and Add. MSS. 9305, f. 114; and 9306, ff. 175, 197.

[2] Add. MSS. 32,471, ff. 2, 6, 15. Comms. Journs. May 20th, 1659.—Pepys's 'Diary.'

the possession of a Navy fit to meet any combination that was likely to be arrayed against it. Their forethought was justified. The Commonwealth found Great Britain weak at sea, but left it with a naval reputation second to that of no power in the world.

The additions to the Navy during the eleven years are here given alphabetically, it being premised, however, that the list[1] is very probably incomplete, especially as regards small craft and vessels taken for a short time only into the service :—

—	* Built. † Bought. ‡ Taken.	Length of Keel.	Beam.	Depth in Hold.	Draught.	Nett Tons.	Guns.	—
		Ft. in.	Ft. in.	Ft. in.	Ft. in.			
Accada . . .	† 1656	..	..	..	..	..	10	
Adam and Eve .	‡ 1652	..	..	..	..	200	20	Sold, 1657.
Advantage. . .	‡ 1652	..	..	..	..	..	26	Sold, 1655.
Advice	* 1650	100 0	31 2	12 3	15 7	516	48	
Adviser . . .	* 1654	..	..	..	..	..	8	Taken, 1655.
Amity	† 1650	85 0	28 0	14 0	..	354	30	
Antelope . . .	* 1651	120 0	36 0	16 0	..	..	56	{Wrecked off Jutland, 1652.
Arms of Holland .	‡ 1652	..	..	..	..	..	32	{Blown up in W. Ind., 1656.
Assistance. . .	* 1650	102 0	31 0	13 0	15 0	521	48	
Augustine. . .	‡ 1653	100 0	26 0	14 0	14 0	359	26	
Basing. . . .	* 1654	80 0	24 6	10 0	12 0	255	22	{Re-named Guernsey, 1660.
Bear	‡ 1653	106 0	26 6	14 6	14 6	395	36	
Beaver. . . .	‡ 1656	..	..	..	..	..	6	
Blackamoor[1] . .	* 1656	47 0	19 0	10 0	..	90	12	
Black Raven . .	‡ 1653	..	..	..	..	300	38	Sold, 1654.
Bradford . . .	* 1658	85 0	25 6	10 8	12 0	230	28	{Re-named Success, 1660.
Bramble . . .	‡ 1656	..	..	..	..	112	14	
Bridgewater . .	* 1655	116 9	34 7	14 2	17 0	742	52	{Re-named Anne, 1660.
Bristol. . . .	* 1653	104 0	31 1	13 0	15 8	532	48	
Bryar	‡ 1651	..	..	..	..	108	18	
Cagway . . .	‡ 1658	..	..	..	..	60	8	
Call, prize . .	‡ 1652	.	..	..	..	..	8	
Cardiff . . .	‡ 1653	..	..	..	..	..	18	Sold, ca. 1658.
Cat.	‡ 1654	..	..	..	..	..	8	Taken, 1656.
Centurion . . .	* 1650	104 0	31 0	13 0	16 0	531	40	

[1] Or *Blackmoor*. Built for service in Virginia.

---

[1] Compiled chiefly from two lists in Charnock's 'Marine Architecture,' ii. 377, 382 ; the list in ' Archæologia,' xlviii. ; two partial lists in the Sergison Collection ; lists in the Pepysian Library ; and references in the State Papers. The measurements have, in many cases, been checked by those given by Mr. Oppenheim, p. 330, *et seq.* The armament of most of the ships varied from term to term. Numerous other vessels were levied for war purposes ; but those given in the table seem to have all been regularly added to the Navy. For much information as to changes in the names of ships, I am personally indebted to Mr. Oppenheim and Professor Laughton, R.N.

	* Built. † Bought. ‡ Taken.	Length of Keel.		Beam.		Depth in Hold.		Draught.		Nett Tons.	Guns.	
		Ft.	in.	Ft.	in.	Ft.	in.	Ft.	in.			
Cheriton . . .	* 1656	76	0	24	0	10	0	11	0	194	20	Re-named *Speedwell,* 1660.
Chestnut¹ . . .	* 1656	47	0	19	0	10	0	..		90	12	
Church . . .	‡ 1653	..		..		..		..		300	30	
Colchester . . .	* 1654	83	0	25	6	10	0	12	0	287	24	
Concord . . .	† 1650	..		..		..		..		..	26	Sold, 1659.
Convert . . .	‡ 1652	..		..		..		..		..	26	Sold, 1659.
Convertine . .	‡ 1651	..		..		..		..		500	40	Taken by the Dutch, 1666,
Cornelian . . .	‡ 1655	..		..		..		..		100	12	
Coventry . . .	‡ 1658	..		..		..		..		200	20	
Crow . . .	‡ 1652	..		..		..		..		..	36	Sold, 1656.
Cygnet (I.) . .	* 1650	..		..		..		..		..	22	
Cygnet (II.) . .	* 1657	..		..		..		..		60	6	
Dartmouth . .	* 1655	80	0	25	0	10	0	12	0	230	22	
Deptford, shallop .	* 1652	..		..		..		..		..	4	Sold, 1659.
Diamond . . .	* 1652	105	6	31	3	13	0	16	0	547	40	
Discovery . . .	† 1651	..		..		..		..		..	20	Burnt at Jamaica, 1655.
Dolphin . . .	‡ 1652	..		..		..		..		..	30	Disposed of, *ca.* 1657.
Dover	* 1650	100	0	31	8	13	0	16	0	571	40	
Drake	* 1652	85	0	18	0	7	0	9	0	113	14	
Duchess . . .	‡ 1652	..		..		..		..		..	24	Sold, 1654.
Dunbar . . .	* 1656	123	0	46	0	17	2	21	0	1047	64	Re-named *Henry,* 1660.
Eagle	‡ 1650	..		..		..		..		..	12	
Eaglet	* 1655	..		..		..		..		60	8	
Elias (I.) . . .	‡ 1653	101	0	27	6	11	0	14	6	400	36	
Elias (II.) . .	‡ 1656											
Elizabeth, prize .	‡ 1650	..		..		..		..		..	..	Disposed of, *ca.* 1652.
Endeavour . .	‡ 1652	..		..		..		..		..	36	Sold, 1656.
Essex	* 1653	115	0	33	0	13	8	17	0	742	48	Taken by the Dutch, 1666.
Fagons² . . .	* 1654	82	0	24	8	10	0	12	0	262	22	Re-named *Milford,* 1660.
Fairfax (I.) . .	* 1649	116	0	35	8	14	6	17	6	789	64	Burnt at Chatham, 1653.
Fairfax (II.) . .	* 1653	120	0	35	2	14	6	16	6	745	52	
Falcon, flyboat	‡ 1653	..		..		..		..		200	24	Sold, 1658.
Falmouth³ . .	‡ 1652	..		..		..		..		..	20	Sold, 1659.
Fame	‡ 1655	..		..		..		..		90	10	
Fly	?	..		..		..		..		..	6	Disposed of, *ca.* 1652.
Foresight . . .	* 1650	102	0	31	0	13	0	14	6	524	40	
Forester . . .	* 1657	..		..		..		..		230	22	
Fortune (I.) . .	‡ 1651	..		..		..		..		..	..	Taken by the Dutch, 1652.
Fortune (II.) . .	‡ 1653	..		..		..		..		..	26	Sold, 1654.
Fox (I.) . . .	‡ 1651	..		..		..		..		..	22	
Fox (II.) . . .	‡ 1658	72	0	23	0	8	6	10	0	120	14	
Francis . . .	‡ 1658	..		..		..		..		90	10	

¹ Built for service in Virginia.   ² *I.e.,* St. Fagans.   ³ Late Dutch *Rotterdam.*

— ⎧ * Built. ⎨ † Bought. ⎩ ‡ Taken.	Length of Keel.		Beam.		Depth in Hold.		Draught.		Nett Tons.	Guns.	—
	Ft.	in.	Ft.	in.	Ft.	in.	Ft.	in.			
Gainsborough . .	* 1654	100	10	31	10	13	0	15	0	543	40	⎧R e - n a m e d ⎨ Swallow, ⎩ 1660.
Gift Major . .	‡ 1652	90	8	30	8	11	6	13	6	480	26	
Gift Minor . .	‡ 1658	..		..		..		..		120	12	
Gilliflower [1] . .	† 1651	..		..		..		..		530	32	Sold, 1657.
Gloucester . . .	* 1654	117	0	34	10	14	6	18	0	755	50	
Golden Cock . .	‡ 1653	..		..		..		..		..	24	Sold, 1656.
Golden Falcon .	‡ 1652	..		..		..		..		..	28	Sold, 1658.
Golden Lion . .	‡ 1652	..		..		..		..		..	..	Sold, 1653.
Grantham . . .	* 1654	80	0	25	0	10	0	11	6	265	28	⎧R e - n a m e d ⎨ Garland, ⎩ 1660.
Great Charity .	‡ 1650	106	0	28	6	11	10	14	0	400	39	⎰Lost in action, ⎱ 1665.
Greyhound . .	‡ 1657	60	0	26	6	11	6	..		150	20	
Griffin	‡ 1656	..		..		..		..		90	12	
Guinea . . .	† 1649	90	0	28	0	14	0	..		375	30	
Hare	‡ 1653	..		..		..		..		..	12	Wrecked, 1665.
Harp	* 1656	..		..		..		..		..	8	
Hart	* 1657	50	0	14	6	5	6	5	0	55	6	
Half Moon . .	‡ 1653	..		..		..		..		300	30	Sold, 1659.
Hampshire . .	* 1653	101	9	29	9	13	0	14	10	481	38	
Hawk	* 1655	42	0	16	0	8	0	..		60	8	
Heartsease . . .	‡ 1652	..		..		..		..		..	36	Sold, 1656.
Hector	‡ 1653	..		..		..		..		150	30	Sold, 1657.
Hind	* 1655	42	0	16	0	8	0	..		60	8	
Hope	‡ 1652	..		..		..		..		..	26	Sold, 1657.
Hopewell . . .	† 1652	..		..		..		..		..	20	Sold, 1656.
Horsleydown . .	* 1652	..		..		..		..		..	4	Sold, 1655.
Hound	‡ 1652	..		..		..		..		..	36	
Hunter (I.) . .	‡ 1652	..		..		..		..		..	..	⎰Lost in action, ⎱ 1653.
Hunter (II.) . .	‡ 1656	..		..		..		..		50	6	
Indian	‡ 1654	..		..		..		..		..	44	Sold, 1659.
Islip	* 1654	..		..		..		..		..	22	⎧Wrecked off ⎨ Inverlochy, ⎩ 1655.
Jermyn . . .	‡ 1649	..		..		..		..		..	..	⎰Disposed of, ca. ⎱ 1652.
Jersey	* 1654	102	10	32	2	13	2	15	6	560	40	
Jesu Maria . .	‡ 1656											
John	† 1650	..		..		..		..		..	30	⎰Disposed of, ca. ⎱ 1652.
John Baptist . .	‡ 1653	..		..		..		..		..	12	Sold, 1656.
Katherine . . .	‡ 1653	..		..		..		..		..	36	Sold, ca. 1658.
Kentish . . .	* 1652	107	0	32	6	13	0	15	0	601	40	
King David . .	‡ 1653	..		..		..		..		..	12	Sold, 1654.
Kingsale . . .	‡ 1656	..		..		..		..		90	10	
Langport . . .	* 1654	116	0	35	7	14	4	17	0	781	50	⎧R e - n a m e d ⎨ Henrietta, ⎩ 1660.
Lark	‡ 1656	..		..		..		..		80	10	
Laurel	* 1651	103	0	30	1	15	0	..		489	38	Wrecked, 1657.
Leopard . . .	* 1659	109	0	33	9	15	8	17	0	636	44	

[1] Ex-*Archangel*, taken by Prince Rupert, but recaptured and purchased.

—	* Built. † Bought. ‡ Taken.	Length of Keel.		Beam.		Depth in Hold.		Draught.		Nett Tons.	Guns.	—
		Ft.	in.	Ft.	in.	Ft.	in.	Ft.	in.			
Lichfield . . .	‡ 1658	..		..		.		..		200	20	Re-named Happy Entrance, 1660.
Lily (I.) . . .	?	.		..		..		..		..	8	Disposed of, ca. 1652.
Lily (II.) . . .	* 1657	..		..		..		5	0	60	6	
Little Charity . .	‡ 1653	..		..		..		..		500	30	Sold, 1656.
Little President .	‡ 1651	..		..		..		..		..	12	Sold, 1657.
Lizard	‡ 1653	..		..		..		..		100	16	
London . . .	* 1656	123	6	41	0	16	6	18	0	1050	64	Blown up near the Nore, 1665.
Lyme	* 1654	117	0	35	2	14	4	18	0	769	52	Re-named Montagu, 1660.
Maidstone . . .	* 1654	102	0	31	8	13	0	16	0	566	40	Re-named Mary Rose 1660.
Maria	‡ 1658	..		..		..		..		120	12	
Marigold . . .	‡ 1650	..		..		..		..		..	30	Sold, 1658.
Marigold, hoy .	‡ 1653	32	0	14	0	7	0	7	0	42		
Marmaduke¹ .	† 1652	..		..		..		..		400	32	
Marston Moor . .	* 1654	116	0	34	6	14	2	17	0	734	52	Re-named York, 1660.
Martin . . .	* 1652	64	0	19	4	7	0	..		92	14	
Martin, prize . .	‡ 1651	..		..		..		..		..	..	Disposed of, ca. 1653.
Mary, prize . .	‡ 1650	..		..		..		..		500	36	Sold, 1657.
Mathias . . .	‡ 1653	..		..		..		..		500	38	
Mayflower . . .	† 1651	..		..		..		..		..	20	Sold, 1658.
Merlin	* 1652	75	0	18	0	7	8	9	0	105	14	Taken by the Dutch, Oct. 1665.
Mermaid . . .	* 1651	86	0	25	2	10	0	12	0	289	22	
Middelburg . . .	‡ 1652	..		..		..		..		..	32	Disposed of, ca. 1657.
Minion . . .	?	..		..		..		..		..	6	Disposed of, ca. 1652.
Monck	* 1659	108	0	35	0	13	11	16	0	703	52	
Nantwich . . .	* 1654	86	8	26	4	10	4	12	6	319	28	Re-named Breda, 1660.
Naseby	* 1655	131	0	42	0	18	0	11	0	1229	80	Re-named Royal Charles, 1660.
Newbury . . .	* 1654	117	0	35	0	14	5	17	6	765	52	Re-named Revenge, 1660.
Newcastle . . .	* 1653	108	6	33	1	13	3	16	0	631	44	
Nightingale . .	* 1651	86	0	25	2	10	0	12	0	289	22	
Nonsuch, ketch .	† 1654	27	0	15	6	6	0	..		60	8	Taken March, retaken April, 1659.
Norwich . . .	* 1655	81	0	25	0	10	6	12	0	246	22	
Oak	‡ 1652	..		..		..		..		..	..	Lost in action, July, 1653.
Old President . .	‡ 1651	..		..		..		..		..	..	Sold, 1665.
Old Success . .	‡ 1649	..		..		..		..		380	34	
Orange-Tree . .	‡ 1653	..		..		..		..		300	26	Sold, 1655.

¹ Taken by Prince Rupert, but re-taken and bought into the service.

—	* Built. † Bought. ‡ Taken.	Length of Keel.		Beam.		Depth in Hold.		Draught.		Nett Tons.	Guns.	—
		Ft.	in.	Ft.	in.	Ft.	in.	Ft.	in.			
Ostrich . . .	‡ 1653											
Oxford . . .	* 1656	72	0	24	0	10	0	11	0	240	22	
Paradox . . .	‡ 1651	..		..		..		..		120	12	
Parrot . . .	* 1657	..		..		..		5	0	60	6	
Paul	‡ 1652	84	0	26	0	9	6	10	6	290	22	
Peacock . .	‡ 1651	..		..		..		..		..	..	Sold, ca. 1658.
Pearl	* 1651	86	0	25	0	10	0	12	0	285	22	
Pelican . . .	* 1650	100	0	20	8	15	4	..		..	38	{Burnt at Portsmouth, 1656.
Pelican's Prize .	‡ 1653	..		..		..		..		..	34	Sold, 1655.
Pembroke . . .	* 1655	81	0	25	0	11	6	12	0	269	22	
Peter	‡ 1652	..		..		..		..		..	32	Sold, 1653.
Plover (I.)[1] . .	‡ 1652	..		..		..		..		..	..	{Sunk in action, Feb. 1653.
Plover (II.) . .	‡ 1653	..		..		..		..		..	26	Sold, 1657.
Plymouth . . .	* 1653	116	0	34	8	14	6	17	0	741	54	
Portland . . .	* 1653	105	0	32	11	12	10	16	0	605	44	
Portsmouth . .	* 1650	99	0	28	4	14	2	15	0	422	38	
Portsmouth, shallop	‡ 1655	..		..		..		..		..	4	{Taken, July, 1655.
President[2] . . .	* 1649	102	9	29	6	12	6	15	6	445	42	{Re-named Bonaventure, 1660.
Preston . . .	* 1654	101	0	30	0	13	0	16	0	550	40	{Re-named Antelope, 1660.
Primrose . . .	* 1651	86	0	25	2	10	0	12	0	..	22	{Lost on the Seven Stones, 1656.
Princess Maria .	‡ 1652	..		..		..		..		..	36	{Wrecked on the Goodwin, 1658.
Raven (I.). . .	‡ 1652	..		..		..		..		..	36	{Taken by the Dutch, April, 1654.
Raven (II.) . .	‡ 1656	..		..		..		..		..	6	Sold, ca. 1658.
Recovery . . .	‡ 1651	..		..		..		..		..	26	Sold, 1655.
Redhart, pink . .	‡ 1653	..		..		..		..		55	6	Sold, 1654.
Red Horse, pink .	‡ 1655	..		..		..		..		..	10	Sold, 1658.
Renown . . .	‡ 1653	..		..		..		..		..	20	Sold, 1654.
Reserve . . .	* 1650	100	0	31	1	12	4	15	6	513	40	
Richard . . .	* 1658	124	0	41	0	18	0	20	0	1108	70	{Re-named Royal James, 1660.
Roe	* 1655	..		..		..		..		60	8	
Rose	* 1657	50	0	14	0	5	6	5	0	55	6	
Rosebush . . .	‡ 1653	..		..		..		..		300	34	
Ruby	* 1651	105	6	31	6	13	0	16	0	556	40	
Samson . . .	‡ 1652	..		..		..		..		..	32	Sold, 1658.
Samuel . . .	?	..		..		..		..		..	6	{Disposed of, ca. 1652.
Sapphire . . .	* 1651	100	0	28	10	11	9	13	6	442	38	{Run ashore by her captain, 1671.
Satisfaction . .	‡ 1651	..		..		..		..		220	26	
Scout	?	..		..		..		..		..	6	{Disposed of, ca. 1652.

[1] Late Dutch *Morgenstar*.   [2] Also called *Great President*.

——	* Built. † Bought. ‡ Taken.	Length of keel.		Beam.		Depth in Hold.		Draught.		Nett Tons.	Guns.	——
		Ft.	in.	Ft.	in.	Ft.	in.	Ft.	in.			
Seahorse . . .	‡ 1654	..		..		..		..		..	26	Sold, 1655.
Selby	* 1654	85	6	25	8	10	0	12	0	299	22	{Re-named Eagle, 1660.
Sophia. . . .	‡ 1652	..		..		..		..		300	26	
Sorlings [1] . . .	‡ 1654	..		..		..		..		250	28	
Sparrow . . .	‡ 1653	..		..		..		..		60	12	Sold, 1659.
Speaker . . .	* 1649	116	0	34	9	14	6	17	0	778	64	{Re-named Mary, 1660.
Spice	?	..		..		..		..		..	6	{Disposed of, ca. 1652.
Star	† 1650	..		..		..		..		..	12	{Disposed of, ca. 1652.
Stork	‡ 1652	..		..		..		..		..		
Sun	‡ 1652	..		..		..		..		..	12	Sold, 1654.
Sussex	* 1652	..		..		..		..		..	46	{Blown up at Portsmouth, 1653.
Swallow . . .	* 1657	..		..		..		5	0	60	6	
Swan	‡ 1652	..		..		..		..		..	22	Sold, 1654.
Swiftsure . .	* 1653	116	0	37	4	14	10	18	0	740	60	{Taken by the Dutch, 1666.
Taunton . . .	* 1654	100	6	31	8	13	0	16	0	536	40	{Re-named Crown, 1660.
Tiger's Whelp. .	‡ 1649	..		..		..		..		..		Sold, ca. 1658.
Torrington . .	* 1653	116	8	34	6	14	2	17	0	738	52	{Re-named Dreadnought, 1660.
Towing Galley [2] .	* 1659	..		..		..		..		..	1	
Tredagh [3] . . .	* 1654	117	3	35	2	14	5	..		771	50	{Re-named Resolution, 1660.
Tresco . . .	‡ 1651	..		..		..		17	0	..	..	Wrecked, 1651.
Tulip	‡ 1653	..		..		..		..		..	32	Sold, 1657.
Violet	‡ 1652	98	0	28	0	11	0	12	6	400	44	
Vulture . . .	‡ 1656	..		..		..		..		100	12	
Wakefield . . .	* 1656	74	0	23	6	9	9	11	6	235	26	{Re-named Richmond, 1660.
Waterhound . .	‡ 1652	..		..		..		..		..	32	Sold, 1656.
Welcome . . .	‡ 1652	..		..		..		..		400	36	
Westergate . .	‡ 1653	86	0	24	6	11	6	13	0	270	34	Sold, 1657.
Wexford . . .	‡ 1655	..		..		..		..		130	14	{Re-named Dolphin, 1660.
Weymouth . .	‡ 1651	..		..		..		..		120	14	
Wildman . . .	‡ 1652	..		..		..		..		..	16	Sold, 1657.
Winsby . . .	* 1654	104	0	33	2	13	0	17	0	607	44	{Re-named Happy Return, 1660.
Wolf	‡ 1656	..		..		..		..		120	16	
Worcester . . .	* 1651	112	0	32	6	14	0	16	0	629	48	{Re-named Dunkirk, 1660.
Wren	‡ 1653	..		..		..		. ..		250	12	Sold, 1657.
Yarmouth . . .	* 1653	105	0	33	0	13	3	17	0	608	44	

[1] Ex-*Royal James*, Royalist privateer, Capt. Richard Beach. Taken near Les Sorlingues, or Scilly Isles.
[2] For the defence of the Medway.   [3] *I.e., Drogheda.*

The *Constant Warwick*, built in 1646, and purchased by
Parliament in 1649,[1] is popularly supposed to have been the first
frigate constructed in a British yard. She was not a frigate in the
modern sense, and several vessels very similar to her were added to
the Navy while she was still a privateer, cruising for the profit of
the Earl of Warwick, Peter Pett, and others. But she and other
craft of 1646 marked the beginning of a progressive tendency in
naval architecture. It lay in the direction of making ships of
medium size less high out of water, of finer lines, and of longer
proportionate keel than before, and of so obtaining faster vessels and
steadier gun platforms. The developments in this direction continued under the Commonwealth ; but they did not go very far, and

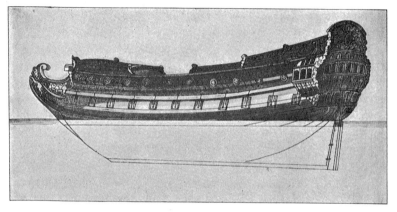

THE COMMONWEALTH SHIP "SPEAKER," 64. BUILT 1649. RENAMED "MARY," 1660.

(From Tomkins's engraving in Charnock.)

nothing closely approximating to the Nelsonian idea of a frigate was
produced until the eighteenth century. Another beneficial advance
was a very considerable reduction in the amount of external decora-
tion conferred upon men-of-war. Figure-heads and stern-carvings
were still allowed, and there was carving round the ports ; but the
expenditure on such luxuries was limited. The regulation dress of
a Commonwealth man-of-war was black, with the carvings gilt.
As yet, not more than two boats seem to have been carried by any
ship. These were a pinnace, of a maximum length of 29 feet, and
a skiff, of a maximum length of 20 feet. A third boat, the long

[1] See list of ships added to the Navy under Charles I., pp. 10, 11.
[2] Add. MSS. 9306, f. 132.

boat, of a maximum length of 35 feet, was never carried inboard, but was towed astern. The two smaller boats were hoisted in and out, not by means of davits, but by means of tackles on the main and fore-mast shrouds.

The large and rapid increase of the ships of the Navy during the Commonwealth taxed the resources of the State dockyards to the utmost. Many vessels were consequently laid down and built at private yards at Blackwall, Ratcliff, Rotherhithe, Limehouse, Woodbridge, Horsleydown, Wapping, Yarmouth, Wivenhoe, Lydney, Bristol, etc.

Ships were rated as follows : first-rates, of 80 guns and upwards ; second-rates, of 52 and less than 80 guns ; third-rates, of 44 and less than 60 guns ; fourth-rates, of 32 to 50 guns ; fifth-rates, of 12 to 32 guns ; and sixth-rates, smaller craft. The distinction between the rates was not as yet very closely drawn, and did not strictly and exclusively depend upon tonnage and number of guns carried ; but classification on the lines of common sense and obvious convenience became more and more usual as the years went on. A regular establishment [1] of guns for each rate was prescribed in 1655, but was never fully enforced.

The first Navigation Laws in England date from the Act of 1381–82 (5 Rich. II. c. 3). The policy represented by this Act was not of English invention, but was suggested by the previous action of foreign nations. It was persisted in and developed under Henry VII. and Elizabeth. But not until the temporary fall of the monarchy did it become an important factor in determining the relations of the country with other powers. As soon as Parliament could find the necessary leisure, amid the pressure of domestic troubles, it enacted, in 1646, that no one in any of the ports of the plantations of Virginia, Bermuda, Barbados, etc., should suffer any goods or produce of the manufacture or growth of the plantations to be carried away to foreign ports except in English ships. In 1650 it was further enacted that no foreign ships whatsoever should trade with the plantations in America except with a regular licence. And in 1651 the most famous measure of the series, " Cromwell's Navigation Act," was passed. By this Act the prosperity of Holland was dealt a very serious blow, for it was declared that no goods or commodities whatsoever of the growth, production, or manufacture of Asia, Africa, or America should be imported into

---

[1] S. P. Dom. ciii. 94.

either England or Ireland, or into any of the plantations of Great Britain, except in British-built ships, which were owned by British subjects, and of which the master and three-fourths of the crew belonged to Great Britain. It was additionally provided that no goods of the growth, production, or manufacture of any country in Europe should be imported into Great Britain except in British ships, owned and navigated by British subjects, or in such ships as were the real property of the people of the country or place in which the goods were produced, or from which alone they could be, or most usually were, exported.[1] These enactments, levelled at the Dutch carrying trade, were the cause of the first Dutch War. Other enactments, following the same lines, had much to do with provoking the second and third Dutch Wars, under Charles II., and

the wars of American Revolution and of 1812, under George III.

It has been already noted that by an order of February 22nd, 1649,[2] the St. George's Flag, a flag exactly similar to the present admiral's flag, was made the national ensign. At the same time it was directed that every man - of - war should

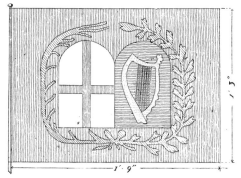

COMMONWEALTH FLAG.

(From the Original at Chatham Dockyard.)

carry on her stern an escutcheon containing in one compartment a red cross, and in another a harp. This escutcheon seems to have suggested as a flag of command, instead of the Union, a flag bearing the arms of England and Ireland in two escutcheons on a red field within a compartment *Or*. In the case of a vice or rear-admiral, the compartment seems to have been unornamented. In that of an admiral, it was encircled by a laurel wreath.

A variant of this flag is still preserved in an old chest in the house of the Admiral Superintendent at Chatham. Through the kindness of Staff-Commander J. E. Coghlan, R.N., I am enabled to illustrate and describe it. It measures 21 inches by 15 inches. The field of the flag is red; the encircling wreath is green; the

[1] Macpherson, ii. 430, 442–444.   [2] S. P. Dom. Interreg. i. 62.

English escutcheon bears the red St. George's Cross on a white ground, and the Irish escutcheon bears a yellow seven-stringed harp on a blue ground. I take this to have been an Admiral's boat flag. It may, however, have been a Jack.

There is also evidence that during the Commonwealth, red, white, and blue ensigns with St. George's cantons, bore sometimes a harp on the fly. A Dutch medal commemorative of the death of Admiral M. H. Tromp shows such a flag. In 1653 the Generals-at-Sea, in addition to their flags of command, flew pennants at the main; and the Vice and Rear-Admirals flew their respective colours, red, white, or blue, at the fore and mizzen. From May 18th, 1658, says Mr. Oppenheim,[1] " the standard of the General of the Fleet was to bear the arms of England, Scotland, and Ireland, ' with His Highnes' escutcheon of pretence, according to the Great Seal of England.' The Jack for admirals was to consist of the arms of England and Scotland united, ' according to the ancient form,' with the harp added, ' according to a model now shown.' "

By the Treaty of April 5th, 1654, it was agreed " that the ships of the Dutch, as well ships of war as others, meeting any of the ships of war of the English Commonwealth in the British Seas, shall strike their flags and lower their topsails, in such manner as hath ever been at any time heretofore practised under any form of government." [2] The right of the flag, thus formally acknowledged, was afterwards generally conceded, though not always with grace. When Blake was at Cadiz a Dutch officer also lying there kept his flag struck ʂo long as the great Englishman remained. On the other hand, Jacob van Wassenaer,[3] in 1657, when going down Channel with thirty sail, refused to strike to the *Dragon* and *Colchester*, and only when these ships threatened to engage him until they should sink did he comply " in a great rage."

---

[1] ' Admin. of Roy. Navy,' 370.

[2] See Anderson : ' Orig. of Commerce,' ii. 423.

[3] Having been Lord of Obdam, he is usually known in England as Obdam van Wassenaer, or simply Obdam.

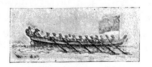

CHAPTER XXI.

MILITARY HISTORY OF THE NAVY, 1649–1660.

L. CARR LAUGHTON.

The Royalist fleet—Rupert's command—Piracy in the Channel—The Parliamentary Generals-at-Sea—Rupert at Kingsale—Relief of Dublin—Rupert's voyage south—Attitude of John IV. of Portugal—Position of the Parliament—Position of Charles—Blake follows Rupert—His fleet—Proceedings off Lisbon—Blake reinforced by Popham—Hostilities against Portugal—English victualling in Spanish ports—Blake's force weakened—Rupert's escape from the Tagus—Blake and Lalande—Penn to take the place of Blake—Destruction of the piratical squadron—The *Marmaduke*—Penn's instructions—A new era in the Mediterranean—Further movements of Rupert—Mutiny of the *Revenge of Whitehall*—Penn's cruise—Edward Hall—Precautions against the Royalists—The Royalist privateers—Reduction of Scilly—Ayscue's West India expedition—Reduction of the Isle of Man—Reduction of Jersey and Guernsey—Reprisals against France—Ill-feeling between Holland and England—Preparations for war—Causes of the First Dutch War—The Navigation Act—The Pawlett reprisals—Tromp and Blake off Dover—Explanations and recriminations—Maritime resources of the two countries—Withdrawal of the Dutch ambassadors—Return of Ayscue from the West Indies—His meeting with the Dutch off the Lizard—Tromp's attempt on Ayscue in the Downs—Blake and the herring busses—Tromp superseded—Popularity of the war in England—De Ruijter as Tromp's successor—Battle off Plymouth—Subsequent movements of the fleets—Destruction of Vendôme's squadron before Dunquerque—Defeat of Badiley off Elba—The balance of force in the Mediterranean—Cutting out the *Phœnix*—De With in command—Battle of the Kentish Knock—Factions in the Dutch fleet—Results of the English victory—Relations with Denmark and Sweden—Dispersal of the English fleet—Tromp at sea again—Battle off Dungeness—Dejection and demands of Blake—The position at Leghorn—Defeat of Appleton—The Mediterranean left to the Dutch—The command of the English Channel—Battle off Portland—The Protectorate, and the hopes of the Dutch—Movements of the fleets—Meeting off the Gabart Sand—Battle of June 2nd and 3rd, 1653—Blockade of the Dutch ports—Battle of the Texel—Junction of Tromp and De With—Death of Tromp—Retreat of De With—Losses and rewards—The fate of the blockade—The peace—Relations with Denmark, with Portugal, and with France—The French privateers—Capture of Beach—France and Spain bid for Cromwell's alliance—Hostilities against Spain—Penn and Venables to the West Indies—Penn's fleet—Failure at Hispaniola—Jamaica taken—Return of the Generals—Goodsonn in the West Indies—Blake to the Mediterranean

—Blake at Tunis—Spain declares war—Blockade of the Spanish coast in 1656—
Stayner and the Plate fleet—Santa Cruz de Tenerife—Death of Blake—John
Stoakes in command—"That famous rover, Papachino"—Fall of Dunquerque—
Troub'e in the Sound—Montagu sent to bring Charles II. to England.

 THE death of Charles I. put an end to any hopes
that may have been entertained by the Navy of
a reconciliation between King and Parliament, and, by
widening the breach, determined the ultimate fate of
the Royalist fleet.

While the ships which had revolted from Parliament
still lay in Hellevoetsluis, Prince Rupert[1] was appointed
to the command; a reservation, however, of the rights of
Lord High Admiral being made in favour of the Duke of York.

Rupert's sea command was most eventful. By his commission
he was absolute; by the nature of the service before him he was
fettered both in respect of his ill-paid mutinous crews, and in having
to cater for the Royalist exiles in Holland. The squadron represented the investment of such money as the exiles could scrape
together. Charles himself wrote to Rupert at Kingsale: "Being
totally destitute of means, we intend to provide for the satisfaction
of our debts out of the proceeds of the goods in the ships lately
taken."[2]

In 1648, Warwick had blockaded the revolted ships in Hellevoetsluis till November. On his withdrawal, it was decided that the
Royalist fleet should go to Ireland to help Ormonde. On the way it
was to plunder as much as possible, for such a course would harm
the "rebels," and was, to the loyal party, an indispensable means of
livelihood.

But the fleet could not sail, the men deserting daily from
a service where neither pay nor provisions seemed forthcoming.
Rupert acted, however, with vigour; he sold the brass guns of the
Antelope, which, with the value of the Queen of Bohemia's jewels,

---

[1] Prince Rupert, son of the Elector Friedrich V., sometime King of Bohemia,
and of Elizabeth, eldest daughter of James I. Born, 1619, at Prague. Served on
shore during the Civil War. In 1649 commanded a semi-piratical squadron in the
name of Charles I. Served as a flag-officer in the second Dutch war. Conjointly with
Albemarle, commander-in-chief, 1666, and greatly distinguished himself. Vice-
Admiral of England, 1672. Commander-in-chief in the third Dutch war. Governor
of Windsor Castle. One of the first Fellows of the Royal Society. Of high scientific
attainments. Died, 1682, in London. Buried in Henry the Seventh's Chapel at
Westminster.

[2] Warburton, 'Hist. of the Cavaliers,' iii. 308. *Cp.* Cal. S. P. Clarendon, ii. 421.

served to fit for sea two "frigates," the *Roebuck*, 14, Captain Marshall, and the *Guinea*, 30, Captain Thomas Allin.[1] These returned shortly with two prizes which enabled him to equip the whole squadron;[2] and on January 21st, Rupert, in the *Constant Reformation*, weighed and steered for the Channel. With him at that time were the *Convertine*, Prince Maurice, Vice-Admiral; the

H.R.H. PRINCE RUPERT, DUKE OF CUMBERLAND, P.C., K.G., BARRISTER-AT-LAW, F.R.S., VICE-ADMIRAL OF ENGLAND.

(From the portrait by Sir P. Lely.)

Swallow, Sir John Mennes, Rear-Admiral; the *James*, prize; and the *Charles, Roebuck, Pelican,* and *Guinea*. His original fleet had, to a great extent, melted away. The *Crescent* had been retaken

[1] Thomas Allin. Born, 1612. Commanded under Prince Rupert, 1649-50. Commanded in Mediterranean, 1664. Engaged the Dutch Smyrna Convoy and was knighted, 1665. Flag-officer during the second Dutch war. Reduced the Barbary States, 1669. Controller of the Navy, 1670. Commander-in-chief in the Channel, 1678. Died, 1685.

[2] Warburton, iii. 275.

almost at once, and other ships besides those that sailed with Warwick had deserted. The *Antelope*, it has been seen, was dismantled ; the *Blackamoor Lady* could not sail for want of £100.[1]

The *Antelope* never did sail. In the spring a party of seamen from the *Happy Entrance*, the senior officer's ship in the Downs, made a raid over to the Dutch coast, and surprising her, still in Hellevoetsluis but now ready for sea, immediately destroyed her. Such few men as were in her could offer no resistance.[2]

Rupert meanwhile, in company with three outward-bound Dutch East Indiamen, passed the Strait of Dover. Moulton was lying in the Downs with the *Happy Entrance, Constant Warwick, Satisfaction*, and a " frigate " or two besides. That he did not attack was due possibly to a misconception of the strength of Rupert.[3] The Princes reached Kingsale and collected there all the buccaneers of Munster, together with such Dunquerquers as would join them for the time being. By liberal offers of pay and prize-money they contrived also to enlist a certain number of men. The result was felt immediately. Complaint was made from Bristol that no ship could pass into the Channel in daylight, and the Governor of Youghal wrote that Rupert's fleet was twenty-eight strong.[4] At the beginning of February, Penn fell in with two of these ships, the *Mary Antrim* and another. The fight that ensued was well maintained by the Irish cruisers. Penn's ship, the *Lion*, lost both mizzen and bowsprit, while the *Mary Antrim* continued the fight till she had eleven men killed.[5] At that time a ship was sent from Ireland to bring the Prince of Wales, as Charles was still called by many men in England, out of Holland. This ship, the *Santa Teresa*, Captain Francis Darcy, failing in the object of her journey, and being unwilling to return empty handed, stayed out till July for a Channel cruise ; but in that too she was unlucky, for she fell a victim to the *Garland* and *Nonsuch*.[6]

As the piracy increased, so also did the Parliament's desire to make a speedy end of Rupert. At first the newly-appointed Generals-at-Sea, Popham, Blake, and Deane,[7] thought that the case

---

[1] Hyde to Rupert from the Hague, 28th February.

[2] Cal. S. P. Dom. 1649–1650, pp. 105, 206, and Whitelocke Memorials, 396.

[3] Warburton, iii. 281.

[4] Hist. MSS. Com. 13 Rep. App. 1, pp. 509, 510.   [5] *Ib.*

[6] Cal. S. P. Dom. 1649–1650, 17th July.

[7] This is the order of their appointment. Blake had served on land under Popham and may even have been suggested by him for this service.

would be met by adding somewhat to the fleet in Irish waters under
Ayscue and Penn, while Popham himself commanded in the Downs.
But though the Irish fleet did good service, and its captains, notably
James Peacock, of the *Tiger*, sent in many prizes ;[1] yet, when
Rupert was shut up in Kingsale, it appeared that the one fleet could
not at once do the regular work of the station, involving at the time
much hard service, and also maintain the blockade. Consequently,
on May 22nd, Blake and Deane appeared off Kingsale in the *Triumph*,
having with them the *Leopard, Nonsuch, Constant Warwick, Happy
Entrance*, and others. Their well-appointed squadron was stronger
than was needed, and they were presently able to send a ship or
two back to the Downs to assist against the North Sea pirates.

Royalist hopes were already on the wane in Ireland. Ormonde
was indeed besieging Dublin, but in May, Ayscue[2] and Penn[3]
brought relief to that town, and soon afterwards, Jones beat
Ormonde under its walls.[4] This, coupled with Cromwell's bloody
victories, made it very clear to the Princes that Kingsale would soon
cease to shelter them ; but still, as often, sheer good luck helped
Rupert. A heavy north-easterly gale drove the blockading fleet far
to leeward, and gave him the long-desired chance of slipping out.
He escaped with the loss of three of his squadron.[5]

The Parliament soon had news of him. He had gone to the
south, plundering all he met. There was no Mediterranean
squadron, and the Irish fleet could no longer reach him ; nor could
any reliance be placed on the fact of his being a public enemy.
The Moorish pirates throve in spite of their being *hostes humani
generis ;* and, moreover, Europe had not as yet decided whether
King or Parliament would be the winner. It happened, therefore, that when the Royalist fleet with its prizes appeared off
the mouth of the Tagus, and demanded admission to the river,
John IV. of Portugal readily granted all that was asked. He, in
his new-found independence, was so weak as to be in urgent need

---

[1] Cal. S. P. Dom. 1649–50, pp. 201, 235, and often. Among the prizes taken at
this time were the *Guinea* and the *Charles* of Rupert's ships.

[2] George Ayscue. Born probably about 1615. Knighted by Charles I. Captain,
1646. Made Admiral of the Fleet in the Irish Seas, 1649. Commanded in the West
Indies. Engaged De Ruijter off Plymouth, August 16th, 1652. Vice-Admiral (B.) in
the action of June 3rd, 1665. Admiral (W.) and taken prisoner by the Dutch, 1666.
Supposed to have died about 1674.

[3] Hist. MSS. Com. Rep. 13, App. 1, pp. 66, 67.

[4] At Rathmines.

[5] Granville Penn, i. 292.

of an ally. In Rupert, or rather in the sovereign whom Rupert
represented, chance had sent one to his hand.

With the Royalist fleet gone from Ireland, but with much still
to be done there on land, Cromwell offered Blake a command
on shore. But Blake, having the choice,[1] preferred the sea, and
remained on his station till the end of the year. For so long as
Rupert's movements were unascertained, careful precautions were
taken, a far greater force being kept up than had been previously
maintained. Thinking that Rupert might make Scilly his headquarters, Popham[2] sent a small but strong squadron to cruise off
the Lizard. It was under the command of Captain Edwaid Hall
in the *Leopard*, and included the *Happy Entrance*, Captain
Richard Badiley, the *Adventure*, Captain Andrew Ball, and Captain
Hackwell in the *Bonaventure*. But Hall, like Penn in 1651 in the
Mediterranean, could get no sight of his enemy.

When news came that Rupert was to the southward, all unusual precautions were abandoned. Blake was recalled to Plymouth
to superintend the fitting out of the fleet that it now became
necessary to send to Lisbon. Vice-Admiral Penn was left to
command on the Irish station, which still demanded a capable
head ; and it was subsequently decided that Popham should take a
reinforcing squadron to Blake in the course of the spring.

At this period the infant Commonwealth was in no enviable
position. So odious is the name of Regicide, that in no case could
the envoys of the Parliament have been welcome. But " the difficulties of the English agents abroad were the greater because agents
for the late King, who had been sent with proper credentials, and
who had transferred their allegiance to Charles II., were resident in
several parts."[3] And, apart from such difficulties as these, Parliamentary agents had to face the very real danger of assassination at
the hands of the embittered Royalists.

With the Royalists still on their hands, and with Ireland in a
state of tumult, the Parliamentarians had need of caution. Against
the Dutch they had already many causes of complaint, and, in
spite of the reluctance of the Prince of Orange to grant more than
passive support to Charles, the unfortunate murder of Dorislaus
brought the countries still nearer to an open rupture. Charles

---

[1] Cal. S. P. Dom. 2nd October, 1649.
[2] *Ib.* 14th November, 1649.
[3] Cal. S. P. Dom. 1649–1650, p. xxxv.

spoke of throwing in his lot with Ormonde and Inchiquin, and William of Orange gladly helped on a course that would relieve him of so dangerous a presence. But the three ships that sailed from Holland got no farther than Jersey, where Sir George Carteret held Castle Elizabeth; and there the Irish project was abandoned on receipt of the news of the revolt of Munster to the Parliament.[1]

In March, 1650, Charles returned to Breda, whence, in June, he went to Scotland. He had hoped for help from France, but Mazarin found one civil war at home enough and had no desire to meddle in another abroad. The French ambassador in England was told in plain words that the recognition of the Commonwealth was essential before business could be transacted[2] and when that recognition did not appear to be forthcoming, and English trade was impeded, Parliament ordered reprisals which, in all but the name, resulted in war. Coupled with the help which Rupert had found at Lisbon, and the action of the Tsar of Moscovy in driving the English from his dominions, this action on the part of France showed that the Commonwealth had to face a hostile Europe. Her instinct of self-preservation was appealed to, and this " drove England to become a maritime power such as she had never before been.[3] The Parliament saw where its strength should lie, and fell to increasing the Navy, with such good results that its sea power speedily became an important factor in the policies of Europe. Basnage wrote[4]: " La république d'Angleterre eut un sort assez singulier; c'est qu'elle devint redoutable dès sa naissance, et avant même que son autorité fût affermie. Les princes se liguèrent presque tous avec le Parlement, et abandonnèrent Charles II. à sa mauvaise fortune." And though it is probable that Basnage regarded the Parliament as the representative of the army which had made it supreme, yet the immense rise of England during this period was wholly due to her Navy. This is amply illustrated by the fact that, save to fight the Battle of the Dunes before Dunquerque, in 1658, no English troops served on the Continent so long as the Commonwealth lasted.

The equipment of the fleet at Plymouth was forwarded with all speed, and on January 17th Blake received his instructions. He was to command in chief as general of the southern expedition,[5] and

---

[1] Gardiner, i. 207.   [2] August 23rd; Gardiner, i. p. 200.   [3] Gardiner, i. 331.
[4] Basnage, ' Annales des Provinces Unies,' p. 193.   [5] Thurloe, i. 134.

his main object was to be to seek out Rupert and destroy him. If any Power proved so ill-advised as to shelter his enemy, Blake was to point out that Rupert and his crew were mere pirates—" piratæ et latrones, hostes humani generis "—that they had stolen the ships which composed their squadron ; and that, having no legal right in those ships, which were the property of the Parliament, they were not entitled to sell them.

When Generals-at-Sea were first appointed, it was the custom to hold closely to the letter of the regulation that required the presence of two of their number,[1] and it is not unlikely that Popham would have been sent out with Blake had his presence not been necessary before Dunquerque.[2] It has already been seen that it was the Parliament's intention that he should follow Blake to the south as soon as he was free. Parliament had received advice, in January, that the Dutch, in consequence of a territorial quarrel with the Portuguese in Brazil, intended to employ twenty ships off Lisbon during the year.[3] This belief seems to have contributed to the strength of our squadrons, and certain it is that Blake, with no Dutch squadron to watch, found himself undisputed master at sea. Cromwell could ill afford the risk of any semblance of weakness. He therefore sent, and maintained, a force more than equal to all possible adverse chances. Danger from Rupert was provided against : so was the contingency of trouble with the Dutch. Blake was likewise in a position to teach international law to the King of Portugal, should need arise, as well as to create a favourable impression upon the French and Spanish courts.

But there was no difficulty then with Holland. The Dutch were quite content, for the time being, that Portugal should embroil herself for the sake of Rupert, who merited scant affection on their part. In the following year the Prince recognised the growth of Republicanism consequent on the death of William of Orange, by including Dutch vessels in the objects of his piracy.[4]

On or about 14th February, 1650, Blake sailed. His fleet was composed as follows [5] :—

---

[1] Penn, i. 289.

[2] Cal. S. P. Dom. January 24th, 1650–1651.

[3] *Ib.* January 26th. The ships were not sent.

[4] Warburton, iii. 275.

[5] S. P. Dom. Int. 1. 123, 316, 5th March, 1649–1650, and a list appended to the ' Declaration of Prince Rupert,' a 4to. pamphlet, 1650.

Ships.	Commanders.	Men.	Guns.
1. *George*	{Robert Blake, General . . . . / Captain Charles Thorowgood . . }	280	50
2. *Leopard*	Robert Moulton, senr., Vice-Ad. .	180	48
3. *Bonaventure* . . .	Captain John Harris	180	37
4. *Happy Entrance* . .	„ Richard Badiley, Rear-Ad.	180	40
5. *Adventure*	„ Andrew Ball	130	36
6. *Assurance*	„ Benjamin Blake . . .	150	33
7. *Expedition*	„ Abraham Wheeler . . .	120	26
8. *Providence*	„ John Peirce	120	27
9. *Tiger*	„ James Peacock	150	32
10. *John*	„ John Saltonstall . . .	130	32
11. *Constant Warwick* . .	„ Robert Moulton, jun. . .	140	31
12. *Merchant,* " frigate " . .	„ Nicholas Park	109	28
13. *Cygnet,* fireship . . .	„ William Wheatley. . .	30	8
14. 10*th Whelp,* „ . . .	„ Robert Banes	30	8
15. *William,* ketch . . .	„ Bartholomew Yates . .		
16. *Patrick,* „ . . .	„ William Kennedy . . .	..	10

He arrived off Lisbon on March 10th, and would have proceeded up the Tagus to seek Rupert, had not the forts opened fire on him.[1] Unable to at once solve the difficulty, Blake anchored in the open roadstead of Cascaes Bay, and demanded that the Princes, who were ready to start on a cruise, should be forced to put to sea.[2] His demand was refused, and for the next few months each side was busy trying to convince the king that its opponents were rebels.

In view of the strength of Blake's fleet, the position of John IV. was the more difficult; for Rupert, though he had with him a squadron which, in point of mere numbers, was almost equal to Blake's, was, in all other respects, severely handicapped. To begin with, his men were mutinous, and desertions were so frequent,[3] that, shortly before, he had thought fit to hang ten at the yard-arm in order to terrorize the rest. He was also so terribly short-handed, that, at one time, report went abroad that he had but forty men in his flagship,[4] a vessel whose complement should have been about three hundred. Such men as he had were a motley band of adventurers, drawn together more by the hope of prize-money [5]

---

[1] Gardiner, i. 331.

[2] Warburton, iii. 300.

[3] Whitelocke, 28th February, 1649–1650.

[4] *Ib.* April 10th, 1650.

[5] For the table by which prize money was to be distributed, *vide* Warburton, iii. 288, 289. Prize-money before being divided into three parts for owners, for victuallers, and for officers and crew, was subjected to a deduction of $\frac{1}{15}$ for Charles, and another of $\frac{1}{10}$ for the Admiral.

than by the offer of high monthly pay,[1] the receipt of which was
by no means to be counted on.

A list of Rupert's squadron, drawn up by some one in Blake's
fleet off Lisbon,[2] can be proved to be fairly accurate. According to
this authority it consisted of thirteen vessels, mounting about four
hundred guns; but only five of the ships had been at Hellevoetsluis,
and, of these, the *Blackamoor Lady*, 18, was sold at Lisbon. The
other four, the *Constant Reformation*, *Convertine*, *Swallow* and
Roebuck, were the only ships of Rupert that had been built as
men-of-war. The remaining ones were prizes.

The first demands of Blake met with no acquiescence from the
king. It was, therefore, decided at a council of war, held on board
the *George*, on March 23rd, to send Moulton as ambassador to the
Portuguese court.[3] His demands were for restitution of, or leave to
seize, all vessels under Rupert's command, or, failing that, for an
engagement, on the part of the king, to force the Princes to put to
sea; and, failing that again, for leave to come into the river on
giving an engagement not to attack.

Although the demands against Rupert were refused, Blake gained
leave to shelter from a heavy gale in Oeiras Bay, but was called
upon to leave the river when the weather moderated. This was
scant concession, and was made not with any intention of deserting
Rupert, but with the natural desire of avoiding an open breach with
the English until they should have allowed the Brazil ships to pass.[4]
But Rupert was not satisfied of his ally's intentions. He knew that
factions ran high at the Portuguese court, and, wishing to be on the
safe side in case the king should give way, he made ready to try to
force a passage out.[5]

The fleets were still in the Tagus when, at the beginning of
April, two French ships-of-war appeared off the port. They knew
Rupert was there, but of Blake they knew nothing. With the
intention of saluting his Royal Highness, the captains went aboard
the flagship at the mouth of the river. This was, of course, Blake's
ship, the *George;* and Blake, perfectly well aware that they had
meant to join with Rupert, ordered their detention, pending instruc-

---

[1] Touching the scale of pay, it is worth recalling that when Rupert offered twenty-
four shillings a month, the Parliament raised the pay of men sent against him to
twenty-five shillings. See p. 98.

[2] Appended to Rupert's declaration to the King of Portugal.

[3] Hist. MSS. Com. Rep. 13, App. 1, pp. 520, 521.

[4] Warburton, iii. 302.   [5] *Ib.* 303.

tions from home.[1] But the time to quarrel with France had not, at that date, arrived, and the Frenchmen were eventually released. Although the squadrons did not meet, watering parties from the ships did. Scuffles on shore were constantly taking place, each side claiming to be the aggrieved party. Rupert accused the Parliamentarians of laying a plot to kidnap himself and his brother, and retaliated for the imagined ill-faith by an undoubted attempt to blow up the *Leopard*.[2] It is sufficiently well known that Rupert's complex nature had always a leaning towards scientific and chemical studies, and that he subsequently devoted years of enforced leisure to their pursuit. On this occasion he sent a couple of negroes and one of his seamen, in Portuguese dress, alongside the English vice-admiral in a shore boat. They carried with them what purported to be a barrel of oil; but the barrel really held an infernal machine, to be fired by a pistol attachment, the trigger of which could be pulled by a string passing through the bung. The travestied seaman, however, coming alongside, and finding the lower deck ports closed, "uttered an exclamation" in English. It at once appeared that there was some deceit. He was seized, and the barrel was given a respectful investigation. Yet harshness to Rupert's followers was no part of Blake's policy, and the man was not punished.

Meanwhile, in England, the summer guard had been made ready, and the ships had been appointed to the various home stations;[3] but the determination to send Popham south to join Blake necessitated the detachment of the following squadron :— [4]

Andrew	Edward Popham, Admiral and General.
Resolution.	Captain William Wildey.
Phœnix	„ William Brandley.
Satisfaction	„ John Lambert.
America	
Great Lewis	
Merchant	Merchant ships.
Hercules	

On the 13th or 14th May,[5] 1650, Popham sailed. His instructions from the Council of State[6] supplemented those which had been

---

[1] Nicholls, S. P. p. 7.   [2] Warburton, iii. 305.
[3] Whitelocke, 428, and list in S. P. Dom. Int. I. vol. 123, p. 315. The numbers were forty-seven men-of-war, and twenty armed merchant ships.
[4] Thurloe, S. P. i. 144, 145 ; S. P. Dom. Int. I. 123, p. 297.
[5] Cal. S. P. Dom. 1650, p. 161.   [6] *Ib.* p. 122.

already given to Blake, and were binding on both Generals. They differed from the earlier instructions in giving distinct orders for the arrest of French ships, and in granting power to attack the King of Portugal if he still persisted in supporting the revolted fleet.

A curious point to notice with regard to the first outbreak of hostilities against Portugal, is that it occurred before Blake received the authority which Popham was bringing out. On May 21st[1] the fleet for Brazil sailed out of the river, and was promptly stopped by Blake. It was found that with it were nine English ships laden with Portuguese goods. These were detained, and the rest were allowed to proceed. According to statements subsequently made by Popham, Blake acted thus because he believed that the French intended to send a force to Lisbon to help Rupert, and because he expected Popham to bring him authority to seize Portuguese goods and ships.[2] It has been seen that he was not mistaken.

Popham joined Blake on May 26th, yet found nothing more to do than to join in a dreary blockade. For two months nothing was done, but, on July 25th, Rupert, with a considerable fleet, consisting largely of Portuguese and French vessels, sailed out to avenge the detention of the Brazil ships. The wind was fresh from the E.S.E., and Rupert was almost up to the blockading fleet before the Portuguese admiral weighed. As Rupert complained afterwards, "his anchor fluke had too good a hold."[3] Then the wind shifted, and Rupert, by the Royalist account, could not come up.[4] He anchored off the Cachopo shoals, and did not move thence till Blake had been reinforced.

Blake and Popham's report to the Council of State was to a somewhat different effect.[5]

"We stood with them, they keeping the wind of us. Our fleet was of ten sail, together with the nine Brazil ships. Having got a reasonable berth from the shore, we haled our foresails to the mast. The enemy still kept the wind of us, the French admiral with four fireships leading, the *Reformation* being a mile astern. Then the wind shifted to the south, whereon we tacked and gained the wind. We bore away large on the Frenchmen and exchanged some shot with him, as did also the *Phœnix*.

[1] Gardiner, i. 334, and Cal. S. P. Dom. p. 428. The Admiralty judges subsequently upheld Blake's action, *vide* S. P. Dom. Int. vol. xvi. 78.
[2] *Ib.* p. 438.
[3] This admiral, and his successor, were nominees of Conde del Miro, of whom Rupert was profoundly jealous. Miro represented the party which saw that a policy of peace with the Parliament was the better one to follow.
[4] Warburton, iii. 310.
[5] Hist. MSS. Com. Rep. 13, App. 1, pp. 521–523.

But as fast as we bore upon him, he bore away large in toward the harbour; and Rupert likewise, his mizzen always haled up. We followed, but having a lee shore, a lee tide and night coming on, drew off in 10 fathoms at the South Hetchoopes." [1]

Next day Rupert was under Fort St. Julian, and refused to move; at night, the *Assurance* was sent in " to alarume them," and was fired on by the forts. On the 28th, Rupert, though he had the wind of Blake, still refused to engage, and in the evening went into the river at the sight of eight ships which had joined his enemy. These were a squadron which had been detached to Cadiz for water. They were under the command of Badiley, and on their return from Cadiz had fallen in with, and fought, a French squadron of king's ships, whereof they had sunk one.

Blake and Popham determined, with their increased fleet,[2] to attack Rupert in Oeiras Bay; " but next day they had all gone up the river, and our plan to fall on them came to nought."

The *Constant Warwick* was at that time on her way from England with instructions, dated July 13th, for a strict blockade to be maintained till Rupert should be driven out. At the same time it was suggested that as the Brazil Fleet had sailed, the generals, by sending some ships to the Azores, might doubtless intercept it. But the generals regretted that the scheme was impracticable. By August 15th the nine Brazil prizes were judged unseaworthy and were sent to England.[3] In spite of the inevitable anger of Parliament at the prospect of a rich prize being missed,[4] Blake decided that the best which he and his colleague could do would be to see that the Brazil Fleet did not get in ; and, with that object, as autumn came on, the blockaders drew farther off from the land.

During July, Blake had insisted on the need of fresh ships.[5] It was very difficult to keep the vessels in repair when the nearest ports at which they could career were San Lucar and Cadiz on the south, and Vigo to the north. But he received no further reinforcement. The squadron under Penn, which was ordered for the autumn, did not sail till the work on the coast had been done.

---

[1] The name Cachopo became with the English Hetchoopes, Catchups, Heckups, etc. Oeiras Bay was written either Wyers or Weyres.

[2] Blake had then eighteen ships and the nine Brazilmen. With Rupert were twenty-six ships and eighteen small craft.

[3] Petition of the masters of these ships for pay while in the service of the State, Cal. S. P. Dom. November 13th, 1650.

[4] Thurloe, S. P. i. 156.   [5] *Ib.* 611 and 620.

On September 7th, Rupert again came out, " to cut capers," as
Nelson might have put it. He plied off the harbour mouth with
thirty-six ships, while there were actually with the Generals only
ten.[1] A thick fog prevented much from being done, but Rupert, in
the *Reformation*, happening to stumble upon the *George*, the
Phœnix, and the *Expedition*, had his foretopmast shot away before
the mist hid him from sight.[2]

A week later, on September 14th, the long-expected Brazil Fleet
hove in sight and was at once attacked by Blake. Blake reported
the matter thus:[3] "I made towards the Admirall, whoe being to
nimble, I fell on the rereadmirall, being a ship of noe less force,
and had above 3 howres dispute with him, it blowing very much
wind, so that wee could not use our loure tire." At length the
rear-admiral struck, having sustained heavy loss. Then the "Vize-
admirall was burnt, being first boarded by the *Assurance* who saved
most of the remainder of his men."

Seven ships were either taken or destroyed, and then Blake,
with his whole fleet, bore up for Cadiz. He was a welcome guest
there in view of his late achievement, for the enmity between Spain
and Portugal was very bitter. It was indeed owing to this that
Blake had been allowed to victual in Spanish ports;[4] and the feud,
combined with an appreciation of England's strength, kept the
two great countries at peace. Looking to the diametrically opposite,
but equally bigoted, religious sentiments of England and Spain, it
was clear that there could be no thorough and permanent alliance.

Popham returned to England and resumed command in the
Downs; and on October 14th, Blake formed a squadron of four
of his least seaworthy ships and sent it home under Badiley in
charge of the four prizes taken in September. Badiley picked up
twelve sail of merchantmen for England from Leghorn, and reached
the Downs with his convoy on November 9th.[5]

Blake was left with seven ships; he himself was in the *Bonaventure*, the others being the *Leopard*, *Phœnix*, *Expedition*, *Elizabeth*,
Constant Warwick, and *John*.[6]

There was now nothing to keep Rupert in Lisbon. The coast

---

[1] Hist. MSS. Com. Rep. 13, App. 1, p. 536. Blake to C. o. S.

[2] The Portuguese never came near the enemy. Rupert asserted that their admiral
towed a sheet anchor overboard to stop his way.

[3] Hist. MSS. Com. Rep. 13, App. 1, 536, 537.   [4] Gardiner, i. 341.

[5] Hist. MSS. Com. Rep. 13, April 1st, p. 541.   [6] *Ib.* pp. 537, 639.

was clear, and since September 14th, the king's estimate of the value of Rupert's presence had fallen rapidly. The Royalist view was that if the Portuguese had victualled Rupert's ships earlier, the seizure of the Brazil Fleet would not have taken place. When, however, because the squadron had become worse than useless, the victualling was pushed on, Rupert sailed with six ships, apparently all that he could man, on October 12th. In the words of the Royalists,[1] " being destitute of a port, we take the Mediterranean sea for our harbour, poverty and despair being companions and revenge our guide."

Rupert's ships were not destined to be left to their piracies for long. After passing down the coast and making a few captures, they passed the Straits. Blake had news of them and weighed from Cadiz at about the time when they must have passed him. On his way to Gibraltar he fell in with a French ship.

As Whitelocke[2] tells a pretty story about this capture, a story wildly improbable but currently accepted, it is well to see what Blake said of the affair. The accepted version is to the effect that Blake summoned the French captain on board and asked him : " Would he surrender his sword?" On being answered " No !" he bade him return on board his ship and make the best fight he could. But after two hours the captain came in to him and, kissing his sword, delivered it up. Blake's letter to the Council says : " On October 20th, being four or five days off the Straits' mouth, we met a French man-of-war who, after some dispute, yielded on quarter. There was in her thirty-six brass guns and one hundred and eighty men, and the captain was Chevalier de Lalande, chef d'escadre, brother to him that was sunk by the *Adventure* frigate."[3]

On November 2nd the Council of State wrote[4] that, hearing that " Rupert with his piratical crew," was got abroad, and that the Brazil Fleet was returning homewards,[5] they were sending out Penn with four ships, all that could at that time be got ready. With Penn, who was to command in chief, Blake was to leave his best sailing light vessels and then to hasten home.

---

[1] Warburton, iii. 313.   [2] *Ib.* p. 462.

[3] Hist. MSS. Com. Rep. 13, App. 1, pp. 538, 539. The letter is far more detailed in its statements than most of Blake's, and is directly corroborated by a letter of Saltonstall to Coytmore (*Ib.* p. 543), which mentions the capture, but records no heroic details.   [4] Thurloe, S. P. i. 166.

[5] Homewards, *i.e.* to England. It was known in England October 15th, that the sugar ships had been captured. Nicholls, S. P. p. 27.

Penn was a capable seaman, and Blake possibly was not. But it is not an occasion for regret that the Royalist squadron was dealt with by Blake before Penn's arrival.

Blake, passing along the coast, had news of Rupert at Malaga, and there heard that he was at Velez Malaga. But Rupert and Maurice had parted company from the rest of their force off Cape de Gata, and had chased a large ship, the *Marmaduke*, of London, towards the Barbary shore. On the morning of November 6th they were up with her and opened fire. She did not strike till disabled by the loss of her mainmast.[1]

At Velez Malaga, Blake found that the Royalists had destroyed two English ships, the master of one of which, Morley, was an object of Rupert's particular detestation as being a regicide.[2] On the next day, November 3rd, the *Roebuck* was taken off Cape Palos; on the 4th, the *Black Prince*, "the *John* being ready to board him,"[3] ran ashore, took fire, and blew up three leagues east of Cartagena. Counting prizes, there were four[4] Royalist vessels left in Cartagena Bay. The accounts of what happened are very conflicting; but this much is certain, that Blake followed them into Cartagena Bay, and that not one of them ever came out.

Blake said they had been driven ashore by a storm and lost.[5] Saltonstall said that they had run themselves ashore for fear of the Parliament's ships; and this, in the main, is corroborated by Cadenas, who told Parliament that Blake had agreed not to harm them till he should receive formal permission, but that the ships tried to escape and were driven ashore. By Warburton's account,[6] one, the *Henry*, was taken; but it is possible that the *Henry* was the *Roebuck* renamed.

In any case it must have been a disappointment to Blake to have been so near Rupert himself and yet to have missed him. By strange irony, on the very day when the squadron was destroyed, the Council wrote to Blake complaining of the cost of the fleet,

---

[1] Warburton, iii. 317.

[2] Hist. MSS. Com. Rep. 13, App. 1, p. 547. Account of the proceedings of November 2nd–5th, given to Parliament by Cadenas, the Spanish ambassador.

[3] *Ib.* p. 543; Saltonstall, of the *John*, to Coytmore, and *cp.* Heath, Chron. 275, 276.

[4] The *Convertine* was not one of these; she seems to have been left unmanned at Lisbon, whence she was afterwards restored to the Parliament. As the *Roebuck* was taken, it will be seen that not one ship of those then destroyed had ever belonged to the Navy of England.

[5] *Ib.* 540, Blake to King of Spain.   [6] *Ib.* iii. p. 322.

recalling Blake, and bidding him try to make a profit on the
expedition by keeping a sharp look out for prizes on the journey
home.[1] When the news of his success reached them, they hastened
to change their minds and wrote an appreciative letter, bidding him
stay where he was and finish what he had so well begun.[2] That
letter, dated December 24th, can never have reached Blake. He
was back in England by the middle of February. On the 13th, he
was thanked by Parliament for his " great and faithful service,"
being voted also the more substantial gratification of £1000.[3]

Even before the news from Cartagena reached England, it had
become evident that the Parliamentary star was in the ascendant.
Vane, writing to Cromwell[4] at the end of December, said : " The
seven ships left with Colonel Blake . . . are very likely to be the
total ruin of Rupert's fleet, and a great terror to the French. This
hath made the Spaniard solemnly to acknowledge us. Portugal
likewise stands knocking at the door, but we pause upon it a little.
The French and Dutch, as conceived, will not sit out long, unless
they are resolved to sit out for altogether ; which we hope they will
think on twice before they resolve on it." In other words, Blake's
fleet had raised the Commonwealth to a recognised position in
Europe.

Blake's entry into the Mediterranean marks the beginning of a
new era, that of English influence in those waters.[5] The Council
adhered to the new policy, and the Mediterranean station, though
for a time neglected, was never afterwards for long abandoned.

Partly as a substitute for Blake's force against Rupert,[6] partly,
too, for the continuation of Blake's policy, a squadron was collected
for Vice-Admiral William Penn. The winter guard had been
already formed.[7] It was now called upon to supply ships for Penn,
who, after waiting some time for the completion of the *Fairfax*, 52,
which was to have been his flagship, sailed without her from
Spithead on November 30th. Though his squadron was nominally
eight strong,[8] he sailed with only five, the *Centurion, Swiftsure,
Foresight, Pelican,* and *Guinea.*[9] He was, however, joined by the

---

[1] Thurloe, S. P. i. 167.   [2] *Ib.* p. 163.

[3] In the C. o. S. minutes for 15th March following occurs the entry " The Admiralty
Committee to consider where the £1000 ordered for General Blake may be had."

[4] Nicholls, S. P. pp. 40, 41.   [5] Gardiner, i. 341.

[6] G. Penn, i. 324, 327.   [7] Granville Penn, i. 302–304.

[8] Cal. S. P. Dom. 25th October, 1650.

[9] Hist. MSS. Com. Rep. 13, App. 2, p. 69.

Fairfax and others in January, 1651; and these, with such "frigates" as Blake had left to him, brought his fleet above its originally intended proportions.

His instructions were to go at once to the Azores on the chance of finding homeward-bound Portuguese treasure-ships there. Not finding them, he was to follow Rupert, and to act against the French in the Mediterranean. He went to the Azores, but found nothing. Blake, as has been seen, had already picked up the Brazil trade. Accordingly, he steered for the Mediterranean, and passed the Straits on March 29th, 1651.

Rupert and Maurice, meanwhile, had been lying in Toulon doing their best to collect a squadron. They bought one ship, another joined them, and the *Marmaduke* prize was fitted as a man-of-war and renamed the *Revenge of Whitehall*. Their squadron then included the *Constant Reformation, Swallow, Revenge of Whitehall, Loyal Subject;* and *Honest Seaman*.[1] Penn did his best to get information, but from first to last was never near the Princes.

There is little need to follow the course of events in the Mediterranean. Rupert, when he was ready to sail, gave out that his intentions were for the Archipelago; so eastward Penn promptly went. Having thus easily disposed of his opponent, the Prince left Toulon on May 7th, passed Gibraltar, and steered to the south. His real desire was to go to Virginia and the West Indies, where the Royalist interest was still strong; but the mutinous attitude with which his crews greeted the news forced him to go instead to the Azores. The rovers gained little there. Few prizes were made, and there sprang up a heavy gale in which the flagship sank. Rupert himself was saved, and a mere handful with him, but three hundred and thirty-three are said to have gone down in the *Constant Reformation*.[2] The *Loyal Subject* was also lost.

Owing to the peace with Parliament, the Portuguese in the Azores would have nothing to do with the Royalists; yet the discontented crews refused to face the Atlantic voyage, and Rupert had to resolve to look for the homeward-bound East Indiamen. But luck now was against him. He did not make the Canaries in time,

---

[1] Warburton, iii. 325.

[2] Warburton, iii. p. 333, says that the crew perished heroically. The ship sprang a leak and foundered slowly, and, as all the long boats towing astern had been lost, no help could be given. Rupert was however saved by a small boat from the *Honest Seaman*. At 9 P.M. the ship with her steadfast crew, "burning two firepikes to give us notice of their departure, took their leave of the world."

and when at last, after refitting at Cape Blanco, he persuaded his
men to follow him to the west, he had with him but two ships and
a few unarmed prizes. Of the three ships which had escaped from
the Azores, the *Revenge of Whitehall* was carried to England by a
portion of her crew.

The story of her transfer to the Parliament shows daring of no
common order.[1] When the ship came into Plymouth Sound on the
last day of May 1652, Coxon, who had brought her home, was
ordered to draw up a narrative of the affair. He showed how, when
the ship had been beating up to the northward on the African coast,
seven officers of merchant ships, pressed from prizes to serve in her,
had decided on revolt. The project was one of extreme difficulty,
and was possible only because the squadron was scattered in order to
let nothing pass it. By degrees they sounded the crew, and having
increased their number to twenty-five Englishmen out of a total of
one hundred and fifteen, the rest being chiefly Frenchmen and
negroes, they watched for their chance. When it came—and it was
slow in coming, for the officers of the ship suspected something—
the captain, Marshall, was attacked and overpowered. Then ensued
a stiff fight with hatchets. No firearms could be used for fear of
bringing Rupert down on the ship, but the conspirators had taken
precautions accordingly. Many of the Royalists were wounded,
and the French, who cried for quarter, were put ashore. But
even then there remained against the mutineers a majority of
more than two to one. Constant watch had to be kept, and
during the five weeks for which the passage lasted Coxon's anxiety
never slept.

Rupert meanwhile made the West Indian Islands and found that
he had come too late. Ayscue had been there before him, and the
Parliament's authority was assured.

Again he met with a terrible storm. He himself had a narrow
escape of being dashed ashore by night on one of the Virgin Islands.
When morning dawned it was found that Prince Maurice, in a
prize named the *Defiance*, had disappeared. Nothing was ever
known of his fate, but there is little doubt that he perished close
under the southern shore of Anagada. Nor did Maurice die alone.
Of the great ships, the *Swallow*, in which was Rupert, alone was
left; and with her, leaking and foul, accompanied by only two

---

[1] S. P. Dom. Int. vol. xxiv. C0.

prizes, the royal corsair ended his long cruise at Nantes in the spring of 1654.[1]

While these varied and evil chances were befalling Rupert, quest was still being made for him in European waters. Penn, as has been seen, had started eastward on a wild goose chase. It was not till he reached Malta on the 25th July,[2] 1651, that he learnt how he had been tricked. Rupert was then reported to be off Cadiz,[3] and this necessitated a return to the neighbourhood of Gibraltar. Nothing of importance was done on the way to Malta and back. The Tunisians and Algerines treated Penn with incivility, refusing even to sell him provisions, but he did not dream of exceeding his instructions on their account. On August 6th "the *Foresight's* foretopmast was split from head to heel with a clap of thunder."[4] Three weeks later Penn met a Dutch admiral, who gave him false news of Rupert.

On September 25th, Penn heard that Rupert was at the Azores. He did not, however, make any attempt to follow him, but contented himself with keeping his ships at the Straits' mouth to intercept him on his return. An appreciation of Rupert's boldness does not seem to have entered into Penn's composition. Like others, he had not the least suspicion of Rupert's West Indian voyage ; and there can be little doubt that, had the Royalist fleet gone thither at once, instead of wasting time, the Parliamentary cause in the New World would have suffered heavily.

Cornelis Tromp was in Malaga in October, 1651, while Penn lay near Gibraltar ; and the English admiral seems to have been exercised in his mind as to how to behave to Tromp. English and Dutch were, as yet, no more than mutually suspicious. But both had realised the value of their interests in the Mediterranean and had determined to protect their trade ; and both were acting, or were intending to act, against the African pirates.[5] The difficulty arose out of the English war of reprisals with the French. This obliged Penn to seize everything French that he could lay his hands on, whereas the Dutch were at peace with France and their men-of-

---

[1] The *Swallow* was the last of the revolted ships. She was laid up at Nantes, and it was intended to refit her. But she was too far spent and never put to sea again.

[2] G. Penn, i. 313, remarks that Penn's was the first man-of-war squadron to penetrate so far.

[3] G. Penn, i. 353.   [4] *Ib.* 356.

[5] Basnage, 214, and ' Vie de Corneille Tromp,' p. 9. The Dutch had concluded a peace with Sallee at the end of January, 1651.

war were as ready to convoy French-owned goods as any others. But the rest of Penn's commission, until he reached Falmouth on March 18th, 1652, passed off uneventfully enough. He did indeed believe that Tromp was collecting men-of-war to take a convoy to France, yet there was no collision; and when Dutch ships met the English squadron, they were so much inferior in force that they did not dare to refuse to salute the flag.[1]

The English Mediterranean trade was well protected at that time. Sailing shortly after Penn, Captain Edward Hall passed the Straits with a convoy a few days before Penn had come thither from the Azores.[2] His work was chiefly of a nature to leave little trace, but one legacy left behind by him was pregnant enough of results. By seizing a French ship in a Tuscan port he angered the Grand Duke, who complained to Parliament. No satisfaction was given. Parliament wrote that as accounts differed widely, and as their real wish was for peace, they thought that the end would be best attained by letting the matter sleep.[3]

Appleton[4] in the *Leopard* went up the Straits on similar duty soon after Hall, and like his predecessor annoyed the Duke of Tuscany. He, with Richard Badiley, who went out in December, 1651, was left in the Mediterranean to represent English rights during the Dutch War, while Hall, with his far more adequate squadron, was withdrawn.

During 1650 there was still the possibility of help reaching the Royalists from abroad. An English squadron was constantly employed on the east coast of Scotland, and, though it failed to intercept either Montrose or Charles, it at least caused the lengthening of the Prince's passage to three weeks, and, by co-operating with the Parliamentary army that started north in June,[5] had considerable influence on the Scots War. Dunquerque too was busy,[6] and gave ample employment to ships in the Narrow Seas. So dangerous indeed did the Dunquerquers threaten to become, that a blockade of the port was instituted, and it was from this service that Popham

---

[1] G. Penn, i. 365, 386.   [2] Lediard, p. 535.

[3] Hist. MSS. Com. Rep. 13, App. 1, p. 622.

[4] Save for his service from this time until the beginning of 1653, all in the Mediterranean, Henry Appleton is utterly unknown. It is probable that he was a merchant skipper; it may also be possible to identify him with a Mr. Appleton who had served as lieutenant of the *Jonas*, hired merchantman, in the Rhé expedition of 1627.

[5] Gardiner, i. 288.   [6] G. Penn, i. 294; Cal. S. P. Dom. 23rd August, 1649.

was withdrawn to join the fleet off Lisbon. It was truly a time of
difficulty for peaceful traders, for, besides the accepted dangers from
Dunquerquers, from French cruisers,[1] and, in the East Indies, from
the Dutch, the home seas were full of Royalist privateers from the
islands.

With regard to the Dutch, the period was one of embassies and
negotiations; but Parliament was loth to take the high hand. The
East India Company was warned "that as soon as any ship's
company brings the tidings of injury offered, they," must "put the
thing into way of proof in the Admiralty, that complaint may be
made thereof to the States."[2] For the moment, diplomatic action
was preferred. But against the Royalists another method was
adopted. In the Isle of Man, the Earl and Countess of Derby; in
Scilly, Sir John Grenvile; and in the Channel Islands, Sir George
Carteret, still held out for the king. And in addition, Parliament
had to deal with Royalist influence in the Colonies.

On the establishment of the Commonwealth, one of the first
pieces of work which the Council of State purposed to take in hand,
was the reduction of the islands.[3] Scilly was the most important
of these stations, for cruisers from the islands could ply on the
Soundings and levy toll on all homeward-bound trade, English and
Dutch alike. The Council realised as early as April, 1649, that " it
would be a great service to take Scilly,"[4] and the Generals-at-Sea
were informed of the decision. But the Generals-at-Sea were too
busy then with Rupert, who, before the blockade of Kingsale, seems
to have made some attempt at concerted action with Grenvile.[5] So
the matter dragged on until the spring of 1651, when suddenly
Marten Tromp appeared off Scilly with a squadron.[6] On April 1st
the Council wrote to Blake and Ayscue to hurry to Scilly and watch
Tromp's movements. Tromp had demanded reparation and, getting
none, proceeded to declare war[7] against Grenvile, as his instructions
permitted. But Parliament could allow no such thing. Scilly in
Dutch hands would be far more dangerous than it was in Royalist
possession. Blake and Ayscue sailed at once in a squadron which

---

[1] Gardiner, i. 339. At the end of October 1650, it was estimated that the French
privateers had taken 5000 tons of English shipping, and goods to the value of half a
million sterling.

[2] G. Penn, i. 301.   [3] Cal. S. P. Dom. Int. 1649, p. 6.

[4] C. o. S. Minutes, 24, April 16th, 49, in S. P. Dom. Int.

[5] Warburton, iii. 289.   [6] Basnage, 215; Thurloe, S. P. i. 177.

[7] Whitelocke, 17th April, 1651.

had been prepared for Ayscue to take to the West Indies. Tresco and Bryer were seized, and the walls of the main stronghold where Grenvile held out in St. Mary's were breached.[1] This, combined with a rigorous blockade,[2] forced the governor to come to terms, and the islands were surrendered on 2nd June, while he retained his liberty.

Even before this service, short as it was, had been completed, Ayscue for some reason left his command. He was at once ordered to return,[3] and did so; and, as soon as the work was finished, he received instructions to refit his squadron and carry out his original orders.[4]

The Caribbee Islands belonged to the Earl of Carlisle, who in 1647 had leased his rights to Lord Willoughby of Parham.[5] Prince Charles at the Hague gave Willoughby a commission to govern in his name, and with this Willoughby had sailed in February, 1650, taking out a similar commission to Sir William Berkeley, the Royalist Governor of Virginia.

On reaching Barbados, Willoughby found that party spirit ran high, and that the Cavalier faction was in the ascendant and had cleared the island of Roundheads.[6] Some of these Roundheads reached England, and, no doubt, their representations helped to fix the determination of Parliament. Ayscue left England 8th August, and arrived at Barbados with seven ships. He at once attacked, and Willoughby, after a stubborn defence, capitulated upon favourable terms. Ayscue granted Lord Willoughby his freedom, an act of leniency which seems to have been remembered against the admiral in the following year.

When Barbados had fallen, no further resistance was made. Nevis, St. Kitt's, and Virginia, submitted to the Parliament, and Ayscue was at liberty to return to England, which he reached in May, 1652.

In his absence, Jersey and the Isle of Man had been reduced. In the case of the latter, after an expedition had been organised and troops landed, no resistance was offered. Captain Anthony Young, in the *President*, challenged Man, and met with defiance.[7] The Earl of Derby was not in the island at the time, but his countess retired

---

[1] Cal. S. P. Dom. Int. 23rd May, 6th June, 1651; Whitelocke, 464–467.

[2] 'Elenchus Motuum,' p. 77.   [5] Gardiner, i. 350.

[3] Cal. S. P. Dom. 10th May, 1651.   [6] *Ib.* 352.

[4] *Ib.* 10th June, 1651, and 8th July, 1651.   [7] Whitelocke, 486.

to Peel Castle, and was preparing to hold out when she was forced by her own men to capitulate.

The Isle of Man was reduced in October, and only Jersey and Guernsey were left. But Jersey had become more formidable in proportion as other refuges had been withdrawn from the Royalists. Innumerable piracies are recorded of the Jersey men,[1] and as early as April of the year 1651, the Lord General had been requested to consider how and when the reduction was to be.[2] Troops were held in readiness, but on 1st August were countermanded. Next day they were ordered to proceed. Jersey, it was thought, " will feel security, and the expedition will advance easier." During September, Blake at sea and Colonel Heane on land reduced the islands, and penned Carteret in Elizabeth Castle. The surrender could not be long delayed, for the castle was quite cut off, and Carteret's garrison was large.[3] A bombardment was opened and was replied to. The castle was well stocked with munitions of war; and that the capitulation occurred so early as December 12th was due in great part to the mutinous disposition of the rabble which the Governor had within the walls. It was said at the time that he had with him Frenchmen, Danes, Germans, Swiss, Scots, Hollanders and Irishmen. With the fall of Castle Elizabeth, resistance ended. Five days later, Castle Cornet in Guernsey surrendered, and Charles had no longer a foot of land to receive him throughout the whole of what he claimed as his dominions.

Relations between England and France, it has been seen, were by no means satisfactory. The war of reprisals was carried on with vigour, and many of the ships of the Navy saw service therein. The *Fairfax*, for instance, a new ship of fifty-two guns, fought two or three severe actions in the Channel with French cruisers,[4] and Penn brought home thirty-six French prizes from the Mediterranean. In addition to this, in December, 1650, Ormonde, Inchiquin and many other refugees from Ireland went over to the Duke of York, and thus largely increased the Royalist strength in France,[5] to which country the Stuarts then, as afterwards, looked for their chief support.

Much has been written on the one side and the other to prove

---

[1] Whitelocke, pp. 464–494.   [2] C. o. S. Minutes, 24th April, 1651.

[3] Whitelocke, 485, says that he had four thousand men.

[4] Cal. S. P. Dom. 1650, pp. 312, 313; Whitelocke, 26th July, 28th August, 9th September, 1650.

[5] G. Penn, i. 309.

each of the combatants responsible for the first Dutch war. It is impossible to adopt conclusions without a consideration of the facts on which they rest. In considering these, it will be best to follow the chronological sequence of these events.

One of the most important features of the history of James I. and Charles I. was the growth of enmity between England and Holland. The Dutch held in their hands a great majority of the carrying trade of the world. They were, therefore, the rivals in commercial enterprise of England, seeing that she was likely to prove the most formidable competitor. And in this connection it must not be forgotten that England's rivalry was doubly dangerous, for not only was she able to compete in the markets, but she could at will all but close the trade routes of Dutch shipping. This was a cause of ill-feeling. Another cause was the disputed question of the herring fisheries, which had never been settled. During the Civil War in England it had, indeed, been allowed to drop out of sight ; but it was not dead, and it began to reassert itself in proportion as the power of the Commonwealth became established.[1]

In the spring of 1651, it became obvious that both countries were preparing for a struggle. Orders were given in England to hasten forth the summer guard, but the order was the less to be remarked because there was no lack of ordinary work for the fleet to do. The action of Holland was more suspicious. To allay the feeling aroused in England by the intelligence of great preparations in the Netherlands, the three Dutch ambassadors signed a memorial for presentation to Parliament. In this they admitted that a fleet of one hundred and fifty ships, over and above those already at sea, was being made ready, but they maintained that there was no hostile intent against the Commonwealth. The force, they explained, was needed for the police of the seas and the protection of trade.[2] The most lucid exposition of English scepticism that occurs bears a date subsequent to the war, and takes the form of a charge brought against the States.[3] "It is showed how you made a league defensive and offensive with France, a league *de non offendendo* with Spain, a league defensive with Sweden and Denmark, and a defensive league with Denmark against Sweden and all other nations ; and therefore it did appear that you had in the preparation of that navy no real intention of peace with us, but the contrary."

[1] Whitelocke, 487.   [2] Hist. MSS. Com. Rep. 13, App. 1, p. 636.
[3] Thurloe, S. P. i. 291.

Consequent on the death of the Prince of Orange, Parliament proposed a closer alliance of the two republican governments, but the scheme was such as would have given to England a preponderance. The Dutch were not prepared for this, nor would they accept a clause by which they should make England's enemies their own.[1]

Mutual suspicion continued to grow, and was by no means allayed by Tromp's appearance off Scilly. On June 20th, 1651, the negotiations were broken off and the English ambassadors recalled. The chief determining cause came from England. On October 9th, very shortly after the final ruin of the Royalist hopes by the "crowning mercy" of Worcester, was passed the famous Navigation Act.

The Dutch, of course, assumed that the blow was struck primarily at them; and doubtless it fell far more heavily on them than on others. But the gain to England was so evident that the passing of this Act could not be attributed only to a spirit of vindictiveness against the States. Hollanders in London tried to negotiate, but were met with a statement of grievances, beginning with the death of Courthope and the massacre of Amboyna, and the losses of the Muscovy and Greenland companies, and continued down to the support given to Charles at the Hague, the murder of Dorislaus, and the insults that had been heaped upon the Parliament's ambassador St. John.

No settlement was arrived at. None, perhaps, was expected. Letters of marque had already been granted, and in November, 1651, the Pawlett Reprisals began. The heirs of Robert and William Pawlett obtained leave to make reprisals on the Dutch for damage done to the extent of £29,170; and two vessels put to sea under Captains Smith and Stanton.[2] Complaint was immediately made at the Hague, and one more point was added to those already in dispute. On the other hand, England demanded the repayment of money advanced by Elizabeth for the fortresses of Flushing and Briel,[3] which had weakly been restored by James I.

While arming their great fleet the Dutch issued an edict that none of their seamen should serve abroad.[4] All was then ready for war, which began without formal declaration, on the old and most convenient claim of the honour of the flag. The Dutch were at least as desirous for war as were the English, and probably more so, for they had more to gain. The request for a closer alliance had been shelved, and the Parliamentary demands, though heavy and distasteful, did not go beyond what was legally due. Holland could not go to war because her old debts were called in. She could, however, find a pretext for a war, and in the event of a happy issue thereof, escape for ever from making restitution.

The Navigation Act was rigidly enforced, and many Dutch vessels were confiscated, not without loud protests from their owners. A large fleet of Dutch men-of-war was reported [1] to have appeared on the eastern coast in February, to have used rough treatment towards the English, and to have demanded the restoration of confiscated vessels. News, too, was received that Ayscue had found many Dutch ships openly engaged in an illegal trade with the Royalist colonies; and had seized eleven at Barbados; [2] and that Penn in the Mediterranean and on the Portuguese coast had made various captures of a like nature. [3]

On May 12th, 1652, Captain Anthony Young, in the *President*, accompanied by two other "frigates," fell in off the Start with a small squadron of a dozen ships. [4] Taking them to be Ayscue's vessels, he stood towards them, but, on coming up, discovered that they were homeward-bound Dutch merchant ships, convoyed by three men-of-war wearing flags as admiral, vice-admiral, and rear-admiral. The Dutch admiral, on being summoned, struck his flag and held his course, but the vice-admiral who followed him refused point-blank, bidding Young come aboard and strike it himself. Young naïvely sent his master aboard, only to meet with a further refusal. On this the *President* ranged up on the Dutchman's weather quarter and again called on him to strike. The vice-admiral refused, and Young at once gave him a broadside, which was as promptly returned. The Dutch admiral hauled his wind—the wind seems to have been north-west—and tried to weather Young, who found himself obliged to put his helm down to prevent the admiral from getting out to windward of him and boarding. Meanwhile, Captains Chapman and Reynolds had fired on the rear-admiral astern. They now came up with the vice-admiral, but, as they overhauled him, the Dutchman struck his flag, and the rear-admiral did the like.

---

[1] Whitelocke, p. 498.   [2] *Ib.*   [3] G. Penn, i. 391, 392.

[4] The main authority for the engagements off the Start and off Dover is the collection of evidence and declarations published as a pamphlet in June, 1652, under the title of "The Answer of the Parliament of the Commonwealth of England to three papers delivered by the Lords Ambassadors Extraordinary . . . of the United Provinces." *Cp.* Basnage, 253.

Young demanded that the vice-admiral should be sent into port with him to make good the loss to the "frigates." To that the admiral said that so long as the dispute concerned the flag alone he did not interfere, but that he would resist to the uttermost any interference with the possession of the ship.

Nothing further was done. Young, who had lost one man killed and four wounded, wrote, "I do believe I gave him his bellyful of it; for he sent me word he had orders from the States, that if he struck he should lose his head; but at length he did strike, which makes me conceive he had enough of it." Whitelocke,[1] who repeats many hearsay reports, records that the Dutch admiral offered in explanation the suggestion that his vice-admiral was drunk. When he goes on to say that after the fight the Hollanders gave Young "such loving salutes, confessing their faults, and so they parted good friends," he rather discredits his story.

This action, unimportant in itself, very soon had a most important result. On May 18th, Bourne was lying in the Downs in the *Andrew*, 42 guns, with the *Triumph*, 42; the *Fairfax*, 52; *Happy Entrance*, 32; *Centurion*, 40; *Adventure*, 38; *Assurance*, 32; *Greyhound*, pinnace, and *Seven Brothers*, hired merchantman; nine ships in all. Suddenly the Dutch fleet, forty-two strong, appeared on the back of the Goodwins. When it reached the South Sand Head, Marten Harpertszoon Tromp,[2] who was in command, sent two ships into the Downs to Bourne. Bourne, by special leave from Blake, was then, as commander-in-chief, wearing a flag at the main. From this Tromp at first supposed that Blake himself was present. These two ships came into the Downs and saluted the flag. The captains went on board the flagship, and explained that Tromp's presence was involuntary; that it was due to foul weather, which made it impossible for him to lie longer before Dunquerque, where he had lost many anchors and cables; and that all he desired was shelter. Bourne answered that Tromp would best show his sincerity by getting away from the coast as soon as possible.

Meanwhile Tromp dropped anchor in Dover road. He had not gone into the Downs because he did not wish "to breed dispute about the flag, inasmuch as he had no order to take it down." It

---

[1] Whitelocke, 508.

[2] Marten Harpertszoon Tromp. Born, 1579, at Briel. Admiral of Holland, 1639. Is said to have been victorious in thirty-three actions. Killed in the battle of July 31st, 1653.

was not, therefore, to be expected that he would strike it to the
Castle. He did not. The Castle fired a shot or two to call his
attention to the fact, but all the heed he paid was to exercise his
small-arm men in volley firing continually throughout the day.

Blake, meanwhile, was in Rye Bay with the main part of the
fleet, consisting of his own ship, the *James*, 48; *Victory*, 42;
Garland, 34; *Speaker*, 64; *Star*, 12; *Martin*, 36; *Ruby*, 40;

MARTEN HARPERTSZOON TROMP, LIEUTENANT-ADMIRAL OF HOLLAN

(*From Dalen's engraving, after the portrait by J. Jœvens.*)

Sapphire, 38; *Portsmouth*, 38; *Mermaid*, 22; one other, and a
hired merchantman. At the first sight of Tromp, Bourne had
made up his mind that there was danger of an attack, and
besides clearing his ships for action, had sent an express to Blake
asking him to come at once to his support. The wind on the 18th
was at north-east, and Blake soon received the message. He
weighed at once, and wrote to Bourne to join him. This message

reached the Downs by 10 A.M. on the 19th, by which time the Dutch, at the sight of Blake beating up towards them against an easterly wind, weighed together and stood closehauled towards Calais.

Bourne, who had been lying all night with two "frigates" posted between himself and Tromp, weighed about mid-day when the tide served. When he was off the South Foreland, the Dutch suddenly went about and bore down on Blake, who was then near Folkestone, Tromp, in the *Brederode*, leading.

As Tromp drew near, Blake, already cleared for action, fired a gun for him to strike his flag. As this had no effect, it was followed by another, and by a third, to the last of which Tromp made answer with a broadside.[1] This was promptly returned, and, Tromp "having put abroad the bloody flag under his Holland's colours," other ships engaged as they came up.

Tromp, according to his captains, when he altered course, "came through the whole body of his fleet," and bore directly down on Blake. To the impulsive nature of this attack was due the straggling line which the Dutch fleet presented at the moment of impact. The fight at once grew hot in the van; Blake was supported by several of his heaviest ships, although a few were so far to leeward that some time passed before they could come up. The Dutch, on their part, being greatly superior in numbers, would have surrounded the English van had not Bourne come up almost simultaneously with his nine ships and fallen impetuously on the enemy's straggling rear.

The battle thus joined raged till dark. In the van the heavier English ships held their own, sustaining considerable damage, but inflicting heavy loss. From time to time boatloads of the Kentish fishermen joined the fleet with admirable spirit, and helped to fight the guns.[2] For the time it was not seen who held the advantage, but in the morning it appeared that Bourne had taken two ships from among those cut off by him, viz., the *St. Laurens* and the *St. Maria*. The latter was abandoned by her captors as being in a sinking condition; she drifted to seaward, and on the morning of the 20th was discovered dismasted by the Dutch, who carried her

---

[1] Though Dutch writers, as Basnage, 253 ('Vie de Corneille Tromp,' 17), show Tromp to have claimed that Blake fired the first broadside, there is little doubt about the matter. In the examinations before Cromwell the Dutch captains taken in the engagement corroborated the version given by every Englishman concerned.

[2] Whitelocke, 509.

into port. Her crew, however, had been put on board Lawson's
ship, the *Fairfax*.

The advantage, then, was distinctly with the English, who had
lost no ship. Of the English vessels, the flagship *James* had suffered
the most heavily, both as being first into action and as being the
chief object of the Dutch attack. In her there were six men killed,
nine or ten desperately wounded, and twenty-five wounded " not
without danger." She had received seventy great shot in the hull

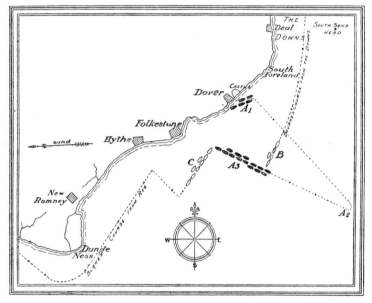

THE BATTLE OFF DOVER, MAY 19TH, 1652.

A 1. Tromp in Dover Road.
A 2. Point at which Van Sanen fell in with Tromp.
A 3. Tromp attacking, at 4 P.M.
C. Blake attacked, at 4 P.M.
B. Bourne falling on the Dutch rear, at 4.30 P.M.

NOTE.—Groups, and not single ships, are represented in the above plan.

and masts, her mizzen mast had been knocked overboard, and her
sails and rigging were cut to pieces.

Such was the fight. As it had been preceded by no declaration
of war, it was necessary for each commander to explain the part
which he had taken.

The narrative which has been given shows what was Blake's
share, while Tromp's conduct was explained by evidence which was

taken at the official inquiry held at Dover. From this it appeared that Tromp had originally no intention of attacking. In appointing him to command the fleet, the States General had examined him on the question of the salute to the English flag. It was customary, had been the reply of Tromp, to make the salute, especially when the Dutch force chanced to be the weaker; and, upon this, Tromp had been dismissed with instructions to protect trade, to keep off the English coast, and to do nothing discreditable to his country. Whether to strike his flag or not, he himself was to decide when occasion should arise.

This explains every incident up to the moment when Tromp changed course. What occasioned this was the sudden arrival of a vessel from the westward, which joined the Dutch fleet, and sent a boat aboard Tromp. In her was Captain Joris van Sanen, who had been present off the Start a week before, and who added the information that, near the Parliament's ships, to leeward, lay a squadron of rich trading vessels, which were homeward bound to Holland, and in imminent danger of being searched. From English sources we hear very little of these few ships, save the mere statement that they proceeded on their course that same morning. It is, however, certain that they were not molested

It may, then, be accepted without hesitation that Tromp had at first intended to avoid any dispute by keeping clear of the English flag ; that to gain this end he had weighed from Dover on Blake's approach, but that he altered his course and bore down to engage on receiving the news of Captain Young's action. To claim, as Tromp himself did in his letter to the States,[1] that he weighed, stood over towards Calais, received news of the search of merchant vessels when he was in mid-channel, and that, as he steered towards them, he "fell in with" the English fleet under Blake, is to outrage belief. On the face of it, it is absurd to think that Tromp—the foremost naval commander of his age and a thorough seaman—could "fall in" by accident with a fleet of the presence of which he had learnt the day before, and which he had seen beating up towards him before he weighed from Dover that morning.

Another argument often repeated on Tromp's behalf[2] is that, had his intentions been hostile, he would have crushed Bourne in the Downs on the 18th before Blake could support his subordinate. This, too, is a fallacy. Bourne had "the later tide of ebb in hand,"

[1] 'Vie de Corneille Tromp,' p. 17.   [2] Basnage, 253.

and a fresh north-easterly breeze was blowing.   To beat into the Downs was not impossible, for Captains Thijssen and Allers [1] actually did so; but for the Dutch fleet to do so against the lee tide, and under fire from Bourne's heavily-armed squadron, would have exposed it to a certainty of heavy loss before any effective answer could be made.

On the night of the 19th the Dutch lay with lights burning, whilst Blake was repairing damages off Hythe.   On the 20th the enemy was standing over towards the French coast, and Blake went on to Dover, whence he passed into the Downs.

Here it is necessary to insert a few words concerning the maritime resources of the two countries.   The first point that will draw attention is that in the subsequent battles, with scant exception in home waters, enormous fleets were employed.   But when we hear that Tromp, or Monck, or another commander, took the sea with a fleet of one hundred or one hundred and twenty sail, we must bear in mind how such fleets were formed.   In England, of course, there was, at the opening of the war, a Navy large and rapidly increasing.   But, in May, 1652, the number of first, second and third rates did not rise in all above twenty ships, though there were many ships of less force.   Owing to the system of buying into the service prizes and suitable merchantmen, it is extremely difficult to be sure what was the regular establishment at any given time.   The foregoing number, however, is approximately accurate.   But this was only a small part of the available force.   In days when a merchant ship was beset with dangers from legitimate foe and illegitimate pirate at every turn, she was built far more stoutly than mere seaworthiness demanded.   She carried guns, and could be pierced to carry more.   Thus the State could form a large fleet by the speedy but effective process of laying an embargo on the country's outward-bound trade, and refusing to allow it to proceed till from it there had been chosen all such craft as promised to prove effective against the enemy.   This, then, is what was done.   The impress of ships was as regular and as indispensable as the impress of seamen.

But when these ships had been impressed it is not to be supposed that they were usually to be compared with vessels of the first, of the second, or even of the third rate.   They were, for the most part, of inferior size, of from three hundred to five hundred

[1] 'Vie de Corneille Tromp,' 16.

tons' burthen; and rarely did they mount more than about thirty guns.

With the Dutch the case was exactly similar, save, perhaps, that our primary resources were greater. In mere number of merchant ships that could, on occasion, be taken into the country's pay, the Dutch had an advantage. But with number the advantage ended. Their vessels were even smaller than the English merchantmen, with the exception of a few East Indiamen, which seem to have carried about fifty guns; and, from their tendency to sink upon receiving a comparatively small amount of ill-treatment, these would seem to have been of slighter scantling and inferior workmanship.

Till the last few months of the war there was in the Dutch fleet no vessel superior to Tromp's ship, the *Brederode*, of fifty-six guns, and about eight hundred tons. This state of things does not compare at all favourably with that existing in the English Navy. The Dutch admirals, after each engagement, made regular complaint to the States General that it was useless to send them out so long as there were in the English fleet twenty vessels better than their best. And in this they seem to have been guilty of very little overstatement, as will be seen from the subjoined table of their ships which were ready to join the fleet at sea in March, 1654, and which would, it was claimed,[1] with a very few more, place the Navy on a better footing by half than it had ever before been on.

DUTCH NAVY LIST, 10TH MARCH, 1654.[2]

SHIPS MOUNTING	BELONGING TO OR BUILT IN				Total Number.
	Zeeland.[1]	Rotterdam.[2]	Amsterdam.[3]	Hoorn.[4] Enkhuizen. Medemblik.	
From 24 to 28 guns . . .	3	none	1	none	4
„ 30 „ 38 „ . . .	16	7	26	20	69
„ 40 „ 48 „ . . .	8	6	18	7	39
50 guns and upwards . . .	2	4	3	none	9

[1] Of these, four, including two 48-gun ships, were new.
[2] The eight greatest were new. These included one 60-gun ship. No other in the list mounted more than fifty-four guns.
[3] Fourteen of the greatest were new.
[4] Nine new, including all of more than forty guns.

The Dutch Navy then, in 1652, was comparatively small, the more so because many ships had been sold after the Peace of

[1] Thurloe, S. P. ii. 319.   [2] *Ib.* ii. pp. 78, 79.

Münster; and few of them mounted as many as forty guns.
Merchantmen were armed, but they were in every way inferior.
They were small; they carried few guns—from twenty-two to
twenty-eight—and those of small calibre; and the numbers of their
crews were scanty. Naval tactics at that period were in their infancy. The line of
battle proper was not yet invented, though, in the course of the war,
some sort of line formation was developed; and the distinction of
the "ship of the line" was unthought of. So far as a commander
had any theory as to the fighting of a fleet action, it was founded on
the subdivision of the fleet into squadrons, each with its own flagship. Round the flagship the ships of the squadron rallied, keeping
clear of one another by sheer exercise of seamanship. When, as in
time of panic, that failed, the confusion and disaster were appalling.
During the whole of the First Dutch War this system held its
ground. It was, indeed, found to answer well enough, for the
flagship was generally the most powerful vessel in her part of the
field, and, as such, could give help to the smaller fry that clustered
round her. The glaring defects of the system did not appear till
after the great battle of June 1-4, 1666.

The details of the rise of squadronal subdivision cannot be
investigated here. Briefly, the system had been adopted from the
Mediterranean as eminently satisfactory in the organisation of large
fleets. It is first met with in the Cadiz Expedition of 1625,[1] and in
some degree in the expedition to Rhé in 1627. The Blue, at that
time, had preceded the White. With the advent of the Commonwealth it fell into the third place.

In London the news of the battle created an uproar, and had not
a guard been placed over the house of the Dutch ambassadors in
Chelsea, there is little doubt that they would have fallen victims to
the fury of the mob.

With the Parliament it had been no unlooked-for thing that a
battle should be fought; but that the collision should have come
so soon, and at a time when the chances of peace seemed to be
improving, was of the nature of a surprise. In the crisis, however,
the Government behaved with dignity. To its former demands it
added a claim for the reparation of all damage done by hostilities,[2]
for which it held the States wholly responsible. When reparation

---

[1] S. P. Dom. Charles I. vii. 50.
[2] 'Vie de Corneille Tromp,' pp. 51, 52.

had been made, hostilities should cease and negotiations for an alliance might be reopened. But Pauw[1] shirked the ultimatum, and, when the Council of State insisted on an answer, the ambassadors withdrew.

Parliament at once proceeded to prepare still further for the struggle. Merchant ships were called in for the service of the State. It will have been noticed that on 19th May only two were serving with the Downs fleet. And a proclamation was issued for the impressment of all seamen between the ages of fifteen and fifty years in the south-eastern counties.[2] At the opportune moment Ayscue reached England from Barbados, dropping anchor in Plymouth Sound on May 26th. He did not return empty-handed. With him were thirty-six prizes,[3] taken in virtue of the Navigation Act, chiefly from the Dutch.

Blake now received instructions to attack the Dutch East India fleet and to disturb the enemy's herring fishery and Eastland trade.[4] His fleet was largely increased, and a careful survey was made of it as it lay in the Downs. While this was taking place, the Channel and North Sea cruisers were busy. Blake himself seems to have found time to intercept a Dutch convoy; but the only incident of much note was an engagement in June between the *Tiger*, Captain James Peacock, and another " frigate," with two Dutch men-of-war on the coast of Holland. Of the two Hollanders, one was carried by boarding, but afterwards sank, and the other was run ashore.[5]

Seeing that Blake's absence to the northward would leave the mouth of the river wholly unprotected, it was decided that Ayscue should be called from Plymouth to take up his station in the Downs.[6] But Ayscue, while still in the west, received news of the approach of the Dutch outward-bound Portuguese trade, consisting of about forty merchantmen, convoyed by a few men-of-war. His own squadron seems at that time to have consisted of eleven ships, the *Marmaduke*, which joined him at Plymouth from Rupert's flotilla, being not yet added to the Navy. Ayscue himself was in the *Rainbow*,[7] and with him were the *Amity*, Captain Pack, second in command, the *Happy Entrance*, and the *Tiger*.[8] The rest of his

---

[1] Adriaan Pauw, Heer van Heemsted, Pensionary of Holland and Ambassador Extraordinary to the Parliament.

[2] Cal. S. P. Dom. 24th May, 1652.   [3] Whitelocke, 509.

[4] Clarendon S. P. Cal. ii. 743; C. o. S. to Blake, 10th June, 1652.

[5] 'Col. Rostr.' 98; Whitelocke, 510.   [6] C. o. S. Minutes, 15th June, 1652.

[7] Cal. S. P. Dom. 1650, p. 455.   [8] *Ib.* 417, 500.

ships were either prizes bought into the service, or hired merchant-men,[1] so that the total strength of the squadron was not great.

Chasing to the westward, Ayscue came up with the Dutch off the Lizard on June 12th, and, after a sharp fight, took half-a-dozen of them,[2] and sent them into port.

Immediately afterwards he went to the Downs and dropped anchor near Blake on the 20th. War was in the air, and further hostilities were expected at any moment, so that the mere noise of the inter-change of salutes was enough to send abroad the report of a further engagement.[3] Such vessels as had been made ready for sea since the battle off Dover had been sent to the fleet, the result being that Blake had thirty-nine men-of-war, two fireships, two shallops, and eighteen merchantmen,[4] while Ayscue's squadron was still in the condition in which it had returned from Barbados. The two forces remained quite distinct, for Ayscue, though subordinate to Blake, continued to exercise the duties of an independent command.

When Blake sailed north on June 27th it was at once seen how dangerously weak Ayscue was. Efforts were made to send ships to him,[5] but three only—the *Vanguard, Success,* and *Pelican* [6]—were able to join him before the news of the presence of Tromp made it impossible for others to venture to quit the river.

On the breaking off of negotiations, Pauw, returning to Holland and fully posted in the positions and strength of the English squadrons, fell in with Tromp near Schouwen on July 3rd.[7] He gave him all the information possible, and pointed out the weakness of Ayscue, urging that he should be attacked in the Downs before Blake's return. Tromp, not sorry to see an opportunity of atoning for his defeat, fell in with the scheme the more readily as the wind which promised it success made it a matter of great difficulty for him to follow Blake. Ayscue's ships were only sixteen, possibly only fourteen, in number, whereas there were with the enemy ninety-two.[8] Of these latter, six were fireships, two were galliots, and ten were small "frigates" mounting eight or ten guns. Of the rest, twenty were "good and firm ships" of from thirty to forty guns, and the rest "of the middle size," meaning, in all likelihood,

[1] Cal. S. P. Dom. 1651, p. 261.   [2] 'Col. Rostr.' 98.
[3] Whitelocke, 512.   [4] Hist. MSS. Com. Rep. 13, App. 2, p. 69.
[5] C. o. S. Minutes, July 4th, 1652.   [6] *Ib.* June 28th, 1852.
[7] 'Vie de Corneille Tromp,' 60.
[8] Whitelocke, 514. The list is possibly not accurate, but at least it is typical of a Dutch fleet of the time.

hired merchantmen. A partial attack was made, the Dutch being to the north of Ayscue and having the wind fair to come into the Downs. The attempt failed, however, partly because the English had drawn close in shore and were protected by gun platforms run out towards the sea from Deal Castle,[1] but chiefly because of a fortunate shift in the wind.

Tromp, Evertsen, and Floriszoon, in command of the Dutch fleet, had now nothing left to do but to seek Blake. But in this too they were unfortunate. At the very time when they were threatening Ayscue in the Downs, Blake was making short work of the herring fleet. Of the thirteen small " frigates " that served it for a guard he took or sank twelve, while of the busses themselves about a hundred were taken, the rest being scattered.[2] The busses, with 1500 men on board, were set free : the other prizes returned to England with Blake. No explanation has been offered for Blake's action, but it would seem likely that, as his intention was to keep the sea for some time, this leniency was due to his reluctance to weaken the fleet. That so many prisoners had been set free was not acceptable news in England.

But in spite of the simultaneous presence of the two fleets on the fishing grounds, no action resulted. On 26th July, when the fleets were in sight of one another,[3] a heavy gale sprang up from the north-west and blew all that night. Blake, who was inshore, managed to find shelter with but little damage, but Tromp's fleet felt the full force of the storm. It was scattered over the North Sea, and when morning dawned Tromp could collect no more than thirty-nine ships, with which, and with two or three East Indiamen which he had met, he returned home. Of the ships that parted company most were disabled, many were lost. This was the crowning misfortune of Tromp's commission. He had failed to protect trade ; he had brought about an open rupture, for which it suited his country to hold him to blame ; his attempt on Ayscue in the Downs had been unsuccessful, and he brought home but a bare half of his fleet.

A town mob is never reasonable, and in Tromp and Pauw the mob at the Hague saw the men who were responsible both for the war and for its ill success. The States General too turned upon Tromp, who was suffered to lay down his command.[4]

---

[1] Cal. S. P. Dom. 11th July *sqq.*; 'Vie de Corneille Tromp,' 61.
[2] 'Columna Rostrata,' 99.   [3] Basnage, 258.   [4] *Ib.*

England had fared proportionately well and the war was popular. The English cruisers brought in a great number of prizes; indeed, it is said that in the course of the war no less than 1700 were taken. But, save in fleet actions, the capture of men-of-war was of rare occurrence. A "frigate" of twenty-six guns, the *Rotterdam*, was taken in the Channel at this time and was sent into Falmouth. There was urgent need of ships, and, renamed the *Falmouth*, she was at once added to the Navy.[1] It is probable that this ship was one of a small Dutch squadron stationed near the Soundings to warn homeward-bound merchantmen of the war, and to send them to Holland north about.

That the Council of State was jealous of English prestige is shown by a decree that letters of marque should be granted to no ship of less than twenty guns and two hundred tons; but this it was found necessary to withdraw.[2] With Blake's return, Ayscue was appointed to command "the guard for the Channel and those seas."[3] Captain William Haddock, in the *Vanguard*, was his vice-admiral, and Pack his rear-admiral. His fleet had been increased to nearly forty sail, but even that did not seem strong enough, and on August 15th Blake was advised[4] to support the Western Guard.

Meanwhile De Ruijter[5] had been appointed in Holland to supersede Tromp. Tromp's politics were not likely to bind his arm, but he was known to be an Orangeman, and that fact, while the Loewenstein faction was in power, made his retirement desirable. De Ruijter himself was a man of moderate politics, though an adherent of the party in power; but he had seen too much service to be ignorant of the bitterness of the party spirit afloat. Thus, when the command was offered to him, it was with great difficulty that he could be induced to accept it, and he did so at length

---

[1] Cal. S. P. Dom. 19th July, 1652.

[2] *Ib.* 1652, July 10th and August 23rd. Possibly as a result of this edict, we find the Levant Company petitioning on August 2nd for state protection, and professing inability to fit out privateers.

[3] *Ib.* pp. 335, 339 *sqq.*

[4] *Ib.* August 15th. It so happened that on that day there was not a quorum of members present. The result was that the Council could not command Blake, but could only advise him to go.

[5] Michiel Adrienszoon De Ruijter, the greatest naval leader of his century. Born, 1607, at Flushing. Served at sea in all ranks from seaman to Liutenant-Admiraal-Generaal. Commanded in 1641 against Spain. Served in all three of the wars with England. Died, April 29th, 1676, in consequence of a wound received in action with the French off Messina. As great in private as in public life. Biography by Klopp (1852).

protesting against the insufficiency of the fleet.[1] He left port with
no more than seventeen ships in all, his own ship, the *Neptune*,
mounting only twenty-six guns. This made reinforcements imperative, for he would attempt nothing before his number had
reached twenty-nine, including six fireships. He had instructions
to wait for and convoy some fifty merchantmen, and, expecting
them, he reached Calais about August 3rd, only to receive news of
Ayscue's presence, and, with it, a grossly exaggerated statement of
his force. How many and what ships Ayscue had with him cannot
be determined; but this much is certain, that he had not, as
De Ruijter had been led to suppose, twelve of the first rate and
eight of the second, for of the two rates together there were then
but six representatives in our Navy.

De Ruijter was joined on August 11th by eight men-of-war
bringing to him the merchantmen from the Texel : and it is well to
point out in this place that of these merchantmen, of which many
were East Indiamen, there were few that were not heavily armed.
Thus reinforced he proceeded down Channel, and five days later met
Ayscue off Plymouth.

In point of strength the fleets seem to have been well matched.
It is impossible to speak exactly as to the numbers, inasmuch as no
two accounts agree; but approximately Ayscue had thirty-eight
ships and eight small craft,[2] while De Ruijter, it is known, had
thirty men-of-war besides small craft. The difficulty is to decide
how many of the Dutch merchantmen took part in the engagement. A moderate estimate makes this number about twenty, and
in Dutch writers evidence abounds that divers of these acquitted
themselves extremely well.[3]

Of the action, as an engagement between fleets, nothing can be
said. The chronicles are full of isolated heroic actions of single
captains, but the only detail of any value that is preserved is that
the wind was at north-east;[4] and even this is discounted by our
ignorance of the course which Ayscue was steering and of how he
bore when sighted by the Dutch. All that can be said with
certainty is that the fight began at about one o'clock and continued
till dusk; that the contest was stubborn; that no formation was
attempted on either side, and that both countries claimed a victory.
As between fleets of men-of-war the advantage lay with neither;

---

[1] 'Vie de De Ruijter,' 17, 18.   [3] 'Vie de De Ruijter,' 20 ; Basnage, 259.
[2] 'Col. Rostr.,' 100.   [4] *Ib.* 18.

but inasmuch as De Ruijter was able to continue his course without the loss of his convoy, while the English were too much shattered to pursue, it must be allowed that the great Dutchman had effected his purpose.

De Ruijter did not accompany his convoy beyond the Soundings, but returned eastward from the neighbourhood of Scilly on September 12th.[1] Blake meanwhile had been sent westward to support Ayscue and to secure the Channel during the time when the Western Guard lay in Plymouth Sound refitting. In the late engagement both fleets had suffered heavily, though neither had lost a ship. The Dutch vessels, it was claimed, had been for the most part badly damaged in the hulls, while Ayscue's ships had lost spars and rigging. Both seem to have lost many men. On the English side the most serious loss was that of Pack, the rear-admiral, who had a leg carried away by a round shot and soon afterwards died. His successor in the post was Joseph Jordan.[2]

This battle was almost the last piece of active service that Ayscue saw under the Commonwealth. He continued afloat for a month or two during the reorganisation of the fleet, but we find him constantly summoned to attend meetings in October of the committee for trade and foreign affairs,[3] and after that time he was relieved of his command. The reason for this is shrouded in obscurity, but it has been generally supposed that the Council of State took the step owing to his success having fallen short of their expectations. It is not impossible that such was the case, but Ayscue was, even during his retirement, held by the bulk of his countrymen to be a most capable commander. He had, moreover, "extraordinary power with the seamen," and seems to have been popularly spoken of as likely to succeed Blake in the chief command when the General was subsequently lying ill and wounded ashore.[4]

---

[1] 'Vie de De Ruijter,' 20.

[2] Cal. S. P. Dom. 23rd August, 1652. Joseph Jordan. Born, 1603. Captain of the *Cæsar*, 1642. Rear-Admiral of the Irish squadron, 1643–44. Rear-Admiral with Penn in the Mediterranean, 1651–52. Vice-Admiral (B.) in the first Dutch war. Rear-Admiral in Blake's expedition against the Barbary States, 1654. Served, chiefly as a flag-officer, throughout the second Dutch war. After Lawson's disablement Vice-Admiral (R.), 1665. Commanded an attack on the Dutch in the Thames, 1667. Vice-Admiral (B.) at Solebay, 1672. Died, 1685. Buried at Hatfield.

[3] Cal. S. P. Dom. 1652, pp. 441, 458, 462.

[4] Clarendon S. P. Cal. ii. 1307, July 29th, 1653. This letter adds, " Cromwell cannot trust Ayscue," as being the chief reason why Ayscue did not command at sea that summer. This might be passed over as the vapouring of an enthusiastic Royalist, were it not that other information seems to confirm it.

When Blake reached the west in the *Resolution*, he joined to himself such of Ayscue's squadron as were ready for sea. On September 14th, taking with him the main part of the fleet, he parted company, leaving Penn on the Devon coast with about fifteen sail. Next day, with the wind at W. by N., Penn's scouts sighted two Dutch flyboats ;[1] and immediately afterwards the whole Dutch fleet, numbering from thirty-five to forty sail, was seen to windward. Blake, it was supposed, and as was afterwards proved to be the case, was in Torbay, yet Penn was ready to fight as soon as he could reach the enemy. But the Dutch, having the weather gauge, availed themselves of it to shun an engagement, their reason (besides the knowledge that the main body of the English fleet was not far off) being that they had suffered considerably in the fight with Ayscue, and had but recently been still further damaged by a severe westerly gale which had caught them near Scilly.[2]

All that day the Dutch kept the wind, and Penn held his squadron well together, confidently expecting an attack. It was a thick dirty night that followed, with the wind blowing hard from the west, and about midnight some firing was seen on the weather quarter of the *James*. Penn at once tried to come up, thinking the Dutch had fallen upon his stragglers, but he lost sight of the ships engaged, and till morning did not know what had happened. At eight A.M. he was joined by seven ships from Blake in Torbay, and at about the same time Captain Sanders, of the *Assurance*, came aboard and told him the meaning of the guns which had been fired in the night. At about midnight, he said, he saw to the north of him a great ship bearing away to the eastward. As she would not stay, he made a running fight of it with her till his course brought him down on the whole Dutch fleet, when he hauled his wind. The Dutch fleet had passed in the night and was steering east.[3] For a while Penn could not believe that " they would have been so poor and low-spirited ; " but, when conviction came, there was nothing left to do but to join Blake and follow them.

Anxiety in the west, whether for the safety of the Isle of Wight,[4]

---

[1] G. Penn, i. 440 *sqq*.   [2] 'Vie de De Ruijter,' 21.

[3] Dutch writers, as in 'Vie de De Ruijter,' 21, have claimed that, so far from seeking to slip past, De Ruijter was actually in pursuit of the English squadron. A Dutch captain who had been made prisoner on September 28th had been present on that occasion, and gave Penn an account of it which agrees with that in the text. Penn, i. 439.

[4] Thurloe, S. P. i. 214 ; C. o. S. to Governor of the Island.

or for the welfare of British commerce, was for the time being at
an end.

Blake meanwhile had not been idle. Besides fighting the Dutch,
it fell to his lot to ensure the freedom of the Channel from the
depredations of French privateers ; and on September 5th he was
offered a chance of striking heavily against French resources.[1] The
Spaniards had lost Dunquerque six years earlier, and were now
making strenuous efforts to regain it. If no relief came, it was
believed that the French could not hold out ; but Vendôme appeared
with a strong squadron of men-of-war convoying troops and munitions for the town. It made little difference to England who held
Dunquerque, but, considering the state of affairs in the Mediterranean, it was essential to stand well with Spain, the more so as
such an end could be gained at the expense of France. At the right
moment, then, Blake, with his vastly superior force, swept down on
Vendôme's relieving squadron, and in a running fight so handled it
that a few days later the town fell. Of the men-of-war engaged
Blake took seven, besides two small craft. What became of the
transports is not stated, but the intention was to keep them out of
Dunquerque, and that end was most certainly gained.

This affair made a good deal of noise at the time, the King of
Spain expressing to Parliament his gratitude for an attack which
had laid Dunquerque at his mercy, and Louis XIV., on the other
hand, adding to his former complaints against the letters of reprisal,
which were then in force, a very definite statement of his grievance.[2]
It was, urged his ambassador, an unheard-of thing that a nation
should extend letters of marque so as to cover the property of an
allied prince. Such an action was tantamount to a declaration of
war. When he went on to say that England might at least show
gratitude to France, which had not interfered in the Civil War
though in a position to do so, it is impossible to believe that his
words carried conviction to any man who knew that the policy of
the English Navy had been " to keep foreigners from fooling us."

During the summer of 1652 there were many minor actions in
which the balance inclined distinctly in England's favour. In August
Blake and Penn both made valuable captures of laden merchantmen
from the West Indies and the Straits,[3] but against this the Dutch

[1] Cal. S. P. Dom. 1652–1653, p. 504 ; Whitelocke, 518 ; ‘ Columna Rostrata,’ 105 ;
Basnage, 264.

[2] Hist. MSS. Com. Rep. 13, App. 1, pp. 661, 663, 666.   [3] ‘ Col. Rostr.,’ 105.

could claim the capture of two small men-of-war, the *Fortune* and the *Hart*. Of these two the former seemed to the Council to have been too easily surrendered, and an order was therefore made[1] that the wages of her crew should not be paid until it was found out who had cried for quarter, and till the offender was punished. The *Hart*, on the other hand, had been gallantly fought, and had yielded at length only to the greatly superior force which three Dutch ships brought against her.[2] The *Hart* was a marked ship. There had been a heavy blot against her name on the Navy List, in the shape of the record of her mutiny; and doubtless her stubborn defence was an effort to wipe this out. Francis Darcy, the Royalist, who had been captured in the previous year, had headed the rising,[3] and, with a few men, had surprised such of the crew as were averse to his project of carrying her over to the Duke of York at Dunquerque. The resistance had been overcome, and sail had been made on the ship, but, before they were many leagues on their journey, the seamen had thought better of the bargain and had insisted on returning to Harwich. The ringleaders had been "made an example of," and the wages of the other guilty persons had found their way into the Chest at Chatham.

Everywhere the course of the war was favourable to England, save only in the Mediterranean, where her interests were being distinctly neglected. When Penn returned with his squadron, the total force left on that station was represented by the few ships with Appleton and Badiley. The ships being so few in number, in view of the local strength of the Dutch, could in no case have taken the initiative; but, being divided into two commands, they were doubly feeble.

As early as June, before the rupture, and therefore long before the news of the breach had reached the Mediterranean, Longland wrote from Leghorn[4] showing his anxiety. The Dutch were supporting the French, and they were in such force that nothing could be undertaken against them. They had, in point of fact, a squadron of eighteen men-of-war lying before Toulon, while the total English force consisted of eight ships, the *Leopard*, *Constant Warwick*, *Phœnix*, *Paragon*, *Elizabeth*, *Adventure*, and two armed merchantmen. Individually, however, as the result proved, the English

---

[1] Cal. S. P. Dom. 1652 ; C. o. S. to Navy Commissioners, 23rd August.
[2] *Ib.* and Whitelocke, 516.   [3] *Ib.* 1650, March 2nd, 4th, 9th, etc.
[4] Cal. S. P. Dom. 1652, p. 293.

vessels were superior to the Dutch, many of which were merchant-men, unsatisfactorily armed, and undermanned.

On July 8th the war was formally proclaimed in Holland, and a few days later, before the English in the Mediterranean had news of the breach, Joris Catz, in command of the Dutch squadron off Toulon, moved with fourteen ships to Leghorn, where Appleton was lying, and closed the port.[1] He injured his chance, however, by trying to prevent the unloading of the merchantmen which Appleton had convoyed thither, for this action ensured the opposition of the Grand Duke, who, by a complaint to the States General, brought about Catz's dismissal.[2] Van Galen, who went out overland, at once set to work in earnest. Appleton, save for the despatch of the *Constant Warwick* to apprise Badiley of the turn of events and to reinforce him somewhat, was content to accept the blockade passively. Van Galen left only four ships to watch him, while with the rest he cruised to intercept Badiley. Had it been possible for the Council of State to respond immediately to Longland's appeal of July 12th and to send the twelve " frigates " which had been asked for, there is little doubt that the situation would have been saved. The Grand Duke of Tuscany, indeed, was friendly, and made a direct offer of help, but it was not to be supposed that he could do more than guarantee the safety of his ports against attack.[3]

Badiley, on being joined by the *Constant Warwick* at Cephalonia, made the best of his way towards Leghorn. He hoped that, by touching at no port on the way, he might arrive before the Dutch expected him, and that he might thus avoid the blockading ships and join with Appleton. This was not the case. When he passed Monte Cristo, on August 27th, he found the Dutch squadron, ten strong,[4] lying between that island and Elba.

Badiley had with him, besides his own ship the *Paragon*, 42, the *Constant Warwick*, 30, Captain Owen Cox, the *Elizabeth*, 38, and the *Phœnix*, 38, with which he was convoying four Levant merchantmen. On the 27th the wind was light, and the squadrons could not come to close action.[5] The merchantmen made no

[1] Basnage, 263 ; Cal. S. P. Dom. 1652, p. 330.	[2] ' Vie de Corneille Tromp,' 73.
[3] Hist. MSS. Com. Rep. 13, App. 1, p. 656.
[4] Cal. S. P. Dom. 13th September, 1652 ; Basnage, 263. Whether this squadron numbered ten or eleven ships is a small point, but the weight of evidence is in favour of ten. There is no proof that Van Galen was reinforced before the fight, and it is known that of an original force of fourteen ships he left four to watch Leghorn.
[5] S. P. Dom. Int. vol. xxiv. 120, 125, 125 (i.) ; which are Badiley's and Appleton's official reports.

attempt to offer help, considering that their own safety was the point under discussion; and they made the best of their way into Porto Longone. Badiley hoped for some help from Appleton, but Appleton declared that he was too ill to leave port—an excuse which Badiley refused to accept, alleging that, even if such were the case, he might at least have sent his vessels. The four ships were thus 'eft to fight it out by themselves; and, as all accounts agree, they made a right gallant defence.

The calm gave the English some little help, by keeping three of the enemy out of action; and, although the odds were still two to one, Badiley did not despair. He decided that, as his ship was the heaviest, it would be best that she should meet the brunt of the attack, and accordingly he bade his consorts take up their stations under his stern. This, he says, the *Constant Warwick*, and apparently the *Elizabeth*, did with satisfactory results, but the *Phœnix* remained too far off to allow of any support being given to her by the others. The manœuvre may be looked upon as one of the earliest attempts at the formation of a line; but as the ships were so few in number, it is at least likely that Badiley merely intended to collect his squadron into a compact group for mutual support, with a reservation to himself of the post of honour in the van.

The *Paragon* drew the fire of the three Dutch flagships,[1] which engaged her within pistol-shot; and she continued throughout in the heat of the fight, being always well supported by the *Constant Warwick*, whose captain, Owen Cox, was, by his record, a man of more than ordinary valour. Little mention is made of the *Elizabeth*, but she seems to have been somewhat to leeward of, and screened by, the two first-named ships. That she was closely engaged may be taken for granted, in view of the balance of force in favour of the enemy, but though she did not come off by any means free, her loss was slight compared with that sustained by the *Paragon*.

The *Phœnix*, wrote Badiley, was taken in a strange and sudden manner, and would not have been thus lost had she fallen astern of the *Paragon* as ordered. A heavy ship of the enemy's ran her aboard, and, owing to her want of a forecastle, captured her. Badiley, however, declared that he had four ships close aboard him at the time, so that it may reasonably be doubted whether he was

---

[1] Any Dutch squadron, however small, bore in separate ships flags as of admiral, vice-admiral and rear-admiral. Such was the case even in Young's action of May 12th, although there were but the three Dutch ships present.

in a position to say what happened. The accepted account of the loss [1] has nothing unlikely in it. It shows that a Dutch ship which was closely engaged with Badiley, lost her mainmast, and hauled out of the fight. The *Phœnix*, seeing this, ran alongside of her, and boarded, but, while she was thus left empty and defenceless, a second Dutch ship in turn boarded the *Phœnix*, and took her without resistance. The boarding-party from the *Phœnix* had no means of retreat, and, being overpowered, was killed or taken.

With evening the fight came to an end; and the remaining English ships, torn and shattered, and with all, or nearly all, their

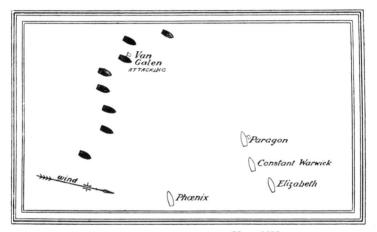

THE ACTION OFF ELBA, AUGUST 28TH, 1652.

NOTE.—No accounts of the fight contain details that make the preparation of an exact plan possible ; but the conjectural plan given above will explain how the *Phœnix* was taken, and how the *Elizabeth* escaped the brunt of the attack.

ammunition expended, were towed into Porto Longone.[2] The *Paragon's* loss was twenty-six men killed, including her principal officers, and fifty-seven wounded. She had received fifty great shot in her hull, many between wind and water; and hardly a spar was sound.[3] The other ships had suffered only less heavily. The Dutch loss was represented by three captains killed,[4] besides very many of their men. Two ships also had lost their mainmasts, and the whole squadron was hardly in a position to keep the sea.

The enemy managed, however, to follow Badiley to Porto Longone, where they would have made an attack on him at once

[1] 'Columna Rostrata,' 103 ; Whitelocke, 520.   [3] Badiley to Navy Committee.
[2] 'Vie de Corneille Tromp,' 76.   [4] 'Vie de Corneille Tromp,' 77.

had they not met with opposition from the governor.[1] The next expedient tried was to attempt to bribe the governor, but he not only proved incorruptible, but also allowed the English to land guns and make batteries on shore for their protection,[2] whereupon the Dutch withdrew.

This left Badiley free to quit the port: and he availed himself of the opportunity to go over and concert matters with Appleton at Leghorn. There he found that Appleton and Longland had been doing their best to persuade merchant ships to volunteer for the service, but with singularly little success.[3] Everywhere they met with the answer, that the merchant captains had no orders from their owners, and could not act without them—all of which was doubtless true to a certain extent, as was the further objection that, even if taken up, the ships, owing to the small numbers of their crews, would not be efficient for war. And Appleton was not the sort of commander to attract men to the service, especially when the prospect was one of hard blows and deferred pay. He was a man absolutely without tact, and unpopular alike with officers and men. Badiley found him engaged in a quarrel with one of his captains, but contrived to smooth over the difficulty to such good effect that some progress at last began to be made.

Two merchant ships were taken up and equipped in Leghorn; and then a much-cherished project was carried into execution. This was no other than the recapture of the *Phœnix*—an affair which was much spoken of, both at the time and afterwards, and which was destined to have important results.

The Dutch had at once careened and refitted their prize; and she now lay in the outer road at Leghorn ready for sea, and under the command of Cornelis, son of Marten Tromp. To the English in the port, she, with the English ensign trailing in the water astern, was a continual eyesore; and it is hardly to be wondered at that an effort should have been made for her recovery. To surprise her did not promise to be difficult, and Badiley, Longland and Appleton had the less hesitation about doing so, in violation of a neutral port, seeing that the Government at home was aware of the scheme.[4] After all, they argued, the affair could be carried through without

---

[1] 'Vie de Corneille Tromp,' 76.
[2] Longland to Navy Committee, October 11th.
[3] S. P. Dom. Int. xxv. 44, 46, 56, 60.
[4] Blackborne to Longland, October 22nd.

the use of firearms, and, so long as there was no noise, there would
be no insult to the Grand Duke. Such was a theory which had
been laid down by the elder Tromp, and which it was now convenient for the English to adopt.

Accordingly they chose their occasion—the night of the 20th of
November—which was, in the calendar style, St. Andrew's Day.
By good luck the night was extremely dark, so that there was
little fear of the attackers being seen by the other Dutch ships. In
command of the expedition went Captain Owen Cox.[1] He took with
him eighty men in three boats, fourteen with himself, the rest with
lieutenants Young and Lynn; and all were armed with hatchets and
cutlasses, besides which they carried bags of flour for the purpose of
blinding the Dutch. Twice the boats were separated in the dark,
but at the third attempt they reached the *Phœnix,* and boarded. It
was then almost daybreak, and, as the Dutch had been keeping high
festival the night before in honour of the saint, the watch was not
too well kept.

There was practically no resistance. Tromp himself, who was
entertaining a brother officer in his cabin, saw that there was
nothing to be done, and firing a pistol at the boarders as they broke
in, rushed to the cabin window and jumped out. It is possible that
he dropped into the longboat, which would be towing astern: in any
case he was picked up. The English at once made sail, and the
ship, thanks to her recent careening, was soon beyond pursuit.[2] She
rejoined her squadron at Elba, and was there blockaded by the
enemy.

The Dutch were more formidable than ever in those waters, for
they had withdrawn from the neighbourhood of Messina a squadron
which had been stationed there to intercept Badiley, and had joined
it to the ships already cruising between Leghorn and Elba, thus
bringing the total numbers of the blockading force up to twenty-
seven sail.

The recapture, in spite of the precautions taken, gave serious
offence to the Grand Duke, who refused to be convinced by the
English arguments that there had been no violation of his port.
Neither had Appleton improved matters by violence which his men
had offered to a sentry on the Mole.[3] The affair was looked upon

[1] S. P. Dom. Int. xxv. 65; Appleton to Navy Committee, 22nd November
' Vie de Corneille Tromp,' 82.
[2] *Ib.*   [3] Grand Duke of Tuscany to Badiley, 25th November.

as a most serious insult, and for that reason it became necessary to remove Appleton from his command, leaving him, however, his captaincy of the *Leopard*.[1] Badiley was appointed Commodore of the two squadrons.

It is now necessary to revert to affairs in the Narrow Seas, as well to avoid anticipating events as to explain the further action taken by the Grand Duke.

De With,[2] meanwhile, had put to sea with the main fleet of the Dutch. He was intensely unpopular with the men, but his ability and courage were undoubted, and his politics were those of the party then in power.[3] His orders were to take De Ruijter under his command, for which reason he proceeded at once to the Narrows, knowing that the western fleet would be due there in a few days.

On September 11th he showed himself at the South Sand Head, this being the first intimation the Council had of his being at sea. The Council at once wrote to warn Blake and Ayscue[4] of his presence, but it has been already seen that the English Western Guard had failed to intercept De Ruijter. The junction took place in due course off Calais on September 22nd, the number of ships brought out by De With being forty-four. The first duty that was incumbent on the Dutch admirals was to hold a survey of their fleet,[5] which was in many ways ineffective ; and when this had been done it was discovered that ten men-of-war and five fireships were quite unfit for service. After these had been sent home, with instructions to the captains to refit with the utmost speed and to come out again, the total of the united fleet was sixty-four sail,[5]

---

[1] Hist. MSS. Com. Rep. 13, App. 1, 662 ; ditto to Parliament. Appleton was arrested, and by order of the Grand Duke was confined for a few days until set at liberty owing to Badiley's representation that he would be punished by his own country.

[2] Witte Corneliszoon de With, after serving the Dutch West India Company, fought under Piet Hein and Tromp. He fell in action in 1658.

[3] *I.e.* Strongly republican.

[4] C. o. S. Minutes, September 12th. The exact date of Ayscue's retirement is unknown, but it is usually placed directly after the battle off Plymouth, which, as this order shows, was not the case. Further, there is no proof of the supposition that his retirement was due to ill-success. This is indeed contradicted by the fact of his having received a pension. It is far more natural to suppose that the committee for foreign affairs had presented an adverse report on the Royalist tendency exhibited by him at Barbados. G. Penn, i. 457 ; Cal. S. P. Dom. 1652, pp. 441, 458, 462. *See* also p. 157.

[5] *Ib.* The English report of it was fifty-nine sail, and a few small craft. Blake's fleet was slightly superior in numbers, but very greatly so in the force of individual ships. There were no vessels in the Dutch fleet to compare with the *Sovereign* or *Resolution*, and but few that were a match for the *Fairfax, James, Andrew*, and other second-rates present.

with which, inferior though he knew them to be, De With felt that he was bound to seek out the enemy and give battle at once. He had come out to better the work done by Tromp, and it was clearly his duty as well as his inclination to endeavour, by success in a general engagement, to clear the sea of the many cruisers that pressed so heavily on Dutch commerce.

The English fleet that had collected from the westward, with the exception of some of Ayscue's ships which were refitting, joined the force in the Downs, and weighed to seek the Dutch early on the morning of September 28th, 1652.[1] The force passed the North

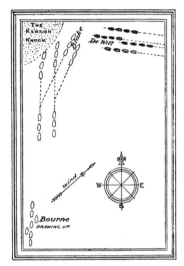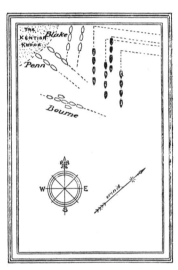

TWO PHASES OF THE BATTLE OF THE KENTISH KNOCK, SEPTEMBER 28TH, 1652.

English, white.   Dutch, black.

Foreland with a fresh westerly breeze; and at about noon the Dutch hove in sight. The wind shifted to the south-west and fell light, and the greater part of Blake's fleet was left some distance astern, " by reason of their late weighing from the Downs." Blake, in the *Resolution*, and Penn, the vice-admiral, were well up with the enemy, who were standing west close-hauled on the port tack; but as some little time would elapse before Bourne, the rear-admiral, could come up with the rest of the fleet, Blake refrained from attacking.

The enemy, meanwhile, was hove-to close under the lee of the

[1] Penn to Bishop. Blake to C. o. S. in G. Penn, i. 446–453.

Kentish Knock, which lies at the north-east end of the Long Sand, about . fifteen miles north-east from the North Foreland. The English came upon them somewhat as a surprise, and De With, having no time to hold a council of war, had to rest content with sending advice vessels round the fleet. Nevertheless, his position was one of strength, the ships being drawn up so close to the shoal that there was little chance of the English weathering them without grounding. Just before the action De With was seen to leave his own ship, a forty, and go on board the largest of the East India-men, which mounted fifty-six guns. The *Brederode*, Tromp's old ship, was in the fleet, but her crew refused to receive the new admiral on board,[1] and showed a spirit which boded ill for any chance of Dutch success. The Dutch fleet was organised in four squadrons : De Ruijter had the van, W. C. de With the centre, G. de Wildt the rear ; and J. Evertsen,[2] with the fourth, formed a reserve.[3] De With held the chief command, but De Ruijter also wore his flag at the main, in virtue of the independent command which he had exercised before the junction.[4]

As the vessels from astern drew up, Blake and Penn with the leading ships ran down to attack the Dutch van; "but," wrote Penn, "it pleased God to disappoint us, being aground upon a sand supposed the Kentish Knock. It was reasonable smooth, and for my part, I did not feel her strike. . . . The *Sovereign* was near musket-shot without us, and struck several times." Others of the heaviest ships also grounded, while yet others held on with Blake. The fight in the van was hot. Two Dutch ships were dismasted at the outset. De With, whether to come to a general engagement the sooner or to avoid for a time the two or three heavy ships with Blake, whose course was taking him somewhat to leeward, tacked all together and stood south. As the Dutch came up with the English rear, Penn and the ships with him contrived to cast free from the shoal and fell in amongst them, thus turning to advantage what had threatened to be a grave mishap. To quote Penn again:[5] "We were forced to tack our ship to clear ourselves of the sand ; and, indeed, it fell out better for doing execution upon the enemy, than we could have cast it ourselves ; for, as the Dutch fleet cleared

---

[1] Penn, i. 447.

[2] Jan Evertsen, brother of Cornelis Evertsen "the Old," who was also in the fleet. Served as flag-officer under M. H. Tromp, De Ruijter, and Wassenaer van Obdam. As Lieut.-Admiral, fell in the battle of July 25th, 1666.

[3] 'Vie de Corneille Tromp,' 78.   [4] Penn, i. 453.   [5] *Ib.* 447.

themselves of our General, he standing to the northward and they to the southward, we fell patt to receive them, and so stayed by them till the night caused our separation."

Penn, together with Bourne, completed what Blake had begun. By night the Dutch were beaten and discouraged, yet De With had no thought of retiring. He could not return beaten to Holland without forfeiting his command, and he was, in addition, a man of that stubborn type which is very slow to recognise defeat. Unhappily, his captains were not all of the same way of thinking, and many of them chose the occasion to exhibit their political prejudice. In the morning it was found that some twenty of them were at a distance to eastward of the fleet; and though further action was contemplated, these men refused to come within range. A council of war was held, and De With was eager to re-engage, although De Ruijter and Evertsen, men of known valour and reputation, did their best to prevent his risking the safety of the vessels that remained with him. They pointed out that many of the ships were crippled, and that so many men had been lost as seriously to impair their efficiency ; and they spoke also, doubtless, of the disaffection existing in the fleet.[1]

Early in the day the wind was light and treacherous, so that the English were unable to bring on more than a partial engagement; but when, at about noon, a northerly breeze sprang up in favour of the Dutch, they were able easily to avoid coming to close quarters, and though for a while " they seemed to stay," at about three they set their mainsails, and what else they could carry, and made for their own shores. The English followed, but drew off at nightfall lest they should get among the shoals of the Dutch coast. In the morning the Dutch were hull down, and as it seemed impossible to come up with them, it was determined by a council of war [2] to return to the Downs for victuals, of which there was great need.

The actual duration of the engagement can have been little more than three hours, and it is not to be expected that very many ships were captured. The English loss was singularly slight, both in men and in ships, but the Dutch had, not unnaturally, been far more roughly treated. Two vessels at least were taken, of which one, the *Mary*, of 30 guns, served through the rest of the war in the English Navy. The second, also a 30-gun ship, was found to be so riddled

---

[1] Basnage, 260, 261.　　　　　　　　[2] Penn, i. 449.

with shot that she could not be kept afloat, and was consequently abandoned and allowed to sink.

De With, on his return, inveighed bitterly, and not without justice, against his captains; but he could effect nothing. Their very number, if not their political friends, shielded them from punishment.

With the English, after this, all was for a time prosperous in the Narrow Seas. The Dutch dared not appear outside their ports, and the small cruisers reaped a golden harvest. On October 18th, the *Tiger*, Captain James Peacock, a man well used to North Sea cruising, and his small squadron, put into Yarmouth with twenty prizes.[1] Of these, one, the *Morgenstar*,[2] was a man-of-war which had been taken after stiff fighting. The *Tiger* had not lost a man, while the Dutchman had suffered heavily.

Another result of the victory was that the batteries overlooking the Downs, that had been run up in July for the protection of the anchorage, were now looked upon as useless and were dismantled. This was a mistake for which England was destined to pay a price, and that soon; for in Holland there was little thought of peace. The successes of the English were either not recognised or were regarded as merely local and temporary. Nor is this to be wondered at when we consider how little the burden of the war pressed upon the people. Johan de Witt[3] was at the helm of the state, and so excellently did he manage the country's finances that no loan was called for in consequence of the war till June, 1654.

In the belief that the States must soon submit, or that in no case would anything further be attempted that year, the Council of State proceeded to disperse the fleet. Captain Andrew Ball, in the new second-rate, *Antelope*, was sent with a squadron of eighteen ships to the Sound, where there was urgent need for the presence of a force, owing to an embargo having been laid by the Danes on about twenty English merchantmen, and to the capture by the Dutch of two or three ships in the Eastland trade.[4] The actual loss of these Baltic ships was less important at that time than it

---

[1] S. P. Dom. Int. xxv. 18.

[2] Added to the Navy as the *Plover*, Oct. 30th, 1652.

[3] Johan de Witt. Born at Dordrecht, 1625. Opponent of the House of Orange. Leader of the burgher republican aristocracy. Grand-Pensionary, 1653–1672. With his brother, Cornelius, murdered by a mob, Aug. 20th, 1672. Life by Simons, 1832–1836.

[4] Cal. S. P. Dom. 29 Sept. 1652; Whitelocke, 522.

would have been a few years earlier,[1] for the extension of England's colonies allowed her to buy timber and pitch in other markets; yet the position in the Sound was serious.

The arrest of four Swedish ships from the west coast, in the belief that they were Dutchmen disguised, challenged danger from Sweden. Their release, however, coupled with the Swedish jealousy of the Danes, joined Sweden for a while to English interests.[2] The Danes were useful allies to Holland. Not only did they supply very many men to the Dutch navy, but also they were bound, by the receipt of a subsidy, to maintain a squadron of twenty men-of-war for the Dutch service.[3]

And here it will not be amiss to say that Charles imagined that he discovered in the war another means of regaining his kingdom. Representing that Rupert was in the Mediterranean with a strong squadron,[4] he offered his alliance to the Dutch. But the Dutch would have none of it. Setting aside the question of what value they may have attached to the Royalist declarations, they knew full well that such an alliance would make a reconciliation with Cromwell impossible.

Ball was unfortunate. On September 30th, before anything could be done, a severe storm struck the squadron, and the *Antelope* was driven ashore and lost, though the commodore and most of the crew were saved. The rest of the squadron weathered the danger, and returned to England, picking up a number of prizes on its way.[5]

Such was the history of the Sound squadron. Of the other squadrons detached, one, of twenty sail, was sent north under Penn for the convoy of colliers; another, of twelve sail, was sent to Plymouth for the guard of the western Channel; a further division was busy refitting in the river; and, with yet another, the Council decided to comply with Longland's repeated requests for an accession of force.[6] A squadron of twelve frigates was ordered for this purpose, and Captain James Peacock, who, with the *Tiger*, had for some years done excellent service in the Narrow Seas, was appointed to command it. The re-appearance of the Dutch fleet, however, and the reverse sustained by the English arms, compelled the

---

[1] 'Elenchus Motuum,' ii. 174.   [2] Basnage, 287; Whitelocke, 520.

[3] Basnage, 286–295; Colliber, p. 108, adds that the Danish king made the restoration of Tromp one of his conditions.

[4] *Ib.* 298.   [5] 'Col. Rostr.' 108.

[6] Cal. S. P. Dom. 1652, p. 498; C. o. S. Minutes, November 18th.

Council to rescind the order for Peacock's sailing, and to employ both the ships and their commander nearer home.

Meanwhile, in Holland, it was recognised that, if surrender was not to be thought of, some great effort must be made to relieve the harassed commerce of the country. Since the fight off the Kentish Knock, matters had been many times worse than before it, and what this must have meant will appear when it is recalled that on September 22nd, before the defeat, it had been necessary formally to restrict all sailings of merchantmen to those of organised fleets under the convoy of men-of-war.[1]

A huge Dutch fleet of three hundred merchantmen was lying ready to sail. Great efforts were made to ensure its safety, and a fleet was equipped and sent to sea under Tromp and Jan Evertsen, with De Ruijter as vice-admiral, and Pieter Floriszoon as rear-admiral. De With was to have held a vice-admiral's command, but had to be left sick ashore.[2] The fleet, by Dutch accounts,[3] consisted of seventy-three men-of-war and a few fireships and small craft, while with Blake at the time in the Downs there were, from causes already explained, no more than thirty-seven, with two or three small tenders.[4]

Tromp left his merchantmen on the Flamand coast, and appeared with all his fighting ships at the back of the Goodwin on November 29th. Blake, after holding a hasty council of war, weighed and stood with him to the southward.

It is impossible now to say exactly why Blake took this step, so contrary to his usually well-considered methods. Many reasons have been suggested, and of these the oldest, that Blake had to defend the river at any cost, is obviously the most fallacious, for Blake's course took him to leeward of the river's mouth. It is possible that Blake recalled how this same Tromp had, in the case of Oquendo, turned the Downs into a rat-trap, and that, in view of the demolition of the batteries that had protected Ayscue, the anchorage was held to be unsafe. It is also possible that the thickness of a November day led him to misjudge the quantity or quality of the enemy's fleet.[5] The action certainly was not due to a mere chivalrous spirit that held itself in honour bound to accept every proffered challenge.

---

[1] 'Vie de De Ruijter,' 24.   [2] *Ib.*

[3] *Ib.* and Basnage, 261.   [4] 'Col. Rostr.' 109.

[5] Cal. S. P. Dom. 1652, 541, shows that he had lately heard of a large Dutch merchant fleet at sea.

Not until he was under way does Blake seem to have realised
what force he had to meet. The wind, too, which, at the time of
weighing had been at S.W., veered and made return to the Downs
impossible. For awhile it was variable, but soon it settled in the
north-west and blew too strongly to admit of fighting,[1] so that with
evening Blake anchored in Dover Roads, Tromp lying some two
leagues to leeward, *i.e.*, close off the South Sand Head. With
the morning of the 30th both weighed, and, as Blake still kept
the wind, both steered parallel courses along the shore. There
was no engagement till the fleets came off Dungeness, when the
trend of the coast brought the English van down upon the Dutch.

There resulted a partial engagement, in which the leading English
ships were terribly outnumbered. It is probable that many Dutch
vessels were too far to leeward to help, while it is but too certain that
English captains in the rear availed themselves of the wind to keep
out of action [2] The reason for their doing so is hard to discover.
Had they been mere merchant captains the case would be easily
understood ; but the evil system of employing merchant captains to
fight battles had been remedied somewhat, and the offenders in this
case commanded ships of the regular Navy and were, in some cases
at least, men of known courage.[3] The only reason that can be
suggested is that they had received Royalist bribes ; but as the
evidence taken on their examinations is not forthcoming, this must
remain a theme for speculation.

Such ships as were engaged fought desperately, foremost among
them being the *Triumph*, with Blake on deck. She was resolutely
seconded by Lionel Lane in the *Victory* and John Mildmay in the
Vanguard, and against Evertsen and De Ruijter these ships fought
from about one o'clock till dark. As Tromp came into action a most
gallant attack was made on him by Captains Robert Batten in the
Garland, a third rate, and Hoxton,[4] in the hired merchantman
Bonaventure. The *Brederode* was laid aboard on both sides and was
extremely hard pressed, but Evertsen, drawing up, took the pressure
off her and captured the *Bonaventure*, with the loss in killed and
wounded of the major part of her crew, among whom fell the
captain. Tromp himself proved far more than a match for the

---

[1] G. Penn, i. 458; Blake to C. o. S. December 1st.   [2] *Ib.*
[3] *E.g.* Young and Taylor.
[4] This is the spelling of Blake's official report. *Cp.* Cal. S. P. Dom. 1652..451.
The name is often misspelt, Hoxon, Axon, Ackson, Achson, Hookson, etc.

Garland, which before being taken had lost her captain and sixty men killed,[1] out of a company of one hundred and fifty.

Blake did his best to relieve these two ships, but, owing to the loss of his foretopmast and mainstay, found himself unable to get near them till too late.[2] In the attempt the *Triumph* was herself placed in danger, being boarded on both sides at once; but she managed to shake off her assailants and to rejoin the rest of the fleet. Besides the *Garland* and *Bonaventure*, the English loss amounted to three ships sunk, while the Dutch lost only one, which was accidentally blown up.

Blake went to Dover Roads and thence into the Downs. Tromp, for his part, lay for two or three days off Dungeness refitting, and was thus in a position to intercept vessels coming round from the western ports. On the night of December 1st, one of these, the *Hercules*, hired merchantman, fell into the Dutch fleet and was at once taken. Tromp next picked up his convoy and took it as far as Rhé, where he lay to wait until the homeward-bound trade was ready for his escort back.[3]

Blake was extremely dejected by his defeat. In reporting the result of the battle to the Council of State, he wrote:—[4]

" I am bound to let your Honours know that there was much baseness of spirit, not among the merchantmen only, but many of the State's ships ; and, therefore, I make it my earnest request, that your Honours would be pleased to send down some gentlemen to take an impartial and strict examination of the deportment of several commanders. . . . And I hope it will not be unreasonable for me, in behalf of myself, to desire your Honours, that you would think of giving me, your unworthy servant, a discharge from this employment, so far too great for me . . . that so I may be freed from that trouble of spirit which lies upon me, arising from the sense of my own insufficiency."

But Blake was far too valuable a servant to lose, and the Council refused to receive his commission back again. It thanked him for his efforts, and it at once acceded to his demand for a commission of inquiry.[5] The results of this inquiry were threefold : a considerable increase in the material force of the fleet, including the building of thirty new frigates; the removal from their commands,

---

[1] Basnage, 261.

[2] Blake to C. o. S. December 1st in G. Penn, i. 458–460.

[3] It is to this time that tradition assigns the fabulous broom at Tromp's masthead. There is no mention of it in any writer, Dutch or English, Royalist or Roundhead, until it appears as a vague report in the *Daily Intelligencer* for the 9th March following (No. 113). A broom at the masthead being a sign that the ship wearing it is for sale, it is possible that the story was started as a joke by some one who had seen Tromp refitting and selling his prizes at St. Martin's.

[4] Blake to C. o. S. 1st December.　　[5] G. Penn, i. 461, *sqq.*

and the committal to the Tower, of various captains,[1] including Saltonstall, Taylor, Young, Brown, and Chapman; and the giving of orders that, to avoid desertion and delay, seamen should be kept in their ships while the ships lay in port, and that merchant skippers should no longer be allowed in action to command their own vessels.[2]

What could be done was done to make the fleet ready to meet Tromp on his return. But the sum total of preparations in England did nothing to help the cause in the Mediterranean; and, unfortunately, it was imperative to turn over again to the main fleet the squadron which had recently been appointed to go thither with Peacock.

At Leghorn and Elba the position remained practically unchanged. In the one port the Dutch held Appleton, and in the other was Badiley. At neither place had the English succeeded in taking up for the service more than a very few ships. The force at the beginning of the new year[3] was thus distributed: with Appleton, in the *Leopard*, 50, at Leghorn, were the hired merchantmen *Bonaventure*, *Samson*, *Mary*, *Peregrine*, and *Levant Merchant;* with Badiley in Porto Longone were his old four ships, *Paragon*, *Phœnix*, *Elizabeth*, and *Constant Warwick*, together with two merchantmen which had been recently added.

Life in the Mediterranean convoy service, the Straits fleet as it was called, cannot have been pleasant during the Dutch War. Not only was the enemy present in vastly superior force, but since the re-taking of the *Phœnix* it was becoming more and more doubtful whether the squadrons would be allowed to go on sheltering themselves in port until the relief force should arrive. The fact is that the Grand Duke was bitterly affronted by the capture, and that no amount of polite negotiation could appease him unless restitution were made. When the news of Dungeness came and he began to think that the Dutch would prove victorious everywhere, he saw fit to conciliate them. Refusing all apologies, he insisted that the English must either accept his terms or leave his port, and to this ultimatum he attached a time limit. Apparently in expectation of the sailing of Appleton's squadron, the Dutch massed their whole

---

[1] G. Penn, i. 469, 471.

[2] *Cp.* Penn's letter to Cromwell, June 2nd, 1652, advising this step and other improvements.—G. Penn, i. 466.

[3] Dates are given in the old style, but the year is reckoned from January 1.

force off Leghorn, leaving Badiley free to come out. This Badiley, who, in preparation for the worst, had concerted a scheme with Appleton, immediately did; and he proceeded to Leghorn to effect, if possible, a junction of the squadrons. Divided, the two English forces were despicable; united, they might be able to offer a good resistance; for the Commonwealth ships were superior to nearly all that the Dutch had on the station.

The plan agreed upon was, that as soon as Badiley should appear off Leghorn, Appleton should weigh to meet him. If the wind should be on shore, and in Badiley's favour, the Elba squadron was to keep to windward till the very moment when Appleton should reach the Dutch fleet; and it should then try to break through and join him. But if the wind should be off shore the ships in Leghorn were to avoid getting into action till the Dutch should have attacked or should be on the point of falling on Badiley.

On the 4th March, 1653, when Badiley presented himself, the wind was off shore. Van Galen made a feint of attacking him, and possibly by this move induced Appleton to weigh too soon. The Dutch indeed claim so much in his honour. But as we know Appleton to have been, though personally brave, but an addleheaded commander, it is far more likely that he mistook the purport of his instructions and hastened to attack with no clear conception of how long he would have to fight unsupported. As soon as they saw his sails let fall, the Dutch recalled the ships, and pushed forward towards Badiley; and if Appleton then saw his mistake it was too late to remedy it. The wind was fresh. The harbour faces somewhat northerly, and to the north of it there projects the Mallora shoal for some five miles from the coast.

Appleton's only possible plan, then, was to run down before the wind. This brought him into action while Badiley was still some miles to leeward. The action began with a great disaster. At the very outset the *Bonaventure* received a shot in her magazine and blew up, and at the same time a round shot it is said from the *Bonaventure*, shattered Van Galen's leg. The remaining English ships were surrounded, and one only, the *Mary*, succeeded in fighting her way through and joining Badiley. The other four were taken after a stubborn defence. In Appleton's own ship, out of two hundred men, there were one hundred and fifty killed and wounded, yet Appleton declared that, even so, he was forced into a surrender by his men when his own wish was to blow up the ship.

There was nothing left for Badiley to do. As he came up he saw the last of the four ships taken, and therefore laid his course back to Elba. The Dutch made no serious effort at pursuit. They were, in fact, too much cut up to be able to do so. Badiley went from Porto Longone to Messina, and thence home, rightly judging that his small remaining force was useless in the Mediterranean. When he reached the Downs in May, he found that he had but anticipated an order for his recall.

For a few weeks after November 30th the Channel swarmed with Dutch cruisers, but by the end of the year the English Navy was able to resume the control pending the return of Tromp. It

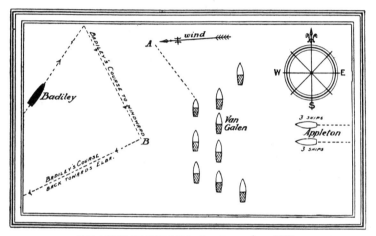

THE ACTION IN LEGHORN ROAD, MARCH 4TH, 1653.

A. Point reached by three of Van Galen's ships when feinting against Badiley. From it they rejoined the squadron.
B. Point at which the *Mary* joined Badiley.

was seen to be essential to meet him on his homeward journey, and by a victory to gain back that supremacy which Dungeness had shaken.

How far the supremacy had been re-established even before the main fleet put to sea is curiously attested by a letter addressed to the Parliament in January, 1653.[1] The Genoese had ordered two ships to be built in Holland for the protection of their commerce against pirates. These were now ready to sail, but, as there was the danger of their falling a prey to the English in the Channel, the Genoese petitioned for a free pass out to be granted to them;

[1] Hist. MSS. Com. Rep. 13, App. 1, p. 669.

which alone is strong evidence that the Dutch superiority in the Narrow Seas was already a thing of the past.

On February 10th, Penn was appointed to command,[1] as vice-admiral of the fleet,[2] twenty-two men-of-war and nine merchant-men, constituting the White squadron. But Monck and Deane were associated with Blake in the command, and Monck elected to go to sea as Admiral of the White. Penn therefore became Admiral of the Blue, while John Lawson,[3] to whom the post of rear-admiral of the fleet [4] really belonged, was made Vice-Admiral of the Red.

The flagships then wore the distinctive flags of the following commanders :—

Red . . .	*Triumph,*	62	. . .	The Generals, Blake and Deane.
	Fairfax,	64	. . .	John Lawson, Vice-Admiral.
	Laurel,	38	. . .	Samuel Howett, Rear-Admiral.
White . .	*Vanguard,*	56	. . .	General Monck.
	Rainbow,	58	. . .	James Peacock, Vice-Admiral.
	Diamond,	40	. . .	Roger Martin, Rear-Admiral.
Blue. . .	*Speaker,*	64	. . .	Wm. Penn, Admiral.
	Victory,	60	. . .	Lionel Lane, Vice-Admiral.
	Assistance,	48	. . .	John Bourne, Rear-Admiral.

As is suggested by this list, some of the most powerful vessels afloat, notably the *Sovereign* and *Resolution*, first rates, and the *James*, second rate, were absent from the fleet as the result of injuries sustained at the Kentish Knock.

Tromp, having some two hundred merchantmen to convoy home, would have been glad to get this charge off his hands before falling in with the enemy. Accordingly when he received news from the States General that the English fleet was ready for sea, he made haste to pass the Channel. But on February 18th, in the morning, "to his amazement," as we are told, he discovered the English fleet to the number of eighty sail, standing south on the starboard tack. The wind was fresh at W.N.W., and, his fleet being about equal to the English, he at once decided to engage. He had indeed

---

[1] Hist. MSS. Com. Rep. 13, App. 2, p. 85.

[2] In other words, as Admiral of the White squadron.

[3] John Lawson. Born about 1616. Originally the Anabaptist master of a collier. Served ashore and afloat during the Civil War. Commanded the *Centurion* in North Sea, 1650. Commanded *Fairfax*, 1652. Rear-Admiral of England. Vice-Admiral (R.) in the action off Portland, 1653. Admiral (B.) in the actions of June and July, 1653. Vice-Admiral of England, 1653. Knighted, 1660. Reduced the Barbary States, 1661. Vice-Admiral (R.) 1665. Mortally wounded in the action of June 3rd, 1665, and died on June 25th. Buried at St. Dunstan's-in-the-East.

[4] In other words, Admiral of the Blue.

every advantage, and an inspection of the relative positions of the
fleets will show that the arrangement of the English was such as to
invite attack.

Here we may pause for a moment to congratulate the English
Navy on the happy chance that had decided Deane to remain with
Blake in the *Triumph*, when he might have elected to command the
Blue squadron as Monck did the White. Monck had allowed
himself to fall four or five miles to leeward with his whole squadron.
But Penn remained to windward with the Blue squadron ahead of
the Generals, and actually with Blake were not more than ten or a

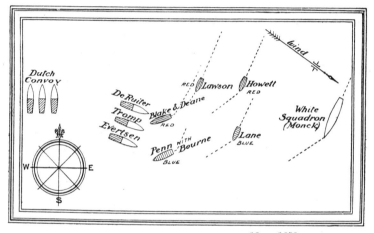

THE BATTLE OFF PORTLAND, FEBRUARY 18TH, 1653.
The Fleets at the moment of Impact.
NOTE.—Groups, and not single ships, are represented in the above plan.

dozen ships. Lawson was a short distance astern of the *Triumph*,
and about a mile to leeward.

It was of course open to Blake to run to leeward and form his
line on the lee squadron, but rather than risk any semblance
of giving way, he elected to fight where he was, thus making it
necessary for a part of the fleet to sustain the action for a considerable time before the leewardmost ships could support it. The attack
was bound to fall upon Blake and Penn, and it was possible for
Tromp to throw the bulk of his force on either.

Tromp was not slow to seize the opportunity. With his fleet
in three divisions, or possibly four, he ran down to engage, leaving
his convoy some four miles to windward. Of the engagement that
followed details are sadly lacking, but as far as can be ascertained,

Tromp commanded in the centre, De Ruijter on the left and Jan Evertsen on the right. The Dutch centre attacked Blake directly, and immediately pressed him very hard. De Ruijter passed on and bore in among Blake's ships from the north, while Evertsen was to the southward and threatened entirely to surround him. It was at this point, when the danger was already most serious, that the great advantage of having trained seamen in command at least of part of the fleet appeared.

Penn, like Blake, hauled to the wind to meet the attack, and opened fire on Evertsen, who was then on his starboard bow. Evertsen held his course, and Penn, to avoid being cut off from the Red squadron, tacked at once, passed through the opposing Dutch squadron and joined the few ships which were, with the Generals, engaged against Tromp. Lawson, meanwhile, had also shown his ability. If he should haul on a wind as Penn had done, he saw that De Ruijter could interpose between him and the Generals, while still keeping up the severity of the attack. He therefore bore away, with the wind abeam, till he had made enough southing to be able, by tacking, to fetch the main body of the enemy. And this he did, following the Blue squadron very closely when it crashed into Tromp's rear.

Meanwhile, part at least of Evertsen's squadron ran down to leeward, and engaged Monck and the White squadron within a couple of hours from the beginning of the battle. Some of the ships of the lee line, not improbably the stragglers of the Red and Blue squadrons, by dint of sailing close-hauled on the starboard tack, were by four o'clock in a position to weather the Dutch main body. But in the van, where the ships were massed most thickly and where both Tromp and Blake were, the fighting had been of a very stubborn order, and the Dutch were left in no position to withstand the attack of comparatively fresh ships. Accordingly, both for this reason and to avoid the possibility of the English stretching to windward enough to fall upon his convoy,[1] Tromp drew out of action and rejoined the merchantmen. In the van the battle was over for the day, but to leeward the fighting continued till dark.

Details of Monck's share in the action are almost entirely wanting, but as Mildmay, the captain of his ship the *Vanguard*, was killed, we can at least be certain of the truth of the statement that he was engaged towards evening.

[1] 'Vie de Corneille Tromp,' 94.

In the Red and Blue squadrons the loss was heavy; and as the *Triumph* was first into action against overwhelming numbers, and was for a while unsupported, she suffered extremely. Her captain, Andrew Ball, was killed; so, too, was the Generals' secretary, Sparrow; Blake himself was badly wounded in the thigh by a splinter; and of men put ashore dangerously wounded, fifty-five were from her and the *Worcester* alone.[1] The *Triumph*, too, was much damaged, and lay till the morning refitting. Other vessels were so much shattered that they had to be sent into Portsmouth, after contributing men to make up the complements of some that had lost most heavily.

Among these ships were the *Assistance*, 48, Rear-Admiral John

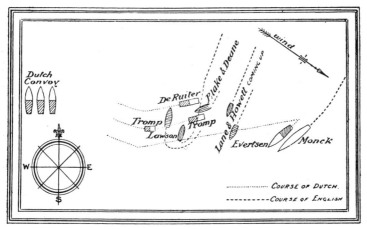

THE BATTLE OFF PORTLAND, FEBRUARY 18TH, 1653.

The Fleets engaged.

NOTE.—Groups, and not single ships, are represented in the above plan.

Bourne; the *Oak*, 32, Captain Edwin, and the *Advice*, 48, Captain Day. Bourne himself was wounded in the head, and the three ships lost so many men in the action, besides contributing to Blake at its close, that they must have reached port all but unmanned. They were all, as was officially reported, "so disabled as to be unfit for service till repaired." [2]

Both the *Oak* and the *Assistance* were taken by the Dutch but afterwards re-won; so, too, was the *Prosperous*, 40. Boarded by De Ruijter, the last named, cleared her deck, her men then

<hr />

[1] Cal. S. P. Dom. 23 February, 1653.   [2] Cal. S. P. Dom. 1652–1653, p. 174.

following the Dutch on board their own ship. A second attempt was made and she was carried, but, the *Martin* coming up, she was re-taken.[1] Her loss, of course, was great, and among the dead was John Barker, her captain.

The English lost but one ship, the *Samson*, which they found to be in a sinking condition. Button, her captain, and most of the crew were dead, but the survivors were taken out before the ship was allowed to founder. It is claimed by the Dutch that the *Speaker* put into port much damaged,[2] a thing most probable in itself, but quite unsupported by official record.

Of the Dutch,[3] one was taken and sent dismasted into port. This was the *Struisvogel*,[4] Captain Adriaen Cruick;[5] but others were destroyed. The Dutch confessed to three ships sunk and one blown up,[6] and it is fairly certain that some others were burnt.[7]

Where Tromp himself had been the English had suffered so heavily that he may have naturally exaggerated the damage done to the entire fleet. When morning dawned, it was found that he had passed to leeward and was running up Channel before the wind with his fleet in crescent formation between the English and his convoy. Towards two o'clock the greater part of the English fleet came up with the Dutch off the Isle of Wight, the wind having fallen light, and "had warm work, till night parted" them.

The event proved the necessity for Tromp's manoeuvre, though his action certainly gave the Generals the impression that they were pursuing a beaten fleet. But Tromp's first duty was to bring his convoy safely home, and not to risk such loss as would leave it unprotected.

Ammunition ran very short in the Dutch fleet, and only the fitful lightness of the wind on the 19th prevented the English from reaping their harvest. The fighting was partial, but heavy. De Ruijter withstood the attack time after time, and, towards night, entirely dismasted and riddled with shot, had to be taken in tow.[8] What the day's loss was is uncertain, but Lawson, with a few of the quicker-sailing "frigates," contrived to cut off from the right wing two or three men-of-war and a handful of merchantmen. It

---

[1] Willoughby to C. o. S. February 20 ; S. P. Dom. xxxiii. 72.

[2] 'Vie de Corneille Tromp,' 91; G. Penn. i. 478.

[3] The prisoners sent into Portsmouth were so numerous that it was hard to know how to dispose of them. S. P. Dom. xxxiii. 72.   [4] *I.e. Ostrich.*

[5] 'Vie de Corneille Tromp,' 91.   [6] *Ib.* 94.

[7] Cal. S. P. Dom. 1652–1653, pp. 174, 175.   [8] 'Vie de Corneille Tromp,' 95.

is probable that the Dutch estimate, viz., two men-of-war, with ten or twelve merchantmen taken, is right.[1] Disorder crept in as the convoy lost faith in the men-of-war. Many vessels turned their heads towards the French coast, some few escaping into Le Hâvre.

At night the Generals steered their course by the Dutch lights with a steady breeze at W.N.W. The next day's action is well described in the official report.

" On the 20th, about nine in the morning, we fell close in with them with some five great ships and all the frigates of strength, though very many could not come up that day; and seeing their men-of-war somewhat weakened, we sent ships of less force that could get up amongst the merchantmen." The Dutch, who were now past Beachy Head, standing towards Boulogne, turned some merchantmen out of the fleet for a bait. The scheme failed to draw off the English who, hauling to windward, fought on till dusk. They were then ten miles from Gris Nez, " so that, had it been three hours longer to-night, we had probably made an interposition between them and home, whereby they might have been obliged to have made their way through with their men-of-war, which at this time were not above thirty-five." [2] That they were so few was due in great measure to the flight of some twenty who had fired away all their powder.[3]

At night the English anchored three leagues from Gris Nez, which bore N.E. by E.; and the enemy lay in-shore to leeward. This step was taken by the advice of the pilots, who pointed out that, with a lee tide, the Dutch would be unable to weather the point.[4] But, in the morning, not one Dutch ship remained in sight. After refitting, the English weighed on the night of the 21st, and on the 27th made Stokes Bay.

Monck and Deane's estimate that the enemy had lost seventeen or eighteen men-of-war, is certainly an exaggeration. Only four were admitted by the Dutch to have been taken,[5] and only four were brought in.[6] This agreement disposes us to accept the Dutch statement that only five were sunk,[5] though two or three more at least seem to have been burnt. The number of merchantmen taken

[1] ' Vie de De Ruijter,' 30; *cp.* S. P. Dom. Int. xxxiii. 88, 89.
[2] *Cp.* Basnage, 300.   [3] ' Vie de Corneille Tromp,' 97.
[4] The Generals to the Speaker, 27th February. G. Penn, i. 476.
[5] ' Vie de De Ruijter,' 31.   [6] S. P. Dom. Int. xxxiii. 72, 89.

is stated variously at from thirty to fifty, but no official list was ever made.[1]

Of English ships, only the *Samson* miscarried, though three more were quite disabled. To these three the Dutch added a fourth, the *Fairfax*, which they asserted was purposely burnt as unfit for service. This was not so, however; the burning was due to criminal negligence, but was accidental.[2]

There was much to be done before the fleet could be again ready, but a commission was appointed[3] and the work was energetically taken in hand. There had been good ships absent from Portland, but of them the *Resolution* and the *James*, as well as others, were now made ready. Yet the old difficulty of raising mariners continued, and again recourse had to be had to drafting large bodies of soldiers to the fleet.[4] That men were so hard to obtain was due partly to the smallness of their pay, but chiefly to the difficulty which they experienced in getting any pay at all. This led not only to mutiny and riot at home, but also to the presence in the Dutch fleet of many Englishmen who, doubtless, like the Scots and Irishmen in the same service, salved their consciences with the reflection that they were fighting for their lawful king against a pack of rebels. Many such were taken in the battle off Portland; and the extreme need of men is typified by the reluctance of the Council of State to hang those whom it was possible to press for service against their former friends.[5]

Blake's wound proved severe. A month after he had been put ashore, his doctor wrote from Portsmouth : "General Blake, I hope, mends, but . . . *de senibus non temere sperandum*," a sentiment which shows how altered is the conception of old age, for Blake was but fifty-three. His general health, too, was bad, so bad that the Royalists hoped that he would never go to sea again.[6]

On April 20th, 1653, Cromwell dissolved the Rump and usurped the supreme authority, a change to which the Generals-at-Sea and the captains adhered,[7] though the Royalists tried to persuade themselves that it was otherwise.[8] The Dutch, who were thinking

[1] 'Vie de De Ruijter,' 31; 'Col. Rostr.' 115; Basnage, 300; G. Penn, i. 479, 480; Clar. S. P. Cal. ii. 997, 1002.

[2] Cal. S. P. Dom. 1652–1653, 231, 255–257.

[3] C. o. S. Minutes, February 26th.

[4] *Ib.* March 16th, April 8th; Penn to Admlty. Com. April 9th, etc.

[5] *Ib.* March 4th.   [6] Clar. S. P. Cal. ii. 1082.

[7] G. Penn, i. 489–191.   [8] Clar. S. P. Cal. ii. 1121.

of peace, hoped much from the change,[1] but the Pensionary de Witt soon found how little it affected the war. Negotiations, indeed, were opened with Cromwell, but so little did they advance, the basis still being the Hague articles of 1651, that the Dutch ambassadors were advised to conclude, if possible, a secret treaty with France.[2] Denmark was apprised of this, for just then it was essential for Holland to maintain cordial relations with a country which had twenty-two men-of-war ready for sea.[3] Of these ships as well as of a further squadron of equal force, the Dutch hoped to derive the benefit. They had, it is true, themselves already ordered heavier ships to the number of thirty, but none of them were ready.

In Holland, the questions of rewards and punishments, of refitting, of finding men and making provision for the wounded, gave at least as much trouble as in England.[4] Partly owing to increases of pay, partly to individual enterprise, the fleet was manned. It put to sea under Tromp, who sailed north about with a large outward-bound convoy and returned at once by the same way and on the same duty.

Monck and Deane were on the Zeeland coast to intercept him, but, though the fleets came very near one another, they failed to meet; and the English contented themselves with ravages on the fishing and coasting trade.[5] They also made, in May, an abortive attempt on the shipping in the Vlie;[6] and the Dutch on the 14th tried to come into the Downs.

The whole Dutch fleet was there under Tromp, De Ruijter, De With, Jan Evertsen, and Floriszoon; and it was decided at a council of war that, when both entrances should have been closed, the whole of the five squadrons would attack together.[7] This was, in fact, a suggested repetition of the treatment meted out to Oquendo fourteen years before.

But both the Downs and Dover Roads were empty. Even Badiley and the Straits fleet, which had but recently returned to England, were not to be found; and Tromp withdrew under a heavy fire from Dover Castle. On the coast of Flanders he heard from the fishermen that the English fleet had been seen off Nieuwpoort, and

[1] Whitelocke, 531; 'Col. Rostr.' 116, 118.
[2] Basnage, 303, 306.
[3] Thurloe, S. P. i. 244, 248.
[4] Basnage, 301; 'Col. Rostr.' 123.
[5] Basnage, 307; 'Vie de De Ruijter,' 34.
[6] 'Col. Rostr.' 124.
[7] Basnage, 307; 'Vie de De Ruijter,' 34.

he at once went in search of them.   On June 1st the English lay in
Yarmouth Roads, where they received advice that the Dutch fleet
was near the coast ; but the thickness of the weather prevented any
meeting that day.   They weighed, and anchored next tide two miles
outside the Gabart [1] Sand, Orfordness bearing N.W. about five
leagues.   On the following morning at daybreak, the Dutch fleet
was sighted two leagues to leeward,[2] bearing S.S.W., the wind
being in the north-east.[3]   Tromp had come down a S.W. wind on
May 31st with the intention of interposing between the English and

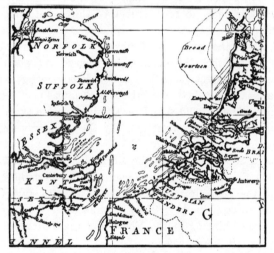

THE STRAIT OF DOVER, AND PART OF THE NORTH SEA.

From a chart in the *London Magazine.*

the river, and on June 1st had been anchored four leagues N.E.
of the North Foreland.   The battle, therefore, that followed,[4] was
sought for by both nations.   On its result depended in no small

---

[1] In old accounts the spelling of this name is Gaber, Gober or Gable.

[2] Monck to Admlty. Comrs. in G. Penn, i. 491.

[3] 'Vie de De Ruijter,' 34 ; Basnage, 307.

[4] This battle has suffered from a multiplicity of names, due chiefly to the neglect
of historians to follow the movements of the fleets, but in no small degree to the
great expanse over which the action was fought.   However, Lowestoft is certainly a
misnomer ; so too are Nieuwpoort and Dunquerque when stated as being the scene of
the opening fight.   If the name is to be other than purely chronological—and perhaps
June 2nd is too near June 1st to allow of that—it must be called after either the
Gabart, from the point of sighting, or the North Foreland, which is not far from where
the first day's battle began.

degree the result of the war. Then, for the first time, did the full strength of each country take the field ; and then, for the first time, were disadvantages, whether of convoy or of a hated commander, absent from the Dutch.

The Dutch fleet, according to Tromp's report, was of ninety-eight sail of men-of-war together with six fireships,[1] while the English, as appears from the subjoined contemporary list, consisted of one hundred men-of-war and five fireships.[2]

The English Fleet of the 2nd and 3rd June, 1653.

(The ships appear to have been even more than usually overgunned. Compare the Table, pp. 107–112.)

The Red Squadron.

Ships.	Commanders.	Men.	Guns.	Ships.	Commanders.	Men.	Guns.
Resolution . .	The Generals	550	88	Heartsease . .	Thomas Wright, Captain	150	36
Worcester . .	George Dakins, Captain	220	50	Hound . . .	Jonah Hide, ,,	120	36
Advice . . .	Jeremy Smyth, ,,	180	42	†Anne and Joyce	William Pile, ,,	119	34
Diamond . .	William Hill, ,,	180	42	London . . .	Arthur Browne, ,,	200	40
Sapphire . .	Nicholas Heaton, ,,	140	38	†Hannibal . .	William Haddock, ,,	180	44
Marmaduke .	Edward Blagg, ,,	160	42	Mary . . .	Henry Maddison, ,,	120	37
Pelican . .	Peter Mootham, ,,	180	40	†Thomas and⎫	John Jefferson ,,	140	36
Mermaid . .	John King, ,,	100	26	William . .⎬			
†Golden Fleece .	Nicholas Forster, ,,	180	44				
†Loyalty . .	John Limbry, ,,	150	34	Speaker . .	Samuel Howett, R.-Adm.	300	56
†Society . .	Nicholas Lucas, ,,	140	44	Sussex . . .	Roger Cuttance, Captain	180	46
†Malaga Mer-⎫	Henry Collins, ,,	140	36	Guinea . . .	Edmund Curtis, ,,	150	34
chant .⎬				Tiger . . .	Gabriel Sanders, ,,	170	40
Martin . .	John Vessy ,,	90	14	Violet . . .	Henry Southwood, ,,	180	40
3 fireships . .	. . . .	90	30	Sophia . . .	Robert Kirby, ,,	160	38
				Falmouth . .	John Jeffreys, ,,	100	26
Triumph . .	James Peacock, V.-Adm.	350	62	†Four Sisters .	Robert Becke ,,	120	30
Laurel . . .	John Stoakes, Captain	200	48	†Hamburg Mer-⎫	William Jessel ,,	110	34
Adventure . .	Robert Nixon, .,	160	40	chant .⎬			
Providence .	John Peirce, ,,	140	33	Phœnix . .	Henry Eaden ,,	120	34
Bear . . .	Francis Kirby, ,,	200	46				

The White Squadron.

Ships.	Commanders.	Men.	Guns.	Ships.	Commanders.	Men.	Guns.
James . . .	William Penn, Adm. .	360	66	Gillyflower .	John Hayward, Captain	120	32
Lion . . .	John Lambert, Captain	220	50	Middelburg .	Thomas Withing, ,,	120	32
Ruby . . .	Robert Sanders, ,,	180	42	Raven . . .	Robert Taylor, ,,	140	38
Assistance . .	William Crispin, ,,	180	40	†Exchange . .	Jeffery Dare, ,,	120	32
Foresight . .	Richard Stayner, ,,	180	42	Globe . . .	Robert Coleman, ,,	110	30
Portsmouth .	Robert Danford, ,,	170	38	†Prudent Mary	John Taylor, ,,	100	28
†Anne Piercy .	Thomas Ware, ,,	120	33	†Thomas and⎫	Andrew Rand, ,,	125	34
Peter . . .	John Littleton, ,,	100	32	Lucy . . .⎬			
†Exchange . .	Henry Tedman, ,,	100	30				
Merlin . .	George Crapnell, ,,	90	12	Andrew . .	Thomas Graves, R.-Adm.	360	56
†Richard and⎫	Eustace Smith, ,,	180	46	Assurance . .	Phillip Holland, Captain	160	36
Martha. .⎬				Crown . . .	— Thompson, ,,	140	36
†Sarah . . .	Francis Steward, ,,	140	34	Duchess . .	Richard Seafield, ,,	90	24
†Lissa Merchant	Simon Baily ,,	160	38	Princess Maria	Seth Hawly, ,,	170	38
1 fireship . .	. . . .	30	10	Waterhound .	Giles Shelly, ,,	120	30
				Pearl . . .	James Cadman, ,,	100	26
Victory. . .	Lionel Lane, V.-Adm. .	300	60	Reformation .	Anthony Earning, ,,	160	40
Centurion . .	Walter Wood, Captain	200	42	†Industry . .	Ben Salmon ,,	100	30
Expedition .	Thomas Foules, ,,	140	32				

† These ships were hired armed merchantmen.

[1] 'Vie de Corneille Tromp,' 126.   [2] G. Penn, i. 491 (corrected by W. L. C.).

THE ENGLISH FLEET OF THE 2ND AND 3RD JUNE, 1653—*continued.*

The Blue Squadron.

Ships.	Commanders.	Men.	Guns.	Ships.	Commanders.	Men.	Guns.
George . . .	John Lawson, Adm. . .	350	58	*Crescent* . .	Thomas Thorowgood. .	115	30
Kentish . .	Jacob Reynolds, Captain	180	50	†*Samuel Taboat*	Joseph Ames	110	30
Great Presi-	Francis Park, ,,	180	40	†*Benjamin* . .	Robert Sparks, Captain	120	32
dent . . .}				†*King Ferdi-*	Richard Paine, ,,	140	36
Nonsuch . .	Thomas Penrose, ,,	170	40	*nando* . .}			
Success . . .	William Kendall, ,,	150	38	*Roebuck* . .	Henry Fenn, ,,	100	30
Welcome . .	John Harman, ,,	200	40				
Oak. . . .	John Edwin, ,,	120	32	*Rainbow* . .	Will. Goodsonn, R.-Adm.	300	58
†*Brazil* . . .	Thomas Heath ,,	120	30	*Convertine*. .	Anthony Joyn, Captain .	210	44
†*Eastland Mer-*	John Walters ,,	110	32	*Amity* . . .	Henry Pack ,,	150	36
chant . .}				*Dolphin* . .	Robert Davis ,,	120	30
†*Adventure*. .	Edward Greene ,,	160	33	*Arms of Hol-*	Francis Mardrig ,,	120	34
†*Samaritan* .	Shadrach Blake ,,	120	30	*land* . . .}			
1 fireship . .	. . . .	30	10	*Tulip* . . .	Joseph Cubitt ,,	120	32
				†*Jonathan* . .	Robert Graves ,,	110	30
Vanguard . .	Joseph Jordan, V.-Adm.	390	56	†*Dragoneare* .	Edward Smith ,,	110	32
Happy Entrance	Richard Newbery, Captain	200	43	†*William and*	Nathaniel Jesson ,,	120	36
Dragon. . .	John Seaman, ,,	260	38	*John* . . .}			
Convert . .	Philip Gethings ,,	120	32	*Nicodemus*. .	William Ledgart ,,	40	12
Paul . . .	Anthony Spatchurt, ,,	120	38	†*Blossom* . .	Nathaniel Cock ,,	110	30
Gift. . . .	Thomas Salmon, ,,	130	34				

† These ships were hired armed merchantmen.

The battle that ensued not only went far to decide the result of the war, but, owing to the tactical principle involved, was one of extreme interest. For both of these reasons it is much to be regretted that the evidence is incomplete, and is involved in a mass of unintelligible contradiction.

On sighting the enemy at dawn of June 2nd, the Generals weighed with their fleet in the recognised three squadrons,[1] and stood towards him. The chief interest of the battle attaches to the first meeting of the fleets, for it is certain that there was some attempt at line formation. Where exactly the meeting took place cannot be told with certainty, for it is not known what course the Dutch held. It seems probable, however, that while the English bore down, the Dutch stood close hauled to the eastward with the wind at N.E., in the hope of presently gaining the weather-gauge.

It has been claimed for William Penn that he had learnt the lesson of the line of battle from Tromp, and had introduced it into the English Navy,[2] a thing which may be possible enough, for Penn was probably consulted freely by the Generals on matters of seamanship and tactics. But Penn's biographer, enthusiastic, but ignorant of naval warfare, grossly overstates his case. He misreads "fought" for the second "fight" in the following quotation:[3] "We must fight in a line, whereas we fight promiscuously, to

---

[1] Cal. S. P. Dom. 1652–1653, p. 104.   [2] G. Penn, i. 399, *sqq.*

[3] Pepys's 'Diary,' 4th July, 1666.

our utter and demonstrable ruine: the Dutch fighting otherwise ;
and we, whenever we beat them." And, referring it to the Four
Days' Battle of June, 1666, he preaches a homily on his text. The
result he arrives at is that the battles of the first Dutch wars were
fought in line ahead, and that the credit was due to William Penn.
The assertion [1] that the tactics of the day consisted in letting ships
of a squadron group themselves round their flagship, he scouts as
ridiculous. The truth would seem to be that both assertions are
wrong and both partly right.

The squadronal subdivision was essential. It was, in fact, the
unit of the fleet. But there was already an appreciation of the line.
There exists distinct evidence in support of the statement that the
ideal formation of the time was, with men of wide seamanship, a
line ahead of small squadrons with the wind abeam. Such progress
as was made in this direction lay, not in regarding the single ship as
the unit. With fleets one hundred strong, that was impossible. It
lay rather in a minuter subdivision. That Marten Tromp was a
man of masterly ability is a commonplace, but explanations of the
operation of his genius are far to seek. It would seem, however,
that the line is due to him ; that the English adopted it from the
Dutch ; and that Tromp in and after 1639 extended the principle by
dividing the fleet into as many as fifteen small subdivisions. [2]

At Portland it is possible to see, in the position of Penn's
squadron, and in his ready movement to support Blake, some
confirmation of this theory. With regard to the battle of June 2nd,
direct evidence is to be had. At the Hague, the estimate of the
English formation was that, " having the wind they stayed on a
tack at half cannon shot for half an hour, until they put themselves
into the order in which they meant to fight, which was in file at
half cannon shot " : [3] and this method of attack was observed on
both days, the English not bearing down to board save when the
enemy fell into great confusion. The only English account which
hints at such formation is that of the chaplain of the *Resolution*, in
which occur the words : "Our fleet did work together in better order
than heretofore, and seconded one another " [4] ; but such silence
seems to prove merely that the formula, " in line ahead," was not as
yet a popular catch-word.

---

[1] Macpherson, ' Hist. of Britain,' i. 74, and G. Penn, i. 400.
[2] ' Vie de Corneille Tromp,' 118.
[3] Thurloe, S. P. i. 277; ' Vie de De Ruijter,' 34. [4] G. Penn, i. 493.

Just before the action began, it was noticed by the Dutch that the divisions of the English fleet were strongly marked, and then De Ruijter, possibly with a lucky slant of wind, weathered Lawson on the English left. Monck and Deane supported Lawson, the latter being killed by a round shot as the *Resolution* got into action ; and Tromp, possibly owing to the English falling somewhat to lee- ward in consequence of the lightness of the wind,[1] also became engaged on the English left.[2] But though the fighting was of a severe nature, a considerable part of each fleet was not able to come into action.

Before three o'clock the Dutch lost a forty-two-gun ship, of De Ruijter's squadron, which was sunk by Lawson,[3] but then the wind, veering, seemed to give them an advantage. The weather-gauge, however, was soon lost owing to confusion in the Dutch fleet. What the confusion was Dutch writers do not say, but as the English were proficient in gunnery, and as the calm day was all in favour of the over-gunned English ships, it is not hard to understand.

Having the wind again the English bore down to attack, and the fight became general all along the line. We have seen how Tromp had been busy on one English wing. That he now fought on the other appears from his falling in with Penn in the *James*. Tromp boarded and was beaten off ; Penn in turn boarded, and was only dislodged by blowing up the decks of the *Brederode*. Again he returned to the attack, but help came to the Dutchman.[4] At six the Dutch bore away before the wind ; and the "frigates" followed till dark, the Dutch losing another ship, that of Cornelis van Velsen, which blew up.[5]

At night Blake joined the fleet with eighteen fresh ships. Tromp had by that time found ammunition running so short, especially with De With and De Ruijter, that he determined to draw back towards the Wielings on the following morning. To do so he steered south with the wind at S.W., the English bearing down to intercept him. At eleven o'clock he was on the point of success when the wind veered to W.S.W., and fell so light that he lay

[1] *Vanguard's* log, G. Penn, i. 530.

[2] Basnage, 307, 308; G. Penn, i. 496.

[3] 'Vie de Corneille Tromp,' 124; 'Col. Rostr.' 125; Tromp to S. G., June 4th in Thurloe, S. P. i. 270.

[4] 'Col. Rostr.' 125, 126.

[5] Thurloe, S. P. i. 270.

helpless under the lee of the enemy, who at once attacked.[1] All that he could do was to gather his scattered ships into some sort of order.[2]

For a while the fight was renewed with vigour, but soon dire confusion fell on the Dutch fleet. Fireship captains scuttled or burnt their vessels and escaped in the boats; vessels ran foul of one another, and either sank or lay at the mercy of the English boarders. Some fled. Tromp fired on the fugitives, but with little or no effect. The Dutch fleet was, in fact, very badly beaten.

The end of the day's work, as stated by the Generals, was as follows: " After four hours' dispute with them they endeavoured what they could to get away from us; but having then a pretty fresh gale of wind, we pressed so hard upon them that we sank and took many, and do suppose that we should have destroyed most of them, but that it grew dark, and being off Ostend, among the sands, we durst not be too bold, especially with the great ships." The English therefore anchored, and saw Tromp go into the Wielings next morning. De With went to the Hague, and openly admitted that the English were masters of the sea; and De Ruijter refused to serve again unless the fleet were improved.[3]

Among eleven prizes brought in,[4] besides small craft, was one towed by the *Happy Entrance*, " a rear-admiral, being far bigger than herself," of twelve hundred tons, and fourteen guns on a tier.[5] About six ships were sunk, two more being burnt or blown up. The prisoners numbered one thousand three hundred and fifty, including six captains, but of the killed and wounded there is no record.

In the English fleet no ship was lost, nor even seriously damaged, though a few vessels were without a bowsprit, and one or two without a head. In men the loss was heavy, one hundred and twenty-six being killed, including Deane and two captains, and two hundred and thirty-six wounded. The Generals' flagship had eighteen killed and eight wounded.

The result of the victory was the closing of the Dutch ports, and

[1] *Vanguard's* Log, G. Penn, i. 531.

[2] Generals to Cromwell, G. Penn, i. 493; Tromp to S. G., June 4, Thurloe, i. 270.

[3] ' Vie de Corneille Tromp,' 132.

[4] The official list, in Penn, i. 494, is so far borne out by Dutch and other statements of losses, that it may be accepted as substantially correct. *Cp.* Cal. S. P. Dom. 1653, pp. 597, 599, etc.; Log of the *Vanguard*, G. Penn, i. 422–540.

[5] Whitelocke, 532.

the maintenance of a rigid commercial blockade.[1] It was Cromwell's intention to keep the whole fleet on the enemy's coast,[2] for, though negotiations were resumed, it was confidently expected that the Dutch fleet would again come out to do battle. Such, indeed, was the Dutch intention. Tromp refitted in the Maas; De With collected a squadron in the Texel. Their design was to do their best to effect a junction and to raise the blockade as soon as they were both ready

Blake did not share in the great fight that ensued. He was put ashore seriously ill, at Solebay, after the former victory, and there was no hope of his serving again for a considerable period. Monck was, therefore, ordered to command in chief for the time alone,[3] he being the only man left afloat of the triumvirate of December, 1652. The Council, hoping for Blake's recovery, delayed the appointment of Penn, who had been suggested by Monck[4] as a colleague, until December 2nd, when Disbrowe was nominated to make up the three. Disbrowe never served afloat. Lawson became admiral of the White in Penn's place, and was succeeded by Badiley,[5] in command of the Blue squadron.[6]

Before the last great battle of the war was fought, there was a resumption of peace negotiations, and it was then that the scheme for a union between the two republics, which had long been in the air, took definite shape. When first advanced by St. John, in 1651, the proposal had been merely for "a more intimate alliance," and on that basis the Dutch had been ready to treat. But St. John's instructions demanded that the Dutch should accept the principle blindly, while they, on their part, refused to consider the scheme in the abstract. Till after the battle of June 2nd and 3rd, 1653, the points of this treaty were never formulated, but, as the result of

---

[1] The history of this blockade is in the *Vanguard's* Log, G. Penn, i. 522-540. It is as colourless as the records of such service are wont to be. The only important capture made was that of two ships from the Sound laden with three hundred and sixty guns for ships then on the stocks.

[2] Hist. MSS. Com. Rep. 13, App. 2, p. 86.

[3] C. o. S. to Monck, 9th July, 1653.

[4] Monck to C. o. S. 2nd June, 1653.

[5] Badiley, on his return from the Mediterranean, had had to meet an attack made on him by Appleton, 'A Remonstrance of the Fight in Leghorn Road,' etc.: London, 1653, fol. He replied in pamphlet form, 'Captain Badiley's Reply to Certain Declarations,' etc. 4to. The best commentary on the matter is this appointment and the shelving of Appleton.

[6] G. Penn, i. 578, 579.

that battle, Cromwell felt that it was possible to make an advance
on all former demands.

Privately at first, publicly afterwards, through the Council of
State, Cromwell put forward his project for a complete coalition.[1]
By this, with the two countries under one government, but with a
great preponderance of material force assured to England, Holland
as an independent state would have ceased to exist. No wonder,
therefore, that the ambassadors drew back in the utmost alarm,
and refused to proceed without consulting the States General. Two
of their number were sent to Holland for that purpose. While
they were at sea there was fought the Battle of Scheveningen.[2]

On July 24th, 1653, Tromp sailed out of the Maas with eighty
men-of-war and five fireships,[3] and, for a few days, plied to and fro
before the mouth of the river. On the 26th, the English off the
Texel noticed that the ships under De With "turned down to the
outer part of the channel, as we conceive, to have got out and away
(in the fog) to join with Admiral Tromp."[4] Accordingly a council
of war was held on the following day, and it was decided that the
whole fleet should weigh " to meet with Admiral Tromp, having an
eye to prevent his conjunction with those in Texel."[5]

The English fleet weighed on the 28th at 8 P.M., and stood north
with the wind at W.S.W. On the following day Tromp was sighted
before noon.[6] The wind was westerly, and, had Tromp held on his
course to the north, he could have weathered the English.[7] But his
immediate business was to draw the enemy from before the Texel,
that De With might come out to join him; and for that day he
would have preferred to decline the engagement. He therefore
tacked, and steered S.S.E., with the English fleet in hot pursuit.

At about five o'clock the sternmost Dutch ships were brought
to action off Katwijk ; and, as other English ships came up, the
fight became pretty general. By about seven o'clock, Monck, who

---

[1] Basnage, 312.   [2] Called by the Dutch the Battle of "ter Heijde."
[3] Thurloe, S. P. i. 392 ; De With to S. G., 1st August, 1653. The English official
report stated the numbers as ninety-seven sail, whereof ninety were men-of-war.
Penn said they were eighty-three men-of-war four fireships strong. G. Penn, i. 506.
[4] *Vanguard's* Log, July 26th.   [5] *Ib.* July 27th.
[6] Monck to President of C. o. S. 31st July. G. Penn, i. 501, says that Monck's
scouts discovered a fleet about nine, that he stood towards it, and that two hours later
he made it out to be the Dutch fleet.
[7] *Vanguard's* Log, July 29th. The wind was light and fickle. Tromp seems to
have had a breeze at S.W. and to have tacked when it veered to W.N.W. ' Vie de
Corneille Tromp,' 138 ; Basnage, 313.

in the *Resolution,* had fallen somewhat to leeward, supported by
Jordan, in the *Vanguard,* came into action, and it was estimated
that the English ships engaged that night amounted to thirty sail.[1]
The Dutch rear was supported by the whole fleet,[2] and the fighting,
though without order, was very severe. Darkness put an end to the
combat, and left the fleets to prepare for the further struggle that
was expected on the morrow. In the Dutch fleet De Ruijter and
Cornelis Evertsen, "the Old," suffered most, both having lost
topmasts;[3] and two ships were sunk.[4] The loss in men must
have been heavy, if we may judge from the sixteen or seventeen
killed and twenty-five dangerously or severely wounded on board the
Resolution alone.[5]

Tromp had not succeeded in avoiding an engagement and in
keeping his fleet intact; but he had avoided a decisive battle, and he
had drawn the English from before Texel, thus leaving free exit for
De With.

At night the English held on their course towards the south,
thinking that they had the Dutch under their lee; but with daybreak
of the 30th it was found that the enemy was to windward.[6] All
that day it blew hard between W. and N.W., and both fleets had
enough to do to haul off the lee shore. Very little was done in
consequence. Early in the morning, Tromp, in the *Brederode,* with
a few ships of his squadron, stood south till he was within range, and
then fired a few guns;[7] but when Monck and Jordan tacked towards
him he went about and rejoined his fleet.[8] The English followed,
making as much northing as the wind would allow. They seem, however, to have made little progress, for when the Texel ships joined
the enemy that afternoon, both fleets were off Scheveningen. De
With brought twenty-seven men-of-war and four fireships, and the
numbers of the united fleet rose to about one hundred and twenty.[9]
The English fleet was roughly the same as that which had fought
the battle of the 2nd and 3rd of June; but a few ships had been
withdrawn for refit, and, although as many as could be made ready,
and others besides, had been sent out, the fleet was not quite at its

[1] Monck to the President of the C. o. S. 31st July.
[2] Tromp to States General, 29th July; 'Vie de Corneille Tromp,' 138, 139.
[3] Basnage, 313.   [4] G. Penn, i. 506.
[5] Monck to President of C. o. S. July 31st.   [6] *Ib.*
[7] *Vanguard's* Log, July 30th.   [8] 'Vie de Corneille Tromp,' 140.
[9] De With to States General, 1st August; Thurloe, S. P. i. 392.
[10] *Vanguard's* Log, *e.g.* July 7th and 23rd.

former force.[10] De With reported that it numbered ninety sail of men-of-war, with twenty-six victuallers and small craft.

The fleets were within about half a mile of one another in the evening, the English being to westward of the Dutch ; but the weather continued too heavy for an attack to be made, and at night it blew harder than ever from the N.N.W.

By the morning, the wind, which had fallen considerably, was blowing from the south.[1] The English, who were a mile and a half to windward, off Scheveningen, bore down to attack, and at seven o'clock began the last and bloodiest fleet engagement of the war.[2]

The Dutch fleet was again in its usual formation of five squadrons, Tromp being on the right wing, and Jan Evertsen in the centre.[3] As the English bore down, the enemy stood up to windward to meet them, and within a few minutes from the firing of the first shot, shortly before 7 A.M., the battle grew general.

Again we have no record of the disposition of the ships or squadrons, but again, on good evidence,[4] we can affirm that the English fleet was drawn up in a line of squadrons. Jordan wrote : " About seven in the morn, my General tacking to meet them, each division followed. Most of the enemy weathered us, but the rest were scattered." And this is all that can be told of the opening of the fight. It appears, however, that the Dutch broke through the English line, instead of weathering the whole fleet, and that foremost among them was the *Brederode*. She was engaged with the Blue squadron, and, for a time, received so little support,[5] that, by a concentrated fire, she suffered heavily. There was little wind, and the furious cannonade kept up by Tromp shrouded his ship from sight in a dense veil of smoke. When this cleared away, the signal for a council of war was flying. Such flag-officers as could go on board hastened to do so, and there they found the lifeless body of their great commander—the only admiral under whom all others had been content to serve—the adored of the seamen, the bravest and most skilful enemy then known to the English Navy. From a

---

[1] *Vanguard's* Log, *e.g.* July 31st.

[2] Basnage, 314 ; De With to States General ; 'Vie de Corneille Tromp,' 140.

[3] Hoste, p. 78, claims that the fleets fought in parallel lines.— " The English when first discovered," he says, " were drawn up in a line four leagues long, and stretching N.N.E. and S.S.W." The *Vanguard's* Log shows us that the English fleet was, at the time named, anchored before the Texel, while Hoste infers that it was under way. Of the many inaccurate accounts of this battle, there is none more grossly incorrect than his, which is demonstrably wrong in every particular.

[4] *Vanguard's* Log, July 31st.   [5] 'Vie de Corneille Tromp,' 141.

ship of Goodsonn's division of the Blue squadron a musket-bullet
pierced his heart.[1]

It was decided to keep Tromp's flag flying, and not to let the
knowledge of his death become general. This was done both to prevent the dismay which such news would spread in the Dutch fleet,
and to avoid giving the English any encouragement; and so well
was the secret kept that Monck was not aware of the enemy's great
loss until the battle was over.[2] It was agreed that Jan Evertsen
should assume the command, and with this resolution the Dutch
admirals returned to their ships and continued the fight with un-
abated vigour. With the main part of the Dutch fleet to windward,
the battle raged until one o'clock. De Ruijter's ship, the *Lam*, 40,

DUTCH MEDAL COMMEMORATIVE OF M. H. TROMP, 1653.

(From an Original kindly lent by Capt. H.S.H. Prince Louis of Battenberg, G.C.B., R.N.)

was riddled with shot, had only her mizzen left standing, and of a
crew of one hundred and fifty, lost forty-three killed and thirty-five
wounded. In this condition she was towed into the Maas, as also
was Jan Evertsen.[3] Many other Dutch ships were in nearly as bad
a state, and not a few sank amongst the enemy; but no vessels were
taken on either side. It has been said that Monck purposely refrained from taking prizes and prisoners, because he did not wish the
movements of his fleet hampered or its strength diminished. There
is no evidence that he forbade the giving of quarter,[4] and it is most

---

[1] It was said that the captain of the ship whence the shot was fired was instantly
slain. 'Vie de Corneille Tromp,' 142. Such was not the case. No captain of
Goodsonn's was killed, though one, Cubitt, was wounded.

[2] Monck to the President of the C. o. S. August 1st.

[3] 'Vie de Corneille Tromp,' 153.   [4] Burchett, 384; 'Col. Rostr.' 133.

improbable that he did so; but judging from the result, he may have advised his captains that the destruction of the enemy's fleet, not prize money, should be the object of their endeavours. In point of fact, not only was quarter given, but very many men were taken up from sinking ships by the English, and were brought back as prisoners.

The English meanwhile had not escaped without heavy loss. As has been seen, for a long time the enemy had the wind; and well did they use it. The *Oak* was burned; the *Worcester*, grappling the *Garland*, formerly taken from the English, burnt to the water's edge together with her enemy. Fireships were sent down on the English flagships. Two grappled the *Triumph*, bearing the flag of Peacock, Vice-Admiral of the Red, and placed her in a position of extreme danger. The fire gained a good hold, and panic seemed to be setting in. The Dutch maintained a heavy fire on the burning ship, and a third fireship was sent against her.[1] But Peacock remained cool in the midst of the danger, and his men stood to their guns. The third fireship was beaten off; the grappling irons of the others were cast loose; and, with great difficulty and danger, the flames were got under; but not before the brave Peacock had been most severely burned.[2] In the same way the *Andrew* was attacked and half burned, Rear-Admiral Graves and many men perishing by fire before help was received and the fire quenched.

The enemy was in no danger in this fight of running short of ammunition, for a supply of many thousands of rounds had been brought out to them by the fishermen.

At about one o'clock the English, apparently taking advantage of a shift of wind, weathered the enemy. Those of the Dutch fleet that had stayed to leeward in the morning were now some way off and refused to come into action; but the Dutch hoped again to weather the English and the main body did not yet give way. The attempt, however, failed. As De With, who, with Floriszoon, had taken up the command, wrote:[3] "We could not get the wind of the enemy and divers of our ships are far off, so I have thought

---

[1] 'Vie de Corneille Tromp,' 143.

[2] A medal, now rare, was given for this service. It is oval, and bears on the obverse the picture of a sea fight and the words, "For eminent service in saving y.ᵉ *Triumph* fiered in fight wᵗʰ yᵉ Duch in July 1653." On the reverse side are the arms of the three kingdoms suspended from an anchor. Peacock unhappily died as the result of his burns.

[3] De With to States General, August 1st.

good to temporize and retire. Afterwards we showed our sides again to the enemy towards the south-west," but an hour later De With, with thirty ships, was covering the flight of many recreant captains. Very unwillingly did he retire, still fighting bravely and firing on the fugitives: "Had they been hanged for doing the like before," said he, "they had not now again done this." The English, despite their losses, were now in overwhelming force: a vice-admiral's ship was sunk alongside the *Brederode*,[1] which, in her turn, was with great difficulty kept out of the hands of the English. The battle lasted till eight at night, when the retreat became a flight, the ships setting their mainsails and what they could carry.[2] The English pursued till midnight, when they hauled off the shore. On August 1st, Monck's advice-vessels watched the Dutch run into the Texel, whereon the English fleet bore up for home, made Yarmouth on the 4th and went into Solebay on the 5th.

In ships the English had lost the *Oak*, the *Worcester*, and a fire-ship:[3] in officers and men the loss was heavy, though it cannot be stated accurately. Penn put it at two hundred and fifty killed, and seven hundred wounded;[4] but many unofficial estimates exceeded his. The following captains were killed:—[5]

Andrew	Thos. Graves (R.-Adm. of White).
Golden Cock . . .	Captain Edward Chapman.
William	„ John Taylor.
Mayflower, merchant . .	„ William Newman.
Prosperous	„ Crisp.
Phœnix	„ Owen Cox.

and the wounded included—

Triumph	{ James Peacock (Vice-Adm. of Red), mortally.
Laurel	Captain John Stoakes.
Dragon	„ John Seaman.
Portland	„ William Rous.
Assurance	„ Philip Holland.
Tulip	„ Joseph Cubitt.

How many ships the Dutch had lost it is impossible to say. De With[6] put the loss at fourteen, but Dutch writers assert that five of these, including the *Garland*, got into port very much damaged. The English, on the other hand, insisted that they had destroyed

[1] Monck to President of C. o. S. July 31st. The sunken ship was C. Evertsen's, "the Old."

[2] *Vanguard's* Log, July 31st; 'Vie de Corneille Tromp,' 145.

[3] Monck to President of C. o. S. July 31st.

[4] G. Penn, i. 504.   [5] Heath, 348.   [6] De With to S. Gen., August 1st.

twenty or thirty,[1] Heath putting it at twenty-six. Of the enemy's loss in men it is equally difficult to speak, but it included eight captains killed, and five, including Cornelis Evertsen, Vice-Admiral of Zeeland in his brother's squadron,[2] taken, besides some 1300 men, who were brought to England. In Holland, August 17th was observed as "a day of fasting and prayers."

After all, the details of the losses[3] are unimportant. What is important is that though the English were too much shattered to keep the sea in August, the Dutch were in no state to offer any further resistance on a large scale ; and that though the war dragged on till the following year, the decisive blow had been struck and had made the enemy anxious for peace on any terms.

On August 6th, Parliament voted to Blake and Monck chains of gold to the value of £300 each, and to Penn and Lawson others worth £100. That the award was made to Blake, who had been absent from the last great battle, shows that these chains were given for services in the whole war rather than in one particular action.

The temporary raising of the blockade was a great relief to the Dutch, though bought at so high a price ; and the outgoing trade at once sailed north convoyed by De With with forty ships of war, which by degrees were increased to seventy-six.[4] But by the middle of August, the English North Sea fleet of about forty-five sail resumed, under Lawson, its duties on the Dutch coast,[5] and kept a sharp look out for De With's return from the Sound. The fleets did not come into contact. De With received the Eastland trade from its convoy of fourteen Danish men-of-war, and, having added to it merchantmen that had gathered from all parts to the northern waters, he avoided Lawson, and brought the whole of that enormous fleet, some four hundred sail,[6] safely into the Zuider Zee.

This piece of Dutch good fortune was followed, however, by a severe mishap to De With's fleet, which, riding off the Texel, was struck at the end of October by a heavy three days' gale from the N.W. which destroyed or dismasted half of it.[7]

---

[1] Penn's report in G. Penn, i. 504.

[2] 'Vie de Corneille Tromp,' 118. This was Cornelis Evertsen, "the Old," brother of Liut.-Admiraal Jan Evertsen. Served later under De Ruijter. Fell on the first day of the Four Days' Fight, 1666, having the rank of Lieut.-Admiral.

[3] For various estimates, *see* G. Penn, i. 504, *sqq.* ; also Thurloe, i. 412, 415, 440.

[4] 'Vie de Corneille Tromp,' 159.

[5] Thurloe, S. P. i. 440 ; Whitelocke, 545.

[6] 'Vie de De Ruijter,' 43.

[7] 'Vie de Corneille Tromp,' 160 ; Whitelocke, 549.

The blockade was not formally renewed, both belligerents [1]
confining themselves to the interception of isolated ships and small
squadrons of merchant vessels. In December, Monck took the
fleet, refitted, from the river to the Downs, but did nothing beyond
sending out cruisers.[2] There is no need to follow in detail the
many recorded captures of that autumn and winter, for the fate of
the war was decided; but a few single ship actions call for passing
mention.

On November 15th, the *Nonsuch*, 38, came much damaged into
Plymouth, with her boatswain and trumpeter dead, and her
lieutenant, master, chaplain, and many others wounded.[3] Cruising
near the Soundings she had fallen in with, and brought to action off
the Lizard, a Dutch man-of-war. She reported other Dutchmen on
the station; and the *Assistance* with a consort put to sea to meet
them.

At sea the English Navy lost no ship to the enemy. Two
vessels, however, came to grief, the *Lily* being wrecked near
Weymouth in September, and the *Sussex* being blown up by her
own powder at Plymouth in December. The latter loss was by far
the more serious, especially seeing that fifty men perished with
the ship.

In December, the *Phœnix* carried Whitelocke, as ambassador, to
Sweden, and no sooner had she put him ashore and got well into
the North Sea than she fell in on the 21st with the Dutch Baltic
trade, seventy-two sail, going home. Foster at once attacked, but
without success. He had four men killed and eleven wounded; was
utterly dismasted; and had to get to England as best he could,[4] a
task which seems to have employed him for nearly a fortnight.

In January, 1654, the *Sapphire*, Captain Nicholas Heaton,
brought in the *Walcheren*, man-of-war, and in February a Dutch
twenty-gun ship was captured by the *Amity*. Other small fights in
home waters, were reported from time to time, till the conclusion
of peace on 5th April.

It is enough to say that all Cromwell's terms, including the
Navigation Act, the right of the flag, the claims for damages,[5]
compensation for Amboyna, and the exclusion of the Prince of

---

[1] Whitelocke, 545–549.　　　[2] *Ib.* 557, 562.　　　[3] S. P. Dom. Int. xli. 150.
[4] Foster to Admlty. Ctee. Cal. S. P. Dom. 3rd January, 1654.
[5] Pulo Ron was restored and £900,000 damages paid. The Amboyna claim was
settled for a trifling sum. Basnage, 349.

Orange were accepted.[1] The peace was a very hard one; but the Dutch were fortunate in that one point, the demand for a union of the two countries, had been abandoned. Holland was allowed to continue to exist as a separate nation.

Vastly though the peace improved the Protectorate's[2] position, France was still glad to see it concluded, knowing that, if the war continued, England's power at sea would become so great that there would be no resisting it. Speaking for the Royalists, Hyde wrote to Nicholas, " the news of the treaty has struck us all dead."[3]

It was a time for the settling or readjustment of quarrels. The war had been against Denmark as an ally of Holland, and Denmark was of course included in the peace. The ships which had been detained in the Sound were restored, and Holland was made responsible for the damage, to the extent of £140,000, which had been done to English trade by the Danes.[4]

The dispute with Portugal was also brought to a close, the terms being those which had been proposed in April, 1651.[5] The main demands had been : (1) the restoration of goods and prisoners ; (2) punishment for all who had aided Rupert in his outrages ; (3) the payment of the cost of the Lisbon expedition of 1650, subject to the deduction of the value of the sugar ships seized ; (4) the making good of all damages done by Rupert from Lisbon, and the restoration of all prizes of his made in Portuguese harbours. The proclamation of peace was delayed ; and the money was not actually paid till June, 1656.[6]

The quarrel with France remained on much the same footing as during the war. Reprisals were made far more vigorously by the English than by the French, for to the latter a reconciliation was the more essential. To avoid an open breach with Cromwell, Charles was requested to leave Paris. This he did, going to Cologne, and intriguing thence.[7]

The position of Cromwell thus assured, the suppression of privateering was the only essential naval work to be taken in hand. With the French the scuffles continued, and, though it would seem

---

[1] Basnage, 338, 339.

[2] 'Instrument of Government' and the Induction of Cromwell as Protector : December 16th, 1653.

[3] Clarendon, S. P. Cal. ii. 1693.

[4] Whitelocke, 573 ; Basnage, 349.

[5] S. P. Dom. Int. I. 89, pp. 24–29.

[6] Whitelocke, 638.

[7] Basnage, 352, 358, 399.

that the English were in most cases the aggressors,[1] the French corsairs were really troublesome.

Blake and Penn were ordered to consider how best to deal with the corsairs of Brest; and a squadron of six ships was made ready for the service, other vessels being ordered to watch the mouth of the Channel.[2] But the report of the pilots was to the effect that a rigid blockade of Brest was, from the prevalence of westerly winds, impossible,[3] so that the ships were sent to the neighbourhood of Ushant, there to do as best they could. The "admiral" of the Brest privateers bore the name of Beach,[4] a name which suggests that he was English; and his capture was the main object. It was not long delayed. At the end of February he was brought to action by the *Falmouth*, Captain Mill, but for the time escaped. In the early days of March he fell in with the *Portsmouth* and *Constant Warwick*. The two ships chased, but the *Portsmouth* soon dropped astern. The *Constant Warwick*, however, came up with him before dark and kept company with him all night. In the morning at six o'clock Beach opened fire; but by 2 P.M., with twenty men out of a crew of two hundred, killed, and with five feet of water in the hold, he cried for quarter. He was taken into Plymouth with his ship, the *Royal James*, a vessel pierced for forty-two guns, but then mounting only thirty.[5] The prize was added to the Navy as the *Sorlings*, in memory of her capture near Les Sorlingues, or the Scilly Islands.[6]

The blow went a long way to finish the matter, for on board Beach's ship there happened to be at the time of capture a number of captains of privateers belonging to Brest. It would seem, however, that Beach was presently set free, for in August, 1657, he had returned to his old trade.[7]

Little more trouble came from Brest, though the course of French reprisals was not completely stopped until after the conclusion of a peace and the signature of a commercial treaty with France on 3rd November, 1655. When Penn sailed on the West Indian expedition, which forms one of the main features of the year

---

[1] 'Col. Rostr.' 139, 140; Cal. S. P. Dom., 1st February, 1654.

[2] Cal. S. P. Dom. 1653, 1654, p. 568.   [3] *Ib.* 4th February, 1654.

[4] He was apparently the Royalist Richard Beach who in 1661 was appointed to the *Crown*, and, after having served as a flag-officer and been knighted, died Controller of the Victualling Accounts in 1692.—W. L. C.

[5] Whitelocke, 567; Cal. S. P. Dom. 1654, p. 38.

[6] *Ib.* p. 337.   [7] S. P. Dom. Int. clvi. 1.

1654, he took with him very definite instructions from Cromwell to act against the French,[1] and the peace was not concluded till after his return.

Before proceeding to relate the great undertakings which were set on foot in 1654, it remains only to notice the appointment of John Bourne to sail in the *Essex* in command of a squadron of six ships destined for the protection of the Newfoundland fisheries.[2]

France and Spain had at length begun to bid for Cromwell's favour; and France, with an offer of Dunquerque, when it should once more be taken from Spain, carried the day.[3] Cromwell could, however, have easily kept peace with both as he had done for so long. No one in Europe wished to quarrel with him; and there were more ambassadors at that time at the English Court than had been seen there for many a long year.

To account for Cromwell's determination to make war on Spain, it is necessary to consider the state of affairs at home.[4] The rule of Cromwell was the rule of a conqueror. The success of the Dutch War was largely responsible for his installation, and, when the excitement of that had subsided, it became evident that to many the Instrument of Government was bitterly distasteful. Foremost among them were the sterner Republicans, and, of course, the Royalists. These were but two of many factions from which trouble might be anticipated; and it was imperative to divert public attention from home politics. And by far the best, most natural, and most popular way in which Cromwell could do this would be by waging a lucrative and successful foreign war.

As has been seen, Cromwell had to choose an adversary. That he chose Spain was due partly no doubt to the ostensible reason, of her religious oppression and cruelty;[5] but chiefly to the wealth to be obtained from her. But in estimating the motives for the step it must not be forgotten that our West Indian colonial expansion had brought us more and more into contact with Spain, and that a settlement of all questions thus arising with her had to be attempted sooner or later. And, taking advantage of the old doctrine of "no peace south of the line," the war might be waged elsewhere than in Europe until a formal declaration should become convenient.

---

[1] G. Penn, ii. 25.   [2] Cal. S. P. Dom. 1654, p. 241, 3rd July.
[3] Basnage, 400.   [4] *Ib.*
                    [5] G. Penn, ii. 21.   Cromwell to Penn.

The armament of two fleets was openly pushed forward during the summer, one destined for Blake, who was at length restored to health, the other for Penn.[1] But the objective of each was kept in profound secrecy, and both France and Spain were painfully anxious to see where the blow would fall.[2]

In the course of that summer, Penn, always a Royalist at heart, but loyal to the national interest so long as the war lasted, wrote to Charles at Cologne that he was prepared to place at his Majesty's disposal the fleet which he was about to command, if a secure port could be named in which to deliver it.[3] But Charles, though, according to Clarendon, he received a very similar offer from Venables, who was to command the soldiers during the expedition, could not name a port.[4] He desired the officers to continue their enterprise, and to wait a favourable opportunity. It will be not amiss to say that Penn and Venables were not in one another's confidence. This is enough to show what need Cromwell had to think of diverting men's minds.

Penn's commission was dated October 9th. After enumerating Spanish outrages in America, assaults on planters, and the like, it went on to suggest that the King of Spain's object then was "the ruin and destruction of all the English plantations, people, and interest in those parts."[5] Penn and Venables were therefore appointed for the express purpose of attacking that monarch in the West Indies. Besides dealing with his shipping, they were authorised to land men upon any of the dominions and possessions of the King of Spain in America.[6] The continuance of reprisals against France was also part of their care, as well as the maintenance of the provisions of the Navigation Act.

In view of the experience of this expedition, it is important to remember that neither Penn nor Venables[7] was chained to a hard and fast plan.

An advance squadron was despatched as soon as it was ready;[8] and, a little later, on Christmas Day, 1654, Penn weighed from Spithead. The force was composed of thirty-eight ships and four

---

[1] The comprehensive account of this expedition is in Granville Penn, ii. 1–142. This is the first history of the business written from original documents.

[2] Hepworth Dixon, 'Blake,' 271. [3] G. Penn, ii. 14.

[4] Clarendon, iii. 576. [5] G. Penn, ii. 21, *sqq.*

[6] *Ib.* 24. [7] *Ib.* 28.

[8] Hist. MSS. Com. Rep. 13, App. 2, p. 88; and *Swiftsure's* Log, Dec. 20th, in G. Penn, ii. 56, *sqq.*

small craft, with three thousand soldiers. A further regiment was
to be enrolled at Barbados, and arms were to be there embarked.

PENN'S FLEET FOR THE WEST INDIES.[1]

Rates.	Ships.	Seamen.	Soldiers.	Guns.	Captains.
2	*Swiftsure*	350	30	60	{ William Penn, General. { Jonas Poole, Captain.
2	*Paragon*	300	30	54	W. Goodsonn, Vice-Admiral.
3	*Torrington*	280	30	54	George Dakins, Rear-Admiral.
3	*Marston Moor*	280	30	54	Edward Blagg.
3	*Gloucester*	280	30	54	Benjamin Blake.
3	*Lion*	230	30	44	John Lambert.
3	*Mathias*	200	30	44	John White.
3	*Indian*	220	30	44	— Terry.
4	*Bear*	150	30	36	Francis Kirby.
4	*Laurel*	160	30	40	William Crispin.
4	*Portland*	160	30	40	(Richard) Newbery.
4	*Dover*	160	30	40	Robert Sanders.
4	*Great Charity*	150	..	36	Leonard Harris.
4	*Heartsease*	70	160	30	Thomas Wright.
4	*Discovery*	70	160	30	Thomas Wills.
4	*Convertine*	75	200	30	John Hayward.
4	*Katherine*	70	200	30	Willoughby Hannam.
5	20 ships for transports	1145	{ 1830 { 38 { horses)	352	
6	*Martin*, galley 4 small craft.	60	..	12	William Vesey.

The outward passage was good, and Barbados was reached on
January 29th. It was found that the Dutch were engaged in an
illicit trade with that colony, and eight Dutch ships were seized;[2]
but it was found to be impossible to raise the expected reinforcements there, or to find the desired arms.[3] By one method or
another, however, the land force was at last nearly doubled,[4] and
while the force still lay at Barbados, a regiment of one thousand
two hundred seamen was formed, and Goodsonn, the vice-admiral,
was appointed by Penn to command it ashore as colonel.[5]

The fleet sailed from Barbados on March 31st, 1655; and, after
touching at and raising troops in Antigua, Montserrat, Nevis and
St. Kitts,[6] reached Hispaniola, the primary object of attack. On
April 13th the fleet made San Domingo, and the greater part of the

[1] Granville Penn, ii. pp. 17, 18. (Corrected by W. L. C.)
[2] Commissioner Butler to Cromwell, February 7th.
[3] Winslow to Thurloe, March 16th.
[4] Hist. MSS. Com. Rep. 13, App. 2, p. 21.
[5] G. Penn, 73, 74.
[6] Butler to Cromwell, June, 1655.

army, four thousand strong, landed with Venables ten leagues to leeward of the town, the fleet, with the remainder of the force, keeping under way to the eastward.[1] The men who went ashore carried three days' provisions, but no entrenching tools; and as Venables presently discovered this want, and many other deficiencies, much time was wasted. On the 14th the remaining troops were landed, also to leeward of San Domingo, inasmuch as no landing could be found to windward; and meanwhile some of the lee division of the fleet exchanged frequent shots with the town.[2]

The success of the affair depended entirely on Venables and the army. Penn had brought him to the chosen landing-place, and supplied him with everything he demanded from the ships. All that Venables had to do was to march forward with seven thousand men and capture the town. Penn lay with eleven ships, including both the second-rates, within shot, ready to stand closer in and batter the forts when the army should approach the town;[3] but on the 25th the troops were disgracefully beaten and Venables refused to make any further attempt.

It is needless here to enter into a defeat which concerns only the land service; but in extenuation of Venables's failure on the occasion, it is fair to point out that he was seriously unwell, and that his troops were an undisciplined rabble.[4] What little credit can be assigned to any one is due to the regiment of seamen, who, when the army was in full flight under the walls of San Domingo from a small party of Spaniards and negroes that had burst upon them from an ambush, stood its ground and beat the enemy off.[5]

Penn offered to support the army with the fleet if another attack should be made, but he found in the land officers a disinclination to trust themselves to their men, "for they would never be brought to stand."[6] Yet, as the fleet and army could not go home empty-handed, an attempt upon Jamaica was decided upon.

Penn himself was eager that Hispaniola should be again attempted, and offered to stand off to sea for a few days with the army on board, to allow the enemy to disperse, and, then returning, to try to surprise the town. But again he was refused.

---

[1] *Swiftsure's* Log, April 13th.
[2] Butler to Cromwell, June, 1655.
[3] Butler to Cromwell; and *Swiftsure's* Log, April 18th, *sqq*.
[4] He had also embarrassed himself by allowing his wife to accompany him.
[5] *Swiftsure's* Log, April 28th; Venables to Montagu, May 26th.
[6] *Ib.* 30th.

On May 4th the fleet left Hispaniola, and reached Jamaica on the 10th. Penn went on board the *Martin*, a galley drawing little water, and led the way in, saying that "he would not trust the army if he could come near with his ships."[1] Other small vessels followed the *Martin* under the walls of the fort, while the larger ships anchored in the harbour. A brisk cannonade was maintained between the *Martin* and the fort, until the boats had set the troops ashore; when the Spaniards ran without waiting for an attack. Venables did not land till he saw that no resistance had been offered, and, though the boats came cheering close past the *Martin*, on board which he was, "he continued walking about, wrapped up in his cloak, with his hat over his eyes, looking as if he had been studying of physic more than like the general of an army."[2] The town surrendered next day, and the whole island by the 17th.

Penn and Venables stayed for a month, seeing to the pacification of the island, and sending cruisers along the Spanish main.[3] They then resolved to return home with the chief part of the fleet.[4] There was good reason for this step, for provisions were hard to come by at Jamaica; the fleet might be useful nearer home; the army needed the fleet no longer; and, lastly, the enemy had no great naval strength in those waters. Accordingly Goodsonn was appointed to command-in-chief,[5] while Dakins went home with Penn. The ships left on the station were the[6] *Torrington, Martin, Gloucester, Marston Moor, Laurel, Dover, Portland, Grantham, Selby, Hound, Falmouth,* and *Arms of Holland,* with three brigs and a dogger.

. On May 25th, a disaster befel the fleet.[7] The *Discovery* took fire in the steward's room, and burned till the fire reached her powder, when, having one hundred and twenty barrels on board, she blew up "with a very terrible blow," putting the *Swiftsure,* which rode next her, in great danger.[8] The loss was the greater because many provisions, as well as the *Swiftsure's* lower deck guns, had only that day been transferred to her. Most of the guns, however, were soon recovered.

On June 25th, Penn left Jamaica and sailed for England, hoping

[1] Butler to Cromwell, June, 1655.   [2] G. Penn, ii. 32.
[3] Hist. MSS. Com. Rep. 13, App. 2, p. 91.
[4] *Swiftsure's* Log, May 24th.   [5] Thurloe, S. P. iii. 582.
[6] *Ib.* 584.   [7] *Swiftsure's* Log, 25th May.
[8] The accident seems to have been due to careless drawing of the brandy which, in lieu of beer, was carried by the ships of the expedition.

to fall in with the Spanish Havana fleet before he should pass the
Florida Channel. But the flota was never sighted,[1] and the only
event of note before the fleet reached home, was the loss of the
Paragon, which took fire at sea on July 13th, and was burnt with
a loss of one hundred and ten men. After a passage retarded by
calms, the fleet dropped anchor at Spithead on August 31st. Penn
himself at once went round to Chatham, whence on 11th September
he was summoned to attend before the Council, as was Venables on
the 20th. Both were examined, chiefly on the resources of Jamaica,
of which they spoke highly;[2] and both were at once committed to
the Tower. √

It is rather hard to guess why this step was taken. Certainly
it was not due, in Penn's case, to the failure at San Domingo, for
Cromwell very well knew the importance of what had been accomplished. It is possible to suppose that Cromwell was aware of
Penn's correspondence with the Royalists. The same may possibly
have been the case with regard to Venables,[3] though the confinement of the latter was well merited by his gross mismanagement.
The imprisonment was not for long. Penn was released[4] on
making an abject submission.

Meanwhile, Goodsonn was acting energetically enough, if with
no startling effect. On 31st July he left Jamaica to go over to the
mainland with his squadron. He wished to surprise Rio Hacha,
but was so much delayed by the shoal water that the attempt
became useless, as the Spaniards had ample warning to carry off all
treasure. The same was the case at Santa Marta; but there,
though he got little plunder, he sacked the town and captured
thirty guns. Before returning to Jamaica, he attempted Cartagena,
where six ships lay, but could do nothing.[5] During the winter, the
force suffered somewhat from sickness, but in March, Goodsonn
wrote that the soldiers were " fit to clear the island of Spaniards
and make it secure for the planters," who were yet to come; and
that " the fleet are in a prosperous condition and ready to embrace
any action they may be put upon."[6]

On April 5th, 1656, Goodsonn sailed again, this time for a five

[1] Penn to Goodsonn, 24th July.
[2] Thurloe, S. P. iv. 28.
[3] G. Penn, ii. 14, 15 and 135, *sqq.*
[4] Cal. S. P. Dom. p. 396, 25th October, 1655.
[5] Thurloe, S. P. iv. 159; Goodsonn to C. o. S.
[6] *Ib.* 600–602; Goodsonn to Cromwell.

months' cruise,[1] leaving eight or nine of the heaviest ships behind him. He lost nothing, but gained nothing, the second cruise being as little successful as the former. He did not remain at sea so long as he intended, but returned to Jamaica at the end of May, possibly because he had heard that the Spaniards at Cartagena intended to land one thousand men on the island.[2]

There Benjamin Blake, who had been acting as vice-admiral, quarrelled with Goodsonn, probably on some point of command, and, rather than be court-martialled, resigned his commission and went home. Goodsonn took no steps against him, but furnished Thurloe with the facts of the case, to be used only in the event of Blake's trying to vindicate himself.[3]

In August, finding that several ships were unfit to remain abroad, he decided to return home. He moved his flag from the *Torrington*, first to the *Marston Moor*, and afterwards to the *Mathias*, in which he sailed for England, where he arrived, in very bad health, on 18th April, 1657.

In the Channel and North Sea little had been done in the interval beyond checking the privateers and enforcing the Navigation Act; so that the two years' command held by Lawson in the Downs was uneventful.

But Blake had, in the meanwhile, still further added to his great name.

On September 29th, 1654, he had sailed for the Mediterranean, with instructions to continue reprisals against the French, to curb the African pirates, and, in general, to take charge of the English interests which had been so sadly neglected during the Dutch War.

His fleet, as originally formed, consisted of the following ships[4] (see next page), together with five smaller craft.

Of the destination and purpose of Blake's fleet, nothing was known in Europe; and speculation was busy. At Paris it was believed that the intention was to attack the Duke of Guise, who was then preparing for his expedition to Naples. "However, Guise escaped this pull," says a Paris news letter.[5]

Spain, which had been anxious while the fitting-out was in progress, was lulled to security when it was found that Blake's course was not to the westward. Blake's orders, indeed, were to

[1] Thurloe, S. P. 748.
[2] *Ib.* iv. 695.
[3] *Ib.* v. 154.
[4] G. Penn, ii. 150, 151 (corrected).
[5] Thurloe, S. P. iii. 41, ii. 653.

Ships.	Men.	Guns.	Captains.
George	350	60	{Robert Blake, General. {John Stoakes, Captain.
Andrew	300	54	Richard Badiley, Vice-Admiral.
Unicorn	300	54	Joseph Jordan, Rear-Admiral.
Langport	260	50	Roger Cuttance.
Hampshire	160	34	Robert Blake.
Bridgewater . . .	260	50	Anthony Earning.
Foresight	160	36	Peter Mootham.
Worcester	240	46	William Hill.
Plymouth	260	50	Richard Stayner.
Kentish	170	40	Edward Witteridge.
Diamond	160	36	John Harman.
Taunton	160	36	Thomas Foules.
Ruby	160	36	Edmund Curtis.
Newcastle	180	40	Nathaniel Cobham.
Amity	120	30	Henry Pack.
Mermaid	100	22	James Ableson.
Pearl	100	22	Ben. Sacheverell.
Maidstone	140	32	Thomas Adams.
Princess Maria . . .	150	34	John Lloyd.
Elias	140	32	John Symonds.

be friendly with Spain. There was to be no war in Europe till Cromwell should have stolen a march "beyond the line;" and an alarm might have resulted in the non-sailing of the Havana fleet. Till well on into the next year, when Penn's proceedings were known, Blake maintained cordial relations, and received civility and support, in Spanish harbours. There was good reason for this, however, when it appeared that the fleet was intended to do Spain the excellent service, which she could never undertake for herself, of reducing the pirates. How little a rupture was expected is shown by a letter from the Dutch ambassador in France to the States General. This expresses a belief that the English fleet was intended to enter the Spanish service.[1]

After touching at Cadiz,[2] Blake went on to Leghorn, where, it is said, he extorted compensation from the Grand Duke for the expulsion of Appleton. But evidence of this is wanting, nor can it be proved that he received 60,000 ducats from the Pope as amends for the sale of Rupert's prizes in the Papal States.[3]

From Leghorn, Blake had intended to sail for Trapani and thence to Tunis ; but on receipt of news that Tunis Bay was full of men-of-war bound eastward for the service of the Sultan, he altered

---

[1] Thurloe, S. P. iii. 102.　　　　[2] Whitelocke, 591.

[3] Campbell, ii. 43 ; Ludlow, ii. 507. Most of Blake's letters for this period are lost, but in such as remain there is no reference to any important doings either at Leghorn or at Civita Vecchia.

his plans and proceeded to Tunis direct. On February 7th he arrived,[1] and at once sent on shore a paper of demands. But, though the Bey professed anxiety to conclude a firm peace, no restitution was obtainable. " On this we sailed to Porto Farina,[2] where the men-of-war lay blockaded by our frigates. We found the ships unrigged, their guns planted, and a camp formed ashore. An attack seemed difficult. We had only five days' drink, and were not satisfied that our instructions allowed of our attacking. We therefore sailed off leaving the *Plymouth, Kentish, Mermaid, Foresight, Newcastle* and *Taunton* for that service."

Blake went to Cagliari to get drink and to make up his mind as to an attack. On March 14th he wrote[3] that his intention was to sail with the first fair wind, and endeavour " to bring the business . . . to an end." On March 18th he returned to Tunis, and found the Bey more intractable than before. The English were not allowed even to buy bread ; and remonstrance was met by a request that Blake should cast his eyes on the forts and ships.[4] Blake did look at the forts and ships, and determined to attack them. When, with reference to this operation, it is said that Blake was the first to use ships against forts, a partial truth only is told. But he was the first to do so on a large and successful scale.

There were nine vessels lying unrigged in Porto Farina on April 4th[5] when the attack was delivered. The harbour itself is a small bay in the left bank, and at the mouth, of the Medjerda ; and is almost closed to the south by a spit of land which is a continuation of the left bank of the river, and which runs back on itself. On the spit of land was a fort mounting twenty guns, and along the shores of the bay were other works. Opposite the town were the ships. Blake divided his fleet into two divisions, the lighter to attend to the ships, the heavier to batter the forts.

Standing into the harbour with a gentle breeze, the ships took up their stations in perfect order under a severe fire. There were two advantages in Blake's favour. The first and main one was the enormous superiority of the English gunners, a superiority which was not taken into consideration by the Tunisians. The second was fortuitous. The breeze that had brought Blake into the harbour

---

[1] Thurloe, S. P. iii. 232. Blake to Thurloe.
[2] Or El Bahira.
[3] Thurloe, S. P. iii. 232. Blake to Thurloe.
[4] *Ib.* iii. 390.
[5] 'Columna Rostrata,' 141.

continued to blow steadily towards the town, enveloping the enemy in a dense cloud of smoke.

Soon the forts were breached, and the guns dismounted; and then came the second part of the work. The boats were manned, and, under the command of Stoakes, pulled straight for the ships, and boarded. The enemy was sufficiently demoralised to make no great resistance. The ships were set on fire, and the squadron drew out of the bay to the roads. The loss of twenty-five Englishmen killed and forty-eight wounded shows that the enemy's fire had not been very deadly; yet it had been a most gallant action, the difficulty of which is apt to be under-estimated by reason of its complete success. Blake's doubts as to what the Protector would think of the engagement were set at rest by the receipt of a very gracious letter.[1]

Meanwhile, in Spain, doubt as to what Penn's movements might be was followed by certainty.[2] There was no further need of disguise, and Blake received orders to cruise off Cadiz for the interception of the Plate fleet, and to prevent the sending of reinforcements to the West Indies. At Madrid it was believed that, by his orders, he was authorized to act against Spain from August 1st,[3] a belief borne out by his not attacking a Spanish fleet on July 15th, and by his subsequent capture of two rich Dunquerquers early in August. Such, however, was not the case. He received his orders in July,[4] and did not attack on July 15th purely because the weather and the condition of his fleet, which was very foul and defective,[5] made it impossible. He stationed himself off Cape St. Mary to try to intercept the incoming Plate fleet, but had to give up the cruise in the autumn. Besides the state of his ships he had his own health to consider; and by his instructions a large measure of discretion had been allowed to him.[6] He therefore left the coast, and reached home on October 9th.

In addition to the more visible results of the work done, which included an agreement with Algier, and the affair at Tunis, he had accomplished something else of importance. He had reinstated the English flag in the Mediterranean, and had shown that the time had come when the Navy recognised its duties for the protection of

---

[1] Thurloe, S. P. iii. 547.

[2] *Ib.* iii. 417, 609, 610; Whitelocke, 602.

[3] Thurloe, iii. 698, 718.

[4] Thurloe, S. P. iii. 547.   Cromwell to Blake.

[5] *Ib.* iii. 611, 620.

[6] Thurloe, S. P. i. 724.

traders, and would no longer systematically leave them to fight their own battles to the best of their power.

The peace with France, October 3rd, 1655, was followed a month later by a commercial treaty; and there was no longer any difficulty on hand save that with Spain. And this, after mutual reprisals towards the end of 1655, resulted in the formal declaration of war by Spain in February 1656.

At the beginning of the new year Blake asked for a colleague; and, by Cromwell's choice, Edward Montagu [1] was appointed, and the fleet again sailed for the Spanish coast. Blake and Montagu were in the *Naseby;* and Lawson was appointed on January 25th to sail as vice-admiral in the *Resolution.* But before the fleet left England he was suddenly removed from his command on political grounds. His old command in the Downs had been given to Badiley.

There is no need to follow minutely the doings of the fleet on the Spanish coast in 1656; for the record of a blockade is marked by few striking incidents so long as the enemy elects to stay in port. One incident of note there was, but in that Blake and Montagu did not share. When they, with the major part of the fleet, had left the neighbourhood of Cadiz and gone to Oeiras Bay for water and provisions, the Spanish West India fleet appeared on the coast.

Stayner, in the *Speaker,* was lying off Cadiz with a squadron of six " frigates " when the fleet was reported. In his own words :—[2]

"In the evening (8th September) we espied eight sail some five or six leagues to the westward of Cadiz, we using the best means that we could to meet with them next day, which we did; it being little wind at N.E. It was nine of the clock before we came up with them; but having a fresh gale in the night, all but we and the *Bridgewater* were to the leeward, and could not come up to us. It proved to be the Spanish fleet come from the West Indies, which were four of the King of Spain's three merchantmen, and one prize, a Portuguese. We engaged the fleet, but being within four leagues of Cadiz, could not stay for our ships; but we, the *Bridgewater* and *Plymouth* engaged them, and had a sharp dispute, some of us. But the admiral being the smallest ship, we slighted her, for we conceived there was some policy used in the flag; by which means, the admiral and the Portuguese prize got into Cadiz. The vice-admiral, and one more, we sunk, and burnt two; we took one. The captain of her, which we have on board, saith she hath in her two millions of silver. The vice-admiral hath as much, I do believe. The *Plymouth* chased another, who came ashore near St. Peter's; but it seems they had no silver in her. The ship we took is as good as all the fleet besides. The other, that Captain Harman hath taken, is very

---

[1] Or Mountagu, afterwards First Earl of Sandwich.

[2] Stayner to the Generals, G. Penn, ii. 155, 156.

rich; but little silver in her. Both the prize and our ship are sorely wounded, both in masts and hull. There is no news, only I believe the fleet will follow us; the galleys came out. . . . . This is all; only there is a loss of men in some ships, the number I know not."

The action thus modestly and hastily reported, was, from the quantity of treasure sent to England, quite enough to make the war popular. Much as we may congratulate Stayner on the happy event, it is impossible to avoid sympathy for the Spanish vice-admiral. His ship, which had fought for six hours before taking fire,[1] had on board the Marques de Badajos, who with all his family was returning from Lima, whereof he had been Governor for many years. Husband and wife, one son and a daughter were burned, and the rest were left destitute.

Montagu in the *Speaker*, with others of the great ships, convoyed the treasure home. The captor went with him, but rejoined the fleet in the spring. The resolution voted in Parliament on October 1st " that the war with Spain was taken on just and necessary grounds, and the Parliament doth approve thereof," [2] was probably due to the new argument presented on the war's behalf.

Blake, though broken in health, stayed out during the winter with the remainder of the fleet to endure the hardships of the blockade. But it was not until Stayner had rejoined in the spring that Blake received news of the treasure-ships which Blake wished to intercept. He at once weighed, and on April 20th was off Santa Cruz de Tenerife, where the fleet, sixteen in number, was discovered moored in the harbour.[3] At the entrance to the bay stood a strong castle, while round it lay a fringe of smaller forts mounting four or six guns each, and connected with one another by a breastwork manned with musketeers. The Spaniards were aware of the threatened attack; they had strengthened the defences, landed the silver, and kept their men continually on board the ships which were held in readiness to sail. It was intended to make no further attempt to get to Spain that year, and the fleet was provisioned for its return to the Indies.[4] And the dangers from the many heavy guns both in the ships and ashore were intensified by other circumstances.

As Nelson found in later days, the wind at Tenerife is nearly always foul for an attack on the harbour. Either it blows off shore,

[1] G. Penn, ii. 157.   [3] Heath, 391.
[2] Whitelocke, 643.   [4] S. P. Dom. cliv. 104.

squally and patchy, involving ships in the risk of being becalmed within range; or there blows dead into the harbour a steady breeze with which it is very easy to get in, but impossible to get out. With such a wind there could be no such thing as partial failure : there could be no drawing back.   Either Blake must win a complete victory, or he must be annihilated.   Few men would have taken the risk ; and the daring necessary to such an action raised Blake's name higher than it had ever stood before.

The Spaniards had ten ships drawn up in a semicircle at the bottom of the bay off the town, and the six greatest galleons were moored in line opposite to the entrance to the harbour.   Doubtless Blake saw what the Spaniards did not, that the six masked the fire of the ten.

On the morning of April 20th, with a sea breeze and a flowing tide, Blake stood in to the bay.   His plan was simplicity itself ; to destroy the ships and castles before the tide turned, and to trust to the ebb to take him out.   Stayner led, with instructions that his division should attack the galleons while Blake dealt with the forts. Accordingly the *Speaker, Bridgewater, Providence, Plymouth* and the other vessels which were with the vice-admiral bore down on the galleons, and, as they closed with them, came up to the wind and anchored broadside to broadside.   To have attempted to anchor by the stern between these ships for the purpose of raking them, would have exposed the attackers in their turn to a raking fire from the ships inshore.   As Blake must have foreseen, the fight raged chiefly round the galleons.   The whole six were taken ; but, as soon as the forts realised that they had passed into English hands, they opened a heavy fire on the prizes.   Blake gave orders to burn them. This was done, and the smaller vessels too were set in flames. Then with the ebb the English had already begun to drift out, when a steady land breeze at S.W., an occurrence of the utmost rarity among those islands, sprang up.   The English loss was forty killed and one hundred and ten wounded, and the *Speaker* was rendered unfit for service.   How many men the Spaniards lost it is impossible to say.   Heaven itself fought for the English, as Blake might have said.   The breeze took them all the way back to Cadiz, where they lay till the great seamen received permission to go home.

On July 17th,[1] leaving many of the ships under Captain Stoakes

[1] S. P. Dom. Int. clvi. 17 ; Robert Clarke to Admlty. Com.

to finish off the work, whether against Spain or against the pirates, Blake set sail for England. But he never saw home again, strong as was his desire to live till he could be put ashore. His health had been permanently shattered by the hard life of the sea, with the added malady of a scorbutic fever, and he died on board the *George* on August 7th, 1657, at the entrance to Plymouth Sound. He had not the glorious end of Nelson, but, like Nelson, he fell only when his work had been brought to completion. The naval history of the period is, with small exceptions, the story of his life ; and to him more than to any man had been due the success of the Navy and the uplifting of his country. " He was a man of as much gallantry and sincerity as any in his time, and as successful." [1]

Four days after Blake died Richard Badiley. [2]

Just before he left the station, Blake had received instructions to afford help to the Portuguese, should any attempt be made on their coasts by the Spaniards. [3] Stoakes narrowly watched Cadiz, where, after Blake's departure, a great fleet of forty-two sail lay fitting for sea ; [4] but he noticed little progress ; and at the end of November, the Spanish vice-admiral took fire and was burnt. This stopped preparations altogether; and Stoakes, keeping ten sail with him, sent the rest home under Jonas Poole, his vice-admiral. [5]

With the ten, namely the *Lyme*, Captain Stoakes, admiral ; *Fairfax*, Captain Whetstone ; *Phœnix*, Captain Thomas Bonn ; *Tredagh*, *Jersey*, *Torrington*, *Dover*, *Tiger*, *Yarmouth*, and *Malaga Merchant*, Stoakes passed the Straits. In January, 1658, he was at Leghorn, taking measures against piracy ; and he intended to go at once to Tunis " to make peace if possible. If not, then to do damage." [6] His plan involved the keeping of three " frigates " cruising to the north of Sicily ; and thus he had only six with him. Unlike Blake, he felt called upon to resent paying a price for such captives as the Bey should liberate ; [7] and he would have fought had his force been stronger. But with six weak ships he could do nothing against the rebuilt forts, and eight ships of war which lay in Porto Farina. He did, however, conclude a satisfactory treaty with the Bey. [8] His fleet varied considerably in the course of his long command, and in November, 1658, three of his ships,

[1] Whitelocke, 664.   [2] *Ib.*   [3] Cal. S. P. Dom. 1657, p. 368.
[4] S. P. Dom. Int. clvii. 64.   Stoakes to Adlty. Comtee.
[5] *Ib.* 145.   [6] *Ib.* clxxix. 13.
[7] *Ib.* 88.   [8] *Ib.* clxxxii. 35.

the *Phœnix*, the *Bristol*, and the *Hampshire*, cruising between
Sicily and Sardinia, met " that famous rover, Victorio Papachino,
the prince of Spanish pirates.[1]　He was so confident as to give
us chase, taking us for three Bacallao men.　We chased him for
nearly seven hours before we could bring him by the lee, and
would not have effected it then had not his sails been all shot to
pieces.　The force of his vessel is ten guns and some pedereros.[2]
She sails well, on which account Papachino always kept her full
of men for the purpose of boarding.　She had but one hundred and
sixteen men when taken, Captain Kempthorne having killed and
spoiled the rest.　The news of his being in our hands is very
welcome in this place, and the French are no less joyful than
ourselves."

Such was the style of the effective work done by Stoakes ; who
sailed for home on July 29th, 1659, and dropped anchor in the
Downs on September 16th.

In northern waters there was little of note for English ships to
do at this time.　The fighting that delivered up Mardijk and
Dunquerque to England did not affect the Navy.　A fleet of twenty-
six ships was present at the time off Dunquerque for blockade duty,
but its service was confined chiefly to passive endurance during
the severe winter of 1657–1658.

There was, throughout the period of the Protectorate, continual
trouble in the Sound ; but England was able to avoid being drawn
into the eddies.　In the spring of 1657, war broke out between the
Danes and Sweden ;[3] and Holland was looked to to help the Danes,
who were somewhat severely pressed.　This, owing to want of instructions, the Dutch fleet did not at first do ; but on receipt of
orders from the States General, it subsequently took the part of the
Danes.　Thus it was that early in November, 1658, there was fought
in the Sound that extremely bloody battle in which the Dutch were
indeed victorious, but with the loss of De With and Floriszoon
killed.　Soon afterwards England joined with Holland to force a
peace on the combatants.　It agreed with the interests of neither
that the Baltic should become a Swedish lake with a prohibitive
toll.

Ayscue went out in autumn, 1658, as naval adviser to the
Swedish king, but saw no active service.　Goodsonn went as

---

[1] S. P. Dom. Int. clxxxiii. 96, clxxxiv. 9.　Bonn to Adlty Comnrs.
[2] *I.e.* " patereros."　　　　　　　　　　　　[3] Basnage, 480, *sqq.*

Ayscue's vice-admiral and brought the fleet home that winter when bad weather would not allow it to be kept out longer. In 1659 a fleet was again sent to the Sound, the commander-in-chief being General Montagu, and the vice-admiral, John Lawson. But Montagu, at the end of 1659, had a greater interest in home politics than in the future of the Baltic trade. Accordingly he abandoned the Sound, when the rival kings seemed likely to accept the joint ultimatum, and returned to England, which was then in the throes preliminary to the Restoration. But the right moment had not yet arrived, and he was forced to abandon the command, which was taken up by Lawson, with the style of vice-admiral. When the Restoration was finally decided upon, Montagu was deputed to bring the King to England. Charles was at the Hague, and the reason the Dutch had for inviting him thither when the Restoration had become imminent, was that they had begun to fear the consequences of their long period of hostility to him, and to feel that a little timely conciliation might not be amiss.

On May 12th, Penn was ordered, as General,[1] to command the fleet in chief till he should meet with Montagu. To the latter the command was then delivered up, and, with Lawson as vice-admiral, the Restoration fleet put over to Holland.

[1] Hist. MSS. Com. Rep. 13, Ap. 2, p. 100.

CHAPTER XXII.

CIVIL HISTORY OF THE ROYAL NAVY, 1660–1714.

Social life in the Navy—Naval diarists—Henry Teonge—A chaplain's kit—Salutes—
Drinking—Punishments—Christmas at Sea—Signals—Sickness and mortality—
Thomas Pocock—Nathaniel Taubmann—Richard Allyn—Lower deck profanity
—The government of the Navy—Victualling—The command of the fleet—
Promotion—The Navy List—Distinguishing pennants—The entry of officers—
Naval pay—Table money—Gratuities for wounds—Seamen's wages—The Press
—Bounties—Registration of seamen—Greenwich Hospital—Medals—The Marines
—The Duke of York's reforms—Sheathing with lead—Captains' journals—Dis-
tillation—The Judge Advocate—The Surgeon-General—The Board of Longitude
—Improvements in shipbuilding—Superiority of foreign models—The naval revival
of 1686—The Navy at the Revolution—List of ships—Establishment of guns and
men—The Cushee Piece—The bomb-ketch—The "Machine"—Navigation Acts—
The Law of Wrecks—Dockyards and docks—Buoying and lighting—The Eddystone—Marine surveying—The Union with Scotland.

ANGEL OF CHARLES II.

(*From Ruding's 'Annals
of the Coinage of Great
Britain.'*)

A FAR better picture of social life in the
Royal Navy can be obtained from such
sources as diaries, private logs, and autobio-
graphical memoirs written by observant naval
officers, than from such more precise but drier
authorities as letters on service, official logs, and
records of courts-martial. The period of the
Restoration was the golden period of the English
diarist; and the age that saw Pepys and Evelyn
recording from day to day their impressions of
things seen and heard on shore, saw also more than one careful
observer setting down memorials of daily life on board ships of the
Navy.

The most interesting of the naval diarists of the epoch now
under review is the Rev. Henry Teonge, who, born on March 18th,
1621, had been first a cavalier, then rector of Alcester in Warwick-
shire, and of the neighbouring parish of Spernall, and then, like other
poor clergymen of the day, a fugitive from his creditors. It was
to avoid his duns that in 1675 he went to sea as a naval chaplain.

In that capacity he made two cruises, leaving his son Henry, vicar of Coughton, as his *locum tenens*. In 1679 he returned home for the last time; and on March 21st, 1690, he died. Teonge was with Narbrough's expedition of 1675–76 for the chastisement of the Barbary pirates; and his notes on that affair possess considerable historical value; but the chief importance of his diary [1] arises from its obviously faithful and detailed reflex of social life in the Navy in the last quarter of the seventeenth century. Some account of naval manners and customs, as pictured in this volume, is therefore offered to the reader.

The naval chaplains of the time, like the surgeons, were partially paid out of deductions made from the monthly wage of every seaman, the chaplain receiving a groat, and the surgeon twopence, in respect of each man. The *Assistance*, to which Teonge was first appointed, was a fifty-six gun [2] fourth-rate, carrying two hundred men. His next ship, the *Bristol*, was of the same force and rating. His third ship, the *Royal Oak*, was a sixty-four gun third-rate, carrying three hundred and ninety men; so that the chaplain's monthly income from the groats was, in the *Assistance* and *Bristol*, about £3 6s., and in the *Royal Oak*, about £6 10s. In addition, he received ordinary seaman's pay at 19s. a lunar month. Teonge's whole income from the Navy, per year of thirteen months, was, consequently, about £55 in the two smaller ships, and about £96 in the larger vessel; and as he was victualled while afloat, and was at the same time free from the attentions of his creditors, and leading an enjoyable life, it is not difficult to understand that the position had great attractions for an impecunious country parson.

That he was exceedingly impecunious when he left Spernall is evident from his diary. He carried all his kit on his body and in an old sack. His mare was so out of condition that, upon reaching London, he sold her, " with saddle, bridle, and bootes, and spurrs," to his landlord for 26s., "upon condition that if 26s. was sent to him in a fortnight's time, the mare might be redeemed, but the other things lost." His wardrobe was correspondingly poor; yet he had to pawn part of it in order to supply himself with a small sea

---

[1] The 'Diary of Henry Teonge,' chaplain on board his Majesty's ships, *Assistance*, *Bristol*, and *Royal Oak*, anno 1675 to 1679. London, 1825.

[2] This was her then nominal force. The number of guns as well as of men actually carried by this, and all other ships of the seventeenth century, varied from time to time.

bed, pillow, blanket, and rug. Teonge does not say how he obtained
his appointment, but he owed it, no doubt, to some extent to the
favour of Captain William Holden,[1] of the *Assistance*. Both
Holden and his lieutenant, Henry Haughton, welcomed the chaplain in London, " with bottells of claret, etc. " ; and on the night
when Teonge joined his ship, which lay in Long Reach, he records
that he " dranke part of 3 boules of punch (a liquor very strainge
to me) ; and so to bed in a cabin so much out of order, that when
I thought to find my pillow on the topp, I found it slipt between
the coards and under the bed."

The ship left Long Reach on June 2nd, and next day was at the
Nore. Until the buoy there was reached, the *Assistance* must have
been a pandemonium of drunkenness and immorality, for there were
many seamen's wives and sweethearts on board, punch and brandy
were drunk, and the song, " Loath to Depart,"[2] was sung ; " so that
our ship was that night well furnished, but ill man'd ; few of them
being able to keepe watch, had there beene occasion."

While the *Assistance* lay in the Downs, Teonge was enabled to
add to his scanty kit. " And here," he says, " I might tell you what
Providence putt into my hands ; which, though littell worth of
themselves, yet were they of greater use to him that then wanted
almost every thing. Early in the morning I mett with a rugged
towell on the quarter deck, which I soone secured ; and soone after,
Providence brought me a piece of an old sayle, and an earthen
chamber pott." These few words strangely illustrate the difference
between both the two chaplains, and the internal economy of
men-of-war of 1675 and of to-day, and are, perhaps, as suggestive
as any in the diary.

On his first Sunday at sea, Teonge held no service, " by reason
of the buisnes of the shipp." On his second, " I preached my first
sermon on shipboard, where I could not stand without holding by
boath the pillars in the steerage ; and the captain's chayre and
others were ready to tilt downe, sometimes backwards, sometimes
forward. All our women and olde seamen were sick this day ; I was
only giddy." The last of the women seem to have been sent ashore
at Dover on the following Monday week, after having been about
three weeks on board. Their departure was honoured " with

---

[1] Teonge calls him Houlding.

[2] The tune of this song was used in the Navy as a trumpet-salute to persons of rank
on quitting a vessel.

3 cheares, 7 gunns, and our trumpetts sounding," the tune on this occasion probably being the one known as " Mayds, Where are your Hearts ? "

This was by no means the first useless expenditure of powder on the cruise. Several days earlier, a merchantman at the mouth of the Thames had taken no notice of the man-of-war as she passed out ; whereupon, says Teonge, " Wee give him a shott, make him loare his top-gallant (*id est*, putt off his hatt to us) ; and our gunner presently goes on board of him, makes him pay 6*s*. 6*d*. for his contempt, abateing him 2*d*. because it was the first shott." And enormous quantities of powder were wasted later. Indeed, questions concerning salutes and guns were very burning ones in those days. On one occasion, when a Dutch man-of-war was sighted, Captain Holden " commanded to tack upon her, which they soone perceiving (like a cowardly dogg that lys downe when he sees one com that he feares), loares not only his top sayle, but claps his sayle to the mast, and lys by. This satisfys us, as unworthy of so pittifull an onsett, and we keepe on our course as before. Yet I can not forget the words of our noble captain, viz., ' I wish I could meete with on that would not vaile his bonnett, that I might make woorke for my brethren at White Hall ' ; meaning officers that were out of employment." In the Channel, some East Indiamen were fallen in with. " Each of them salute with 5 gunns, and we answer accordingly ; the last gave us 7 ; and each give us one back, but the last gave us 3." At Plymouth, " we salute the Castle with 9 gunns, they answer with as many ; wee returne our thanks with 3 more." The *Assistance* convoyed six vessels bound for Tangier. Captain Holden, in due course, dined on board one of them, which, when he left her, gave him five guns, for which the man-of-war returned three. Compliments were, in fact, usually returned with two guns less, when both parties were British ; but foreigners were expected to return gun for gun. Ships, on parting company, fired three guns.[1] On joining a senior officer, they fired five, the senior returning three, and the other vessel again returning one. A British consul received five guns,[2] and a salute from the trumpets of, " Mayds, Where are your Hearts?" An over-obsequious Venetian, who saluted with eleven guns, was snubbed by having only five returned to him,

---

[1] But on parting company with Narbrough, the *Assistance* fired eleven, and gave three cheers, Narbrough answering with eleven, and the *Assistance* replying with five.

[2] But the consul at Scanderoon received seven—possibly as a personal compliment.

The King's birthday was celebrated with thirteen guns,[1] "the last with a shott in her." Yet there were noisier and more costly displays than these. When Narbrough entered Malta, the Knights gave him forty-five guns, and the salutes and returns lasted for "almost two howers." Again, upon the conclusion of the arrangement with Tripoli, the town fired all its guns, and each of Narbrough's ships returned twenty-one. On St. George's Day, at the drinking of the King's health, twenty-five rounds were got rid of. And, at the funeral of a captain, the ship fired forty guns, and certain Dutch ships, which were in company, fired at "least one hundred."

There was an excessive amount of drinking in his Majesty's ships. It was usual, on Saturday evenings, to "end the day and weeke with drinking to our wives in punch bowles," and to drink as well to the King; and Teonge never omitted to take his share on these occasions. When land was sighted, the fact was celebrated in "severall boules of punch drank round about the ship." And, when little of importance was doing, we find in the diary such entries as, "Nothing to-day, but drinke to our friends in England in racckee at night."

There are many notices concerning naval punishments. On June 24th, 1675, Teonge writes: "This day 2 seamen, that had stolen a piece or two of beife, were thus shamed; they had their hands tyd behind them, and themselves tyd to the maine mast, each of them a piece of raw beife tyd about their necks in a coard, and the beife bobbing before them like the knott of a crevatt; and the rest of the seamen cam one by one and rubd them over the mouth with the raw beife; and in this posture they stood 2 howers." On September 28th, 1675: "This morning one of our men, viz., Skinner, a knowne coockould, for goeing on shoare without leave, had his legs tyd together, his hands tyd to a greate rope, and stood on the syd of the ship to be hoysted up to the yard arme, and from thence to dropp downe in to the water 3 times; but he lookeing so very pittifully, and also by the gentlemen's intreatys to the captaine for him, who alleaged that he had injurys enough already, as haveing a wife a whore and a schold to injure him at home, *ergo*, had the more need to be pittyed abroad, was spared." On January 29th, 1676: "This day, David Thomas, and Marlin the

[1] This was in 1675. In 1676 the senior officer fired eleven guns, and other ships either nine or seven.

coock, and our master's boy, had their hand stretched out, and with their backs to the rayles, and the master's boy with his back to the maine mast, all looking on upon the other, and in each of their mouths a maudlen-spike, viz., an iron pinn clapt cloese into their mouths, and tyd behind their heads ; and there they stood a whole houre, till their mouths were very bloody ; an excellent cure for swearers." On August 4th, 1678 : "Isaac Webb stood tyd to the geares [1] an houre, and had *speculum oris* placed in his mouth, for saying to a seaman in the captain's hearing, 'Thou lyest, like a sonn of a whore.'" And, twelve days later, "A seaman had 29 lashes with a cat of 9 tayles, and was then washt with salt water, for stealing our carpenter's mate's wive's ring." This last entry was made while the *Bristol*, in which Teonge was then serving, lay at Spithead. Signs are not wanting that whenever ships of war were in home waters, there were plenty of women on board ; and it would even appear that they also were subjected to punishment ; for under June 18th, 1678, when the *Bristol* was in the Downs, is the suggestive note : "The scolding woman was well washt to-day."

All the above punishments, save perhaps the one which was remitted at the last moment, were fanciful ones, imposed at the discretion of the commander, and not prescribed by written regulations. The serious punishments which seem to have been officially recognised at the time, were known as the capstan, the bilboes, and ducking ; and they are thus described by the author of the 'Diologicall Discourse of Marine Affaires' [2] : "A capstan barr being thrust through the hole of the barrell, the offender's armes are extended to the full length, and soe made faste untoe the barr croswise, having sometymes a basket of bulletts or some other the like weighte, hanging abowt his necke, in which posture he continues untill he be made either to confesse some plotte or cryme whereof he is pregnantlie suspected, or that he have received such condigne sufferinge as he is sentenced to undergoe by command of the captaine" . . . "The punishment of the bilboes is when a delinquent is putt in irons, or in a kind of stocks used for that purpose, the which are more or lesse heavy and pinching, as the qualitie of the offense is proved against the delinquent" . . . "The

---

[1] Or "jears" : an assemblage of tackles whereby the lower yards of a ship are hoisted to, or lowered from, their usual stations.

[2] Harl. MSS. 1341.

ducking att the mayne yarde arme is when a malefactor, by having
a rope fastened under his armes and abowte his myddle and under
his breatche, is thus hoysed upp to the end of the yarde, from
whence he is againe vyolentlie lett fall intoe the sea, sometymes
twyse, sometymes three several tymes one after another ; and if the
offense be verye fowle, he is alsoe drawne under the verye keele of
the ship, the which is termed keel-haling ; and whilst hee is thus
under water a great gunn is given fire righte over his head ; the
which is done as well toe astonish him the more with the thunder
thereof, which much troubleth him, as toe give warning untoe all
others toe looke out, and toe beware by his harmes."

Of the observance of Christmas Day at sea, Teonge wrote in
1675 : "At 4 in the morning our trumpeters all doe flatt their
trumpetts, and begin at our captain's cabin, and thence to all the
officers' and gentlemen's cabins, playing a levite at each cabine
doore, and bidding good morrow, wishing a merry Christmas.
After they goe to their station, viz., on the poope, and sound
3 levites in honour of the morning. At 10 wee goe to prayers and
sermon : text, Zacc. ix. 9. Our captaine had all his officers and
gentlemen to dinner with him, where wee had excellent good fayre ;
a ribb of beife, plumb puddings, minct pyes, etc., and plenty of
good wines of severall sorts ; dranke healths to the King, to our
wives and friends, and ended the day with much civill myrth." On
Christmas Day, 1678, at Port Mahon, fresh beef could not be
obtained, " yet wee had to dinner an excellent rice pudding in
a greate charger, a speciall piece of Martinmas English beife, and
a neat's tongue, and good cabbidge, a charger full of excellent fresh
fried fish, a douzen of woodcocks in a pye, which cost 15*d.*, a couple
of good henns roasted, 3 sorts of cheese, and, last of all, a greate
charger full of blew figs, almonds, and raysings ; and wine and
punch gallore, and a douzen of English pippins."

Of signals, Teonge says very little ; but he gives us the sailing
orders of Captain Holden to his convoy, and Sir John Narbrough's [1]
signals for desiring to speak to the captains in his fleet. Holden's
orders were the usual convoy orders of the time, and as they
illustrate the awkwardness of the prevailing system, they may find
a place here : —

[1] Sir John's commission at the time was that of " commander-in-chief," but he was
only a commodore.

Sayling Orders, June 20, 1675, between his Majesty's ship Assistance, *under the command of Capt. William Holden, and the other ships then under his conduct.*

" 1. If wee weigh in the day time, wee will loose our fore top-sayle, and fyre on gun. If in the night, wee will fire on gun, and put forth a light in the fore top-mast shrouds : which light is to be answered by every ship in the same place.

" 2. If wee tack in the night, wee will put out two lights, on in the mizen shrouds, the other in the fore shrouds, of equal hight.

" 3. If we anchor in the night, we will fyre on gun, and put out a light in the mizen shrouds, which light is to be answered in the sam place.

" 4. If we lye by in the night, or try, or hull, by reason of bad weather, wee will fyre on gun, and put out two lights in our mizen shrouds of equall hight, which lights are to be answered : and when we make sayle, wee'l make the signe as for weighing in the night.

" 5. If wee should chance to see any ship in the night, the discoverer is to fyre a muskett, and to make false fyres. And if we should not know on another, the hayler shall ask, ' What ship is that ? ' The other shall answer, Royall Highness ; and the hayler shall say, ' Prosper.'

" 6. If any be opressed by reason of carrying sayle, he is to hang out a light att bowsprett end, and to fyre a gun, and to make false fyres now and then, till he be assisted.

" 7. If any spring a leake, or be in distrese by day, let him make a weft, and halle up his sayles that his weft may be seene, whereby to repayre to him. If in the night, to fyre on gun, and to put out 4 lights of equall hight.

" 8. If it prove foggy weather by night or day, we must ring our bells, and fyre a musket now and then. And in dark nights, each ship to carry a light.

" 9. No ship shall presume to goe a head of the light in the night.

" 10. If any loose company in foule weather, and meete again, those to windward shall let run theire topsayles, and those to leeward shall hall up theire foresayles, and mizens if they are abroade.

" 11. If wee loose company between this and Plimworth, our rendisvouse is at Plimworth : if between that and Tangeare, Tangeare."

Narbrough's signals [1] for speaking his captains were as follows :—

Pennant at—						To speak—
Mizzen peak	.	.	.	.	.	All captains.
Main topmast head	.	.	.	.	.	*Dragon.*
Fore topmast head	.	.	.	.	.	*Newcastle.*
Mizzen topmast head	.	.	.	.	.	*Success.*
Mizzen topsail yard arm		.	.	.	.	*Swallow.*
Fore yard arm	.	.	.	.	.	*Assistance.*
Fore topsail yard arm	.	.	.	.	.	*Dartmouth.*
Main yard arm	.	.	.	.	.	*Diamond.*
Cross-jack yard arm	.	.	.	.	.	*Mary Rose.*
Mizzen topsail yard arm		.	.	.	.	*Roebuck.*
Spritsail head	.	.	.	.	.	*Portsmouth.*
Spritsail yard arm	.	.	.	.	.	*Yarmouth.*
Boom on the quarter	.	.	.	.	.	Tripoli prize.
Half up ensign staff	.	.	.	.	.	*Anne and Christopher.*
Boom on the stern	.	.	.	.	.	*Homer.*
Ensign staff	.	.	.	.	.	*Wivenhoe.*

[1] These signals were issued on August 12th, 1675, from on board H.M.S. *Henrietta*, at sea before Tripoli. Notes appended to them directed that in the event of a captain

Teonge's diary throws a somewhat ghastly light upon the sanitary conditions prevailing in the Navy of his day. The causes of the mortality, which occasionally more than decimated ships' companies within a few weeks, seem to have been mainly bad food and water, absence of anti-scorbutics, insufficient clothing, personal dirtiness, and exhalations from the bilge, or from other decaying matter in the hold. Here are some of the chaplain's entries when the *Royal Oak* was at Port Mahon, and on her way thence to England, in 1679:—

Feb.   7. "This day I buried two out of our ship: John Parr and John Woolger. I think they were little better than starved to death with cold weather."

Feb.   9. "I buried our captain's cabin boy, Imanuell Dearam."

Feb. 11. "I buried Samuell Ward, who had layn sick a longe time."

Feb. 26. "This day I buried John Wilkinson, the carpenter's mate."

Mar.   5. "I buried Izaak Maule, a Sweade."

Mar.   6. "And this day I buried Samuell Massy."

Mar.   9. "This day I buried in the sea William Watson, belonging to the carpenter's crue."

Mar. 12. "Here (at Formentera) was buried William Foster of the carpenter's crue."

Mar. 19. "Brave Captain Antony Langston,[1] dyed a very little after ten o'clock this night."

Mar. 22. "I buried Francis Forrest, as 'tis said eaten to death with lyce."

Mar. 23. "I buried Joseph Pearson."

April 6. "I buried Isaac Webb out at the gunn-roome porte."

May   1. "I buried John Johnson out of the gunn-roome porte."

May   2. "I buried Henry Johns out of the gunn-roome porte."

May   3. "I buried Rich. Dell, as before."

May   7. "I buried Thomas Smith."

May   9. "I buried John Horsenayle."

May 12. "I buried Mr. Richard Cooling in a coffin."

May 16. "I buried William Wattson."

---

being sick, he was to send to the flag-ship, in response to the signal, his lieutenant or next officer: that, in case of separation, Tripoli was to be the rendezvous; and that the ultimate rendezvous, for vessels unable to keep the sea, would be Malta.

All the signals were to be made with "my pendant." This was probably a red one. Admiral Russell, later Earl of Orford, adopted this system in an order of May 6th, 1691, but used red, white, and blue pennants in twenty-five different positions, whereby he was enabled to make signals to seventy-five different ships. Russell also made other signals upon the same principle. If, for example, he wanted a particular ship to chase to windward or leeward, he made the signal for her captain, and also showed a red or a blue flag in the mizzen rigging. His system rendered fleet manœuvres possible. It was largely based upon a system applied by H.R.H. James, Duke of York, about 1665, and embodied in "The Duke of York's Fighting Instructions," as drawn up by Sir W. Penn.

[1] Of the *Royal Oak*, to which he had exchanged from the *Bristol* on January 16th. He was succeeded by Captain Roome Coyle.

May 25. "I buried Jeffery Tranow."
May 30. "I buried Joseph Bryan. And we sent to shoare 32 sick men
        pittifull creatures."
May 31. "The muster-master mustered us, and wanted above 60 men that
        were on the bookes, all dead at sea."

This was fearful mortality, for the ship's complement was only
three hundred and ninety officers and men. At the end of the
nineteenth century a death-rate, even at sea, of twenty-five or thirty
per thousand per annum is accounted enormous; but if we take
the recorded deaths in the *Royal Oak* during the four months
ending May, 1679, we find the death-rate to have been in the
proportion of not less than one hundred and sixty-five per one
thousand per annum. Yet it does not appear that she was an
exceptionally unhealthy ship, and it is almost certain that Teonge
failed to specifically mention each death that occurred during the
period.

There are other chaplains' diaries of about the same time.
One was written by the Rev. Thomas Pocock, chaplain of the
Ranelagh in 1704, and father of Admiral Sir George Pocock.
Extracts from this, which remains in MS., are printed as an
appendix to "Memoirs Relating to the Lord Torrington" (Camden
Society, 1889). Another was written and published by the
Rev. Nathaniel Taubmann, who was in the Mediterranean in
1708–9. A third, quoted by the editor of Teonge's diary, was
written by the Rev. Richard Allyn, chaplain of the *Centurion*
in 1691–2. From this last is taken the following amusing extract,
illustrative of the character of the seamen of the time :—

"April 21st, 1692 . . . . Tho' the wind was so boisterous, yet the running about of
shot, chests, and loos things about the ship, made almost as great a noise as that (viz.
the wind). We had about 16 or 17 buts and pipes of wine in the steerage, all which
gave way together, and the heads of one of them broke out. We shipped several great
seas over our quarter as well as wast. Sometimes for nigh the space of a minute the
ship would seem to bee all under water, and again sometimes would seem fairly to
settle on one side. The chests, etc., swim'd between decks, and wee had several foot of
water in the hold. In short, the weather was so bad, that the whole ship's company
declared that they thought they had never seen the like, and that it was impossible for
it to be wors. Notwithstanding, all our ports were neither caulked nor lin'd, want of
doing which was supposed to have occasioned the loss of the *Coronation*.[1] During the
dreadful season I quietly kept my bed, tho' very wet by reason of the water that came
into my scuttle. The behaviour of our Puggs [2] at this time was not a little remarkable;

---

[1] The *Coronation*, a second rate, Captain Charles Skelton, was lost off Ram Head
on September 3rd, 1691.
[2] Puggs, seamen.

some few of them would pray, but more of them curs'd and swore lowder than the wind and weather. I can't forbear writing one instance of this nature, and that is in the story which was told me the next morning of George the caulker, and old Robin Anderson. Poor George, being very apprehensive of his being a sinner, and now in great danger of his life, fell down upon his marrow bones, and began to pray: ' Lord, have mercy upon me! Christ have,' etc., and so on to the Lord's Prayer. All the while old Robin was near him, and, between every sentence, cry'd out : ' Ah, you cow! Z——ds, thou hast not got the hart of a flea! ' Poor George, thus disturbed at his devotion, would look over his shoulder, and, at the end of every petition, would make answer to old Robin with a ' God d——n you, you old dog! can't you let a body pray at quiet for you, ha ? A plague rot you! let me alone, can't yee ? ' Thus the one kept praying and cursing, and t'other railing, for half an hour, when a great log of wood by the rowling of the ship, tumbled upon George's legs, and bruised him a little ; which George, taking up into his hands, and thinking it had been thrown at him by old Robin, let fly at the old fellow, together with an whole broadside of oaths and curses, and so they fell to boxing. I mention this only to see the incorrigible senslesnes of such tarpawlin wretches in the greatest extremity of danger."

One of the first acts of Charles II. after the Restoration was to revive the office of Lord High Admiral in favour of his brother, Prince James, Duke of York. When the Duke, in consequence of the passing of the Test Act, ceased to hold it, the office was put into commission, and so remained until the accession of James II., who became his own minister of marine. After the Revolution [1] a new Board of Admiralty was appointed, and successive commissions ruled the Navy until 1702. For a short time in 1708, Queen Anne personàlly directed the affairs of the service. A new Lord High Admiral was then appointed, but in 1709 the office was once more put into commission, and so continued for upwards of a century. Lists of the Lords High Admiral and First Commissioners of the Admiralty, as well as of the Principal Officers of the Navy, Secretaries of the Admiralty, Commissioners of the Navy, etc., during the period under review, are appended :—

HEADS OF THE ADMIRALTY :—	
4 June 1660. James, Duke of York, Lord High Admiral.	14 May 1679. Sir Henry Capel, Kt., First Lord.
14 June 1673. Charles II.	14 Feb. 1680. Daniel Finch, later Lord Finch, and Earl of Nottingham and Winchelsea, First Lord.
9 July 1673. Prince Rupert, First Lord.	

---

[1] Early in the new reign there was passed a declaratory Act (2 W and M, sess. 2, c. 2), which is the authority for the present constitution of the Admiralty Board. It declared that " all and singular authorities, jurisdictions, and powers which, by Act of Parliament or otherwise," had been "lawfully vested" in the Lord High Admiral of England, has always appertained, and did and should appertain, to the Commissioners for executing the office for the time being, "to all intents and purposes as if the said Commissioners were Lord High Admiral of England."

1685. James II.
8 Mar. 1689. Admiral Arthur Herbert, later Earl of Torrington, First Lord.
20 Jan. 1690. Thomas Herbert, Earl of Pembroke, First Lord.
10 Mar. 1692. Charles, Lord Cornwallis, First Lord.
15 April 1693. Anthony Cary, Viscount Falkland, First Lord.
2 May 1694. Admiral Edward Russell, later Earl of Orford, First Lord.
21 May 1699. John Egerton, Earl of Bridgewater, First Lord.
4 April 1701. Thomas Herbert, Earl of Pembroke, First Lord.
26 Jan. 1702. Thomas Herbert, Earl of Pembroke, Lord High Admiral.
20 May 1702. George, Prince of Denmark, Lord High Admiral.
29 Oct. 1708. Queen Anne.
29 Nov. 1708. Thomas Herbert, Earl of Pembroke, Lord High Admiral.
8 Nov. 1709. Admiral Edward Russell, Earl of Orford, First Lord.
4 Oct. 1710. Admiral Sir John Leake, Kt., First Lord.
30 Sept. 1712. Thos. Wentworth, Earl of Strafford, First Lord.

SECRETARIES OF THE ADMIRALTY :—

1673. Samuel Pepys (Clerk of the Acts from 1660).
1689. Josiah Burchett.

TREASURERS OF THE NAVY :—

1660. Capt. Sir George Carteret, Bt., R.N.
Arthur Annesley, Earl of Anglesea.
1671. Sir Thos. Osborne, Bart., afterwards Duke of Leeds.
1673. Sir Edward Seymour, Bart.

Anthony Cary, Viscount Falkland.
1689. Admiral Edward Russell.
1693. Sir Thomas Lyttleton, Bart.
1710. Robert Walpole, afterwards Earl of Orford.
1711. Charles Cæsar.
1714. John Aislabie.

COMMISSIONERS :—

1686. (*See names on p.* 243.)

CONTROLLERS OF THE NAVY :—

Oct. 1688. Capt. Sir Richard Haddock, Kt., R.N.
Feb. 1714. Rear-Adm. Sir Charles, Wager, Kt.

SURVEYORS OF THE NAVY :—

30 Sept. 1668. Sir John Tippets, Kt.
25 June 1692. Edward Dummer.
25 Sept. 1699. Daniel Furzer.
9 Sept. 1706. William Lee (conjointly with Furzer until May 1713, when Lee became Commissioner at Portsmouth).

CLERKS OF THE ACTS :—

Oct. 1688. James Southern.
Nov. 1689. Charles Sergison.
Feb. 1701. Samuel Atkins.

CONTROLLER OF THE TREASURER'S ACCOUNTS :—

1691. Dennis Liddell.

CONTROLLERS OF THE VICTUALLING ACCOUNTS :—

Oct. 1688. Vice-Adm. Sir John Berry, Kt.
Jan. 1690. Rear-Adm. Sir Richard Beach, Kt.
Mar. 1692. Samuel Pitt.
Mar. 1699. Adm. Sir Clowdisley Shovell, Kt.
Aug. 1704. Benjamin Timewell.

CONTROLLERS OF THE STOREKEEPERS' ACCOUNTS :—

1688. Capt. Sir Wm. Booth, Kt., R.N.
Mar. 1689. Capt. Harry Priestman, R.N.

June 1690. Vice-Adm. Sir John
    Ashby, Kt.
June 1693. Capt. Thomas Will-
    shaw, R.N.
Sept. 1702. Henry Greenhill.
Jan. 1704. Capt. Thomas Jennings,
    R.N.

EXTRA COMMISSIONERS :—

Jan. 1691. Rear-Adm. Sir Geo.
    Rooke, Kt.
Jan. 1691. John Hill.
Mar. 1693. Rear-Adm. Sir Clowdis-
    ley Shovell, Kt.
Sept. 1693. Capt. George St. Loe,
    R.N.
Mar. 1694. Vice-Adm. Matthew
    Aylmer.
Mar. 1695. James Southern.
Dec. 1696. Benjamin Timewell.
Feb. 1701. George Tollet.
July 1702. Anthony Hammond.
Nov. 1702. Vice-Adm. Sir Thos.
    Hopsonn, Kt.
Feb. 1705. Capt. Sir Wm. Gifford,
    Kt., R.N.
July 1712. James Hunter.
Nov. 1713. Capt. Isaac Townsend,
    R.N.
Nov. 1713. Capt. Lawrence Wright,
    R.N.

COMMISSIONERS AT H.M. DOCKYARDS,
    ETC. :—

Chatham :
Oct. 1688. Sir Phineas Pett, Kt.

Oct. 1689. Sir Edward Gregory, Kt.
April 1703. Capt. George St. Loe,
    R.N.

Portsmouth :
Oct. 1688. Rear-Adm. Sir Richard
    Beach, Kt.
April 1690. Captain Thomas Will-
    shaw, R.N.
Mar. 1692. Benjamin Timewell.
April 1695. Henry Greenhill.
June 1702. Capt. Sir Wm. Gifford,
    Kt., R.N.
June 1705. Capt. Isaac Townsend,
    R.N.
May 1713. William Lee.

Plymouth :
Dec. 1691. Henry Greenhill.
April 1695. Capt. George St. Loe.
    R.N.
April 1703. Capt. Wm. Wright, R.N.
Feb. 1704. Henry Greenhill.
July 1708. Capt. Wm. Wright, R.N.
June 1711. Capt. Rich. Edwards,
    R.N.

Deptford and Woolwich :
Oct. 1688. Balthasar St. Michell.
Aug. 1702. Henry Greenhill.

Kinsale :
Mar. 1695. Benjamin Timewell
May 1702. Capt. Lawrence Wright,
    R.N. (to 1713).

Lisbon :
Feb. 1704. Capt. Wm. Wright, R.N.

The victualling, which had been conducted " upon account " up
to the Restoration, was placed by Charles II. in the hands of Denis
Gauden as contractor. In 1668, two responsible persons approved
by the King were associated with this gentleman ; but the system
did not give satisfaction, and on December 10th, 1683, Commissioners
of Victualling were appointed, with power to contract for provisions,
and to appoint clerks and purveyors.[1] The first commissioners
were, Captain Sir Richard Haddock, Kt., R.N., Anthony Sturt,
John Parsons, and Nicholas Fenn.

The supreme command of the fleet was entrusted by James II.,
at the close of his reign, to George Legge, Lord Dartmouth, who

[1] Pepys's MSS., 'Nav. Precedents,' 48.

may be regarded as the first of the Admirals of the Fleet. Arthur Herbert, Earl of Torrington, took his place after the Revolution. But as yet there was no regular succession ; and the position was an office rather than a rank. On two or three occasions under William and Mary the command was placed in commission. George Rooke was made Admiral of the Fleet in 1696. Rooke was followed in 1705 by Sir Clowdisley Shovell, who perished in 1707. Sir John Leake, Kt., was appointed to the post in 1708, and Matthew Aylmer, afterwards Lord Aylmer, in 1709, Leake again taking the place in 1710, and Aylmer supplanting him once more later. Both Leake and Aylmer died in 1720, and it was not until after that time that flag officers were permanently promoted to the rank of Admiral of the Fleet. Nor, until 1718, was it ordered that captains, if duly qualified for flag-rank, should be promoted by seniority. Writing to Rooke in 1703, Prince George of Denmark said : " Upon making the flags last year, all my council were of opinion that the Crown never tied itself to seniority in choosing their officers." [1]

(1)

Admiralty Office,
July 1. 1700.

A LIST of the Names of such Lieutenants who served in His Majesty's Fleet , during the late War, One hundred whereof will from time to time be Entituled to Half-Pay, during their being out of Employment a-shoar, according to their Seniorities, and His Majesty's Establishment in that behalf, Dated the 18th of April, 1700.

Lieutenants Names.	Dates of their First Commissions.	Which of them are now Employ'd, and how.
Humphry Parker	11 April 89	First Lieutenant of the Worcester.
Samuel Tilley	20 June 89	
Nath Brown.	23 Aug. 89	First Lieutenant of the Carlisle.
Clempson Cave	27 Jan. 89	23d Dec. 1699. Leave given him to go into the Merchant Service
Henry Cremer	13 Febr. 89	
Nath. Fogg	25 Febr. 89	
John Tucker	30 Mar. 90	In the Merchant Service
Gustavus Lang	13 April 90	
Elias Waffe	1 May 90	First Lieutenant of the Tilbury.
John Pepys	3 May 90	
Jacob Fletcher	4 May 90	First Lieutenant of the Glocester
John Jephcott	26 June 90	
Jof. Berry	26 June 90	
Edward Manning.	1 Aug. 90	Midshipman Extra. in the Queenbrough.
Robert Dobson	12 Aug. 90	First Lieutenant of the Salisbury.
Thomas Mead	2 Dec. 90	
Nath. Hubbard	16 Dec. 90	
William Sharp	31 Dec. 90	Second Lieutenant of the Portland.
John Hart	9 Jan. 90	
Jonathan Denn	19 Jan. 90	
Matthew Tate.	13 Febr. 90	Third Lieutenant of the Chichester.
Owen Serle	16 Febr. 90	5 June, 1700. Had Leave given him to go into the Merchant Service.
		A Edward

PAGE OF OFFICIAL NAVY LIST, 1700.

(From the original in the Author's Collection.)

Yet already the Navy List had begun to assume much of the character which now distinguishes it. From the year of the Restoration there was an official recognition of the seniority of captains, according to the dates of their first commissions as such.[2] From

---

[1] Printed in Charnock, ii., 302.

[2] This naturally tended to the encouragement of a spirit of professional pride, and to the maintenance of naval traditions. Soon after the Revolution, also, naval officers'

about the year 1667 the separate and subordinate rank of Master and Commander[1] began to be conferred. From the Revolution there exist lists of Captains, Masters and Commanders, and Lieutenants, according to their seniority, and from the commencement of the eighteenth century or thereabouts such lists appeared from time to time in printed form. Reproductions of portions of two of these are given. One, dated April 18th, 1700, and issued from the Admiralty in the following July, is entitled, "A List of the Names of such Lieutenants who served in His Majesty's Fleet during the late War, One hundred whereof will from time to time be Entituled to Half-Pay, during their being out of Employment a-shoar, according to their Seniorities, and His Majesty's Establishment in that behalf." Among the lieutenants who figure in this list, and of whom the junior is Thomas Mathews, later the gallant but unfortunate commander-in-chief in the Mediterranean, there are many who are noted as "In the Merchant Service," or as "Had Leave given him lately to go another Voyage in the Merchant

(5)

27 May 1700.

A Lift of the Names of such Captains who Served in His Majesty's Fleet, during the late War, Fifty whereof will from time to time be Entituled to Half-Pay, during their being out of Employment on Shoar, according to their Seniority, and His Majesty's Establishment in that behalf, Dated the 18th day of April 1700.

Persons Names.	Date of First Commission as Captain.	Rate	For what Ship.	Which of them now Employ'd.
Munden John	23 July 88	6	Half-moon Prize	Commands off Sally.
Cornwall Woolfran	23 Aug 88	4	Dartmouth	
Fairborne Stafford	30 Aug. 88	5	Richmond	Gone to Newfoundland.
Myngs Chriftopher	3 Sept. 88	6	Sophya Prize	Captain of the Naffau.
Graydon John	9 Sept 88	6	Saudadoes	
Leake John	24 Sept. 88	5	Firedrake Bomb	
Robinfon Robert	26 Sept. 88	4	Crown	Captain of the Chichefter.
Ley Thomas	24 Octob 88	5	Mermaid Firefhip	Captain to the Admiral.
Foulks Symon	22 Dec. 88	5	Affurance	Captain of the Bedford.
Greenhill David	5 Mar 88	5	Cadiz Merch't Fir fhip	
Granvill John	1 2 Mar. 88	4	Advice	
Dilks Thomas	8 April 89	5	Charles Firefhip	Captain of the Bridgewater.
Coal Thomas	10 April 89	5	Pearle	
Bokenham William	7 May 89	5	Saphire	
Beaumont Bazill	21 May 89	5	Centurion	
Warren Thomas	28 May 89	5	John of Dublin Firefhip	Captain of the Harwich.
Jennings Thomas	29 May 89	5	Alexander Firefhip	Captain of the Revenge.
Hicks Gafper	30 May 89	4	Arch-Angel Hired	
Good Edward	6 June 89	3	Briftol	
Haughton Henry	13 June 89	3	Kent 2d Capt	
Martin Henry	16 June 89	4	Berwick	
Avery John	16 June 89	4	Sampfon Hired	
Robinfon Henry	17 June 89	5	Nonfuch	
Syncock Robert	27 June 89	5	Pearle	
Wilhart James	4 July 89	5	Europa Hired	
Whetftone William	30 July 89	4	Saphire Hired	
Price John	30 July 89	5	Kingfifher	
Jennings John	16 Nov. 89	4	Succefs Hired	
Fitz-Patrick Rich'd	Jan. 89	4	Affurance	Captain of the Defiance.
Main John	4 Febr. 89	5	Guarland	
Robinfon Thomas	5 Febr 89	5	Succefs Hired	
Kirkby Richard	7 Febr. 89	5	Richmond	
Crawley Thomas	7 Febr. 89			

B
Edwards.

PAGE OF OFFICIAL NAVY LIST, 1700.

(From the original in the Author's Collection.)

---

clubs began to flourish. Kempthorne, Holmes, Ashby, Berry, and Jennings, are known to have belonged to one which met on Tuesdays at the "Mitre," on Cornhill, as early as 1674. 'Brit. Fleet,' 496.

[1] Robert Best, appointed "Captain and Master" of the *Orange Tree* on September 13th, 1667, is usually supposed to have been the first to receive this commission: but it appears to have given him regular captain's rank and seniority; and separate commander's rank was possibly not introduced until a little later.

Service," etc. Several also are returned as serving as " midshipmen
extra." From these statements we get a glimpse of the existence
of an evil which has always afflicted the naval service after the
conclusion of any great war—the difficulty of obtaining employment.
Another list is made up of Captains' and Commanders' Lists, dated
August 18th, 1704. A third list is "A List of the Names of such
Captains who Served in His Majesty's Fleet, during the late War,
Fifty whereof will from time to time be Entituled to Half-Pay,
during their being out of Employment on Shoar, according to their
Seniority, and His Majesty's Establishment in that behalf," and is
dated, like the first-mentioned list, April 18th, 1700. It is noteworthy that several captains in this list are returned as serving at
the time as lieutenants in various ships of his Majesty. Thus,
John Balchen, afterwards the Admiral Sir John Balchen who went
down in the *Victory*, in 1744, though a captain of July 25th, 1697,
is said to be doing duty as first lieutenant of the *Burford*.

By an order of 1674, captains officiating as commodores in
command of squadrons were directed to wear a large red distinguishing pennant. This was the origin of the broad pennant, as it
is now called.

The entry of officers was modified by regulations of 1676. The
preamble to these ran as follows : " Whereas out of our royal desire
of giving encouragement to the families of better quality among our
subjects to breed up their younger sons to the art and practice of
navigation, in order to the fitting them for further employment in
our service, we have for some time past been graciously pleased at
our extraordinary charge to admit of the bearing of several young
gentlemen to the end aforesaid on board our ships, in the quality of
volunteers." These volunteers, called " volunteers by order," or
" King's Letter boys," were from that time forward regularly
entered at an age not exceeding sixteen years, and were paid £24 per
annum. But, in the meantime, entry in the old less regular ways
also continued. Among early King's Letter boys were Byng, Earl
of Torrington, and Sir John Norris. The regulations of 1676 were
followed by additional ones of 1677, which provided, among other
things, that candidates for a lieutenant's commission must be not
under twenty years of age, and must have served for three years at
sea, one of the years being served as midshipman. They also
provided for the examination of the candidate. In 1703, the period
of preliminary service was increased to six years : and in 1728, when

the institution of the King's Letter was abolished and the Naval Academy at Portsmouth was established, the candidates were ordered to be examined by the Navy Board, instead of by three naval officers. Thenceforward, no one could lawfully become a commander, R.N., unless he had first passed as a lieutenant; and no one could lawfully become a lieutenant without previous qualifying service. Still, for many years afterwards, the legal provisions were often more or less openly evaded. And, until 1794, the readiest way of entering upon the career of a naval officer was not by joining the Naval Academy, but by becoming the " servant " of an admiral, or captain, or by being rated as A.B., O.S., or even landsman.

Half-pay to a limited number of captains was granted in 1673, and to certain masters, in 1675; and in 1693 it was ordered that all flag-officers, and all captains of 1st, 2nd, 3rd, 4th, and 5th rates, and fireships, and the first lieutenants and masters of 1st, 2nd, and 3rd rates, who had served for a year in the same capacity in ships of those rates, or who had been in a general engagement, should have half-pay while on shore. At the same time, the sea-pay of officers was largely increased, but in 1700 it was again reduced, and a new scale of half-pay was adopted. The old and the revised scales were :—

		Full Pay.		Half-Pay.	
		1693.	1700.	1700.	
		£ s. d.	£ s. d.	£ s. d.	
	Admiral of the Fleet . .	6 0 0	5 0 0	2 10 0	
	Admiral.	4 0 0	3 10 0	1 15 0	
	Vice-Admiral	3 0 0	2 10 0	1 5 0	
	Rear-Admiral	2 0 0	1 15 0	17 6	
	Captain to the Admiral of the Fleet	2 0 0	1 15 0	17 6	
per day	Captain of a 1st rate . .	1 10 0	1 0 0	10 0	to 20 seniors, with war service.
	„ „ 2nd „ . .	1 4 0	16 0		
	„ „ 3rd „ . .	1 0 0	13 6		
	„ „ 4th „ . .	15 0	10 0	8 0	to 30 next senior, with war service.
	„ „ 5th „ . .	12 0	8 0		
	„ „ 6th „ . .	10 0	6 0		
	Lieutenant of 1st or 2nd rate	6 0	5 0	2 6	to 40 seniors, with war service.
	Lieutenant of 3rd, 4th, 5th, or 6th rates	5 0	4 0	2 0	to 60 next senior, with war service.
per month	Master of a 1st rate . .	14 0 0	9 2 0		
	„ „ 2nd „ . .	12 12 0	8 8 0	3 10 0	to 15 seniors, with war service.
	„ „ 3rd „ . .	9 7 4	6 6 0		
	„ „ 4th „ . .	8 12 4	5 12 0		
	„ „ 5th „ . .	7 15 0	5 2 8	2 16 0	to 15 next senior, with war service.
	„ „ 6th „ . .	6 12 0	4 13 4		
	Surgeon	5 0 0	5 0 0		

Table money to flag-officers was first allowed in 1664. It was granted to captains in 1686.[1] Gratuities for wounds were first given to captains in 1666. In the year last named, also, the proportion of servants to flag-officers was regulated. In 1693, the proportion of servants was revised and reduced, and it then stood : Admiral commanding-in-chief, 10 ; other flag-officers, 8 ; captains of 1st or 2nd rates, 6 ; captains of 3rd or 4th rates, 5 ; captains of 5th or 6th rates, 4.

There were, of course, in those days, no equivalents to the modern Colonial cadetships ; yet, from a very early period, the Navy was, at least to a slight extent, officered by persons of Colonial birth or training, and the entry of such was, in various ways, encouraged. Captain Robert Fairfax (November 15th, 1690), was a New

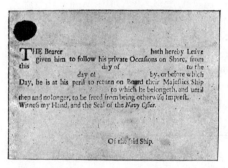

SEAMAN'S PASS AGAINST IMPRESSMENT, 1691.

(*From an original in the Author's collection.*)

[The seal in the corner is that of the Navy Office].

Englander. So was Captain Richard Short, his contemporary and friend. Captain Wentworth Paxton (April 7th, 1694), was another New Englander. And in 1706 a commission of vice-admiral was granted to Lieut.-Colonel Rhett, a gentleman of Charleston, who distinguished himself against the Spaniards. Some years later, in 1745, Mr. John Rous, master of an American privateer, was promoted by Sir Peter Warren to be a commander, R.N., as a reward for special services, and was subsequently posted.

The wages of seamen were not altered ; but various inducements were from time to time offered with the object of rendering the service more popular. For example, in 1672, a bounty of six weeks' pay was given to men entering themselves on board 1st and 2nd rates, and one of a month's pay to those entering themselves on board 3rd rates.[2] And in 1706, acts for the better manning of the

---

[1] By instructions dated July 15th, 1686, many admirable reforms were introduced with a view to the encouragement of officers of all ranks.

[2] On the other hand, it was directed in 1667 that men absenting themselves from vessels that were fitting should have 2s. 6d. for each day of absence deducted from their pay, and that the fines should be given to the men who remained on duty.

fleet provided, among other things, that conduct-money should be allowed, and that seamen turned over from one ship to another should receive the wages due in the former ship. But the press had to be continually made use of ere ships could be manned. Copies of two interesting passes entitling their holders to immunity from the press, are reproduced here. An Act of 1696 provided a new form of encouragement to the service. Its object was to establish a register for 30,000 seamen, who were to be in readiness at all times for the work of the Royal Navy, and who were to receive a premium or bounty yearly of 40s. each. It was ordered that none but such registered seamen were to be promoted to warrants or commissions in the Navy, and that such seamen, besides being entitled to a double share in prizes, should, if maimed or super-annuated, be admitted to Greenwich Hospital, where also, if they were killed on service, their widows and children should be entitled to relief. The Act was repealed in 1710.

But the greatest of all encouragements to seamen offered during the period under review were those held out to them by the establishment of Greenwich Hospital.

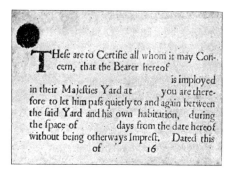

DOCKYARDMAN'S PASS AGAINST
IMPRESSMENT, 1691.

(From an original in the Author's collection.)

[The seal in the corner is that of the Navy Office.]

The project of founding a hospital for disabled seamen is attributed to Queen Mary, who was deeply impressed with the sufferings of the men wounded at the battle of La Hague ; and it was in 1694 that by letters patent the King and Queen devoted to the purposes of a national naval hospital " all that capital messuage lately built or in building by our Royal uncle King Charles the Second, and still remaining unfinished, commonly called by the name of our palace at Greenwich," together with the adjacent land. The motives and objects of the foundation are well set forth in the preamble to the Registered Seamen's Act of 1696, whereby a contribution of 6d. a month towards the maintenance of the Hospital from the wages of all seamen,

whether of the Royal Navy or mercantile marine, was made
obligatory :—

"Forasmuch as the strength and safety of this and other of H.M. realms and
dominions do very much depend upon the furnishing and supplying of H. M. Royal
Navy with a competent number of able mariners and seamen which may be in readiness
at all times for that service; and whereas the seamen of this kingdom have for a long
time distinguished themselves throughout the world for their industry and skilfulness
in their employments, and by their courage and constancy manifested in engagements
for the defence and honour of their native country; and for an encouragement to
continue this their ancient reputation and to invite greater numbers of H.M. subjects to
betake themselves to the sea, it is fit and reasonable that some competent provision
should be made that seamen who by age, wounds, or other accidents shall become
disabled for future service at sea, and shall not be in a condition to maintain themselves
comfortably, may not fall under hardships and miseries, may be supported at the public
charge, and that the children of such disabled seamen, and also the widows and children
of such seamen as shall happen to be slain or drowned in sea service, may, in some
reasonable manner, be provided and educated."

The King did, however, not limit his bounty to the grant of the
site ; he himself bestowed £2000 a year on the new foundation, and
invited his subjects to follow the example thus set by adding their
contributions ; and in the museum at Greenwich is still to be seen
the autograph roll of benefactors who have left a record of their
benevolence.[1] The architectural designs were by Sir Christopher
Wren, who supplied them gratuitously.

The management of the foundation was vested in Commissioners
who were nominated by the Crown. The government and discipline
of the hospital were eventually entrusted to a Master and Governor,
a Lieutenant-Governor, a Treasurer, four Captains, and eight Lieutenants, R.N.[2] Among the Governors have been Rodney and Lord
Hood ; among the Lieutenant-Governors, Captains William Locker
and Sir Richard Pearson, R.N. ; among the Captains, James Cook,
the navigator, figures ; and among the Treasurers have been John
Evelyn, the diarist, Sir Charles Saunders, and Lord Bridport. By
the early days of 1705 there were one hundred pensioner inmates.
The first of all these to enter, John Worley by name, is commemorated by a portrait, attributed to Sir James Thornhill, which
still hangs in the Painted Hall. In 1707, the benefits of the

---

[1] See a bicentenary article in the *Times*, July 14, 1894.

[2] The annual salaries of these were: Governor, £1000; Lieut.-Governor, £400;
Treasurer, £200; Captains, each, £230; Lieutenants, each, £115. There were also on
the staff, one clerk to the Governor at £50, and three clerks to the Treasurer, one at
£100 and two at £50. In addition, there were two chaplains, a physician, a surgeon, a
steward, a cook, nurses, etc.

hospital were extended to foreigners who had served two years in British ships of war, privateers, or merchantmen ; and unclaimed or forfeited prize-money, together with a percentage of all naval prize-money, was granted by Parliament to the establishment. An Act of 1710 directed that any seaman in the merchant service, who had been disabled in defending or taking a ship might be eligible for the hospital.

As in earlier periods, medals were very sparingly distributed, and there seem to have been no instances whatsoever of their having been officially given to seamen. For Rear-Admiral Dilkes's destruction of French shipping near Granville, in 1703, Queen Anne ordered gold medals to be struck for presentation to the admiral and officers ; but this is almost the sole example of the kind.

One of the most interesting and important naval innovations of the time was the establishment of a marine force. The origin of this force may be traced to the creation, on October 28th, 1664, of " The Duke of York and Albany's Maritime Regiment of Foot," [1] which was placed under the command of Sir William Killigrew, Bart., a nephew of George Monck, Duke of Albemarle. Upon the accession of James II., in February, 1685, the regiment was re-named " Prince George, Hereditary Prince of Denmark's Regiment of Foot," and on February 28th, 1689, it was disbanded. Early in the next year, two new regiments were raised, and called the First and Second Marines. These regiments were increased to four in 1698, under Colonels William Seymour, Edward Dutton Colt, Henry Mordaunt, and Thomas Brudenall. They again were disbanded in 1699. [2] The forces of 1664 and 1690 were, to a certain extent, connected one with another, several officers who had served in the original regiment serving in the later organisations, and there being, therefore, a certain continuity, if not of existence, at least of tradition. But to the end of the seventeenth century, the Marines in England were, to a large extent, experimental. At the beginning of the eighteenth, under Queen Anne, with the advantage of the experience already gained, the Marines were once more revived, and while still in their infancy, gained for themselves a reputation by their behaviour at the capture of Gibraltar.

The seventeenth century regiments were far from being un-

---

[1] Also called " The Admiral's Regiment."
[2] Edye : ' Hist. Records of the Royal Marines,' *passim.*

distinguished. Among their officers were Piercy Kirke, who was later colonel of the Old Tangier Regiment, "Kirke's Lambs," John Churchill, who became the great Duke of Marlborough, George Rooke, the victor of Malaga, Sir Clowdisley Shovell, and Sir William Jumper. Moreover, detachments of the regiments did good service in several of the actions of the second and third Dutch wars, and of the war with France. It should be added that, as early as 1666, provision [1] was made for land-officers (*i.e.* Marine officers, or, in their default, officers of troops serving as marines) to be borne in ships of all rates, except the 5th and 6th, and that cabins were allotted to them. In 1st and 2nd rates there was to be cabin accommodation for two, and in 3rd and 4th rates for one. There was no general regulation of cabins for subordinate naval officers until 1673, so that if, as it would appear was the case, a subaltern of Marines afloat in a 2nd rate in 1666 had a cabin to himself, he was probably better off than several naval officers of equivalent rank.

Among the general naval improvements of the time, many, for the most part of an administrative nature, were due to the energy and activity of H.R.H. James, Duke of York, and of Samuel Pepys. Among practical improvements that deserve mention here, a leading place should be given to the encouragement of the practice of sheathing ships, to better their speed, and to preserve their bottoms. Sheathing with lead had been usual in the Spanish Navy since the middle of the sixteenth century, and had been employed in the case of British merchant shipping for several years ere it was utilised for British men-of-war. The first ship of the Royal Navy to be so treated was the *Phœnix*, which was taken in hand at the desire of Charles II., and which was afterwards very favourably reported on. This was in 1670. Among ships to be lead sheathed soon afterwards, were the *Dreadnought, Henrietta, Mary, Lion, Bristol, Foresight, Vulture, Rose, Hunter, Harwich,* and *Kingfisher.* But the lead was not always applied in such a manner as to prevent the setting up of galvanic action between it and the ironwork of the ship ; several shipwrights were privately against the innovation ; Sir John Narbrough and other officers were dissatisfied with it, and it was at length discontinued. [2] The next proposal for the

---

[1] Add. MSS. 9311.

[2] See 'The New Invention of Mill'd Lead,' London, 1691; and 'An Account of several new Inventions and Improvements now necessary,' London, 1691. Sir William Petty was probably concerned in the preparation of both these little books.

preservation of ships' bottoms, was brought forward in 1696 by a gentleman who invented a composition, which was applied to the *Sheerness*. These efforts to deal with one of the most troublesome naval problems of the age, were unsuccessful; but they led to further experiments which, in the eighteenth century, attained their object.

From 1686, officers commanding his Majesty's ships were ordered to deposit perfect copies of their journals with the Secretary of the Admiralty; in the previous year, the earliest patents were granted for a process of rendering salt water fresh by distillation; in 1695, the brass box compass was first supplied to ships of the Royal Navy; in 1660, a Judge Advocate of the Fleet was for the first time appointed; and the office of Surgeon-General of the Fleet, by warrant from the Lord High Admiral, was created in 1664.

The very end of the reign of Anne witnessed the passing of an Act[1] which was destined to greatly influence and benefit the science of navigation. It provided for the offer of a reward to such person or persons as should devise a method for the discovery of the longitude at sea. Sir Isaac Newton and Dr. Halley suggested the Bill. Commissioners were appointed for judging proposals and conducting experiments. These, upon satisfying themselves of the reality or probability of the discovery, were directed to certify their opinion to the Commissioners of the Navy, who were authorised to make out a bill for any sum, not exceeding £2000, such as the Commissioners of Longitude might deem necessary for the making of experiments. If the discoverer of the longitude should determine it to one degree, or sixty geographical miles, he was to be rewarded with £10,000; if to two-thirds of a degree, with £15,000; and if to half a degree, with £20,000. To this offer, the world owes the invention and perfection of the chronometer; although the Act of Anne did not bear fruit until many years after it had been passed.

There were several improvements in shipbuilding. In 1663 and 1664, it was observed that Dutch and French built two-deckers of from sixty to seventy guns, carried their lower tiers four feet above the water, and could stow four months' provisions; whereas our

---

[1] This Act of 1714 was supplemented by Acts of Geo. II. and Geo. III.; and all the Acts were repealed by a new Act of 1774. Philip III. of Spain had offered a reward for the same discovery as early as 1598; and the States General had soon afterwards followed his example. Burney's edition of Falconer's 'Marine Dictionary,' 243.

corresponding vessels, copied from Dunquerque models, carried their guns but little more than three feet above the water, and stowed provisions for only ten weeks. The shipwrights, Sir Anthony Deane, and Messrs. Shish, Johnson, and Castle, set to work to remedy these imperfections; and there were presently built, among other vessels, the *Warspite* and the *Defiance*, which carried their lower guns four and a half feet above the water, and could stow provisions for six months. Ten years later we copied foreigners again, and again improved upon their work. In 1672–73 we were in alliance with the French; and it was once more noticed that their ships were more beamy, and more battle-worthy in a sea way, than ours. Sir Anthony Deane thereupon took measurements of the *Superbe*, one of the finest of the French seventy-fours, and, in 1674, launched the *Harwich*, which was generally agreed to be the best vessel of her rate then in existence.[1] Up to that time, British men-of-war were usually too narrow in proportion to their length, and, to be made efficient, had to be girdled.[2]

In the later years of Charles II., in consequence, to a large extent, of the Duke of York's deprivation of office by the operation of the Test Act, the Royal Navy fell into a very weakly and unserviceable state. James II., upon his accession, did his best to revive it, but soon discovered that his personal efforts alone would be of but little avail; and therefore, acting upon a suggestion of Pepys, he, in 1686, suspended the ordinary conduct of the Navy

---

[1] Pepys's 'Naval Minutes,' 268.

[2] There is no room for doubt that the French ships were, both then and long afterwards, immeasurably better sailers than the English. Charnock, after justly pointing out that, but for this superiority, it would have been almost impossible in 1708 for Forbin's squadron, in face of Byng's very much larger force, to have left Dunquerque, proceeded to the Firth of Forth, and returned to port having suffered only what, in the circumstances, was ridiculously small loss, goes on to say: "There remains behind a still stronger evidence of this alleged superiority which the French ships possessed in respect of form, over those of the English; and this arises from the particulars of the loss which the enemy sustained on this occasion. It was confined entirely to ships which had once been in the possession of, and had been built by, the English themselves. Of these, the *Salisbury*, of 50 guns, was taken. The *Blackwall*, of the same force, with the *Deal Castle* and *Squirrel*, of 24 guns each, either foundered at sea or were wrecked on the coast of Holland." . . . "It is no less worthy of remark that very few ships captured by the enemy, from the British, have ever continued long the property of their new possessors. If it has so happened that one of them, being in company with others of French construction, has ever fallen in with any English squadron, that ship, almost without exception, has been among those captured, and, most frequently, the first which has fallen." . . . "On the other hand, the recapture of any ship, frigate, or vessel of inferior rate from the British, which was originally French, is a circumstance extremely uncommon." 'Mar. Archit.' iii. 16, 17.

by the Commissioners, and appointed a Commission, partly made
up of the existing Commissioners of the Navy, and partly composed
of fresh blood, for the settlement of affairs, and the putting of the
fleet in order. He also directed £400,000 a year to be paid
quarterly from the Treasury for the furtherance of the objects
in view. The old Commissioners on this occasion were Anthony,
Viscount Falkland, Sir John Tippetts, Kt., Captain Sir Richard
Haddock, Kt., R.N., Sir Phineas Pett, Kt., Admiral Sir John
Narbrough, Kt., James Southern, Rear-Admiral Sir Richard
Beach, Kt., and Sir John Godwin, Kt. The new Commissioners
who were added to them were Sir Anthony Deane, Kt., Captain
Sir John Berry, Kt., R.N., William Hewer, and Balthasar
St. Michell. The Commission did its work with so much activity
and promptitude, that it was found possible to determine it on
October 12th, 1688, by which date the whole Navy, except three
ships, had been repaired or was under repair. There were eight
months' stores in the depôts, and all the vessels under construction
were upon the verge of completion.[1] The result was that at the
Revolution the Navy was much more efficient than it had been for
many years previously.

As the Revolution marks an important epoch as well in naval as
in national history, and as, moreover, owing to the enormous
development of the Navy after that time, it will be impossible, in
this work, to provide space wherein to give full lists of the
fleet at later periods, a state of the Navy as it existed on December 18th, 1688, is here appended.[2] Such a state is given at
length for the last time. Only summaries will be printed of
the states during the eighteenth century, details of particular
ships being, however, supplied as may be necessary for the illustration or elucidation of particular incidents.

---

[1] Pepys's ' Memoirs relating to the state of the Royal Navy,' 1690.

[2] This is compiled mainly from two lists in Pepys's ' Memoirs relating to the state
of the Royal Navy ' ; two lists in Charnock's ' History of Marine Architecture' ; MS. lists
in the Sergison Collection ; contemporary MS. lists in the collection of the author, and
notices in the State Papers. Certain particulars differ from those given for some of
the same ships in the list on pp. 107–112. Alterations in the modes of measurement,
and changes in armament and complement will account for the discrepancies.

Ships.	* Built. † Bought. ‡ Taken.	Length.		Beam.		Depth.		Draught.		Tons.	Guns.	Station or Condition.	Compt.
		Ft.	In.	Ft.	In.	Ft.	In.	Ft.	In.				
First Rates :													
St. Andrew . .	* 1670	128	0	44	0	17	9	21	6	1338	96	In repair	730
Britannia . .	* 1682	146	0	47	4	19	7½	20	0	1739	100	Refitting	780
Royal Charles .	* 1673	136	0	46	0	18	3	20	6	1531	100	In repair	780
St. George . .	* 1667	128	0	42	6	18	6	21	0	1229	96	Refitting	710
Royal James .	* 1675	132	0	45	0	18	4	20	6	1422	100	In repair	780
London . . .	* 1670	129	0	44	0	19	0	20	6	1328	96	,,	730
St. Michael . .	* 1669	125	0	40	8½	17	5	19	8	1101	90	Refitting	600
Royal Prince .	* 1670	131	0	45	10	19	0	21	6	1463	100	{Needing repair}	780
Sovereign [1] . .	* 1637	131	0	48	0	19	2	23	6	1605	100	In repair	815
Second Rates :													
Albemarle [2] . .	* 1680	140	11	44	4	19	7½	21	0	1395	90	,,	660
Coronation [3] .	* 1685	140	0	44	9	18	2	16	2	1427	90	,,	660
Duke . . .	* 1682	..		..		18	9	20	6	1546	90	,,	660
Duchess . . .	* 1679	132	6	44	6	18	3	20	0	1395	90	,,	660
Katherine . .	* 1664	124	0	41	0	17	3	20	0	1108	82	Refitting	540
Neptune . . .	* 1683	139	0	45	8	18	6	21	0	1497	90	In repair	660
Ossory . . .	* 1682	139	7	44	6	18	2	20	0	1395	90	,,	660
Sandwich . .	* 1679	132	6	44	6	18	3	20	0	1395	90	,,	660
Vanguard [4] . .	* 1678	126	0	45	0	18	1½	20	0	1357	90	,,	660
Victory (reblt.) [5]	* 1665	121	0	40	0	17	0	19	0	1029	82	{Needing repair}	530
Windsor Castle	* 1678	143	0	44	0	18	3	20	0	1462	90	In repair	660
Third Rates :													
Anne [6] . . .	* 1678	128	0	40	0	17	0	18	0	1089	70	,,	460
Berwick . . .	* 1679	128	0	40	0	17	0	17	0	1089	70	,,	460
Breda [7] . . .	* 1679	124	6	39	10	16	9	18	0	1055	70	,,	460
Burford . . .	* 1679	140	0	40	10½	17	3	18	0	1174	70	,,	460
Cambridge [8]. .	* 1666	121	0	37	10	16	4	17	6	881	70	Channel	420
Captain . . .	* 1678	138	0	39	10	17	2	18	0	1164	70	In repair	460
Defiance . .	* 1675	117	0	37	10	15	10	17	6	890	64	Channel	390
Dreadnought [9] .	* 1654	116	0	34	6	14	2	16	6	732	62	,,	355
Dunkirk . .	* 1651	112	0	33	4	14	0	17	0	662	60	{Commissioning}	340
Eagle [10] . . .	* 1679	120	0	40	6	17	0	18	0	1047	70	In repair	460
Edgar . . .	* 1668	124	0	39	8	16	0	18	4	994	64	{Commissioning}	445
Elizabeth [11] . .	' * 1679	137	6	40	11½	16	8½	18	0	1108	70	Channel	475
Essex . . .	* 1679	134	0	40	0	16	9½	18	0	1072	70	In repair	460
Exeter . . .	* 1680	137	0	40	4	16	9	18	0	1070	70	,,	460
Expedition . .	* 1679	120	0	40	9	17	0	18	0	1059	70	,,	460
Grafton [12] . .	* 1679	139	0	40	5	17	2	18	0	1174	70	,,	460
Hampton Court [12]	* 1678	131	0	39	10	17	0	18	6	1105	70	{Commissioning}	460
Harwich [13] . .	* 1674	123	9	38	10	15	8	17	6	993	70	In repair	420
Henrietta [14] . .	* 1654	116	0	35	7	14	4	17	0	781	62	Channel	355
Hope . . .	* 1678	124	5	40	0	16	9	10	6	1058	70	In repair	460
Kent . . .	* 1679	134	10	40	2	16	9½	18	0	1067	70	{Commissioning}	460
Lenox . . .	* 1678	131	0	39	8	17	0	18	0	1096	70	In repair	460

[1] Accidently burnt, 1696.
[2] Renamed *Union*, 1711.
[3] Wrecked off Ram Head, 1691.
[4] Sunk in the Great Storm, 1703.
[5] Condemned, 1690.
[6] Destroyed after the Battle of Beachy Head, 1690.
[7] Blown up at the siege of Cork, 1690.
[8] Wrecked near Gibraltar, 1694.
[9] Foundered off the N. Foreland, 1690.
[10] Lost off the Scillies, 1707.
[11] Taken by the French, 1704.
[12] Taken by the French, 1707.
[13] Wrecked off Mount Edgecumbe, 1691.
[14] Lost near Plymouth, December, 1689.

Ships.	* Built. † Bought. ‡ Taken.	Length.		Beam.		Depth.		Draught.		Tons.	Guns.	Station or Condition.	Compt.
		Ft.	In.	Ft.	In.	Ft.	In.	Ft.	In.				
Lion (reblt.) .	* 1658	108	0	35	4	15	6	17	6	717	60	In repair	340
Mary . . .	* 1649	116	0	35	0	14	6	17	0	777	62	Channel	355
Monck . . .	* 1659	108	0	35	0	13	11	16	0	703	60	Refitting	340
Monmouth . .	* 1668	118	9	36	10	15	6	18	0	856	66	{Home, to} pay off	400
Montagu (reblt.)	* 1675	117	0	36	6	15	0	17	4	829	60	In repair	355
Northumber-land [15] . .	* 1679	137	0	40	4	17	0	18	0	1050	70	,,	460
Royal Oak . .	* 1674	125	0	40	6	18	3	18	8	1107	74	{Needing} repair	460
Pendennis [16] .	* 1679	136	9	40	1	17	0	17	0	1093	70	Channel	460
Plymouth . .	* 1653	116	0	34	8	14	6	17	0	742	60	,,	340
Resolution [15] .	* 1667	120	6	37	2	15	6	17	0	885	70	,,	430
Restoration [15] .	* 1678	123	6	39	8	17	0	18	0	1032	70	In repair	460
Rupert . . .	* 1666	119	0	36	3	15	6	17	0	832	66	{Home, to} pay off	400
Stirling Castle [15]	* 1679	133	11	40	4	17	3	18	0	1114	70	In repair	460
Suffolk . . .	* 1680	138	0	40	6	16	9½	18	0	1066	70	,,	460
Swiftsure . .	* 1673	123	0	38	8	15	6	17	6	978	70	,,	420
Warspite . .	* 1666	118	0	38	9	15	6	17	6	942	70	{Commis-} sioning	420
York [15] . . .	* 1654	115	0	35	0	14	2	16	6	749	60	Channel	340
FOURTH RATES :													
Advice . . .	* 1650	100	0	32	2	12	3	15	0	544	48	,,	230
St. Albans . .	* 1687	107	0	32	10½	13	3	15	9	615	50	,,	280
Antelope . .	* 1653	101	0	31	0	13	0	16	0	516	48	,,	230
Assistance . .	* 1650	102	0	32	0	13	0	15	6	555	48	Jamaica	230
Assurance . .	* 1673	107	6	34	0	14	0	16	6	680	50	Channel	280
Bonadventure .	* 1683	102	6	32	2	12	4	15	6	561	48	,,	230
Bristol . . .	* 1653	104	0	31	0	13	8	15	8	534	48	,,	230
Charles, galley .	* 1676	114	0	28	6	18	7	12	0	492	32	{ Home, } paying off	220
Centurion [17]. .	* 1650	104	0	31	0	13	0	16	0	531	48	Channel	230
Constant War-wick [18] . .	† 1649	90	0	28	2	12	0	12	8	379	42	,,	180
Crown . . .	* 1654	100	0	31	7	13	0	16	0	535	48	Channel	230
St. David [19]. .	* 1667	107	0	34	9	14	8	16	8	685	54	,,	280
Deptford . .	* 1687	108	0	33	6	13	11	15	6	644	50	,,	280
Diamond . .	* 1651	105	6	31	3	13	0	16	0	548	48	,,	230
Dover . . .	* 1654	100	0	30	8	13	0	16	0	530	46	,,	182
Dragon . . .	* 1647	96	0	30	0	12	0	15	0	470	46	Sallee	220
Falcon . . .	* 1666	88	0	27	0	12	0	13	0	349	42	{ Home, } paying off	180
Foresight . .	* 1650	102	0	31	0	12	9	14	6	522	48	Channel	230
Greenwich . .	* 1666	108	0	33	9	14	6	15	0	654	54	,,	280
Hampshire . .	* 1653	101	9	29	9	13	0	14	5	479	46	In repair	220
Happy Return [18]	* 1654	104	0	33	2	13	0	17	0	609	54	Refitting	280
James, galley .	* 1676	104	0	28	1	10	2	12	0	436	30	In repair	200
Jersey [20]. . .	* 1654	132	0	32	1	13	6	15	0	556	48	Channel	230
Kingfisher . .	* 1675	110	0	33	8	13	0	13	0	663	46	Refitting	220
Mary Rose [21] .	* 1654	102	0	32	0	13	0	16	0	556	48	{ Home, } paying off	230

[15] Lost in the Great Storm, 1703.
[16] She had been lost in October 1689 on the Kentish Knock.
[17] Lost off Plymouth, December, 1689.
[18] Taken by the French, 1691.
[19] Had sunk at Plymouth in November 1689. She was weighed and made a hulk.
[20] Taken in the W. Indies, 1691.
[21] Taken by the French, July 1691.

Ships.	*Built. †Bought. ‡Taken.	Length.		Beam.		Depth.		Draught.		Tons.	Guns.	Station or Condition.	Compt.
		Ft.	In.	Ft.	In.	Ft.	In.	Ft.	In.				
Mordaunt[22]	† 1683	101	9	32	4½	13	0	16	0	567	46	Channel	230
Newcastle[23]	* 1653	108	0	33	1	12	2	16	0	628	54	„	280
Nonsuch[24]	* 1668	88	3	27	8	10	10	13	0	368	42	„	180
Oxford	* 1674	109	0	34	0	15	6	17	8	670	54	Refitting	280
Phœnix	* 1671	90	0	28	6	11	2	13	0	389	42	Channel	180
Portland	* 1652	105	0	33	13	13	0	16	0	608	50	„	240
Portsmouth[25]	* 1649	100	0	29	6	12	6	16	0	463	46	„	220
Reserve[23]	* 1650	100	0	32	10	12	8	..		576	48	Home, paying off	226
Ruby	* 1651	105	6	31	6	13	0	16	0	530	48	Channel	230
Sedgemoor[26]	..	..		..		..		..		..	48	Sallee	240
Swallow	* 1653	100	10	32	0	12	0	15	0	549	48	Channel	230
Sweepstake	* 1666	..		..		..		..		336	42	Commissioning	80
Tiger (rebuilt)	* 1681	104	0	32	8	13	8	15	6	590	48	Channel	230
Tiger Prize[27]	‡ 1678	..		..		..		..		649	46	Commissioning	200
Woolwich	..	..		..		..		..		716	54	Channel	280
FIFTH RATES:													
Rose	* 1674	75	0	24	0	10	0	12	6	229	28	New England	105
Sapphire	* 1675	86	0	27	0	11	0	13	2	333	32	Sallee	135
SIXTH RATES:													
Drake	* 1652	85	0	18	0	7	8	9	0	146	16	Jamaica	65
Dumbarton[28]	‡ 1685	77	8	22	1	10	0	11	0	191	20	Virginia	70
Fanfan	* 1665	44	0	12	0	5	8	5	6	32	4	In repair	30
Greyhound	* 1672	75	0	21	6	9	0	8	6	184	16	„	75
Lark	* 1675	74	0	22	6	9	2	9	0	199	18	Channel	85
Soldadoes	* 1673	74	0	21	6	10	0	9	6	180	16	„	75
BOMBS:[29]													
Firedrake	* 1648	..		..		..		..		202	12	„	75
Portsmouth	* 1674	59	0	21	1	9	0	7	6	133	10	In repair	35
Salamander	* 1687	..		..		..		..		110	10	„	35
FIRESHIPS:													
Cadiz Merchant[30]	† 1688	..		..		..		..		320	12	Commissioning	45
Cygnet	† 1688	..		..		..		..		100	6	Channel	30
Charles	† 1688	..		..		..		..		90	6	„	20
Charles and Henry	† 1688	..		..		..		12	0	120	6	„	25
Dartmouth[31]	* 1655	80	0	25	10	10	0	12	0	265	..	„	55
Eagle	† 1654	85	6	25	6	10	0	12	0	305	12	Guard, at Sheerness	45
Elizabeth and Sarah	† 1688	..		..		..		..		100	6	Channel	25
Guardland	* 1654	81	0	24	6	10	0	11	6	263	..	„	50
Guernsey	* 1654	80	0	24	0	10	0	12	0	245	..	„	50
Half Moon[3?]	..	..		..		..		..		..	8	„	35
Mermaid	* 1651	86	0	25	0	10	0	12	0	268	..	Commissioning	50
Owner's Love	..	..		..		..		..		217	10	Commissioning	40

22 Bought from Lord Mordaunt.
23 Lost in the Great Storm, 1703.
24 Taken by the French, 1693.
25 Had been taken by the French.
26 Included by Pepys by error. She had been lost in St. Margaret's Bay in January 1689.
27 Taken from the Algerines.
28 Taken from the Earl of Argyle.
29 Each of these carried two mortars.
30 Expended at La Hougue, 1692.
31 Lost off Mull, November 1690.

Ships.	* Built. † Bought. ‡ Taken.	Length.		Beam.		Depth.		Draught.		Tons.	Guns.	Station or Condition.	Compt.
		Ft.	In.	Ft.	In.	Ft.	In.	Ft.	In.				
Pearl . . .	* 1651	..		..		..		..		260	10	Channel	50
Richard and John . . }		..		..		..		..		..	..	„	20
St. Paul [32] . .	‡ 1679	74	0	25	9	11	2½	14	0	260	10	„	45
Richmond . .	* 1655	72	0	23	6	9	9	11	6	211	..	„	
Roebuck . . .	† 1688	..		..		..		..		80	6	„	16
Rose, Sallee prize[33]	‡ 1684	64	0	23	0	10	2	10	8	180	..	?	
Samson . . .	† 1678	78	0	24	1	10	8	12	0	240	12	{Guard, at Sheerness}	50
Sophia [34] . .	‡ 1685	72	3	20	1	9	6	11	0	243	6	Channel	22
Speedwell . .	† 1688	..		..		..		..		120	8	„	25
Supply . . .	† 1688	..		..		..		..		70	6	„	20
Swan . . .	† 1673	74	0	25	0	10	0	11	0	246	6	„	22
Thomas and Elizabeth[35] .}	† 1688	..		..		..		..		184	10	{Commis- sioning}	40
Unity . . .	† 1688	..		..		..		..		120	6	Channel	25
Young Spragge[36]	† 1673	46	0	18	0	9	0	8	6	79	10	{Guard, at Ports- mouth}	20
Hoys:													
Delight . . .	* 1680	55	5	18	5½	8	6¾	..		100	..	In repair	4
Lighter . . .	* 1672	28	0	18	0	7	6	6	6	65	..	„	3
Marigold . .	* 1653	32	0	14	0	7	0	7	0	33	..	„	5
Nonsuch . .	* 1686	53	8¾	18	10½	8	4¾	..		81	..	„	5
Transporter .	* 1677	66	9	17	0	10	11	..		70	..	„	5
Unity, horseboat	..	58	6	15	9	6	5	6	0	40	..	„	4
Hulks:													
Arms of Hoorn.	† 1673	106	0	30	3	12	0	18	0	516	..	„	8
Arms of Rotter- dam[37]. . }	‡ 1673	119	0	39	6	18	9	18	6	987	..	„	7
French Ruby .	‡ 1666	112	0	38	2	16	6	18	6	868	..	„	4
St. George . .	* 1622	116	0	38	0	14	10	18	0	891	..	„	2
Leopard . . .	* 1659	109	0	33	9	15	0	17	3	645	..	Sallee	33
Maria Prize [38] .	‡ 1684	..		..		..		..		120	..	Gibraltar	
Pontoon . . .	*1678–80	70	0	14	0	6	0	4	0	80	..	„	3
State-House [39] .	‡ 1667	90	0	30	4	11	6	15	0	440	..	In repair	4
Ketches:													
Deptford . .	* 1665	52	0	18	0	9	4	8	4	89	10	Virginia	40
Kingfisher . .	† 1684	47	9	15	6	8	5½	7	3	61	4	Jersey	15
Quaker . . .	† 1671	54	0	18	2	9	0	9	6	94	10	Channel	40
Smacks:													
Royal Escape .	† 1660	30	0	14	3	7	9	7	0	34	8	In repair	10
Little London .	* 1672	26	0	11	0	5	8	4	0	165	2	„	2
Sheerness . .	* 1673	28	0	11	6	6	0	5	6	18	2	„	2
Shish . . .	* 1670	38	0	11	0	6	6	5	6	18	..	„	2
Tow-Engine .	† ..	..		..		..		..		10	..	„	2
Yachts:													
Charlotte . .	* 1677	61	0	21	0	9	0	7	10	143	8	„	20
Cleveland . .	* 1671	53	4	19	4	7	6	7	6	107	6	Channel	30
Fubbs . . .	* 1682	63	0	21	0	9	6	7	10	148	12	„	40
Henrietta . .	* 1679	65	0	21	8	8	3	8	9	162	8	In repair	20
Jemmy . . .	* 1662	31	0	12	6	6	0	3	6	25	4	„	4
Isabella . . .	* 1683	60	0	18	11	8	11½	7	9	114	8	Channel	30

[32] A Dutch vessel recovered from the Algerines.
[33] Also called *Sallee Rose.*
[34] Taken from the Earl of Argyle.
[35] Expended at La Hougue, 1692.

[36] Bought from Adm. Sir Ed. Spragge.
[37] A Dutch East Indiaman.
[38] Taken from Sallee.
[39] *I.e., Stadthuis,* taken from the Dutch.

Ships.	* Built. † Bought. ‡ Taken.	Length.		Beam.		Depth.		Draught.		Tons.	Guns.	Station or Condition.	Compt.
		Ft.	In.	Ft.	In.	Ft.	In.	Ft.	In.				
Isle of Wight .	* 1673	31	0	12	6	6	0	6	0	25	4	In repair	5
Katherine . .	* 1674	56	0	21	4	8	6	7	9	135	6	Channel	30
Kitchen . . .	* 1674	56	0	21	4	8	6	7	9	125	6	„	30
Mary . . .	* 1677	66	6	21	6	8	9	7	6	166	6	„	30
Merlin . . .	* 1666	53	0	19	6	6	0	7	4	109	6	⎰Guard, at⎱ Ports- mouth	30
Monmouth . .	* 1666	52	0	19	6	8	0	7	3	103	6	Ireland	20
Navy . . .	* 1673	48	0	17	6	7	7	7	1	74	6	Guernsey	20
Queenborough .	* 1671	31	6	13	4	6	6	5	9	29	4	In repair	4

NOTE.—A full list of the losses during the period 1688-1714 will be found in the Appendix to Chap. XXIV., p. 535.

The first approach to a regular establishment of men and guns in the Navy was devised in 1677, when, upon the recommendation of the Navy Board and certain officers, it was decided to build thirty new ships, viz., one first-rate, nine second-rates, and twenty third-rates. This establishment was as follows :—

Guns.	1st Rates.	2nd Rates.	3rd Rates.	Men per Gun.
Cannon (42 prs.)	26	..	..	8
Demi-Cannon (32 prs.)	..	26	26	6
Culverins (18 prs.)	28	26	..	5
12-prs.	..	..	26	4
Sakers	44	36	14	3
3-prs..	2	2	4	2
	100	90	70	

In addition to the men per gun, the first-rates had complements of 296, the second rates of 262, and the third-rates of 160,[1] subsequently reduced to 150. Towards the end of the period, 1660–1714, guns began to be denominated only according to the weights of their shot, and the names cannon, culverins, etc., disappeared.

The improvements in ordnance were, upon the whole, unimportant ; and it is necessary to here mention but one of them. This was the introduction of the gun known as the cushee piece, a short weapon throwing a small shell or carcase instead of an ordinary shot. It was the invention of Richard Leake, Master Gunner of

---

[1] Derrick's ' Memoirs of the Royal Navy,' App. 28, p. 270.

England, and it seems to have been first employed in action by his son, Commander John Leake, of the *Firedrake*, at the battle of Bantry Bay.

The bomb-ketch became, after the Revolution, a feature in almost every English fleet. " Machines," or " infernals," were also introduced for a time as substitutes for the older fireships, but were soon discredited. Some notice of these will be found in the succeeding chapters.[1]

The policy illustrated by the Navigation Act of the Commonwealth was persisted in under Charles II. In 1660,[2] an Act was passed providing that all colonial produce should be exported in English vessels ; that no man might establish himself as a factor

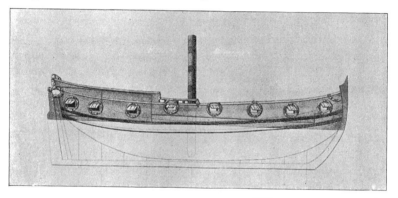

AN ENGLISH BOMB KETCH OF 1692.

(After Charnock's copy of the original draught.)

in the colonies ; and that various sorts of colonial produce could be exported only to England and her dependencies. In 1663, it was enacted that the colonies should receive no goods whatsoever in foreign vessels. And in 1672 the Navigation Act of Charles II. prohibited the introduction of nearly all goods except in English ships manned by crews of which at least three-fourths were English.

In the last year of Anne, the law of wrecks was amended, the statute, 3 Edward III., being confirmed, and it being further enacted that in case either the Queen's or merchants' ships, riding at anchor near the wreck, should neglect to give assistance upon its being demanded, the commander of any such ship snould forfeit

---

[1] And especially on p. 476*n*.   [2] 12 Car. II. c. 18.

£100 to the owners of the vessel in distress. And to encourage the rendering of assistance, there was provision for the payment, as salvage, of rewards by the owners, and, in default, for the detention of the ships and goods pending satisfaction. Under George I., this Act was made perpetual.

In 1691, one dry and two wet docks were ordered to be constructed at Portsmouth. About three years later new docks and storehouses, as well as several official residences, were built at Plymouth.[1] Money for building a wharf and further storehouses at Portsmouth was voted in 1704; and in 1710 the purchase of land was authorised to facilitate the better fortification of the Royal Yards at Portsmouth, Chatham, and Harwich. In 1693 there was a project to utilise Falmouth as a naval port, and to build docks there; yet, though the harbour was surveyed with this view, nothing further seems to have ever been done in the matter.

The marking, buoying, and lighting of the coasts received much attention. In 1694, for example, the Gilkicker mark, near Gosport, was erected, and the Horse buoy was moored at Spithead. In 1691, Mr. Walter Whitfield had suggested to Trinity House the erection of a lighthouse on the Eddystone, to be built at his expense, in return for certain dues granted by patent from the Crown. This lighthouse was designed and constructed by Mr. Henry Winstanley, of Littlebury, Essex, and a light was first shown from it in October, 1698. In 1699, Winstanley strengthened the tower, and increased its height from eighty to one hundred and twenty feet. He was in the building when the great storm of November 26th, 1703, swept it away. Its place was presently taken by a structure designed and completed by Mr. John Rudyerd, a silk mercer of Ludgate Hill, assisted by two shipwrights, Messrs. Smith and Norcott, of Woolwich Dockyard. This tower, which was of wood, built around a basic core of granite, was ninety-two feet high to the top of the ball; and a light, supplied by twenty-four candles, the five largest weighing two pounds each, was first shown from it on July 28th, 1708. The lighthouse survived until 1755, when it was accidentally burnt down.

The art of marine surveying made great progress, and many excellent charts, especially of home waters, date from the period under review. Among the most noted cartographers were Captain Christopher Gunman, whose name is commemorated in the

---

[1] Plymouth Citadel had been rebuilt under Charles II.

Gunman Sand, which he discovered on May 31st, 1670, and which lies off Dover; and Captain Greenville Collins (1679), whose charts are extremely numerous and accurate.

The Union with Scotland, effected on May 1st, 1707, revived and rendered permanent an arrangement which had already subsisted for a short time under the Commonwealth, but which had ceased at the Restoration. The two kingdoms were made one, under the title of Great Britain ; the few vessels [1] composing the Scots Navy became British, and the already blended national ensigns of the two countries were, by proclamation of July 8th, 1707, ordered to be worn by the vessels of all British subjects, in the form of a canton on a red flag, the Jack itself being reserved as the peculiar distinction of Queen's ships.

[1] The ships taken over, with their commanders, were the *Edinburgh,* Thomas Gordon; the *Glasgow,* James Hamilton; and the *Dumbarton Castle,* Matthew Campbell. All were small and of little importance.

CHAPTER XXIII.

campagne au large—Loss of the *Coronation*, etc.—Projected invasion of England —Supposed disaffection in the fleet—The Battle of Barfleur, May 19th, 1692—Death of Carter—Tourville's able tactics—Chase of the French—Destruction of French ships at Cherbourg and La Hougue, May 22nd and 23rd, 1692—The command again in commission—The disaster to the Smyrna convoy—Decline of the French navy—The war against commerce—Loss of the *Sussex*, etc.—Russell winters in the Mediterranean—Russell in the Channel—The Treaty of Rijswijk—The Navy during the Peace—Rooke's expedition to Copenhagen in 1700—The War of the Spanish Succession—Death of William III.––The war in America—Benbow in the West Indies—His action with Ducasse, August 20th to 24th, 1702—Misbehaviour of some of Benbow's captains—Death of Benbow—Wager in the West Indies—Capture of the *San Josef*—Misbehaviour of some of Wager's captains—The war in Europe—The attack on Cadiz, 1702—Causes of the failure—The galleons at Vigo—Rooke at Vigo Bay, October 12th, 1702—Gallantry of Hopsonn —Shovell in the Mediterranean—The Great Storm of 1703—Barcelona bombarded —Rooke and the French fleet—Capture of Gibraltar, 1704—Behaviour of the Marines—Battle off Velez Malaga, August 13th, 1704—Leake in the Mediterranean —Siege of Gibraltar—Peterborough and Shovell in the Mediterranean—Capitulation of Barcelona—Surrender of Cartagena—Storming of Alicant—Norris at the mouth of the Var—Siege of Toulon—Death of Shovell—Reduction of Minorca—Byng, Whitaker and Baker in the Mediterranean—Norris captures Cette and Agde—Jennings in the Mediterranean—Treaty of Utrecht—Results of the war.

MEDAL COMMEMORATIVE OF THE ENGLISH CLAIM
TO THE DOMINION OF THE SEA, 1665.

(*From an original kindly lent by H.S.H. Captain
Prince Louis of Battenberg. R.N.*)

THE comparatively brief period of English history included between the restoration of Charles II. in 1660, and the death of Queen Anne in 1714, witnessed the outbreak and conclusion of no fewer than four great naval wars. The earliest of these was the Second Dutch War, which, begun informally very soon after the Restoration, assumed a regular and official character at the commencement of 1665, and was terminated in 1667 by the Treaty of Breda. In the course of it, England had as her opponents Holland and France, and fought without allies. The next was the third Dutch War, of 1672–73. In this conflict England had the co-operation of France. The third was the war of the Grand Alliance, begun in 1689, terminated by the Treaty of Rijswijk in 1697, and waged by England, Holland, the Empire, and Spain against France. The fourth and last was the war of the Spanish Succession, declared in 1702, and ended by the Peace of Utrecht in 1713. Again, England, Holland, and the Empire, as well as several minor powers, were ranged against

France, which had the support of the majority of the Spanish people, and of Cologne, Bavaria, and Mantua.

The naval operations of each of these wars may be divided into two categories. There were, first, the operations of fleets, operations which had a distinct and immediate influence upon the spirits and *moral* of the whole body of combatants, and so upon the issue of the strife; and there also were the operations of small detached squadrons and of single ships, operations which, although of much interest and importance in themselves, did not form any essential part of the strategic campaign, and did not materially affect the final result.

For the sake of convenience, and in order, so far as possible, to present the really essential story of each war in a consecutive form, the two categories of operations will be separately dealt with — the major operations in this, and the minor operations in the following chapter. For the same reasons a similar distinction will be made, whenever it may appear to be desirable, in the case of the wars that have taken place since 1714. It is believed that the clearness and continuity of the main narrative could not but suffer by a frequent introduction of episodal scenes which, no matter their intrinsic attractiveness, have no easily definable bearing upon the general issue, and that such scenes will be more fitly treated of apart.

The peace of 1654 had brought the first Dutch War to a conclusion but had not destroyed the ill-feeling between England and the Netherlands. The Dutch had been obliged to acknowledge the English claim to the honour of the flag, to submit to the irksome provisions of the Navigation Act, and to undertake to exclude members of the House of Orange from the office of Stadtholder and from the Admiralship of Holland. Their trade had also suffered most severely. On the other hand, England had not secured any effective satisfaction for the massacre of Amboyna. Thus there were left many smouldering sparks which awaited but a breath to fan them into flame. The breath was applied very soon after the Restoration. Complaints reached England of high-handed action by the Dutch East and West India Companies, of the seizure of English ships, of interference with English trade in remote regions, and of omission on the part of the Dutch to carry out certain stipulations of the treaty—notably, those for the handing over of Cape Coast Castle, on the Gold Coast, and of Pulo Ron, in the East India Archipelago. These acts of the Dutch led to the making of reprisals, chiefly under the direction of Commodore (afterwards Admiral Sir) Robert Holmes, an account of whose proceedings will be found in the next chapter.   The tension between the two countries was intensified, on the one side, by the discovery of a Dutch project for seizing Cormantyne, an English fort, and, on the other, by the English capture of New Amsterdam, now New York, which Holmes took, not merely by way of reprisals, but also in

H.R.H. JAMES, DUKE OF YORK, LORD HIGH ADMIRAL
(AFTERWARDS JAMES II.).

(After the portrait by Sir G. Kneller.)

virtue of a claim of old standing.   Still further friction was occasioned by the desertion by the Dutch Admiral De Ruijter of the English Admiral Sir John Lawson at a moment when the two were about to co-operate against the Algerine pirates; by De Ruijter's counter-reprisals on the African coast and on the high seas; and, finally, by Admiral Sir Thomas Allin's attack upon the Dutch Smyrna fleet off Cadiz.   In this action, as will be shown later,

Captain Pieter van Brakel, senior officer in charge of the Dutch convoy, was killed. War, in consequence, was declared by the Dutch—who had encouragement from France—on January 14th, and by the English on February 23rd, 1665. France, after some hesitation, went to the active assistance of her ally a year later, and on January 16th, 1666, also declared war against England.

Both sides displayed extraordinary energy in their preparations. Holland arrested both ships and men belonging to the Dutch East India Company, and laid an embargo on all other craft; but, with a view to creating sympathy among British merchants, she presently released such English and Scots vessels as had been seized in Dutch harbours at the outbreak of hostilities. The English administration worked feverishly to make good the numerous faults and deficiencies which were revealed by the crisis, and, in the meantime, repaid the diplomatic generosity of the Hollanders by freeing such Dutch ships as had been seized in British ports.

Of the two grand fleets the British was the first to be ready. It consisted of 109 men-of-war, including "frigates" and armed hired vessels, and twenty-eight fireships and ketches, mounting in all 4192 guns, and having on board 21,006 seamen, marines, and soldiers. The flag officers in command were: the Lord High Admiral, H.R.H. James, Duke of York, K.G., with Sir William Penn as Captain of the Fleet, in the *Royal Charles*, 80, Captain John Harman, and Admirals H.R.H. Prince Rupert (White) and Edward Montagu, Earl of Sandwich (Blue); Vice-Admirals Sir John Lawson (Red), Sir Christopher Myngs[1] (White), and Sir George Ayscue (Blue); and Rear-Admirals Sir William Berkeley (Red), Robert Sansom (White), and Thomas Tyddiman[2] (Blue).

This fleet, sailing on April 21st, proceeded with as little delay as possible off the Texel, within which the Netherlands fleet was assembling; and it began a blockade of the Zuider Zee and of the neighbouring coasts, chiefly with a view to cutting off home-coming Dutch vessels, but with the subsidiary design of engaging the Dutch off their own shores should they venture to put to sea. The Duke

---

[1] Christopher Myngs. Born probably about 1620. Was a captain during the first Dutch War. Knighted by Charles II. Vice-Admiral (W.) in the action of June 3rd, 1665. Killed on June 4th, 1666.

[2] Thomas Tyddiman. Born probably about 1620. Captain of the *Resolution*, 1660. Acting Rear-Admiral in the Channel, 1664. Flag-officer in most of the actions of the Second Dutch war. Knighted, 1665. Led the attack on Bergen, 1665. Died, 1668.

of York cruised on and off for more than a fortnight, capturing a
number of merchantmen ; and then, his fleet having suffered somewhat from bad weather, especially on May 8th, he drew off.   His
desire appears to have been, ere he returned to England, to intercept
Vice-Admiral M. A. De Ruijter, who, as has been seen, had been
making counter-reprisals on the West Coast of Africa, and who was

JACOB VAN WASSENAER, LORD OF OBDAM, LIEUTENANT-ADMIRAL OF
HOLLAND AND WESTVRIESLAND.

(After the engraved portrait by J. Suijderhoef.)

supposed to be homeward bound ; but provisions fell short, and the
Duke had to forego his intention and anchor off Harwich, and in the
mouth of the Thames.

In the meantime a formidable Dutch fleet had been got together.
It consisted, in addition to several vessels which were ultimately left
behind, of 103 men-of-war, seven yachts and dispatch vessels, eleven
fireships, and twelve galliots, mounting in all 4869 guns, and having

on board 21,556 officers and men.[1] It was divided into no fewer
than seven squadrons[2] of nearly equal strength, each made up
of three divisions. The squadron commanders, in the order of
their seniority, were: Jacob van Wassenaer, Lord of Obdam, Commander-in-Chief, in the *Eendracht*, 76 ; Lieut.-Admiral Jan Evertsen,
Lieut.-Admiral Egbert Meussen Cortenaer Lieut.-Admiral Augustus
Stellingwerf, Vice-Admiral Cornelis M. Tromp,[3] Vice-Admiral
Cornelis Evertsen,[4] and Vice-Admiral Volkhard Adriaensze Schram.
Each of these had under him two junior flag-officers, or captains
acting as such; so that, in the battle which ensued, the extraordinary number of twenty-one Dutch and nine British flags flew.

The Dutch put to sea on May 13th and 14th, and, a few days
later, Obdam, who cruised in the neighbourhood of the Dogger
Bank, was able to report to his Government that, on the evening of
May 20th, he had sighted several vessels which he had at first
supposed to be the English fleet ; that he had approached them and
found them to be English-Hamburg merchantmen, convoyed by a
man-of-war of thirty-four guns ; and that he had captured all. The
ships, he said, were laden with pitch, hemp, tar, cables, cable-yarn,
planks, iron, copper, copper wire, cloth, etc., and were very valuable
prizes. The number of vessels taken was, according to the English
accounts, ten, inclusive of the man-of-war ; but some Dutch writers[5]
claim that twenty-two prizes were made. Obdam himself does not
in his dispatch mention any specific number.

This capture involved a very serious loss, not only to the
merchants concerned, but also to the British Government, which
was still largely dependent for naval stores upon the countries lying
on and near the shores of the Baltic, and which, at the moment,
had the greatest need of such supplies. The disaster consequently
caused much outcry, and led to the fleet being immediately hurried
again to sea. It weighed from the buoy at the Gunfleet on May 29th,

---

[1] List in the Rijks Archief. A second official Dutch list gives the number of
officers and men as 21,631.

[2] The Dutch squadrons were thus distinguished :—(1) flag at the main ; (2) flag
at the fore ; (3) flag at the mizzen ; (4) yellow pennant ; (5) red pennant with white
stripe ; (6) white pennant with red stripe ; (7) blue pennant with yellow stripe. List
in the Rijks Archief.

[3] Cornelis Martenszoon Tromp, son of the great Admiral M. H. Tromp. Born
1629. Created a baronet by Charles II., March 25th, 1675. Liutenant-Admiraal-
Generaal of Holland and Westvriesland. Died, May 22nd, 1691.

[4] " The Old."

[5] *E.g.* Van den Bosch : ' Leven van J. van Wassenaer.'

and lay for the night off Aldborough, where the Duke seems to have received news that the enemy was not far from him. The fleet subsequently proceeded to Southwold Bay, where it anchored at 6 A.M. on June 1st.

Obdam, if the *personnel* of his force had been better than it was, might have followed the retiring English to their coasts early in May, and dealt them a serious blow ere they were once more ready for sea; but he realised that the discipline of many of his ships was bad, that jealousy existed among his officers, and that some of the impressed vessels of the East India Company were not to be depended upon. He, therefore, had no desire, even at the end of the month, to force an action until such time as he should find himself more advantageously situated. But his Government, which did not see things with his eyes, ordered him to keep close in with the English coast, and to find and engage the foe;[1] and he obeyed.

At mid-day, consequently, on June 1st, it was reported to the Duke of York in Southwold Bay that the enemy was about six miles to the E.S.E.; whereupon the commander-in-chief weighed and put to sea. There is much contradictory evidence as to the direction of the wind at the time. It is probable, however, that it was favourable to the Dutch, and that Obdam's only reason for not attacking at once was that his ships were scattered, and that he desired to enable the whole of his force to come up. He consequently kept away to seaward during the afternoon and night. On the morning of June 2nd, he was visible about five miles to the S.E., and at 8 A.M. Lowestoft was eight miles to the N.W., and the enemy had closed to a distance of three miles or less. But that day there was no farther approach until towards evening. The wind then shifted from E. to S., later veering to S.W. by W.,[2] with the result that, at about 2.30 A.M. on June 3rd, the fleets were some fourteen miles N.N.E. of Lowestoft, and the English had the weather-gauge.

Prince Rupert led the van, the Duke the centre, and Sandwich the rear. At 3.30 A.M. the action began, and it would appear that the two fleets, each in line ahead, passed one another on opposite tacks in the set manner of the time, though some accounts declare that they passed through one another. Having passed, each turned

---

[1] Dispatch of May 29th; Aitzema, 446.
[2] Coventry's report to the Duke of York says S.W.

sixteen points and renewed the encounter. The Dutch seem to
have altered course in succession, their van remaining their van,
their centre their centre, and their rear their rear; but the English
altered course simultaneously, so that, at the second passage, their
rear became their van. The Dutch in vain strove to gain the
weather-gauge; and it was probably owing to these efforts that at
about 1 P.M., in the course of the second or a subsequent passage,

CORNELIS TROMP AS LIEUTENANT-ADMIRAL OF THE MAZE.

(After the engraved portrait by A. Blotelingh.)

[This represents him as he was at the time of the third Dutch war. A portrait of him in
his old age will be found at p. 320.]

Sandwich's squadron found itself mixed up with the Dutch centre,
and, either by accident or by design, broke through it, so cutting
the enemy's fleet into two parts. It is likely that it was by accident, for the English accounts admit that by that time, owing to the
smoke, there was great confusion, and that friendly vessels narrowly
escaped firing into one another. Indeed, there is no doubt that,
after a certain time had elapsed, order on both sides almost ceased to
exist, and the action degenerated into a gigantic *mêlée*.

In the course of the struggle, Opdam, in the *Eendracht*, 76,[1] found himself close to the Duke of York in the *Royal Charles*, 80 ; and the two commanders-in-chief promptly and hotly engaged one another. The *Eendracht* attempted to board the *Royal Charles*, but without success. She nevertheless plied her broadside so well and continuously that the Duke was in the greatest danger of being sunk

EGBERT MEUSSEN CORTENAER, VICE-ADMIRAL OF HOLLAND, WESTVRIESLAND.

(From the engraving by Jan Kralinge.)

or of having to surrender. Charles Berkeley, first Earl of Falmouth, Mr. Boyle, second son of the Earl of Burlington, and Lord Muskerry, with others, were killed at the Duke's side by a single chain-shot, and his Royal Highness was covered with their blood, and even,

---

[1] This was her nominal force, though English writers call her an 80 and even an 84. Her real force was only three 36-pounders, twenty-two 24-pounders, fourteen 18-pounders, twelve 12-pounders, and twenty-two 6-pounders : total, seventy-three guns. List in Rijks Archief.

according to one account, slightly wounded in the hand by a splinter from Mr. Boyle's skull. But, at the height of the fight, the *Eendracht* suddenly blew up, only five souls out of four hundred and nine who had gone into action in her escaping with their lives. It is probable that the accident was occasioned by the ignition of some loose cartridges and the extension of the flames to the powder-room, but popular tradition in Holland ascribes the catastrophe to another cause, and declares that a negro servant of Obdam fired the magazine from motives of revenge.

The explosion, and the loss of their commander-in-chief,[1] increased the confusion of the Dutch, many of whom began to give way and to put before the wind. Yet some of the squadrons, and numerous individual ships, still gallantly held their ground. Jan Evertsen assumed the chief command, but the news of his having done so did not reach Cornelis Tromp, who, knowing of the death of Obdam, and presently learning also that Cortenaer[2] had succumbed to a wound in the thigh, and that Stellingwerf had been killed by a ball through the body, imagined himself to be the senior surviving officer, and took command of so much of the fleet as remained near him. As late as two days afterwards Tromp wrote to the States-General that he did not know what had become of Evertsen. There can surely be no better proof of the disorganisation of the Dutch.

Yet, with certain disgraceful exceptions,[3] they fought magnificently. Captain Bastiaen Centen, in the East India Company's ship *Oranje*, 76, pressed the *Montagu*, 52, very hard, and, according to Dutch reports, even had possession of her for a time, until she was retaken by the *Royal James*, which lost her captain, James Ley, third Earl of Marlborough, and Charles Weston, third Earl of Portland, a volunteer on board, during the fight. The gallant *Oranje* subsequently caught fire, and her brave commander, who

---

[1] There is a fine monument to Obdam in the Groote Kerk at the Hague.

[2] There is a monument to Cortenaer in the church of St. Laurens, Rotterdam.

[3] The *Nagelboom* and *Hilversum* were shamefully surrendered. The *Carolus Quintus* was betrayed by her mutinous crew. In consequence of misbehaviour, three captains were subsequently sentenced to be shot; three were publicly degraded; two more were dismissed the service; and the master of Cortenaer's ship was made to stand on a scaffold with a halter round his neck, and was afterwards banished. Captain Laurens Heemskerk, of the *Vrede*, who was condemned in contumacy, later vindicated the sentence of his judges by assisting Sir Robert Holmes in August, 1666, and by serving against his country on board the French flagship at Solebay in 1672. 'Nederl. Zeewezen,' ii. 34, 35; 146, 147; 302.

was saved from her ere she blew up, ultimately died of his wounds. Captain Jan de Haen, in the *Stad en Landen*, 56, actually took the *Charity*, 46, and eventually carried her into port as a prize. It is but fair to say, however, that the *Charity* had first been sadly mauled in succession by the *Liefde*, 70, *Elf Steden*, 54, and *Cruijningen*, 58, and that, before she was boarded, about ninety of her people escaped from her and later reached the shore.

But the day was lost ; and such minor incidents as the blowing up of the poop of the *St. George*, or the fatal wounding of Vice-Admiral Sir John Lawson, who had been detached after some Dutch ships which were making off, failed to revive the spirits of the enemy, even for a moment. By 7 o'clock, P.M., the Dutch were in full flight. Jan Evertsen, and the vessels with him, made for the mouth of the Maas. Tromp and his ships, in somewhat better order, made for the Texel. It was when each man, conscious of defeat, was thinking mainly of himself, that two serious disasters occurred. On one part of the scene of action, the *Maarseveen*, 78, *Ter Goes*, 30, and *Svanenburg*,[1] all belonging to different squadrons, ran on board one another, and were set on fire, and destroyed. On another part, four ships, the *Prins Maurits*, 53, *Coeverden*, 56, *Utrecht*, 48, and one more, similarly fouled one another, and being caught, while still interlocked and unmanageable, by an English fireship, were all burnt.

According to Sir William Coventry's report[2] to the Lord High Admiral, the prizes taken and already brought into British ports, were as follows :—

SHIPS.	GUNS.	MEN.
Carolus Quintus	54	230
Hilversum	60	290
Delft	32	130
Yacht, *De Ruijter*	18	80
Jonge Prins	36	160
Mars	50	200
Nagelboom	54	225
Wappen van Zeeland . . .	44	180
Bul	36	150

But to these should be added the *Huis te Swieten*, 70 guns, 300 men, the *Geldersche Ruijter*, 48 guns, 180 men, the *West Vriesland*,

---

[1] The *Svanenburg* is not mentioned in the official lists of the fleet in the Rijks Archief, but all accounts agree that she was present, and that she perished as here stated.

[2] Written in London on June 13th. Sir William was secretary to the Duke.

50 guns, 260 men, and probably one more, making fourteen in all, besides four which were abandoned after capture, in consequence of their unseaworthy condition. About fourteen in addition seem to have been destroyed. If this estimate be correct, the total loss of the Dutch was about thirty-two sail. Their loss in officers and men was about 4000 killed and 2000 taken.

The British loss was, in comparison, very slight. That the *Charity* was taken is admitted by all. The Dutch claim to have also taken the *John and Mary,* but nothing else. Of killed, there were only about 250, of wounded, about 340 ; and the Dutch cannot have carried off more than about a couple of hundred prisoners at

MEDAL COMMEMORATIVE OF THE DUKE OF YORK'S VICTORY OFF
LOWESTOFT, JUNE 3RD, 1665.

(From an original kindly lent by H.S.H. Captain Prince Louis of Battenberg, R.N.)

most. But the victory cost the lives of two British flag-officers and three captains, Vice-Admiral Sir John Lawson,[1] Rear-Admiral Robert Sansom,[2] Captain James, Earl of Marlborough,[3] of the *Royal James,* Captain Robert Kirby,[4] of the *Breda,* and Captain James Ableson,[5] of the *Guinea.*

But for the pertinacity of Tromp, who covered the retreat, the Dutch would have suffered still more severely. Two other causes

---

[1] Was wounded in the knee. The injury was at first not considered to be serious, but gangrene supervened, and Lawson died at Greenwich on June 29th.

[2] Had commanded the *Mary Rose* and later the *Dunkirk* in 1664, in which year also he had served as rear-admiral under Prince Rupert.

[3] Had commanded the squadron sent to take possession of Bombay. He fell in his forty-sixth year.

[4] Had previously commanded the *Ruby* and the *Constant Warwick.*

[5] Had previously commanded the *Bear* and the *Expedition.*

contributed to save them from utter destruction. One was that, after the action, it blew hard towards the dangerous Dutch coasts, and that the victors, according to Colliber, had expended all their fireships. The other was the failure of the English to press the pursuit. This is thus accounted for by Bishop Burnet :—

"After the fight, a Council, of War was called to concert the method of action when they should come up with them. In that Council, Penn, who commanded under the Duke, happened to say that they must prepare for better work the next engagement. He knew well the courage of the Dutch was never so high as when they were desperate. The Earl of Montagu, who was then a volunteer and one of the Duke's court, told me it was very visible that made an impression upon him, and all the Duke's domestics said he had got honour enough : why should he venture a second time ? The Duchess had also given a strict charge to all the Duke's servants to do all they could to hinder him to engage too far. When matters were settled, they went to sleep, and the Duke ordered a call to be given him when they should get up with the Dutch fleet. It is not known what passed between the Duke and Brouncker, who was of his bed-chamber, and then in waiting ; but he came to Penn, as from the Duke, and said the Duke ordered the sail to be slackened. Penn was struck with the order, but did not go about to argue the matter with the Duke himself, as he ought to have done : but obeyed it. When the Duke had slept, he, upon his waking, went out upon the quarter-deck, and seemed amazed to see the sails slackened, and that thereby all hope of overtaking the Dutch was lost. He questioned Penn upon it. Penn put it upon Brouncker, who said nothing. The Duke denied he had given any such order; but he neither punished Brouncker for carrying it nor Penn for obeying it. He, indeed, put Brouncker out of his service ; and it was said that he durst do no more. Brouncker was so much in the King's favour and in the Mistress's. Penn was more in his favour after that than ever before ; which he continued to his son after him, though a Quaker : and it was thought that all that favour was to oblige him to keep the secret."

The catastrophe was, for the moment, very demoralising to the Hollanders. There were regrettable public demonstrations ; and in their angry excitement the people were unable to discriminate between those who had done well and those who had done ill. Jan Evertsen, against whose personal and professional character nothing was ever seriously alleged, was mobbed at the Briel, and being flung into the water, barely escaped with his life. Disgusted at such treatment, he temporarily withdrew himself from the service, in which he was ultimately to perish very gloriously.

But the Dutch Government, although it was torn by faction, did not similarly lose its self-control. On the contrary, it at once began the most strenuous efforts to repair damages, and to fit a new fleet for sea. Cornelis Tromp expected to be entrusted with the command of the reorganised force ; and, indeed, he deserved the distinction ; but De Ruijter, a greater than he, was on his way home, and would soon be available ; and the States very wisely overlooked the considerable claims of Tromp, and trusting that the latter's patriotism would outweigh his personal feelings, kept open the appointment for De Ruijter. Tromp afterwards co-operated on several occasions with his chief, but the affair caused great bitterness, and the two gallant seamen, even while working side by side for their country, were thenceforward prevented by their personal differences from co-operating to the best advantage.

On the English side there was even greater dispatch. The Duke of York and Prince Rupert having hauled down their flags, the Earl of Sandwich assumed the chief command of a fleet which sailed from Southwold Bay on July 5th. Arriving off the Texel, the Earl satisfied himself that there was no likelihood of the Dutch

NAVAL REWARD OF CHARLES II., 1665.

(From an original kindly lent by H.S.H. Captain Prince Louis of Battenberg, R.N.)

being ready to come out for some considerable time. He therefore turned his attention to the making of dispositions which he hoped would result, firstly, in the interception of De Ruijter, who was known to be on his way home from America by way of the north of Scotland, and secondly, in the capture or destruction of certain Dutch Smyrna and East India ships, which had taken refuge at Bergen, in Norway.

Sandwich missed De Ruijter, who, with his squadron, returned, and safely anchored at Delfziel late in July. The Earl also failed at Bergen, whither he detached Rear-Admiral Sir Thomas Tyddiman[1] (Red) to carry out his scheme. An account of Tyddiman's action will be found in the next chapter. De Ruijter put to sea to convoy

[1] He had been knighted for his share in the victory of June 3rd.

the Bergen ships to a Dutch port; but, although he reached them
without mishap, he lost several of them on the way back. Particulars of this affair, and of other captures made by the fleet under
Sandwich, will also be found in the next chapter. The year 1665,
indeed, witnessed no second important action; and after France, at
the beginning of 1666, had joined the Dutch, the English grand
fleet was placed under the combined command of Prince Rupert and
the Duke of Albemarle, Sandwich, who was under a cloud on
account of alleged peculations, accepting the post of Ambassador
to Spain.

Authorities differ as to the exact constitution of the two fleets
which were pitted against one another in the summer of 1666, but
careful comparison seems to indicate that the strength of the
opponents was as follows :—

	ENGLISH.	DUTCH.
Ships of above 90 guns . . .	2	—
„ from 80 to 90 guns . . .	2	2
„ „ 70 to 80 „ . . .	7	11
„ „ 60 to 70 „ . . .	14	21
„ „ 50 to 60 „ . . .	25	18
„ „ 40 to 50 „ . . .	22	19
„ „ 30 to 40 „ . . .	8	13
„ under 30 guns	—	1
Fireships	?	9
Yachts, ketches, etc.	?	8

Thus, excluding small craft, the English, under Prince Rupert
and the Duke of Albemarle, disposed of 80 ships, which mounted
4460 guns and carried 21,085 officers and men; while the Dutch,
whose force was under De Ruijter, Cornelis Evertsen,[1] and Cornelis
Tromp, disposed of 85 ships, which mounted 4615 guns and carried
21,909 officers and men.

When, therefore, on May 29th, Rupert and Albemarle arrived in
the Downs, their joint command was so little inferior to the
command of De Ruijter, who was still in port, that, after the
experiences of the previous year, it may well have appeared to
unprejudiced onlookers as if, granting to the English a continued
superiority in discipline, the Joint Admirals had little to fear from
their distinguished enemy.

But a strategical blunder, for which neither Rupert nor Albemarle
was responsible, imperilled the whole position. France, as has been
said, had thrown in her fortunes with the Dutch, and had declared

[1] " The Old."

war on January 16th. News, which subsequently proved to be false, reached London that a French fleet of thirty-six sail, under the Duc de Beaufort, was on its way from the Mediterranean, and was, indeed, already approaching the mouth of the Channel, with a view to joining hands with De Ruijter; and upon the receipt of this news, Charles II. at once ordered Rupert to detach himself to the westward with the White Squadron, or about one-third of the

GEORGE MONCK, DUKE OF ALBEMARLE, K.G., ADMIRAL AND GENERAL-AT-SEA.

(*From W. T. Mote's engraving after the portrait by Sir P. Lely.*)

English fleet. The Prince was to lie off the Isle of Wight, where he would probably be reinforced by about ten vessels from Plymouth, and was to see to it that the anticipated junction was not effected.

Says Mahan: "A position like that of the English fleet, threatened with an attack from two quarters, presents one of the subtlest temptations to a commander. The impulse is very strong to meet both by dividing his own numbers, as Charles did; but, unless in possession of overwhelming force, it is an error, exposing both divisions to be beaten separately." Rupert and Albemarle together had eighty ships wherewith to oppose De Ruijter's eighty-five. The Dutch superiority was not so marked as to rob the English of a reasonable prospect of victory. But Rupert having been detached with about twenty-four ships to meet the ten from Plymouth, Albemarle was left with only about fifty-six in face of a gallant foe who was more than half as strong again. Charles's order, then, was a fatal error. If he had directed both Rupert and Albemarle to fall upon De Ruijter, or at least to blockade him; or even if he had directed both of them to proceed westwards, and to crush the supposed squadron of De Beaufort, his strategy, leaving contingent questions aside, would have been defensible; but there is no excuse to be found for his division of an inferior force holding an interior position.

The order from London reached the fleet as soon as the latter arrived in the Downs, and Prince Rupert accordingly parted company,[1] with a fair easterly wind at his back. The same wind which was thus favourable to him also favoured De Ruijter, who left port, and had got as far as a point nearly midway between Dunquerque and the Downs, when the breeze changed to south-west, and the weather became somewhat thick. He therefore anchored. This was in the early morning of June 1st.

As he lay, his rear, under Tromp, was to the south-east, and consequently somewhat to windward of his centre, which was under his own immediate eye; and his van, under Evertsen, was to the north-west, and so still more to leeward than he himself was. Almost dead to windward was the Duke of Albemarle, who was sighted at about 9 o'clock, A.M., and who sighted his enemy at much the same time. Albemarle weighed, and, although so inferior in force, determined to attack with energy, trusting that, by retaining the wind, he might always be able to avoid committing himself too far. Unhappily, his windward position proved to be a distinct disadvantage, inasmuch as, the sea being lumpy, it prevented many of his vessels from using their lower tier of guns, or, in other words, their heaviest metal. Opening the lower ports on the leeward side resulted in the flooding of the batteries and in danger to the ships.

Having approached, Albemarle stood along the irregular Dutch line on the starboard tack, leaving the van and centre (the Dutch

---

[1] Leaving, however, the flag-officers of the White Squadron behind with Albemarle.

proper right and centre) out of gunshot, and passing on until he was abreast of the rear (the Dutch proper left).   He advanced in column —a formation most difficult for a large number of vessels to preserve in a satisfactory manner—and the consequence was that, when he came abreast of Tromp, he had but about five-and-thirty ships close up with him and well in hand, the remaining twenty straggling and tailing out so as to afford little support either to him or to one another.   Albemarle, nevertheless, put his helm up and ran down upon Tromp, whose ships, cutting their cables, made sail on the same tack, and stood across towards the French coast, hotly

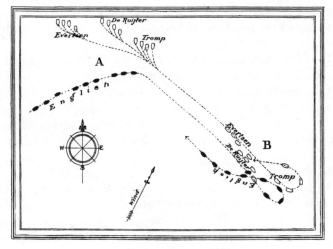

THE FOUR DAYS' FIGHT, 1666.

A. The attack on June 1st (the first day).
B. The conclusion of that day's action.

engaged.   The Dutch centre and van also weighed or cut their cables, and followed on the same course, but, being far to leeward, did not get into action until about noon.

When the action had continued in this fashion for nearly three hours, Albemarle, probably because he found himself too close to the shore, seems to have ordered his ships to put about together so as to return on a north-west course.   This evolution turned what had been the English rear into the van ; and the van, thus newly constituted, presently got into furious action with De Ruijter and the comparatively fresh Dutch centre.   No doubt the English ships had already suffered severely.   This new encounter threw the head of the column into some confusion, of which De Ruijter knew how to take advantage; and presently three or four of the English ships found themselves cut off from their line and surrounded. One of these was the *Swiftsure*, bearing the flag of Vice-Admiral Sir William Berkeley [1] (W), a promising officer of only seven-and-twenty years of age. Badly disabled, the *Swiftsure* was boarded simultaneously from several quarters; yet Berkeley would not surrender, and he continued fighting, almost alone, until, receiving a ball in the throat, he staggered back into his captain's cabin and flung himself on to a table, where he was found dead. His body met with the most generous treatment from the Dutch, who, on June 30th, despatched to England a highly laudatory letter, and offered either to return the remains or to bury them with honour in Holland. Besides the *Swiftsure*, a hired vessel, said to have been of 60 guns, and the *Loyal George*,[2] 44, were surrounded and taken, chiefly by the efforts of Captains Hendrik Adriaensze, Jacob Andries Swart, and Willem van der Zaen.

Rear-Admiral Sir John Harman (W), in the *Henry*, was also cut off and surrounded; and, he being in a short time completely disabled, one of the enemy's fireships grappled him on the starboard quarter. He was, however, soon freed by the almost incredible exertions of his lieutenant,[3] who, having in the midst of the flames loosed the grappling-irons, swung back on board his own ship unhurt. The Dutch, bent on the destruction of this unfortunate vessel, sent a second fireship, which grappled the *Henry* on the port side and set her sails on fire. This caused so much panic that about fifty of the crew jumped overboard. Harman, however, drew his sword, and, running among the people, threatened to kill the next man who should endeavour to leave the ship, or who should fail in his duty; and thus order was restored and the flames were got under, not, nevertheless, until a topsail-yard, in falling, had broken Harman's leg. A third fireship approached, but the *Henry*, with her lower-deck guns, sank her. Cornelis Evertsen then bore up for the crippled vessel, and the Dutch admiral hailed Harman to surrender, promising him quarter. " It has not come to that yet,"

---

[1] Third son of Sir Charles Berkeley, of Bruton, who became in 1665 Lord Fitzharding. Sir William was brother of that Earl of Falmouth who had fallen in the action with Obdam in the previous year, and whose Irish title reverted to his father.

[2] The *Loyal George* was also hired.

[3] Thomas Lamming. For this service he was made captain of the *Ruby*. His subsequent career is unknown.

shouted Harman in return; and with his next broadside he killed the gallant Evertsen and freed himself. In spite of the injuries to his ship he succeeded in carrying her into Harwich, and by the following evening he had so far refitted her that, oblivious of his broken leg, he put to sea again, hoping to be back in time to see the conclusion of the fight. But ere he could rejoin\ the fleet the action was over.[1]

Evertsen and Berkeley were not the only flag-officers to fall on that bloody first day of the great Four Days' Battle. Rear-Admiral[2] Frederick Stachouwer also perished. Tromp was dismantled, and had to shift his flag; De Ruijter himself fared almost as ill; and on each side two or three ships were sunk or blown up and several captains were killed.

Albemarle continued on the port tack, taking the remnants of his battered column past the division of Evertsen, very few ships of which had been able to get into action, owing to their leewardly position at the commencement. The battle continued until about 10 P.M. Towards the end of the day Albemarle, according to one of De Ruijter's dispatches,[3] anchored in order to collect his ships, although this is scarcely credible. He is said, however, to have weighed again as the Dutch neared him; and there is no doubt that, after firing had ceased, the bulk of his fleet was well to the west, or west-north-west of the enemy.

Captain Mahan considers that, " the merit of Monck's attack as a piece of grand tactics is evident, and bears a strong resemblance to that of Nelson at the Nile. Discerning quickly the weakness of the Dutch order, he had attacked a vastly superior force in such a way that only part of it could come into action; and though the English actually lost more heavily, they carried off a brilliant prestige, and must have left considerable depression and heart-burning among the Dutch." [4]

For some time during the night Albemarle stood off on the port tack repairing damages. The Dutch, occupied in the same way, were in no condition to pursue. In the morning of June 2nd, the English returned to continue the engagement. They found the enemy on the port tack, the original van leading. The Dutch were

---

[1] From particulars in Campbell, ii. 353, 354; Kennet. iii. 281; and Charnock's 'Biog. Navalis': said to be taken in part from Harman's own narrative.

[2] The Dutch title is Schout-bij-nacht.

[3] To the States-General, dated the morning of June $\frac{4}{14}$.

[4] 'Inf. of Sea Power upon Hist.' 121.

at first to windward, but, by a little manœuvring, Albemarle's ships, which were the more weatherly and the better handled, presently regained the weather-gauge. There were that day in the English line forty-four ships, and in the Dutch about eighty; and the wind was as before, though there was less of it.

The two fleets passed one another on opposite tacks, the English being in good order, but the Dutch overlapping, and being in places crowded together, so that the fire of many ships was partially or wholly masked. Tromp, who commanded the rear of the long Dutch column, noticed this when the heads of the columns were still nearly abreast of one another; and, as he had plenty of time for the execution of the manœuvre, he chose, upon his own responsibility, to go about and so ultimately to gain the wind of the English van. This independent and, indeed, insubordinate action, would have greatly added to the anxieties of the Dutch commander-in-chief, even if it had not been complicated by the almost simultaneous vagaries of part of the Dutch van. On Tromp's behalf it may be said that, although he did wrong, he erred from pure love of fighting and with the mistaken idea that he was acting for the best. But two other insubordinate flag-officers in the van quitted the line from very different motives. To De Ruijter's dismay they kept broad off from the centre of the English column, and, while apparently endeavouring to get away, not only exposed themselves to be raked, but also threw the whole Dutch line into confusion. De Ruijter, threatened with the general disruption of his command, and anxious to succour Tromp, had no alternative but to keep broad off also, and then to haul up for the protection of the rear, standing back to it on the starboard tack.

The whole English force was for a time concentrated upon Tromp, who, by his own act, was separated from his friends, and who suffered severely. But, as De Ruijter returned to the rescue, Albemarle had to relinquish the attack for fear lest the Dutch might gain the wind of him. He seems to have continued his course for a short period on the starboard tack, and so to have caused a lull in the action. During this, Tromp went on board De Ruijter, and, though he was cheered by the people, he seems to have been very coldly received by his chief.

While the Dutch were still in great disorder Albemarle appears to have put about and repassed them, they lying huddled together like a flock of sheep. But he was too weak and disabled to press such slight advantages as the situation offered him. When, however, De Ruijter had again formed some sort of line, the English once more went about and passed him, the Dutch commander-in-chief, now at the extreme rear of his column, losing his main-top-mast and mainyard in the encounter. Yet once again did Albemarle put about; but when, this time, he had passed the enemy, the Duke had had enough of it, and he continued towards the north-west or west, being, in point of fact, in full retreat. The Dutch pursued in a long straggling line, De Ruijter's flagship, on account of the damages which she had sustained, finally dropping out of sight in the rear.

The second day had been but little less costly than the first. Each side had lost about three ships sunk, burnt, or blown up; and Tromp's dangerous adventure had sacrificed the life of the vice-admiral of his squadron, Abraham van der Hulst.[1]

On the third day, the wind being easterly, Albemarle continued his retreat to the westward, maintaining good order, sending his most disabled ships ahead, and himself bringing up the rear with such vessels—about twenty-eight in number—as were still in fair fighting trim. The object of the English admiral was to avoid a general renewal of the engagement until he should succeed in effecting a junction with the squadron of Prince Rupert. By sacrificing three hopelessly mauled craft, which would have delayed his progress, and which he burnt, he attained his end; for the Dutch, though they pursued closely, did not venture to molest him, probably because they were themselves in very evil plight. During the retreat, however, the English suffered a severe loss. The *Royal Prince*, 90,[2] bearing the flag of Admiral Sir George Ayscue (W.), ran aground on the Galloper, and being surrounded by the enemy,[3] and attacked simultaneously by two fireships, had to strike after she had lost about one hundred and fifty killed. Tromp, who was at the time on board the ship of the Dutch Rear-Admiral Isaac Sweers, received the surrender, and was very desirous of carrying the prize to Holland, but, at De Ruijter's orders, she was burnt.

At about the same time a fleet of some twenty sail was

---

[1] There is a monument to Van der Hulst in the Oude Kerk at Amsterdam.

[2] Her armament was, at the time, fourteen 48-pounders, fourteen 32-pounders, thirty 24-pounders, sixteen 12-pounders, and fourteen 6-pounders. She had on board a quantity of treasure.

[3] Ayscue, in his letter to the King, from Loevestein, on June 10th, says that other English vessels were also surrounded.

sighted to the westward. The Dutch at first took it to be the expected French force under the Duc de Beaufort. Had it really been that force Albemarle's fate would have been sealed. Happily it was Rupert's division. De Jonge [1] suggests that it was the knowledge of this fact which induced De Ruijter to order the burning of the *Royal Prince*. Towards nightfall the two English squadrons once more united. Under Albemarle and the Prince there were then about fifty-eight or sixty sail, and under De Ruijter, about seventy-eight fit for action.

On the morning of June 4th, the wind blew once more from the south-west, and was very fresh. The action recommenced all along the line on the port tack, the English being this time to leeward. For a couple of hours the two fleets ran thus, firing furiously. During that period two

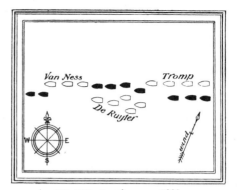

THE FOUR DAYS' FIGHT, 1666.
June 4th. Position I.

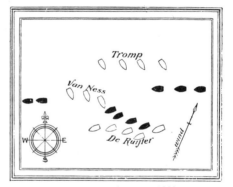

THE FOUR DAYS' FIGHT, 1666.
June 4th. Position II.

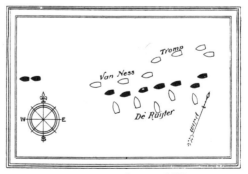

THE FOUR DAYS' FIGHT, 1666.
June 4th. Position III.

NOTE.—In the above plans, groups, and not single ships are repesented.

[1] 'Nederl. Zeewezen,' ii. 78.

Dutch vessels seem to have been burnt, and at the end of it—perhaps, as Mahan suggests, owing to the superior weatherliness of the English—great part of each line had broken across the original course of the other, so that many of the Dutch were to leeward. There was consequently much confusion. De Ruijter, with his largest group, was still to windward, and Albemarle, with his largest group, was still to leeward; but the other groups were scattered, some of each side being to windward and some to leeward. The Dutch Rear-Admiral Jan Jansze van Nes, with fourteen ships of the van, was rashly pursuing three or four English vessels which, under a press of sail, had gained the windward of the head of the enemy's column. Tromp, with the Dutch rear, was to leeward of De Ruijter and of the main body of the English. (Position I.) By carrying sail he overhauled Van Nes and brought him back, passing round the English centre. In the meanwhile, however, De Ruijter and Albemarle, in hot action, were both beating to windward, so that Tromp and Van Nes came up to leeward of the Dutch centre, with the English centre between them and it. (Position II.) Seeing the situation, De Ruijter signalled the ships about him to keep away before the wind. This manœuvre broke up the English centre, through which passed the Dutch centre, probably in a very irregular line abreast. (Position III.) For a short space the fight was hot. Then ship by ship, sorely shattered, the English gained a windward position, and comparative safety; for by that time it blew half a gale. Albemarle was in no condition to attack again, though he seems to have followed the enemy for some distance. As for the Dutch, apart from the fact that they were to leeward, they were, no doubt, quite exhausted, besides being well satisfied with the success which they had gained.[1]

Concerning the losses on each side, it is difficult to arrive at a definite conclusion owing to the conflicting nature of the various accounts. The Dutch appear to have had about six or seven vessels sunk or burnt, and two thousand officers and men killed or wounded.

[1] The chief printed authorities for the Four Days' Fight are: Van den Bosch, 'Leven van De Ruijter'; 'Mémoires du Comte de Guiche'; Aitzema, 'Leven van C. Tromp'; Brand, 'Leven van De Ruijter'; De Jonge, 'Leven van Evertsen'; Pepys's 'Memoirs'; 'Memorials of Sir W. Penn'; certain letters of De Witt; Sir W. Temple, 'Observations'; Swinnas, 'Eng. Nederl. en Munst. Krakeel.'; the Dutch account in 'Rev. Mar. et Col.,' lxxxii. 137; Gumble, 'Life of Monck'; Sir John Harman's Account; Skinner, 'Life of Monck'; 'Lettres et Mém. du Comte d'Estrades'; Philip's continuation of Heath's Chronicle; Parker, 'Hist. of Own Time'; 'A True Narrative,' etc. London, 1666, fol.

The English undoubtedly lost very much more heavily. In addition to the *Royal Prince* burnt, and the *Swiftsure* and *Loyal George* taken, they certainly lost the *Essex*, 58, *Clove Tree*, 62, *Convertine*, 54, *Bull*, 40, *Spread Eagle* and *Little Katherine*, all of which were carried home by the Dutch, besides two or three other ships which struck, and eight or ten more which were sunk or blown up; and the number of their killed and wounded, placed by Lefèvre-Pontalis, in his Life of Jan de Witt, at five thousand, is probably not exaggerated. Moreover they lost between two and three thousand prisoners. The death of Berkeley on the first day has been already noted. The English also lost another flag-officer

DUTCH MEDAL COMMEMORATIVE OF THE FOUR DAYS' FIGHT, 1666.

(From an original kindly lent by H.S.H. Captain Prince Louis of Battenberg, R.N.)

in the person of Vice-Admiral Sir Christopher Myngs, who had his flag in the *Victory*, and who fell on the fourth day. Van den Bosch narrates that, having received a ball through the throat, this gallant officer remained on deck a good half-hour, compressing the wound with his fingers in order to stop the flow of blood, until a second shot struck him in the neck and killed him. Among the English commanders who fell during the long battle were Captains John Coppin of the *St. George*, Peter Mootham, of the *Princess*, Walter Wood, of the *Henrietta*, Henry Terne, of the *Triumph*, Philemon Bacon, of the *Bristol*, Thomas Whitty, of the *Vanguard*, Roger Miller, of the *Plymouth*, John Chappel, of the *Clove Tree*,[1] and Jeffery Dare, of the *House of Sweeds*.[2]

[1] Late *Nagelboom*, Dutch prize.   [2] Late *Huis te Swieten*, Dutch prize.

The English had been badly beaten but their *moral* had not suffered. The battle had demonstrated that their discipline and seamanship were better than those of the enemy ; and it encouraged them to hope that, against a Dutch foe of approximately equal numerical strength, they would be victorious. The Hollanders, on the other hand, had no ground for any extreme elation. They had, it was true, won a battle, but it was against a fleet which, although of very inferior force, had sustained one of the longest fights in the history of naval warfare, had inflicted no insignificant amount of damage, and had not been crushed. Both sides, in consequence, felt that a decisive result had not been arrived at. Albemarle and Rupert still commanded a "potential" fleet, and, so long as they commanded it, the Dutch had the real problem of the war still unsolved before them.

Yet, in spite of their consciousness of the very partial nature of their advantage, the Dutch must have been astonished at the celerity with which the battered English squadrons were refitted, reinforced, and sent to sea again. Not until about July 15th had the Dutch themselves any considerable fleet ready for action ; and then, although they had embarked troops with the object of effecting a landing somewhere on the British coasts, the attitude of the English prevented them from making any attempt of the kind, and the soldiers were put ashore again. Had the Duc de Beaufort joined with the expected French squadron, De Ruijter might have deemed himself strong enough to essay an invasion ; but Louis XIV. was no very ardent ally, and his ships failed to appear when they would have been most useful.

The greater part of the English grand fleet was assembled off the mouth of the Thames by July 22nd, on the evening of which day it anchored at the Gunfleet, the enemy being then also at anchor about eighteen miles to the N.N.E. On the morning of the 23rd both fleets weighed, but, owing to calms, could not approach one another. On the following night it blew very hard, with lightning and thunder, and some damage was done, especially to the English.

As before, Albemarle and Prince Rupert were in joint command on the English side, both having their flags in the *Royal Charles*. The White Squadron was under Admiral Sir Thomas Allin, and the Blue under Admiral Sir Jeremy Smyth. With them were Vice-Admirals Sir Joseph Jordan (R.), Sir Thomas Tyddiman (W.),

and Sir Edward Spragge (B.); and Rear-Admirals Sir Robert
Holmes (R.), Richard Utber (acting W.), and John Kempthorne
(acting B.). On the day of the action the fleet seems to have
consisted of 81 ships of the line and "frigates," carrying 4460 guns,
besides about 18 fireships.[1]

The Dutch were under the supreme command of Admiral M. A.
de Ruijter, who had under him Lieut.-Admirals Aert Jansze van Nes,
Cornelis Tromp, Jan Corneliszoon Meppel, Tjerck Hiddes de Vries,
and Jan Evertsen, who, in response to the call of his country, had
returned to the service upon the death of his distinguished brother.
The other flag-officers who had served in the previous action served
again, Isaac Sweers being promoted to the place of the dead Van
der Hulst, and Captain Willem van der Zaen taking Sweers's place
as Rear-Admiral. The vacancy caused by the death of Stachouwer
was filled by the promotion of Captain Govert 'T Hoen. On the
day of the action the Dutch fleet included 88 ships-of-the-line and
"frigates," 10 yachts or dispatch vessels, and 20 fireships, mounting
in all 4704 guns.[2] The Dutch, therefore, had a distinct, yet not a
great, apparent superiority.

During the 24th the Dutch seem to have kept the wind, and the
English to have in vain manœuvred to obtain it. The night found
the two fleets in the broad part of the estuary of the Thames,
between Orfordness and the North Foreland, the Dutch being to
the N.E., and the wind blowing generally from the northward, but
varying from N.N.E. to N. As early as 2 A.M. on the morning
of Wednesday, the 25th, St. James's Day, Rupert and Albemarle,
who had anchored, weighed; and from that hour until about
10 A.M. the fleets slowly approached one another. Particulars of
the manner of approach are both scanty and, to some extent,
conflicting. The English seem to have been in line of battle close
hauled or a point large on the port tack, Sir Thomas Allin's
squadron leading; the Dutch, in line of battle with the wind on
the port quarter, or steering about six points large, Evertsen's
squadron leading; and, as they closed, the wind veered to N.W.
It is evident that the Dutch line was ill-formed, so much so, indeed,
that to some observers it looked as if bowed into a half moon :
and, while the van and centre were crowded, there was a con-

[1] From lists in 'Holl. Mercurius'; 'Kort en Bondigh Verhael'; Aitzema; the
Rijks Archief; and contemporary English publications.
[2] De Jonge, i. 787.

siderable interval between the centre, under De Ruijter, and the rear, under Tromp. On the other hand it is probable that the English line was as regular as a line of such length—five or six miles at least—could be. The regularity of the English line during that war often extorted the admiration of foreign and even of hostile critics.

It was about 10 A.M. when the leading vessels of the two columns arrived within gunshot of one another. Allin, as he thus came up, engaged Evertsen and the Dutch van, the squadrons holding parallel courses on the port tack, and the Dutch being to windward. In a similar manner the English centre, as it came up, engaged and went away with De Ruijter and the Dutch centre. But when Smyth, with the English rear, came up with Tromp, the latter, always fond of independent action, and anxious, it may be, to distinguish himself above his chief, put before the wind and broke through just ahead of the English rear, thus, as on a previous occasion, separating himself by his own act from his friends. To De Ruijter, who wrote bitterly to the States-General of Tromp's conduct,[1] it appeared that his subordinate had allowed his squadron to fall far astern of its station, and to be cut off by Smyth; but the balance of evidence tends to show that, though Tromp was often headstrong, perverse, and insubordinate, he never, by deliberate remissness, postponed action for an instant, and that, on this July 25th, as usual, he erred rather on the side of excess of rashness than of that of either slothfulness or prudence.

From the moment when Allin joined battle with Evertson, and went away in hot action with him, to the time when Tromp quitted the Dutch line, two hours, or thereabouts, elapsed. It was then noon, and the wind had, since 11 A.M., blown again from the northward. Tromp's was the strongest of the Dutch, and Smyth's was the weakest of the English squadrons; and, if only Tromp's manœuvre had been executed at the order, or even with the full comprehension, of De Ruijter, it might, from some points of view, be defended. But De Ruijter was only mystified. Tromp and Smyth, engaged in more or less confused *mêlée*, eventually went away on the starboard tack, and were presently lost to sight in the direction of the English coast; while the two vans and centres, broadside to broadside, headed nearly due east.

The English van from the first asserted its superiority over

[1] Dispatch of July 26th.

the Dutch van. The latter fought magnificently, and, in a very
brief period, lost no fewer than three flag-officers—Jan Evertsen,
Tjerck Hiddes de Vries, and Rudolf Coenders ; but it was overpowered, and at one o'clock was in full flight to the eastward.
The English centre had a more difficult and prolonged task
before it, for, as usual, De Ruijter and the captains under his
immediate command behaved most stubbornly and gallantly. The
English commanders-in-chief had to shift their flag ; the *Royal
Katherine* and *St. George* had to haul out of action; and De Ruijter's
flagship, the *Zeven Provinciën*, was entirely dismasted after a hot
and savage conflict with Sir Robert Holmes in the *Henry.* At
4 P.M. the Dutch centre gave way ; but both squadrons were by
that time in a terrible plight, and for some hours they seem to have
drifted together to the southward, too mauled and exhausted to
continue any kind of general action. Towards night the English
recommenced the engagement ; but by that time De Ruijter had
to some extent re-formed his squadron, and, having stationed Vice-
Admiral Adriaen Banckers, with twenty of the least damaged ships,
at the rear of his line, began a masterly retreat. The battle continued in a desultory way during the night, and became brisk again
on the morning of the 26th ; but the wind being then strong from
the N.E., and the shallows close at hand, the pursuit was at last
discontinued. Before the retreat began Banckers's first flagship,
a vessel of 60 guns, and a ship called the *Sneek van Harlingen*, 50,
had been abandoned and burnt.

In the meantime the two rears had been closely engaged to the
westward. Dutch accounts have it that Smyth continually gave
way, and that he did so designedly, in order to further separate
the Dutch rear from the van and centre. Tromp, and Meppel, who
was with him, certainly seem to have had at first the best of the
conflict, for they burnt the *Resolution*, 64 ; and it is maintained on
their behalf that, having gained the wind, they chased throughout
the night of the 25th. Yet, be this as it may, on the morning
of the 26th, Smyth had the wind once more, and was in chase of
Tromp, who had somehow learnt in the interval that his friends
had suffered defeat, and that part of them had taken refuge in the
Wielings. Smyth chased hard all day. Rear-Admiral Govert 'T
Hoen was killed. In the evening Albemarle and Rupert, far to
leeward and unable to interfere, saw Tromp flying for his ports,
with Smyth at his heels. At 11 P.M. on the 26th the English

van and centre anchored off the Dutch coast. On the following morning, when Smyth rejoined, he reported that his enemy had escaped, and, with such shattered force as remained to him, was safe behind the shoals.

Such was the St. James's Fight, or, as some have called it, the second battle of the North Foreland. It was a brilliant and decisive English victory. The Dutch lost about twenty ships,

REAR-ADMIRAL SIR ROBERT HOLMES, KT.

(*From the original in the possession of Lord Heytesbury.*)

four thousand killed, and three thousand wounded, and, in addition to the four flag-officers already mentioned, numerous captains, including Ruth Maximiliaan, Hendrik Vroom, Cornelis van Hogenhoeck, Hugo van Nijhoff, and Jurriaan Poel. The victors, on the other hand, lost only the *Resolution* and two or three fireships,[1]

---

[1] Although De Ruijter, in his dispatch of July 26th, says that two English ships had been seen to sink, and that two more had been burnt.

and a relatively small number of men.[1] No flag-officers fell, and the only captains who lost their lives seem to have been Hugh Seymour, of the *Foresight*, John Parker, of the *Yarmouth*, Joseph Sanders, of the *Breda*, Arthur Áshby, of the *Guinea*, and William Martin of the hired East Indiaman *London*.

The Dutch dismissed Tromp,[2] superseding him by Willem Joseph van Ghent, a colonel of marines. They also punished several inferior officers who were thought to have misbehaved themselves. De Ruijter, on the other hand, was generally recognised to have conducted himself with prudence and ability, and was allowed to retain his command. From Louis XIV. he received the military order of Saint Michel, in diamonds, and a gold medal.

The victory gave the complete command of the sea to the English. They anchored for a time in Schooneveld, one of the favourite anchorages of the Dutch fleets, and then moved slowly up the coast, making captures everywhere, and thoroughly alarming the country. As they went northward the renegade Dutch captain, Laurens Heemskerk, informed the commanders-in-chief that on the islands of Vlieland and Ter Schelling there were valuable magazines and stores, and that within them lay nearly two hundred sail of richly laden merchantmen, some lately arrived from abroad and some waiting for an opportunity to sail ; and that they were convoyed by only two men-of-war. A council of flag-officers determined that these should be immediately attacked, and confided the conduct of the affair to Rear-Admiral Sir Robert Holmes (R.), with, as his immediate second in command, Captain Sir William Jennings.

To Holmes were entrusted nine men-of-war of the lower rates, with five fireships and seven ketches. Three hundred men for the venture were specially chosen from each squadron of the fleet, two-thirds of them being soldiers and marines under Sir Philip Howard, and one-third seamen.

At 7 A.M. on August 8th this little squadron parted company from the rest of the fleet, and betook itself to an anchorage about three miles outside the first buoys marking the channel into the Vlie, the strait, that is, separating the two islands from one another. Thence the Rear-Admiral sent in the *Fanfan*, ketch,

---

[1] Some accounts, indeed, place the number at only three hundred.

[2] Tromp returned later to the service and greatly distinguished himself.

which, presently returning, reported that ships, as described by
Heemskerk, were indeed within.   Holmes determined to attack
the vessels before dealing with the storehouses ashore ; and, leaving
the *Advice* and *Hampshire*, two of his largest craft, outside the
buoys to attend to any sail that might escape him, he weighed
with the rest of his force, and, not without difficulty, for the
wind was contrary, made his way into Ter Schelling Road, where
he anchored the *Tiger*, in which he had entered, and shifted his
flag to the *Fanfan*.   Signalling for his captains to come on board,
he gave them the plan of operations, and ordered the *Pembroke*,
which drew less water than the other ships, to proceed with the
fireships and make as quick work as possible of the Dutch
vessels.

Captain Henry Browne, of the *Richard*, at once made for and
grappled the larger of the two convoying men-of-war, and soon
burnt her.   The second man-of-war, threatened by another fireship,
cut her cables and backed on to a sand-bank, where she was taken
a little later by some of the boats of the squadron and also burnt.
Each of the other fireships grappled one of the largest of the
merchantmen.   By that time the Dutch were in confusion, and
Sir Robert, taking advantage of it, sent in Sir William Jennings,
with all the available boats of the squadron, to complete the
disaster.   The officers in charge were ordered not to plunder,
but only to destroy; and so well did they carry out the duty
that, in a very short time, about one hundred and seventy ships [1]
were delivered to the flames.   About a dozen only escaped by
running up into a creek where the boats could not follow
them ; and even these few were damaged.   The affair was spoken
of for years afterwards in England as " Sir Robert Holmes, his
Bonefire."

On the following day men were landed without opposition on
Ter Schelling, the chief village of which was plundered, and, with
a number of storehouses, set fire to and partially burnt.   The
damage done afloat and ashore was enormous, and the value of
the property destroyed was estimated at the equivalent of at least
£850,000.   A previous attempt upon Vlieland had been abandoned
owing to the state of the weather.   The total English loss during
these operations did not exceed about twelve men killed or wounded,
and four or five fireships, which were very profitably expended.

---

[1] De Jonge says " not fewer than a hundred and forty."

Sir Robert Holmes promptly re-embarked his men and rejoined the fleet, which, after making a few more prizes on the coast, returned to its ports.

The effect of these proceedings was to prompt the Dutch to strain every nerve to restore their prestige ; and almost as soon as the English had withdrawn to their own coasts De Ruijter was once more at sea. He sailed on August 26th with eighty-one men-of-war, thirteen fireships, and several other craft, and on the 30th was off the North Foreland, the English fleet being in Southwold Bay. De Ruijter had instructions to endeavour to effect a junction with the long-delayed squadron of the Duc de Beaufort, which was reported to have left La Rochelle ; and he therefore stood across to look into Calais and Boulogne. The English followed close with about one hundred sail ; and a general action would have resulted had not a violent storm ended the battle almost ere it had begun. Van den Bosch [1] asserts that on this occasion the Dutch Admiral Sweers took an English man-of-war [2] and set her on fire, but no confirmation of the story is obtainable from English sources. He also asserts that De Ruijter lay for some time off Boulogne awaiting De Beaufort, the English having previously retired to Portsmouth in consequence of the bad weather. There is some doubt as to the sequence and inter-dependence of events ; yet it seems to be certain that De Ruijter had no mind to risk an action before being joined by his French allies ; that the storm relieved him from a very dangerous situation ; and that, in the event, the English were obliged to withdraw to St. Helens and he to Dunquerque. He is said to have so deeply taken to heart the dilatoriness of the French that he contracted a fever. To recover his health he entered the Maas, and went for a short time to Amsterdam.

De Beaufort's conduct exactly reflected the hesitating and undecided policy of his master, Louis XIV. who, though the ally of Holland, was extremely unwilling to be of any practical use to that country, and who was, moreover, loath to risk any part of the new fleet which Colbert had created for him. De Beaufort had with him, or on the point of joining him, at La Rochelle a very considerable force, and, as this was the first great fleet ever

[1] ' Levens der Zeehelden.'
[2] Said by De Jonge, ii. 150, to be the *Loyal Charles*, 56. If this be so, she was a hired vessel.

collected by France, the following list of it, taken from Guérin, should be of interest :—

Ships.	Guns.	Men.	Ships.	Guns.	Men.
St. Philippe[1]	74	600	*St. Antoine*	30	200
Royale[2]	56	400	*Elbeuf*	34	230
Dauphin	56	350	*Vierge*	34	200
St. Louis	56	400	*Lion d'Or*	30	250
Reine	56	400	*Postillon*	8	80
César	52	350	*Ligournois*	24	250
Jules	40	250	*Vendôme*[4]	72	600
Thérèse	60	350	*Diamant*	60	400
Hercule	40	300	*Rubis*	50	400
Soleil	38	230	*Triomphe*	40	300
St. Joseph	34	230	*Mazarin*	40	300
Dragon	36	250	*Mercœur*	36	230
Palmier	36	230	*Beaufort*	36	230
Ecureuil	38	230	*Infante (II.)*	30	200
Etoile de Diane	36	250	*Victoire*	30	230
Françoise	36	230	*Hermione*	30	200
Notre Dame	36	230	*Hirondelle*	30	220
Croissant d'Afrique	36	230	*Dunquerquois*	24	200
Soleil d'Afrique	34	232	*Bourbon*	50	400
Ste. Anne	16[3]	120	*N. D. des Anges*	16	150
Infante (I.)	22	80	*Grand Charles*	34	130

With 15 fireships.

[1] Flag of De Beaufort, Capt. Gabaret.
[2] Flag of Vice-Adm. the Chevalier Paul.
[3] Commanded by the celebrated Châteaurenault.
[4] Flag of the great Abraham Duquesne.

This force, or even part of it, might have been of great assistance to De Ruijter, but De Beaufort, hampered by continually changing orders, and influenced by his personal anxiety to be as far away as possible from Colbert de Terron, who had been given some sort of control over him, never brought it farther northward than Dieppe, and then returned to Brest. In the course of these movements the *Rubis*,[1] losing her friends, and mistaking an English squadron for a French, fell in with Sir Thomas Allin off Dungeness, and was captured with but little difficulty on September 18th. Colliber[2] relates that six French and Dutch vessels were in her company at the time, and that two of the Dutch were driven ashore and burnt. The *Rubis*, as the *French Ruby*, was added to the Navy, as also was the *Victoire*, taken during the same year, and renamed the *French Victory*.

The negotiations on the subject of the return of the body of Sir William Berkeley, who had fallen in the Four Days' Fight,

[1] Captain de la Roche. She figures in the above list. Some English accounts exaggerate her armament at the time of her capture to 54 and even to 70 guns.
[2] 'Columna Rostrata,' 187.

paved the way to overtures for a peace between England and the States; and presently Sweden offered her services as mediator. Both parties were tired of the war, and in May, 1667, a conference to consider the terms of an arrangement was opened at Breda; but, as Mahan[1] puts it, Charles, " ill disposed to the United Provinces, confident that the growing pretensions of Louis XIV. to the Spanish Netherlands would break up the existing alliance between Holland and France, and relying also upon the severe reverses suffered at sea by the Dutch, was exacting and haughty in his demands. To justify and maintain this line of conduct he should have kept up his fleet, the prestige of which had been so advanced by its victories. Instead of that, poverty, the result of extravagance and of his home policy, led him to permit it to decline; ships in large numbers were laid up, and he readily adopted an opinion which chimed in with his penury, and which, as it has had advocates at all periods of sea history, should be noted and condemned here." This opinion, as expressed by Campbell, was, " that as the Dutch were chiefly supported by trade, as the supply of their navy depended upon trade, and, as experience showed, nothing provoked the people so much as injuring their trade, his Majesty should therefore apply himself to this, which would effectually humble them, at the same time that it would less exhaust the English than fitting out such mighty fleets as had hitherto kept the sea every summer." Charles was further persuaded by his mother that any elaborate preparations on his part would dispose the States to think that he was not sincerely desirous of peace. The result was that, instead of commissioning a grand fleet of about a hundred sail, the King ordered out two small squadrons only to undertake the summer service for 1667.

The Grand Pensionary, Johan de Witt, disliked the prospect of peace because, as he admitted to D'Estrades, then French Minister to Holland, peace would render him less necessary and so diminish his authority; because it would be favourable to the interests of the House of Orange, to which he was opposed; and because, during the war, he had done unconstitutional acts for which, though they had been done with the best objects, he might be called to account in peace time.[2] These feelings, and

---

[1] 'Influence of Sea Power,' 131.
[2] 'Méms. du Cte. d'Estrades,' iii. 393, 483, 521. *See also* iv.

the temptation afforded to him by Charles's negligence, determined
him to utilise certain information which he had acquired in 1666
concerning the shoals and channels at the mouth of the Thames,
and to deal a sudden blow at England in that quarter. Louis XIV.
was apprised of the project and undertook to direct the Duc de
Beaufort to co-operate in its execution. In pursuance, however,
of his former ambiguous policy, he seems to have made this promise
merely in order to encourage the Dutch to strike, and when they
had perfected all their preparations and were finally committed to
the adventure, he conveniently forgot to keep it.

De Witt went warily to work. Instead of at once preparing
such a force as was necessary for the attainment of the object in
view, he assembled a comparatively small fleet of a score of ships,
with four fireships and a few galliots, ostensibly for the chastisement of Scots privateers; and in April he sent it to sea under
Van Ghent, the ex-colonel of marines, with about one hundred
and fifty sail of merchantmen in convoy. Van Ghent, after seeing
his charges clear of danger, entered the Forth, and on May 1st
appeared before Leith. An attempt on the part of a division
under Captain Thomas Tobijas [1] to ascend the Firth and burn the
shipping there was unsuccessful, and the Dutch contented themselves with an unsystematic bombardment of Burntisland, and
with the capture of six or seven small prizes, with which they
presently returned home to participate in De Witt's main project.

The operations of Van Ghent served to blind England and to
conceal the preparation of the more formidable fleet which was
destined for the attempt upon the Thames. This was collected
in the Texel, whence it sailed on May 27th for Schooneveld, and
thence, on June 4th, for England. On the night of the 4th, being
not far from the mouth of the Thames, it encountered bad weather
from the S.W., and suffered some damage; but the wind soon
moderated, and the fleet anchored a few miles from land. At
that time it consisted of only 54 ships of the line, with small
craft, but on the 6th it was joined by a Friesland contingent under
Lieutenant-Admiral Hans Willem van Aylva, another ex-colonel,
who had been promoted to the vacancy occasioned by the death
of Hiddes de Vries; and the united force then comprised 64 ships
of the line and "frigates," 7 armed dispatch yachts, 15 fireships,

---

[1] Two of whose subordinate captains were subsequently punished for dereliction of
duty. De Jonge, ii. 164.

and 13 galliots, mounting 3330 guns, and having on board 17,416 officers and men.   On the evening of June 7th, De Ruijter moved up to, and dropped anchor in, the King's Channel, and that night communicated the plan of operations to the flag officers, who, on the following morning, explained it to their captains and to the military officers who were to be employed.   Chief among the latter was Colonel Thomas Dolman.

The plan was briefly as follows.   The main body of the fleet was to lie in Thames mouth, while a squadron passed up as far as the Hope, and then returning, entered the Medway, doing what damage it might to English property and shipping, and seizing Sheerness, the defences of which were at the time in an unfinished condition.   De Ruijter, who was to remain with the reserve, would, in the event of the appearance of the enemy in force, fire two guns as a signal for the recall of the detached squadron.

This squadron was made up of two ships of 60 guns, six of 50, four of from 40 to 45, and five of from 32 to 36, with five armed yachts, most of the fireships, and all the galliots; and it was entrusted to the command of Lieutenant-Admiral Van Ghent. Although he had little or no experience of naval affairs, he was elected, firstly, because he was an Amsterdam officer, and the Amsterdam contingent was the strongest in the fleet, and secondly, because it was thought that, for the peculiar operations which were contemplated, military experience would be scarcely less serviceable than naval.   Van Ghent thereupon shifted his flag from the *Groot Dolphijn*, 84, to the *Agatha*, 50.   With him went Cornelis de Witt, who accompanied the expedition as plenipotentiary, and who had been enjoined by his brother, the Grand Pensionary, to watch all the operations in person, and not to let Van Ghent out of his sight.   Van Ghent's vice-admiral was Jan de Liefde, and his rear-admiral David Vlugh.   Both were tried seamen of courage and resource.   Van Ghent's flag-captain was Hendrik van Vollenhoven.

The detached squadron started up the river early on the morning of June 9th.   The tide was flowing, but the wind was from the S.W., so that little progress was possible, and Van Ghent presently anchored again.   Later in the day, however, the wind changed to S.E., and, while Van Ghent weighed and proceeded, De Ruijter, with the main fleet, took advantage of the opportunity to come up as far as the Middle Ground.

There were English ships in the Hope and near Gravesend, but towards evening the wind dropped; and Van Ghent failed to reach them ere they effected their escape to narrower and safer waters. He anchored for the night a little below Gravesend, and on the morning of the 10th fell down the river again. De Ruijter reinforced him with ten men-of-war and two fireships, and at noon Van Ghent entered the Medway, an English "frigate"[1] and some fireships slipping their cables and fleeing before him towards Chatham. Captains Jan van Brakel, Pieter Magnussen, and Eland du Bois were ordered to bombard Sheerness Fort, while Colonel Dolman[2] landed with soldiers and marines; and in an hour and a half the place was evacuated by its defenders under Sir Edward Spragge, who retreated up the river and established himself in a battery near Gillingham, nearly opposite Upnor Castle, where later he rendered excellent service.

Two yachts and some boats were sent up the Medway to sound the channel and were ordered to return as soon as they should sight any English ships; and De Witt and Van Ghent decided to prosecute the affair on the following day.

The appearance of the Dutch, and especially the capture of Sheerness, threw the English Court into consternation. The Duke of Albemarle with some land forces hurried to Chatham, where panic reigned and all was in confusion. The dockyard officials were more concerned for themselves and their private property than for the fate of the ships, docks, and stores. It was most difficult to secure workmen. Half the population had fled. Albemarle, however, managed to sink some ships[3] below Gillingham, and to lay a strong iron chain across the river immediately above them. This chain had long before been prepared for the defence of the upper reaches of the Medway, but does not seem to have been properly stretched and moored until Albemarle took it in hand. Nor was it protected until, by great exertions, he placed a small battery on shore at each end of it, and stationed the *Unity*[4] just outside its eastern extremity. He had to contend with scarcity of labour and the anxiety of the civilian population to hurry elsewhere; yet he succeeded not only in accomplishing this

---

[1] The *Unity*.
[2] A renegade English republican.
[3] Two large vessels and five fireships.
[4] C. de Witt calls her the *Jonathan*. Disp. of June 13th.

work and in strengthening the defences and garrison of Upnor
Castle, but also in to some extent blocking the river above the chain,
so as to impede the progress of the Dutch should they burst through
the lower obstructions. Immediately above the chain, with their
broadsides commanding it, he moored the *Carolus Quintus* and
the *Mathias*, and a little above them the *Monmouth*. He directed
the *Royal Charles*, 100, one of the finest ships in the Navy, which
lay near the *Monmouth*, to be towed farther up the river, but, owing
either to misunderstanding or to the lack of boats, the order was
never carried out. Finally, he ordered a Dutch prize, the *Slot van
Honingen*, which had been renamed the *Mary*, to be sunk in a
certain specified position, but, owing to the ignorance or the carelessness of the pilots, she was run aground in the wrong place and
could not be brought off again. Above all these defences lay in
order the *Royal Oak, Loyal London, Old James, Katherine, Princess,
Geldersche Ruijter* (renamed *Golden Ruyter*), *Triumph, Rainbow,
Unicorn, Henry, Hilversum*, and *Vanguard*, the last named being just
below Rochester Bridge. Abreast of the *Mary*, and again abreast
of the *Loyal London, Princess*, and *Old James* respectively, there
were batteries on shore ; but several of these defences were not in a
tenable condition, and some had not even all their guns mounted.

The Dutch do not appear to have advanced on the 11th. They
however sent up towards Gillingham a division consisting of four
men-of-war, three armed yachts, and two fireships ; and at 7 A.M.
on the morning of June 12th Van Ghent's squadron weighed, and,
with a fresh N.E. breeze, began to make its way up the Medway.
Captain Jan van Brakel in the *Vrede*, 40, accompanied by the
fireships *Susanna*[1] and *Pro Patria*, led the van ; and while the
Vrede engaged, boarded, and carried the *Unity*, the fireships made
for the chain. The *Susanna* charged it without effect, but the
Pro Patria, Captain Jan Danielszoon van De Rijn, broke through
it and at once placed herself alongside the *Mathias*, which she
set on fire, and which quickly blew up. By that time several fireships and other craft had crowded through and had got out their
boats. Van Brakel, who had quitted the *Vrede* for the *Schiedam*,
a craft of less draught, boarded the *Carolus Quintus*, after she had
driven off two fireships, took her, and turned her guns upon the
land batteries at each end of the chain. These he soon silenced,

---

[1] De Jonge calls her *Susanna*. Some contemporary dispatches indicate, however,
that her name was *Schiedam*.

and then a party of Dutch landed and blew up a magazine attached to one of the batteries.

By this time De Ruijter himself had arrived upon the scene. During the rest of the operations his barge, and the boats of the other Dutch flag officers, were frequently engaged with both the

STERN CARVING FROM H.M.S. "ROYAL CHARLES," 100.

(*Captured by the Dutch in the Medway in 1667, and now preserved in the Rijks Museum at Amsterdam.*)

The following is a translation of the Dutch inscription upon the above: "These arms decorated the *Royal Charles*, of 100 guns, the largest ship in the English Navy; which, with several other vessels, was captured during the glorious operations in the river of Rochester in the year 1667, under the chief command of Lieut.-Admiral M. A. de Ruijter, and the Regent, C. de Wit. In the same year she was brought into the Maas; and in 1673 she was broken up at Hellevoetsluis."

ships and the batteries. The *Royal Charles*, which had but thirty-two of her guns mounted, was the next vessel to be captured, and as soon as she had struck, and the *Agatha* had passed the chain, the flag of the States was hoisted in the English three-decker, which thenceforth became Van Ghent's flagship for the rest of the day.

Efforts were made by the defence to tow or warp away the *Monmouth*, which was only partially rigged, but she fell foul of the *Mary*, which had been grounded, as above mentioned, in the wrong position, and was taken and set fire to.

The scene at that moment to be witnessed below Chatham has not often been paralleled in naval history. In some respects it resembled the scene at Toulon in December, 1793, and in others, the scarcely less imposing scene in the Bay of Navarin in October, 1827. The river was full of moving craft and burning wreckage ; the roar of guns was almost continuous ; the shrieks of the wounded could be heard even above the noise of battle, the clangour of trumpets, the roll of drums, and the cheers of the Dutch as success after success was won ; and above all hung a pall of smoke, illumined only, as night closed in, by the gleam of flames on all sides and the flashes of guns and muskets.

In the night several of the Dutch ships took the ground. On the 13th it was decided to attack the vessels lying higher up, above Upnor Castle. That work, however, commanded by Major Scott, and the battery under Sir Edward Spragge, nearly opposite to it, proved to be very formidable obstructions to the continued progress of the enemy. The Dutch, it is true, after a hard struggle, succeeded in setting fire to the *Royal Oak*, the *Loyal London*,[1] and the *Old James*,[2] but when they had done so they were in no condition to do more ; and neither the sunken *Katherine*, yet a little higher up, nor the scuttled *Vanguard* at Rochester Bridge, was needed to bar the channel. The enemy had expended all his fireships except two, and dared go no farther. On the 14th, therefore, he retired, carrying off with him the *Royal Charles* and the *Unity*, and rejoined his main body at the mouth of the Medway.[2]

The English defence was hampered by the fact that, owing to the parsimonious policy of the Government, most of the ships in the Medway were partially dismantled, all were but one-half or one-quarter manned, and some were actually laid up in ordinary

---

[1] In the case of the *Loyal London* and the *Old James*, the flames were ultimately extinguished.

[2] Swinnas ; Penn ; Pepys ; Albemarle's Report ; Journal of Van Brakel ; Journal of Van Nes ; Life of De Ruijter in 'Levens der Zeehelden,' pt. ii. ; 'Kort en Bondigh Verhael' ; printed letters of De Ruijter, Van Ghent, and De Liefde ; Reports of C. de Witt ; Parker's 'History of Own Time' ; Gumble's 'Life of Monck' ; 'Mems. of J. Sheffield, Duke of Buckingham' ; State Letters of Roger, Earl of Orrery ; Arlington, Letters ; Coke's 'Detection' ; Basnage ; Le Clerc ; Neuville ; Ludlow, 'Memoirs,' etc.

at the time of the attack. Yet there can be no doubt that, in spite
of the enormous difficulties of the situation, the English fought
stubbornly. A land officer, Captain Dowglass, who had been
ordered on board the *Royal Oak*, and directed to hold her to the
best of his ability, perished gallantly with the ship when at length
the enemy succeeded in burning her. " Never," he declared, upon
being advised to retire, " shall it be told that a Dowglass quitted
his post without orders." [1] The total Dutch loss does not appear
to have exceeded one hundred and fifty men. The English must
have suffered very much more severely.

At the mouth of the Medway the Dutch fleet was reinforced by
a Zeeland squadron of five large men-of-war and five fireships under
Lieutenant-Admiral Adriaen Banckers, and, soon afterwards, by a few
other vessels, which brought up the total strength in sail of the line
and " frigates " to eighty-four. Thereupon Van Ghent was detached
with eighteen ships and " frigates," a storeship, and three galliots,
to meet and convoy some home-coming East Indiamen. Another
squadron, under Vice-Admiral Cornelis Evertsen, " the Younger," a
son of Jan Evertsen, was ordered to cruise between Harwich and the
Foreland. A third squadron, under Rear-Admiral Van der Zaen,
was stationed between Harwich and the King's Channel. As for
the bulk of the fleet under De Ruijter, it remained for several days
before Queenborough, and then, anticipating danger from fireships,
moved to the mouth of the Thames. During that time an efficient
blockade of the river was maintained, and the price of coals in
London rose from 15*s*. to 140*s*. a ton, the price of other sea-borne
products rising in proportion. A reconnaissance up the Thames as
far as the Hope showed the Dutch that the channel had there been
effectively obstructed by means of sunken ships, among which,
according to Van den Bosch, were the *Huis te Swieten* and the
Phœnix, and that heavy batteries had been erected [2] on both banks.
Meanwhile, De Ruijter looked anxiously for the arrival and co-
operation of the Duc de Beaufort, whose assistance at that juncture
might have brought England to her knees. But it was not the
policy of Louis XIV. to crush Charles for the benefit of the
Netherlands ; and not only did De Beaufort stay quietly at anchor

---

[1] Sir W. Temple to Lord Lisle ; 'Works,' ii. 40.

[2] Chiefly by the exertions of Capt. Sir John Griffith of the Duke of York's
Maritime Regiment, who was Governor of Gravesend Fort.   S. P. Dom. Car. ii. cciv.
42, and Ent. Bk. xxiii. 433.

at Brest, but also it presently appeared that there was so amicable
a private understanding between England and France that Holland
had nothing further to hope from the latter.

On the evening of July 1st the bulk of the Dutch fleet anchored
off Aldborough, and at dawn on the 2nd it weighed, and, after
having proceeded for some time to the northward, tacked, stood
again to the south, and passed Orfordness at about 7 A.M., bent
upon attacking Harwich.[1] At 1 P.M. the greater part of the force,
which consisted of forty-seven sail, besides tenders, drew in within
half gunshot of the shore near Felixstowe Cliffs, but out of reach of
Landguard Fort, and, getting out its boats, threw ashore about three
thousand men, two thousand of whom lost no time in delivering two
successive assaults on Landguard Fort. The first was repulsed after
three-quarters of an hour's fighting; the second, after about a
quarter of an hour only; and finally, the enemy, after losing about
one hundred and fifty men, retired, leaving their scaling-ladders
behind them in their haste.

In the meantime the thousand or twelve hundred men who had
been left near the place of landing were attacked by the trained
bands under James, third Earl of Suffolk. The struggle with them
was continued in a desultory manner until about 10 P.M., when the
routed Dutch returned from the attack on the fort. The enemy
then managed, though with considerable loss, to re-embark. Just
after he had done so, a detachment of five hundred foot, under
Major Legge, arrived from Harwich. The fight, however, was then
over; and it is neither Legge nor the Earl of Suffolk who must be
credited with the honour of having saved Landguard. The credit is
due to Captain Nathaniel Darell of the Duke of York and Albany's
Maritime Regiment of Foot, and to his gallant marines. Darell,
who was Governor of Landguard, and who was slightly wounded on
the occasion, had, but a month before, been represented to the
king and council as a malignant Papist and an incompetent. Well,
indeed, did he vindicate himself.[2] The family of Darell-Blount, of
Calehill, Kent, still possesses one of the ladders abandoned by the
Dutch. The attack on shore was commanded by the same renegade
Colonel Dolman who had captured the fort at Sheerness.

---

[1] Sir Joseph Jordan with a small squadron then lay in the Stour; but his force was
far too weak to justify him in leaving it, in face of so powerful a force.

[2] *London Gazette*, 1–4 July, 1667; Hill's 'Nav. Hist.' 510; Pepys's 'Diary' (Ed.
1848), iv. 107; S. P. Dom. Car. ii. ccviii. 72; Brandt, 'Leven van De Ruijter,' 563.

Having returned to the mouth of the Thames, De Ruijter divided his fleet into two squadrons, one of which he retained under his own orders, and the other of which he entrusted to Lieutenant-Admiral Aert Jansze van Nes. With his own squadron, and accompanied by Cornelis de Witt, he entered the Channel and excited much alarm upon the south coast of England. He appeared before several ports, including Portsmouth, and captured several vessels, but he made no very serious attempts upon any place, and encountered no English fleet during his cruise.

The squadron of Van Nes, left to blockade the Thames, had a much more eventful experience. Here is a summary of a journal of its proceedings printed in Van den Bosch's Life of De Ruijter :—[1]

" On July 13th we sailed six leagues, and saw the Naze N.W. by W. four miles from us. We were then forty-three sail in company, part men-of-war, part fireships, and part victuallers. On the 14th, the wind blew so hard from the N.E. that we had to take in all sail, but happily the fleet suffered no damage. On the 18th, two victuallers parted company to the S.S.E. On the 21st, eight men-of-war, eight fireships, and eight victuallers left us to join the Admiral-in-Chief ; but, on the other hand, Vice-Admiral Enno Doedes Star appeared with nine ships and twenty-one Flamand merchantmen, and presently joined us with eight of the men-of-war. . . . On the 23rd, we learnt from two vessels laden with prisoners that up the river lay five English men-of-war and twenty fireships. At about 9 o'clock, six of our men-of-war, under Vice-Admiral Star, pushed up and anchored a little above 'Blacktyl,' while fifteen men-of-war and thirteen fireships, under Lieut.-Admiral Van Nes, Lieut.-Admiral Meppel, and Vice-Admirals Sweers and Schram, advanced further. . . . At noon we heard a heavy cannonade and saw several ships burning. On the morning of the 24th, our vessels came in sight again. Towards 4 o'clock our people recommenced firing briskly, and so matters went on until late in the evening. On the 25th, our vessels returned, having expended all their fireships and burnt seven English craft ; but the enemy was then where our ships had lain. In the afternoon the English came down somewhat lower, but we, having the advantage of the east wind, advanced towards them . . . and they retired, although they still had a strength of five men-of-war, thirteen fireships, and many small craft. At dawn on the 26th, with a light E.N.E. wind, we weighed and made towards the island of Sheppey. At about 10 A.M., twenty-three or twenty-four English vessels came down [2] the river on the flood, and set upon us. . . . There were fifteen or sixteen fireships and a couple of ' frigates ' of 16 or 20 guns. The rest were small. Capt. Naelhout (of the *Harderwijck*) had two fireships on board of him, but drove them off with great courage and small loss. Rear-Admiral Jan Matthijsse was also assailed by one, but happily got free from her. Our advanced ships fired on them so hotly that they gave way, and drifted over towards Sheppey. . . . Our boats chased two of their fireships, one of which ran aground on Sheppey, and was set on fire, though her people escaped, while the other took refuge in an inlet. The other three fireships before mentioned passed through our fleet without doing harm, . . . but two of their ships caught fire and were burnt before our eyes. . . . On the 28th of July we left the river once more. . . ."

---

[1] ' Levens der Zeehelden,' pt. ii.
[2] This is apparently an error. This little English squadron came up the river, and was last from Harwich.

It is possible that the above account may not have been intentionally coloured, but it is certainly incorrect in many particulars and incomplete in others. On the 23rd, when the Dutch got up to the Hope, they encountered a small squadron,[1] which had been placed under the orders of Sir Edward Spragge, who, however, had not then arrived to take command. Van Nes attacked; and, although he had to expend twelve or thirteen fireships in destroying six or seven English vessels, he was successful in driving the enemy under the guns of Tilbury Fort. But on the 24th, when Sir Edward had arrived, the English attacked, and obliged the Dutch to retreat, with the loss of their last fireship; and on the 25th Sir Edward still followed them, though at a distance, and does not appear to have been repulsed. He anchored, however, at about 5 A.M., when the tide began to make up river, weighing and following again at 1 P.M. On the 26th, Sir Joseph Jordan, with his twenty small vessels from Harwich, entered the Thames. He seems to have fought the enemy as he passed in to join Sir Edward ; but it is just possible that, taking advantage of the shoals, he passed in without fighting, and that he did not engage until he and Sir Edward were united.

The commanders of several of the English fireships which had been stationed to defend Gravesend unhappily misbehaved themselves in a very disgraceful manner on this critical occasion. Of their officers, one, William Howe, of the *Virgin*, was sentenced by court-martial[2] to be shot, and was executed on November 18th ; and three, Joseph Paine, of the *Blacknose*, Anderson Gibbons, of the *John and Elizabeth*, and Ralph Mayhew, of the *Blessing*, were ignominiously dismissed the service.[3]

After quitting the Thames, the Dutch hovered off the coasts and created alarm in various quarters ; but ere they had time to undertake any other venture of importance, the signature of the Treaty of Breda[4] put an end to the war. This settlement, which was

---

[1] Of five "frigates," seventeen fireships, and some small craft.

[2] C. M. November 4th, 1667.

[3] C. M. November 11th, 1667; *Gazette*, No. 208. The sentence on each was that he was "to be sent on board the *Victory Prize* at Deptford, on the 18th of the same month, where he was to have a halter put about his neck, and a wooden sword broken over his head : he was then to be towed through the water at a boat's stern, from the ship to Deptford Dock, a drum beating all the time in the boat, and to be rendered incapable in future of any command." Gibbons, in addition, was sentenced to be triced up by the arms during the punishment of the other two.

[4] July 31st, 1667.

a tripartite one, executed between England on the one hand, and Holland, France, and Denmark on the other, provided, among other things, for the restoration of St. Christopher, Antigua, and Montserrat to England, and of Acadia, now Nova Scotia, to France ; for the retention of New York and New Jersey by England, and of Surinam by Holland ; and for a modification of the Navigation Act in favour of the Dutch. But the Honour of the Flag in the British seas was confirmed to England.

France had already shown a desire to get possession of the Spanish Netherlands and Franche Comté. Soon after the conclusion of the Treaty of Breda, Holland, England, and Sweden formed an alliance, with the object of checking Louis XIV., ere his power should become too great. This alliance, of which Holland

MEDAL COMMEMORATIVE OF THE PEACE OF BREDA, 1667.

(From an original kindly lent by H.S.H. Prince Louis of Battenberg, R.N.)

was the moving spirit, exasperated France. She, however, appeared to yield, and then set to work to plot the destruction of the United Provinces. There was much sympathy between the English people and the Dutch, but more between Charles and Louis ; and the latter was soon able to break up the alliance, and to conclude an offensive league with Charles. Charles, in fact, was bribed, firstly, by actual payments of money; secondly, by promises of Netherlands territory, and thirdly, by Louis's concession that, in the coming war afloat, an English officer should command in chief. Having come to this arrangement, Charles lost no time in provoking a conflict.

A yacht having been directed to bring home the wife of Sir William Temple from the Continent, her captain was ordered to deliberately place himself in the way of a Dutch fleet at sea, and,

if it did not strike, to fire at it. Van Ghent, who commanded the
Dutch fleet, was treated in this outrageous manner, but pocketed
the insult. Then came a demand on the part of England for more
specific recognition by Holland of the English sovereignty of the
seas. The Dutch evinced an obvious desire to preserve peace, but,
perceiving that all concessions would be useless, they, as a precautionary measure, commissioned seventy-five ships of the line,
and a number of smaller vessels, in February, 1672. This was all
the excuse that Charles II. needed. On March 12th, without any
declaration of war, Sir Robert Holmes, by order, waylaid and
attacked the Dutch home-coming Smyrna and Lisbon convoys;[1] on
March 19th, Charles declared war, and on March 27th, Louis XIV.
did likewise.

The war which followed was not, as the previous war had been,
a maritime war only. France, the most formidable military nation
in Europe, pressed the Republic continually by land; and, had it
not been for the naval genius of De Ruijter, and for the masterly
manner in which he utilised the sea power of his sorely-tried
country, Holland must have collapsed under the terrible ordeal to
which she was exposed.

"The naval war," says Mahan, "differs from those that preceded it in more than
one respect, but its most distinctive feature is that the Dutch, except on one occasion
at the very beginning, did not send out their fleet to meet the enemy, but made what
may properly be called a strategic use of their dangerous coast and shoals, upon which
were based their sea operations. To this course they were forced by the desperate odds
under which they were fighting ; but they did not use their shoals as a mere shelter ;
the warfare they waged was the defensive-offensive. When the wind was fair for
the Allies to attack, Ruijter kept under cover of his islands, or at least on ground where
the enemy dared not follow ; but when the wind served so that he might attack in his
own way, he turned and fell upon them. There are also apparent indications of tactical
combinations on his part of a higher order than have yet been met ; though it is
possible that the particular acts referred to, consisting in partial attacks amounting to
little more than demonstrations against the French contingent, may have sprung from
political motives. . . . There is, however, an equally satisfactory military explanation
in the supposition that, the French being yet inexperienced, Ruijter thought it only
necessary to contain them while falling in force upon the English. The latter fought
throughout with their old gallantry, but less than their old discipline ; whereas the
attacks of the Dutch were made with a sustained and unanimous vigour that showed a
great military advance. The action of the French was at times suspicious ; it has been
alleged that Louis ordered his admiral to economise his fleet, and there is good reason
to believe that towards the end of the two years that England remained in his alliance
he did do so." [2]

The first object of the allies was to effect a junction of their

---

[1] *See* Chap. XXV.

[2] 'Influence of Sea Power upon History,' 144, 145.

fleets; the next was to utilise the combined force for the making of
a descent upon the coast of Zeeland, and so for assisting the
operations of the French army which had entered the Netherlands,
and which Louis XIV. commanded in person.

The French fleet destined for co-operation with the English,
consisted of thirty-three ships of the line and "frigates," eight
fireships, and four storeships, mounting 1926 guns, and having on
board 10,966 officers and men. It was commanded-in-chief by
Jean d'Estrées, Vice-Admiral of France, an officer who, until 1668,
had been a lieutenant-general in the army, who knew little or
nothing of naval affairs, and who was an incapable leader. He
hoisted his flag in the *St. Philippe*, 74. The second in command
was Abraham Duquesne, an able and experienced seaman, but
a quarrelsome man, who was jealous of D'Estrées, and whom
D'Estrées seems to have hated. He had his flag in the *Terrible*, 70.
As *chefs d'escadre*, or commodores, under these two officers, were
Captains Treillebois de La Rabesnière, in the *Superbe*, and Des
Ardens, in the *Tonnant*. Tourville, whose name came into
prominence twenty years later, commanded the *Sage*, 50.

The English fleet seems to have consisted of 65 ships of the line
and "frigates," 22 fireships, and a considerable number of ketches
and small craft, mounting 4092 guns, and having on board 23,530
officers and men. Its commander-in-chief was H.R.H. the Duke
of York, Lord High Admiral, in the *Prince*. As usual, the fleet
was organised into three squadrons, the Red, or centre, the White,
or van, and the Blue, or rear; but on this occasion the White
squadron consisted of the French contingent, D'Estrées taking the
place and functions, and hoisting the flag, of the Admiral of the
White. The Admiral of the Blue was Edward, Earl of Sandwich,
in the *Royal James*. Among the other English flag-officers were
Sir Joseph Jordan, in the *Sovereign*, Sir John Harman in the *Royal
Charles*, and Sir John Kempthorne in the *St. Andrew*. There
seems to have been no love lost between the English and their
allies, and Dutch writers relate that English prisoners declared after
the battle that they had no ill-feeling against the Hollanders, but
would have been delighted to fight the French. In this case the
inherent weakness of a fleet formed of ships of two or more nationalities was intensified by the facts that the English did not trust
the French, and despised them as seamen, and that the French,
besides being jealous of one another, were jealous of the English.

The Dutch, on the other hand, were, at sea if not ashore, united and disciplined as they had never been during the previous war. Their fleet, according to a list prepared by Cornelis de Witt, who accompanied it as Plenipotentiary of Their High Mightinesses, consisted of 75 ships of the line and "frigates," 36 fireships, and 22 yachts and small craft, mounting 4484 guns, and having on board 20,738 officers and men. The commander-in-chief was the great De Ruijter;[1] Lieutenant-Admiral Adriaen Banckers commanded the van or left; Lieutenant-Admiral W. J. van Ghent commanded the rear or right; and among the other flag-officers were Vice-Admirals Cornelis Evertsen,[2] De Liefde, and Sweers, and Rear-Admirals Jan Jansze van Nes, Jan den Haen, and Jan Matthijsze.

The strength of the two fleets, omitting small craft other than fireships, was therefore :—

	Allies.	Dutch.
Ships of the line and " frigates " . .	98	75
Fireships	30	36
Guns	6,018	4,484
Officers and men	34,496	20,738

Knowing of the contemplated junction between the French and English forces, the United Provinces made great exertions to fit out their fleet in time to enable it to strike at the latter in the mouth of the Thames ere the French should arrive from Brest. Says Mahan :—

"The wretched lack of centralisation in their naval administration caused this project to fail. The province of Zeeland was so backward that its contingent, a large fraction of the whole, was not ready in time; and it has been charged that the delay was due, not merely to mismanagement, but to disaffection to the party in control of the government. A blow at the English fleet in its own waters, by a superior force, before its ally arrived, was a correct military conception; judging from the after-history of this war, it might well have produced a profound effect upon the whole course of the struggle."

---

[1] In his favourite flagship the *Zeven Provinciën*, a vessel that deserves to rank with Nelson's *Victory*. Built at Delfshaven, and carrying eighty guns, she first went to sea in 1665, De Ruijter's flag being then hoisted in her. She served through the second and third Dutch wars, but was no longer his flagship when De Ruijter received his fatal wound at the battle of Agosta. She suffered severe damage at La Hougue, and seems to have been broken up in 1694. 'Nederl. Zeewezen,' i. 638, 642 ; ii. 488, 568 ; iii. 305, 685.

[2] Cornelis Evertsen, "the Younger," son of Liut.-Admiraal Jan Evertsen. Served in the second war with England. Led a squadron at Solebay and in other actions of the third war. Commanded in the West Indies. Died, 1679.

D'Estrées early in May reached Portsmouth, where he was
presently joined by the English fleet; and a little later the allies
put to sea in company. De Ruijter at length sailed, and, in the
North Sea, captured the *French Victory*, 38.[1] On May 19th, he
fell in with the allied fleets[2] about twenty-four miles E.S.E. of
the Gunfleet, but, though anxious to engage them, he lost sight
of them in consequence of the thickness of the weather. The
Duke of York and D'Estrées, instead of following up the enemy,[3]
anchored in Southwold Bay, or Solebay, then apparently a considerable indentation on the Suffolk coast, but now, owing to
changes in the conformation of the shore, no bay deserving of the
name. The land runs nearly north and south. The fleets were
anchored almost parallel with it, the French squadron, or proper
van, being to the south, the Blue squadron, under Sandwich, being
to the north, and the Red squadron, under the Duke of York
himself, being in the centre. Captain Christopher Gunman, who
was serving as Master of the *Prince*, wrote in his 'Journal,' on the
26th, " we received intelligence that the Dutch were gone off our
coast over to their own."

We do not know how the wind was when they anchored, but
it is recorded that on May 27th it blew stiffly from the N.E.,
and that Sandwich, being that day, with other flag-officers, at a
council of war on board the *Prince*, ventured to suggest that, as
matters were, the fleet was in danger of being surprised upon a
lee shore, and that, in his opinion, they ought to weigh and put
to sea. The Duke, however, instead of taking the advice, seems
to have hinted that the Earl's very praiseworthy caution was the
effect not so much of prudence as of apprehension. In a very few
hours Sandwich's prescience was amply vindicated. The failure of
others to take advantage of it probably cost the gallant Earl his life.

A little before three o'clock the report of guns was heard in
the fleet, and soon afterwards a French craft, which had been on
the look-out in the north-east, came back before the wind with all

---

[1] Ex-*Victoire*, taken from the French in the previous war.

[2] S. P. Dom. ii. B. C. 309. Gunman, in his 'Journal,' says that although the
Allies were to the windward of the enemy, when the fleets sighted one another on the
19th, they made no effort to attack, deeming that they could not get up with the
Dutch in time to fight an effective action that day.

[3] It is asserted (S. P. Dom. ii. B. C. 309) that the Allies were in sight of the Dutch
on May 21st, the day before they anchored in Solebay. Gunman's 'Journal' confirms
this, and adds that the Dutch stood to the southward; so that the Allies seem to have
deliberately refrained from taking the offensive.

sail set to report the approach of the enemy from that quarter. The Allies had many boats ashore with watering parties and were taken quite unawares. Sandwich's squadron, which was to windward, cut its cables with great promptitude and stood out on the starboard tack—probably in consequence of some previous orders from the Duke of York, or possibly in response to a signal from the commander-in-chief; but in spite of the fact that Sandwich was early engaged, and that he did his utmost to hold the attention of the Dutch, the allied fleet seems to have been only saved from destruction by the wind dropping. But for that the enemy's fireships would have got into the body of the fleet while it was still in confusion.

De Ruijter's fleet, which came from the E.N.E., was in two grand divisions of line abreast. The advanced division consisted of eighteen ships of the line or "frigates," accompanied by a large number of fireships. The second, or main division, consisted of the bulk of the fleet, and was commanded on the left by Banckers, on the right by Van Ghent, and in the centre by De Ruijter himself.

The Duke of York, like Sandwich, stood out on the starboard tack, that is, to the northward; but D'Estrées, either misapprehending the directions of the commander-in-chief, or acting in pursuance of previous orders from Paris, stood out on the port tack, that is, to the south-east; so that an ever-widening gap immediately opened out between the French and their English allies.

De Ruijter, in the previous war had experienced the value of a French alliance, and, no doubt, appreciated at its proper worth the indifferent French seamanship of that day. Moreover, it is possible that he may have suspected that D'Estrées had been directed to run no great risks. He therefore detached Banckers with a comparatively small force to hold in check the 33 French ships, and, with the rest of his fleet—probably about 50 or 55 sail of the line and "frigates," besides most of his fireships—made for the 65 ships of the allied centre and proper rear.[1]

While the wind was light, falling almost to a calm, the allied centre, with the assistance of its boats, got into some kind of order. When the wind freshened again it blew from the S.E.,

[1] Some English historians claim that after this separation of the forces, the Dutch were to the English in the proportion of three to two. This claim seems to be untenable. The Dutch were then, apparently, still inferior in numbers.

thus giving the English more sea room to the northward. D'Estrées kept away, and was not pressed by Banckers, who, although he had the wind, contented himself with a distant cannonade ; yet, owing no doubt to some extent to Colbert's order to the French admiral to make his report as favourable as possible, French historians, almost without exception, describe their countrymen as having borne a very important share in the action, and as having greatly distinguished themselves. It will be sufficient, in support of this, to quote the following from Guérin : [1]

"The White squadron . . . received Banckers with valour. . . . The Vice-Admiral of France, who had been directed at all hazards, while economising the naval forces of the kingdom, to make a demonstration sufficient to save the honour of the royal flag, certainly fulfilled in a most satisfactory way the second part of his orders ; and in consequence of the ardent bravery of his captains, he was led even farther than the Court would have wished him to go. . . . The French retook the English ship *Katherine* which the enemy had captured, and prevented the capture of another English vessel commanded by Lord Ossory. The ship commanded by Captain de Valbelle was specially noticed by the English for the generous devotion with which she hastened to the assistance of all the allied vessels that were endangered. She could not prevent the loss of the *Royal James*, 100, bearing the flag of the Admiral of the Blue," etc., etc.

Most of this is pure imagination. The French kept as much as possible out of the fight ; and, although Commodore Treillebois de La Rabesnière was fatally wounded, and Commodore Des Ardens lost a leg—although the French even lost two ships—the White squadron, if it escape the charge of cowardice, must be convicted either of treachery or of the grossest incapacity on the part of its leaders. The French had no hand in the retaking of the *Katherine* ; they were never, after the battle had begun, in a position to affect, either one way or the other, the fate of the *Victory,* the Earl of Ossory's ship ; and Captain de Valbelle's activity, if exerted at all, was exerted at such a distance from the allied centre and rear as to be far beyond the notice of English officers. After the action D'Estrées and Duquesne quarrelled as to the behaviour of the latter ; and, to pacify the former, Duquesne was superseded, although no judgment was passed upon his conduct.

When Sandwich, with the English rear, had been for a time hotly engaged with the Dutch rear, or right, under Van Ghent, the English centre, under the Duke of York, got into equally hot action with the Dutch centre under De Ruijter. Sandwich, in the *Royal James,* soon found himself gallantly and closely attacked by Captain

[1] ' Hist. Marit. de France,' iii. 220–222.

Jan van Brakel in the *Groot Hollandia*, a ship of much inferior force, which, it appears, had left, or been detached from, the Dutch centre, and had joined Van Ghent. Brakel behaved in the most brilliant manner, and his vessel eventually lost no fewer than 150 killed and 50 wounded out of her complement of 300;[1] but the *Groot Hollandia*, which was a 60-gun ship only, must have been eventually overpowered by the *Royal James*, a 100-gun three-decker, had not the latter been

EDWARD MONTAGU, EARL OF SANDWICH, ADMIRAL AND GENERAL-AT-SEA.

(From J. Cochran's engraving after the portrait by Sir P. Lely.)

presently attacked as well by two fireships and by Van Ghent in person. Sandwich defended himself against these for two hours, sinking the fireships and killing Van Ghent; but, at about noon, a third fireship[2] grappled the *Royal James* and set her on fire.

---

[1] 'Generale Lijst van de Dooden,' in C. de Witt's Journal, and letter of Carel Jans to the Plenipotentiary.

[2] Commanded by the same Jan Danielszoon van De Rijn who had broken the chain in the Medway.

Sandwich held his ship to the last, and then, according to what seems to be the most probable account, entered a boat, accompanied by his son-in-law,[1] in order to go to another vessel. The boat, however, overcrowded by the number of people who flung themselves into her, sank, and all on board were drowned. Contemporary feeling blamed Sir Joseph Jordan, the vice-admiral of the Earl's squadron, for the death of Sandwich, alleging that Jordan quitted his own chief at a critical moment in order to support the Duke of York who was hard pressed. Captain Richard Haddock, who commanded the *Royal James*, and who survived, in a letter to the Duke of York, wrote : "Some short time after, Sir Joseph Jordan . . . passed by us, very unkindly, to windward, and with how many followers of his division I remember not, and took no notice of us at all." This certainly seems to give some tinge of truth to popular opinion ; but it is fair to add that Jordan had previously received certain special directions from the Duke, and appears to have engaged to support him ; and that the fact of Jordan having kept the wind on the occasion in question subsequently enabled him to break the Dutch centre and to throw it into considerable confusion. After the action he was promoted. On the other hand he was not again employed afloat. The Earl's body, picked up a few days afterwards, was recognised by the George [2] and star on the coat, and was ultimately buried with great ceremony in Henry the Seventh's Chapel at Westminster.

The fight made by Sandwich and the ships of his immediate following, and the death of Van Ghent, demoralised the Dutch rear, which, for a time, retired almost out of action. This allowed the English Blue squadron as a body to join the English Red and to concentrate upon De Ruijter and the Dutch centre, which suffered very severely. The battle continued until 8 or 9 P.M., but towards its conclusion the Dutch rear rejoined the commander-in-chief ; and, as the French made no move to assist their allies,[3] the Dutch were at length able to withdraw to the northward.[4]

---

[1] Sir Philip Carteret.   [2] Exhibited at the R. N. Exhib. 1891.

[3] Hoste, however, says that D'Estrées contemplated tacking and breaking through Banckers's squadron so as to rejoin the English. Had he tried this manœuvre, the result would probably have been most disastrous to him, and, as Mahan thinks, would in all likelihood have overwhelmed him with a fate similar to that of the Spanish admiral off St. Vincent in 1797.

[4] They still, nevertheless, hovered near, for Christopher Gunman's 'Journal' of the 29th, after stating that the *Prince* and ships in company had stood that morning to the northward, continues : "The Dutch, seeing no more of our ships than so small a

Claimed both by the Dutch and by the Allies as a victory, the battle
of Solebay was, in reality, a drawn fight. The Allies held the field
and made a prize; but the Dutch effected their main object, which
was to prevent or delay their enemy from crossing the North
Sea and co-operating with the French in the Netherlands. It
must be admitted also that the action added to the already great
fame of De Ruijter, who confessed that he had never before been
present in so hard fought and obstinate an engagement.

The losses on both sides were heavy. The Dutch ship
Stavoren, 48, Captain Daniel Elsevier, was taken; and the
Jozua, 60, Captain Jan Dick, was sunk by gunshot.[1] Strange
to say, Van Ghent was the sole Dutch officer of high rank who
was killed outright, though Captain Joost Michiels Cuijcq, of the
Windhond, subsequently died of his wounds. Among the wounded
were Banckers, Engel de Ruijter, son of the Dutch commander-
in-chief, Brakel, and many other officers of distinction. The loss
of private men was very serious, though not so serious as on
the side of the English. The gallant Sandwich was the only
English flag-officer to fall, but a number of captains perished
in the performance of their duty. Willoughby Hannam, of the
Triumph; Geoffrey Pearce of the *St. George*; Sir John Cox,[2] First
Captain of the *Prince*; Sir Frescheville Holles, of the *Cambridge*;
John Waterworth, of the *Anne*; the Hon. Francis Digby, of the
Henry, and Captain Ezekiel Yennis, of the *Alice and Francis*,
fireship, were among these. Digby, besides being a captain in
the Royal Navy, was a captain in the Duke of York and Albany's
Maritime Regiment of Foot (the Marines of that day), and is
remarkable as having been the first naval officer to hold the double
commission. Yet another captain, R.N., Walter Perry, who,
however, at the time of the action, was serving in a lieutenant's

---

number, came after us: but we, coming up with our own ships, so that we were then
about 80 sail of ships, did tack upon them, which when they saw, and we coming near
that they could see what number of ships we had, they stood away from us for their
own coast as fast as they could, E.S.E. and S.E. by E." Indeed, the action would
have been renewed that day had not a fog come on after the "Blody Flagg" had
actually been hoisted by the Duke.

[1] On the following day the Dutch also lost the *Westergoo* which accidentally
blew up.

[2] Sir John Cox was First Captain, or Captain of the Fleet; Captain John Nar-
brough was flag-captain; and Captain Christopher Gunman served as Master of the
Prince. After the death of Cox, Narbrough was made Captain of the Fleet, and
Gunman, flag-captain.

capacity in the *Royal James*, lost his life. How severely the
Marines suffered may be gathered from the fact that out of twelve
captains on the strength of the Duke's regiment, four, namely,
Thomas Bennett, Thomas Bromley, Roger Vaughan, and Francis
Digby above-mentioned, were killed. Writing to Lord Arlington's
secretary, and referring to this battle, Captain Silas Taylor, of
Harwich, said: "Those Marines of whom I soe oft have wrote
to you behaved themselves stoutly."[1] This, so far as is known,
is the first application of the term "Marines" to the military
force which, a few years earlier, had been specially raised for
service afloat; and it is therefore of much historical interest.

The total English loss in officers and men has been estimated

FRENCH MEDAL COMMEMORATIVE OF THE BATTLE OF SOLEBAY, 1672.

*(From an original kindly lent by H.S.H. Captain Prince Louis of
Battenberg, R.N.)*

at 2500. The Duke of York was obliged, in the course of the
action, to shift his flag to the *St. Michael*, and later, to the *London*.
Besides the *Royal James*, another ship was blown up, and two
vessels were sunk. The *Royal Katherine* was captured, but quickly
retaken, though her captain,[2] with others of her people, remained in
the hands of the Dutch.[3]

The successes of the French on land had by this time brought
the Netherlands to a deplorable condition. Owing to lack of
ammunition great part of the fleet had to be laid up. Owing to

---

[1] S. P. Dom. Car. ii. B. 310.   [2] Sir John Chicheley.

[3] 'A True Relation,' etc., in a letter from Henry Saville (1672, fol.); 'Mems.' of
John, Duke of Buckingham, ii.; Ludlow's 'Memoirs,' iii.; Parker's 'Hist. of Own
Times'; Arlington's Letters; 'Mems.' of Sir John Reresby; Neuville, 'Hist. de Holl.';
Basnage, 'Anns. des Provs. Unies.'; Letters of C. de Witt and De Ruijter; Brand,
'Leven v. De Ruijter'; Van den Bosch, 'Levens der Zeehelden'; Sketches by W. van
de Velde, who was present, etc. etc.

lack of credit the States could discount their bonds only at 30 per cent. of their nominal value. It was thought right to offer to treat, and commissioners were sent to London for that purpose. But Charles II. made demands which were inadmissible; his representatives behaved disingenuously; and the negotiations were quickly broken off. The failure to secure peace caused something very much like a revolution in Holland, and led to the fall of the party of the De Witts [1] and the election of William Prince of Orange as Stadtholder, Admiral, and General of the provinces of Holland and Zeeland, and as Admiral and General of all the other provinces.

The battle of Solebay had sufficed to delay, but not to prevent, the allied fleets from crossing to co-operate with the French. The fleets actually crossed in June, with a large body of troops on board. De Ruijter with such ships as were still in commission, kept among the shoals and preserved a watching attitude; and as the English and French could not induce him to venture out and give battle, they first blockaded the coast and then made preparations for a landing in force on the island of Texel on July 4th. But a storm defeated the intention and forced the Allies to sea; and, for reasons which are not very apparent, the project was thereupon abandoned.

No other naval operations that had great influence upon the issue of the war took place during the year 1672. There was much activity both in the East and in the West Indies; but the transactions there were scarcely of a nature to demand notice in this chapter, and will be more fitly described in the next.

In 1673 the passing of the Test Act rendered it impossible for Roman Catholics to retain offices of profit or trust under the Crown; and one of the results was the resignation by the Duke of York of the post of Lord High Admiral, and, indeed, of his position in the Navy. No new Lord High Admiral was appointed, but Prince Rupert was given authority almost equivalent to that of a modern First Lord of the Admiralty (though the King himself had the largest share in the management of the department), and was entrusted with the chief command of the fleet.

The divided administration was extremely prejudicial to the welfare of the service. The fleet was not ready for sea until long after it should have sailed. Sir Robert Holmes, one of the best flag-officers of the day, was not employed, chiefly because he was

[1] And very speedily to the murder of the De Witts themselves.

in favour with the Duke of York ; and, although Prince Rupert
applied for Holmes as one of his seconds, Sir Edward Spragge was
appointed instead to that post, and was then, without any explanation being vouchsafed to the Prince, despatched on a confidential
mission to the Court of France, whence he returned only just in
time to hoist his flag ere the fleet put to sea. Friction and delay,
indeed, allowed the Dutch, in spite of the enormous difficulties with
which they had to contend, to send out their main fleet before
the English had a proper fleet collected; and, but for Prince Rupert's
personal energy, the enemy would probably have assumed the
offensive, and have repeated the descent which they had made upon
the Thames and Medway at the close of the Second War. When,
in April, the Prince learnt that the Dutch were purposing to block
the mouth of the river by sinking hulks laden with stones in the
channels, and that they had the necessary vessels in readiness, he
hastily got together such ships of moderate size as were in a condition to go to sea, and made a demonstration [1] which prevented the
execution of the project, although the enemy actually entered the
mouth of the river for the purpose on May 2nd. The Dutch
thereupon returned to Schooneveld. They had previously failed
in an attempt to intercept the English home-coming convoys from
the Canaries and Bordeaux.

As before, the object of the Allies was, if the Dutch could not
be brought to action, then to blockade the enemy, to make a
descent on the coast of Holland, and to land troops. The
manner in which De Ruijter met this intention was masterly in
the extreme.

After the Allies had joined forces, King Charles and the Duke
of York visited the combined fleets on May 19th. The English
contingent, consisting apparently of 54 ships of the line, about
8 " frigates," and 24 fireships, was under Prince Rupert, as commander-in-chief, in the *Royal Charles*, and Sir Edward Spragge,
Admiral of the Blue. The other flag-officers were Vice-Admirals
Sir John Harman (Red), and Sir John Kempthorne (Blue) ; and
Rear-Admirals Sir John Chicheley (Red), and Thomas Butler,

---

[1] ' An Exact Relation,' etc. (1673, 4to.), states that at that time the French at Brest
declined to come out until the English were in the Channel ; and that Prince Rupert,
from the Thames, in defiance of the enemy, who was riding at the Gunfleet, passed
through the passage called the Narrow—and this, too, against the wind ; which so
surprised the Dutch, that, seeing the end of their lying there lost, they sailed back
again to their own ports.

Earl of Ossory (Blue). The French contingent was composed of
27 ships of the line, 2 " frigates," and 18 fireships, and was under
Admiral Jean, Comte d'Estrées, in the *Reine*, 104 ; Vice-Admiral
des Ardens, in the *Terrible*, 70, and Rear-Admiral the Marquis
de Grancey, in the *Orgueilleux*, 70. The Allies consequently
disposed of 81 ships of the line, 10 " frigates," and 42 fireships,
besides dispatch vessels and other small craft.

The Dutch had but 52 ships of the line, 12 " frigates," and
25 fireships, in addition to small craft. These were under De
Ruijter, as commander-in-chief, Cornelis Tromp, who had been
reinstated in the service and given the post vacated by the death
of Van Ghent, as commander of the van, and Adriaen Banckers, as
commander of the rear.

About May 20th the Allies sailed. They had on board a number
of troops ; and 6000 additional soldiers lay at Yarmouth, ready to
be embarked and transported to Holland in the event of the Dutch
suffering a decisive defeat. On the 25th the Dutch were sighted
at their anchorage in Schooneveld ; but first a calm and then
heavy weather prevented any steps from being taken to bring them
to action until the morning of the 28th.

The line of the Dutch coast near the mouth of the Schelde
runs N.E. and S.W. The wind that day was S.S.W., and was
favourable, therefore, both for entering and for leaving the anchorage
in which De Ruijter lay. Prince Rupert sent in a light draught
squadron of 35 vessels, with 13 fireships, to tempt the Dutch to
come out. This force comprised both French and English craft ;
yet, strange to say, it appears not to have been placed under the
orders of a flag-officer ; and the evidence tends to show that some,
if not all, of the captains concerned were in doubt as to which of
them was the senior. De Ruijter needed no drawing. He had
already shortened in his cables, and he was consequently able to
weigh with a rapidity that surprised the Allies. While they crowded
back in confusion towards their main body, the Dutch, in excellent
order, pressed after them ; and a general engagement resulted
much sooner, in all probability, than Prince Rupert had anticipated.

De Ruijter, in his dispatch, distinctly says that Des Ardens
was with the Red squadron under Prince Rupert, and that De
Grancey was with the Blue squadron under Spragge ; and, although
certain French historians indignantly deny that any such arrangement was adopted, there seems to be no doubt that, with a view

to prevent the French from holding aloof, as at Solebay, their
ships were formally mixed up with those of the English, and that,
just as there were French vessels in the squadrons of Prince Rupert
and of Spragge, so were there English vessels in the White squadron
under D'Estrées. This distribution was perhaps judicious so long
as every captain realised and clearly admitted his subordination
to the flag under which he was temporarily acting; but the lack
of proper organisation in the advanced division, and its hasty
retirement before the out-coming Dutch, had the effect of adding
to each squadron at the last moment a number of ships which did

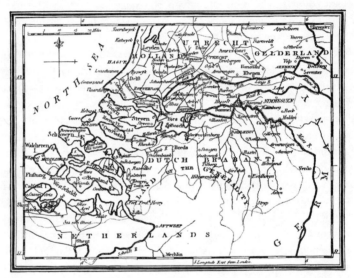

THE SOUTHERN NETHERLANDS.

not properly belong to it, and which, it may be, did not recognise
their adventitious relation to it. Every craft, as she fell back,
took refuge with that squadron which happened to be the easiest
for her to reach; and so the confusion of the advanced division
communicated itself to some extent to the main fleet. This was
of no small advantage to the Dutch, who derived further benefit
from the fact that, since the advanced division as it withdrew was
between them and the Allies, the latter dared not for some time
fire, for fear lest they should injure their friends.

Owing to these and other causes, the allied line was not fairly
formed when, at about noon, the Dutch began the action. It is

impossible to follow in detail the manœuvres of the two fleets. Tromp's impulsive valour got him into difficulties; and, as usual, he managed to separate himself from his fellow admirals. His first flagship the *Gouden Leeuw*, Captain Thomas Tobijas, was disabled, and narrowly escaped being burnt by a fireship, which, by direction of Sir William Reeves, captain of the *Edgar*, had been laid alongside of her. He then shifted his flag to the *Prins te Paard;* and, upon that vessel being seriously damaged, to the *Amsterdam*, finally removing it to the *Comeetstar*.[1] De Ruijter, with the greatest gallantry, rescued him from the consequences of his rashness, and, in the course of the day, deliberately broke the line of the squadron of D'Estrées. Captain George Legge, later Earl of Dartmouth, distinguished himself in the *Royal Katherine* by taking the Dutch ship *Jupiter*, which, however, was presently retaken. Spragge also, and Lord Ossory, behaved brilliantly; and the French fought well. But the action, though bloody, was indecisive; and at night De Ruijter, who had no intention of being drawn far from the shoals, anchored again within the sands, about two miles W.N.W. of Westkapelle, while the Allies brought to about two miles N.W. by W. of him.[2] No ships changed owners, and neither English nor Dutch seem to have had any vessels larger than fireships burnt or sunk; though, on the night following the battle, the Dutch *Deventer*, 70, which had behaved magnificently under Captain Willem van Cuijlenburgh, especially in action with the French *Foudroyant*, 70, Captain Jean Gabaret, and which had been almost knocked to pieces, foundered at her anchors, carrying down with her most of her people, including her commander. But the French had two ships sunk, besides five or six fireships.[3]

The loss of life was greater on the side of the Allies than on that of the Dutch. In both fleets the loss of officers was particularly heavy. The Dutch lost Vice-Admiral Volkhard Adriaensze Schram, Rear-Admiral David Vlugh, and Captains van Cuijlenburgh and

---

[1] Tromp's letter to his sister, written on the following day, is characteristic: "Dear Sister," it runs, "yesterday we went into the dance, and God be praised, we are sound, and have enjoyed ourselves like kings. I am in my fourth ship, the *Comeetstar*, and mean to have a fine dance to-day. We make the French run, so that they have to set sky-scrapers and everything else; and, if things go on to-day as before, I trust that our prayer and that of all our friends will be heard, and that we shall be freed from tyranny. Adieu. Courage. Things are bound to go well."

[2] The wind seems to have been then W.S.W.

[3] S. P. Dom. Car. ii. B. 335, f. 262.

Jacob van Bergen; the French lost Captains Rocuchon, Ozée-Thomas, de Tivas, and Serpault. And the English lost Captains William Finch, of the *York*, Thomas Foulis, of the *Lion*, and John Tempest, of the *Sweepstake*.

The Allies, of course, had but very limited facilities for repairing damages, whereas the Dutch were at home, and had the resources of their country immediately behind them. The Allies, moreover, had to be on their guard, both by night and by day, when the wind was favourable, for another sortie by De Ruijter; whereas the latter, who had no reason to apprehend attack, could choose his own time for moving, and could rest his men in the interval. It was, therefore, the duty of the Allies to be ready for instant action, upon penalty of being surprised with results far worse than those which had followed the battle of May 28th.

Prince Rupert apparently realised the situation. On the evening of June 3rd, the wind coming from off the land, he made certain preparations, and afterwards sat up during the entire night. But Spragge was more negligent. On the following morning, when there was a strong breeze from the north-east, he went with Lord Ossory on board the commander-in-chief, and either remained so long, or had such difficulty in getting back again, that when, at 11 A.M., De Ruijter weighed and began to come out, the English Blue squadron had to wait for its admiral.

The accounts of this, the second battle of Schooneveld, are confusing and even contradictory. So far as can be gathered, the French were again mixed with the English, the Blue, or rear, being to windward, and the White, or van, being to leeward of the allied centre. Finding his crew somewhat slow in weighing, Prince Rupert cut his cable, and the example was probably followed by other ships of his own squadron; so that the allied centre was quickly under sail. The White also seems to have weighed quickly. But the Blue, delayed by the absence of Spragge and Ossory, was some time behind the other squadrons, so that when Prince Rupert signalled to make sail on the starboard tack upon a north-westerly course, with a view to drawing the Dutch away from their coasts, the Blue squadron still lay in some confusion to windward. At length, however, the whole of the allied fleet was in motion, though not in good order. The Blue had the van position and the White the rear, the natural formation being thus reversed. The Dutch made no difficulty about following their enemy, yet

necessarily took some time to come up with him, and at first the
action was at long range only; but by 5 P.M. all the squadrons were
hotly engaged, Tromp holding his course with Spragge, De Ruijter
with the Prince, and Banckers with D'Estrées; and each squadron
plying its opponent broadside to broadside. So the action continued,
save when De Ruijter made an ineffectual effort to pass through the
allied centre, until about 10 P.M. Soon afterwards, apparently, the
Dutch stood to the south-east, and next morning the two fleets were
out of sight of one another. It is clear that De Ruijter believed,
even as late as June 7th, when he sent off his dispatch on the
subject, that, after he had quitted the Allies in the darkness, they
had held on their course for the English coast; but Prince Rupert's
dispatch to Lord Arlington, while admitting that the Dutch altered
course at about midnight, declares that at 2 A.M. the Allies altered
course also, and pursued until 6 A.M.[1] It may be safely assumed
that, had the Allies been in a condition to do otherwise, they would
not have permitted their enemy to retire without following him very
closely indeed, and that they would not have allowed a period of at
least two—possibly as much as four—hours to elapse, ere they made
after him at all. On the other hand, De Ruijter's withdrawal is
perfectly consistent with the Dutch claim that the Allies had somewhat the worse of the encounter; for the Dutch were, and had
been ever since Solebay, acting in pursuance of a well-defined
strategical policy, which demanded that they should not venture far
from their own coasts, and should, after each engagement, return as
quickly as possible to the comparative security of their shoals.

Neither side could, however, affect to make very much of the
affair. The Dutch lost no ships, and, though they had several
badly damaged, they had but 216 officers and men killed, and
285 wounded. The Allies likewise lost no vessels, other than
fireships, and their loss in men seems to have been about the same
as that of their opponents. But the English had to lament the
death of Captains Richard White, of the *Warspite*, and Richard
Sadlington, of the *Crown*. D'Estrées, after the action, complained
bitterly of the conduct of Spragge; and Tromp, of that of his
vice-admiral, Isaac Sweers; but the latter quarrel was smoothed
over by the Prince of Orange, and Sweers served again with
gallantry, and, as will be seen, died for his country only a few
weeks afterwards.

[1] S. P. Dom. Car. ii. B. 335, f. 19.

The Allies did not attempt to at once resume their station off the Dutch ports. On the contrary, they returned to their own harbours to refit and refresh, the English reaching the Nore on June 8th, and the French proceeding to Brest and Rochefort. Scarcely had the English anchored ere a Dutch squadron of observation, under Rear-Admiral Jan den Haen, appeared off the mouth of the Thames. Den Haen reported that on the 12th the bulk of the fleet lay between Queenborough and Gravesend, that great efforts were being made to get it ready for sea again as rapidly as possible, and that a very large body of troops was waiting to be embarked in it with a view to a new attempt upon the coast of Holland. The Dutch were still more active; and their fleet, refitted and reinforced, sailed on June 23rd, and was off Harwich on the evening of the 25th. But some infectious disease, apparently the plague, almost immediately broke out in most of the ships, and De Ruijter had to return.

King Charles and the Duke of York visited the fleet in the Thames on June 13th, and did their utmost to further the preparations; but delays of one kind and another supervened; the French fleet did not rejoin until the middle of July; and not until July 17th, did the Allies put to sea. In the English fleet was a large number of soldiers.

The strength of the forces collected for what proved to be the final battle of the war was, according to what seem to be the most trustworthy accounts :—

	English.	French.	Total Allies.	Dutch.
Ships of the line and frigates	62	30	92	75
Fireships	..	..	28	22
Ketches, yachts, etc.	..	..	23	18
			143	115

The English and Dutch commanders-in-chief and flag-officers of squadrons were the same who had served in the two actions off Schooneveld; and D'Estrées still commanded the French contingent, but, in addition to Des Ardens, he now had with him, as *chefs d'escadre*, De Martel, and the celebrated Châteaurenault.

All Dutch accounts have it that De Ruijter put to sea at about

the same time as the Allies, sighted them on the evening of
July 20th, and subsequently offered them battle; but that they
declined it, and that he, fearing lest a change of wind or any other
cause might prevent him from getting back to his own coasts in
time to be of use in their defence, once more proceeded to his old
anchorage in Schooneveld. English accounts mention this statement only to deride it; but in the Rijks Archief there is a copy of
a letter of De Ruijter, addressed to the Prince of Orange, under date
of August 2nd (July 23rd), 1673, and as this letter corroborates the
statement, and, indeed, was, no doubt, the original authority
for it, the fact of the fleets having sighted one another must be
credited.[1]

The allied fleet stood on and off near the mouth of the Maas,
threatening to effect a landing near Briel, and then proceeded off
Scheveningen, where the threats were renewed. But the Dutch,
though the whole country was terribly alarmed, were prepared for
an attack. Moreover, the presence on the spot of the Prince of
Orange inspirited the defence, while the presence in Schooneveld,
only sixty or seventy miles to the southward, of a "potential" fleet,
under so able a man as De Ruijter, must have inclined the allied
admirals to think twice ere beginning an operation which they
might not have time to complete without being disturbed by
interference from seaward.

The Prince of Orange presently ordered the Dutch fleet to sail
in search of the enemy, and on July 28th it weighed from Schooneveld, and moved up to Scheveningen, whence the Allies had shortly
before departed, heading to the N.N.E. The Dutch authorities on
land were in doubt as to whether De Ruijter's immediate services
would be more usefully devoted to convoying some very valuable
home-coming East Indiamen that were daily expected, or to
fighting the enemy; but the Prince of Orange, who was in no
doubt on the subject, determined in favour of fighting, and on
August 2nd, visited the fleet, and, on board the *Zeven Provinciën*,
discussed with the naval chiefs the course to be pursued. On the
morning following the Dutch fleet weighed again; but almost
immediately afterwards a strong gale sprang up from the N.W.,
and, lasting for several days, prevented any progress from being
made. Not until the 7th could De Ruijter proceed for the neighbourhood of the Texel, where the Allies were reported to be; and

[1] *See also* 'Nederl. Zeewezen,' ii. 399–401; and 'Leven van De Ruijter,' 835–837.

not until 10 A.M. on the 10th were the two fleets in sight of one
another. The wind was then from the E., and the Dutch were
heading N.N.W. The Allies at once headed S.S.W. Later in the
day the wind veered to N.W., and, as this gave the Allies the
weather-gauge and the choice of the method of attack, De Ruijter
kept very close to the beach, so that the enemy dared not approach
him; and in the evening turned to the southward, so as to avoid
being cut off from his base in Schooneveld. In the night, the
wind again shifted, this time to E.S.E., giving the Dutch the
weather-gauge; and, at daybreak, De Ruijter stood down into action.

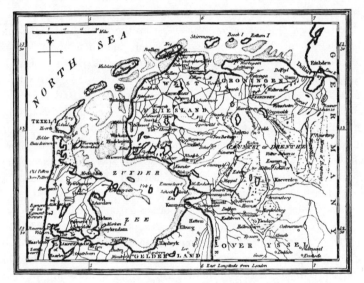

THE NORTHERN NETHERLANDS.

The battle which ensued is known in Holland as that of Kijkduin,
and in England as that of the Texel.

The Allies were on the port tack, the French, who formed on
this occasion a squadron by themselves, leading, Prince Rupert
being in the centre, and Spragge's squadron forming the rear. The
Dutch also were in three squadrons; but, while the squadrons of
the Allies were equal, or nearly equal, in numerical strength, the
Dutch van, under Banckers, consisted of only ten or twelve ships,
the other two squadrons, under De Ruijter and Tromp respectively,
each consisting of thirty-two or thirty-three. As in previous en-

counters, De Ruijter decided, if possible, to simply hold the French in check, and to fall with somewhat superior force upon the English. He therefore sent Banckers against D'Estrées, and attacked the van and rear with about sixty-five ships to the English sixty-two. The battle, so far as the French were concerned in it, was not of long duration, and may be very briefly described in Captain Mahan's words :—

" M. de Martel," he says, " commanding the van of the French, and consequently the leading sub-division of the allied fleet, was ordered to stretch ahead, go about, and gain to windward of the Dutch van, so as to place it between two fires. This he did!; but, as soon as Banckers . . . saw the danger, he put his helm up and ran through the remaining twenty ships of D'Estrées' squadron with his own twelve—a feat as creditable to him as it was discreditable to the French—and then, wearing, stood down towards De Ruijter, who was hotly engaged with Rupert. He was not followed by D'Estrées, who suffered him to carry this important reinforcement to the Dutch main attack undisturbed." [1]

Prince Rupert, while engaging De Ruijter, kept away, with a view to drawing the Dutch from their own shores ; and De Ruijter followed him. Thus the centre became separated by a considerable distance from the van. This separation supplied D'Estrées with a pretext for not further co-operating with his commander-in-chief ; yet it did not prevent Banckers, a seaman of a very different type, from presently joining De Ruijter.

Sir Edward Spragge, in the rear, seems to have felt it incumbent upon himself to wait for Tromp and the Dutch rear. He therefore hove to, and, of course, drifted quickly to leeward, thus as effectively —though from different motives—separating the rear from the centre, as D'Estrées had separated the van. Tromp, when he came up, drifted away with him in hot and close action. Tromp and Spragge were men of kindred kidney, brave, rash, and insubordinate, and they seem to have delighted in this personal conflict. The *Royal Prince*, Spragge's first flagship, soon became disabled, and the admiral shifted to the *St. George*, which in her turn, after about four hours' fighting, was reduced to the condition of a wreck. Tromp was similarly obliged to shift from the *Gouden Leeuw* to the *Comeetstar*. Spragge was removing to a third ship, the *Royal Charles*, when a round shot struck his boat and sank her. Before this happened the wind shifted, and a heavy shower of rain fell, brought down probably by the firing.

Prince Rupert, in the meantime, was terribly pressed by De

---

[1] ' Infl. of Sea Power,' 153.

Ruijter, reinforced by Banckers. De Ruijter, thus strengthened, had at least two-and-forty ships to Rupert's two-and-thirty. In spite of the confusion of the battle, the great Dutch admiral still had his squadron well under control, and was able to utilise it to the best tactical advantage, for he cleverly cut off the rear sub-division [1] of the allied centre, by detaching eight or ten ships; and

SIR CORNELIS TROMP, BART., COUNT VAN SYLLISBURG, LIEUTENANT-ADMIRAL-GENERAL OF HOLLAND AND WESTVRIESLAND.

(*From a Dutch engraved portrait of about* 1690.)

then, with his remaining two-and-thirty, or thereabouts, surrounded the remaining two-and-twenty of the English. Never, perhaps, did a commander of inferior forces handle them with greater tactical ability, or more skilfully create for himself a temporary local superiority. It speaks well for the steadiness of Rupert's officers and men that the van and centre sub-divisions of the Red squadron

[1] Under Rear-Admiral Sir John Chicheley, (R.)

were not crushed.   In time, after losing heavily, they managed to
extricate themselves; and then Prince Rupert, anxious to reunite
with Sir John Chicheley, and seeing that Spragge's squadron was
still in difficulties, ran down towards his rear, De Ruijter following
him on a parallel course, but neither centre firing, possibly, as
Mahan suggests, because ammunition was threatening to fall
short.   At 4 P.M. the centres and rears reunited, and, a little later,
the action recommenced and continued until 7 P.M.

Towards the end of the day De Ruijter made great but vain
efforts to destroy the disabled *Royal Prince*, which, however, was
saved by the interposition of the Earl of Ossory.   The combat
seems to have ended in consequence of the approach of the French.
De Ruijter withdrew, not actually victorious, yet with every reason
to feel satisfied; for he had freed the Dutch ports from blockade,
and had reduced the Allies to such a condition that they had no
further thought of landing troops on Dutch soil.[1]

Neither side lost any ship of importance.   The English yacht
Henrietta was sunk, and several fireships were expended; but there
were no prizes.   The loss of officers was, however, heavy; and,
especially among the English, many of whose ships were full of
troops, the number of men killed and wounded was considerable.
In addition to the gallant Spragge, Captains Richard Le Neve,[2]
of the *Edgar*, John Hayward, senior,[3] of the *Royal Charles*, Sir
William Reeves,[4] of the *Sovereign*, John Rice, of the *Marigold*,
fireship, and Francis Courtnay,[5] of the *Dunkirk*, fell.   The French
lost Captain d'Estival, of the *Invincible*.   The Dutch lost two vice-
admirals, Jan de Liefde and Isaac Sweers, and Captains Jan van
Gelder, a son-in-law of De Ruijter, David Sweers, Hendrik Vischer,
and Dirck Jobse Kiela.

Prince Rupert blamed D'Estrées and Spragge for the indecisive
nature of the action; D'Estrées blamed Prince Rupert for having
run to leeward.   De Martel, in a letter to Colbert, did not hesitate to
call D'Estrées a coward, who was unworthy of his country; and, for

[1] Rupert's Dispatch: S. P. Dom. Car. II. B. 366, f. 432.
[2] He was also a captain in Prince Rupert's Maritime Regiment. He was, as his
monument in Westminster Abbey testifies, but twenty-seven when he died. He had
previously commanded the *Phœnix* (1671) and *Plymouth* (1672).
[3] An old officer, who had commanded the *Plymouth* at the time of the Restoration.
[4] Had distinguished himself as captain of the *Essex*, when she was taken in the
Four Days' Fight in 1666, and on numerous other occasions.
[5] Captain, 1666, when he was appointed to the prize *Golden Ruyter*.

his pains, he was sent to the Bastille for two years. The result was in no sense creditable to the allied commanders; and although Spragge and Tromp, in their insubordinate fashion, fought admirably, and Prince Rupert and most of the English commanders behaved with great gallantry, the real heroes of the day were undoubtedly De Ruijter and Banckers.

Before the autumn of 1673 the common political hostility of England and Holland to the ambitious plans of Louis XIV. had begun to create so powerful a bond of union between the two countries that even commercial rivalry was powerless to keep them apart. In England the sympathies of the people had been for years rather with the Dutch than with the French; the former had proved themselves brave enemies, the latter had exhibited themselves as untrustworthy, if not treacherous, allies; and the accession to power in Holland of the House of Orange contributed much towards removing the chief differences which had estranged the governments of the two great maritime nations. Charles II., in consequence, became somewhat more flexible in his demands; and, after a little negotiation, peace between England and the States was concluded at Westminster on February 9th, 1674.

The provisions of the treaty were particularly advantageous to England. The Right of the Flag was formally and fully admitted by the Dutch; arrangement was made for the settlement of disputes connected with trade to the East Indies; places taken by either side during the war were to be restored; and the States agreed to pay an indemnity of 800,000 crowns. A subsidiary treaty stipulated that neither party should assist the enemies of the other, and that the English regiments in the French service should be suffered to die out, no further recruiting being allowed for them. On December 1st following, a treaty of commerce was concluded between the two countries, and in 1677 the Anglo-Dutch alliance was cemented by the marriage of the Princess Mary of York to William, Prince of Orange.

During the remainder of the reign of Charles II., and the whole of the reign of James II., the fleet was not called upon to carry out any further warlike operations of first-rate importance. Such minor undertakings as the Royal Navy was from time to time concerned in will be found described in the next chapter. But the events of the Revolution of 1688 brought the fleet once more into intimate connection with the fortunes and fate of the country; and, although there was, happily, no fighting at sea upon that occasion, the share borne by the Navy, and by naval officers, in effecting, or at least in facilitating, the accession to power of William and Mary cannot be here passed over in silence.

The most useful English naval allies of the Prince of Orange were Admiral Arthur Herbert, afterwards Earl of Torrington, who, having opposed the repeal of the Test Act, had been dismissed from all his employments, civil as well as military; and Captain Edward Russell, afterwards Admiral the Earl of Orford. The latter was particularly active during the period immediately preceding the Revolution, and served as messenger between the Prince and his supporters in England. The former became William's professional adviser in Holland, and eventually commanded the fleet which convoyed the new sovereign to Torbay.

Towards the end of his reign, James II. had brought the fleet to a high point of material efficiency; but he had so conducted himself that, although he was still popular in the service as a naval officer, as a monarch he excited very little loyalty. The Royal Navy was, as a body, strongly opposed to Roman Catholicism; yet, upon its becoming known in England that William, the Protestant champion, was preparing to invade the country, James not only appointed a Roman Catholic officer, Sir Roger Strickland, Rear-Admiral of England, to the command of the active fleet, but also sent priests on board the ships, and encouraged the celebration of Mass there. By thus identifying his cause with that of a religion which was not that of the majority of his subjects, he committed a great political error, and, from the first, prejudiced his prospects. Officers and seamen were antagonised, the priests narrowly escaped physical ill-treatment, and it became exceedingly difficult to bring up the complements of the ships to their proper strength, men who would gladly enough have fought for their country being in the highest degree unwilling to strike a single blow, even indirectly, for the advancement of popery.

This, however, was not James's only error. When, early in June, 1688, Strickland's squadron was ready for sea, it was kept upon the English coast, instead of being sent to observe the ports of Holland. At first it was allowed to idle in or about the Strait of Dover, with its cruisers plying northward to Orfordness, and south-eastward to Boulogne. As the danger increased, the squadron moved to the Nore, and then to the Gunfleet. Not until

September did James appear to realise that Strickland was not the commander-in-chief to lead English officers and men at such a crisis. Admiral the Earl of Dartmouth was then appointed to the position, the King relegating Strickland to the second post, and, a few days later, entirely superseding him in favour of Vice-Admiral Sir John Berry. These changes, however, were made too late. Distrust and discontent, combined with private influences judiciously exerted, had by that time completely sapped the allegiance of almost half the officers; and although the fleet at the Gunfleet, towards the end of October, made a noble show, it is doubtful whether one-third of it would have offered any determined resistance to Herbert and the Dutch, had they then provoked a battle.

Forty men-of-war, eighteen fireships, and three yachts or other small craft were with Dartmouth; but there were cabals in every forecastle, and political meetings in nearly every captain's cabin; and when Sir William Jennings, one of James's most thorough adherents, and a few other officers of similar unquestioning loyalty to the King, proposed at a council of war that the fleet should cross the North Sea and there watch the motions of the Dutch, the project met with little support.

It may be that it was because James suspected the true condition of affairs afloat that he attempted so little with the fleet. He cannot but have been discouraged by the fact that outbreaks in the royal dockyards and revolts in Jersey and Guernsey occurred at the very moment when the attitude of the fleet and of the maritime population was of the utmost importance to him. Yet it is astonishing that he so easily resigned himself to a passive policy, and, still more, that he did not call in the aid of his ally the French king, whose fleet had, by that time, become a fine fighting machine, very different from what it had been in the last Dutch war. The Earl of Sunderland, however, is reported to have advised his master that the one thing which it was quite certain that Englishmen would not suffer was French interference in their affairs.

William collected his fleet at the mouth of the Maas. As finally constituted, it consisted of fifty ships of the line, twenty-five " frigates," twenty-five fireships, and about four hundred transports, containing 4092 horse and 11,090 foot. Lieut.-Admiral Cornelis Evertsen, "the Youngest," son of Cornelis Evertsen, "the Old," commanded up to October 17th, the other flag-officers and all the captains being Dutch. On October 17th Admiral Arthur Herbert

hoisted his flag in the *Leijden*, 62, and assumed supreme control:
William himself went on board the *Briel*, 30, on the 19th; and in
the following night the fleet put to sea. On the 20th the wind was
first N. and then N.W., and very heavy weather prevailed, so that
on the 21st the whole force returned to the Maas and anchored off
Briel and Hellevoetsluis. It did not sail again until November 1st,
when the intention was to make the Humber and to effect a landing
there; but the plan was altered, and, with a wind blowing briskly
from the E.S.E., the fleet crossed almost to within sight[1] of
Dartmouth's squadron off the Shipwash, near the Gunfleet.

The weather and his position were such that Dartmouth could
not weigh in chase; and Herbert proceeded down Channel. Dart-

MEDAL COMMEMORATIVE OF THE LANDING OF WILLIAM III., 1688.

(From an original kindly lent by H.S.H. Captain Prince Louis of Battenberg, R.N.)

mouth was unable to pursue until the 4th. On that day the Dutch
came to a determination to land part at Dartmouth and part at
Torbay; but in the night, owing to the incompetence of the pilots,
the fleet overshot both places. The fault was, however, corrected
by the wind, which shifted from E. to S.W., and which, while aiding
the Dutch to return, impeded their pursuers. William landed at
Torbay on November 5th. Dartmouth, who had been driven back
to the Downs, and who, upon sailing again and getting as far as
Portland, was once more driven back to Spithead and St. Helens,
soon realised that the cause which he had undertaken to defend was
lost. He unwillingly held a council of his officers, sent ashore such

---

[1] A few of the transports were actually seen by the English through the fog which
prevailed.

commanders as were Roman Catholics, and agreed to an address to William. By the middle of December he had made his full sub-mission ; and, before the end of the year, the Navy everywhere had formally adhered to the new order of things.[1]

At the time of the accession of William and Mary the young French navy had reached a pitch of development to which it had never previously attained, and to which it did not for many years attain again. The intelligence and energy of Colbert had created a splendid fleet, which was numerically equal, if not superior, to the combined fleets of England and Holland ; and the officers and men of the service had learnt experience in the best schools of the day, fighting at one moment with the Dutch against the English, and at another, with the English against the Dutch. Nor had the French navy been without its successes. If it had not defeated the great De Ruijter, it had at least slain him.

Yet Louis XIV. failed to seize the magnificent opportunities which came to him in consequence of the growth of his naval strength. When he could have crushed England and Holland at sea he allowed his attention to be diverted landwards ; and his enemies, profiting by his omission in the critical years 1689 and 1690, took measures which soon deprived him of his temporary superiority.

France was already at war with the Empire, with Sweden and with Spain, when the policy of the Prince of Orange caused her to plunge into active hostilities with the Netherlands also. There is little doubt that she could, had she so chosen, have prevented William's expedition to England ; but, instead of endeavouring to do so, she wasted her strength on shore. Not until William was established in his new kingdom did Louis move so much as a single ship in the interests of his ally and co-religionist, the fallen James II. Even then France did not declare war against England, but con-tented herself with personal hostility to the Prince of Orange, apparently believing that England, far from ranging herself behind

---

[1] Authorities for the expedition of William : Burnet, i. 703 ; Evertsen's General Orders of Oct. 16–26 ; Scheltema, 'Mengelwerk,' iii. ; Letters of A. van Citters ; Letters of Will. III. ; *Holl. Mercurius;* 'Mems. relating to the Lord Torrington' (Byng); 'An Impart. Acct. of . . . the Life . . . of Torrington' (Herbert), 1691 ; Herbert's Instructions of Oct. 17th ; Lutterell, 'Relat. of State Affairs,' i. ; Dalrymple, 'Mems. of Grt. Brit. and Ireland'; Wagenaar, 'Vaderl. Hist.,' xv. ; d'Avaux, 'Négocia-tions'; 'Notul. der Admiraliteiten,' 1688 and 1689 ; 'Mems. of Sir J. Reresby'; Quincy, 'Hist. Milit.,' ii. ; Bohun, 'Hist. of the Desertion'; Hornby, 'Caveat agst. the Whigs'; 'Life of Capt. Stephen Martin' (Nav. Rec. Soc.); Le Clerc, 'Hist. des Provs. Unies'; 'Mems. of Jno. Duke of Buckingham'; Falle, 'Hist. of Jersey.'

him, regarded him as an invader, and was still at heart true to James II. But, in pursuance of his policy of alliance with the exiled king, Louis, when at length he did move his fleets, behaved generously, if not altogether wisely. He fitted out at Brest thirty ships of the line and seven "frigates," which conveyed James and 5000 troops to Kingsale, where the ex-King landed on March 12th, 1689, and the men two days later. Nearly all Ireland, except Ulster, was opposed to the Prince of Orange; and, for the moment, the prospects of James looked rosy.

As soon as news of this expedition reached England Admiral Arthur Herbert was ordered to take command of a fleet which was being collected at Portsmouth, and was directed to hasten to Ireland with part of the force, leaving the rest to follow as it became ready for sea. In pursuance of his instructions, Herbert sailed for Cork with twelve vessels in the first half of April; but, finding that the French had quitted the coast, he cruised in search of them off Brest and at the mouth of the Channel, and, still failing to discover the enemy, headed again for the south of Ireland. By that time more ships from Portsmouth had joined him. On April 29th he sighted a considerable fleet, which, however, he soon lost again. On the 30th he looked into Baltimore, and, seeing nothing there of the enemy, came to the conclusion that the French must be to the westward of him. He therefore bore away with an east wind for Cape Clear. In the evening he had the satisfaction of sighting the fleet of which he was in search. It was standing into Bantry Bay. Herbert lay in the offing for the night, and in the morning stood in after the foe.

This French fleet, consisting of twenty-four ships of the line, two "frigates," and ten fireships, had left Brest to carry to Ireland a quantity of stores and ammunition, and was under the orders of Louis François de Rousselet, Comte de Châteaurenault,[1] as Lieutenant-Général, in the *Ardent*, 66, with the *chefs d'escadre* Jean Gabaret, in the *Saint-Michel*, 56, and Forant, in the *Courageux*, 56, as second and third in command. In addition to the force which had come directly from Brest, there were in the Bay three "frigates" under Captain Duquesne-Mosnier, who had been left behind by the previous expedition in order to serve the interests of James on the Irish coast. One of them was commanded by an

[1] Born 1637; Lieutenant-Général, 1688; Vice-Admiral of the Levant, 1701; Marshal of France, 1703; died 1716.—Jal, 'Ab. Duquesne.'

English officer who had adhered to the late king in his misfortunes.
The whole French force upon which Herbert descended consequently amounted to twenty-four ships of the line, few of which
apparently mounted more than sixty guns, five " frigates," and ten
fireships. The fleet with Admiral Herbert on the day of the action
was as follows :—

ORDER OF BATTLE OF THE ENGLISH FLEET IN THE ACTION OFF BANTRY BAY.[1]

Rate.	Ship.	Guns.	Men.	Commanders.
3	*Defiance*	64	400	Capt. John Ashby.
4	*Portsmouth* . . .	46	220	Capt. George St. Loe.
3	*Plymouth* . . .	60	340	Capt. Richard Carter.
4	*Ruby*	48	230	Capt. Frederick Froud.
4	*Diamond* . . .	48	230	Capt. Benjamin Walters.
4	*Advice*	48	230	Capt. the Hon. John Granville.
3	*Mary*	62	365	Capt. Matthew Aylmer.
4	*St. Albans* . . .	50	280	Capt. John Layton.
3	*Edgar*	64	445	Capt. Clowdisley Shovell.
3	*Elizabeth* (flag of) Adm. Herbert. .	70	460	Capt. David Mitchell.
3	*Pendennis* . . .	70	460	Capt. George Churchill.
4	*Portland* . . .	50	230	Capt. George Aylmer.
4	*Deptford* . . .	54	280	Capt. George Rooke.
4	*Woolwich* . . .	54	280	Capt. Ralph Sanderson.
5 [1]	*Dartmouth* . . .	36	150	Capt. Thomas Ley.
4	*Greenwich* . . .	54	280	Capt. Christopher Billop.
3	*Cambridge* . . .	70	400	Capt. John Clements.
4	*Antelope*	48	230	Capt. Henry Wickham.
3	*York*	60	340	Capt. Ralph Delavall.
	FIRESHIPS.			
5 [2]	*Firedrake*	12	65	Commander John Leake.
5 [3]	*Soldadoes* . . .	16	75	Capt. Francis Wyvill.
[2]	*Salamander* . . .	10	35	Commander Thomas Crawley.

[1] In the previous year the *Dartmouth* had been classed as a fireship.
[2] The *Firedrake* and *Salamander*, though here classed as fireships, were really bombs. The former carried six patereroes in addition to her guns. The latter had two mortars.
[3] The *Soldadoes* had been classed in the previous year as a sixth-rate. Besides her guns she seems to have carried ten patereroes on this occasion.

As Herbert went into the Bay on the morning of May 1st,
Châteaurenault, who, according to French accounts, would have
attacked earlier had he not desired to first land as many troops and
stores as possible, weighed to meet the English. The latter, being
to leeward, experienced some difficulty in working up towards the
French, who, bore down in excellent order and began the engagement at about 10.30 A.M. When the English commander-in-chief
saw the force of the enemy, and realised how disadvantageous

[1] Compiled mainly rom the list in ' Memoirs relating to the Lord Torrington,' 37,
compared with MS. official List of Commissions of Captains in Author's coll.

for his own fleet would be an action to windward in waters so
narrow, he put about and went out of the Bay under easy sail, so as
to be able to manœuvre, with a view, if possible, to gain the wind,
and so as to bring his very indifferent line into something like order.
The line was improved; but, owing to the caution of the French,
the wind could not be gained. The action continued, however,
until about 5 P.M., and, in the course of it, the French ship
Diamant, 54, commanded by the Marquis de Coëtlogon, was most
seriously damaged by an explosion of ammunition which had been
accumulated in her captain's cabin. Towards the end of the battle
the English had been so worsted that, but for two facts which told
accidentally in their favour, Châteaurenault would, in all probability,
have decisively defeated them. One was the absence of the French
fireships, which were still landing stores in the Bay. The other was
the jealousy with which the *chefs d'escadre* Gabaret and Forant
regarded Châteaurenault, who was much their junior in point of
service. These officers tacitly refused to press the advantage; and
at length the French commander-in-chief found it prudent to tack
and stand again towards the shore. Having completed his mission
he returned to Brest on May 8th. In consequence of the battle,
war between England and France was immediately declared.

Admiral Herbert, who thus narrowly escaped a crippling disaster,
made for Portsmouth. His fleet had lost one captain, George
Aylmer, one lieutenant, and ninety-four men killed, and about three
hundred officers and men wounded. The English had not been so
inferior as to render their action a brilliant one: the French success
had scarcely been so pronounced as to be entitled to the name of
victory; yet apparently both nations were satisfied. When King
William visited Portsmouth a few days later he created Herbert
Baron Herbert of Torbay and Earl of Torrington, knighted Captains
Ashby and Shovell, presented each seaman with a gratuity of ten
shillings, and made special provision for the widows of Captain
Aylmer and others who had fallen. These royal attentions from the
new monarch, to servants of the fidelity of many of whom he was
still in much doubt, were, perhaps, politic; but it can hardly be said
that they were all fully deserved.[1]

---

[1] Herbert's Disp. of May 2nd; *London Gazette*; Jal, 'Abraham Duquesne,' ii.
'An Impart. Acct. of the Life of Torrington'; Chandler's 'Debates'; 'Mems. relating
to the Lord Torrington' (Byng); 'Life of Capt. Stephen Martin'; MS. List of
Commissions in Author's coll.

A little later, Torrington, reinforced by a Dutch contingent and by a squadron under Vice-Admiral Killigrew, cruised for a time on the French coast, but presently returned owing to lack of provisions, and especially beer, having accomplished nothing.

Before proceeding to Portsmouth, Admiral Herbert detached the *Deptford*, 54, Captain George Rooke, as commodore, and the *Antelope*, 48, Captain Henry Wickham, to the northward, to pick up other vessels, and with them to carry out certain special services. Londonderry was hard pressed by the Jacobites ; Major-General Piercy Kirke, with a body of troops, was waiting in Cheshire to go to its relief, and Rooke's first duty was to facilitate this important operation. The commodore anchored in the Clyde about May 10th, and thence sent word to the expeditionary force, which lay in the mouth of the Dee, to join him off Cantire. The junction was not fully effected until the beginning of June, but on or before May 22nd, the *Greyhound*, 16, Captain Thomas Gillam ; *Kingfisher* (ketch), 4, Commander Edward Boys ; and *Henrietta* (yacht), 8, Commander Sir William Sanderson, met Rooke at the appointed rendezvous, and subsequently co-operated with him, pending the arrival of Kirke's transports, in dispersing some malcontents on the small islands of Gigha and Kara. On June 8th, the transports, convoyed by the *Bonaventure*, 48, Captain Thomas Hopsonn ; *Swallow*, 48, Captain Wolfran Cornewall ; and *Dartmouth*, 36, Captain John Leake,[1] and apparently also by the *Portland*, 50, Captain Thomas Ley, appeared off Cantire, and the expedition set sail for Loch Foyle ; but it was driven by stress of weather into Rathlin Bay, and there detained until the middle of the month. When at length it reached Loch Foyle, Kirke, who, perhaps, in consequence of his previous experience in the Marines, had been given charge of some of the vessels, made a reconnaissance up the river, and was so impressed by the boom and the shore defences wherewith the Jacobites below Londonderry had barred the stream, that he decided to await reinforcements ere attempting to succour the garrison. Rooke thereupon entered Lough Swilly, where he annoyed the enemy ; and then cruised off the coast in search of some small French vessels which he knew to be in the neighbourhood ; but he was at length advised that

---

[1] John Leake. Born, 1656. Captain, 1689. Relieved Londonderry. Commanded the *Eagle* at Barfleur, 1692. Rear-Admiral, 1702. Vice-Admiral, 1703. Knighted, 1704. Commanded the van at Malaga. Commander-in-chief in the Mediterranean, 1705–07. Admiral, 1707. Admiral of the Fleet, 1708. First Lord of the Admiralty, 1710. Died, 1720.

Kirke had altered his mind.[1] He therefore returned with the
Deptford and *Dartmouth*, and again confided the latter to Kirke's
orders.

Among the ships belonging to the convoy in Lough Foyle were
the *Mountjoy*, of Derry, Micaiah Browning master, and the *Phœnix*,
of Coleraine, Andrew Douglas master. The two gallant skippers
volunteered to endeavour to force their way up, and to the *Dartmouth* was assigned the honour of accompanying them. On
July 28th, under a heavy fire, the *Mountjoy* led the perilous
attempt. Batteries played upon her and her consorts ; musketry
fire rained upon the ships from both banks : but the *Mountjoy* struck
the boom and broke it. The elasticity of the mass of cables, chains,
and spars caused her, however, to recoil, and she drifted on to a
mudbank, while the *Phœnix* entered through the gap. The *Mountjoy*, nevertheless, was not far behind her consort. As soon as he
found himself aground, Browning fired a broadside into the nearest
body of the enemy. The concussion of this brought the ship off,
and she also passed the boom, though with the loss of her brave
master. The *Dartmouth* had rendered valuable aid in covering the
merchantmen and in assisting to sweep the banks of the river with
her guns, and at ten o'clock that night the three ships, not much
the worse for their adventure, reached Derry quay and began to
unload their welcome stores. On the night of July 31st the
discomfited Jacobites burnt their camp and abandoned the siege.

Captain Rooke continued to cruise in the neighbourhood of
the North Channel, and on August 13th, he escorted transports
carrying Schomberg's army to Belfast Lough, and so facilitated the
capture of Carrickfergus. With the ridiculously inadequate force at
his disposal, he made admirable arrangements, and kept careful
watch from Malin Head as far south as Dublin and the Isle of Man.
From time to time he received small reinforcements ; and early in
September he found himself able to divide his little squadron,
leaving part in the North to co-operate with the army there, and
going south with the remaining ships. On September 16th, he made
an attempt to burn the Jacobite shipping in Dublin Bay, but was
driven off by a gale. Two days later he was off Cork, and under a
heavy fire, took possession of the principal island in Queenstown
Harbour. Owing, however, to the condition of most of his vessels,

---

[1] This was in consequence of the receipt of positive orders from Marshal Schomberg.
See MS. in Nairne Coll., Bodleian Library.

he was unable to prolong his cruise; and on October 13th, he anchored in the Downs.[1]

Rooke's services on this occasion were undoubtedly of much value, yet they are here described at greater length, perhaps, than their intrinsic importance deserves. They illustrate how thoroughly mismanaged was the French naval campaign; and it is on that account that they chiefly merit attention. France was superior at sea; she had inflicted a severe check, if not a positive defeat, upon the principal English naval force in home waters; she had the ball at her feet. Yet, although, very soon after Bantry Bay, she had afloat a larger fleet than ever, she failed to apply it in the locality where it might easily have produced a decisive effect upon the fortunes of her ally, James II. She might have captured Rooke and his little squadron, ensured the fall of Londonderry, prevented Schomberg from landing in Ireland, and established herself, at least for a time, in almost unchallenged possession of the Irish Sea and its approaches. Instead, she contented herself with sending a few impotent small craft to the true sphere of action, and with allowing the bulk of her naval forces to make a useless promenade in the Channel.

England, however, was guilty of not less glaring strategic mistakes at this critical moment in her history. When war was declared, it was known in London that there was a strong French naval force at Toulon, and that this would make an effort to join hands with the fleet in Brest; yet no serious efforts were made to stop the threatened concentration, and, ere the summer of 1689 was over, a squadron of twenty ships of the line, four "frigates," eight fireships, and several storeships passed round unchallenged from the Mediterranean to the Atlantic. Tourville,[2] who thereupon assumed command there, then had at his disposal no fewer than sixty-two ships of war, and thirty fireships, besides other vessels in proportion. More ships still remained at Toulon, and although the government of William did attempt to prevent them from passing the Strait of Gibraltar, there was, as will be seen, so much delay and mismanagement, that the French effected their object with very little difficulty.

At the time of the Revolution there was no English naval force of any moment in the Mediterranean. Towards the end of 1689,

---

[1] *Gazette*; Buchan's letter in Nairne MSS.; 'Life of Sir John Leake'; 'Hist. de la Révol. d'Irlande'; 'Hist. of Red. of Ireland'; Walker, 'True Acct. of the Siege of Londonderry'; 'MS. Mems. of Sir G. Rooke'; 'Life of Sir G. Rooke.'

[2] Anne Hilarion de Cotentin, Comte de Tourville; born 1642; Vice-Adm. of the Levant, 1689; Marshal of France, 1693; died 1701; Jal, 'Dict. Crit. de Biog. et d'Hist.'

the government decided to send one thither; and a considerable squadron was told off for the purpose. To the command of this, Vice-Admiral Henry Killigrew was ultimately appointed. He had Mediterranean experience, having served as senior officer of the few vessels that were on the station previous to and immediately after the accession of William and Mary. But, while the squadron was still being collected, the government received from its ally, the King of Spain, a request that it would furnish an escort from Flushing to Corunna for a princess whom his Majesty had just previously married by proxy. In spite of the strain upon the naval resources of the country, it was rightly or wrongly deemed politic to grant the request, and a second squadron, ultimately entrusted to Admiral Edward Russell, was prepared for the purpose. In this squadron were included some of the ships which were eventually to be under Killigrew, and Russell was directed, after accomplishing his complimentary mission, to send them on from Corunna to Cadiz.

Russell's squadron was the first to depart. It sailed on December 1st, 1689, for Flushing; but, owing to the unreadiness of the royal bride, to contrary winds, and to other causes, it did not reach Corunna until March 16th, 1690. There, the grounding of one of the ships caused additional delay, but at length the Mediterranean contingent parted company for Cadiz; and Russell, returning, anchored at Spithead on April 28th.

Killigrew was appointed to his command on December 28th, 1689, but did not succeed in getting away from Torbay until March 7th, 1690. He had with him one second-rate, four third-rates, seven fourth-rates, one fifth-rate, and two fireships, and was to pick up at Cadiz one second-rate, and two third-rates detached thither by Russell. Moreover, he was joined by a Dutch contingent under Lieutenant-Admiral Philips van Almonde. He was directed firstly to convoy the outgoing trade; and then, with the greater part of his force, to watch the French in the Mediterranean, to protect British interests there, and, in case the Toulon ships should evade him and pass the Strait of Gibraltar, to follow them. He reached Cadiz on April 8th, but was obliged to remain there for some time in order to repair certain of his ships which had suffered in a storm. On May 9th, he heard simultaneously from Alicant, Malaga, and Gibraltar that the Toulon squadron had been seen from each of these places. Some of his ships were still not ready for sea; but he sailed on the 10th, with one second-rate, two third-rates, four fourth-rates, two fifth-rates, and two Dutch ships of the line, and next day was joined by other vessels which had been detached to Gibraltar. These brought up his strength to one second-rate, three third-rates, six fourth-rates, two fifth-rates, and two fireships, besides five Dutch ships.

Acting on information, he stood over to Ceuta and Tetuan, but found there nothing of importance. Returning towards the Spanish side, he sighted ten ships to the northward of him. These were the French. French writers say that they offered battle, and that Killigrew refused it. The weight of evidence shows, however, that Killigrew chased them for twenty-four hours, and failed to come up with them only because all his vessels were foul. Indeed, as he was in superior force, it is altogether improbable that he wilfully neglected any measure that might have brought on a general action. But, after losing sight of them, he certainly failed to follow them up with all possible energy. The result was that they joined the already large French force in the Channel in time to contribute to the result of the battle of Beachy Head, and that he did not reach Plymouth until after that battle had been fought. When he at length arrived, so great was the panic that he was hastily ordered into Hamoaze, lest his squadron should be carried off by the triumphant enemy.

Nor was this the extent of English mismanagement. The grand fleet was further weakened by the detachment of Sir Clowdisley Shovell, with a small squadron, to convoy King William to Carrickfergus ; and Shovell, like Killigrew, was consequently unable to take part in the great action of 1690. In the meantime, such force as was in Irish waters did not prevent a French division under D'Amfreville from conveying six thousand French troops to Cork, and from safely carrying back thence to Brest about the same number of Irish soldiers.

What has been written will go far to explain why, when the

Notes to Table on opposite page.

[1] Flag of Vice-Admiral Sir John Ashby (R.).
[2] Flag of Admiral Lord Torrington, Commander-in-Chief.
[3] Flag of Rear-Admiral Rooke (R.).
[4] Flag of Vice-Admiral Sir Ralph Delavall (B.).

[5] The English fireships were :

Centre.
Wolf, Thos. Urry.
Vulture, Jas. Moody.
Roebuck, Isaac Townsend.
Dolphin, Wm. Vickars.
Owner's Love, Thos. Heath.
Speedwell, John Mason.
Hound, Thos. Foulis.
Spy, Fredk. Weighman.

Rear.
Fox, William Stone.
Thomas and Elizabeth, Thos. Marshall
Charles, Anthony Roope.
Griffin, Clifford Chamberlain.
Hawk, Wm. Harman.
Cygnet, Robert Willmot.
Hunter, Thos. Kercher.
Cadiz Merchant, David Greenhill.

THE ORDER OF BATTLE OF THE FLEETS IN THE ACTION OFF BEACHY HEAD.

ANGLO-DUTCH FLEET.

Van—White.

Ships.	Guns.	Commanders.
Wapen van Utrecht	64	Decker.
Wapen van Alkmaar	50	Calf.
Tholen	60	Calis.
West Vriesland	82	(V.-Ad. van Callenburgh.)
Prinses Maria	92	(R.-Ad. Gilles Scheij.)
Castricum	50	Kuijper.
Agatha	50	Van der Zaan.
Stad en Landen	52	Abraham Taelman.
Maagd van Enkhuizen	72	Van der Poel.
Noord Holland	46	Swaen.
Maagd van Dordrecht	68	Anthonij Pieterson.
Hollandia	74	(Lt.-Ad. Corn. Evertsen.)
Veluwe	68	(R.-Ad. Jan van Brakel.)
Provincie van Utrecht	50	Jan van Convent.
Maze	64	Jan Snellen.
Vriesland	64	Philips van der Goes.
Elswout	50	Noortheij.
Reijgersberge	74	A. F. van Zijll.
Gekroonde Burg	62	(V.-Ad. C. van de Putte.)
Noord Holland	72	(R.-Ad. Jan Dick.)
Veere	60	Moselman.
Cortienne	50	A. den Boer.
*And four fireships.		

Centre—Red.

Ships.	Guns.	Commanders.
Plymouth	60	Richard Carter.
Deptford	50	William Kerr.
Elizabeth	70	David Mitchell.
Sandwich[1]	90	?
Expedition	70	John Clements.
Warspite	70	Stafford Fairborne.
Woolwich	54	James Gother.
Lion	60	John Torpley.
Rupert	66	George Pomeroy.
Albemarle	90	Sir Francis Wheler.
Grafton	70	Henry, Duke of Grafton.
Royal Sovreign[2]	100	John Neville.
Windsor Castle	90	George Churchill.
Lenox	70	Hon. John Granville.
Stirling Castle	70	Anthony Hastings.
York	60	Thomas Hopsonn.
Suffolk	70	Wolfran Cornewall.
Hampton Court	70	John Layton.
Duchess[3]	90	Thomas Gillam.
Hope	70	George Byng.
Restoration	70	William Botham.
*Constant Warwick	36	John Beverley.
*And eight fireships.[5]		

Rear—Blue.

Ships.	Guns.	Commanders.
Anne	70	John Tyrrel.
Bonaventure	48	John Hubbard.
Edgar	64	John Jennifer.
Exeter	70	George Mees.
Breda	70	Matthew Tennant.
St. Andrew	96	Robert Dorrell.
Coronation[4]	90	John Munden.
Royal Katherine	82	Matthew Aylmer.
Cambridge	70	Simon Foulks.
Berwick	70	Henry Martin.
Swallow	48	Benjamin Walters.
Defiance	64	John Graydon.
Captain	70	Daniel Jones.
*And eight fireships.[5]		

FRENCH FLEET.

Van—Blue at the Fore.

Ships.	Guns.	Commanders.
Fier	68	De Relingues.
Fort	52	De La Harteloire.
Maure	52	De La Galissonnière.
Eclatant	64	De Septesmes.
Conquerant	70	(V.-Ad. de Villette-Mur[çai.)]
Courtisan	62	De Pointis.
Indien	50	De Roussel.
Trident	52	De Ryberette.
Hardi	58	Des Gouttes.
Saint-Louis	56	De La Roque-Persin.
Excellent	56	De Montbron.
Pompeux	74	d'Aligre.
Dauphin Royal	110	(Ad. Châteaurenault.)
Ardent	62	d'Infreville de St. Aubin.
Bon	52	De Digoin du Palais.
Fendant	52	Treillebois de la Vigerie.
Courageux	60	De Sévigné.
Couronne	58	(R.-Ad. de Langeron.)
Ferme	54	De Vaudricourt.
Téméraire	52	Du Rivau-Huet.
*Solide	48	De Ferville.
*Alcion	44	Jean Bart.
*Eole	50	Du Tast.
*And six fireships.		

Centre—White at the Main.

Ships.	Guns.	Commanders.
Brusque	50	De Recours.
Arrogant	54	Chev. des Adrets.
Arc-en-Ciel	44	De Sainte-Maure.
Henri	62	d'Amblimont.
Souverain	80	(R.-Ad. de Nesmond.)
Brillant	66	De Beaujeu.
Neptune	46	De Forbin.
Sans Pareil	58	De La Rongère.
Fidele	46	De Forbin Gardanne.
Diamant	56	De Serquigny.
Sérieux	56	De Bellefontaine.
Tonnant	70	Marquis de La Porte.
Soleil Royal	98	(Ad. Comte de Tourville.)
Saint-Philippe	80	Marquis de Coëtlogon.
Marquis	80	DeChâteau-Morand.
Furieux	60	Desnots.
Fortuné	58	Pallas.
Apollon	56	Bidault.
Saint-Michel	54	De Villars.
Entreprenant	56	De Sebeville.
Magnifique	76	(V.-Ad. d'Amfreville.)
Content	56	De Saint-Pierre.
Vermandois	58	Du Chalard.
Cheval Marin	40	d'Amfreville.
Fougueux	58	De Saint-Marc.
*Faucon	44	De Montbault.
*And six fireships.		

Rear—White and Blue at the Mizzen.

Ships.	Guns.	Commanders.
Comte	40	De La Roche-Courbon- [Blenac.]
Vigilant	52	De Chalais.
Parfait	62	De Machault.
Triomphant	70	(R.-Ad. de Flacourt.)
Bourbon	62	d'Hervault.
Vaillant	48	De Feuquières.
Duc	48	De Pallières.
Capable	54	De La Boissière.
Brave	54	De Champigny.
François	46	d'Hailly.
Agréable	58	De La Motte-Genouillé.
Grand	80	De Cogolin.
Belliqueux	74	(Ad. Victor Marie Des Francs. [d'Estrées.])
Prince	56	Baron des Adrets.
Prudent	52	Des Herbiers.
Modéré	50	Des Augers.
Fleuron	54	De Chabert.
Aimable	70	Du Magnon.
Intrépide	80	(V.-Ad. Jean Gabaret.)
Glorieux	60	De Bellei-le-Erard.
Illustre	66	De Rosmadec.
Terrible	74	Pannetier.
*Léger	44	Du Rouvroy.
*And six fireships.		

Vessels thus indicated * were not in the line of battle.   For notes to Table see opposite page.

Anglo-Dutch fleet, under Torrington and Cornelis Evertsen,[1] met the greatest fleet which France up to that time had ever sent to sea, the former was notably weaker than the latter. The fleets which thus met are shown in Table on p. 335 *ante*.

The strength of the line-of-battle on each side was, therefore:—

	ANGLO-DUTCH.		FRENCH.	
	Ships.	Guns.	Ships.	Guns.
Van	22	1374	20	1214
Centre . . .	21	1410	25	1518
Rear. . . .	13	912	23	1390
	56	3696	68	4122

This was, no doubt, a considerable disparity, for the French had in line 22 per cent. more ships than the Allies, although, on the other hand, the Anglo-Dutch vessels averaged about six more guns apiece than the vessels of Tourville. At Trafalgar, Nelson was proportionably quite as inferior to Villeneuve and Gravina, yet he fought them and beat them. It is fair to bear in mind that, while at Trafalgar it was the smaller force that enjoyed the great advantage of being of a single nationality, at Beachy Head it was the larger. At Beachy Head, nevertheless, the odds against Torrington were not heavy enough to justify him in looking upon victory as hopeless.

Tourville quitted Brest on June 13th, 1690. Torrington at that time lay in the neighbourhood of the Isle of Wight, awaiting, and from day to day receiving, reinforcements of English and Dutch ships. Indeed, his force did not attain its full strength until very shortly before the battle which was fought at the end of the month. In that age it was still customary for the belligerent powers to withdraw their grand fleets from sea at the beginning of winter, and to send them out again at the beginning of summer. Navies, in fact, like armies, habitually went into winter quarters. Yet, although by the middle of June the ordinary season for the resumption of hostilities was already several weeks old, and although Torrington

[1] Cornelis Evertsen, known first as "the Youngest," and later as "the Younger," son of Lieut.-Admiral C. Evertsen, "the Old." Distinguished himself in the Second War with England, especially in the affair of the Smyrna fleet, at Solebay, and in the West Indies. Accompanied William III. to England. Led the van at Beachy Head. Died Lieut.-Admiral of Zeeland, 1706.

knew very well that a large armament was getting ready to fall upon him, the port of Brest was altogether unwatched, and not a single English cruiser was on the look-out to the westward of St. Helens. On June 20th, the French were off the Lizard; on the 23rd, they were off St. Alban's Head. Not, apparently, until then did Torrington become fully aware that they were anywhere near him. On that day he weighed and stood off shore to the S.E., anchoring again late in the afternoon, with Culver Cliff bearing S.W. by S., about six or seven miles. At five on the following morning he weighed again, with a fresh gale from the N.E. by N., and stood away S.E. by E. In the evening he again anchored, with Culver Cliff bearing nearly W.N.W. At 5 A.M. on the 25th, he once more weighed, and exercised the fleet at tactics until 9 A.M., when, the wind having veered to S.S.E. and a thick fog having come on, he anchored, Dunose being W.N.W., about fifteen miles.

Half an hour later a "frigate" came in with her topgallant sheets flying and her guns firing. This was the signal for the approach of the enemy in force. The fleet at once weighed, the wind being S.S.E., and stood to the eastward; and, soon afterwards, the French were sighted to the westward. In the afternoon, the Blue squadron was ordered to lead towards the foe; but although a shift of wind gave the Allies the weather-gauge, no action resulted. Indeed, it was decided, at a council of war, that the fleet was too weak to engage the enemy; and a dispatch to that effect was sent by express to Queen Mary, who, in the absence of King William in Ireland, was at the supreme head of affairs. That night both fleets anchored. On the 26th, still in full sight of one another, they drew into line; but the wind dropped, and rendered an attack by either side impossible. In the evening, with a light breeze from N.W., Torrington stood up Channel, the French following him at a distance of about twelve miles. And so, now anchoring, now weighing, now sighting, and now losing sight of the French, the English slowly withdrew, until the evening of the 29th, when dispatches arrived containing explicit orders for the French to be fought. Next morning, when there was a fresh gale from about N.E., and Beachy Head lay ten or twelve miles to the northward, Torrington, who was to windward, formed his fleet in order of battle, and bore down in line abreast upon the enemy, van upon van, centre upon centre, and rear upon rear. The French, who were on the starboard tack, heading N.N.W., awaited the onslaught with their head-sails aback.

The allied van, consisting of the Dutch contingent under Evertsen, was the first part of the fleet to get within range. As it did so, the ships of which it was composed hauled their wind together on the starboard tack—on a parallel course, that is, with the course of the enemy—and then, hotly engaging, edged towards and pressed the French van with the greatest gallantry and determination, backing and filling as the enemy did.

Torrington, with the allied centre, did not take an equally direct course for the enemy, but, at first stood more to the southward, as if with the intention of cutting off the French rear. When, however, Ashby who, with his division, was imitating the example

DUTCH SHIP OF THE LINE "HOLLANDIA," 74. BUILT IN 1683.

Flagship of Lt.-Adm. Cornelis Evertsen (III.) at Beachy Head.

(*From the drawing by A. L. van Kaldenbach.*)

of Torrington, observed how great a gap was growing between the centre and the Dutch, he altered his course in such a manner as to lessen the interval somewhat, and Torrington stood after him, Rooke duly standing after Torrington. Each of the three divisions of the allied centre kept well together ; but when at length both fleets were heading in roughly parallel lines to the N.N.W., there were considerable spaces not only between the three divisions of the allied centre, but also between the centre and the van, and between the centre and the rear.

Delavall, with the allied rear, meanwhile engaged the French rear very closely, in spite of its largely superior force, and backed and filled to keep abreast of it in the most deliberate and pertinacious manner.

By accident or design, the centre of the long French line, which seems to have been very correctly formed and preserved, so far as the distances between the ships were concerned, was bowed or sagged to leeward. That fact may have suggested to Torrington the design, which he must be supposed to have abandoned soon after it was conceived, of concentrating upon, and cutting off, the enemy's rear. The plan of action which apparently he next adopted, and which he pursued throughout the early part of the engagement, was to keep the allied centre, or at least the centre and rear of his own

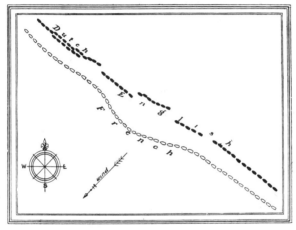

THE BATTLE OFF BEACHY HEAD.

June 30th, 1690.

squadron, at long gunshot to windward, with a view to preventing Tourville from tacking and doubling upon Delavall's squadron. But this plan was a faulty one. It did not prevent the head of the French Blue squadron, when the Dutch had been for some time engaged, from going about and so placing the Dutch between two fires; nor did it prevent the head of the French White squadron, when it had severely mauled Ashby, from pushing forward to complicate the perplexities of the gallant but unfortunate Evertsen. The Dutch might have held, and, indeed, did for some time hold, their own against the three divisions of Châteaurenault; but when these three divisions were reinforced by the divisions of De Nesmond and of Tourville himself, the Dutch, overpowered and engaged on

z 2

both sides simultaneously, were exceedingly hard pressed. But for a calm which opportunely befell, they would, in all likelihood, have been destroyed.

During the calm, the French centre got out its boats in order to tow more ships into action. The Allies, on the other hand, shrewdly dropped anchor with all sail set, Torrington first placing himself between the Dutch and the enemy. The result was that when the ebb tide made strongly to the S.W., the French, who had not anchored, were gently carried out of gunshot, and not until they were three miles from the Allies did they anchor also.

So ended the battle of Beachy Head, or, as the French style it, of Bezeviers. The Dutch had begun firing at about 9 A.M.; Delavall's squadron had attacked the French rear at 9.30 A.M.; and the allied centre had opened at long range at about 10 A.M. It was 1 P.M. when part of the French van doubled upon the Dutch; about 3 P.M. when the wind fell;[1] and about 5 P.M. when the Allies anchored. The loss of officers and men had naturally been considerable; but, thus far, the only vessel lost was one, apparently small, belonging to the Dutch. For want of anchors, she had drifted among a mass of French vessels, and had been taken or sunk. Numerous ships of the Allies were, however, in a perilous condition, owing to loss of spars or to shot-holes between wind and water.

Torrington, in his official dispatch, dated from off Beachy Head on July 1st, said :—

"What the consequence of this unfortunate battle may be, God Almighty only knows; but this I dare be positive in, had I been left to my liberty, I had prevented any attempt upon the land, and secured the western ships, Killigrew, and the merchantmen. . . . Had I undertaken this of my own head, I should not well know what to say ; but its being done by command will, I hope, free me from blame."[2]

It is, undoubtedly, always somewhat unfair to a naval commander-in-chief when a superior authority, at a distance from the scene of operations, undertakes to direct the details of his strategy and to force his action.[3] Torrington had desired not to fight, and

---

[1] Torrington's dispatch says that the calm came on after the action had lasted two hours. The times here given are taken from 'Mems. relating to the Lord Torrington (Byng); and from Dutch and French accounts, and most of them are corroborated by the evidence at the court-martial.

[2] S. P. Dom. (K. Will's Chest), B. 7, f. 161.

[3] While the late Admiral Sir Geoffrey Phipps Hornby was still on the active list of the Navy, and when there appeared to be some chance of difficulties with a foreign

had been, rightly or wrongly, of opinion that he could best serve his country's cause by avoiding a decisive battle, pending the arrival of reinforcements. His views, as expressed by himself, were : " Whilst we observe the French, they cannot make any attempt, either upon ships or shore, without running a great hazard, and, if we be beaten, all is exposed to their mercy."[1] Weeks afterwards he declared : " Had I fought otherwise, our fleet had been totally lost, and the kingdom had lain open to an invasion. . . . As it was, most men were in fear that the French would invade, but I was always of another opinion, for I always said that, whilst we had a fleet in being, they would not dare to make an attempt."[2]

One may not challenge the sincerity of Torrington's beliefs ; nor is it necessary to attack, as many of his contemporaries did, the honesty of his motives. Yet it is possible that, upon at least two important points, the admiral was wrong. It may be that he over-rated the menace of what he called his " fleet in being." A fleet merely " in being " is not, of necessity, a menace at all. It is not a menace unless it be also " potential," and by " potential " is implied " able and ready to act up to the limit of its strength at the required moment and at the required point." At the time of the descent of William III., Dartmouth's fleet, though certainly "in being," was in no sense " potential." In the first place, it was prevented by the weather from placing itself in the position where it could have acted with effect ; in the second place, it was so disaffected that, had it been offered battle, it would not have acted up to the limit of its strength at the required moment. Torrington's fleet, as a body, was willing enough to do its best against the enemy, as was amply proved by the conduct, at Beachy Head, of the Dutch, and of Ashby's and Delavall's portions of the command. But it might have easily happened, had the French chosen to attempt a sudden landing, that Torrington could not have reached the

---

Power, it was intended that, in case of a fleet having to be sent to the enemy's coast, a cable ship should accompany it, paying out cable as she went, in order that Whitehall should always be able to communicate with the commander-in-chief. The Author asked Sir Geoffrey his opinion of this arrangement : " I think," he said, " that a commander-in-chief thus tied to the Admiralty would be at a grave disadvantage, as he would be liable to be controlled by men ignorant of the state of affairs at the scene of action. If I were that commander-in-chief, therefore, I suspect that you would hear of the cable breaking, soon after the fleet had left port." Yet, if not used to unduly control a commander-in-chief, a cable to a fleet in wartime might surely be invaluable.

[1] Letter to Nottingham.					[2] Torrington's defence.

threatened spot in time to prevent it. The enemy might have elected to run the risk, in view of the discontent and readiness for counter-revolution which were supposed to prevail in England. The weather, moreover, might at any moment have given the French an opportunity of snapping up Killigrew, Shovell, and the incoming merchantmen, or of evading Torrington and making for Scotland. It was probably these aspects of the situation that struck Queen Mary and her advisers, and that induced them to order Torrington to fight as soon as he should have the advantage of the wind. It is not so important to discuss whether Torrington's views or the government's views were the juster, as it is to determine what was Torrington's duty in the position in which he found himself after the receipt of the Queen's commands.

Three courses were open to him. He might have taken upon himself the grave responsibility of disobedience. A Nelson would have done that, had he been absolutely convinced in his own mind that to fight was to imperil his country. Or he might have fought the fight of the forlorn hope, firing as long as he had a plank beneath him. A Nelson would, in certain circumstances, have been capable of that also. "Though," said Nelson, "we are but eleven to eighteen or twenty, we won't part without a battle." And again : " By the time the enemy has beaten our fleet soundly, they will do us no harm this year." The third course was to compromise, by obeying the letter, and disobeying the spirit of the order. This course Torrington adopted. He fought, but he did not fight with all his might. He did not throw his whole heart and strength into the encounter. He still adhered to his own conclusion that, after all, to preserve a " fleet in being " was the great point to be aimed at. He was defeated and driven into the Thames; yet no French invasion followed. It is scarcely conceivable that if he had fought with less reserve, and had done much more injury to the enemy than he actually did, the apprehended invasion would have been in any way facilitated. But it is conceivable that if he had swept aside his own prejudices, and looked only and with a single eye to damaging his foe to the utmost, he might have won one of the most brilliant and decisive victories in naval history. Even had he failed, the French would have been little less complete masters of the Channel than they actually became.

At 9 P.M. on the evening of the battle, the tide changed, and the Allies weighed and stood to the eastward, with the most seriously disabled ships in tow. Next day it was decided at a council of war to destroy these ships rather than hazard an engagement for their protection. Tourville pursued, but, instead of ordering a general chase, preserved his line of battle. If he had been less deliberate, he would have taken many prizes. Yet his pursuit was close enough to induce the Allies to carry out their decision as regards many of the disabled vessels. Off Dover the pursuit was abandoned, and on July 9th, the Allies, still in great confusion, anchored at the Nore, and, lest they should be followed, prepared to remove the buoys at the mouth of the river.[1]

In this battle the French lost no ship, and but one officer of rank. Their loss in men was considerable, but much inferior to that of the Allies. They claim to have destroyed, or caused the destruction of, no fewer than fourteen Dutch and English vessels, and to have taken one ship. Neither in the Dutch nor in the English archives is there, however, anything to substantiate this claim. Of the allied ships of the line, not more than eight or nine appear to have been lost, among them being the *Anne*, 70, which was beached near Winchelsea, and burnt by her captain, John Tyrrel ; the *Wapen van Utrecht*, 64, which sank after the action ; the *Maagd van Enkhuizen*, 72, the *Tholen*, 60, and the *Elswout*, 50. If other vessels were destroyed, they were probably Dutch fireships which were expended in the ordinary course. Among the English officers who perished were Captains William Botham of the *Restoration*, and George Pomeroy[2] of the *Rupert*. Captain John Jennifer of the *Edgar*, who was badly wounded, lingered until early in the following year. Three Captains of Marines, Erasmus Philips, of the *Hampton Court*, John Barrington, of the *Restoration*, and Thomas Mitchell, of the *Anne*, were also killed. Among the Dutch officers who fell were Rear-Admirals Jan van Brakel and Jan Dick, and Captain Noortheij.[3]

---

[1] Lediard says that, although an order to that effect was given, the buoys were not actually taken up.

[2] Pomeroy, though mortally wounded, did not die until July 10th, 1690.

[3] Authorities for the events of the Battle of Beachy Head: Minutes of the Court Martial, Dec. 8th, 1690; Torrington's Disp. in S. P. Dom. (K. Will's Chest), B. 7, f. 161 ; 'Mems. relating to the Lord Torrington' (Byng), 43–51; 'Reg. van den Lt.-Adm. C. Evertsen'; Evertsen's Report in Rijks Archief : Ships' Pay Lists in P.R.O.; MS. List of Commissions in Auth.'s coll.; 'Relat. du Commis. Castigny' (of *Triomphant*) in Arch. de la Mar. Franç.; 'Reasons for the Tryal,' etc. (1690); Lists of Ships in De Jonge, iii., App. ; Hoste, 'L'Art des Armées Navales'; Richer, 'Vie de Tourville,' 'Vie de V. M. d'Estrées'; various tracts in Roy. Lib. at Amsterdam;

The effect upon the country of the intelligence of the defeat was somewhat tempered by the news, which arrived almost simultaneously, of King William's victory on the Boyne on July 1st. Nevertheless, there was a great, and, all things considered, not unnatural outcry against Torrington.

On July 8th, the French fleet stood for a time towards its own coasts; but on the 27th, it was off Berry Head, and subsequently entered Torbay. Some of its small craft made a raid on Teignmouth, and burnt a few ships there. On July 29th, the enemy was off Plymouth, and on August 5th, off Ram Head; but Tourville then withdrew, and the panic occasioned by his mastery of the Channel gradually subsided. It is difficult to understand why Louis XIV. did not press his advantage. The shattered fleet of the Allies was, it is true, still "in being," but if an invasion had been seriously attempted in the early days of July, it is extremely probable that, for several weeks, it would have met with little, save on shore, to jeopardise its success.

Torrington, leaving the command to Ashby, landed soon after he had entered the river. He was presently sent to the Tower, and a commission was ordered to Sheerness to inquire into the circumstances of the late miscarriage. In December, the commander-in-chief was tried by a court-martial, over which Vice-Admiral Sir Ralph Delavall presided; but, although he was unanimously acquitted, and returned to London on December 11th in his barge with his flag still flying, he was superseded and never again employed. He was a gallant man, and, undoubtedly, he had acted throughout with the best intentions. Seignelay reproached Torrington's adversary, Tourville, with being "brave of heart and coward of head." The description seems to apply even more accurately to Torrington himself, whose main fault arose out of the fact that when William's necessities called for the services of genius, the services of no more than fair ability were forthcoming.

The allied fleets having been refitted and reinforced, the chief command was entrusted in August to three officers conjointly,

---

Méms. du Cte. de Forbin' (1729); Sylvius, 'Saken v. Staat en Oorlog'; Chandler's 'Debates'; Wagenaar's 'Vaderl. Hist.'; *London Gazette*; Holl. *Mercurius*; 'Nauwkeurig Verhaal' (Rotterdam, 1690); Journ. of H. of Comms.; 'Hist. and Proc. of H. of Lords,' i. and ii.; Sue, 'Hist. de la Mar. Franç.'; Guérin, 'Hist. Mar. de France'; Evertsen family papers; Letters of A. van Citters; 'The Account given by Sir J. Ashby,' etc. (1691); Richer, 'Jean Bart'; Vanderest, 'Jean Bart.'

Sir Richard Haddock, Henry Killigrew, and Sir John Ashby. As
the season advanced the heavier ships were laid up. Most of
the rest were employed in conveying troops to Ireland, where a
small squadron, under Captain the Duke of Grafton, as senior
officer, was left to assist in operations against Cork.[1] The main
body of the fleet returned to the Downs in October, and then
dispersed to its ports for the winter, only a cruising force remaining
in commission under Rear-Admiral Sir Clowdisley Shovell. In
December Admiral Edward Russell was appointed Admiral of the
Fleet.

The year 1691 saw very little fighting on a great scale afloat, and
is mainly remarkable in naval annals as having witnessed Tourville's
brilliant strategical operations, which are remembered in French
history as his *campagne au large*, or deep-sea cruise.[2] Russell, joined
by the Dutch, was at the head of about one hundred sail of the line.
Tourville had few more than seventy. He nevertheless sailed
from Brest in June, and, during nearly the whole of the summer,
managed to remain in or off the chops of the Channel, and to
harass English trade without once allowing his opponent to bring
him to action. "The actual captures," says Mahan, "made by
Tourville's own fleet were insignificant, but its service to the
commerce-destroying warfare of the French, by occupying the
Allies, is obvious." Moreover, while the Allies were drawn elsewhere, French convoys passed safely to and from Ireland.
Tourville captured some merchantmen homeward bound from
Jamaica, but missed the far richer Smyrna convoy, which reached
Kingsale without mishap and was thence escorted into the Channel
by Russell.

After Tourville had returned to Brest, the Allies went to
Torbay to refresh their men, and then cruised again for a short
time. In the autumn, as was usual in those days, the heavy ships
withdrew for the winter, only small craft continuing to keep the
sea. The withdrawal was very disastrous to Russell's command.
A storm overtook the English fleet and scattered it as it was
endeavouring to bear up for Plymouth in thick weather. On
September 3rd, the *Coronation*, 90, having first been totally dismasted, foundered with her captain, Charles Skelton, and almost

---

[1] For the siege of Cork, see Chap. XXV.
[2] Tourville's dispatches in the Archives de la Marine ; Hoste, 'Traité des
Evol. Nav.'

all her crew, off Ram Head; and the *Harwich*, 70, went ashore
and became a wreck under Mount Edgcumbe. The *Royal Oak*,
74, and *Northumberland*, 70, grounded, but were fortunately got
off again, and many other vessels, Dutch as well as English, very
narrowly escaped disaster.[1]

Early in 1692 King William, always anxious to prosecute the
war on land, went to Holland. In March the ex-King James
went to Cape La Hougue, where transports had been collected,
and a large mixed force had been assembled in readiness to embark
and to attempt an invasion of England. Queen Mary, who, during
her husband's frequent absences on the Continent, was the active
head of the government, pressed forward the preparation of the
fleet, and caused a large camp to be formed near Portsmouth
under the command of General Thomas Tollemache.[2]   Russell
was again appointed Admiral of the fleet. Delavall, who had come
back from Cadiz, whither he had escorted a squadron of merchantmen, was sent to scout off the French coast; and Rear-Admiral
Richard Carter, with a small force, was also dispatched on a
cruise in the Channel. As soon as the greater part of the
main fleet was ready it proceeded to Rye Bay;[3] a large Dutch
contingent joined it on May 9th; and on the 11th the united
squadrons sailed to the westward. On the 13th, off St. Helens,
they were reinforced by the divisions of Carter and Delavall; and
on the 15th a council of all the English and Dutch flag-officers
was held.

At that time there was in England a very prevalent belief that
many officers of the Royal Navy were disaffected to the House
of Orange, and would seize an early opportunity for abandoning
its cause and deserting to James and Louis. The belief, for which
there seems to have been remarkably little basis, probably originated
with, and was disseminated by, impulsive English Jacobites, who
imagined that, without some such encouragement, the ex-King and
his French allies would never be induced to essay a bold stroke.
Lord Melfort either credited it, or supposed it politic to affect to
credit it; and he represented to Louis in specific terms that Rear-

---

[1] Home Off. Recs., Admiralty, 10; Burchett, 448, 449.

[2] In most contemporary documents, this gallant officer is called Talmash.

[3] The rapid assemblage of the fleet was much facilitated by the energy of Russell,
who, contrary to the advice of the pilots, quitted the Downs with a very scant wind,
and successfully carried his heavy ships past the dangers of the Goodwins and the
Varne.

Admiral Carter and certain captains were among those who would actively assist in the restoration of the fallen dynasty. It is doubtful whether Louis placed any faith in the story; nor, perhaps did Queen Mary, to whose ears rumours of intended treachery filtered, attach much importance to the tale; yet she deemed it right to apprise Russell of what she had heard. Her Majesty's communication, sent

EDWARD RUSSELL, EARL OF ORFORD, VISCOUNT BARFLEUR,
ADMIRAL OF THE FLEET.

(*From Vertue's engraving after the painting by T. Gibson.*)

through the Secretary of State, was discussed at the council of war on May 15th; and, in reply, all the flag-officers and captains in the fleet signed an address in which the Queen was assured of their loyalty and devotion.[1]

Tourville, as in the previous years, was the French commander-

---

Gazette, 2767; 'Mercure Hist. et Pol.' xii. 646.

in-chief. The long accepted belief that he had received from Louis definite orders to fight the Allies upon meeting them, is, apparently, without foundation; but it is true that reflections which had been made upon his conduct of operations in 1690 and 1691 had decided him to take risks such as his own uninfluenced judgment would have bidden him avoid. His state of mind was known at the French Court. It was there realised that, with a view to restoring a reputation which he wrongly fancied to be tarnished, he would probably essay some desperate stroke; and, as it was believed that he might be ignorant of the accomplished junction of the Dutch with the English, two separate dispatches were sent to him to inform him of that fact, and to desire him, in consequence, to avoid an action. Neither reached him, and thus it was that he fought the brilliant but disastrous battle of Barfleur. After waiting in vain for a squadron which he expected from Toulon under Admiral Victor Marie d'Estrées, Tourville quitted his anchorage in Bertheaume Bay, and, with such inadequate force as he had, entered the Channel on May 17th.

The fleets which were about to meet were very disproportionate in every respect, and may be thus summarised :—

		ALLIES.			FRENCH.	
		Flag-officers.	No. of Ships.		Flag-officers.	No. of Ships.
Dutch.	Van.	Vice-Adm. G. van Callenburgh . R.-Adm. P. van der Goes . . . Vice-Adm. G. Scheij . . . . Lt.-Adm. P. van Almonde . . R.-Adm. J. G. Muijs . . . . Vice-Adm. C. van de Putte . . R.-Adm. Geleijn Evertsen . .	36		M. de Nesmond . . Lt.-Genl. d'Amfreville M. de Relingues . .	14
English.[1]	Centre.	R.-Adm. Sir C. Shovell. . . Ad. of the Fleet E. Russell . Vice-Adm. Sir R. Delavall. .	31		M. de Villette-Murçai. Comte de Tourville . M. de Langeron . .	16
	Rear.	Vice-Adm. Geo. Rooke. . . . Adm. Sir J. Ashby. . . . . R.-Adm. R. Carter	32		M. de Coëtlogon . . V.-Adm. Gabaret . . M. Pannetier . . .	14
		Total ships of the line .	99		Total ships of the line .	44
		"Frigates" and fireships	38		"Frigates" and fireships	13
		Guns.	6756		Guns	3240

[1] As the constitution of the English portion of the allied fleet is of more special interest, it is given in detail. The following was its intended constitution; but a few of these ships did not join until after the action, and, on the other hand, the *Portsmouth*, 46, Capt. John Bridges (2); the *Soldadoes*, 16, Capt. Wm.

FLAGS.

CENTRE OR RED SQUADRON.

Admiral of the Fleet, Edward Russell } *Britannia.*
Captain of the Fleet, David Mitchell }
Vice-Admiral, Sir Ralph Delavall . *Royal Sovereign.*
Rear-Admiral, Sir Clowdisley Shovell *Royal William.*

SHIPS.	GUNS.	CAPTAINS.
Plymouth	60	John Maine.
Ruby	50	George Mees.
Cambridge	70	Richard Lestock.
Oxford	54	James Wishart.
Sandwich	90	Anthony Hastings.
Royal William	100	Thomas Jennings.
Breda	70	David Lambert.
Kent	70	John Neville.
St. Albans	50	Richard Fitzpatrick.
Swiftsure	70	Richard Clarke.
Hampton Court	70	John Graydon.
F.S. *Phaeton* . . 8	..	Robert Hancock.
F.S. *Fox* . . 8	..	Thomas Killingworth.
F.S. *Strombolo* . 8	..	Thomas Urry.
F.S. *Hopewell* . 8	..	William Jumper.
Grafton	70	William Bokenham.
Restoration	70	James Gother.
Greenwich	54	Richard Edwards.
London	96	Matthew Aylmer.
Britannia	100	John Fletcher.
St. Andrew	96	George Churchill.
Chester	48	Thomas Gillam.
Eagle	70	John Leake.
Rupert	66	Basil Beaumont.
Elizabeth	70	Stafford Fairborne.
F.S. *Flame* . . 8	..	James Stewart.
F.S. *Roebuck* . . 8	..	Francis Manly.
F.S. *Vulture* . . 8	..	Hovenden Walker.
F.S. *Spy* . . . 8	..	John Norris.
Burford	70	Thomas Harlow.
Centurion	48	Francis Wyvill.
Captain	70	Daniel Jones.
Devonshire	80	Henry Haughton.
Royal Sovereign	100	Humphrey Sanders.
Royal Katherine	82	Wolfran Cornewall.
Bonaventure	48	John Hubbard.
York	60	Robert Deane.
Lenox	70	John Munden.
St. Michael	90	Thomas Hopsonn.
F.S. *Extravagant* 10	..	Fleetwood Emes.
F.S. *Wolf* . . . 8	..	James Greenaway.
F.S. *Vulcan* . . 8	..	Joseph Soanes.
F.S. *Hound* . . 8	..	Thomas Foulis.

FLAGS.

BLUE OR REAR SQUADRON.

Admiral, Sir John Ashby . . . . . . *Victory.*
Vice-Admiral, George Rooke . . . . . *Neptune.*
Rear-Admiral, Richard Carter . . . . *Duke.*

SHIPS.	GUNS.	CAPTAINS.
Albemarle	90	Sir Francis Wheler.
Resolution	70	Edward Good.
Monck	60	Benjamin Hoskins.
Expedition	70	Edward Dover.
Chatham	50	John Leader.
Windsor Castle	90	Earl of Danby.
Neptune	96	Thomas Gardner.
Royal Oak[1]	74	George Byng.
Advice	50	Charles Hawkins.
Northumberland	70	Andrew Cotten.
Lion	60	Robert Wiseman.
F.S. *Half-moon* . 8	..	John Knapp.
F.S. *Owner's Love* 10	..	John Perry.
F.S. *Cadiz Merchant* . 12	..	Robert Wynn.
F.S. *Lightning* . 8	..	Lawrence Keek.
Berwick	70	Henry Martin.
Defiance	64	Edward Gurney.
Montagu	62	Simon Foulks.
Warspite	70	Caleb Grantham.
Adventure	44	Thomas Dilkes.
Vanguard	90	Christopher Mason.
Victory	100	Edward Stanley.
Duchess	90	John Clements.
Monmouth	66	Robert Robinson.
Edgar	72	John Torpley.
F.S. *Speedwell* . 8	..	Thomas Simonds.
F.S. *Griffin* . . 8	..	Robert Partridge.
F.S. *Etna* . . . 8	..	Richard Carverth.
F.S. *Blaze* . . . 8	..	Thomas Heath.
Stirling Castle	70	Benjamin Walters.
Dreadnought	64	Thomas Coall.
Crown	50	Thomas Warren.
Suffolk	70	Christopher Billop.
Woolwich	54	Christopher Myngs.
Ossory	90	John Tyrrel.
Duke	90	William Wright.
Cornwall	80	Edward Boys.
Essex	70	John Bridges (1).
Deptford	50	William Kerr.
Hope	70	Henry Robinson.
F.S. *Thomas and Elizabeth* . 10	..	Edward Littleton.
F.S. *Vesuvius* . . 8	..	John Guy.
F.S. *Hunter* . . 8	..	Thomas Rooke.
Charles Galley 32	..	Joseph Waters.

[1] Joined after the action.

Having sent ahead some "frigates"—the lighter and faster part of his fleet—to reconnoitre the French coast and watch the motions of the enemy, Russell sailed on May 18th. At 3 A.M. on the morning of Thursday, the 19th, when he was off Cape Barfleur,[1] the *Chester* and *Charles Galley*, which were then scouting to the westward, fired guns, and made the best of their way towards the flag. Upon arriving within signalling distance, they reported that the enemy was in sight. The wind was S.W., and, the French being

Prower; the *Greyhound*, 16, Capt. Wm. Kiggens; the *Reserve*, 48, Capt. Thos. Crawley; and the *Hawk*, fireship, Capt. Wm. Harman, which may have been picked up by the fleet while cruising, seem to have been added.

[1] When the French were sighted the Cape bore S.W. by S., about 21 miles.

to the south-west of the Allies, Tourville had the option whether
he would or would not engage. He had not received the order
to avoid an action ; he believed that he was expected to fight ; and
mortification at the manner in which his previous proceedings
had been criticised inclined him to the combat. Moreover, he
seems to have been at first quite ignorant as to the overwhelming
strength of the Allies, and to have supposed that not more than
five and forty ships were opposed to him. He therefore ordered
his whole fleet to keep away together for the enemy, who, heading
S.S.W., awaited him on the starboard tack in the natural order,
the Dutch, that is, being in the van, and Ashby, with the Blue

MEDAL COMMEMORATIVE OF THE ACTIONS OFF CAPE BARFLEUR
AND LA HOUGUE, 1692.

(From an original kindly lent by H.S.H. Captain Prince Louis of Battenberg, R.N.)

squadron, occupying the rear. Supposing for a short time that
the French might stand to the northward, Russell had signalled
his own rear to tack ; but when, soon after 4 A.M., he saw the
enemy standing to the southward and preparing to form line on
the same tack as the Allies, he annulled the order ere Ashby had
gone far towards obeying it. Tourville indeed accepted the
challenge in the handsomest manner, when he might have discovered a dozen excellent reasons for declining it.

"When," says Mahan, "they were within easy range, the
French hauled their wind on the same tack, keeping the weather-
gauge. Tourville, being so inferior in numbers, could not wholly
avoid the enemy's line extending to the rear of his own, which

was also necessarily weak from its extreme length ;[1] but he avoided Torrington's error at Beachy Head, keeping his van refused,[2] with long intervals between the ships, to check the enemy's van, and engaging closely with his centre and rear." Thus formed, the two lines headed from N.N.E. towards S.S.W. Russell was not entirely satisfied with his own line, which was completed at about 8 A.M. He calls it an "indifferent" one. Tourville's line was also ragged, but the resolute manner in which his ships bore down was remarked by all.

Russell's last order, ere the action began, took the shape of directions to Admiral van Almonde to endeavour to weather the enemy as soon as possible. It was about 10.30 A.M. when the French centre hauled its wind and opened fire on the Red squadron at three-quarter musket shot; and, it falling calm almost immediately afterwards, the Dutch could not, for the time, do much towards carrying out the desires of the commander-in-chief. Nevertheless several of their ships succeeded in getting into close action, and the *Zeven Provinciën*, De Ruijter's famous flagship, had that day nineteen killed and fourteen badly wounded, while the *Admiraal Generaal* lost nine killed and thirty wounded, among the latter being Rear-Admiral van der Goes.

The hottest fighting, however, was in the centre ; and at 1 P.M. Tourville, in the *Soleil Royal*, was observed to be towing off to windward with his sails and rigging badly damaged. At about 2 P.M. the wind, such as there was of it, shifted to N.W. by N., and five fresh and almost untouched French ships of D'Amfreville's squadron thereupon ranged themselves three ahead and two astern of the *Soleil Royal*, and, in the most devoted manner, endeavoured to relieve her. The chief opponents of the group thus formed were the *Britannia*, *London*, and *St. Andrew ;* and, for an hour, these ships, and others near them in the line, were very hotly engaged. All day it had been misty, and, soon after three, a fog began to gather very thickly over the scene of action. This caused much confusion on both sides, and it was doubtless in consequence of it that the *Sandwich* drove through the remnants of the French line, and, in the heavy fire which was turned upon her from all sides, lost her captain, Anthony Hastings. Before the fog became so thick as to oblige all ships to cease firing, Shovell's division had doubled upon the *Soleil Royal* and her immediate supporters ; and it is

[1] *I.e.* its attenuation.   [2] *I.e.* at long gunshot to windward.

not, therefore, astonishing that when Tourville's ship next became visible she still was towing out of action to the northward. The *Britannia* and other vessels attempted to tow after her, the wind having again dropped; but soon the fog once more shrouded everything.

At about 5 P.M. a light breeze sprang up from the eastward, and the weather became a little less thick. The French were then discovered heading west; and as much of the allied fleet as could be communicated with was ordered in chase. There was a partial renewal of the battle until about 8 P.M., when the

BARFLEUR, LA HOUGUE, AND CHERBOURG.

fog, denser than ever, put an end for the night to all combined action.

It was when this fog was at its worst that Rear-Admiral Carter's division of the allied Blue squadron by hazard fell in with the main body of the flying enemy, and, for half an hour, engaged it in the ever-growing darkness. Carter was the officer whose loyalty and good faith had been most peculiarly suspected. Other officers had been believed to be disaffected; but rumour had charged Carter with being corrupt and treacherous as well. That night he silenced for ever those who would have impeached his honour. A shot struck him, and, as he realised that death had come to him, he said to Wright, his flag-captain : " Fight the ship as long as she will swim." Later, both fleets anchored.[1]

The morning of Friday, the 20th, broke foggy ; but at 8 A.M. the Dutch, who were to the southward of the Commander-in-Chief, sighted the enemy, and, the weather lifting a little, and the wind being E.N.E., a general chase was ordered. The French crowded to the west. At 11.30 A.M. the wind, which remained light, changed to S.W., and at 4 P.M., unable to make head against the tide, both the French and the Allies anchored. At 10 P.M., the tide then favouring, they weighed again with a freshening breeze. At midnight the *Britannia* lost her foretop-mast, which had been

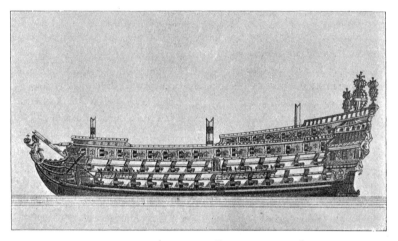

TOURVILLE'S FLAGSHIP, " LE SOLEIL ROYAL."

(From the drawing by A. L. van Kaldenbach.)

wounded on the previous day ; and the Red squadron waited for the damage to be made good, while the Blue squadron and the Dutch continued the chase.

On the 21st, the chase was prosecuted as before, the fleets anchoring when the tide was against them, and weighing when it was favourable. In the course of the morning, Tourville hauled down his flag in the *Soleil Royal* and transferred it to the *Ambitieux*, 92, which already carried the flag of De Villette-Murçai. He did this because he foresaw that, looking to the position into which

---

[1] A pension of £200 a year was settled on Carter's widow.—Admlty. Min. of Oct. 9th, 1692.

she had been driven, the *Soleil Royal* must go ashore unless the wind changed ; and at about 11 A.M., in fact, the three-decker took the ground near Cherbourg, and her masts were cut away by her people. Vice-Admiral Delavall was therefore ordered to take command of enough ships to deal with the stranded flagship and with several vessels which hovered near her, and to send the rest of the craft which were with him to join the main body of the fleet. Towards evening a large force of French was seen entering the Bay of La Hougue, and at night the Allies dropped anchor just outside.

In the meantime, Sir Ralph Delavall found with the *Soleil Royal*, in Cherbourg Bay, two more large ships of the line. Transferring his flag to the *St. Albans*, he took with him the *Ruby* and two fireships, and went in to reconnoitre ; but being met with a hot fire, retreated. On the following day, Sunday, the 22nd, he sent in his boats and three fireships, covering them with the guns of his larger vessels.[1] The attack was stoutly opposed both by the ships and by a fort on shore ; but Commander Thomas Heath, of the *Blaze*, succeeded in burning the *Soleil Royal*, 106 ; Commander James Greenaway, of the *Wolf*, destroyed the *Triomphant*, 74 ;[2] and the boats disposed of the *Admirable*, 90. Commander Thomas Foulis, of the *Hound*, had his ship set on fire by hostile shot ere he could get sufficiently near to the *Soleil Royal* to grapple her.

The main body of the fleet spent the greater part of Sunday, the 22nd, in working, as far as possible, into the Bay of La Hougue, near the head of which twelve large French ships were seen to have taken refuge. Twenty other French ships, chased by Ashby and some of the Dutch, saved themselves by running through the dangerous Race of Alderney, and so getting into St. Malo. Yet five more escaped to the eastward, and four are said to have rounded Scotland ere they again entered a French port. But the twelve in the Bay of La Hougue never quitted the asylum which they had been obliged to seek.

On Monday, the 23rd, Vice-Admiral Rooke,[3] with several men-of-war and fireships, was ordered to destroy the French shipping in the bay. The enemy, however, had hauled the vessels so close

---

[1] Among these Delavall specifies the *Reserve*, but it is not quite certain that she belonged to the fleet at the time.

[2] Delavall, in his dispatch, calls this ship the *Conquérant* ; but the *Conquérant* was apparently not destroyed. The true name appears, no doubt, in the French accounts. *See* p. 356.

[3] Rooke shifted his flag for the occasion to the *Eagle*.

in shore that only small craft could approach them.[1] The boats of the fleet were then got out, and, with the fireships, they burnt six French ships that night. The troops destined for the invasion of England assisted in the defence; and so shallow was the water into which some of the ships had been run that the French cavalry rode right down among the English and Dutch boats, and some of the troopers were actually pulled from their chargers by the seamen's boathooks. On the English side there was very little loss. On the following morning the boats were sent in again to complete the destruction, and the remaining six men-of-war were all fired. Several transports and storeships, which had taken refuge up a

MEDAL COMMEMORATIVE OF THE BURNING OF FRENCH SHIPS AT
LA HOUGUE, ETC., 1692.

(From an original kindly lent by H.S.H. Captain Prince Louis of Battenberg, R.N.)

creek, were also given to the flames; and the ex-King James, who witnessed the whole spectacle, experienced the mortification of seeing his hopes of an invasion of England, and of a re-acquisition of a crown, annihilated, and the finest ships of his only ally rendered for ever harmless. Until far into the nineteenth century the weather-worn ribs of some of those ships were still visible at low spring tides in the Bay of La Hougue. In March, 1833, numerous relics were recovered from the wreckage. They are now preserved in the Musée de la Marine in Paris.

Russell's detailed dispatch, describing the affair, and dated from Portsmouth on June 2nd, informed Nottingham that sixteen French

---

[1] They were also well covered by the fire of forts.

men-of-war had been destroyed, and professed to give the names of fourteen of them.[1] The Commander-in-Chief seems to have been mistaken both as regards the number and as regards many of the names. Papers in the French archives show that, in addition to the three ships already mentioned as having been destroyed near Cherbourg by Delavall, the French lost the following twelve vessels of the line ; and there is apparently no ground for supposing that any other craft, except fireships, transports, and storeships, met their fate either during, or as a consequence of, the six days' operations :— [2]

St. Louis	.	.	56	*Tonnant*	.	.	70
Fort	.	.	52	*Terrible*	.	.	74
Gaillard	.	.		*Fier*	.	.	68
Ambitieux	.	.	92	*Bourbon*	.	.	66
Magnifique	.	.	76	*Merveilleux*	.	.	92
St. Philippe	.	.	80	*Foudroyant*	.	.	90

Tourville and his captains had made a most gallant defence, and had, indeed, done wonders, seeing that, when night fell after the battle of Cape Barfleur on May 19th, they had not lost a single ship. Had Barfleur had no morrow, the action would have been a French triumph ; for, although much of the allied line was never fully engaged, the French fought from beginning to end against enormously superior forces. The battle presents no very interesting tactical features, but it pointedly illustrates the strategic maxim that the best place in which to attack a naval enemy is close to his own shores. Credit is due to Russell for the promptitude with which, in face of difficulty, he arranged his junction with the Dutch ; but it can scarcely be contended that at Barfleur, and during the subsequent movements, he could, with his greatly superior fleet, have well done much less than he did. He won a victory of vast importance, yet of no particular brilliancy. Tourville lost a very small amount of reputation in the encounter, and Russell gained as little.[3]

[1] Dutch accounts also over-estimate the French loss in ships of the line, putting it at seventeen or eighteen sail.

[2] The English fireships expended were the *Half-moon, Cadiz Merchant, Blaze, Thomas and Elizabeth, Phaeton, Fox, Hopewell, Extravagant, Wolf,* and *Hound.*

[3] Lutterell, 'Relat. of State Affairs,' ii. ; 'Mémoires de Forbin'; 'Adm. Russell's Letter,' etc. (1690 fol.); Almonde's Disp. of May 24th ; Delavall to the Earl of Nottingham of May 22nd ; Burnet's 'Hist. of Own Time,' ii. ; 'Mercure Hist. et Pol.' xii. ; Kennet, iii. 639 ; Oldmixon, 'Hist. of the Stuarts,' ii. ; 'Hist. Milit.' ii. ; *London Gazette* ; 'Life of K. Will.'; Burchett, 'Memoirs'; Reincourt, iii. ; 'Mems. of

Admiral Russell, leaving Sir John Ashby and Vice-Admiral van Callenburgh off the French coast, returned to St. Helens. It was hoped that the French ships, which had taken refuge in St. Malo, would come out, and, endeavouring to get into Brest, would be intercepted; but the expectation was disappointed. A retaliatory descent upon the French coast was next projected; yet, although enormous preparations were made, and great sums of money spent, lack of decision in high places, and general mismanagement, led at length to the abandonment of the scheme.

In the following year Russell, who had had differences with the Earl of Nottingham, was not employed; and on March 18th, 1693, the command of the grand fleet for the ensuing summer was put into commission, and entrusted to Henry Killigrew, Sir Clowdisley Shovell, and Sir Ralph Delavall, who acted jointly in a single flagship flying the Union at the main. A great many vessels hoisted the pennant; a large Dutch contingent joined, and vast plans were discussed; but owing to dilatoriness, confusion, and contradiction of orders, bad organisation, and deficient intelligence, no good was effected, and a serious disaster was suffered.

A huge flotilla of merchantmen—English, Dutch, German, Danish, and Swedish—bound chiefly for the Mediterranean, and generally spoken of as the Smyrna fleet, had for some time been awaiting a safe opportunity to leave the Channel and pass the Strait of Gibraltar. It was determined that the grand fleet should escort these ships some leagues to the south-west of Ushant, and should then return, leaving Vice-Admiral Rooke, who had been knighted by King William on February 16th, to convoy them farther on their voyage. The French Court had good intelligence of what was going forward, and, with a view to intercept this rich flotilla, Tourville, with about seventy ships from Brest, and Victor Marie d'Estrées, with about twenty ships from Toulon, were ordered to make rendezvous in Lagos Bay, and there to lie in wait. Though

Russell'; 'Observats.' of M. de Crisenoy; Letter of James to Louis; Russell's short Disp. of May 20th; Daniel, 'Hist. de la Mil. Franç.'; De Larrey, 'Hist. de France'; 'Not. der Admiraliteiten,' 1692; Papers of Scheij Family; Dalrymple, 'Mems. of Grt. Brit. and Ireland,' i.; Richer, 'Vie de Tourville'; Contin. of Aitzema, iv.; 'Europ. Mercurius'; MS. List of Commissions in Auth.'s coll.; 'Méms. de Villette-Murçai'; 'Méms. de Berwick' (1778); Papers of Tourville, Gabaret, D'Amfreville, Coëtlogon, and 'Ordres du Roi,' in the Archives de la Marine; 'Life of Capt. Stephen Martin'; Extrs. from Rooke's Journal (Charnock, i. 405); 'Bull. de la Soc. de l'Histoire de la France,' 1877.

Tourville proceeded thither with all his force, very little suspicion was awakened in England. The sailing of D'Estrées was however, reported soon after it had taken place. In the meantime, the Smyrna fleet, numbering four hundred sail, more or less, had quitted the Channel. On the evening of June 6th, Sir George Rooke, with his valuable charge, parted company and proceeded, while the Joint Admirals and the main force returned, and dropped anchor in Torbay on June 21st. Two days later, rumours having arrived that the two French fleets were out, and had effected a junction, it was determined to put to sea again and follow the convoy. But difficulties, real or imaginary, arose, and in the result the fleet did not sail. If it had sailed at once, it would still have been much too late to avert the catastrophe. Dispatches, intended to warn Sir George of his danger, were actually sent after him ; but they also were too late.

The men-of-war with Rooke were as given below :—

CONVOY FOR THE SMYRNA FLEET, JUNE, 1693.

SHIPS.	GUNS.	COMMANDERS.	SHIPS.	GUNS.	COMMANDERS.
Royal Oak [1]	64	Gerard Elwes.	[3] *Admiraal Generaal* [4]	84	
Breda [2]	62	?	[3] *Gelderland* . . .	72	Andries Stilte.
Monmouth	58	Peter Pickard.	[3] *Zeeland*	64	Philip Schrijver.
Lumley Castle (hired).	56	George Meester.	[3] *Wapen van Medem-*		
Monck	52	Stafford Fairborne.	*blik*	64	Juriaan van der Poel.
Lion	52	Thomas Gardner.	[3] *Oost-Stellingwerf* .	52	
Loyal Merchant (hired)	50	Philip Harris.	[3] *Nijmegen*. . . .	50	
Princess Anne (hired).	48	William Wakelin.	[3] *Schiedam*	50	W. van Rechteren.
Tiger Prize. . . .	48	Robert Sincock.	[3] *Wapen van De*		
Woolwich	46	Christopher Myngs.	*Schermer* . . .	44	
Newcastle	46	John Baker.	*Salamander*, bomb .	10	Thomas Pindar.
Chatham	44	John Leader.	*Susanna*, bomb . .	..	?
Smyrna Factor (hired)	40	Edward Littleton.	*Dispatch*, brig. . .	..	James Peacock.
Sheerness	28	John Norris.	*Speedwell*, fireship .	8	Thomas Simonds.
Lark	16	Peter Wotton.	*Vulture*, fireship . .	..	William Lindsey.
			Muscovia Merchant, storeship. . . .	..	Daniel Parsons.
			[3] Two fireships.		

[1] Flag of V.-Adm. Sir George Rooke.
[2] Flag of R.-Adm. Thomas Hopsonn. He apparently acted also as captain.
[3] Dutch.   [4] Flag of R.-Adm. P. van der Goes.

Dropping from time to time such vessels as were bound for intermediate ports, Rooke, with a fair wind, kept his course towards the Strait. He encountered nothing to warn him of his danger. On June 15th, he ordered the *Lark* into Lagos Bay to obtain news ; but, going close in shore, she was becalmed, and so failed to carry out her instructions. On the 16th, two of the look-out ships ahead of the fleet discovered and engaged two Frenchmen ; but, seeing other French ships under Cape St. Vincent, they deemed it prudent to retire and report to the Vice-Admiral. Rooke proposed to lie to until the enemy's strength should be ascertained, but he allowed himself to be over-persuaded by his captains; and the squadron proceeded. At daybreak on the 17th, ten sail of French men-of-war were seen and chased, and a French fireship was taken. The crew falsely declared that only fifteen French ships of the line were in the neighbourhood; but, by noon, Sir George could count eighty. Sixteen of these showed a disposition to attack, whereupon the English men-of-war stood off towards the convoy. Van der Goes advised that an engagement should be avoided; and Rooke, though much doubting whether this could be done at so late a stage, took all possible measures to get away without fighting, and, at the same time, directed such of the convoy as might be able, to endeavour, during the night, to take refuge in San Lucar, Faro, or Cadiz. But the enemy's van pursued closely, and, in the evening, brought the rearmost ships of the convoy and some of the Dutch men-of-war to action. Thereupon Captains Schrijver and Van der Poel, who found themselves to leeward of the foe, very gallantly tacked towards the shore, drawing the enemy after them, and deliberately sacrificing their ships in hopes of saving the rest. They made a most desperate defence, and partially accomplished their object, but were at length taken. In the meantime, the convoy was so much dispersed that on the morning of the 18th, Sir George, who had stood off all night with a fresh N.N.W. gale, found but fifty-four vessels near him. That day a few French still hung about him. On the 19th, after having discussed the situation with his officers, the Vice-Admiral made for his rendezvous off Madeira.

The amount of damage done by the enemy was presently found to be extremely serious. In addition to the two Dutch ships of the line, about ninety-two of the merchantmen were taken, burnt, or sunk, the value of the whole being estimated at upwards of a million sterling. Rooke's prudence, and the fact that some of Tourville's orders were not properly obeyed by his captains, saved, however, the greater part of the convoy. Nor was Tourville able to do such damage as he did without embroiling himself with the Spanish authorities at Malaga, Cadiz, and Gibraltar, in each of which ports some of the convoy had taken refuge. The blame for the disaster lay not with Rooke but with the authorities at home. They appear to have had no proper machinery for obtaining early intelligence of the enemy's movements, and to have been, for the time, incapable either of deciding or of acting with the promptitude necessary in time of war. How far the Joint Admirals must be held responsible is doubtful. When their conduct was called in question, they were successfully defended in Parliament; but it is obvious that the system of three-headed command was inherently bad ; and the experiment of commissioning Joint Admirals of the Fleet was, fortunately, never repeated, save once, under somewhat different conditions, in 1705.[1]

The remaining years of the War of the League of Augsberg witnessed no great sea battles, nor any single maritime event of the first importance. Such minor operations as were undertaken will be found described in the next chapter. After the battle of La Hougue the direct military action of the allied navies was exerted in three principal ways, namely, in attacks upon the French ports; in threatening the left flank of the French advance into Spain up to the moment when William became disposed to peace; and in protecting sea commerce. It was not exerted in the destruction of fleets, for the reason that, after 1693, Louis XIV. commissioned every year fewer and fewer ships of the line, and that France gradually, for the time, relinquished the dream of maritime supremacy. The warfare against the French coasts produced little except local effect; but the threatening of the flank of the French advance in Spain also drove Tourville into Toulon, kept him there, and saved Barcelona until England and Holland ceased to desire a prolongation of hostilities. As for the protection of sea-borne commerce, it was so indifferently managed that, although the allied fleets remained in almost unchallenged possession of the seas, the damage wrought by French privateers ultimately had an important influence in bringing the sea nations to wish for peace. Upon this subject Captain Mahan makes some observations which must be quoted.

"The decay of the French fleet," he points out, "was gradual, and . . . the moral effect of its appearance in the Channel, its victory at Beachy Head, and gallant conduct

---

[1] Authorities for the affair of the Smyrna fleet : Burchett, 'Mems.' 185, etc.; *Gazettes*, No. 2888, 2893, 2894, 2895 ; Corr. of Will. III. and Heinsius; Littleton's Letters in 'State of Europe,' July and Aug. 1693 ; Le Clerc, 'Hist. des Provs. Unies,' iii. 426 ; 'Life of Sir G. Rooke'; 'Merc. Hist. et Polit.' xv. 332; De Quincy, 'Hist. Milit.' ii. 703; Du Mont, 'Méms.'; Letter of Wolffsen, Dut. Resid. in Portug.; Disps. of Schrijver and Van der Poel ; Disps. of Consul Amia, and of Schonenberg ; Richer, ' Vie de Tourville '; Burnet, 'Hist. of Own Time,' ii. 115, etc.; 'Hist. de la Mil. Franç.' ii. 492 ; 'Notul. der Adm. van Amsterdam '; 'Europ. Mercur.' July, 1693 ; Forbin, 'Méms.' i. 340 ; Disps. of Tourville, D'Estrées, Coëtlogon, Renau and Gabaret, in Arch. de la Marine, etc.

at La Hougue remained for some time impressed on the minds of the Allies. This impression caused their ships to be kept together in fleets, instead of scattering in pursuit of the enemy's cruisers, and so brought to the latter a support almost equal to an active warfare on the seas. Again, the efficiency of the English Navy . . . was low, and its administration perhaps worse ; while treason in England gave the French the advantage of better information. . . . In truth, it was immediately after La Hougue that the depredations of cruisers became most ruinous ; and the reason was twofold ; first, the allied fleet was kept together at Spithead for two months and more, gathering troops for a landing on the Continent, thus leaving the cruisers unmolested ; and, in the second place, the French, not being able to send their fleet out again that summer, permitted the seamen to take service in private ships, thus largely increasing the number of the latter. The two causes working together gave an impunity and extension to commerce-destroying which caused a tremendous outcry in England. ' It must be confessed,' says the English naval chronicler, ' that our commerce suffered far less the year before, when the French were masters at sea, than in this, when their grand fleet was blocked up in port.' But the reason was that the French, having little commerce and a comparatively large number of seamen, mainly employed in the fleet, were able, when this lay by, to release them to cruisers. As the pressure of the war became greater, and Louis continued to reduce the number of his ships in commission, another increase was given to the commerce-destroyers. ' The ships and officers of the royal navy were loaned, under certain conditions, to private firms, or to companies who wished to undertake privateering enterprises, in which even the cabinet ministers did not disdain to take shares ' ; indeed, they were urged to do so to please the King. . . . The commerce-destroying of this war, also, was no mere business of single cruisers : squadrons of three or four up to half-a-dozen ships acted together under one man. . . . Still, as the war went on and efficiency of administration improved, commerce-destroying was brought within bounds. At the same time, as an evidence of how much the unsupported cruisers suffered, even under these favourable conditions, it may be mentioned that the English report fifty-nine [1] ships of war captured against eighteen admitted by the French during the war, a difference which a French naval historian attributes, with much probability, to the English failing to distinguish between ships of war properly so-called, and those loaned to private firms. Captures of actual privateers do not appear in the list quoted from. . . . The results of the war of 1689–1697 do not therefore vitiate the general conclusion that ' a cruising, commerce-destroying warfare, to be destructive, must be seconded by a squadron warfare, and by divisions of ships-of-the-line, which, forcing the enemy to unite his forces, permit the cruisers to make fortunate attempts upon his trade. Without such backing the result will be simply the capture of the cruisers.' . . . Notwithstanding their losses, the sea nations made good their cause." [2]

The chief work of the main fleets of the Allies during the period 1694-1697 may be very briefly summarised.

Sir Francis Wheler departed for the Mediterranean, as commander-in-chief there, in the last days of 1693. He had under his charge a considerable fleet, and a convoy, and was instructed to look

---

[1] These are Burchett's figures. He puts the English loss during the war at 50 men-of-war mounting 1112 guns, and the French loss at 59 men-of-war mounting 2244 guns. For a nominal list of English losses, see the Appendix on pp. 535–537. This is probably more correct than Burchett's figures. It is impossible to compile a list of the French losses.

[2] ' Infl. of Sea Power upon Hist.' 194–196.

out off Cadiz for the home-coming Spanish Plate fleet, so as to ensure its safe arrival in port. He was also directed to provide for the security of convoys returning from Spain and the Mediterranean ; then to proceed as far as Malta with such merchantmen as were bound for the Levant ; and, having detached ships to show the flag before Algiers, Tunis, and Tripoli, to join the Spanish fleet and annoy the enemy until the returning Levant ships should require his escort back to the Channel. He carried out the first part of his commission ; but, when about to enter the Mediterranean in company with a Dutch contingent under Admiral Callenburgh, he encountered a very heavy gale, with haze and violent rain. In this storm, which occurred on the 18th and 19th of February, 1694, the following English ships of war, besides many merchantment, were unhappily lost :—

Ship.	Tons.	Guns.	Commanders.	Compt.	Lives Lost.
Sussex	1203	80	Charles Hawkins .	550	548
Lumley Castle (hired)	. .	56	George Meester . .	280	130
Cambridge . . .	881	70	John Ward . . .	420	100
Serpent, bomb . .	260	18	Abraham Colfe . .	65	15
William, ketch . .	. .	10	. . . . . .	50	15
Mary, ketch . . .	. .	10	. . . . . .	50	16

Sir Francis Wheler and Captain Hawkins both perished with the *Sussex.* Captains Ward and Meester were saved. Commander Colfe's fate is unknown, but his name disappeared from the Navy List at the same time as his ship. Rear-Admiral John Neville succeeded to the command of the squadron, but was not able to prevent a French fleet from Brest from passing the Strait of Gibraltar on May 4th and proceeding to join the force at Toulon.

In the meantime, the command of the grand fleet of the Allies had been conferred upon Admiral Edward Russell, who, leaving part of it under Sir Clowdisley Shovell at St. Helens for the purposes of the projected attack on Brest,[1] sailed to the chops of the Channel, and there learnt that the Brest fleet had quitted port on April 15th, and that a large French convoy, bound east, lay in Bertheaume Bay. He detached Captain Peter Pickard, in the *Monmouth,* with two or three ships, to deal with this convoy, and himself returned to

---

[1] *See* next chapter.

St. Helens. Thence, when the arrangements for the attack on Brest had been matured, the whole fleet sailed. On the night of June 5th, 1694, it separated, one part under Admiral John Lord Berkeley of Stratton (B.), making for Brest, and the other, under the Commander-in-Chief, keeping on to the southward.

Russell was in due course joined by Rear-Admiral Neville, the Dutch contingent under Callenburgh and Geleijn Evertsen, and a small Spanish squadron ; and he entered the Mediterranean, reaching Cartagena on July 13th. The combined French fleets had been off the Spanish coast in the neighbourhood of Barcelona, but, hearing of the approach of the Allies, they withdrew to within the Isles of Hyères, near Toulon. Thus the situation in Catalonia, where the French were actively operating on shore, was rendered somewhat less difficult for the Spaniards. But it was foreseen that, upon the withdrawal of the Allies, the French fleet would return to the coast, and Russell was therefore urged to winter in the Mediterranean. The Commander-in-Chief insisted that this was out of the question, and, after having been as far north as Barcelona, he steered for Malaga with the intention of going home. At Malaga, however, he received orders from the Admiralty directing him to continue upon the station, and to make his winter headquarters at Cadiz.

The decision of the home government was both wise as regards the strategic conduct of that campaign, and important as regards the general policy of the country. The fleet went northward again to Alicant ; the French lay quiet ; and England definitively laid the first foundations of her position as a Mediterranean power. That winter the ships refitted at Cadiz. For some years afterwards England had no permanent naval base of her own in or near the great inland sea, but when she had once realised that the keeping of a large force there was beneficial to her interests, and that it gave her enlarged opportunities of offensive defence, it became inevitable that she should sooner or later seek to acquire bases for the furtherance of her new policy. She had already for a time held Tangier, but that was before she had learnt her lesson. Her adoption of something like a deliberate and steady attitude with respect to the Mediterranean dates only from 1694.

In the spring of 1695, Russell cruised off the east coast of Spain, and to Sardinia ; in August he co-operated in a fruitless attack upon Palamos, which was in the hands of the French ; and in September he returned to England with part of his command, leaving the rest of it at Cadiz in charge of Rear-Admiral Sir David Mitchell (R.), pending the arrival of Admiral Sir George Rooke (W.), who had been appointed to supersede him. Rooke reached Cadiz on October 16th. Rooke did not deem the force at his disposal adequate either in numbers or in condition for active operations against the French, and withdrew the whole of it into Puntal Road for the winter. Tempted, however, by news that some French vessels were in Lagos Bay, he detached Sir David Mitchell, with eight of the cleanest vessels and two fireships, in search of the enemy; but in vain. In January he was directed to return home, unless he had reason to believe that the French were likely to put to sea in strength not greatly superior to his own; and on April 22nd, 1696, he entered the Channel. Had he been properly reinforced, he might, and doubtless would, have considerably annoyed the enemy; but the government of the day apparently thought the spasmodic bombardment of French Channel ports[1] more important than the maintenance of the command of the sea; and in consequence, vessels which might otherwise have been detached to Rooke, were employed, under Lord Berkeley of Stratton, in various adventures which had but little real influence upon the course of the war.

Early in 1696, Admiral Russell took command of a fleet which had been gathered in the Downs in view of an apprehended French invasion from Dunquerque and Calais; and in April a division of this fleet bombarded Calais.[1] In the course of the same month, Rooke, having returned from the Straits, superseded Russell, and received instructions to do his best to prevent any fleet from Toulon from entering one of the northern ports of France. His force, however, was relatively small, his ships were undermanned, and many of the vessels which he had brought from the Mediterranean were not in a condition for service. The French from Toulon, with forty-seven ships of the line, consequently got round to Brest ere he was in a position to intercept them; and, although he was soon afterwards joined by a Dutch contingent, he had to content himself with lying in Torbay, and depending upon his cruisers to give him early information of any further French movements. Soon afterwards Rooke was recalled to his duties at the Admiralty, and the post of Admiral of the Fleet was entrusted to Lord Berkeley of Stratton.

During the early summer, Lord Berkeley and his subordinates, as will be seen in the next chapter, inflicted some annoyance upon

[1] *See* next chapter.

the French Atlantic seaboard; yet an opportunity of attacking a large French fleet which lay in Camaret and Bertheaume Bays was allowed to pass unutilised. Lord Berkeley, dying on February 27th, 1697, was succeeded in command of the main fleet by Sir George Rooke.[1] But owing to mismanagement, lack of organisation, and deficiency of intelligence, a French squadron under Châteaurenault succeeded in putting to sea from Brest with impunity; and, beyond the convoying of the trade, little real service was effected. Ships, when they were most needed, were found to be foul; they were seldom fully manned and never properly provisioned. There were few flag-officers who were willing to assume the responsibility of initiative; and although the Treaty of Rijswijk, concluded on September 11th, 1697, terminated the war in a manner satisfactory to the Allies, and flattering to King William, it is hardly to be contended that, during the eight years' struggle, the English Navy added much to the reputation which it had acquired under Cromwell and Charles II.

By the treaty, France acknowledged William to be King of England, and Anne to be his successor, and undertook to withdraw its assistance from the ex-King James. France also surrendered all conquests made by her since the Treaty of Nijmegen, and placed the chief fortresses of the Netherlands in the hands of the Dutch.

During the peace the Navy was far from being inactive. The cruises of Rear-Admiral Benbow in the West Indies, of Captain Thomas Warren in the East Indies, and of Captain John Munden in the Mediterranean, contributed greatly to the repression of piracy. The operations of these officers, and of others who were elsewhere employed up to the time of the outbreak of the next war, do not, however, call for detailed description in this chapter, and need be but briefly treated of in the next. Of rather more importance was Admiral Sir George Rooke's expedition to the Baltic in the year 1700.

A difference which had arisen between Sweden and Denmark threatened to involve other powers as well; and it was deemed advisable by the governments of England and Holland to intervene promptly in order to preventing a serious conflagration. It was determined, on the one hand, to assist Sweden, and on the other,

---

[1] Rooke, while in command, fell in, off the coast of France, with a fleet of Swedish merchantmen, and, rightly judging it to be loaded with property belonging to the enemy, captured it all. Sweden protested; even England disapproved; but Rooke was firm; and eventually all the ships were condemned as lawful prizes. A most useful lesson was thus taught to neutrals.

to obtain fair treatment for Denmark; and with these ends in view, a combined fleet of English and Dutch men-of-war under Rooke, as commander-in-chief, and Lieutenant-Admiral Philips van Almonde, proceeded to Gothenburg, where it anchored[1] on June 8th. Sir George later entered the Sound, and on July 6th, joined the Swedish fleet; whereupon the Danes, who had previously betrayed a disposition to challenge an action at sea, retreated to Copenhagen, and there established themselves behind sunken vessels and booms, protected by numerous guns, not only on shore but also upon floating stages. It was thought impracticable to force the harbour, but the Danish fleet was bombarded for some hours at long range. Little damage being effected, the King of Sweden landed towards the end of July with a body of troops and prepared to lay formal siege to the city. Happily, however, the differences were composed ere the siege could be actually begun. This early example of armed intervention in the interests of the peace of Europe led to the signing of the Treaty of Travendal on August 18th, 1700.[2]

Very soon afterwards a new cause of quarrel arose between France and the Allies. Charles II., the last Spanish king of the Habsburg dynasty, died on November 1st, 1700. The Spanish crown was thereupon claimed by Louis XIV., on behalf of his grandson Philip, Duke of Anjou, and, some time later, by the Emperor Leopold I., on behalf of his son Charles. England and Holland ultimately sided with the Empire, and the question of the inheritance presently brought about the War of the Spanish Succession. But hostilities did not immediately result; for, finding that Parliament was indisposed for war, King William formally recognised Philip,[3] and contented himself with fitting out a considerable fleet as a measure of precaution against the further ambitions of France. By the first week of July, 1701, Sir George Rooke was at Spithead in command of a large force, and in August and September he cruised in the Channel. On September 20th, he returned to St. Helens, and was ordered thence, with his heavier ships, to the Downs.

The anticipated further aggressiveness of France quickly showed

---

[1] The fleet anchored in Vinga Sound, close to the town.

[2] 'Life of Sir G. Rooke,' 63, etc.; *Gazette*, No. 3602; Journ. of V.-Adm. C. Evertsen; Disp. of Almonde of July 17th; Resoluts. of the Councs. of War; Corr. of Will. III. and Heinsius; Burnet, 'Hist. of Own Time,' ii. 243; Burchett, 'Nav. Hist.' V. c. iii.; 'Merc. Hist. et Polit.' xxix.; 'Jour. of Sir G. Rooke, 1700–1702,' (Navy Rec. Soc.).

[3] This was before Charles's candidature was put forward.

itself. The ex-King James had died at St. Germain on September 16th, and Louis XIV., who, had he desired peace and been
truly inclined to adhere to the spirit of the Treaty of Rijswijk, would
surely have allowed the event to make no difference to his policy,
seized the opportunity for provoking hostilities by causing Prince
James Edward, the son of James II. and Mary of Modena, to be
proclaimed King of England, Scotland, and Ireland. This action
had an immediate effect upon British public feeling. The English
ambassador was abruptly withdrawn from Paris; and when, at the
end of the year, King William called and met a new Parliament, he
found it ready to assist him in resenting to the utmost the attitude
of Louis. But King William, worn out in the service of his two
countries, did not live to see the beginning of the struggle. He died
at Kensington on March 8th, 1702, and not until May 4th following
was the declaration of war published.

The original policy of William was directed not so much to dis-
puting the claim of Philip to the throne of Spain as to the seizing,
for the benefit of the commerce and colonial ascendancy of his own
dominions, of such portions of the Spanish American possessions as
he could, and to imposing upon the new monarchy such conditions
as would spare England and Holland from any serious diminution
of the commercial privileges which they had enjoyed under the
Spanish Habsburg sovereigns. William's policy, as Captain Mahan
points out, would have directed the main efforts of the sea nations
not upon the Spanish peninsula but upon America; and the allied
fleets might not have entered the Straits. Sicily and Naples were
to go, not to England, but to Austria. "Subsequent causes,"
continues Mahan, "led to an entire change in this general plan."
A new candidate, in the person of Charles, son of Leopold I., was
set up, "and the peninsula became the scene of a doubtful and
bloody war, keeping the Anglo-Dutch fleets hovering round the
coasts, with the result, as regards the sea powers, that nothing of
decisive importance was done in Spanish America, but that England
issued from the strife, with Gibraltar and Port Mahon in her hands,
to be thenceforth a Mediterranean power."

It was while William's original policy was still favoured, and
before the Allies had made up their minds to actively oppose Philip
in Europe, that it was determined to send a squadron to the West
Indies, under Vice-Admiral John Benbow (B.). This squadron,
detached from Sir George Rooke's force in the Channel, consisted

of two third-rates, and eight fourth-rates. It parted company with Sir George off the Scilly Islands on September 2nd, 1701, and was escorted by an Anglo-Dutch division under Rear-Admiral Sir John Munden (R.) and Rear-Admiral Baron van Wassenaer, until it reached a point outside the usual cruising grounds of the European fleets of France and Spain. On October 10th, Munden and Van Wassenaer returned to the Soundings, and Benbow proceeded on his voyage. He reached Barbados on November 3rd, 1701.

There were at that time very few English ships of war in the West Indies, where both the French and the Spaniards were in considerable force; and, as an early outbreak of war was anticipated by all parties, Benbow made it his business, not only to reassure and to support the English islands to the best of his ability, but also to satisfy himself as to the resources and preparations of his possible foes. After looking into Martinique he visited Dominica and Nevis, and on December 5th anchored in the harbour of Port Royal, Jamaica, where he remained for some time, chiefly employing himself in collecting intelligence concerning the movements of the French and Spaniards. At the beginning of May he was reinforced by several vessels from England, under Commodore William Whetstone, who assumed the local rank of rear-admiral on the station. Benbow's cruisers were very active, even before the arrival of news of the commencement of formal hostilities; and, as soon as it was known that the rupture had actually occurred, the Vice-Admiral sent three frigates to endeavour to intercept some storeships which, he learnt, were bound for Havana. At the same time, he detached Rear-Admiral Whetstone with two third-rates, three fourth-rates, and a fireship, to look for a small French squadron which, under M. Ducasse, as *chef d'escadre*, was expected from Brest, at Port St. Louis, now known as Cayes, in Haiti.

Benbow himself left Port Royal on July 11th, intending to follow Whetstone; but, receiving intelligence that the real destination of Ducasse was not Port St. Louis but Léogane, near Port-au-Prince, he proceeded thither, arriving on July 27th. Having taken or destroyed several vessels there, and cruised for a few days in the neighbourhood, he was informed that Ducasse had gone to Cartagena, on the mainland of what is now Columbia, and that he was bound thence to Puerto Bello, in Panama. The news seems to have been incorrect. Benbow preceded, and did not follow, Ducasse towards the Gulf of Darien. Ducasse did

not reach Hispaniola, as Haiti and San Domingo were then
called, until after the English had quitted the island. He was
in inferior force, yet he at once went in search of Benbow; and,
on the morning of August 19th, the two squadrons sighted one
another off Santa Marta, a little to the eastward of the mouth
of the Rio Magdalena. The squadrons were at the time thus
composed :—

ENGLISH.				FRENCH.			
Ships.	Guns.	Men.	Commanders.	Ships.	Guns.	Men.	Commanders.
Defiance .	64	445	Richard Kirkby.	*Heureux*[2] .	68	450	Bennet.
Pendennis	48	230	Thomas Hudson.	*Agréable* . .	50	350	De Roussy.
Windsor .	60	340	John Constable.	*Phénix* . .	60	350	De Poudens.
Breda[1] .	70	460	Christopher Fogg.	*Apollon* . .	50	300	De Demuin.
Greenwich	54	280	Cooper Wade.	*Prince de Frise*	30	..	Lt. de St. An-
Ruby . .	48	230	George Walton.				dré.
Falmouth	48	230	Samuel Vincent.	A fireship .	..	..	Cauvet.
				Three small craft.			
				A transport.			

        [1] Flag of Vice-Admiral Benbow, (B.).   [2] Flag of M. Ducasse, *chef d'escadre.*

The French were under topsails, standing along the shore
towards the west, and were to eastward of the English. Benbow
had previously given out the line of battle with the ships in the
order above noted. As some of the vessels were three or four miles
astern, he made the signal for action, and, under easy sail, awaited
the stragglers. Later in the day, he sent an order to the *Defiance*
and *Windsor*, which betrayed no signs of haste, to make more
sail. Towards nightfall an action began; but, after the *Defiance*
and *Windsor* had received two or three broadsides, they luffed
out of gunshot. When it was dark, firing ceased. Benbow, who
kept company with the enemy during the night, thought to shame
those of his captains who had already misbehaved themselves, by
himself leading, and by changing the order of battle to: *Breda,
Defiance, Windsor, Greenwich, Ruby, Pendennis, Falmouth;* but
on August 20th all the vessels, except the *Ruby*, were far astern
of the flagship, and remained astern during the whole day. Nevertheless the *Breda* and *Ruby* followed the enemy and used their
chase guns as best they could until after dusk.

At daylight on August 21st the *Breda* and the *Ruby* again
began action, this time at close quarters, with the French; and
in the course of the early morning the *Ruby's* spars and rigging

were so much mauled that the *Breda* had to lie to and send boats to tow Captain Walton off. For some time before 8 A.M. the *Defiance* and *Windsor* were within point-blank range of the rearmost ship of the enemy, yet refrained from firing a single gun. In the afternoon the action recommenced; but, although several of the ships astern of him then fired in a desultory way, the brunt of the fighting fell upon Benbow, whose rigging suffered severely, and who had some of his lower deck guns dismounted. The *Breda*, by night as well as by day, kept up the signal for the line of battle; yet, on the morning of August 22nd, the *Greenwich* was about nine miles astern, and, except the *Ruby*, which behaved admirably throughout, the rest of the ships were not in their stations.

In the afternoon the wind, which had been E., shifted to S., and gave the enemy the weather-gauge. The *Breda*, by tacking, fetched within gunshot of the sternmost of the French, and once more engaged them; but she had no support, and she could do very little. On the morning of August 23rd, the French, who were six miles ahead of Benbow, were seen to have detached the *Prince de Frise*. At that time some of the English ships, and especially the *Defiance* and *Windsor*, were four miles astern of station. At 10 A.M., the wind being E.N.E., but variable, the enemy tacked. The *Breda* fetched within short range of two of them and then pursued as well as she could. About noon the *Anne*, galley, an English prize, which was one of the small craft with Ducasse, was retaken. On the other hand, the *Ruby* was found to be so disabled that the Vice-Admiral ordered her to Port Royal. At 8 P.M. the enemy, steering S.E. with a light and variable wind from N.W., was two miles ahead of the *Breda*, which had only the *Falmouth* near her. At midnight the French began to separate.

Very early in the morning of August 24th, the *Breda* and *Falmouth* got up with, and engaged, the sternmost of the enemy; and at 3 A.M., the Vice-Admiral's right leg was smashed by a chain shot. Benbow was carried below; but, soon afterwards, he ordered his cot to be taken to the quarter-deck, whence he continued to direct the fight until daybreak. It then appeared that the French ship [1] which had been immediately engaged was disabled, but that other French ships were coming up to her rescue, with a strong gale from the E. The *Windsor*, *Pendennis*, and *Greenwich*, after running to

[1] The *Apollon*.

leeward of the disabled vessel and each firing a broadside, or part of
a broadside, at her, passed her and stood to the southward. The
Defiance also passed to leeward; and, when the French fired a few
guns at her, she put her helm a-weather, and ran away before the
wind. None of these ships returned into action. The enemy speedily
discovered that the majority of the English captains were not serious
opponents, and, bearing down between their disabled ship and the

VICE-ADMIRAL JOHN BENBOW.

(From W. T. Mote's engraving after the portrait by Sir G. Kneller.)

Breda, badly damaged the latter and towed off the former. The
Breda could not renew the pursuit for some time; but, as soon as
she had refitted, she went again in chase, with the neglected signal
for battle still flying. As it was paid no more attention to than on
the previous days, Benbow directed Captain Fogg to send to each
ship, and to remind her captain of his duty. Upon this, Kirkby, of
the *Defiance,* visited the Vice-Admiral, and urged him to forego

further action. The Commander-in-Chief, desirous of knowing the
views of the other captains, signalled for them also to come on
board. Most of them supported Kirkby; and, realising that in the
circumstances nothing else could be done, Benbow unwillingly
desisted from the pursuit, and headed for Jamaica.

Such is, in brief, the story of one of the most painful and
disgraceful episodes in the history of the British Navy. At
Jamaica, on October 8th, and the following days, Kirkby, Wade,
and Constable were tried by court-martial for cowardice, disobedience
to orders, and neglect of duty. The two former were condemned on
all counts, and were sentenced to death. Constable, acquitted of
cowardice, was convicted on the other counts, and sentenced to be
cashiered, and imprisoned during her Majesty's pleasure. Hudson
would have been tried with these three officers had he not died
on September 25th. Captains Fogg and Vincent were afterwards
tried for having signed a protest against continuing the engagement with the French, although there was a reasonable probability
that, had the action been properly renewed, a victory would have
resulted. They alleged that they had signed the protest solely
because, looking to the previous misbehaviour of the other captains,
they feared lest, upon a recommencement of the action, the *Breda*
and *Falmouth*, being wholly deserted, would fall a prey to the
enemy. Benbow and others bore testimony to the courage and
general good conduct of these two officers, who, in consequence,
were sentenced only to be suspended, and that not until the Lord
High Admiral's pleasure should be known. George Walton, alone
of the English captains engaged, was not tried. He had borne
himself with the most uniform gallantry and loyalty; and he lived
to do much more good service, and to die with unsullied reputation at a green old age, a knight and Admiral of the Blue.[1]

Benbow, a brave and capable, if somewhat unconciliatory
officer, was obliged to have his right leg amputated. The resultant
shock, heightened by fever and by disappointment, overcame his
naturally strong constitution and he died on November 4th, 1702.[2]

---

[1] Authorities for Benbow's proceedings in the West Indies: *Gazettes*, 3862, 3865,
3873, 3878, 3886, 3907; Summary of Benbow's Journ. in 'Comp. Hist. of Europe' for
1702, p. 515; Min. of C. M., Oct. 8th, 1702; 'Acct. of the Trials,' etc. (1703 fol.);
'Hist. de St. Domingue,' iv.; Burchett, 'Nav. Hist.' Bk. V.; 'Merc. Hist. et Polit.'
1702, 657; 'Pres. Cond. of Eng. Navy' (1702); Guérin, 'Hist. Marit.' iv. 155.

[2] Mr. Paul Calton, a son-in-law of Benbow, gave Campbell the following copy of a
letter written by Ducasse to Benbow after the action: "Sir,—I had little hopes, on

Kirkby and Wade, sent home after their most just conviction, were shot at Plymouth on board the *Bristol* on April 16th, 1703. Constable, who was also sent home, either died in prison, or, being released, subsided into ignominious obscurity. Fogg and Vincent were mercifully treated; and it would indeed appear that the punishment of both was wholly remitted by Prince George of Denmark; for Fogg remained continuously in full pay until his death in 1708; and no hiatus appears in the record of Vincent's service until April, 1704, when, after having been in continuous pay for three years, he spent about nine months ashore, and, upon the expiration of that period, was appointed to a ship of superior rate. The conduct of the French in the long action merits all praise. Ducasse went to Cartagena. Returning in the following year to Europe, he was chased by Vice-Admiral John Graydon, but escaped and reached France in safety. France, it is strange to note, made little use of the superiority of force which she enjoyed in the West Indies for some time after Benbow's death.

The remaining events of the war beyond the confines of Europe were chiefly of a subsidiary, although by no means always of an unimportant, character, until 1708; when there occurred an action which, owing to the fact that the Spain of that day drew her treasure almost entirely from her colonies, cannot but have gravely affected the general issue.

Upon the death of Benbow, Captain William Whetstone, with the local rank of rear-admiral, succeeded to the command of the station, where he remained as second after the arrival from England of Vice-Admiral John Graydon. These two officers, and Commodore Hovenden Walker,[1] returned to England in October, 1703. Whetstone was promoted to regular flag-rank in 1704, and knighted in 1705; when he again went to the West Indies as Commander-in-Chief. The proceedings there during the five years ending with 1707, will be found described in the next chapter. In 1707, Commodore Charles Wager was appointed to the station. He left Plymouth on April 10th with a small squadron and a convoy; and he had not been long in the West Indies when he conceived the project of attacking the Spanish galleons which

---

Monday last, but to have supped in your cabin ; but it pleased God to order it otherwise. I am thankful for it. As for those cowardly captains who deserted you, hang them up; for, by God, they deserve it."

[1] He had been detached thither from Cadiz in September, 1702. *See infra*, p. 380.

he knew to be upon the point of sailing from Puerto Bello to Spain. The intended route of these galleons, so he ascertained, was from Puerto Bello to Cartagena, and thence to Havana, where they were to join M. Ducasse, the French *chef d'escadre*, who would convoy them to Europe. Wager detached to the Spanish main as many vessels as he could spare, instructing them to keep him advised as to the movements of the enemy; and, in January, 1708, he put to sea from Jamaica with a force which he deemed just sufficient to cope with the Spaniards ere they should effect their junction with the French.

He cruised for about two months, but then learnt from one of his scouts that the galleons would not sail until May 1st; and,

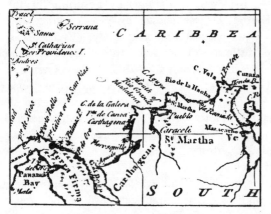

THE COAST NEAR CARTAGENA.

as he had reason to believe that the Spaniards had intelligence of his presence off the coast, and were fully on their guard, he returned to Port Royal. On April 14th, he again sailed, and although his ships suffered severely from the effects of a storm at the beginning of May, he kept the sea with them until May 28th; when, at break of day, he had the satisfaction of sighting two suspicious vessels that were standing in for Cartagena. By noon seventeen sail could be made out. Wager had with him only four; and the enemy, apparently confident in his numerical superiority, held his course without making any additional sail. The English chased, and, towards evening, the Spaniards, finding that they could not weather a small island which lay between them and Cartagena, leisurely formed some sort of a line of battle.

Wager, who had been made a Rear-Admiral on November 19th, 1707, but was not yet aware of his promotion, had his broad pennant in the *Expedition*, 70, Captain Henry Long, and was accompanied by the *Kingston*, 60, Captain Timothy Bridges,[1] the *Portland*, 50, Captain Edward Windsor, and the *Vulture*, fireship, Commander Cæsar Brooks. The enemy's flotilla was made up of the *San Josef*, 64, bearing a pennant at the main, another 64, bearing a pennant at the fore, a 44, bearing a pennant at the mizzen, a 40-gun ship, and eight craft of inferior force. These were in the line. In addition to them there were two French vessels, one of 30, and one of 24 guns, two sloops, and a brigantine, which took no share in the action and which made off ere it commenced. The *San Josef* was in the centre of the line, the other 64-gun ship brought up the rear, and the 44-gun ship led the van.

The Commodore had reason to believe that the whole of the Spanish treasure was on board the three ships bearing pennants. His information proved to be inaccurate ; but, acting upon it, he hailed the *Kingston*, which was near him, to attack the rearmost vessel ; and he sent a boat to the *Portland*, ordering her to attack the vessel at the head of the line. He himself purposed to attack the *San Josef ;* and, seeing nothing for the *Vulture* to do, he directed her to keep to windward.

It was a fine evening, and there was a light gale from the N.N.E. The enemy, to the southward, had tacked, and stood towards the N., to weather the island of Baru. Finding that the *Kingston* and *Portland* did not comply with his instructions, but kept too far to windward, Wager hoisted the signal for the line of battle, and, at about sunset, got within gunshot of the *San Josef* and soon engaged her at close quarters. After an hour and a half's action she blew up.[2] It was then very dark, and from the *Expedition* but one other vessel of the enemy was visible. Wager kept her in view, and by 10 P.M. came up with and engaged her. She turned out to be the 44-gun ship. The *Expedition's* first broadside, which was poured into her stern, disabled her. Wager, who was to leeward, then made aboard in order to get to windward of her, and would, no doubt, have ultimately taken her single-

---

[1] His Christian name is given as Timothy in most of the MS. and other Navy Lists of the time, but the minutes of the court-martial style him Simon ; and in some papers he appears as Thomas. His name was almost certainly Timothy.

[2] Of more than six hundred men on board, only eleven were saved.

handed, even if the *Kingston* and *Portland*, which had thus far
done little or nothing, had not arrived upon the scene. At 2 A.M.,
just as the moon was rising, she struck, and was taken possession
of by Captain Long.

The Commodore remained on deck, and, towards dawn, saw a
large ship on his weather bow and three more sail on his weather
quarter; whereupon he ordered the *Kingston* and *Portland* to proceed in chase. Captains Bridges and Windsor did as they were
ordered, but in the afternoon relinquished the attempt. Wager
then renewed his signal, and the two ships resumed the pursuit.
On the 31st they returned, reporting that they had followed the
second 64-gun ship, and had seen her enter Cartagena; but that
she had led them into such dangerous waters that they had been
obliged to leave her after firing at her. The Commodore was still
refitting his prize when Captains Bridges and Windsor rejoined
him; and, having heard that a galleon had taken refuge behind
Baru, he at once sent the *Kingston, Portland,* and *Vulture* to take
or burn her. They encountered her as she was endeavouring to get
to Cartagena. As soon as she sighted them she went about, ran
herself ashore, and was set on fire by her crew; and the English did
not succeed in saving anything out of her. The squadron, with the
prize, reached Port Royal without further adventure on July 8th.

The loss occasioned to the Spaniards was very heavy. Accounts
as to the treasure in the *San Josef* differ. Some place its total at
as much as thirty millions of pieces of eight; none at less than
five millions. But, unfortunately for the captors, the 44-gun ship
had no government treasure in her. She was mainly laden with
cacao; and, although thirteen chests of pieces of eight and fourteen
pigs of silver were on board, these seem to have been private
property. She was, nevertheless, a very valuable prize. The
64-gun ship which escaped was reported to be nearly as rich as
the *San Josef*. Captains Bridges and Windsor were tried by
court-martial on board the *Expedition* at Port Royal on July 23rd
for neglect of duty, and were sentenced to be dismissed their ships.
Neither was ever again employed.[1]

The remaining occurrences in the West Indies and elsewhere
beyond European waters up to the year 1714 will be dealt with

---

[1] Authorities for Wager's action: *Gazettes,* 4459, 4476; Min. of C. M., July 23rd,
1708; 'Hist. Milit.' vi. 124; 'Merc. Hist. et Polit.' xlv.; Burchett, 'Nav. Hist.' 705;
'Comp. Hist. of Europe' for 1708, 251; Burnet, 'Hist. of Own Times,' ii. 315.

iñ the next chapter. The major operations in the Old World during the War of the Spanish Succession may now be described. At the time of the declaration of war, Thomas Herbert, Earl of Pembroke, was Lord High Admiral. He was to have taken command in person of the main Anglo-Dutch fleet; but the Queen's appointment of Prince George of Denmark to supersede him, and the fact that Pembroke was a civilian, led to the command being eventually entrusted to Admiral Sir George Rooke. It was intended to open the war with an attack in force upon Cadiz, the capture or destruction of which could not, it was felt, fail to greatly cripple the naval resources of Spain. Under Rooke were Vice-Admiral Thomas Hopsonn (R.), Rear-Admiral Sir Stafford Fairborne (W.), and Rear-Admiral John Graydon (B.), together with the five Dutch flag-officers, Lieutenant-Admiral P. van Almonde, Lieutenant-Admiral G. van Callenburgh, Vice-Admiral P. van der Goes, Vice-Admiral A. Pieterson, and Rear-Admiral Jan Gerrit, Baron van Wassenaer. The fleet consisted of thirty English [1] and twenty Dutch ships of the line, besides cruisers, bombs, fireships, storeships, transports, hospital ships, and tenders, which brought up the total number of sail to about one hundred and sixty. On board the ships were embarked 9663 English, and about 4000 Dutch troops under General the Duke of Ormonde, and Major-General Baron de Sparre. On June 19th, 1702, this great fleet weighed from Spithead, and anchored at St. Helens; and, three days later, Rear-Admirals Fairborne and Graydon, with a squadron, were detached to look into Corunna, and, if they found any French ships in that port, to blockade them there.

The main body of the allied fleet, delayed by various causes, some of which might have been easily avoided, did not get clear of the Channel until July 22nd. Fairborne and Graydon found nothing in Corunna; and, after having cruised and taken several prizes, they rejoined Sir George on August 8th. Having communicated with Lisbon, and received intelligence and advice from the English envoy there, the Admiral proceeded, and, on the 12th, anchored in the Bay of Bulls, about six miles from Cadiz. The

---

[1] The English ships of the line were the *Association, Monmouth, Essex, Cambridge, Prince George* (Hopsonn), *Orford, Yarmouth, Grafton, Cumberland, Lenox, Berwick, Triumph* (Graydon), *Torbay, Pembroke, Northumberland, Barfleur, Stirling Castle, Burford, St. George* (Fairborne), *Expedition, Chichester, Swiftsure, Kent, Boyne, Bedford, Royal Sovereign* (Rooke), *Ranelagh, Plymouth, Eagle,* and *Somerset.*

French men-of-war, and the galleys which had lain in the Bay, retired into Puntal Road.

Although two or three councils of war had been held after the fleet had quitted the Channel, there seems to have still been no definite plan of action.   Certain it is that the leaders of the Allies were very much in the dark, not only as to the situation of affairs on shore and as to the state of the garrison and fortifications, but also as to the natural conformation of the coast upon which they were about to attempt a landing; and all this, in spite of the facts that there had been great English expeditions against Cadiz in 1587,

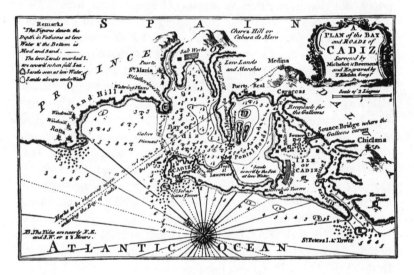

1596, and 1625, and that the adventure had been many months in preparation.   There was, moreover, an ominous lack of energy in the attitude of the Commander-in-Chief.   Fairborne had been for closely following the enemy's ships as they retired into Puntal Road, and had offered to lead the movement; but Sir George Rooke had refused his consent.

Another council of war, held in the Bay of Bulls after the fleet had anchored and Cadiz had been reconnoitred, did not reveal that the allied commanders saw their way clear before them.   Sir Thomas Smith, Quartermaster-General of the Army, had reported after examination that, on the Island of Cadiz,[1] there were three

---

[1] More properly the Island of Leon, on which Cadiz is built.

bays favourable for landing troops; yet it was determined not to
land there. The town was summoned, but the governor civilly
declined to surrender his trust; and again a council of war was
held. At last a landing was effected on August 15th, near Rota,
on the mainland to the north of the island. The Spaniards offered
some resistance, and a heavy swell impeded the operation. Aided,
however, by a covering fire from the *Lenox*, Captain William
Jumper, and from several small craft, the Allies obtained a footing
on shore and drove the defenders from their batteries; and on the
16th, Rota surrendered without further fighting.

In the meantime, yet another council of war was being held
afloat. A scheme, the carrying out of which was to depend upon
various contingencies, was formulated for the bombardment of
Cadiz; but as it was never put into execution, it is unnecessary to
describe it. On the 20th, the town of Puerto Santa Maria, which
had been deserted, was entered. There the army found spoil and
wine in plenty; and, owing to the unwise leniency of Ormonde, and
the evil example of certain other general officers, the men became
completely demoralised, and behaved in the most disgraceful and
abominable manner. Such seamen as had been put ashore
conducted themselves not less shamefully; and it is not surprising
that the violent and licentious proceedings of the champions of
Charles of Austria disgusted all the local adherents of that prince,
and fortified the friends of Philip of Anjou in their hostility to the
other claimant. Fort Santa Caterina, to the southward of Puerto
Santa Maria, surrendered on August 22nd; but, from that day
forward for nearly a month, the time was wasted in negotiations
and further councils of war; and an attempt by the Dutch
troops against Fort Matagorda, at the entrance to Puntal Road,
having failed, and the enemy having fully utilised their opportunities for booming and otherwise obstructing the harbour mouth
and for strengthening their defences, the stores at Puerto Santa
Maria and Rota were destroyed, and on September 15th the army
was re-embarked.[1]

[1] Authorities for the attempt on Cadiz: 'Journ. of Sir G. Rooke' (Navy Rec.
Soc.); *Gazettes*, 3842, 3843, 3845, 3847, 3850, 3858; 'Mems. of Sir Geo. Rooke,' 82;
'Anns. of Q. Anne,' i. 79; Disps. and Journs. of Almonde, in the Rijks Archief;
Limières, iii. 101; Lamberti, ii. 251; Burchett, 'Nav. Hist.' 620, etc.; 'Merc. Hist.
et Polit.' ii. 443; Larrey, iii. 544; 'Comp. Hist. of Europe' for 1702, 312; 'Hist.
Milit.' iii. 702; Burnet, 'Hist. of Own Times,' ii. 330; Oldmixon, 'Hist. of the Stuarts,'
ii. 289; 'Life of Sir G. Rooke,' 68–100; MS. Lists of Captains in Author's coll.; De
Jonge, iii. 578.

At another council of war, held on September 17th on board the *Ranelagh*, the allied chiefs decided not to essay an attack upon any other place in Spain, but to return to England, after detaching to the West Indies, under Captain Hovenden Walker of the *Burford*, a small squadron, and some transports full of troops, which it had been previously determined to send thither. The fleet finally left the neighbourhood of Cadiz on September 19th, and on the 23rd Captain Walker was signalled to part company.

Thus ended this lamentable and wasteful exhibition of hesitation, incompetence and demoralisation. If it had not been happily followed within a short time by an event in which the same allied leaders and their subordinates bore themselves far more creditably, the professional reputations of few concerned in it would have survived the disgrace. It is an episode which, while it may not be forgotten, and while it is full of teaching and suggestiveness, is not pleasant to look back upon. The home authorities and the active commanders were alike to blame. No expedition of the kind can reasonably expect success unless it be properly provided as well with information, intelligence and system as with material resources ; nor can national honour result from any undertaking in the conduct of which indecision, insubordination, brutality and drunkenness are conspicuous. It is refreshing to turn to the subsequent proceedings of Sir George Rooke's command.

It happened that on September 21st several English vessels belonging to the fleet had been sent into Lagos Bay to water. One of these was the *Pembroke*, 60, Captain Thomas Hardy. Her chaplain, a Mr. Beauvoir, was among the officers who went on shore. By accident he encountered, and struck up an acquaintance with, the French Consul, a boastful person, who, in his anxiety to magnify the power of France, injudiciously hinted that, not far off, King Louis, unknown to the Allies, had a considerable force of ships, and that with them, in perfect safety, were certain Spanish galleons which had lately arrived from the Indies. Mr. Beauvoir, a gentleman of much tact, seized an opportunity of obtaining corroborative evidence that M. de Châteaurenault, from Brest, with ships and galleons, was in Vigo Bay. Having secured as much intelligence as possible, he hurried on board, roused Captain Hardy, who was in bed, and told him the news, which was then, by direction of the senior officer, sent off to Sir George Rooke. Hardy, with great difficulty, discovered the fleet on October 6th ; and the allied Admirals, after

having held the inevitable council of war, decided that it was their
duty to attack the enemy.

It should be noted here that the movements of M. de Châteaurenault had already been reported in England, and that the
government had, in consequence, taken measures to advise Sir
George, and had also ordered Sir Clowdisley Shovell, from the
Channel, to reinforce him ; but the news did not arrive from home
until after the information obtained by Mr. Beauvoir had been acted
upon.

Vigo Bay is a roomy opening and excellent anchorage on the
south-western coast of Galicia. Its entrance is sheltered from the
force of the Atlantic rollers by the Isles of Bayona, and at its head,
or eastern extremity, the bay broadens somewhat, and forms the
harbour of Redondela.

Rooke steered for Vigo, dispatching ahead a couple of light
ships which, on the night of October 9th, returned with confirmation of the news brought by Captain Hardy, and with further
intelligence to the effect that the enemy lay in Redondela Harbour.
Early on the following morning, a vessel from Sir Clowdisley
Shovell's squadron also came into the fleet, reporting that Sir
Clowdisley was off Cape Finisterre and had orders to join the
Commander-in-Chief. On the afternoon of October 11th, in hazy
weather, Rooke entered the Bay and anchored off Vigo.

M. de Châteaurenault was not unprepared. Across the narrow
mouth of Redondela Harbour he had drawn a boom of masts,
yards, chains, cables and casks, of great strength. He had strongly
anchored it ; and, near each end of it, he had moored one of his
largest men-of-war.[1] Within the boom he had moored five other
large men-of-war, with their broadsides bearing upon the entrance.
Covering the southern shore end of the boom were a stone fort of
ten guns and a heavy improvised battery or platform mounted with
more guns. Covering the northern shore end was a battery of
twenty guns. The remaining French ships and the Spanish
galleons, lay much farther up ; and, so long as the boom remained
intact, they were well out of gunshot of the Allies. Indeed, the
whole position was very strong.

Upon anchoring, Rooke again called a council of war, at which
it was decided that, seeing that the whole fleet could not be
advantageously employed in such narrow waters, a detachment

---

[1] The *Bourbon* at one end, and the *Espérance* at the other.

only should be sent in, unless necessity should arise for the services of the whole force; and that in the meantime the troops should be landed to co-operate on the south side. A table showing the ships selected for the duty, and showing also the vessels of the enemy, is appended :—

ACTION IN VIGO BAY AND REDONDELA HARBOUR, OCTOBER 12TH, 1702.

ANGLO-DUTCH SQUADRON.			FRANCO-SPANISH SQUADRON.		
Ships.	Guns.	Commanders.	Ships.	Guns.	How disposed of.
Mary	62	Edward Hopsonn.	Fort	70	Burnt.
Grafton	70	Thomas Harlow.	Prompt 8	76	Taken by the English.
Torbay 1	80	Andrew Leake.	Assure 9	66	Taken by the English.
Kent	70	John Jennings.	Espérance	70	Taken and destroyed.
Monmouth	..	John Baker.	Bourbon	68	Taken by the Dutch.
Phœnix (f.s.) . . .	..	?	Sirène	60	Taken and destroyed.
Vulture (f.s.) . . .	..	Thomas Long.	Solide	50	Burnt.
Dordrecht	72	Barend van der Pott.	Ferme 10	72	Taken by the English.
Zeven Provinciën 2 .	92	[Starrenburgh.	Prudent	60	Burnt.
Veluwe	64	Baron van Wassenaer-	Oriflamme	64	Burnt.
A fireship (f.s.) . .	..	?	Modéré 11	56	Taken by the English.
Berwick	70	Richard Edwards.	Superbe	70	Taken and destroyed.
Essex 3	70	John Hubbard.	Dauphin	40	Burnt.
Swiftsure	70	Robert Wynn.	Volontaire	46	Taken and destroyed.
Terrible (f.s.) . . .	..	Edward Rumsey.	Triton 12	42	Taken by the English.
Griffin (f.s.) . . .	..	William Scaley.	Entreprenant . .	22	Burnt.
Ranelagh	80	Richard Fitzpatrick.	Choquante	8	Burnt.
Somerset 4	80	Thomas Dilkes.	Favori (f.s.) . . .	14	Burnt.
Bedford	70	Henry Haughton.	Jesus Maria José .	70	Taken and destroyed.
Hawk (f.s.) . . .	..	Bennet Allen.	Bufona	54	Taken and destroyed.
Hunter (f.s.) . . .	..	Sir Charles Rich, Bart.	Capitana de Assoyes	54	Taken and destroyed.
Slot Muiden . . .	72	Schrijver.			
Holland 5	72	?	Three gunboats . .	..	Burnt.
Unie 5	94	?			
Reigersberg . . .	74	Lijnslager.	Seventeen galleons .	..	Taken or burnt.
A fireship	..	?			
Cambridge	70	Richard Lestock, sen.			
Northumberland 6 .	70	James Greenaway.			
Orford	70	John Norris.			
Pembroke	60	Thomas Hardy.			
Lightning (f.s.) . .	..	Thomas Mitchell.			
Gouda	64	Somelsdijk.			
Wapen van Alkmaar 7	72	?			
Katwijk	72	Beeckman.			
A fireship	..	?			
Association . . .	90	William Bokenham.			
Barfleur	90	Francis Wyvill.			

(These two ships were not in the line, but were assigned to the attack of the forts at the mouth of the harbour.)

1 Flag of Vice-Adm. Thomas Hopsonn (R.).
2 Flag of Vice-Adm. P. van der Goes.
3 Flag of Rear-Adm. Sir Stafford Fairborne (W.).
4 Flag of Adm. Sir George Rooke, Com.-in-Chief.
5 Flags of Lt.-Adm. Callenburgh and Vice-Adm. the Baron J. G. van Wassenaer.
6 Flag of Rear-Adm. John Graydon (B.).
7 Flag of Vice-Adm. Anthonij Pieterson.
8 Commissioned on Oct. 16th as the Prompt Prize by Captain Edward Rumsey.

9 Commissioned on Oct. 16th as the Assurance by Captain John Mitchell.
10 Commissioned on Oct. 14th in the same name by Captain Salmon Morris.
11 Commissioned on Oct. 17th as the Moderate by Captain John Balchen.
12 Commissioned on Oct. 14th as the Triton Prize by Captain William Scaley.

It was also determined at the council that, in order to encourage the men, all the flag-officers should accompany the attack, shifting, if requisite, their flags for the purpose; but it would appear that circumstances afterwards arose to render it desirable for Lieutenant-Admiral van Almonde to remain off Vigo. Rooke spent most of the night of October 11th in passing from ship to ship giving orders, and inspiriting his officers and men; and he certainly did all that lay in his power by such means to ensure the success of the operations on the following day.

Early in the morning of the 12th, the Duke of Ormonde, with two or three thousand men, was landed on the south side of the Bay, and, advancing to the eastward, ultimately took the land works at the south end of the boom. In the meantime, Sir George Rooke ordered the vessels which had been selected to make the attack, to weigh. They did so, forming line in the order given in the table; but when the van had approached within gunshot of the batteries, it fell calm, and they were obliged to re-anchor. Presently, however, a brisk breeze sprang up, whereupon the *Torbay*, which lay nearest to the enemy, immediately cut her cable, and, making all

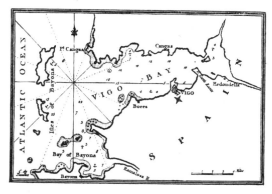

VIGO BAY.

sail, bore up for the boom, under a heavy fire from the foe. The boom gave way at the first shock, and, passing within it, Vice-Admiral Hopsonn anchored between the *Bourbon* and the *Espérance*, and resolutely engaged both of them. The other ships of his division, and the ships of the division of Vice-Admiral van der Goes, had weighed when Hopsonn cut. They came in line abreast upon the remnants of the boom, which, because it was less rigid than at first, and because the briskness of the breeze had temporarily died away, brought them up, and obliged them to laboriously hack their passage through it. But, when the breeze freshened once more, the *Zeven Provinciën* found her way to the opening which the *Torbay* had made, and laid herself on board the *Bourbon*, which she soon forced to strike.

Vice-Admiral Hopsonn, who for some time had had a formidable opponent on each side of him, and had been practically alone, was somewhat relieved by the capture of the *Bourbon*; but he was still in a perilous situation, for he was attacked by a vessel which the French had improvised as a fireship, and he soon found his rigging in flames. It chanced that this vessel was laden with snuff; and when at length she blew up, although she did a great amount of damage, her cargo was thrown in such dense masses over the *Torbay* that it had the effect of partially extinguishing the fire. Hopsonn was further relieved by the covering fire of the *Association*, which had by that time brought her broadside to bear upon the land works on the north side; yet the *Torbay*, which had lost one hundred and fifteen men, killed or drowned, was so battered and burnt as to be almost helpless. The Vice-Admiral had subsequently to transfer his flag to the *Monmouth*, which entered the harbour when the fight was nearly over.

After the action had lasted for little more than half an hour, M. de Châteaurenault found his landworks on the south side carried, his boom cut to pieces, his fireship expended in vain, the *Bourbon* taken, and the allied fleet pouring in upon him: and, despairing of being able to make any further resistance, he ordered his captains to burn their ships, and himself set them the example. Owing, however, to the confusion and haste, the directions were not in every case carried out, and, as may be seen on reference to the table above, many ships fell into the hands of the English and Dutch. Most of the officers and men got ashore and escaped; but about four hundred fell into the hands of the victors; and among these were the Marquis de la Galissonnière, the captains of the *Assuré* and the *Volontaire*, and the Spanish admiral, Don Jose Checon. The victory was most crushing, every vessel in Redondela Harbour being either taken or destroyed. Nor was it a very bloody triumph. The *Torbay* was the only ship of the Allies that suffered heavy loss. The other ships together seem to have lost not more than a dozen killed or wounded; and the French were little worse off. The glory of the day undoubtedly lay largely with Vice-Admiral Hopsonn,[1] who, for his gallantry and great services,

---

[1] Hopsonn at first deemed that any ship attempting the boom must be lost. But Rooke, upon looking at the boom, thought that it had little strength; "so that I ordered Mr. Hopsonn and the rest of the officers to execute their orders." Both officers were mistaken in their first impressions. *See* Rooke's Journal, quoted in Charnock.

was knighted by the Queen on November 29th following, and afterwards granted a pension of £500 a year, with a reversion of £300 a year to his wife, in case she should survive him. His officers and men were also specially rewarded.

The treasure and booty taken were of enormous value, the flotilla of galleons having been the richest which had ever reached Europe from the West Indies. Some of the lading had been removed before the action; but it was estimated that gold, silver and cargo, to the value of thirteen million pieces of eight, fell into the hands of the victors or were destroyed.

The town of Redondela fell to the Duke of Ormonde, but Vigo was not systematically attacked. It was at one time proposed to reduce it, and to leave part of the fleet to winter in the Bay; but

MEDAL COMMEMORATIVE OF THE ACTION IN VIGO BAY, 1702.
(From an original kindly lent by H.S.H Captain Prince Louis of Battenberg, R.N.)

Sir George Rooke opposed the project, and would not remain even long enough to attempt to weigh such ships as had been sunk, or to recover the treasure in the destroyed galleons, his chief reasons being that the fleet would shortly have no more provisions, and would be unable, if the wind changed to the E., to obtain further supplies.

On October 16th, Sir Clowdisley Shovell, with a squadron from England, joined the fleet; on the two following days the troops were re-embarked; and on the 19th, Sir George Rooke, with part of his force, sailed for England, leaving Sir Clowdisley to refit the prizes, save as much treasure and as many guns as possible, and complete the destruction of such vessels as could not be moved. Sir Clowdisley quickly carried out his instructions, effected an exchange of prisoners, and on October 26th began his homeward voyage. While still off Vigo, Captain Francis Wyvill of the *Barfleur*, made prize of the *Dartmouth*, 50, an English man-of-war which had been taken by the French in February, 1695. She was restored to the service and commissioned by Captain Thomas Long, but, as there was already another *Dartmouth*, she was, in memory of the scene of her recapture, named the *Vigo Prize*. The passage home was a stormy one, and the fleet was dispersed ;[1] yet the whole of it, except a prize galleon, and a French vessel which had been taken at sea by the *Nassau*, ultimately reached port in safety.[2]

Ormonde's recompense was the Lord-Lieutenancy of Ireland ; Rooke's, a privy councillorship : but the conduct of the expedition, and especially of the earlier part of it, did not escape severe criticism ; and Sir George's instructions and journals underwent a long examination by a committee of the House of Lords. The report was adverse to Rooke ; yet a vote in his favour was carried, and his behaviour was formally approved. It is to be feared that the verdict of the House was inspired by political considerations rather than by a desire to do strict justice. On the other hand, it must be admitted that Sir George had many personal enemies, and that of these not the least active was Ormonde, who, when he first returned to England, was exceedingly bitter against his naval colleague, though, after receiving the Lord-Lieutenancy, he became less hostile. If Vigo had not so quickly followed upon the fiasco of Cadiz, it is probable that the ministerial influence, strong as it was, would not have sufficed to save Sir George from a disgrace similar to that which a few years earlier had overtaken Torrington. As things stood, Rooke remained Admiral of the Fleet ; and it may be added that at the time of the commencement of fleet operations in 1703, the remainder of the active flag-list was as follows : Admirals, Sir Clowdisley Shovell (W.), George Churchill (B.) ; Vice-Admirals,

---

[1] While on his way home, Shovell was rejoined by the *Dragon*, 50, which, on October 23rd, had lost her captain, Robert Hollyman, in a gallant action with a French sixty-gun ship.

[2] Authorities for the action in Vigo Bay : Rooke's Journal, quoted by Charnock: 'Journ. of Sir G. Rooke' (Navy Rec. Soc.); *Gazettes*, 3858–3863 ; Du Mee, 'Caarte van de Landingh,' etc ; Journal of Almonde, and Disps. of Van der Goes, in Archief van der Marine; Chandler's 'Debates,' iii. ; St. Philippe ; 'Méms. pour l'Hist. d'Esp.' i. 201 ; De Quincy, 'Hist. Milit.' iii. 717 ; Santa Cruz, 'Reflects.' viii. 93 ; Burchett, 'Nav. Hist.' 627 ; 'Comp. Hist. of Europe' for 1702, 388 ; Oldmixon, 'Hist. of the Stuarts,' ii. 291 ; 'Anns. of Q. Anne,' i. 134 ; Burnet, 'Hist. of Own Times,' ii. 322 ; 'Life of Sir G. Rooke ' ; Guérin, iv. 112 ; 'Europ. Merc.' (1702) 315.

Sir Stafford Fairborne (R.), John Graydon (W.), John Leake (B.) ; and Rear-Admirals George Byng (R.), Thomas Dilkes (W.), and Basil Beaumont (B.).

The naval operations of 1703 were not of great importance. Under Sir George Rooke a large fleet cruised in the Channel and the Bay of Biscay in May and June ; and portions of it were from time to time detached on various services ; but, although the enemy was

ADMIRAL OF THE FLEET, SIR GEORGE ROOKE, KT.

(From Bartolozzi's engraving, after a miniature by J. Faber, painted in 1703, when Rooke was fifty-three years of age.)

inconvenienced and his coasts were harassed, no large body of his ships was encountered.

Another great fleet, composed both of Dutch and of English men-of-war, sailed for the Mediterranean on July 1st, under Sir Clowdisley Shovell, with orders to assist the revolted Cévennois, in the south of France ; to do what might be possible towards restoring Sicily and Naples to the House of Habsburg ; to

2 c 2

endeavour to enlist the Algerines, Tunisians, and Tripolitans against France; to settle certain difficulties which had arisen at Leghorn; to convoy the trade; and, generally, to injure the cause of the enemy to the utmost. Sir Clowdisley, whose presence in the Mediterranean had the effect of inducing the French fleet to lie quietly in Toulon harbour, carried out his instructions to the best of his ability; but, having been directed to return to England before the beginning of the winter, he could not remain long enough to confer any permanent benefit upon the cause of the Allies. The expedition was an ill-designed one, and that it accomplished so little was due entirely to the home government, and not at all to Shovell. His cruisers made several prizes, accounts of the taking of some of which will be found in the next chapter. On the other hand, owing to the careless manner in which the ships had been victualled, there was a lamentable loss of life [1] on board the fleet during its absence from England. It arrived in the Downs on November 17th, 1703.

While most of it still lay there, there occurred on November 26th one of the most violent and fatal storms of which we have record. Between eleven and twelve o'clock at night, the gale, which blew from W.S.W. and which was accompanied by thunder and lightning, reached its height; and, until seven o'clock next morning, it did not appreciably moderate. The whole of the south of England suffered; and the damage done in London alone was valued at a million sterling; but the catastrophe is chiefly memorable on account of the terrible losses which it occasioned to the Navy. The following is a list of her Majesty's ships which perished, and of the number of lives sacrificed in each of them. The destruction wrought was, upon the whole, greater than the fleet has ever experienced, before or since, within so brief a period, either in peace or in war; and the magnitude of the disaster is even to this day portrayed in many of the oral legends and traditions of the seafaring populations of Kent and Sussex. (See Table on opposite page.)

Twelve vessels were thus, at one time, totally lost to the Navy. In addition, the *Arundel,* 40, Captain Unton Dering, and the *Lichfield Prize,* 40, Captain Peter Chamberlain, went ashore, but were got off again; and numerous other ships were dismasted or

---

[1] To take an instance: the *Prince George* buried upwards of sixty men in four months, and, although her complement was seven hundred, anchored in the Downs with so few fit for duty that the ship was hardly manageable. ‘Life of Capt. Stephen Martin.’

Ships.	Tons.	Guns	Compt.[2]	Lost.	Commanders.	Fate.
Vanguard . .	1,357	90	..	..,	(Not in commission)	Sunk in the Medway.
Restoration . .	1,032	70	391	391	Fleetwood Emes [3] .	Lost on the Goodwin.
Stirling Castle .	885	70	276	206	John Johnson [3] . .	Lost on the Goodwin.
Resolution . .	..	70	221	..	Thomas Lyell . .	Lost off Sussex.
Northumberland	1,050	70	220	220	James Greenaway [3]	Lost on the Goodwin.
Mary . . .	..	60	272	269	(Rear-Adm. Basil) Beaumont[3] (Edward Hopsonn)	Lost on the Goodwin.
Newcastle . .	628	50	233	193	William Carter [3] .	Lost at Spithead.
Reserve . . .	576	50	222	175	John Anderson. .	Lost near Yarmouth.
Vigo Prize . .	..	50	..	..	Thomas Long . .	Lost at Hellevoetsluis.
Mortar, bomb [1].	..	..	65	..	Baymond Raymond[4]	{Wrecked on the { Goodwin.
Eagle, advice boat	..	18	45	..	Nathaniel Bostock .	Lost off Sussex.
C a n t e r b u r y, storeship . .	..	..	..	?	Thomas Blake [3] .	Lost at Bristol.
				1,519		

[1] The *Mortar*, though stranded on Nov. 27th, was not actually lost until Dec. 2nd.

[2] *I.e.*, number of officers and men apparently borne at the time. The regular complements were, in several cases, higher than those here given.

[3] Perished with their ships.

[4] Captain Raymond, though reported in nearly all histories to have been lost with his ship, is noted in the contemporary lists as having commanded her until Dec. 2nd, 1703 (when she seems to have been finally abandoned) and as having commanded other vessels for many years afterwards. He is believed to have died in 1718.

otherwise seriously damaged. Moreover, the *Vesuvius*, fireship, Captain George Paddon, which was stranded, and for the safety of which most determined efforts were made, had to be abandoned on December 19th. The number actually destroyed has commonly been overstated. As here set forth it is, however, sufficiently serious, and is, moreover, believed to be accurate. The loss of material was quickly made good, and more than made good, thanks to the patriotic action of the House of Commons; and it is satisfactory to be able to add that special provision was made for the families of those seamen who had perished.

A month before the great storm, Sir George Rooke, with a small squadron, had proceeded to Holland, in order to convoy to Spithead, whence he was to be escorted to Lisbon, the Archduke Charles, the candidate of the Allies for the throne of Spain. The *Vigo Prize*, which figures in the above list, was one of the ships of that squadron. Sir George returned to Spithead in December, and King Charles landed at Portsmouth on the 26th.

The first business of the allied fleet in 1704 was to carry King Charles to Portugal. With Sir George Rooke in command, it sailed on January 6th, but was driven back by continuous foul weather.

Sailing again on February 12th, with a very large convoy, it reached Lisbon on the 25th; and King Charles landed a few days afterwards. At Lisbon, on March 2nd, Vice-Admiral Leake, with a further force of ships, and with transports and troops in company, joined the Commander-in-Chief. Sir George, leaving Leake in the river Tagus, departed on a cruise on the 9th to annoy the enemy, and to satisfy himself of the safety of the homeward-bound merchant fleet from the Levant. He returned on April 9th, and found awaiting him orders to proceed up the Straits and to render assistance to the cause of the Allies in Catalonia and the Riviera.

Sir George Rooke left Lisbon towards the end of April with seventeen English ships of the line, four fourth-rates, one fifth-rate, one sixth-rate, and four fireships, besides fourteen Dutch sail of the line, and with some troops under the Prince of Hessen-Darmstadt. He had not long sailed when a French fleet, bound southward, under the Comte de Toulouse,[1] was seen off the mouth of the Tagus. The English minister to Portugal persuaded one of the frigate captains who had been left in the river to follow Sir George with the news; but the Commander-in-Chief, who had already detached a squadron[2] in chase of other French vessels which had been seen off Cape Palos, was far on his way to Barcelona, where, after summoning the Philippist governor of the city to surrender to the representatives of King Charles, he landed troops and Marines on May 19th. Barcelona was bombarded in a desultory way on the 20th; but, it being then thought that a continuation of the operations might alienate King Charles's adherents in the city, the bombardment was stopped, the troops and Marines were re-embarked, and, on the 21st, the fleet weighed and set sail for Nice, which was understood to be in great danger from the French army.

Rooke never reached Nice. On the 27th, his look-out ships reported a fleet, believed to be French, making for Toulon. He tacked and stood after it during the night; and next morning he saw about forty sail ahead of him. Thereupon, as was his custom on all

---

[1] Louis Alexandre de Bourbon, Comte de Toulouse, legitimated son of Louis XIV. and Mme. de Montespan. Born, 1678. Admiral of France, 1683. Commander-in-Chief of the fleet of 1704, with Victor Marie, Comte d'Estrées, as chief of the staff and virtual dry-nurse. Died 1737.

[2] This detached squadron did not get up with the French, who, however, instead of continuing to the northward, whither they were bound to co-operate in the siege of Nice and Villa-Franca, went to Cadiz to join the Comte de Toulouse. On their way thither, they fell in with, and chased, Rear-Adm. Wishart, who was following Sir George, and who safely joined him on May 18th.

such occasions, he called a council of war, which decided that the chase should be continued; but the delay allowed the enemy to increase his distance, and on the 29th, at sundown, the French were within ninety miles of Toulon and almost out of sight. Thinking that they would probably be reinforced, the Commander-in-Chief then relinquished the pursuit and, deterred from proceeding to Nice, steered back towards the Strait of Gibraltar.

A careful examination of the accounts of these events suggests conclusions which are unfavourable to Rooke, but, as the matter was never publicly inquired into, the Admiral's motives can perhaps never be entirely known. At least three days before he sighted the enemy, Rooke, warned by the frigate which had been dispatched after him from Lisbon, had been made aware that a French squadron was on its way round from Brest and would seek to enter Toulon. He had received confirmatory intelligence from other sources; and all the accounts were to the effect that the enemy was in force not superior to his own. Yet he apparently made no attempt whatsoever to find and fight this squadron; and when, by chance, he fell in with it, instead of following it up with energy, he wasted his time over a council of war, and suffered it to escape and accomplish the intended junction with the Toulon fleet. He neglected the advantage given him by the fact that he held an interior position between the French and their port: he sacrificed a magnificent opportunity of winning a complete and possibly an easy victory. But, as on a previous occasion in the course of his career, Fortune, taking no notice of the way in which this spoilt child had spurned her, offered him almost immediately a fresh chance. She had let him retrieve at Vigo the fiasco of Cadiz. Similarly, she let him retrieve at Gibraltar the failure of the Gulf of Lions. Seldom has commander-in-chief, competent or incompetent, been so steadily favoured. Mahan has insisted upon the "luck" of Nelson. The "luck" of Rooke was far more extraordinary. Nelson ever wooed Fortune, and never neglected her; whereas Rooke ever neglected her and never, save as a young officer, wooed her. Rooke commanded at Vigo, but the glory was really not his so much as Hopsonn's. Rooke commanded also at Gibraltar, but again his was not the leading figure. Nelson, commanding at either Vigo or Gibraltar, would, we may be sure, have commanded in a very different and much more immediate manner.

Rooke watered his fleet at Altéa Bay, seizing and destroying a

fort there; and on June 14th he passed the Strait. Off Lagos, on
the 16th, Admiral Sir Clowdisley Shovell's squadron joined.

Shovell had left England in May with belated instructions to
endeavour to intercept the French fleet, bound from Brest to Toulon;
to provide for the safety of the trade; to convoy certain vessels to
Lisbon; and, if he missed the enemy, to reinforce Sir George Rooke.

The Admirals at once held a council of war and decided to look
for the French in the Mediterranean. Rear-Admiral Byng was
first, however, detached to Cadiz to effect an exchange of prisoners.
He rejoined Sir George off Cape Trafalgar on June 29th; but

THE STRAIT AND BAY OF GIBRALTAR.

adverse winds, and then false reports of the presence of a large
French squadron near the Strait, delayed the fleet, which, by
July 17th, had not advanced eastward of Tetuan. In consequence
of suggestions which had been sent to him through the English
minister at Lisbon from King Charles of Spain and the King of
Portugal, Rooke on that day held another council of war, which,
after discussing various projects, determined to make a sudden
attempt on Gibraltar, which at the time was held in the interests
of the French candidate for the Spanish crown. The plan of action
involved the landing to the northward of the town of the English
and Dutch Marines, under the Prince of Hessen, who would sever

communications between the place and the mainland; and the reduction of the fortress by means of the fire of a squadron of ships, placed under the command of Rear-Admirals George Byng and Paulus van der Dussen. The composition and order of battle of this squadron were as follows:—

Ships.	Guns.	Commanders.	
Wapen van Vriesland	64	C. Middagten	
Wapen van Utrecht .	64	— Bolck	
Veluwe	64	R.-Adm.P. van der Dussen	To attack the Old Mole.
Æmelia	66	C. Beeckman	
Veere	60	P. Schrijver	
Katwijk	72	J. C. Ockersse . . .	
Monmouth . . .	70	John Baker	
Suffolk	70	Robert Kirton . . .	
Essex	70	John Hubbard . . .	
Ranelagh [1] . . .	80	John Cowe	
Grafton	70	Sir Andrew Leake . .	To attack the town and
Montagu	60	William Cleveland . .	the south bastion.
Eagle	70	Lord Archibald Hamilton	
Nottingham . . .	60	Samuel Whitaker . .	
Nassau	70	Francis Dove	
Swiftsure . . .	70	Robert Wynn . . .	
Berwick	70	Robert Fairfax . . .	To attack the New Mole.
Monck	60	James Mighels . . .	This division did not sail
Burford	70	Kerryll Roffey . . .	with Rear-Admiral Byng,
Kingston	70	Edward Acton . . .	but crossed with the
Lenox	70	William Jumper . . .	main body, and joined
Yarmouth . . .	70	Jasper Hicks	him on the 22nd.
3 bombs (Dutch).			

[1] Flag of Rear-Admiral George Byng (R.).

On the night of July 20th the Commander-in-Chief signalled to the squadron to proceed. On the following morning the squadron entered the Bay and anchored there. In the meantime, an easterly wind having sprung up, the main body of the fleet had also crossed the Strait. In the afternoon it took up a position in the bight of the Bay, off the rivers Palmones and Guadaranque, and awaited events.

As Byng dropped anchor the town fired; but most of the shot flew over him, though the *Ranelagh's* mainmast was wounded. The ships made no reply, it having been determined not to attack until the Prince of Hessen, with the Marines, should have landed and summoned the place. But the squadron was ordered to warp a little farther out. The Marines, to the number of about eighteen hundred, were then quickly landed on the neck, the only opposition coming from a party of fifty horsemen, who speedily retired with the loss of one trooper. Having posted his men, the Prince of Hessen summoned the governor to declare for Charles III. The Spaniard, after some delay, replied that, having taken the oath to Philip V., he and the garrison would defend the place for that monarch with their lives. On the morning of the 22nd, before this answer had been returned, Byng began to station his vessels for the intended bombardment; but, as it was nearly calm, they had to be warped into their assigned positions. This operation occupied all day, the town occasionally firing, but not being able to interfere with the carrying out of the plan. During the night, while the process of warping in still continued, Rooke, to make some diversion, ordered Captain Edward Whitaker, of the *Dorsetshire*, to man and arm boats, and to destroy a French vessel that lay within the Old Mole; and Byng, at the same time, threw a few shells into the town from his bombs. By daybreak on the 23rd such vessels as had not succeeded in reaching their assigned stations were directed to place themselves to the best possible advantage; and the *Ranelagh* herself pushed close in until there was little if any water under her bottom.

At 5 A.M. the fortress began the action, and the Allies forthwith replied so vigorously that many of the inhabitants immediately fled from the town to points high up the Rock. The smoke soon grew dense, and, as there was little air to carry it off, Byng ordered his ships not to fire unnecessarily and to use only their lower deck guns as being the heaviest. Towards noon he sent word along the line by Captain Edward Whitaker, who had gone on board the *Ranelagh*, that firing was to cease altogether, in order that he might observe what effect had been produced. Whitaker passed southward from ship to ship, until he reached the *Lenox*, which was the nearest ship to the New Mole. From her deck he and Captain Jumper noticed that several of the Spanish guns in that neighbourhood were dismounted or silenced; and, returning to the *Ranelagh*, Whitaker reported this, and suggested that if the boats were manned and armed they might seize that part of the works.

Byng accordingly made a signal for the boats to be got ready, and also dispatched Edward Whitaker to Sir George Rooke with a request for the co-operation of the rest of the boats of the fleet. In the meantime he ordered such boats as he had to proceed to the southward of the head of the New Mole, and to place themselves under the command of Captain Jasper Hicks, the senior officer of

the southern division. Hicks was directed to make the suggested
attack, should it appear to be practicable.

Rooke, upon receiving Byng's message, approved of the design
and sent back word that Edward Whitaker was to lead the attack.
Byng thereupon appointed Captains Fairfax, Mighels, Roffey, and
Acton to assist Captain Edward Whitaker in the attempt upon the
New Mole: but Captains Hicks and Jumper [1] had already proceeded
in pursuance of the Rear-Admiral's earlier orders, and, pressing
ashore with their boats, effected a landing long before the other
captains could come up.

The enemy resisted and sprang a mine,[2] which killed or wounded
a great number of officers and men, and caused so much discourage-
ment that a retreat in the direction of the boats began. Happily

MEDAL COMMEMORATIVE OF THE CAPTURE OF GIBRALTAR, 1704.

(From an original kindly lent by H.S.H. Captain Prince Louis of Battenberg, R.N.)

Captain Edward Whitaker, with more boats, arrived in time to stay
the flight; and from that moment the advance experienced no check.
The English flag was quickly planted on a redoubt half-way between
the New Mole and the town.

When he saw that the landing parties had securely established
themselves, Byng, by direction of Sir George Rooke, went ashore to
Captain Edward Whitaker's position, and summoned the fortress.
At the same time, the Prince of Hessen, advised of what had
taken place, sent in another summons from the northward. In
the evening the governor [3] replied that he would capitulate on the
following morning; and he accordingly surrendered to the Prince of

---

[1] His name is commemorated in Jumper's Bastion.

[2] This mine did as much damage to the Spaniards as to their foes.

[3] Don Diego Salinas.

Hessen, as representing Charles III., on July 24th, and received all the honours of war. The Marines marched in towards evening; and Byng then re-embarked most of his seamen, leaving about two hundred and fifty ashore only pending their relief by additional Marines.

Thus fell this famous fortress, which ever since has been a British dependency. But it should be observed that in 1704 it did not cease to be, in theory at least, an integral part of Spain. It was surrendered by the partisans of Philip V. to the partisans of Charles III.; and if the War of the Spanish Succession had resulted in favour, not of Philip, but of Charles, the place might have ever remained Spanish. Philip, however, was the successful candidate; and when at length, in 1713, the Allies were induced to recognise him, part of the price which he had to pay for peace with Great Britain was the cession to the British of Gibraltar.

It was an important capture, but it was by no means a difficult one. The Spaniards had, it is true, upwards of a hundred guns mounted in it, and the place has always been of immense natural strength. On the other hand, the garrison, at the time of the attack, numbered no more than eighty officers and men,[1] a force obviously insufficient to hold so extensive a position, or even to work one-third of the guns. The Spaniards, taken thus at grievous disadvantage, fought, nevertheless, extremely well; and the Allies were not masters of the fortress until they had lost sixty-one officers and men killed, and about two hundred and sixty wounded. In the former number were included two lieutenants, and in the latter, one captain and seven lieutenants.[2]

Leaving the place in charge of the Prince of Hessen and of the Marines, whose services at Gibraltar are for ever commemorated upon the badge of the British corps, the allied fleets stood over to the coast of Barbary, Rooke having first detached Rear-Admiral van der Dussen, with five sail of the line to Lisbon, and thence to Plymouth, to bring back forces destined for service in Portugal.

[1] This number agrees with the best accounts; but some writers place the garrison at 100, and others at 150 men. The 'Mems. relating to (Byng) Lord Torrington' put the number at 80 only.

[2] Authorities for the capture of Gibraltar: *Gazettes*, 4044, 4045 ; 'Mems. relat. to (Byng) Lord Torrington,' 137–146; and Journ. of Rev. T. Pocock, quoted therein; De Quincy, 'Hist. Milit.' iv. 121; Journs. of Callenburgh, Van der Dussen, and Wassenaer; Letter of Ed. Whitaker, in 'Nav. Chron.' iv. 383; 'Anns. of Q. Anne,' iii. 106 ; Wagenaar, pt. xvii., 225; 'Merc. Hist. et Polit.' xxxvii. 339; 'Hist. of the Stuarts,' ii. 339 ; 'Life of Capt. Stephèn Martin,' 75; 'Hist. and Proc. of Ho. of Lords,' vii. 575.

The ships, after watering at Ceuta, proceeded to Tetuan, and thence, on August 9th, all of them but twelve steered again for Gibraltar. That morning the *Centurion*, which was scouting to the eastward, reported that she could see the enemy in force to windward. After the fleet had been ranged in order of battle, a council of war was held, and it was determined to lie to the eastward of Gibraltar, and if possible, to re-embark half the Marines who were ashore. The French showed no immediate anxiety to engage, their galleys being at the time at Malaga, whither they went to fetch them ; and, in the meantime, a thousand Marines were brought off from the Rock, and the twelve ships which had been left watering, rejoined without interruption. On the 10th and 11th, the Allies plied to windward, seeing nothing of the enemy's fleet, yet occasionally hearing his signal guns. On the 11th, a small French tender was driven ashore a few miles eastward of Malaga, and burnt by her crew. In the afternoon Sir George stood to the N., and at night to the S.E. Still failing to sight the French, and fearing lest they might slip past him to the westward, the Commander-in-Chief again stood to the N., and, early in the morning of August 12th, called another council of war, which decided that, since Gibraltar had but a weak garrison and had not been rendered properly defensible, and since victuallers and other craft had been left ill-protected in the bay there, the fleet should continue the search for the French only until nightfall, and, failing to find them, should then return to the Rock.

The French, however, had by that time picked up their galleys at Malaga, and, never having intended to permanently avoid an action, were already looking for the Allies. They missed and passed by them, owing to Sir George having stood to the S.E. ; and they were thus to leeward, when at about 11 A.M. on the 12th, they were discovered in the N.W. near Cape Malaga, going large, with a small but intermittent gale from the eastward.

Sir George Rooke called in his scouts, formed the line of battle, and bore down, the French simultaneously forming their line, with its head to the southward. Cape Malaga then bore N.N.W. by N., distant about twenty-four miles. In the afternoon the wind dropped, and little progress could be made. Towards night there were small gales from the E., and on the morning of August 13th, the Allies saw the French in line heading as before, about nine miles ahead of them, and lying to to await the attack.

The two lines of battle and the names of the " frigates " and small craft attached to each squadron are fully set forth in the table on the following pages. The allied line would have also included the *Hampton Court*, 70, *Tiger*, 50, *Antelope*, 50, and *Leopard*, 50, had not these chanced to be absent on convoy duties. The two lines, as actually constituted, may be thus summarised :—

	ANGLO-DUTCH.		FRANCO-SPANISH.	
	Ships.	Guns.	Ships.	Guns.
Van	15	1118	17	1184
Centre . . .	24	1722	17	1224
Rear. . . .	12	796	17	1188
	51	3636	51	3596

The total strength arrayed on each side was therefore, as nearly as possible, equal. Outside the line the Anglo-Dutch had more "frigates," and larger ones than their opponents, while, on the other hand, the Franco-Spanish had a large number of galleys which, properly handled, should have been of considerable use in a conflict where the main elements of fighting force were so evenly balanced. These galleys carried from five hundred to seven hundred men apiece; they probably mounted four or six heavy guns in the bows, and all of them were fitted for ramming. Yet they seem to have been very little employed.

"The battle of Malaga," says Mahan, "possesses no military interest, except that it is the first in which we find fully developed that wholly unscientific method of attack by the English which Clerk criticised, and which prevailed throughout the century. It is instructive to notice that the result in it was the same as in all others fought on the same principle. The van opened out from the centre, leaving quite an interval, and the attempt made to penetrate this gap and isolate the van was the only tactical move of the French. We find in them at Malaga no trace of the cautious, skilful tactics which Clerk rightly thought to recognise at a later day. The degeneracy from the able combinations of Monck, De Ruijter, and Tourville, to the epoch of mere seamanship is clearly marked by the battle of Malaga, and gives it its only historical importance."

BATTLE OFF VELEZ MALAGA, AUGUST 13TH, 1704.

ANGLO-DUTCH.

SHIPS.	GUNS.	COMMANDERS.	KILLED.	WOUNDED.
Yarmouth ...	70	Jasper Hicks....	7	26
Norfolk....	80	John Knapp....	15	20
Berwick ...	70	Robert Fairfax ...	23	24
Prince George[1] .	90	Stephen Martin...	15	57
Boyne	80	James, Lord Dursley .	14	52
Newark.....	80	Richard Clarke...	15	32
arland, 50	..	Henry Hobart.		
irebrand, f.s.....	..	Henry Turvill.		
Lenox	70	William Jumper..	23	78
Tilbury....	50	George Delavall ...	20	25
Swiftsure ...	70	Robert Wynn....	13	33
Namur	96	Christopher Myngs..	18	44
Barfleur[2] ..	96	James Stuart....	6	24
Orford	70	John Norris....	6	9
Assurance ..	66	Robert Hancock...	6	14
Nottingham ..	60	Samuel Whitaker ..	7	19
Warspite ...	70	Edmund Loades...	17	44
oebuck, 40	..	Thomas Kempthorne.		
ulcan, f.s.....	..	John Clifton.		
riffin, f.s.....	..	George Ramsey.		
rincess Anne, h.s.	..	Charles Guy.		
Burford....	70	Kerryll Roffey ...	11	19
Monck	60	James Mighels ...	36	52
Cambridge ...	80	Richard Lestock, sen. .	11	27
Kent[3]	70	Jonas Hanway ...	15	26
Royal Oak ...	76	Gerard Elwes ...	20	33
Suffolk	70	Robert Kirton ...	13	38
Bedford	70	Sir Thos. Hardy...	12	51
wallow, 50	..	Richard Haddock ..	1	3
artar, 32	..	John Cooper.		
ightning, f.s.....	..	Archibald Hamilton.		
Shrewsbury ...	80	Josias Crow	31	73
Monmouth ...	70	John Baker	27	67
Eagle	70	Lord Archibald Hamilton	7	57
Royal Katherine[4] .	90	John Fletcher ...	27	94
St. George ...	96	John Jennings ...	45	93
Montagu....	60	William Cleveland ..	15	34
Nassau	70	Francis Dove....	15	26
Grafton	70	Sir Andrew Leake ..	31	66
anther, 50	..	Hon. Peregrine Bertie .	10	16
ark, 40	..	Charles Fotherby.		
ewport, 24	..	George Paddon.		
unter, f.s......	..	Thomas Legg, jun.		
hœnix, f.s.....	..	Edmund Hicks.		
efferies, h.s.....	..	Thomas Robinson.		
are, bomb......	..	?		
error, bomb.....	..	Isaac Cook.		
'm. & Mary, yacht	..	John Robinson.		
Ferme	70	Baron Wyld	25	48
Kingston ...	60	Edward Acton ...	14	46
Centurion ...	50	John Herne	10	33
Torbay	80	William Caldwell ..	21	50
Ranelagh[5] ..	80	John Cowe	24	45
Dorsetshire ..	80	Edward Whitaker ..	12	20
Triton Prize ..	50	Tudor Trevor ...	5	21
Essex	70	John Hubbard ...	13	36
Somerset....	80	John Price	31	62
harles Galley, 32 .	..	Joseph Taylor.		
ulture, f.s......	..	George Fisher.		

FRANCO-SPANISH.

SHIPS.	GUNS.	COMMANDERS.
Eclatant.....	70	De Bellefontaine.
Eole......	62	De Mons.
Oriflamme....	60	F. de Châteaurenault.
St. Philippe[6] ...	92	
Heureux.....	70	Colbert de Sainte-Marc.
Rubis......	56	De Benneville.
Arrogant.....	60	Des Herbiers de l'Etanduère.
Marquis.....	56	De Patoulet.
Constant.....	68	De Sainte-Maure.
Fier[7]......	88	
Intrepide....	84	J. B. Ducasse.
Excellent.....	60	De La Roche-Alard.
Sage	56	De Montbault.
Ecureuil.....	64	Darigny.
Magnifique[8]....	86	
Monarque	88	De Chabert.
Perle	54	Le Mothure.
Anunciada, gall.		
Isabela, gall.		
Sta. Catalina, gall.		
Magdelena, gall.		
Maria, gall.		
Teresa, gall.		
Sta. Rosalea, gall.		
Monica, gall.		
Etoile, 30	..	Gonson.
Hercule, 20	..	De Rouvré.
Enflammé, f.s.		
Dangereux, f.s.....	..	Du Guay.
Turquoise, f.s.....	..	De Soutier.
Furieux.....	60	De La Roche-Courbon-Blenac.
Vermandois....	60	De Béthune.
Parfait.....	74	De Château-Morand.
Tonnant[9]	92	
Orgueilleux	86	De Digoin du Palais.
Mercure.....	54	De Lannéon.
Sérieux.....	58	Desnots de Champmeslin.
Fleuron.....	56	De Grancey.
Vainqueur....	88	Le Bailly de Lorraine.
Foudroyant[10] ...	104	Des Francs.
Terrible.....	96	De Relingues.
Entreprenant ...	58	d'Hautefort.
Fortune.....	58	De Bagneux.
Henri	64	De Serquigny.
Magnanime[11] ...	74	
Lys	84	De Villars.
Fendant.....	58	De La Luzerne.
Patron de la France, gall.		
Favori, gall.		
Duchesse, gall.		
Princesse, gall.		
Couronne, gall.		
Fidèle, gall.		
Andromède, 8.		
Diligence, 6.		
Méduse, 28.......	..	De La Roque-Madère.
Rotterdam, s.s.....	..	De Grandmaison.
Portefaix, s.s.		
Croissant, f.s......	..	Gabaret.
Bienvenue, f.s......	..	De La Rochambert.
Aigle Volant, f.s.	..	De Kervilly.

Vice-Adm. Sir John Leake (B.). } Van.
Adm. Sir Clowdisley Shovell (W.). }
Rear-Adm. Thomas Dilkes (W.)
Adm. of the Fleet Sir George Rooke, Capt. of the } Centre.
et Rear-Adm. Sir James Wishart (B.).
Rear-Adm. George Byng (R.).

[6] Vice-Adm. d'Infreville de Saint-Aubin.} Van.
[7] Lt.-Gen. de Villette-Murçai. }
[8] Rear-Adm. de Belleisle-Erard. }
[9] Vice-Adm. Comte de Coëtlogon.
[10] Adm. Comte de Toulouse; Chef d'État Major,} Centre.
Victor Marie Comte d'Estrées. }
[11] Rear-Adm. de Pointis.

BATTLE OFF VELEZ MALAGA, AUGUST 13TH, 1704—*continued.*

ANGLO-DUTCH.					FRANCO-SPANISH.		
SHIPS.	GUNS.	COMMANDERS.	KILLED.	WOUNDED.	SHIPS.	GUNS.	COMMANDERS.
Wapen van Vries-land	64	C. Middagten . .			Zélande	58	De Serville.
Wapen van Utrecht	64	— Bolck			Saint-Louis . . .	60	De Beaujeu.
Graaf van Albe-marle [1] . . .	64	Visscher			Amiral [3]	92	
Vliessingen . . .	64				Couronne	80	De Champigny.
Damiaten . . .	52				Cheval Marin . . .	54	De Pontac.
Leeuw	64		95	268	Diamant	58	De Rogne.
Bannier	64	J. W. van Ghent .			Gaillard	56	d'Osmond.
Nijmegen	54	H. Lijnslager . .			Invincible	70	Du Rouvroy.
Katwijk	72	J. C. Ockersse . .			Soleil Royal [4] . . .	102	
Unie [2]	90				Sceptre	88	d'Hailly, jun.
Gelderland . . .	72	P. Schrijver . . .			Trident	58	De Modène.
Dordrecht . . .	72				Content	58	De Phelypeaux.
(And some small craft, number unknown.)					Maure.	58	De Saint-Claire.
					Toulouse	62	Duquesne-Mosnier.
					Triomphant [5] . . .	92	
					Saint-Esprit. . . .	74	Duquesne-Guiton.
					Ardent	68	d'Aligre.
					Royal, gall.		
					Conquérant, gall.		
					Gloire, gall.		
					Franciscain, gall.		
					Dorothée, gall.		
					Sta. Clara, gall.		
					Veragua, gall.		
					(Another gall.).		
					Oiseau, 36		De Figuière.
					Galathée, 11.		
					Sibylle, 10.		
					Etna, f.s.		
					Violent, f.s.		
					Lion, f.s.		

[1] Lt.-Adm. Callenburgh.   } Rear.
[2] Vice-Adm. Baron J. G. van Wassenaer.

[3] Vice-Adm. de Sebeville.   } Rear.
[4] Lt.-Gen. Marquis de Langeron.
[5] Rear-Adm. de La Harteloire.

There is much truth in these observations; yet in the present work, which does not exclusively busy itself with the consideration of the influence of sea power upon history, the story of the action cannot be thus summarily dismissed. Nor is it, indeed, devoid of useful suggestiveness. Rooke's journal [1] gives the following account of the proceedings of his fleet :—

"*Aug.* 13*th*, 1704.—This morning we were within three leagues of the enemy, who brought to with their heads to the southward, and formed their line, the wind still continuing easterly. We steered down upon them until ten o'clock, or half an hour past, when, being at little more than a musket-shot distance, I was forced to make the signal and begin the battle; the enemy setting their sails, and seeming to intend to crowd ahead of our van. The fight was maintained on both sides with great fury for three hours. Their van then began to give way to ours, as their rear did afterwards. But several of our ships, as well as mine as of the Rear-Admirals' of the red and white divisions, were forced to go out of the line, some being disabled, but most for want of shot,[2] so that the body of their fleet fell very heavy upon my ship, the *St. George*,

---

[1] Quoted by Charnock, i. 424–426.

[2] For thus leaving the line, several captains were afterwards court-martialled. The verdict justified the necessity for their withdrawal.

Shrewsbury, and *Eagle*, the last of which towed out of the line also, for want of shot two hours before night, so that we were much shattered and disabled. The enemy's line consisted of fifty-two ships and twenty-four galleys ; [1] their ships, most of them, were large. Their line was formed very strong in the centre, and weaker in the front and rear. This defect they endeavoured to supply by their galleys, which were, most of them, posted in those quarters. It has been the sharpest day's service that ever I saw ; and, what was most extraordinary, every officer in the fleet performed their duty without the least umbrage or reflection ; and I never observed the true English spirit more apparent in our seamen than on this occasion. The engagement lasted till about seven o'clock, when the enemy bore away and left us. Most of the masts and yards

ADMIRAL SIR JAMES WISHART, KT.

Captain of the Fleet at the Battle of Malaga, 1704.

(From Bartolozzi's engraving, after a miniature by J. Faber, painted in 1703, immediately after Wishart had been promoted to be a Rear-Admiral.)

in the fleet were wounded to an irreparable degree. . . . Sir Clowdisley Shovell, and the other flag-officers of our front and rear, say the enemy did not behave themselves well in those quarters. I am sure those in the centre did their duty very gallantly and heartily. We lay by all night repairing our defects. At noon, Cape Malaga, N. by E., seven leagues.

" *Aug. 14th.*—This morning the wind backed northerly, and so to the westward. We lay by all night repairing our defects, as did the enemy till the evening ; and then they filled and plied away to the westward. In the evening I called a council of flag-

---

[1] Really fifty-one ships of the line and twenty-two galleys.

officers. I ordered as equal a distribution of shot [1] as I could, to fit the fleet for another day's engagement. At noon, Cape Malaga, N. by E., nine leagues.

"*Aug.* 15*th*.—This morning, about ten o'clock, we had a small breeze easterly, with which we bore up on the enemy till four o'clock in the afternoon. Being within four leagues of them, and being too late to engage before night, I did, by advice of the English flag-officers, bring to with our head to the northward, and lay by all night, and wait[ed] a fresh levant. At noon, Targa Head, S.W. by S., six leagues.

"*Aug.* 16*th*.—This morning, not seeing the enemy or any of their scouts to leeward of us, we concluded that they were put away to the Strait's mouth, so that we bore away W. and W. by N. till six o'clock in the evening. Being hazy weather, and we not sure of our distance from the land, we brought to with our heads to the northward, and lay by with a little wind and a great eastern sea all night. This afternoon the *Albemarle*,[2] a Dutch ship of 64 guns, blew up and lost all her men except nine or ten."

The attempt on the part of the French van to crowd sail ahead and weather the English van was due to the initiative of De Villette-Murçai. Shovell's attempt to prevent the success of this manœuvre led to the opening out of the gap between the van and centre of the English; and this in turn suggested to the enemy the project of endeavouring to cut off the van. But the project failed, chiefly owing to the heaviness of the fire maintained by Shovell's squadron. Shovell afterwards contributed to the relief of the hard-pressed centre by backing astern; and throughout the engagement he greatly distinguished himself both as an able and as a brave officer.

The loss in officers and men was exceedingly heavy. The number killed and wounded in each English ship is given in the table. Two English captains fell, Sir Andrew Leake, of the *Grafton*, and John Cowe, of the *Ranelagh*. The Dutch, who fought with the greatest courage,[3] lost Captain Lijnslager, and, by the accidental explosion of the *Graaf van Albemarle* on the 16th, Captain Visscher. The French and Spaniards lost even more heavily. They had about fifteen hundred people killed, and more than as many wounded, and among the superior officers who were killed or mortally wounded were the Bailly de Lorraine, who acted as a *chef d'escadre*, De Belleisle-Erard, De Relingues, and François de Châteaurenault, a son of the famous Admiral and Marshal of France. But on neither

---

[1] Certain ships had expended most of their shot at the attack on Gibraltar. Sir George seems to have taken no steps towards supplying their deficiency before the action off Malaga. In future actions there will be a much more rapid expenditure of projectiles than in the past; and it will be of great importance to provide means to enable ships to quickly refill their magazines and shell-rooms.

[2] *Graaf van Albemarle.* Adm. Callenburgh was not in her at the time.

[3] Such is certainly the general verdict; yet Byng's 'Memoirs' contain some reflections upon their conduct.

side was any ship taken. The Anglo-Dutch, moreover, had no ship sunk or destroyed in the battle. The French, however, are believed to have lost the *Cheval Marin* and two galleys during the action, and the *Fier, Excellent, Fortuné,* and *Mercure* in consequence of it. The loss of the *Graaf van Albemarle* appears to have been quite unconnected with anything that happened on August 13th.[1]

LIEUTENANT-ADMIRAL GEERIT VAN CALLENBURGH.

(From the engraving by P. Tanjé after the picture by J. Vollevens.)

It was a drawn battle, and as usual, each side claimed it as a victory. The French sang a *Te Deum* in Paris in honour of their

[1] Authorities for the battle of Malaga: *Gazettes,* 4054, 4058; Sir Geo. Rooke's Acct., pubd. by authority; Letter of Sir C. Shovell in 'Comp. Hist. of Europe' for 1704, 456; 'Mems. of (Byng) Lord Torrington,' 147–163, and Pocock's Journal in the Append.; Burchett, 'Nav. Hist.' 677; Ste. Croix, 'Relat. de la Bataille'; Papers of Ducasse, Langeron, D'Estrées, Coëtlogon, etc., in Arch. de la Marine; 'Life of Captain Stephen Martin,' 76–80; Disps. of Wassenaer, and Journs. and Disps. of Callenburgh; 'Europ. Mercur.' July–Dec. 1704, 256; Letter of K. Louis to Noailles; 'Life of Sir

triumph; Queen Anne conferred knighthoods on Rear-Admirals Dilkes and Byng, and on Captain John Jennings, of the *St. George*, whose gallantry had been very conspicuous.[1] But all the solid advantages of the fight seem to have remained with the Anglo-Dutch. At Malaga the enemy, though not defeated, had received sufficient damage to prevent him from then and there making his intended serious attempt to recapture Gibraltar for King Philip; and from that day until the end of the war the French never again allowed their grand fleet to risk a general engagement.

Seeing nothing more of the enemy, the Allies went to Gibraltar, and lay there for eight days to refit and to throw supplies into the place. On August 24th the fleet sailed again, and a few days later it divided, part[2] under Sir George Rooke going home, and part[3] under Sir John Leake, with his flag in the *Nottingham*, 60, remaining in the Mediterranean for the winter.

The party of King Philip quickly discovered that the loss of Gibraltar greatly embarrassed the cause of that prince; and efforts were soon made to retake the fortress. Early in October, Sir John Leake was informed by the Prince of Hessen that the Spaniards, who were to attack the place on the land side, had secured a promise of the co-operation of a French squadron under De Pointis.[4] Sir John sailed from Lisbon, and landed four hundred Marines, and some gunners, carpenters and mechanics at the Rock; but learning that the French were approaching in superior force,[5] he returned to Lisbon to perfect his preparations. Sailing again on October 25th, he entered Gibraltar Bay on the 29th, and had the good fortune to surprise there one "frigate" of forty-two guns, another of twenty-

---

G. Rooke,' 135; Limiers, iii. 166; Chandler's 'Debates,' iii. 353; 'Anns. of Q. Anne, iii. 112; Lamberti, iii. 324; 'Hist. Milit.' iv. 426; 'Hist. of the Stuarts,' ii. 339; Chabaud-Arnault, 'Hist. des Flottes Milit.' 114.

[1] Captain William Jumper, who also was knighted at about the same time, seems to have received the honour mainly in respect of his conduct at Gibraltar, though he was wounded at Malaga.

[2] Five second-rates, twenty-five third-rates, and four fourth-rates, with several small craft.

[3] Two third-rates, nine fourth-rates, four fifth-rates, one sixth-rate, and a fireship. He had also a Dutch contingent under Rear-Adm. van der Dussen.

[4] Jean Bernard Desjeans, Baron de Pointis, born 1645; present at the battle of Beachy Head; commanded a French squadron in the West Indies; was Rear-Admiral of the centre at Malaga; died 1707.

[5] De Pointis, when he reached the Bay, found there, and destroyed, the *Terror*, bomb, Commander Isaac Cook, on October 17th.

four, a brigantine of fourteen, a fireship of sixteen, a storeship laden
with bombs, etc., a tartan, and two vessels which had been taken
from the English. All these were run ashore and destroyed by their
crews. Another "frigate" of thirty guns and a tartan which got
out of the Bay, were chased and taken. The heavier ships of De
Pointis had sailed some days earlier to Cadiz, and were at the time
refitting there. Leake was kept well informed of their movements,

SIR JOHN LEAKE, KT., ADMIRAL OF THE FLEET.

(*From Faber's mezzotint after the portrait by Sir G. Kneller* (1712).)

and knowing that, although he had been slightly reinforced since
Rooke's departure, he was still of inferior strength, he was careful
to make such dispositions as would prevent him from being in turn
surprised. Instead of remaining in the Bay he stood off and on to
the eastward of it, keeping the Rock always in sight. Early in
December he had the satisfaction of watching two convoys of
transports, one in charge of the *Antelope*, and the other in charge

of the *Newcastle*,[1] come in safely, and disembark about two thousand troops and a quantity of stores. Then, feeling that the fortress was in a position to take care of itself for some little time to come, and that his ships needed refitting and cleaning, he sailed on December 21st for Lisbon. On his passage thither he saw nothing of the enemy. De Pointis, indeed, seems to have been somewhat inactive at that time, for on January 29th, 1705, the *Newport* and the *Tartar*, pink, on February 5th, the *Roebuck* and *Leopard*, and on February 7th, the *Tiger*, convoyed further supplies of men and ammunition to Gibraltar, and were not interfered with.

But on February 14th, De Pointis, with fourteen men-of-war and two fireships,[2] returned to the Bay to assist in the prosecution of the siege. News of his arrival was promptly conveyed to Sir John Leake at Lisbon.

Sir John[3] was no longer so weak as to fear the result of an encounter with any foe then in those seas. He had been joined by Rear-Admiral Sir Thomas Dilkes with five third-rates from England; and when he quitted Lisbon on March 6th, he had with him twenty-three English, four Dutch, and eight Portuguese men-of-war. The following is a summary of Leake's proceedings based upon his dispatches dated from Gibraltar on March 31st:—

"On March 9th, at noon, the fleet sighted Cape Spartel, but not having time enough to reach Gibraltar before nightfall, it lay by to avoid discovery from the Spanish shore. The weather was fair until after midnight, when the wind shifted from N.N.W. to S.W., and it became rainy and thick. At about 5.30 A.M. on the 10th, the fleet, being within two miles of Cabareta Point, saw five sail coming out of the Bay. These were chased; and they proved to be the *Magnanime*, 74, *Lys*, 86, *Ardent*, 66, *Arrogant*, 60, and *Marquis*, 66.[4] They made at first towards the Barbary shore, but, finding that they were being gained upon, stood for the Spanish coast. At 9 A.M. Sir Thomas Dilkes, in the *Revenge*, with the *Newcastle*, *Antelope*, and a Dutch man-of-war, got within gunshot of the *Arrogant*, which, after a slight resistance, struck.[5] Before 1 P.M. the *Ardent* and the *Marquis* were taken by two Dutch ships, and the *Magnanime* and *Lys* were driven ashore a little to the westward of Marbella. The *Magnanime*, in which De Pointis had his flag, ran ashore with so much force that all

---

[1] The *Newcastle's* convoy had had one transport taken by the French off Cape Spartel; and some other transports, convoyed by the *Roebuck* and *Greenwich*, had been driven back to Lisbon.

[2] This was part only of his force. In December he had had with him twenty-two men-of-war cruising off Cape Spartel.

[3] Dilkes had brought out to him his commission as Vice-Admiral (W.) and Commander-in-Chief in the Mediterranean.

[4] The gun-power of these ships is otherwise given in the French accounts.

[5] She was added to the Navy, and first commissioned on March 14th, 1706, by Captain Sampson Bourne.

her masts went by the board. She and the *Lys* were subsequently burnt by the French. After the engagement the Allies drew off from the shore, and on the 12th looked into Malaga Road, where the *Swallow* and *Leopard* chased ashore a French merchantman, which was burnt by her crew. The wind continued westerly for some days, and, the weather being bad, the fleet was driven as far as Roquetas, where it anchored for forty-eight hours. It could not get back to Gibraltar Bay until the 31st. At Malaga, on the 29th, it was joined by the *Kent, Orford,* and *Eagle.* The *Expedition* and *Panther,* on the 27th, near Cape de Gata had chased ashore a French merchantman of 30 guns, and had burnt her; and the *Assurance* and *Bedford* had taken two settees. The remaining French ships, which had been at Gibraltar with De Pointis, had been driven from their anchors several days before Sir John's arrival, and were believed to be in Malaga Road when the fleet engaged the other five, whereupon they had cut their cables and made for Toulon."

In consequence of these operations, the siege of Gibraltar was raised. Sir John, returning to Lisbon, was there joined in June by a squadron [1] from England under Admiral Sir Clowdisley Shovell, [2] who assumed the supreme command. Yet "supreme command" was not, technically speaking, the position which Sir Clowdisley enjoyed. Once more, and for the last time, the government had appointed Joint Admirals. Sir Clowdisley was one of these. The other was Charles Mordaunt, Earl of Peterborough, a nobleman who had had some naval experience in the Dutch service, but who had never commanded an English man-of-war. The Earl, however, devoted himself rather to the military than to the naval side of the work that had to be done upon the station; and the management of the naval operations was left almost entirely to Sir Clowdisley.

After cruising for a short time between Cape Spartel and Cadiz, with a view to preventing the junction of French ships from Brest with others from Toulon, the fleet returned to Lisbon, embarked King Charles III., and sailed for the Mediterranean on July 22nd, 1705, with about twelve thousand troops on board. It called at Gibraltar, where Charles was formally received as the lawful King of Spain, and where more troops were picked up; and, having stopped at Altéa Bay to water, it arrived off Barcelona on August 11th.

Barcelona was in possession of the French party, and such of the ships as ventured within range of the batteries were at once fired at. As soon as the Prince of Hessen, who had been reconnoitring the coast in advance of the expedition, had rejoined the fleet, the troops were landed and the place was invested. On September 2nd, the castle of Montjuich was stormed, the Prince of Hessen falling,

---

[1] This squadron included Sir John's old flagship the *Prince George,* to which he at once returned.

[2] Sir Clowdisley had, in the meantime, succeeded Rooke as Admiral of the Fleet.

however, in the assault; on the 9th, the trenches were opened; and
on the 23rd, after a general bombardment, in which the Navy co-
operated on shore as well as afloat, the city agreed to capitulate.
On the 28th, the terms of surrender were formally arranged, and a
few days afterwards the place was occupied. The Earl of Peter-
borough remained with King Charles; a winter squadron, under
Vice-Admiral Sir John Leake and Rear-Admiral Baron J. G. van
Wassenaer, was left in the Mediterranean; and Sir Clowdisley
Shovell, with the bulk of the fleet, returned home, and anchored at
Spithead on November 26th.

Leake's squadron, very badly off for provisions, sailed soon afterwards for Lisbon to refit and fill up with supplies. Owing to foul
weather and other causes, it occupied no less than thirteen weeks
and three days on the passage, "having been reduced in that time
to a biscuit per man a day, and sometimes to half a biscuit, and for
three weeks no bread at all. Water was also wanting some part of
the time, so that many who would have recovered, and did recover
their distemper, perished for want; and it was a most lamentable
spectacle to see some, grown delirious, fall down and die in the
action of feeding themselves. . . . Captain Martin buried fifty men
on board the *Prince George*, besides three times that number in a
dangerous condition, for they had been sickly the whole voyage, so
that, reckoning from the time he sailed with the *Prince George* from
England, he had buried upwards of three hundred men." [1]

As soon as he was again ready for sea, Sir John Leake made an
attempt, which was foiled by the treachery of the Portuguese, to
intercept some galleons bound from Cadiz to the West Indies; and
then, learning from the Earl of Peterborough, who as Joint Admiral
of the Fleet was, though he served ashore, the superior officer, that a
French squadron was off Barcelona, which was besieged by the party
of King Philip, he proceeded for that port. On the way thither,
Leake was joined by successive reinforcements under Commodore
John Price, Sir George Byng, and Commodore Hovenden Walker.
Off Tarragona he was also joined from the shore by the Earl of
Peterborough, who resumed command afloat, and hoisted the Union
at the main in the *Prince George*, though he seems to have left the
active conduct of affairs to Sir John. As the fleet approached, the

---

[1] This awful mortality occurred between March 8th, 1705, and January 16th, 1706,
when the *Prince George*, Leake's flagship, reached Lisbon.—'Life of Capt. Stephen
Martin,' 86.

French squadron before Barcelona withdrew; and on April 30th, 1706, the enemy raised the siege of the city.

Returning down the coast, the Earl of Peterborough again went ashore to prosecute military operations in Valencia; and the fleet, proceeding, received on June 1st the surrender of Cartagena, in which it left a garrison of six hundred Marines. On June 26th, Sir John arrived before Alicant, which was much more stubbornly held on behalf of the French claimant to the Spanish crown. But after the place had been hotly bombarded by a division of ships under Sir George Byng, it was triumphantly stormed on July 28th, on one side by the troops, and on the other by seamen from the fleet, led by Rear-Admiral Sir John Jennings, and by Captains John Evans, of the *Royal Oak*, William Passenger, of the *Royal Anne*, and John Watkins, of the *St. George*. The citadel, defended by the governor, an Irishman named Mahony, held out until August 24th.

Having detached Sir John Jennings with a squadron to Lisbon, Leake, after watering at Altéa, sailed to, and received the surrender of, Ivica and Majorca. Then, leaving Sir George Byng to command the winter squadron in the Mediterranean, he returned home with some of the heavier ships of the fleet and with the Dutch contingent under Baron van Wassenaer.

In the course of the year 1706, the Navy was also active nearer home. A squadron under Vice-Admiral Sir Stafford Fairborne (R.) was employed in the Channel and the North Sea; and a larger force under Admiral Sir Clowdisley Shovell was assembled with a view to effecting a descent upon the French coasts; but, owing to the non-arrival in time of a promised Dutch contingent, and, afterwards, to adverse weather, the project was abandoned, and Sir Clowdisley ultimately proceeded to Lisbon and thence to the Mediterranean. The operations in home waters and elsewhere, both in 1706 and 1707, had, however, comparatively little influence upon the issue of the campaign, and will be more fitly dealt with in the next chapter. The sea-power of the Allies was most tellingly exerted in and about the neighbourhood of the Straits, and it is upon the events of the war in the Mediterranean, therefore, that attention is here concentrated.

Sir Clowdisley Shovell, now sole Commander-in-Chief on the station, sailed from Lisbon on January 7th, 1707, reached Alicant on January 28th, landed there seven thousand troops, and was again at Lisbon on March 11th. Sir George Byng, who had already joined him, was then sent back to Alicant with supplies for the land forces. But, off Cape St. Vincent, Byng learnt that the army, then under the command of the Earl of Galway, had been crushingly defeated at Almanza, and that the remnants of it were retreating upon Tortosa, in Catalonia. Byng consequently hastened on, picking up sick, wounded and stragglers at Denia, Valencia, and elsewhere along the coast, and finally proceeding to Barcelona, where, on May 20th, the Commander-in-Chief joined him. Almanza involved the immediate loss of Valencia and Arragon, and ultimately decided the fate of Spain. It was deemed necessary to make a determined effort to deal a counter-blow at France ; and a combined attack upon Toulon was resolved upon.

An allied army, under the Duke of Savoy and Prince Eugene, was being directed upon that fortress. Sir Clowdisley Shovell, with the fleet, after having called at ports on the Italian Riviera for guns and supplies for the troops, moved along the coast in concert with the military leaders, and, on June 30th, was instrumental in facilitating the passage of the Var by the Allies. This brilliant little piece of service was conducted under the immediate direction of Rear-Admiral Sir John Norris (B.), who, with four English and one Dutch ships of the line, entered the mouth of the river, and, having cannonaded the enemy, landed at the head of six hundred seamen and Marines, attacked in flank the French on the right bank, and routed them, losing only ten men.

In July and August, Sir Clowdisley co-operated in the siege of Toulon. But although the enemy, in the defence of that place, sacrificed about twenty men-of-war by sinking them for the protection of the other vessels in the port, and although the allied fleet did some damage to the works and shipping,[1] the enterprise was perhaps upon the whole less costly to the French than to their opponents, who were presently obliged to raise the siege. Very soon afterwards, Sir Clowdisley, with twelve ships of the line and several small craft, quitted the Mediterranean in order to return home, leaving at Gibraltar Rear-Admiral Sir Thomas Dilkes in command of the winter squadron. Byng and Norris went home with the Commander-in-Chief.

It was Shovell's last service. He got into the Soundings on

---

[1] The following ships in the harbour were reported as destroyed or rendered unfit for service : *Triomphant*, 92, *Sceptre*, 90, *Vainqueur*, 86, *Neptune*, 76, *Invincible*, 70, *Sérieux*, 60, *Laurier*, 60, and *Sage*, 54.

October 22nd ; but that night, in consequence of thick weather, several of the ships of the fleet were lost upon the rocks of the Scilly Islands. Among these was Shovell's flagship, the *Association*, 96, which struck on the Bishop and Clerks, and at once broke up, all on board, including the Admiral, Captain Edmund Loades, Captain of the Fleet, Captain Samuel Whitaker, captain of the ship, and between eight and nine hundred officers and men, perishing.

ADMIRAL SIR CLOWDISLEY SHOVELL, KT.

(From Faber's mezzotint after the portrait by M. Dahl (1702).)

The other ships which were lost were the *Eagle*, 70, with Captain Robert Hancock, and all hands ; the *Romney*, 50, with Captain William Coney, and all hands ; and the *Firebrand*, fireship, whose captain, Francis Piercy, with twenty-four people, was saved. The *Phœnix*, fireship, Captain Michael `Sansom, went ashore, but was got off again ; the *St. George*, 96, Captain James Lord Dursley, also struck, but came off without breaking up. Shovell's body, after having been stripped and buried by the islanders, was recovered and brought to Plymouth by the *Salisbury*, Captain Francis Hosier. It found a final resting-place in Westminster Abbey.

Sir Thomas Dilkes, with the squadron left under his charge, visited Barcelona and Leghorn in the interests of the Allies, but fell ill, and died at the latter place on December 12th, 1707. It was suspected at the time that he had been poisoned; but of this no proof has ever been discovered. The command devolved upon the officer next in seniority, Captain Jasper Hicks, of the *Cornwall*, who, after having convoyed some transports from Italy to Spain, reached Lisbon on March 7th, 1708, to await the arrival from England of Sir John Leake, who had been appointed Admiral of the Fleet, and Commander-in-Chief in the Mediterranean.

Leake, who had left the Channel with a large convoy in his charge, reached Lisbon on March 27th, and sailed again, with thirteen British and twelve Dutch ships of the line, besides transports carrying troops, as well as several small craft, on April 28th, for Barcelona. Off the coast of Catalonia, he captured the greater part of a valuable French convoy of about ninety settees and tartans, laden with supplies for the French army. On May 15th, he anchored off Barcelona, and was joined by four more British vessels of war. Thence he proceeded to Vado to confer with the military leaders of the Allies, and to carry to Spain a princess [1] who was about to marry Charles III. Having returned with her to Barcelona, where he took on board a few Spanish troops, he appeared on August 1st, before Cagliari, which, together with the rest of Sardinia, submitted to King Charles after a very few bombs had been thrown into the city. Leaving Cagliari on August 18th, and reaching Port Mahon, in Minorca, on the 25th, he there took steps to reduce an island which, in after years, was of far more importance than Sardinia to the interests of Great Britain.

The rural population of Minorca and of Mahon itself, was not ill-disposed to Charles III.; but the party of Philip held several strong posts in the island, including Ciudadella, the capital, Fornelle, on the north, and three forts defending the entrance to Port Mahon. Sir John, therefore, lay off the place until he had collected from Majorca and elsewhere sufficient troops for his purpose; and then, on September 3rd, he landed a force of about 2600 men, 1200 of whom,

[1] Elizabeth Christina, of Brunswick.

including a number of Marines, were British. But by that time the season had arrived when, in accordance with precedent, the Commander-in-Chief should return to England, leaving the winter operations to a subordinate officer. Leake, therefore, contented himself with seeing to the completeness of the preliminary measures; and, on September 8th,[1] he sailed for home with seven British and eight Dutch ships of the line. Learning, when he was off Gibraltar, that some French cruisers from Cadiz had been troublesome in that neighbourhood, he detached a few ships to look for them, and, proceeding, reached St. Helens on October 19th.

MINORCA.

Rear-Admiral Sir Edward Whitaker (R.) remained behind to command the winter squadron, and to superintend the reduction of Minorca. He lost no time in detaching the *Dunkirk*, Captain Thomas Butler, and the *Centurion*, Captain William Fairborne, to bombard the fort at Fornelle, which surrendered on September 9th. On the 11th, the garrison of Ciudadella also submitted, and on the 19th, the forts at Port Mahon capitulated and were taken possession of, after an assault delivered on the 17th, in the course of which

---

[1] This is the date given in the 'Life of Capt. S. Martin.' The real date was probably the 6th.

Captain Philip Stanhope,[1] of the *Milford*, galley, was killed, and about forty men were killed or wounded.

Sir Edward spent the rest of the year in attending to the safety of the convoys of the Allies, in putting pressure upon the Pope in order to induce his Holiness to acknowledge Charles III., and in carrying troops.

In the meantime, it had been decided at home to strengthen the winter force in the Mediterranean; and Admiral Sir George Byng (B.) had been dispatched with a fleet from England, to carry the Queen of Portugal to Lisbon, to arrange for the safety of the Portuguese Brazil fleet and the British trade, to leave a detachment in the Tagus under Sir John Jennings, and to proceed to Port Mahon. He anchored in the harbour there on January 12th, 1709; and on February 19th was joined by Sir Edward Whitaker with a large number of troops from Italy. He made an attempt to relieve Alicant, but succeeded only in taking off the garrison when the place fell. He then proceeded for Barcelona, landing General Stanhope and the troops at Tarragona, and calling also at Port Mahon, where Sir John Jennings joined him by order. By the second week in June he had assembled the whole of the Mediterranean fleet, including the Dutch contingent, off the coast of Catalonia. But no measure of importance was attempted, and great schemes were discussed, only to be rejected. A project for a descent upon Cadiz was abandoned, owing to the non-arrival in time of Rear-Admiral John Baker, who, with a convoy of transports, had been dispatched from England to co-operate; and on September 22nd, Sir George Byng quitted the Straits, leaving Sir Edward Whitaker, as before, in command. Byng anchored at Spithead on October 25th.

Whitaker's instructions were to protect the coast of Catalonia, and to intercept the enemy's trade and supplies to the best of his ability. He took many vessels, especially in the neighbourhood of the Gulf of Rosas; and, having cruised very successfully, sometimes with and sometimes without the Dutch and Baker's division, he was at length ordered home, and reached the Channel with a large convoy on June 1st, 1710.

Baker, who had been promoted in November, 1709, to be Vice-Admiral of the Blue, was left behind. He also cruised with success,

---

[1] Younger brother of Genl. Stanhope, who commanded the land forces on the occasion.

until the arrival in the Mediterranean of Admiral Sir John Norris (B.), who had been appointed Commander-in-Chief. Sir John effectively defeated a descent by the enemy upon the island of Sardinia in June, 1710; and many of his detached vessels made prizes. In July he captured the towns of Cette and Agde on the coast of Languedoc, but was obliged to abandon them again within a few days. During the rest of the summer, the autumn, and the ensuing winter, he was continuously active, but was engaged in no enterprise of importance; and in the spring of 1711 he was superseded by Admiral Sir John Jennings (W.).

Charnock observes that "repeated defeat and misfortune had long since convinced the French of the folly of equipping large fleets. These had always been unable to contend with those of the

MEDAL COMMEMORATIVE OF THE REDUCTION OF SARDINIA
AND MINORCA, 1708.

(From an original kindly lent by H.S.H. Captain Prince Louis of Battenberg, R.N.)

allied powers. Their system of naval warfare was completely changed, and they contented themselves with sending out, occasionally, small squadrons and single ships, to keep the spirits of the people alive by the depredations these desultory cruises enabled them to commit on our commerce." There may be two opinions as to whether it would have been folly on the part of the enemy to equip a large fleet and to seriously challenge the dominion of the seas; and even as to whether the French had ever been so decisively beaten as to warrant the conclusion that they could not contend with the Allies. But there is no doubt as to the policy which they actually pursued; and, to continue the quotation from Charnock, "the attention of the British commanders was, therefore, principally directed" to the protection of commerce, and to "properly guarding the reinforcements of troops, as well as stores and provisions, to their several places of destination." Such had been the chief duty of Byng, Whitaker, Baker and Norris, and it was also the chief duty of Jennings; so that the history of the commands of all these officers in the Mediterranean is, upon the whole, comparatively devoid of exciting incident. Jennings remained in the Mediterranean, and followed up with ability and success the monotonous work of his predecessors, until after the conclusion of the Peace of Utrecht, on March 31st, 1713; and in the following November, he went home by land.

The treaty, or, rather, the various treaties, concluded as results of the Congress of Utrecht, secured, among other things, the Protestant succession in Great Britain through the House of Hannover; the expulsion of the Pretender from France; a promise of the permanent severance of the crowns of France and Spain; the cession to Great Britain of Newfoundland, Acadia (Nova Scotia), the Hudson Bay territories, Gibraltar and Minorca; the dismantling of the fortifications of Dunquerque; the retrocession of Lille to France; the handing over of the Spanish Netherlands to the Emperor; and the grant of the crown of Sicily to the Duke of Savoy. But Great Britain's main purpose, the support of the candidature of Charles to the throne of Spain, was frustrated; and so it turned out that her policy of fastening the greater part of her naval forces to the Mediterranean produced, after all, only indirect results. Yet Great Britain benefited enormously, each of her gains being in the direction of the extension and strengthening of her power at sea; and France, although the backer of the successful claimant, came out of the strife exhausted and financially ruined. Holland, also, benefited little. The land war had drained her resources; and during the whole campaign she was never able to supply to the allied fleets the quota of ships which she should have furnished in accordance with her engagements.[1] Austria and Spain benefited, perhaps, still less. The gains of all together were not equal to the gains of Great Britain. Her acquisition of power gave her, as Mahan says, the control of—

" the great commerce of the open sea with a military shipping that had no rival, and, in the exhausted condition of the other nations, could have none; and that shipping was now securely based on strong positions in all the disputed quarters of the world.

---

[1] Lediard. 863 n.

Although her Indian Empire was not yet begun, the vast superiority of her Navy would enable her to control the communications of other nations with those rich and distant regions, and to assert her will in any dispute arising among the trading-stations of the different nationalities. The commerce which had sustained her in prosperity, and her allies in military efficiency, during the war, though checked and harassed by the enemy's cruisers (to which she could pay only partial attention amid the many claims upon her), started with a bound into new life when the war was over. . . . In the War of the Spanish Succession, by her own wise management and through the exhaustion of other nations, not only her Navy, but her trade was steadily built up; and indeed, in that dangerous condition of the seas, traversed by some of the most reckless and ruthless cruisers France ever sent out, the efficiency of the Navy meant safer voyages, and so more employment for the merchant-ships. The British merchant-ships, being better protected than those of the Dutch, gained the reputation of being far safer carriers, and the carrying-trade naturally passed more and more into their hands; while the habit of employing them in preference, once established, was likely to continue."[1]

Yet, even on the British side, the war had been distinguished by few very striking, and by hardly any very brilliant, great successes. It cannot be said that genius had generally directed the operations of her fleets, or that either the organisation or the conduct of her Navy was as good as it might have been. The country merely stuck to its work, and hammered away, often blunderingly and stupidly, but always steadily, until the end. The days of its most brilliant performances were still before it.

[1] 'Infl. of Sea Power upon History,' 224.

GUN PROBABLY OF THE EARLY EIGHTEENTH CENTURY.

(*From a Print in the Royal United Service Institution.*)

CHAPTER XXIV.

MILITARY HISTORY OF THE ROYAL NAVY, 1660–1714.

MINOR OPERATIONS.

The Navy and the Restoration—Marlborough to Bombay—Sandwich to Tangier—
Lawson and the Algerines—Allin and the Algerines—Holmes's reprisals against
the Dutch—Capture of New York—Retaliatory cruise of De Ruijter—Allin and
the Dutch Smyrna convoy—The Second Dutch War—Cruiser actions in the North
Sea—Gallantry of Charles Haward—Danish treachery—Tyddiman repulsed at
Bergen—Actions of 1666—Christopher Gunman—John Torpley of the *Adventure*
—Cruises of Utber and Robert Robinson—Actions of 1667—Berry in the West
Indies—Harman defeats De La Barre—Gallantry of Mark Pearce—Disgrace of
William Seeley—Actions near home—The *Princess* and a Dutch squadron—
Death of Henry Dawes—Arthur Herbert in the *Pembroke*—Privateers—The Navy
during the peace—Allin and the Moors—Actions with the Algerines—John
Kempthorne of the *Mary Rose* — Spragge in the Mediterranean — Death of
Benjamin Young and Argentine Allington — Cowardice of John Pearce and
Andrew Logan—Algerine vessels destroyed in Bugia Bay—Holmes and the
Dutch Smyrna fleet—The Third Dutch War—Bravery of Francis Willshaw—
Thomas Harman, of the *Tiger*—Actions of 1672—Thomas Chamberlain, of the
Dragon—Spragge in the North Sea—Capture of Tobago—Richard Munden takes
St. Helena—Dutch successes in Asia and America—Actions of 1673—The *Tiger*
and the *Schakerloo*—Narbrough to the Mediterranean—Boat action at Tripoli—
Tripoli submits—Depredations of French corsairs—Narbrough and the Algerines
—Death of Thomas Harman—Death of George Canning—Berry to Virginia—
—Death of James Harman — Splendid defence of an Algerine — Narbrough
bombards Algiers—Herbert at Tangier—Curious mistake of the *Swallow*—Actions
in the Mediterranean—Herbert at Algier—The *Adventure* and the *Golden Horse*—
Morgan Kempthorne and eight Algerines—Henry Williams enforces the Right of
the Flag—Loss of the *Gloucester*—Evacuation of Tangier—Piracy in the West
Indies—Cutting out of the *Trompeuse*—Piracy in the East Indies—Cutting out
affair at Mamora—Invasions of Monmouth and Argyle—The Marquis de Fleury—
Rise of Benbow—Recovery of sunken treasure—The Revolution of 1688—French
privateers cut out of Queenstown—Death of Roome Coyle—Capture of Forbin
and Jean Bart—Expedition to Cork of the Joint Admirals and Marlborough—
Death of the Duke of Grafton—Capture of Cork—Burning of the *Breda*—Destruction of French vessels at Dublin—Reduction of St. Christopher and St. Eustatius—
American expedition to Annapolis—Failure of Wright and Codrington at Guadaloupe—Actions of 1691—Loss of the *Happy Return* and *Talbot*, ketch—Early
exploits of Du Guay Trouin—Reduction of Limerick—Wrenn in the West Indies
—Action with Blenac—Death of Wrenn—Loss of the *Norwich, Mordaunt,* and

2 E 2

Edgar—Littleton and the galleons—Recapture of the *Scarborough*—Loss of the *Resolution* and *Restoration*—Actions in the Mediterranean—The Dunquerque privateers—Cruise of Sir T. Hardy—The North Sea—The Mediterranean—Action off Guinea—The Peace of Utrecht.

THE various causes which brought about the return to England of Charles II., in May, 1660, and the restoration of the House of Stuart to the throne, are too numerous and complicated to be here described. It will suffice to say that the King regained his crown largely by the help of the Navy and of naval officers. Monck, who was serving at the time as a land officer, and Edward Montagu and

MEDAL COMMEMORATIVE OF THE EMBARKATION OF CHARLES II. AT
SCHEVENINGEN, IN MAY, 1660.

(From an original kindly lent by H.S.H. Captain Prince Louis of Battenberg, R.N.)

John Lawson, the leaders of the fleet, contributed, indeed, more than any other three individuals towards the re-establishment of the monarchy. Montagu, as has been said, had the honour of actually bringing back Charles, who embarked from Scheveningen, in Holland, on May 26th, 1660, and, convoyed by an English squadron, landed at Dover on May 28th, and, on the following day, reached Whitehall. Monck was rewarded with the dukedom of Albemarle ; Montagu, with the earldom of Sandwich ;[1] and Lawson, with a knighthood.[2]

In the following year, the Princess Katherine of Braganza, daughter of John, King of Portugal, was affianced to Charles II.,

---

[1] July 14th, 1660.   [2] Conferred in Holland before Charles sailed.

and it was arranged that, as part of her dowry, she should bring to
him the town and port of Tangier, on the coast of Marocco, and
the town and island of Bombay. To take possession of the latter,
James Ley, Earl of Marlborough, with the temporary rank of
admiral, and with his flag in the *Dunkirk*, was despatched from
England in command of a small squadron.[1]   The Earl of Sandwich
was commissioned to receive the former from the Portuguese; but
as, at the time, there were differences pending with the Algerines,

GEORGE LEGGE, LORD DARTMOUTH, ADMIRAL OF THE FLEET.

(From Vanderbank's engraving after the portrait by Sir P. Lely.)

on account of their long standing piratical practices, Sandwich was
entrusted with a more powerful force, and was directed to endeavour
to bring Algier to reason before executing his more peaceable work
at Tangier.

---

[1] Marlborough, with five men-of-war, and five hundred troops under Sir Abraham
Shipman, reached Bombay on September 18th, 1662.   Misapprehensions arose as to
how much territory was included in the gift; and Marlborough returned, leaving
Shipman at Angedivah, near Goa.   Shipman died.   His successor, Cooke, finally
accepted the Portuguese view of the questions in dispute, and occupied Bombay.   The
town was handed over to the East India Company in 1668.

Sandwich, accompanied by Sir John Lawson as second in command, sailed from England on June 19th, 1661,. with eighteen men-of-war and two fireships; and on July 29th, he appeared before Algier. Negotiations were begun; but they were presently broken off, and the Algerines fired on the fleet. The English Admiral, whose ships suffered badly in their masts and rigging, quickly came to the conclusion that the forts were too strong for him, and, leaving Lawson to blockade the port, proceeded to Tangier, where, having landed a garrison, he installed the Earl of Peterborough as the first English governor. He afterwards went to Lisbon, where he embarked the Princess Katherine, who landed in England on May 14th, 1662.

Sir John Lawson, who had temporarily rejoined his chief, returned to the Mediterranean to resume negotiations with the pirates, as well of Tunis and Tripoli as of Algier. At Algier he succeeded in redeeming a number of slaves; but, when he demanded the restoration of certain goods that had been seized, the Dey would have nothing further to say to him, and boldly declared war. Lawson almost immediately took an Algerine pirate of 34 guns and 260 men; but, ere he was able to effect more, he was recalled to England, Captain Thomas Allin, with local rank as admiral, and with his flag in the *Plymouth*, superseding him in command of the station. Allin did not do much against the pirates, but, remaining in the neighbourhood of the Straits, was able, as will be seen later, to render service there at the very opening of the Second Dutch War. In the meantime, the proceedings of another English squadron demand attention.

For some years the rivalry between English and Dutch traders in various parts of the world had been very acute. The English charged the Dutch with the non-observance of treaty obligations: each side charged the other with a systematic preference of might to right; and in England the complaints, especially of the Guinea and Royal African Companies, became so loud, even as early as 1661, that, in the course of that year, Captain Robert Holmes, as commodore [1] of a squadron of four small men-of-war, was sent to the African coast to make reprisals. It is unnecessary here to attempt either to attack or to justify the policy of the English Government.

---

[1] He was authorised, while on the station, to wear the Union at the main. For a biog. note of him, see p. 441, *post.*

Holmes, with his small force, could do little ; yet he did enough, during his brief stay on the station, to add to the exasperation of the Dutch without materially improving the situation of his own countrymen. In 1663, with a somewhat stronger force, he was again sent to Africa, and having on his voyage thither [1] possessed himself of papers suggesting, if not establishing, that the Dutch had secret and hostile intentions not only there, but also in North America, he acted with great vigour, and did not hesitate even to exceed the orders which had been given to him before leaving England. Beginning his operations in January, 1664, he captured the island and fort of Goeree, [2] made an energetic but fruitless attack upon Elmina, the best defended Dutch post in that part of the world, and reduced Cape Coast Castle, Ada, and Anamaboe. Then, crossing the Atlantic, and acting finally in conjunction with Sir Robert Carr, he made, in August, 1664, the far more important conquest of Manhattan Island and New Amsterdam, thenceforth known as New York. [3]

As soon as news of these proceedings reached Holland, Admiral De Ruijter, who had thus far been acting with the English against the Moorish pirates in the Mediterranean, received secret orders to leave the station. In pursuance of these, the Dutch Admiral, after obtaining a year's provisions at Cadiz, sailed for the Guinea coast, and promptly undid much of the work that had been done there by Holmes. He took the English fort of Cormantyne, and other posts, though he did not retake Cape Coast Castle. Then he too crossed the Atlantic ; attacked a fleet of merchantmen lying under the protection of forts at Barbados ; made many prizes between the West Indies and Newfoundland; and so returned to the Netherlands. Before he reached home, formal hostilities between England and Holland had been proclaimed, [4] and the first fleet actions of the war had been fought, as narrated in the last chapter.

Yet peace still nominally prevailed, when, on December 19th, 1664, Allin, with eight ships of war under his orders, sighted the Dutch Smyrna convoy coming out of the Straits. It consisted of thirty merchantmen and three ships of war, the whole under Captain

---

[1] On this voyage he made several valuable prizes.

[2] There he took the Dutch ships *Krokodil*, *Vischkorf*, and *Vischer*.

[3] New York was taken partly by way of reprisals, but partly also in pursuance of old claims to possession by right of discovery.

[4] France and Denmark subsequently joined Holland.

Pieter van Brakel. Allin, knowing of the very strained relations existing between the two States, and confident that the actual outbreak of war could not, in any event, be long delayed, vouchsafed no attention to the salute which Van Brakel paid in the prescribed form, and fell upon the unfortunate Dutch without giving them the slightest warning. Not only the men-of-war, but also the merchant-

ADMIRAL SIR THOMAS ALLIN, KT.

(From Vanderbank's engraving after the portrait by Sir G. Kneller.)

men made a very gallant defence. Jan Roelofsze, master of the *Koning Salomo*, fought his ship until she sank, carrying down with her a number of English who had boarded her. Van Brakel, however, fell; the Dutch line was broken; and three of the richest merchantmen were taken. The rest of the convoy sought refuge in Cadiz, and remained there until Allin had quitted the station.

One of the first actions of the war was fought in the North Sea between the English cruisers *Yarmouth*, 44, *Diamond*, 40, and *Mermaid*, 22, and the Dutch cruisers *Eendracht*, 32, and *Jonge Leeuw*, 22, in February, 1665. The vessels seem to have been scouting on behalf of their respective fleets. The Dutch ships, after a brave defence, were taken; and Cornelis Evertsen, "the Youngest," [1] then a young man of three and twenty, in command of the *Eendracht*, became a prisoner: but the victory cost the life of Captain John Golding, of the *Diamond*. At about the same time, Captain Robert Robinson, of the *Elizabeth*, 40, while cruising in the Channel, fell in with a squadron of Dutch merchantmen, homeward bound from Bordeaux, and captured several of them.

The Dutch, also, won some early successes. When, after having appeared off the coasts of Holland in May, the English fleet, under the Duke of York, had to return to its ports for stores, part of the Dutch fleet slipped out of the Texel, and, without difficulty, made itself master of the greater part of a valuable homeward-bound English convoy from Hamburg, as well as of the *Good Hope*, 34, Captain Anthony Archer, which was one of the men-of-war in charge. From the first, the warfare against commerce was waged with exceptional energy by both belligerents; yet, although the English suffered very severely, the enemy suffered probably even more. Among the English officers who, during 1665, were most fortunate in making prizes of Dutch merchantmen and privateers, were Captain Thomas Elliot, of the *Sapphire*, 38, Captain Napthali Ball, of the *Success*, fireship, and Captain Thomas Trafford, of the *Unity*.[2]

Captain Charles Haward, of the *Merlin*, yacht, 14, though less fortunate, distinguished himself to an even greater degree. The story of his gallantry is told in the first number of the *London Gazette*. In October, 1665, he was convoying some victuallers to Tangier, and also had in his company sixteen or seventeen merchantmen, when, on the 13th, five Dutch men-of-war attacked his little squadron off Cadiz. The *Merlin*, being ahead, and the enemy coming up from astern, three of the convoy were taken ere Haward, by tacking, was able to get into action. At length, however, he engaged the entire Dutch force in the bravest and most devoted manner, and succeeded in keeping it occupied for

---

[1] Son of V.-Adm. Cornelis Evertsen, "the Old." He must not be confounded with his contemporary, Cornelis Evertsen, "the Younger," son of V.-Adm. Jan Evertsen.

[2] Possibly the *Eendracht*, 32, taken earlier in the year, and so renamed.

four hours. The remaining part of the convoy was by that time well on its way to the protection of Tangier. Seeing this, the largest of the Dutch ships, the *Karel*, 44, endeavoured to quit the *Merlin* and to cut off the merchantmen and victuallers; but Haward, determined at all hazards to save as many as possible of his charges, ran his little craft on board the Dutchman, and so fought her for yet another hour, until, having but eight men still unhurt, and being himself wounded in two places, he struck. It is satisfactory to be able to add that this plucky officer recovered from his injuries, and, thanks to the chivalry of his captors, was quickly restored to the service of his country.

Of the most successful of the English privateers in the first year of the war were the *Speedwell*, John Tooley, master; the *Lenox*, Edward Lucy, master; and the *Tiger*, William Adrian, master, which, among them, took twelve prizes. A ship called "the *Panther* frigott" was another fortunate cruiser. It is not quite certain that she was a privateer, though it is probable. Certain it is, however, that in the following year her commander, Frescheville Holles,[1] was a Captain in the Navy.

The Duke of York's victory in the early days of June occasioned great anxiety in Holland as to the safety of the homeward bound Dutch East India fleet, which, aware of the outbreak of war, had not dared to enter the Channel, but, passing round by Ireland and Scotland, had with some Dutch ships from the Levant, taken refuge in the harbour of Bergen, in Norway. As the English enjoyed, for the moment, almost undisputed command of the sea, this anxiety was not without reason; yet the ships at Bergen would, perhaps, have never been attacked, but for the fact that Denmark was at that time very jealous of Holland. The King of Denmark, who was also sovereign of Norway, did not feel that he was himself strong enough to fall upon the East India fleet, and so provoke the wrath of the Dutch; but, having talked the matter over with the English envoy at Copenhagen, he agreed to privately further the design, if the English would undertake it and would give him half the spoil, which, it was estimated, would be worth many millions. Denmark was at peace with Holland, and had allowed Dutch shipping to take refuge in the neutral port: yet it was arranged that the neutrality of the port should be violated with impunity, and that Denmark, if called upon to explain, should declare that she would have resisted

---

[1] The same who fell in the battle of Solebay in 1672.

the trespass and protected her guests, had she not feared that Bergen would be destroyed by the English.

It was a contemptible conspiracy. It would, however, have been successful, but for two reasons. The secret instructions which were on their way to the governor of Bergen, and which would have induced him to permit the commission of the intended outrage, did not reach him as early as the English expected. It was known that the governor was aware of the nature of the coming orders; and either it was supposed that he would act in accordance with them, even although he had not actually received them, or it was thought that if the English attacked at once, they would not have to share the spoil with the Danes. Be this as it may: owing to

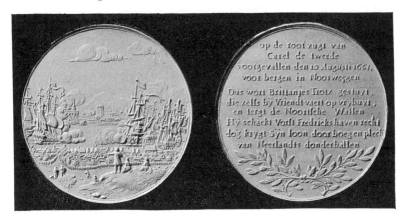

DUTCH MEDAL COMMEMORATIVE OF THE ACTION AT BERGEN, AUGUST, 1665.
(From an original kindly lent by H.S.H. Captain Prince Louis of Battenberg, R.N.)

delay on the one side and to excessive haste on the other, the attack, when made, was resisted.

The Earl of Sandwich, commanding in the North Sea, entrusted the execution of the business to Rear-Admiral Sir Thomas Tyddiman, who, with fourteen sail of the line, three fireships, and four ketches, entered the harbour on the morning of August 3rd, 1665, and anchored there. The Dutch were prepared: the governor, unwilling to play the scoundrel upon his own responsibility, behaved himself like an honest man and fired upon the intruders; and, after several hours of hot action, during which most of his ships suffered severely, Tyddiman slipped his cables and drew off defeated. Many officers and men were unfortunately sacrificed in this affair which, though so disgraceful in its origin, reflected no discredit upon the courage and professional conduct of those engaged. Among the captains who fell were John Utber, of the *Guernsey*, Vincent Pearce, of the *Bryar*, Thomas Haward, of the *Prudent Mary*, Thomas Seale, of the *Breda*, and probably, though this is not quite certain, James Lamb, of the *Anne*.

In 1666 the French, as well as the Danes, who, however, took no very active part in the war, joined the Dutch ; but the earliest of the numerous brilliant small actions of the year was fought, not with any of these, but with the Moors. Captain Henry Osgood, of the *Fox*, 14, being stationed in the neighbourhood of Gibraltar for the repression of piracy, found a large Algerine lying under a fort at Argilla, in February; and, after a gallant struggle of eight hours' duration, succeeded in cutting her out, with a loss of one man only. In April, Captain Jasper Grant, in the *Sapphire*, 38, with the *Dartmouth*, 22, and *Little Gift*, 12, in company, took three well-armed Dutch merchantmen off the Irish coast; and, a few days later, put an end to the career of a very troublesome Flushing privateer. A little earlier, while cruising alone, he had sustained a long and hot fight in the Channel with two Dutch men-of-war, one of 42, and the other of 36 guns. In May, Captain Phineas Pett, of the *Tiger*, 40, fell in with a Zeeland privateer, also of 40 guns. He engaged her, but was killed by one of her first broadsides. His lieutenant, however, continued the action, until, after six hours' contest, the *Tiger* was too severely damaged to be able to prevent her enemy from making off.

More important was a service effected in the same month by Captain Robert Clark, of the *Gloucester*, 58, who, with a small squadron, was stationed off the Texel to observe the motions of the Dutch fleet. On May 15th, he intercepted a Dutch flotilla of twelve ships bound from the Baltic to Amsterdam, and took seven of them. In June, Captain Stephen Sartain, of the *Eaglet*, ketch, captured two rich merchantmen off the French coast. Soon afterwards he was chased by seven French men-of-war, but, taking refuge under the batteries of Jersey, he made so good a defence that, when the enemy, manning and arming boats, endeavoured to cut him out or burn him, the attempt had to be promptly abandoned.

Captain Christopher Gunman, of the *Orange Tree*, 26, distinguished himself on several occasions. On June 29th, being off Guernsey in company with the *Anthony*, privateer, Nicholas

Carew, master, he sighted two vessels. The smaller was chased by Carew, the larger by Gunman, whose 'Journal' thus relates what happened :—

"A litle past 1 in yᵉ afternoone I came upp with him, and itt was a Frenchman wʰ came from yᵉ East Indies, and 1 did ingadge him. He had 26 gunes, and I tore him almost to peces, and about 8 att night he creyd out for quarter, and I gave him good quarter, and exedentally wee did stier on board of him by a mistake of the helme, and my men entred him. He was verie moch shott betwine wind and water. I sent all my carpenters on board of him to endeavour to stop his leakes, but thie cᵈ nott, and about ½ h. past 9 hee did sinke, and I lost of my best men 42, whereof 4 were killed, and I had 7 men wounded : and I saved what men I cᵈ, and about 11 I made saile for Garnesy."

Gunman afterwards cruised at the mouth of the Channel in company with the *French Victory*, Captain Thomas Scott. Here is another extract from his Journal :—

"August 3rd. We found oʳselves to be in the Lat. of 50° 5'; and at noone wee sie 2 saile of shipps, wᶜʰ wee gave chase att. Thie were N.N.W. of us, and wee had then yᵉ wind att S.S.E., and wee went directly afore yᵉ wind uppon them, and putt our shipp in a postewer of warr, and about ½ h. past 3 wee came upp with them, and wee found them to be two Flushing men-of-warr, the one having 36 gunes, the other 40 gunes, and verie full of men, and wee did ingadge them, and thie us, and about 6 o'cl. the Admˡ of them had his maine mast shott by the bord, and a litle after the going doune of the sunn I had my left hand shott away by a great shott from hee that had the 40 gunes, and my maine topmast shott by the board, and then itt was darke, and wee came to the lee for to repaire oure breches, wᶜʰ were many, for wee had nott a whole rope in yᵉ shipp, neither standing nor running, and I had recᵈ 200 great shotts through my sailes, and 7 shotts betwine wind and water, and my boete sonke att my sterne. And wilst I was amending my riggine, and getting upp of another maine topmast, the one of them takes the other in a tow and runes away."[1]

Gunman and Scott chased as soon as they could, but in vain. The Flushingers were clean ships, and were too fast to be come up with. Gunman lost his arm but does not seem to have withdrawn himself, even for a day, from his duties; and, after hastily refitting at Plymouth, the *Orange Tree* was despatched, on September 5th, to cruise to the eastward in search of the fleet. Ere Gunman, on the 9th, anchored off Yarmouth, Isle of Wight, he had taken two more prizes.

The gallantry of Captain William Coleman, of the *Guinea*, 30, also deserves mention. While lying in the Tagus, waiting for a convoy, he learnt that the captain of a French man-of-war, of

---

[1] For this and other matter from Gunman's 'Journal' I am indebted to the Rev. R. E. Cole, Rector of Doddington, who has let me use his copies of the originals belonging to his cousin, Mr. Jarvis, of Doddington Hall, Lincoln.

superior force, also lying there, had publicly boasted that he would follow the English ship, whenever she should leave the port; and would take her. Coleman thereupon gave the Frenchman notice that on the following day he would put to sea. When the *Guinea* weighed, the Portuguese made numerous bets on the result of the expected action, and there was much excitement in the city. Yet, in spite of his pot valour, the Frenchman remained at his moorings; and after standing off and on for three days Captain Coleman had to return for his convoy. On his way home, says Charnock, "he exhibited . . . an extraordinary instance of public spirit" by burning two valuable prizes in preference to reducing the usefulness of his own vessel by manning them. On September 15th, Captain the Hon. Francis Digby, of the *Jersey*, 40, rendered useful service by driving ashore upon their own coast in the Channel, and then burning, four large French vessels, one of which was a man-of-war of 30 guns.

In December, Captain John Torpley, of the *Adventure*, 38, fought two very smart actions. He had sailed from Plymouth on the 17th with five other men-of-war as convoy to a southward-bound fleet. On the 19th he lost all his consorts in a gale of wind, and at daybreak on the 20th he sighted to leeward of him four men-of-war which he not unnaturally assumed to be the vessels with which he had involuntarily parted company. He therefore hoisted his colours and bore down to them. They, deeming the *Adventure* a certain prize, hoisted French colours; and Torpley, hauling as closely to the wind as he could, took to flight. But, as the enemy gained upon him, he presently wore in the most resolute manner to meet the French, springing his foremast in the manœuvre. In spite of this accident, the *Adventure* ran into the hostile squadron, engaged the van ship, brought down her mizzen-mast and main topsail-yard, and passed on to the second, which also quickly had her main topsail-yard shot away. The other ships coming up, a hot action followed and continued for five hours, until a fortunate shot from Torpley blew up the steerage of the French senior officer's ship. In the consequent confusion the *Adventure*, which had received more than five hundred shot in her hull and sails, but which had not so much as a single man hurt, escaped.

On December 31st, before he returned to port, Captain Torpley fell in with three men-of-war belonging to Flushing. He fought them with equal bravery, and with even greater success. One, which attempted to board the *Adventure*, was so badly mauled that she drifted a wreck to leeward, and, it was believed, ultimately sank. The other two, after a long and fierce action, were also driven off; and Torpley, left to himself, made prize of a small Dutch craft which had ventured close up to the scene of combat. Seeing this, the two Dutch ships returned, as if to rescue their fellow-countrymen; but they soon thought better of their project, and abandoned the prize to her fate. In this encounter Torpley had against him one vessel of 32, one of 28, and one of 26 guns. He had his mainmast badly wounded, but only three men hurt.

In the course of the same month Captain Richard Utber, cruising in the Soundings with a small squadron, and with an acting rear-admiral's commission, took a number of prizes, including a Dutch ship of 32 guns.[1] While Utber was thus employed in the Channel, Captain Robert Robinson, of the *Warspite*, was sent, with the *Jersey, Diamond, St. Patrick, Nightingale* and *Oxford* in company, to bring home a fleet of merchantmen from Gothenburg. On December 25th this squadron fell in with a force of five Dutch men-of-war, and, after a short action, captured the *Cleen Harderwijk*, 38, *Leijden*, 36, and *Els*, 36.[2]

The most successful English privateers during 1666 seem to have been the *Anthony*, Nicholas Carew, master; the *Swallow*, Edward Manning, master; and the *Victory*, Edward Lucy (in 1665 of the *Lenox*), master.

The year 1667 witnessed some important operations in the West Indies and on the coast of what is now known as Guiana.

The squadrons of Holland and France had begun to seriously threaten some of the English possessions in the New World. The English had made themselves masters of St. Eustatia, Saba, St. Martin, Tobago, and other islands; but Captain Abraham Crijnssen took Surinam on February 18th, 1667, and later retook Tobago; the French had seized Antigua, St. Christopher, and Montserrat; and Nevis was endangered. Such seems to have been the general situation when, in or about March, Captain John Berry, in the *Coronation*, 56, a hired man-of-war, arrived at Barbados from England. His appearance suggested to the Governor of Barbados the possibility of saving Nevis. Merchantmen were bought and

[1] *Gazette*, 140, 141.
[2] Contemporary English accounts call these prizes the *Cleen Hardeer, Leyden,* and *Eeles*; but the names given in the text seem to be correct. I cannot, however, find a Dutch account of the affair.

hastily adapted for service, and in a short time ten vessels, besides
a fireship, were at Berry's disposal. The French and Dutch [1] are
alleged by English writers to have collected at St. Christopher,
for the intended descent, twenty men-of-war of some force, six
small craft, and six large transports; and Berry is said to have
sailed in time to fall upon the Allies just as they were preparing
to attack; and, after a brisk engagement, which lasted for many
hours, to have driven the enemy to take shelter in Basse Terre,
St. Christopher.[2] Various dates are given for this action. It
took place, perhaps, on May 4th;[3] but it was almost certainly of
a character somewhat different from that above ascribed to it.
According to the Dutch authorities, the Allies sailed, not from
St. Christopher, but from Martinique; and their force consisted,
not of thirty-two, but of eighteen ships, the largest of which carried
thirty guns only. Their immediate object was, moreover, not to
attack Nevis but to meet and beat the English. The English had
twelve ships, not eleven; and some of these were of much heavier
metal than any at the disposal of the Allies. In the result the
Allies were victorious. The French authorities give various versions;
but most of them agree that the Allies had eighteen vessels, and
the English seventeen, of superior force; and all are unanimous
in asserting that the English were defeated, and lost at least three
ships. There is, however, one set of facts concerning which the
English, the Dutch, and the French are not at issue. After the
action the French went to Martinique, and the Dutch to Virginia,
while the English anchored off Nevis, or, in other words, occupied
the field of battle.[4]

In the meantime Rear-Admiral Sir John Harman [5] had been
appointed Commander-in-Chief in the West Indies, and was on his
way out. He had his flag in the *Lion*, 58, and had with him six
other men-of-war and two fireships. Sailing from England in

---

[1] The French were under Le Fèvre de La Barre, and the Dutch under Crijnssen.

[2] The English loss being one ship blown up by accident.

[3] French authorities incline to May 20th, and many English to May 19th.

[4] The difficulty of ascertaining the truth about this action has been materially
increased by the numerous fables which were introduced into a MS. life of Sir John
Berry by the Admiral's brother Daniel.

[5] John Harman. Born probably about 1625. Commanded the *Welcome*, 40, in
the First Dutch War. Captain to the Lord High Admiral in the battle of June, 1665.
Knighted. Rear-Admiral (W.) in that of June, 1666, and was severely wounded.
Served as Vice-Admiral and Admiral in the Third Dutch War. Died in
October, 1673.

March he appears to have reached Barbados on or about June 6th, to have gone thence to Nevis,[1] and, having learnt that the French were still at Martinique, to have discovered them there on June 23rd. The French were twenty-three or twenty-four sail; and Sir John found them lying under three forts, which, as the English approached, fired, but were not replied to. De La Barre, in spite of his superior strength, declined to be tempted out. On the 24th, therefore, the English bombarded and silenced the forts; and, on the 25th, went in, fired eight of the French vessels, including the flagship, sank several others, and, in short, won so complete a victory that only two or three sail of the enemy succeeded in getting away. The English lost no ships, and but eighty officers and men killed and wounded. Surinam was afterwards recaptured from the Dutch by Sir John Harman;[2] but the conclusion of peace prevented further hostilities.

The minor operations near home were numerous, and several of them are noteworthy. On January 5th Captain John Holmes,[3] in the *Lenox*, yacht, met three Dutch vessels off Calais, and took one, burnt a second, and drove ashore the third. On February 3rd the *Deptford*, ketch, 10, Captain Mark Pearce, left Spithead for a cruise off the French coast. At one o'clock on the following day Pearce sighted four sail. Being to windward he stood towards them, whereupon two of them bore away, while the others, hoisting French colours, lay to for him. One proved to be a richly laden merchantman of 400 tons and six guns; the other, a man-of-war of eight guns and fifty-six men, doing duty with a convoy from Le Hâvre. Pearce resolutely engaged both within musket shot for an hour and a half, at the expiration of which the warship made off and her consort struck. The *Deptford*, which had had only one man killed and a few people, including the captain, wounded, pursued the man-of-war, but, as night came on, lost her between Alderney and the Casquets.

An affair of a very different character happened at about the same time near the mouth of the Thames, where the Dutch ships *Delft*, 34, and *Schakerloo*, 28, were doing scouting duty   The

---

[1] Captain Berry returned home when Sir John Harman had been a short time on the station.

[2] It was, however, restored to the Dutch by the treaty. At its capture Captain Thomas Willoughby, of the *Portsmouth*, ketch, lost his life. Sinnamary, in French Guiana, was also taken.

[3] A son of the better known Sir John Holmes.

St. Patrick, Captain Robert Saunders, and the *Malaga Merchant,* Captain William Seeley (or Seale), fell in with them off the North Foreland on February 5th, 1667. Saunders, who was short of his proper complement of two hundred and twenty men, engaged the enemy with spirit, running alongside the *Delft,* and attempting to board her. Seeley, however, instead of rendering assistance, made off, and ultimately took refuge in the Downs; the result being that the *St. Patrick* was presently boarded on the other side by the *Schakerloo,* and, after a fierce hand-to-hand fight, in which Saunders and many of his men were killed, was taken. The *Malaga Merchant* took practically no part in the action; and, for his misbehaviour, Captain Seeley, in pursuance of the sentence of a court-martial, held on board the *Warspite* on February 27th, was shot on board his late ship on March 5th. The following comparison of the gun strength actually engaged on each side shows that, although the Dutch had the more guns, the English had by far the greater weight of metal. The issue, therefore, might easily, in spite even of the defection of Captain Seeley, have been other than it was.[1]

St. Patrick.	*Delft.*	*Schakerloo.*
20 24-pounders.	14 12-pounders.	8 8-pounders.
2 18-pounders.	14 6-pounders.	18 6-pounders.
22 9-pounders.	2 4-pounders.	2 4-pounders.
4 4-pounders.	4 3-pounders.	
48 guns.	34 guns.	28 guns.

Weight of broadside :—

365 lbs.	136 lbs.	90 lbs.

Captain Benjamin Carteret, of the *Pearl,* 26, distinguished himself by his defence of a convoy of colliers bound from Newcastle to London. At 11 A.M. on February 19th, 1667, he fell in with a Dutch man-of-war of fifty guns and three hundred men, which fought him furiously for several hours. During the daytime, the *Little Victory,* another small vessel, which was also with the convoy, was unable, owing to calms, to assist her consort, but towards nightfall she succeeded in getting up; whereupon the Dutchman, badly damaged, made off. In March, Captain Robert Ensome, in the *Constant Warwick,* 30, being bound to Cadiz, encountered and

---

[1] Pepys's 'Memoirs'; 'Not. d. Adm. van Zeeland,' Feb. 13–23, 1667; Charnock, i. 157, 177; 'Kort en Bondigh Verhaal'; 'Not. v. H. H. M.,' Feb. 15–25, 1667: De Jonge, ii. 156. The *St. Patrick* had been built in 1666.

fought, off the mouth of the Tagus, a large Dutch privateer, which, after a short action, made sail and escaped, the *Constant Warwick* being too damaged aloft to be in a condition to pursue. In this affair Captain Ensome was mortally wounded. Towards the middle of the same month, Captain Charles Haward, in the *Guardland*, 28, having, after an obstinate engagement, taken a Dutch ship bound from La Rochelle to Amsterdam, was sighted by a French man-of war of fifty guns, whose captain doubtless expected that the English ship, vastly inferior in force, already mauled by the Dutchman, and encumbered by her prize, would be an easy capture; but Haward, hastily preparing the Dutchman to serve in lieu of a fireship, lay to, and appeared so determined to defend his own, that the Frenchman deemed it wise to bear away.

A most creditable service, rendered by Captain Henry Dawes, of the *Princess*, 52, deserves to be chronicled in his own words. On April 18th, 1667, he sailed from Berwick for Gothenburg.

" On the second day after our departure from Berwick . . . we discovered twenty-five sail of ships, which, upon our nearer approach, about the middle of the Dogger Bank, proved to be seventeen sail of Rotterdam men-of-war, with two fireships and six smacks, steering N.N.W., the wind at S.E. About six in the morning, their rear-admiral, of 64 guns, attended by five frigates of 48 and 50 guns apiece, came up with us, the rear-admiral several times attempting to lay us aboard, with great cries for the States of Holland, but received so warm a welcome that forced him to edge off and keep on the weather quarter. About two in the afternoon, the admiral, of 70 guns, being a good sailor, got close under our lee bow, and two of his seconds on our weather bow, attempting to cross our hawse. Our main-topmast and mizen-yard being shot in pieces, we bore up round and fought our way through them, still keeping them from coming aboard us. The vice-admiral, mounting 66 guns, being sternmost of the squadron, intended then to cross our hawse, having his decks full of men ready to enter; but, our ship bearing round, we brought our broadside to his bow, and, being all laden below with double and bar shot, and above with case and bags [of bullets], our shot did such good execution on them that we brought his foreyard to the deck and laid him by the lee. By five in the afternoon we got clear of all the fleet, and stood to the eastward, they chasing us till night, and then steering on their course. The damage done to our hull was but small, having not received above thirty-eight shot; but our rigging and sails much torn ; only 4 men killed and 9 hurt." [1]

One naturally feels curious about the subsequent career of an officer like Henry Dawes. It was brilliant, indeed, but brief. The *Princess* reached Gothenburg in safety, but, returning, was attacked on May 17th, 1667, off the coast of Norway, by two Danish men-of-war, each of forty guns. After an hour's engagement, Dawes had his left thigh carried away by a cannon shot, and died, saying, "For

---

[1] Dawes's letter, from which this is taken, is printed in Charnock, i. 161, 162.

God's sake, do not yield the ship to those fellows!" After his fall
the *Princess* was successively commanded by the lieutenant, who
lost both legs, and by the master, who was mortally wounded. The
gunner then fought her for three hours, the enemy being within
pistol shot. At length the Danes, having had enough of it, stood
away, and, though they remained in sight until the following
morning, did not endeavour to renew the action. The gallant
Princess anchored at the Nore on May 23rd.

In the neighbourhood of the Straits, the prestige of his country
was well supported by an officer who, in later life, became a famous,
if not a very successful, admiral—Captain Arthur Herbert, of the
Pembroke, 32. One day, in the spring of 1667, he fought a Zeeland
man-of-war of thirty-four guns from 2 P.M. to nightfall. During the
darkness he carried a light, that she might not lose sight of him; and
at daybreak he again bore down upon her; but she avoided him; and
he, the wind blowing strongly from the E., entered Cadiz Bay to
scrape and tallow his ship. While he was thus engaged, the
Zeelander remained in the vicinity, boasting that she had beaten the
Pembroke; but, as soon as the *Pembroke* was once more ready for sea,
Herbert went out, again fought his old antagonist, and drove her to
take refuge in neutral waters. In these actions the *Pembroke* had
only seven men killed and five wounded, nor was she seriously
damaged; but a few weeks later, when returning to England, she
ran foul of the *Fairfax*, off Portland, and sank. The only persons
lost in her were a few who, being sick, could not be moved with
sufficient promptness.

In July, Captain Stephen Akerman, of the *Sorlings*,[1] gallantly
fought two Dutch privateers, one of forty, and the other of thirty-
six guns, near the mouth of the Channel, and not only drove them
off, but also took a merchantman of two hundred tons that was in
company with them. In July and August, Admiral Sir Jeremy
Smyth[2] cruised in the North Sea with a small squadron, and made
numerous prizes; but, while he was at sea, peace was concluded, and
many of his captures had, in consequence, to be returned. The
most successful privateers of this last year of the war seem to have

---

[1] She was wrecked later in the year, but Captain Akerman was acquitted of all
blame (C. M., December 18th), the disaster being due to the pilot.
[2] Commanded the *Advice* in the First Dutch War, and the *Mary*, as a flag-officer,
in the Second. Knighted, 1665. Admiral (B.) under Prince Rupert and the Duke of
Albemarle in 1666. Commissioner of the Navy, 1669. Date of death unknown.

been men who either had already held, or were afterwards to hold, commissions in the Royal Navy. Among these were George Canning, who was given post-rank in 1672, and who, in 1667, commanded a craft called the *Penelope;* Humphrey Coningsby, who had been captain of H.M.S. *Guernsey* in 1663, and who, in 1667, commanded the *Victory*, privateer; and Richard Kegwin, who had previously served in the Navy as a lieutenant, and who, in 1690, captain of H.M.S. *Assistance*, fell bravely while leading his men ashore during the attack on St. Christopher. He cruised, in 1667, in the *Panther*, privateer.

In 1668, the Navy did little active work beyond what was involved in the protection of the fisheries, and the repression of piracy. The *French Victory* and *Speedwell* were dispatched to Iceland to guard the cod ships; and in the North Sea a few other small vessels attended to the interests of the English and Scots herring industry. Admiral Sir Thomas Allin, who, during part of the summer, had cruised in the Channel to observe the French, whose naval preparations were supposed to be somewhat suspicious, sailed in August with a squadron for the Straits; and, off Algier, in October, made so convincing a demonstration of force that the Dey promptly came to an agreement concerning a number of questions which had for some time been in dispute. While thus putting pressure upon the Algerines, Allin detached the *Garland*, Captain Richard Rooth, and the *Francis*, Captain William Bustow, to blockade Sallee. The ships were so fortunate, between September 25th and October 5th, as to drive ashore, and cause the destruction of, one corsair of twenty-two guns, and three corsairs of eight guns, together with three prizes which the corsairs had taken. These successes reduced the navy of Sallee to a single vessel, and were of the highest value in bringing to reason the pirates of that port. Yet, even when the Dey of Algier had signed a treaty, and had professed the utmost anxiety for peace and friendship, some of his cruisers continued to scour the seas and to commit their old enormities. In a smart action with several of these rovers, towards the end of the year, Captain John Hubbard, of the *Assistance*, lost his life.

Sir Thomas Allin, having quitted Algier, visited Naples and Leghorn, and, early in 1669, returned to England, calling on his way upon the Dey, from whom he received renewed assurances that the provisions of the treaty would be scrupulously observed. But as soon as Sir Thomas was clear of the Straits, the Algerines threw off the mask, and began afresh their depredations; so that, ere he had been three months in England, Sir Thomas, with his flag in the *Resolution*, and with eighteen men-of-war, besides fireships and small craft, under his orders, was again dispatched to the Mediterranean. He sailed from Plymouth on July 22nd, arrived off Algier on August 6th, and, finding the Dey intractable, set at once about making reprisals. In the course of these, several actions were fought by detached English ships. On September 7th, for example, Captain John Berry, of the *Pearl*, with the *Portland* and *Nonsuch* in sight, engaged the Algerine ship *Gilt Lime Tree*, 36, and, eventually, being assisted by his consorts, drove her ashore and burnt her.

But the most remarkable engagement of the year was fought by Captain John Kempthorne, of the *Mary Rose*, 48, who, convoying some merchantmen between Sallee and Tangier, was attacked on December 8th by seven Algerine men-of-war. A ballad has not only immortalised, but also, it must be feared, exaggerated the circumstances of the encounter. It is therein asserted that—

> "Two we burnt, and two we sank, and two did run away,
> And one we carried to Leghorn Roads, to show we'd won the day."

The truth seems to be that, after a four hours' fight, Kempthorne beat off all his assailants without losing a single one of the vessels under his charge. Twelve of his men were killed, and eighteen wounded, and the *Mary Rose* was so badly damaged aloft that she had to put into Cadiz to refit. Upon his arrival in England, in the following spring, Kempthorne was deservedly knighted for his valour.[1]

The operations against the corsairs were continued in 1670, in the course of which Allin was, at his own request, superseded by Sir Edward Spragge[2] as Commander-in-Chief in the Mediterranean. In July, being off Cape de Gata in charge of a convoy, the *Advice*, Captain Benjamin Young, and the *Guernsey*, Captain Argentine Allington, fell in with seven sail of Algerine men-of-war, two of which mounted fifty-six guns each, and not one less than forty. In spite of the immense odds against them, the two English ships most gallantly defended their merchantmen during part of two days; and, late in the afternoon of the second day, the enemy drew off, having

---

[1] Charnock, i. 113, 114; Lediard, 593.

[2] Born 1629. Commanded the *Triumph* in the battle of June 3rd, 1665. Knighted. Rear-Admiral (W.), 1666. Vice-Admiral (B.) on July, 25th of the same year. Vice-Admiral (R.) at Solebay. Admiral (B.) in the actions of 1673. Drowned during the battle of August 11th of that year.

taken nothing, and having had more than enough of the fight. Unhappily, both Young and Allington fell in the engagement. At about the same time, the *Holmes*, Captain Henry Clark, drove ashore two Salletines, and chased a third into her port. In the latter part of the year, Captain Clark was again particularly active and successful. On October 5th, he engaged a corsair off Sallee, and drove ashore and destroyed a prize which she had in company; and on October 14th he gallantly engaged two more large Salletines and a prize belonging to them. After ten hours' hot action, one of the pirates and the prize ran ashore, where they capsized. The remaining pirate anchored close in shore, and was there cannonaded, until night came on and she was able to escape. In this fight, Captain Clark, who had two men killed and ten wounded, expended all his ammunition except three rounds.

In the meanwhile, Commodore Richard Beach,[1] who was second in command up the Straits, co-operated most efficaciously with Willem Joseph van Ghent, the Dutch senior officer on the station, the result being that six Algerine corsairs, of from twenty-eight to thirty-four guns apiece, were taken or destroyed on one occasion alone; and numerous other vessels were at various times driven ashore. Sir Edward Spragge, in person, also achieved at least one success. In the month of December, having his flag in the *Revenge*, he was cruising off Formentera in company with the *Little Victory* fireship, 12, Captain Leonard Harris, when, on the 14th, he sighted three sail, two of which were Algerine men-of-war, and the remaining one of which was their prize. Spragge disguised his ship in hopes that the enemy would allow her to come up with them; but in vain. The pirates saw through his device, and the *Revenge* was a heavy sailer. For three days the chase continued. During that period Spragge transferred a hundred of his men and some extra ammunition to the *Little Victory*, which, by means of her sweeps, at length overhauled one of the pirates, a ship of twenty-eight guns, and then so impeded her that the *Revenge* was ultimately able to prevent her escape. The enemy ran herself ashore; but was boarded, and got off undamaged. The other ships, having previously parted company, were no more seen.

Again, in 1671, the active work of the Navy was confined almost exclusively to the Mediterranean. One of the earliest incidents to occur there was, unhappily, of a disgraceful character. On

---

[1] Beach's squadron consisted of the *Hampshire, Portsmouth, Jersey,* and *Centurion.*

March 31st, the *Sapphire*, 38, Captain John Pearce, being on a cruise off Sicily, sighted four sail, which he very hastily concluded to be Algerines. Entirely losing his head, and paying no attention to the remonstrances of the master and of the whole of the ship's company, he ran the *Sapphire* ashore, in order, as he supposed, to save her from capture. She there became a total wreck. If the strangers had really been Algerines his conduct would have been indefensible, but, as they proved to be friends, it was, in addition, contemptible. Pearce and his lieutenant, Andrew Logan, who had abetted him in his foolish cowardice, were tried by court-martial on board the *Bezan*, yacht, in the Thames, on September 17th following, Sir Jeremy Smyth being president; and they were condemned to be shot.

But the shame of these officers was quickly obscured by the gallantry of others. In May, Captain Arthur Herbert (afterwards Lord Torrington), in the *Dragon*, met with and, for nearly three days, fought, two Algerine men-of-war; and although they finally escaped, he behaved himself with the greatest credit.

In the course of the same month, Sir Edward Spragge dealt the corsairs a severer blow than they had experienced for many years. Towards the end of April he had learnt that a number of Algerine pirates lay in Bugia[1] Bay. He proceeded thither with a squadron; but, owing to calms and contrary winds, was not able to make any attack until the night of May 2nd. On that occasion, the *Eagle*, fireship, and all the boats of the squadron, were entrusted to the command of Lieutenant Dominic Nugent, first of the *Revenge*, and were sent in to fall upon the enemy at midnight; but the darkness, and some misapprehension of orders by Nugent's subordinates, caused the enterprise to fail, and the only result was the useless expenditure of the *Eagle*. The attempt was, however, renewed on May 8th, in broad daylight. The pirates, taking full advantage of the delay, had protected themselves by means of a strong boom of spars and cables; but the ships brought to as close as possible under the works on shore; the boats made for the boom, and, in spite of the heavy fire, severed it; and at length, a passage having been opened, the *Little Victory*, Captain Leonard Harris, went in to do her work as a fireship. Harris was dangerously wounded, but Sir Edward Spragge, foreseeing the probability of such an accident, had ordered Henry Williams, a young master's mate, to be at hand to assume the command at a

---

[1] Now Bcugie.

moment's notice ; and Williams, after not only Harris, but also the proper master's mate, and the gunner of the *Little Victory*, had been disabled, brought the business to a triumphant conclusion. Thanks mainly to him and to Lieutenant Edward Pinn of the *Mary*, and Lieutenant John Pearce of the *Dragon*, who commanded boats, the entire Algerine flotilla[1] was destroyed, with a loss on the English side of only seventeen killed and forty-one wounded. Williams, Pearce, and Pinn were deservedly promoted. The effect of this exploit was to cause a palace revolution in Algier, and to induce the new Dey, after a little hesitation, to make peace.[2]   While negotiations were still pending, Captain John Holmes,[3] of the *Diamond*, helped to accelerate them by displaying great activity while cruising in the Strait, where he burnt an Algerine prize and drove ashore an Algerine man-of-war.

Early in 1672, King Charles II. determined to provoke war with the Netherlands, and, if possible, to strike the first blow of the campaign. A very valuable convoy of Dutch merchantmen from the Mediterranean was expected in the ports of Holland. It was decided to intercept this convoy, known as the Dutch Smyrna fleet, and to invent a pretext for attacking it while peace still nominally prevailed. A fleet of thirty-six sail of men-of-war was therefore ordered to be fitted out for the purpose, and to Admiral Sir Robert Holmes[4] was entrusted the somewhat invidious task of falling upon the Dutch, who, it was hoped, would be entirely unprepared.

But the preparations took longer than had been anticipated. In the first days of March, Holmes, with not more than four or five ships—the only ones which had then joined him—was lying outside the Isle of Wight awaiting the rest, when Sir Edward Spragge came

---

[1] The English names of the vessels were *White Horse*, 34, *Orange Tree*, 34, *Three Cypress Trees*, 34, *Three Half-moons*, 28, *Pearl*, 26, *Golden Crown*, 24, and *Half-moon*, 24. Three of their prizes were also burnt. *Gazette*, 627 ; Spragge's Disp. of Sept. 30th.

[2] 'Mems. chiefly Naval,' 200 ; Spragge's Disp. of May 11th ; in ' A True and Perf. Relation,' etc., 1671.

[3] Brother of Sir Robert. He was knighted after the affair with the Dutch Smyrna fleet. Served in the actions of 1673. Rear-Admiral (B.), 1677. Date of death unknown.

[4] Born, 1622. Served Charles I. ashore in the Civil War. Cruised with Prince Rupert, 1649–1650. Commanded a squadron on the Guinea coast, 1660–1661. Reduced New York, 1664. Knighted, 1666. Commanded at Vlieland and Ter Schelling, 1666. Governor of the Isle of Wight, 1669. Commanded against Dutch Smyrna fleet, 1672. At Solebay. Died, 1692. Buried at Yarmouth, Isle of Wight.

up Channel on his way home from the Mediterranean. Holmes made guarded inquiries as to the Smyrna fleet. Spragge said that he had kept company with it for some days, and that it could not be far astern of him. In the circumstances, it was the obvious duty of Holmes to impart his instructions to Spragge, or at least in some way to secure Spragge's co-operation, seeing that his own force was still too weak for the business in hand. But Holmes wanted to have the whole glory and gain to himself, and allowed his brother officer to proceed; so that, when the Dutch very soon afterwards appeared, Holmes had not more than eight ships, besides one or two small craft, wherewith to meet them.

The Dutch convoy consisted of sixty-six sail of merchantmen and six men-of-war, the latter including one ship of fifty guns, two forty-four's, one forty, one thirty-eight, and one very light " frigate." Of the merchantmen, twenty-four were armed, and twelve of them carried twenty guns or upwards. Some of these craft were probably nearly as fit for fighting as many of the smaller of the English ships. Nor were the Netherlanders unsuspicious of what was about to happen to them. Before entering the Channel, they had discussed the risks and debated whether it would not be wiser to endeavour to reach their ports by rounding the North of Scotland. They were, moreover, organised in line-of-battle, Captain Eland du Bois commanding the van, Captain Adriaen De Haese, the centre, and Captain Cornelis Evertsen, "the Youngest," the rear.

Holmes sighted the Dutch off the Isle of Wight on the morning of March 12th, and began the affair by peremptorily ordering De Haese to come on board. De Haese, instead of complying, sent a small craft, commanded by a junior officer, to speak the English Admiral, who greeted him with a broadside from his flagship the *St. Michael*, 90 ; whereupon the engagement quickly became general. Lord Butler (afterwards Earl of Ossory), who was the English second in command,[1] in the *Resolution*, 70, ran alongside Du Bois, while the *St. Michael* tackled De Haese, who fell early in the action. But although the fight went on until sundown, Holmes gained very little advantage, and neither took nor destroyed a single ship.

In the night and early morning he was reinforced by four more men-of-war, and at 9 A.M. on the 13th ; he renewed the fight as

---

[1] The third in command was Sir Frescheville Holles, in the *Cambridge*, 70. He fell on May 28th, 1672, at Solebay.

before. During the earlier part of the day the Dutch held their own very well ; and at noon, when the English made a final effort, Sir Robert had with him but eight ships fit for action, the rest having been sent back to port disabled. This final effort was successful. The Admiral's brother, John Holmes, in the *Gloucester*, 50, reduced the *Klein Hollandia*, 44, Captain Jan Jacobse van Nes, to a state of helplessness, and took her, but too late to prevent her from foundering : other vessels made themselves masters of three of the larger, and one or two of the smaller of the merchantmen ; and, by dark, the rest of the Dutch had been so mauled that they were glad to escape.

They got away without further loss, thanks to the ability and devotion of the surviving captains of the convoying ships. De Haese, as has been said, fell on the first day. His first lieutenant, Tobijas Post, had the presence of mind to keep the pennant flying, and so to conceal the fact of the death of the senior officer until the fight was over. Du Bois lost his left hand. Van Nes, having first been twice wounded, was killed by a round shot ere his ship was boarded. The Dutch defence was extremely gallant : the English attack, though creditable and well sustained, produced far less result than it would have produced had the preparations been better organised, or had Holmes been willing to share the triumph with Spragge. The booty might have been worth a million ; its actual value was probably well under £60,000. It does not appear that any captain fell upon the English side. Sir Robert Holmes himself, however, was wounded. The loss in men was not great.[1]

At the very outbreak of the war, the English outward-bound Mediterranean convoy narrowly escaped a disaster similar to that which had been suffered by the Dutch Smyrna fleet. At a moment when the convoy, which had been dispersed by a gale and had not reassembled, was off the coast of Portugal, the convoying ship, the *Concord*, Captain Francis Willshaw, fell in with a large Dutch squadron, and only avoided capture by gallantly fighting her way through part of it. She was subsequently rejoined by such of her charges as had not put back to England. Another officer who, at

---

[1] Duke of York's Order of Mar. 5, 1672 ; *Gazette*, 660 ; *Holl. Mercur.* ; ' Ontroerd Nederl.' i. 83 ; ' Not. d. Adm. v. Zeeland,' of 26th Mar. (o.s.) etc. ; ' Nederl. Zeewezen,' i. App. xxvi., ii. 251, 256 ; A. Marvell, 'Growth of Popery' ; 'Mems. of John, Dk. of Buckingham,' ii. 11 ; Burnet, ' Hist. of Own Time,' ii. 307 ; Coke's ' Detection,' iv. 61 ; ' Leven v. De Ruijter,' Pt. ii. ; Philips's cont. of Heath's Chron. 582.

about the same time, distinguished himself while on convoy duty, was Captain Thomas Harman, of the *Tiger*, 46. He was escorting a fleet of colliers, bound for the Thames, where coal was already becoming dear, when he was attacked by eight large Dutch privateers; yet, with as much ability as courage, he succeeded in preserving every one of his charges. Some writers have it that he also captured the privateers, but for this statement there seems to be. no authority.

Before the main fleets of the two Powers met, each belligerent adopted the usual methods for keeping itself informed as to the preparations and movements of its adversary, and dispatched small squadrons and detached cruisers to hover off the enemy's coast. Early in May, a squadron of ten sail which, under Captain William Coleman, in the *Gloucester*, 50, was engaged in watching the Dutch ports, narrowly escaped capture; for thirty Netherlands ships were suddenly sent to sea in pursuit of it. Coleman, however, proved himself a particularly able tactician, and conducted so masterly a retreat that, although his rear was for some time continuously engaged, he succeeded in reaching Sheerness without having suffered any noteworthy damage. After the great actions of the summer, the *Bristol*, Captain Charles Wyld, and the *Cambridge*, Captain Arthur Herbert, were sent by the Duke of York on a cruise with similar objects. On July 22nd, being about twelve leagues to the westward of Helgoland, they fell in with the Dutch East India fleet,[1] which they at once attacked. The wind was so fresh that the *Bristol* was unable to fight her lower tier of guns. The action was nevertheless persisted in with much gallantry for several hours, in the course of which Herbert boarded the largest vessel of the enemy, but had to leave her, owing to the excellent manner in which her consorts supported her, and to the fact that the *Cambridge* took fire. The Dutch ultimately got away without loss. In August, the *Mermaid*, Captain John Temple, being on the look-out off the Texel, took a valuable prize; and the *Thomas and Edward*, fireship, Captain John Holmes, the son of Sir John and a nephew of Sir Robert Holmes, captured an Amsterdam ship of 350 tons.

In the month of September some brilliant work was done by ships in charge of convoys. The *Antelope*, Captain Richard White, in charge of a convoy bound to Hamburg,[2] met, on her passage thither,

---

[1] Consisting of ten large ships, four advice boats, and three galliots.
[2] See the Order of Sept. 3rd in the Dk. of York's ' Mems.'

a Dutch convoy, consisting of eleven merchantmen, escorted by one man-of-war of thirty-two, and another of eight guns; and managed, without incurring any considerable loss, to capture two of the merchantmen and the smaller of the convoying vessels. On the 25th of the same month, the *Dragon*, Captain Thomas Chamberlain, lay with a convoy under Berry Head, and was there attacked by two privateers, mounting, one twenty-four and the other eighteen guns. Chamberlain got under way to meet them, and disabled one of them with his first two or three broadsides. She fell to leeward. The *Dragon* then engaged the other, which, as darkness came on, crowded sail and got away. Returning to the crippled ship, Chamberlain hailed her to strike; but she was so unwise as to renew the action; and in a short time she was sent to the bottom.

At that time the Dutch were almost unable to show their flag outside their harbours. Sir Edward Spragge, who, in the *Resolution*, commanded in the North Sea, wrote from off Yarmouth on September 30th: "Since my last, I have taken ten doggers, one buss, and a privateer of eight guns. I am using my best endeavours for the river, having cleared these seas of all fishermen except our own." Captain Thomas Knyvett, of the *Algier*,[1] which seems to have been one of Spragge's detached cruisers, availed himself of an excusable deception to put an end to the depredations of one of the few Dutch privateers that could not be otherwise caught or confined to port. He disguised his ship so as to make her look like a merchantman, and lay off Aldborough in so inviting a situation that the Dutchman deemed him a certain and easy prize. But as soon as the enemy was sufficiently near him, Knyvett triced up his ports, ran out his guns, and delivered so brisk a broadside, that the privateer, in the confusion of her astonishment, hauled down her colours immediately.

On foreign stations little was done during the first year of the war. The *Nightingale*, Captain Henry Clark, was sent to Newfoundland to protect the fisheries there; and captured a small Dutch privateer. Finding no other hostile force on the station, she returned to England in company with the *Adventure*, and, on the way home, took another Dutch privateer and a French merchantman, her prize. The only important colonial expedition of 1672, was one under Captain William Poole,[2] in the *St. David*, with Sir

---

[1] Usually spelt *Argier* in those days.
[2] For this service Poole was knighted. The date of his death is obscure.

Tobias Bridges in command of the troops, against Tobago.[1] It conveyed five or six vessels and but a single regiment of foot. At first the soldiers were landed in an ill-chosen spot, and had to be re-embarked; but, being again landed on December 19th, under cover of the guns of the squadron, and in spite of a heavy fire from the forts and batteries, they established themselves so firmly that the governor capitulated.

About the year 1660, the East India Company had taken possession of, and settled, the island of St. Helena, as some kind of set-off against the Dutch occupation of the Cape of Good Hope. Soon after the outbreak of war, the Dutch seized St. Helena, the English governor and his people, after making some resistance, getting away in English and French ships. News of the loss of the island had not reached England, when in May, 1673, Captain Richard Munden, in the *Assistance*, was sent with three other ships of war and a fireship, to convoy the outward-bound East India fleet. By the time he reached St. Helena he was in want of water, and, perceiving that the Dutch had taken the place, he at once effected a landing on the most accessible side, and, without much difficulty or loss, recaptured the island, which has ever since been a British possession. A day or two later a Dutch ship, the *Europa*, arrived with a new governor for St. Helena. Munden seized her. On a subsequent occasion, five Dutch Indiamen approached the island, and being deceived by the Dutch flag, which the English had hoisted in order to entrap them, two of the richest of them, the *Oliphant* and the *Wapen van Vriesland*, were taken, the others, however, getting off.[2] Munden, with his prizes and a home-coming convoy, returned safely to Portsmouth on August 20th, and on December 8th following was knighted for his services.

But all the colonial events of 1673 were not equally favourable to England. It is true that the Dutch were repulsed in an attempt upon Bombay. On the other hand, thirteen Dutch Indiamen fell in, on August 21st, with an English squadron of ten armed merchantmen, off Masulipatam, and took three of them, losing, however, their vice-admiral, Jan Fredrickszoon, in the action.[3]

---

[1] Called by the Dutch New Walcharen.

[2] 'A Relat. of the Retaking,' etc., 1673 (fol.); Arlington's 'Letters,' ii. 425; Rochefort, 'Hist. Nat. des Antilles'; 'Ontroerd Nederl.' ii. 806; *Holl. Mercurius*, 169 (1673).

[3] 'Ontroerd Nederl.' ii. 811; Lediard, 604. I cannot discover that any of the English ships engaged were regular men-of-war.

Nor was this all. A roving Dutch squadron, which, under Cornelis Evertsen, "the Youngest," and Jacob Binckes, had previously wrought great damage to French interests in the West Indies, cruised northward, and on July 28th, appeared before New York, which, two or three days later, was obliged to surrender to them.[1] The Dutch had originally called it Nieuw Amsterdam. They now renamed it Nieuw Oranje. They had, however, to return it to the English at the conclusion of the war.

Nearer home, several brilliant little exploits were performed in the course of 1673. At the beginning of February, Captain Thomas Hamilton, in the *Constant Warwick*, 36, being about 170 leagues from the Lizard, and in charge of an outward-bound convoy, fell in with a Dutch privateer carrying two tiers of guns, and fought a smart action with her at half pistol shot; but, owing to the roughness of the sea, the *Constant Warwick*, in the endeavour to open her lower ports, shipped large quantities of water. This misfortune, and the leakages occasioned to her by shot-holes, reduced her almost to a sinking condition; and, her powder being all wet, and her rigging badly cut, she was at length obliged to discontinue the engagement. The privateer, glad to escape, seems to have made no further effort to interfere with the convoy. In the course of the same month, Captain John Ashby, in the *Pearl*, 28, while on his return from Jersey, whither he had conveyed a newly appointed governor, Sir Thomas Morgan, encountered a Middelburg privateer of equal force, and after a two hours' fight, reduced her to silence, but was unfortunately unable to take possession of her, the weather being too violent to allow him to send a boat. Next day, however, Ashby had the satisfaction of retaking from another privateer the merchantman *Ruby* of Dartmouth.

On March 10th, about eighty leagues to the westward of Scilly, the *Resolution*, 68, Captain Sir John Berry, which had been detached on scouting duty from the main fleet, captured a Dutch privateer of thirty guns; and on June 8th, at 3 A.M., to the eastward of the Galloper, the *Crown*, 42, Captain Richard Carter, and the *Nightingale*, 18, Captain Joseph Harris, which were returning from a cruise of observation off the coast of Zeeland, sighted three Dutch men-of-war, one carrying forty-four, and the other two carrying each

---

[1] Journal of Evertsen; 'Korte Beschrijving van Nieuw Nederland,' by Lambrechtsen (1818). Few English writers make any mention of this retaking of New York.

thirty guns. At 5 A.M. the English engaged, and for three hours fought as closely as the windward position of the enemy would permit. The Dutch then made off, and for seven hours were chased by the *Crown* and the *Nightingale*,[1] which, however, failed to get up with them.

Peace was agreed to so early in 1674 that there was, happily, little time in that year for further hostilities with the Dutch. Yet, after peace had been signed, two actions deserving of note were performed by officers who, at the time, had not received intelligence of the formal conclusion of the war. One of these was the capture, by Captain John Wetwang, of the *Newcastle*, of a large Dutch East Indiaman of immense value. The other, one of the most gallant performances of the whole campaign, merits a somewhat lengthier description.

Mention has already been made of Captain Thomas Harman, of the *Tiger*, 46. Still in command of that vessel, he was sent to the Mediterranean towards the end of the war. On February 22nd, 1674, the Dutch ship *Schakerloo*, 28, Captain Passchier de Witte, which had been cruising off the mouth of the Strait, entered Cadiz. A few hours later, the *Tiger*, which had been at Tangier, also entered the port. According to local gossip, De Witte had come in because of his unwillingness to meet Harman. Cornelis Evertsen, "the Youngest," who was at the time careening his flagship in the Bay, heard this gossip from the Dutch Consul, and, quite unnecessarily, advised De Witte that, in the circumstances, it was his duty to challenge Harman.

De Witte, an excellent and brave officer, would brook no imputations on his honour; but, looking to his greatly inferior force, he obtained from Evertsen a detachment of seventy officers and men, which, according to the Dutch accounts, brought his total strength up to one hundred and seventy. The *Tiger's* proper complement at the time appears to have been two hundred and twenty-six, but the ship is said to have had only one hundred and eighty-four officers and men on board at the moment, though Evertsen, in his 'Journal,' declares that she had had more than three hundred. On the other hand, the English contemporary reports of the affair

---

[1] In consequence of this action Harris was promoted to the *Constant Warwick*, 36, and the *Nightingale* was given to Captain Edward Pearce, who, on Jan. 16th, 1674, was lost in her with all hands except about thirty, and with a Dutch 12-gun privateer which he had taken on the previous day. The disaster occurred on the Goodwin.

assert that the Dutch ship carried thirty-six guns and about two hundred and seventy officers and men. The gun strength of the *Schakerloo* is here certainly overstated, and it is quite likely that the number of her people is also exaggerated. Be this as it may, at about 9 A.M. on February 23rd, De Witte went out into the Bay, and was presently followed by Harman.

The two ships at once began a hot action at close quarters. Then, as by common consent, they ran alongside one another, and both made attempts to board; but in vain. Again the guns were resorted to; and when the *Schakerloo* was almost in a sinking condition, another English effort to board her met with more success, and the gallant Dutch surrendered after a two hours' fight. The *Schakerloo* had fifty people killed, and seventy, including Captain de Witte, wounded. There could be no stronger testimony to the heroism of the defence. The English loss was but nine killed (four by the bursting of one of the lower-deck guns) and fifteen wounded. Harman received a musket ball under his left eye, but soon recovered from his injury.

I have already characterised this action as one of the most gallant performances of the whole campaign. Yet it seems to me that the chief gallantry was displayed by the Dutch, who, even admitting that they were as strong in numbers of men as their opponents, were undoubtedly very inferior both in number and in relative weight of guns. All the English accounts are so worded as to suggest that the balance of force inclined rather the other way ; and as they are almost unanimous in calling the Dutch ship the *Schaerlaes* instead of the *Schakerloo*, the question has been involved in unnecessary obscurity. It is certain, however, that the ship was the *Schakerloo*, and that she mounted twenty-eight light guns and no more.

Harman took his prisoners into Cadiz. The Spanish governor interceded for them; and Jacob Binckes, with four men-of-war, entering the Bay a few hours afterwards, and threatening, in case of their non-surrender, to sink the *Tiger* as she lay, De Witte and his people were released ere they had spent a night in the English ship.[1] Evertsen, upon his return to Holland, was much censured for having brought about this engagement; and, indeed, to his conduct in the

[1] Disp. from Cadiz, in 'Biog. Naval,' i. 335, 336; Evertsen's 'Journal'; *Holl. Mercurius* for Mar., p. 72; 'Notul. d. Staten v. Zeeland,' of 25 July, 1674; Arlington's 'Letters,' ii. 470; Contin. of Heath's 'Chron.' 595.

affair he owed, in part, the temporary disgrace which soon afterwards overtook him.

The re-establishment of peace afforded the English government leisure to carry out fresh operations against the Mediterranean pirates. In October, 1674, Captain John Narbrough, who had been knighted for his services during the war, was appointed senior officer of a squadron which was got ready for the purpose. He had previously served as a rear-admiral, but on this occasion he held a rank equivalent only to that of commodore and commander-in-chief, although he was permitted to fly the Union at the main of his ship, the *Henrietta*, 62.

Arriving on his station, Sir John, in April, 1675, began negotiations with Tripoli; and, as it quickly appeared that these, unless backed by force, would not be successful, he presently blockaded the port. In June, he destroyed several vessels of the enemy. On August 31st, and the following day, the attempt of a settee to get into Tripoli brought on a lively action between the boats of the squadron and three galleys and a brigantine, which endeavoured to cover the entrance of the settee. The affair ended in the destruction of the settee and the galleys.

Hostilities were continued at intervals as occasion offered. On the night of January 14th, 1676, a very bold attack was made by the boats of the squadron, under Lieutenant Clowdisley Shovell, upon the shipping in harbour; and four vessels,[1] being all that then lay there, were destroyed, without the loss of a single English life. A little later, Sir John landed a party a few leagues from the city, burnt a magazine of timber, and effected other damage. During all this time his cruisers made frequent captures at sea.

Yet still the Dey declined to pay the indemnity which was demanded as one of the most indispensable conditions of peace. In February, the Commander-in-Chief, who had temporarily raised the blockade, and who had transferred his flag to the *Hampshire*, 46, dealt a further blow which brought the pirates to reason. Having a single frigate in company, he fell in, somewhat to the eastward of Tripoli, with four Tripolitan men-of-war, the only large craft that remained in the possession of the enemy. In the action which followed, both sides suffered heavily; but the pirates, who lost about six hundred men killed and wounded, were defeated, and

---

[1] These were a French prize of 20 guns, and (to translate their names) the *Crowned White Eagle*, 50, the *Looking-Glass*, 36, and the *Saint Clara*, 24.

driven into port, the result being that, on March 5th, the Dey signed a treaty by which he agreed to surrender all his English captives, to grant certain privileges to the subjects of King Charles, and to pay an indemnity of 80,000 dollars.

Nevertheless, the matter was not settled. The Tripolitans, irritated at what they conceived to be the pusillanimity of their ruler, rose and expelled him; and it was not until Sir John had returned and threatened to bombard the city that he induced the new Dey to confirm the treaty which had been agreed to by his predecessor.

While these good services were being rendered by the Navy in the Mediterranean, little of importance happened elsewhere. On March 25th, 1675, the *Mary*, yacht, Captain William Bustow, ran upon the Skerries in a fog; and the captain, together with Edward, second Earl of Meath, who was a passenger, the boatswain, and two seamen, perished, the vessel becoming a total loss. In 1676, the activity in the Channel of French corsairs became so troublesome, and satisfaction for their depredations was so arbitrarily withheld, that the relations between the Courts of London and Paris were strained almost to breaking point. It was alleged that no fewer than fifty-three English vessels had been taken by these freebooters since the conclusion of peace with Holland. In the following year, Parliament, on several occasions, addressed the King on the subject, but Charles was too much dependent upon Louis to dare to adopt a patriotic course of action, and England was obliged to stomach, though she did not forget, the insults. The marriage of the Princess Mary, eldest daughter of the Duke of York, to William, Prince of Orange, was celebrated, however, in 1677, and cheered the people as a presage of the approaching downfall of French influence.

The year 1677 witnessed the renewal of operations in the Mediterranean. Sir John Narbrough, with a commission [1] similar to his previous one, and with his flag in the *Plymouth*, 58, was again sent thither, and was ordered to coerce the Algerines, who had grown very bold in their attacks upon English commerce. He arrived upon his station late in the summer, and quickly made several captures and recaptures. The operations, however, outlasted the period of Sir John's command, and the main incidents of them must, therefore, be here chronicled under the respective years in

---

[1] This was superseded on February 15th, 1678, by a new commission constituting him " Admiral of His Majesty's Fleet in the Straits."

which they occurred. Those which happened in 1677, though few in number, included two which were of a particularly gallant character.

Captain Thomas Harman, whose action with the *Schakerloo* has been already described, was, in 1677, still in the Mediterranean, but commanded the *Sapphire*, 34,[1] instead of the *Tiger*. In August he had made himself master of an Algerine man-of-war, whose name was anglicised as *Date Tree*. On September 10th he fell in with another Algerine, the *Golden Horse*, 46, which, in spite of her superior force, endeavoured to avoid an action. Harman, nevertheless, got up with and engaged her; and there was every probability of the English ship capturing or destroying her opponent when, almost simultaneously, the *Sapphire* lost her mainmast, and Captain Harman was mortally wounded. In consequence of these mishaps the pirate got away.

On October 28th following, the *Portsmouth*, 48, was in vain chase of an Algerine man-of-war of thirty-eight guns in the Strait of Gibraltar. The enemy was very fast, and would have easily escaped, had not the noise of the firing attracted the attention of two English ships which were at anchor in the Bay of Tangier. These were the *Charles*, 32, Captain Thomas Hamilton, and the *James*, galley, 30, Captain George Canning. They at once weighed and made sail in order to cut off the pirate, which was commanded by a German renegade, who, knowing that he could expect no quarter, served out unlimited supplies of brandy to his people, and determined to resist to the utmost. The two English ships, having come up with the Algerine and laid her on board, soon obliged the corsairs to quit their upper deck and retire to their main deck guns. But the desperadoes fought these for fully an hour longer, and, even when all their pieces had been dismounted, flung shot into the English boats which were endeavouring to take possession. At length, however, when her captain and upwards of one hundred and sixty of her men had been killed outright, the pirate struck. This success was, unhappily, not gained without the loss on the English side of between twenty and thirty men killed and wounded. Among the killed was Captain Canning.

Outside the Mediterranean, the only important naval event of 1677 was the dispatch to Virginia, early in the year, of a small squadron under Captain Sir John Berry. The Indians had been

---

[1] Later she carried 32 guns only.

threatening the colony, and troops were sent out to deal with them ; but the disturbances had in great measure subsided when Berry arrived, and he soon afterwards returned to England.

In 1678, the Mediterranean was the sole scene of active operations.

The *Guernsey*, 32, Captain James Harman,[1] while cruising under the orders of Sir John Narbrough, on January 19th, 1678, encountered the Algerine man-of-war, *White Horse*, of fifty guns and five hundred men. Neither ship avoided the action, which began, and was maintained, at close quarters. The Algerine made two attempts to board, but was as often driven back. The *Guernsey*, on account of the numerical inferiority of her crew, was unable to make any corresponding effort, but she plied her guns so well that, in course of time, the enemy saw fit to sheer off. The English loss was only nine killed, but among the fatally wounded was the brave Harman. Three musket balls in succession struck him ; yet he remained in command ; and only after a contused blow from a round shot had reduced him to a condition of insensibility, was he carried below. He died three days after the fight.

In March, 1678, Sir John Narbrough himself sank three Algerine men-of-war, and captured a fourth ; and, in April, these successes were well followed up by some of the Admiral's lieutenants. On the 1st of that month, the *Mary*, 60, Captain Sir Roger Strickland, and the *Rupert*, 64, Captain Arthur Herbert, were cruising in company, and sighted an Algerine two-decker, mounting forty, but capable of mounting fifty-four, guns, and carrying four hundred men. The *Rupert* was the first to get up with her, and engaged her singly for a considerable time. Indeed, she may be credited with having subdued her, for as soon as the *Mary* also got up, the enemy struck. She had lost two hundred men. In the *Rupert*, all the officers, down to the boatswain's mate, had been killed or wounded, nineteen people in all being killed, and between thirty and forty wounded. Herbert, by the explosion of some bandoliers which lay on the quarter-deck, was badly burnt about the face, and lost the sight of one of his eyes. The prize, which was taken into the service as the *Tiger*, received an English armament of forty-six guns. Her tonnage

---

[1] A son of Admiral Sir John Harman. His relationship to Captain Thomas Harman, who fell in the *Sapphire*, in 1677, is not clear. Contemporary accounts give the force of the *Guernsey* at only twenty-six guns and a hundred and ten men ; but official lists of the year put it at thirty-two guns and a hundred and fifty men.

was but 649, that of the *Rupert* being 832, so that the Algerine defence was in the highest degree creditable to the "old Turk" who commanded her, and who, previous to her surrender, had caused all her arms to be thrown overboard.

By that time the Algerine navy had been reduced to a very low ebb, and the majority of such ships as still remained to it were confined to port. In August, nevertheless, Sir John Narbrough took two more men-of-war, besides burning twelve Algerine merchantmen ; and soon afterwards he bombarded Algier itself, though the Dey continued obdurate, and declined to agree to any satisfactory treaty. In November, Sir John won a further success. The Dey, disgusted at the inactivity of his fleet, sent to sea nearly all that still existed of it ; but the blockading squadron captured the entire flotilla,[1] after a smart, but not very bloody action, and carried it into Cadiz.

In May, 1679, Sir John Narbrough returned to England with such of his ships as were most in need of repair, and on June 10th he arrived at Portsmouth. The Mediterranean command was left in the hands of Captain Arthur Herbert, who seems to have held local rank as vice-admiral.[2] In November, 1679, Herbert co-operated very effectively, both ashore and afloat, in repelling the attacks of the Moors upon the city of Tangier ; and, for some months afterwards, he remained before the place for its protection. A curious incident in the war with the pirates occurred a little earlier in other waters. Captain Thomas Fowler, in the *Swallow*, 50, being on a cruise near the mouth of the Channel, whither the corsairs often resorted when they were allowed sufficient liberty, sighted, in the month of August, three vessels, which he took to be Algerines. They also took him for an Algerine, and endeavoured to get away, whereupon he chased, and at length drove them all ashore near Ushant. Unfortunately, they proved to be a French trader and two English merchantmen.

In March or April, 1680, while Herbert remained before Tangier, Captains John Wyborn, of the *Bristol*, 48, and William Booth, of the *Adventure*, 40, drove ashore, about five leagues from Tangier, the Algerine man-of-war *Citron Tree*, 32, after a sharp engagement. There were in her many Christians, of whom the *Adventure* saved about fifty, nearly half of whom were English slaves. On April 11th,

---

[1] The translated names of the vessels taken were: *Greyhound*, 42, *Golden Tiger*, 36, *Five Stars*, 36, *New Fountain*, 34, and *Flying Horse*, 32.

[2] He is called vice-admiral in the *Gazette*, Nos. 1412 and 1469. But he was not regularly commissioned as Commander-in-Chief on the station until July 17th, 1680.

the *Adventure*, assisted by the *Hampshire*, 46, Captain Edward Pinn, fought a ten hours' action with four Algerine men-of-war, one [1] of which was driven ashore, and one, the *Calabash*, 28, taken. A third, in her endeavour to get into Sallee, ran on the bar there, and became a wreck. The *Hampshire* had three men killed and nine wounded in this encounter. The same two captains had previously sighted the *Golden Horse*, 46, which was destined to be taken by one of them in the course of the following year; but, owing to a calm, she had escaped for the time by means of her sweeps.

In May, 1680, there was another Moorish attack upon Tangier; and Herbert rendered valuable service by effecting, without much loss, the evacuation of an advanced work called Fort Henrietta, which had to be temporarily abandoned to the enemy. In September, yet another attack was repulsed, largely in consequence of Herbert's activity ashore as well as afloat. A few months afterwards, the Commander-in-Chief was obliged, by the situation of affairs at Algier, to proceed thither. His firmness, and the good work done by his cruisers, eventually brought about a peace, but not until there had been a whole year of further hostilities.

This last year of the war with the Algerine pirates was productive of several gallant actions. On April 8th, 1681, Captain William Booth, of the *Adventure*, 40, fell in with the Algerine ship *Golden Horse*, 46, which had escaped him in the previous year, and which was manned by five hundred and eight Moors and ninety Christian slaves. At 2 A.M. Booth brought his opponent to action, close under Cape de Gata, and the fight continued very hotly until 3 P.M., when the pirate was on the point of surrendering, her mainmast having fallen, and her captain having had his thigh broken. At this critical moment, a strange sail hove in sight. The Algerines took the new-comer to be a friend, and were inspired to fresh exertions. Booth, on the other hand, was correspondingly anxious; for the stranger flew Moorish colours. Yet the *Adventure* steadily continued the combat until nightfall, by which time her determined enemy had one hundred and nine killed, one hundred and twenty wounded, not a mast standing, and six feet of water in the hold. The English ship, though she had suffered much less heavily, was in no state to begin at once an engagement with another foe; and the stranger was, by that time, almost up. The *Calabash*, which had

---

[1] The *Orange Tree*, 28. Booth and Pinn chased her into Tangier Road, where she ran ashore to avoid capture by Herbert's squadron.

been captured in 1680, and which had since been fitted as a fireship, happened to be in company with the *Adventure ;* and, not knowing what better policy to pursue, Booth ordered her to attempt the destruction either of the *Golden Horse* or of the other ship during the night. But the *Calabash's* only boat happened to be staved in, and the order could not be obeyed. This was exceedingly fortunate, for, when day broke, the new-comer hoisted English colours as she bore down. She proved to be the *Nonsuch*, 40, Captain Francis Wheler, and the Algerine, without making the smallest resistance, permitted her to take possession.

Morgan Kempthorne, a son of Admiral Sir John Kempthorno, at that time commanded the *Kingfisher*, 46, on the Mediterranean station. On May 22nd, being apparently off the coast of Sardinia, he sighted eight sail, which turned out to be seven Algerine men-of-war and a small settee. Approaching within pistol-shot, the first ship of the enemy poured a broadside into the *Kingfisher*, and then sprang her luff and stood off to make way for a second, which was followed by a third, and she by a fourth. The *Kingfisher* replied to each to the best of her ability. The fourth ship, which carried the flag of the Algerine admiral, instead of standing off, like her predecessors, fell on board the *Kingfisher's* quarter firing furiously. Captain Kempthorne, after having first received a bullet in the hand, was mortally wounded, and died within a few minutes; but his place was nobly filled by Lieutenant Ralph Wrenn,[1] who beat off the Algerine, which, however, presently filled and laid the *Kingfisher* on board a second time. After a time she fell a little astern and lay there within half pistol shot, while three of her consorts kept on the *Kingfisher's* quarter, and the other three continued a more distant cannonade from windward.

So the fight continued for many hours, the enemy sometimes closing and sometimes drawing off a little. At length they gave up the contest, and quitted the undaunted *Kingfisher*, which, a few days later, got into Naples. She had twice been set on fire; but, looking to the nature and length of the action, which had lasted from 1 P.M. to 1 A.M., her losses were less heavy than might be expected. She had eight killed and thirty-eight wounded. About three months later Wrenn was made captain of the *Nonsuch*, 40, and the *Nonsuch's* captain, Francis Wheler, became captain of

---

[1] Wrenn had been Captain of a fireship in 1677–78, but, probably owing to the difficulty of getting a ship of his own during the peace, served as a lieutenant.

the gallant *Kingfisher*, and, in her, in October, fought and took a large Sallee pirate, which sank soon after she had struck.

In the meantime the *Sapphire*, 34, Captain Anthony Hastings, and the *James*, galley, 30, Captain Clowdisley Shovell, captured in September, after a desperate action, the Algerine cruiser *Half-moon*, 32. Her lieutenant, an English renegade, was deservedly hanged as soon as the prize had been taken possession of. In December Captain William Booth, of the *Adventure*, 40, and Captain Shovell, drove ashore near Mazagran another Algerine corsair, the *Flower-pot*, 34. Thus were the pirates gradually made to see the folly of open resistance to the naval power of England. Their depredations did not altogether cease after the signature of peace ; but they became rarer, and they were, as a rule, promptly disavowed by the Dey.

One other episode of 1681 deserves mention here. Captain Henry Williams, in the *Pearl*, 28, met in the Channel a French armed ship which failed to pay the usual mark of deference to the English flag. After reducing her to a sinking condition he took her, but lost in the action three killed and one wounded.

The year 1682 was a year of peace, and is mainly remarkable for the circumstances which attended the loss of the *Gloucester*, in which the Duke of York was on his way to Leith. The captain of the ship, and senior officer of the escorting squadron, was Sir John Berry ; but the navigation of the vessel had been entrusted to Captain James Aire.[1] The *Gloucester*, in the early morning of May 6th, ran upon the Lemon and Oar,[2] and upwards of one hundred and thirty persons, including Robert, third Earl of Roxburghe, and several other noblemen and gentlemen of the Duke's suite, perished. There is some reason for believing that the ship was deliberately wrecked by Aire, acting as agent for a party of conspirators who desired the death of the Duke of York.[3]

The chief naval event of 1683 was the dispatch of Admiral Lord Dartmouth with a squadron to effect the dismantling and evacuation of Tangier, which, on account of Moorish hostilities, had become a very expensive possession, and which it was deemed imprudent to restore to its original owners the Portuguese. Dart-

---

[1] Spelt also Ayres, Eares, Eyres, and Eyre. He was dismissed the service.
[2] Off Yarmouth.
[3] This view is strongly urged in a memo. (probably by Captain Christopher Gunman) preserved among the Gunman papers at Doddington Hall.

mouth, with his flag in the *Grafton*, and with Sir John Berry as his
second in command, sailed from Plymouth on August 23rd, and,
having razed the fortifications, destroyed or embarked the stores,
and removed such inhabitants as desired to leave, returned early in
the following year. The abandonment of the place has often since
been regretted. Had it been retained, it is probable that long ago
Marocco would have become a civilised and highly developed
country, and it is certain that Great Britain's position in the
Mediterranean would be considerably stronger than it is.

The pirates of Algier and Tripoli continued to profit by the stern
lessons which had been taught them, and caused but little trouble;
but other pirates in more distant waters flourished exceedingly, and
not having received any serious check for a long period, were greatly
in need of one. They were specially in need of it in the West
Indies; and in 1683 Sir William Stapleton, Governor-General of the
Leeward Islands, induced one of the commanders on that station,
Captain Charles Carlisle, of the *Francis*, 20, to proceed in search of
the marauders. On August 1st, Carlisle discovered the most notorious of these freebooters, the *Trompeuse*, at anchor in the road of
St. Thomas, under the guns of a fort. Carlisle ran in and was
saluted not only by a shot from the pirate but also by another from
the work. He therefore sent ashore to remonstrate; but received
only an evasive answer. Determined to persist at all hazards, he
manned and armed his boats that night, and, sending them in, burnt
the *Trompeuse* without loss. He also destroyed two other ships
which had been in league with the pirate.

Two years later, a useful blow was dealt at piracy in the East
Indies. Captain John Tyrrel, in the *Phœnix*, 42, had been dispatched thither in 1684 to assist in the repression of disorders which
had been reported from Bombay, and to protect the trade. On
September 19th, 1685, the *Phœnix*, plying to windward of Bassein,
discovered a strange sail at anchor, and stood towards her; whereupon the stranger weighed and stood away. The *Phœnix* chased,
"and, she proving to be a Zanganian, a sort of piratical people,"[1]
an action resulted. After several ineffectual attempts, a small
boarding party of eleven men, under Lieutenant George Byng,[2]

---

[1] 'Mems. Relat. to the Lord Torrington,' 9.

[2] George Byng, later Viscount Torrington. Born, 1663. Entered the Navy as a
King's Letter Boy, 1678. Captain, 1688. Commanded the *Hope* at Beachy Head,
1690. Rear-Admiral, 1703. Commanded the attack at the capture of Gibraltar,

managed to enter her. More men would have followed but that
the *Phœnix* had too much way on to permit of them doing so.
The pirates, seeing how few they had to deal with, plucked up their
courage and killed or wounded the whole party; but while they
still fought, their ship, which had previously suffered severely, sank
under them. Byng, who had received two deep wounds, and who
could not swim, narrowly escaped with his life. In this fight the
Phœnix lost about seven killed and four wounded. She remained
on the station for some time and appears to have been very active.

Nor did 1685 pass over without necessity arising for further
operations against the corsairs in the Mediterranean. In the course
of these the *Bonaventure*, 48, Lieutenant Stafford Fairborne (*vice*
Captain Harry Priestman, who was sick ashore), *Greyhound*, 16,
Captain Randall Macdonald, and *Lark*, 18, Captain Thomas
Leighton, sent in their boats, on the night of June 12th, to the
harbour of Mamora, and gallantly burnt, under the fire from the
castle, two Salletine pirates, mounting the one thirty-six, and the
other twenty-six guns, besides patereroes. The English loss was
but one man mortally, and five or six men slightly, wounded.

Nearer home, peace was broken by the ill-advised invasions of
the Duke of Monmouth, and of Archibald, ninth Earl of Argyle.
Argyle landed in the Western Highlands from Holland in May,
bringing with him arms and stores, and establishing a depôt in the
castle of Ellengreg, which he hastily fortified. Captain Thomas
Hamilton, in the *Kingfisher*, 46, with two or three vessels in
company, appeared before the castle in June, and very easily made
himself master of it, and of the five thousand stand of arms, the
small park of artillery, and the five hundred barrels of powder
which it contained. Hamilton also captured the three small ships
which formed the luckless Earl's naval force; and, of these, two,
the *Sophia* and the *Dumbarton*, were presently added to the Royal
Navy.

Monmouth landed at Lyme Regis on June 11th, and, proceeding
inland, left in that port the two ships and two transports which
constituted his modest flotilla. These were captured on June 20th
by Captain Richard Trevanion of the *Soldadoes*, 16, who, with

---

1704. Knighted for this and for services at the battle of Malaga. Vice-Admiral, 1705.
Commanded at the capture of Alicant, 1706, and at the battle off Cape Passaro,
1718. Peer, 1721. First Lord of the Admiralty, 1727. Died, 1733.

a small squadron, had been sent after them. Both Monmouth and Argyle were taken while endeavouring to conceal themselves; and they paid the penalty of their rebellion with their lives.

In 1686, the piratical states being still troublesome, and the depredations of a French corsair, the Marquis de Fleury, becoming intolerable, Captain Henry Killigrew,[1] in the *Dragon*, 46, was sent with a squadron to the Mediterranean to protect trade and to deal with the disturbers of it. He did not succeed in taking the Marquis, but he so pressed him as to oblige him to dismantle and abandon his ship at Villa Franca.

The year 1687 was singularly barren of naval events. It nevertheless brought into notice a gentleman who subsequently earned for himself a very honourable naval position. John Benbow, a naval officer temporarily serving as master of a merchantman called the *Malaga Merchant*, being attacked near the mouth of the Strait of Gibraltar by a Salletine cruiser of considerable force, drove her off with great gallantry. This action, which was fought in May, 1687, was only one of several of a similar character; and so strong an impression was created at the Admiralty by Benbow's[2] repeated acts of bravery while in command of vessels not belonging to the Navy that, in 1689, he was rapidly promoted from the rank of master to that of captain, and was given the command of a third-rate, the *York*, 60.

It was also in 1687 that William Phipps,[3] after having induced many noblemen and gentlemen to associate themselves with him in the venture, and having obtained naval co-operation, thanks to the patronage of the Duke of Albemarle, succeeded in recovering from a Spanish wreck, near the Bahamas, silver to the value of £300,000.

The successful expedition of William of Orange in 1688 is described in the previous chapter; and the condition of the Royal Navy at the time of the Revolution is fully set forth in Chapter XXII. It may here be noted that one craft only belonging to the expeditionary force appears to have fallen into the hands of King James's cruisers. This vessel, a not very important

---

[1] On December 8th, 1687, while still on the station, he was badly wounded by the bursting of a gun during an action with a Salletine. He did not return to England until May 5th, 1689.

[2] John Benbow, born, 1653; Master, 1679; Lieutenant, 1689; Captain, 1689; Master of the Fleet at Beachy Head and La Hougue; Rear-Admiral, 1696; Vice-Admiral, 1700: mortally wounded in the action with M. Ducasse, 1702.

[3] *See* note, p. 464, *post*.

one, was taken by the *Swallow*, 48, Captain Matthew Aylmer. She had on board four companies[1] of Babington's regiment of foot.

The Revolution, though practically unopposed in England, was not easily accepted in Ireland; and, moreover, it brought about an almost immediate war with France; so that the Navy quickly found plenty of occupation.

Previous to the battle of Bantry Bay, the *Ruby*, 48, Captain Frederick Froud, was temporarily detached from Admiral Herbert's fleet to look into the Cove of Cork, and to cut out two French vessels which were there fitting to serve as privateers. Captain Froud executed this duty, and then rejoined the flag in time to

MEDAL COMMEMORATIVE OF THE RECOVERY OF SUNKEN SPANISH TREASURE IN THE WEST INDIES, 1687.

(From an original kindly lent by H.S.H. Captain Prince Louis of Battenberg, R.N.)

participate in the action. After the battle, and while Herbert was on his way home, the *Rupert*, 66, Captain Sir Francis Wheler, which was to have formed part of the fleet, but which could not be got ready in time, captured in the Channel a rich merchantman bound from St. Domingo for Brest. Wheler, after carrying his prize into port, was dispatched, with twelve ships of war under his orders, to watch Brest; and, while cruising off that place, took a small French man-of-war which had on board some dispatches from Ireland, and twenty-six storeships and other craft which were bound for Ireland with supplies for James's army there.

The first important single ship action of the war was fought

---

[1] Each of these companies consisted of sixty men.

on May 12th, 1689, by the *Nonsuch*, 42, Captain Thomas Roome Coyle,[1] which was cruising near the Channel Islands. It happened that two Frenchmen, who afterwards attained great distinction, were then engaged in convoying about twenty merchantmen from Le Hâvre to Brest. These were Jean Bart, in the *Railleuse*, 24, and the Chevalier de Forbin, in the *Serpente*, 16. The *Nonsuch* encountered the convoy off the Casquets, the merchantmen fled, and, after a hot action in which Roome Coyle fell, both the *Railleuse* and the *Serpente* were taken. The *Nonsuch* having at the moment no lieutenant on board, her captain's place was taken by the boatswain, Robert Sincock, who, in consequence of the ability with which he brought the action to a conclusion, was promoted, on June 27th following, to be captain of the ship.[2] Bart and Forbin were imprisoned at Plymouth; but they soon made their escape, and were promoted upon their return to be captains[3] in the French navy.

Yet the Channel cruisers were not always so successful. On October 4th, 1689, the *Foresight*, 48, Captain Daniel Jones, *Mordaunt*, 46, Captain John Tyrrel, and *Lively Prize*, a sixth-rate, Captain William Tichborne,[4] fell in with a squadron of twelve French men-of-war to the S.W. of the Scilly Islands; and the *Lively Prize* was taken. And there were disasters elsewhere. The *Deptford*, ketch, 10, Captain Thomas Berry, was lost with nearly all hands on the coast of Virginia on August 26th; and the *Portsmouth*, Captain George St. Loe, was taken on August 9th by a superior French force.

The principal minor expedition of 1690 was one under the Joint Admirals, Haddock, Killigrew, and Ashby, with Marlborough in command of five thousand troops, against Cork. The fleet arrived off what is now Queenstown Harbour on September 21st; and, after a small Irish battery near the entrance had been silenced, the army was landed on the 23rd. On the 29th, Cork surrendered

---

[1] The orthography of this gallant officer's name is uncertain. Charnock has it as it is here given; but an official list of captains in the Auth.'s coll. has "Thomas Roomcoil"; and Prof. Laughton ('Studs. in Nav. Hist.') has "Roomecoyle." "Double-barrelled" names were certainly most unusual in England in the seventeenth century. Roome Coyle was an old officer, his captain's commission dating from 1665.

[2] Captain Sincock died in command of the *Humber* on October 12th, 1702.

[3] "Capitaines de vaisseau." They had previously been commanders (capitaines de frégate).

[4] Captain Tichborne, upon his release, was appointed to the *Crown Prize*, and was lost with her off Dartmouth on February 9th, 1692.

after a general assault, in which Captain the Duke of Grafton, of the *Grafton*, 70, who was serving ashore, received a very severe wound from a ball which broke two of his ribs. Nevertheless, upon the Joint Admirals and the main part of the fleet sailing to return to the Downs, the Duke was left in command. He died on October 9th; and the command then devolved upon Captain Matthew Tennant, of the *Breda*, 70; but the *Breda* unhappily caught fire by accident and blew up, with nearly all hands, on October 12th; and Captain John Crofts, of the *Charles*, galley, 32, became senior officer. Captain Crofts brought back the squadron to England.

Sir Clowdisley Shovell, detached with a squadron, previous to the battle of Beachy Head, to convoy King William to Ireland, cruised for a time in the Irish Sea, and assisted in the reduction of Duncannon Castle. Some of his vessels also did good service in destroying several small French ships that lay in Dublin Bay.[1] Others took the French *Fripon*, 18. On July 18th, 1690, the *St. Albans*, 50, Captain Richard Fitzpatrick (afterwards Lord Gowran), captured off Ram Head a French ship mounting thirty-six guns, after an obstinate fight of four hours. The victors lost only four killed and seven wounded, but the gallant French suffered very severely.

Commodore Laurence Wright, in the *Mary*, 62, had been ordered at the close of 1689 to proceed with a small squadron to the West Indies for the protection of the trade of the Allies, and for the general annoyance of the French.[2] He sailed from Plymouth on March 8th, 1690, with a large convoy, and, after a tempestuous voyage, reached Barbados on May 11th. He refreshed his people, among whom there had been much sickness; collected vessels and land forces under General Codrington and Sir Timothy Thornhill; and, on June 21st,[3] at one o'clock in the morning, disembarked a body of troops in Frigate Bay, St. Christopher. The island was then in possession of the French. The troops fought two smart little actions, and were about to co-operate with the squadron in an attack upon the town of Basse Terre, when the enemy set the

---

[1] This affair took place on April 17th, Captain William Wright, of the *Monmouth*, yacht, specially distinguishing himself.

[2] His instructions are given by Lediard, 644. His force consisted of one third-rate, seven fourth-rates, two fifth-rates, two fireships, and one ketch.

[3] On that day Captain Richard Kegwin, of the *Assistance*, who was serving ashore, was mortally wounded.

place on fire and fled to the hills. The reduction of the island was completed. on July 16th. On the 19th, Wright landed part of the army under Sir Timothy Thornhill on the neighbouring island of St. Eustatius, which surrendered on the 25th without the firing of a gun. On the following day the Commodore returned to St. Christopher, where it was decided to discontinue operations in consequence of the sickness existing among the troops, and the trying nature of the weather. The soldiers were, therefore, carried to Antigua and put into quarters there; and the squadron went to Barbados, where it arrived on August 13th.

By the beginning of 1690 the war had begun to affect the American Colonies; and, in consequence of the large number of French privateers that made Acadia (Nova Scotia) their headquarters, the General Court of Massachusetts fitted out an expedition against Port Royal (Annapolis). A force of about seven hundred men was embarked in small vessels and entrusted to the command of Sir William Phipps, Kt.[1] It sailed on April 28th, took Port Royal and another French settlement in the neighbourhood, and returned on May 30th. Encouraged by this success, the General Court gave Phipps charge of between thirty and forty vessels and a force of two thousand men for an expedition against Quebec. Most of the troops were landed before the town on October 18th, 1690, but they were easily repulsed. On its return to Boston the flotilla was dispersed by a gale of wind. The affair cost New England £40,000.

Upon the conclusion of the hurricane season it was determined by Commodore Wright to attempt Guadaloupe. It had been necessary to detach several vessels; and the available part of the squadron by that time consisted only of the *Mary*, 62, *Tiger*, 48, *Assistance*, 48, *Bristol*, 48, *Antelope*, 48, *Hampshire*, 46, and *St. Paul*, fireship, 10, all of which were more or less unfit for service. To these was presently added the *Jersey*, 48, which arrived in January, 1691, in charge of a convoy. Captain Wright reinforced his command by hiring such armed ships as he could; but in February misunderstandings appear to have arisen between him and General Codrington; and the expedition did not, in consequence, make a fair start until March 21st. Mariegalante, a

---

[1] Born at Pemaquid in 1650, of poor parents. Knighted for his share in the recovery of treasure from a Spanish wreck near the Bahamas in 1687. Governor of Massachusetts, 1691. Died in London about 1695.

French island near Guadaloupe, was taken without difficulty on the 28th; and a landing was effected at Guadaloupe itself on April 21st. The army met with stubborn opposition; and on May 14th, while it was still ashore, the Commodore received news that a French squadron under M. Ducasse was in the neighbourhood. He put to sea in search of it, sighted it, and chased it, but in vain; and, when he returned, it was determined to abandon the effort to reduce the island. A little later, Codrington and most of the troops went, under convoy of the *Antelope* and *Jersey*, to Antigua; and the rest of the squadron made for Barbados. Upon reaching Carlisle Bay, Wright was so ill that he gave up his command and sailed for England.[1] After his return Commodore Ralph Wrenn went out to take his place; but, as Wrenn did not leave Plymouth until December 26th, 1691, he of course did nothing in the West Indies until the following year.[2]

Nearer home numerous small actions were fought in the course of 1691. On January 2nd, Captain John Layton, of the *Montagu* 60, was killed near Ushant in a petty encounter with a French twenty-four-gun privateer, which, after losing between forty and fifty men, was taken and carried into Plymouth. In February, Captain Richard Fitzpatrick (later Lord Gowran), cruising in the *St. Albans*, 50, in company with the *Happy Return*, 54, Captain Thomas Monk, and some privateers, drove ashore two small French " frigates," and captured fourteen out of a fleet of twenty-two French merchantmen off Cape Barfleur, besides driving ashore their convoy, a ship of thirty guns. Later in the year, the *Happy Return* was transferred to the command of Captain Peter Pickard; and, on November 4th, she was unfortunately captured by some privateers off Dunquerque. The *Talbot*, ketch, Captain Charles Staggins, who was mortally wounded, experienced a similar misfortune on July 12th.

Upon the whole, it was not a very satisfactory year for England.

---

[1] Captain Wright was much blamed for having relinquished the attempt upon Guadaloupe, and was never again employed afloat. He served, however, for many years as a Commissioner of the Navy.

[2] The *Jersey*, 48, Captain John Bomstead, while still in the West Indies, was taken by the French on December 18th, 1691, off Dominica. The *Mary Rose*, 48, had been taken on the same station on July 12th, her captain, John Bounty, falling in the action; and the *Constant Warwick*, 42, Captain James Moody, had been captured with her. These were all made prize of by the squadron of the Comte de La Roche-Courbon-Blenac.

Du Guay Trouin, then, though barely eighteen, master of the privateer *Danycan*, 14, landed in Clare, pillaged several huts, burnt a couple of vessels, and got away untouched, in spite of the efforts made by some troops detached from before Limerick.

Yet there were compensations. A little squadron under Captain Thomas Coall, of the *Tiger*, 48, did good service off the coast of Ireland, and contributed to the reduction of ʻLimerick. Another squadron, detached, under Sir Clowdisley Shovell, from the main fleet, hoisted French colours and so got very close in to Brest, where it managed to take or destroy several ships of a convoy. Two or three cruisers under Captain Simon Foulks of the *Montagu*, 60, picked up nine large privateers, besides several small craft, off the Irish coast. Captain James Buck, of the *Charles*, galley, 32, and Captain James Wishart,[1] of the *Mary*, galley, 32, while convoying some vessels to Elsinore in July, fought four French privateers, and retook from them a prize called the *Tiger*, 34, and a smaller craft. And in November, the *Deptford*, 50, Captain William Kerr, in company with another vessel, captured a privateer mounting twenty-two guns.

The proceedings of Commodore Wrenn in the West Indies may now be reverted to. Wrenn sailed from England in the *Norwich*, 48, with the *Diamond*, 48, Captain Richard Cotten,[2] and the *Mordaunt*, 46, Captain Henry Boteler, having on board one hundred and fifty soldiers, and convoying the trade, victuallers, and transports with further land forces. Reaching Barbados on January 16th, 1692, he there found, and assumed command of, the *Mary*, 62, *Antelope*, 48, *Assistance*, 48, *Hampshire*, 46, and *St. Paul*, fireship, 10. He received intelligence that a much larger French fleet than he had previously suspected was in the West Indies; and, anxious for the safety of Jamaica, he detached thither the *Assistance*, *Hampshire*, and *St. Paul*. To strengthen his own small force, he hired a couple of stout merchantmen; and then, learning that a squadron of eight French vessels was cruising of Barbados, and that ten other French ships had been detached elsewhere, he put to sea on January 30th, with the intention of attacking the enemy's

---

[1] James Wishart. Commander, 1689. Captain, 1691. Commanded the *Eagle* at Cadiz and Vigo, 1702. Rooke's Captain of the Fleet at Gibraltar and Malaga, 1704. Rear-Admiral and Knight, 1703. A Lord of the Admiralty, 1710. Admiral, 1713. Died, 1728.

[2] Captain Cotten, who appears to have died on January 28th, 1692, was succeeded by Captain Clinton (or Christopher) Maund, on January 29th.

smaller division ere it should be rejoined by the larger one. He sought in vain for the foe until February 5th, when he returned to Carlisle Bay. The French, it was concluded, had gone elsewhere. Wrenn, therefore, sailed again on February 17th, taking under his convoy such vessels as needed his protection ; and steered for Jamaica, where he purposed to pick up his detached ships, so that, with his whole command, he might meet the enemy's superior force under the most favourable conditions that were possible.

But, ere the Commodore could reach Jamaica, he fell in, on February 21st, off the island of Désirade, with the entire squadron of De La Roche-Courbon-Blenac, consisting of eighteen men-of-war, mounting from forty to sixty guns apiece, two fireships, and five or six small craft. Wrenn's little force was thus made up :—

Ships.	Guns.	Commanders.
Norwich	48	Ralph Wrenn.
Mary	62	Lieut. Richard Wyatt (actg.).[1]
Mordaunt	46	Henry Boteler.
Diamond	48	Clinton Maund.
Antelope	48	Henry Wickham.
2 armed merchantmen.[2]		

[1] Captain Robert Arthur, of the *Mary*, appears to have died on February 17th, 1692, or to have been left ashore on that day at Barbados in a dying state.
[2] One of these was named the *England Frigate*.

Wrenn had to bear away to leeward to range his ships in order of battle, with the convoy to leeward of them. The French were within gunshot all night, but did not attack. On the morning of the 22nd, the enemy having a fresh gale but some of the English vessels being almost becalmed, the French bore down and engaged at 8 A.M. The *Mary* was much pressed by four opponents, but was ultimately relieved by the *Norwich*. The *Mordaunt* and *England Frigate* (Stubbs, master) were also at one time completely surrounded, but fought their way clear. The action continued for four hours, and then ended gradually, as the Commodore began his withdrawal in good order to the southward. He lost no ship ; and, although he was obliged to return to Barbados instead of prosecuting his voyage to Jamaica, he had every cause to congratulate himself upon the manner in which he had behaved in the face of an enemy of thrice his force. He reached Carlisle Bay on February

25th, but, unhappily, died on March 26th following. Part of the squadron, under Captain Boteler, who transferred his pennant to the *Mary*, sailed for England in June.

Of the vessels which remained on the station, the *Norwich*, 48, then commanded by Captain Richard Pugh, was lost with all hands on October 6th, 1692 ; and the *Mordaunt*, then commanded by Captain Francis Maynard, was lost with all hands on November 21st, 1693 ; while the *Diamond*, 48, then commanded by Captain Henry Wickham, was captured by the French on September 20th, 1693. The circumstances of the *Diamond's* loss being such as were not creditable, Wickham was sentenced by court-martial to imprisonment for life. He was released after the accession of Queen Anne, but was never reinstated.

Nearer home, the year 1692 was full of exciting incident. On April 12th a superior French force drove ashore, on the coast of Spain, the *Phœnix*, 42, Captain Jacob Banks. The ship was burnt, to save her from capture.[1] On June 9th, the *Hart*, ketch, Captain David Condon, who fell in the engagement, was taken by the enemy, after having made a gallant resistance.

A few days before this the redoutable Du Guay Trouin, in the *Coëtquen*, 18, accompanied by the *St. Aaron*, 18, Jacques Welch, had put to sea from St. Malo, and had fallen in, almost immediately, with an English convoy, of which he had taken five sail, besides the two small men-of-war or armed ships that formed the escort. The *Hart* seems to have been one of these. Returning, the privateers were chased by an English squadron ; but they escaped into port. The *Coëtquen* put to sea again, and was driven into the Bristol Channel, where she anchored under the lee of Lundy Island. An English sixty-gun ship presently made for the same shelter, but Du Guay Trouin cut his cable, and again got away, owing to good seamanship and superior speed. Before he returned to St. Malo he took a couple of English sugar ships. Captain Robert Partridge of the *Griffin*, fireship, is said to have been killed while fighting his vessel on July 9th ; but particulars of the engagement have not been discovered.

Yet there were successes as well as misfortunes. In July, the *Centurion*, 48, Captain Francis Wyvill, discovered in the Channel three French privateers, of which one only, a vessel of twenty-eight guns, awaited the attack. A very heavy sea was running ; and the

[1] Min. of C. M., July 9th, 1692.

Frenchman was not taken until she had fought for three hours, and had lost, in killed and wounded, sixty out of her two hundred officers and men. Two months later Captain Wyvill was succeeded in the command by Captain John Bridges (2),[1] who, cruising on the East Coast of Scotland, captured three out of six privateers which he fell in with, and carried them into Orkney. In the latter part of this engagement the *Centurion* was assisted by the *Kingfisher*, 46, which had been attracted by the sound of firing.

In October, 1692, the *Deptford*, 50, Captain William Kerr, being in the Channel, took the *Fortune*, 24, a privateer out of Nantes ; and, in November, being in company with the *Portsmouth*, 32, Captain Charles Britiffe, he took the *Hyacinthe*, another craft of the same character. In October also, the *Rupert*, 66, Captain Basil Beaumont, and the *Adventure*, 44, Captain Thomas Dilkes, while cruising together on the Irish station, fought and took two privateers, one mounting twenty-four, and the other eighteen guns, together with their two prizes, and with two merchantmen which were in their company. In the following December, Captain Beaumont, who was then alone, took a very large privateer of thirty-two guns, after a six hours' action ; and Captain Dilkes, in the mouth of the Channel, took two sixteen-gun privateers. It must be admitted, however, that these captures, though extremely useful, reflected but little glory upon the victors. In every case there was a great superiority of force on the English side.

Wrenn had behaved himself admirably, and, if he had failed, he had failed only in consequence of the weakness of the weapons at his command.   Towards the end of 1692 it was determined to place a larger force on the West India Station, and to entrust the command of it to Sir Francis Wheler.[2] On January 9th, 1693, he sailed from Cowes Road with the following force. (See next page.)

Already in the West Indies were the *Diamond*, 48, and *Mordaunt*, 46, the ultimate fate of which has been noted above; together with the *Guernsey*, 28, Captain Edward Oakley, and the

---

[1] There were at that time in the Navy two captains named John Bridges. The senior, a captain of 1679, served after the Revolution in the *Northumberland, Essex*, and *Vanguard* successively, and died on May 24th, 1694. The junior, a captain of 1691, commanded in succession the *Portsmouth, Centurion, Assurance*, and *Deptford*, and seems to have died on May 29th, 1695.

[2] Francis Wheler. Captain, 1680. Knighted, 1689. Commanded the *Albemarle* at Beachy Head. Rear-Admiral, 1693, and Commander-in-Chief in the Mediterranean. Perished off Gibraltar in his flag-ship, the *Sussex*, February 19th, 1694.

Ships.	Guns.	Commanders.	Ships.	Guns.	Commanders.
Resolution [1] .	60		*Mermaid* .	32	William Harman.
Dunkirk . .	52	James Ward.	*Pembroke* .	32	George Warren.
Ruby . .	42	Robert Deane.	*London Mer-*		William Orton.
Tiger . .	42	Thomas Sherman.	*chant*, h.s. }	..	
Advice . .	42	Charles Hawkins.	*Canterbury*, }		Robert Leonard.
Chester . .	42	Thomas Heath.	storeship }	..	
Dragon . .	40	William Vickars.	*Quaker*, ketch	10	John Anderson.
Falcon . .	36	Nathaniel Browne.	1 bomb		
Experiment .	32	James Greenaway.	3 fireships		

1 Sir Francis Wheler was captain of the *Resolution* until February 5th, 1693, previous to which he seems to have had only local rank as a rear admiral. Yet, when out of the Soundings, he wore the Union at the main. His rank as Rear-Admiral of the Blue seems to have dated from February 5th, 1693, but he did not receive the commission until he returned to England in October.

Henry Prize, 24, Captain Richard Finch ; so that upon reaching Barbados, whither he arrived on March 1st, 1693, Sir Francis found a very respectable force under his orders.

The Rear-Admiral determined to attack Martinique; and sent word of his arrival and intentions to General Codrington, Governor of the Leeward Islands, whom he begged to co-operate. With the squadron were the regular regiments of Foulks and Godwin. To these were added local forces, collected from Barbados and neighbouring islands. Having made his preparations, Sir Francis sailed on March 30th, and on April 1st, 1693, anchored in the harbour of Cul-de-Sac Marin. The Rear-Admiral and the military chiefs at once reconnoitred the coast. It was decided to endeavour to effect a landing near Fort St. Pierre, but, pending the arrival of General Codrington, to do no more than harass the enemy. In pursuance of this resolution, all the houses and plantations about Cul-de-Sac Marin and Grande Anse du Diamant were ravaged or destroyed. On the 9th, General Codrington, with his troops, joined the squadron, which sailed on the 12th, and on the 15th appeared before St. Pierre. Unhappily the naval and military leaders failed, as on many previous and subsequent occasions, to act together satisfactorily. Sir Francis, who was supported by Lieutenant-Colonel Colt, was for active measures : Codrington, urging the unhealthiness of the forces, the superiority of the French, the number of disaffected Irish with the expedition, and the rawness of many of the troops, was for withdrawing. This was also the general view; and so, after men and guns had been put ashore, and even after some small successes had been won, the attempt upon Martinique was abandoned.

The expedition proceeded to Dominica, where the ships were

watered and the men refreshed.   At a council of war held there, a proposal to attack Guadaloupe was negatived, and it was ultimately determined to send all the local forces back to their homes.   Sir Francis, who had peremptory orders not to remain in the West Indies after the end of May, went to St. Christopher, where he parted with Codrington, and whence he sailed with that part of the squadron which he had brought from England, for Boston.   This abortive expedition had by that time cost the country the death of upwards of a thousand officers and men by disease, while not more than a hundred and twenty had fallen by the hands of the enemy.

At Boston, Sir Francis discussed with Sir William Phipps, the Governor of Massachusetts, the propriety of an attack upon Quebec ; but it was deemed inadvisable to undertake it, and on August 3rd the squadron quitted Boston.

There is little doubt that Wheler was a good and energetic officer, and that, had he not been hampered by his instructions, and by the opinions of his military colleagues, he would have effected something of importance.   In spite of all his disappointments he still hoped to make himself useful ere his return home ; and he therefore proceeded to Newfoundland with the intention of seizing Placentia. But again the land officers objected.   The French settlement on the Island of St. Pierre was destroyed.   No more, however, was either done or attempted ; and, after taking in wood and water on the east side of Newfoundland, the squadron sailed on September 22nd, reaching Portsmouth on October 18th.

The only other detached squadron that was actively employed during 1693 was one which, towards the end of the year, was selected from the main fleet and entrusted to Captain John Benbow,[1] for the purpose of bombarding St. Malo.   It consisted mainly of vessels of the fourth-rate and below it, and of bombs.   Having made rendezvous at Guernsey, the force appeared before the town on the afternoon of November 16th.   That night the place was bombarded for six hours.   On the 17th and 18th, more bombs were thrown into the town ; and on the evening of the 19th a specially prepared fireship was sent in close under the town wall and there exploded. A considerable amount of damage was done, many houses were

---

[1] Benbow's position in this squadron was anomalous.   He seems, during most of the operations, to have been on board the *Norwich*, 48, Captain Josias Crow, and not to have been himself captain of any vessel.

destroyed, some of the works were razed, a few prisoners were taken ; and on November 22nd the squadron returned to Guernsey.

The year witnessed numerous minor actions. On January 12th, the *Scarborough*, ketch, Captain Thomas Taylor, was captured on the Irish station by the *St. Antoine*, 26, and *Mariana*, 16, two privateers out of Nantes. On the 27th of the same month the privateers and their prize fell in with the *York*, 60, Captain George Mees, and the *Dover*, 48, Captain Edward Whitaker, and were all taken.[1] Whitaker had just previously taken another privateer, the *Lion Eveillé*, 14 ; and Mees, in April, took yet another, the *Prince of Wales*, 14, which had been newly commissioned on behalf of the ex-King James. In June, the *Dover*, 48, then commanded by Captain William Cross, but still cruising on the Irish station, took a thirty-two-gun privateer. On June 17th, the *Sun Prize*, a sixth-rate doing fishery protection duty in the North Sea was taken ; and her captain, Francis Manly, who made a brave defence, was mortally wounded. In July, the *Dolphin*, 26, Captain Thomas Kercher, being off the West Coast of Ireland to intercept supplies from Nantes, most gallantly retook a prize from a French twenty-four-gun privateer. In the autumn, the *Monck*, 52, Captain Stafford Fairborne, and the *Chatham*, 44, Captain John Leader, while returning to Ireland from Madeira, after the unfortunate affair of the Smyrna fleet, made themselves masters of two French merchantmen, each mounting thirty guns, homeward bound with rich cargoes from the West Indies, and having also some troops on board. But there were no actions of striking brilliancy ; and the latter part of the year saw two misfortunes, both of which might apparently have been avoided. On September 20th, the *Cygnet*, fireship, 6, Captain John Perry,[2] was taken in the West Indies in circumstances which were so discreditable that Perry, upon his release, was court-martialled and dismissed the service. And on December 9th, the *St. Albans*, 50, Captain Thomas Gillam, was driven by a storm from her anchorage in Kingsale Harbour, and wrecked on a rock in Sandy Cove. Captain Gillam was on shore when the gale became serious. He endeavoured to reach his imperilled ship in his pinnace, taking with him Captain John Hales, of the *Virgin Prize*, which also lay in the road ; but the boat was staved in against the bows of the *St. Albans*, and both captains

---

[1] The *Mariana* was added to the Navy as the *Mariana Prize*.

[2] Perry afterwards distinguished himself as a hydraulic engineer, and recovered from the Thames a large tract of land in Essex. He lived until 1733.

perished. The major part of the crew of the *St. Albans* happily escaped. In addition to these disasters, there were the several losses already noted as having taken place in the West Indies.[1]

It has been mentioned in the previous chapter that, on the eve of his departure for the Mediterranean, in 1694, Admiral Russell detached Captain Peter Pickard against a large French convoy which was known to be lying in or about Bertheaume Bay. The detached force consisted only of the *Monmouth*, 66, Captain Pickard, *Resolution*, 70, Captain John Baker, and *Roebuck*, fireship, 6, Captain Robert Kirton. The little squadron made the French coast on the morning of May 10th, and soon afterwards discovered a number of ships in Blanc Sablon Bay (the White Sands Bay of old English charts). The enemy at once endeavoured to slip and get under sail. Pickard, therefore, manned and armed his boats in order to deal with the convoy, and himself chased the French man-of-war which had charge of the merchant vessels. The man-of-war, which proved to be the *Jersey*,[2] was forced ashore, and there burnt by her people. In the meantime, the English boats wrought great havoc, carrying or driving ashore about twenty-five vessels in Blanc Sablon Bay, the men-of-war cutting off all escape to seaward. Other vessels in and about Conquêt Bay were similarly dealt with. The squadron then stood into Bertheaume Bay, and took a large merchantman under a heavy fire from the fort there. By 4 P.M. little remained to be captured or destroyed, and as night was coming on, and the weather looked threatening, Captain Pickard withdrew.[3]

The operations of 1694 included a number of attacks on French ports. These attacks were, for the most part, similar in character to

---

[1] The gallant action of an English merchantman should not pass altogether unnoticed here. The *Hannibal*, of London, 36, of 450 tons, Thomas Philips, master, fell in, off Orotava, on November 23rd, 1693, with the *Louis*, of St. Malo, 52, De Gras, master, and fought her for six hours at close quarters, until the Frenchman, having lost his foretopmast, towed away out of action. The *Hannibal*, though too damaged in her rigging to chase, had lost but five men killed and thirty-two wounded. The *Louis*, from the report of an English prisoner who was on board at the time, had lost sixty-three killed and about seventy wounded, out of a complement of two hundred and eighty.

[2] She had been taken in the West Indies on December 18th, 1691. *See* p. 465, *note.*

[3] Two French sloops of war were fired by the explosion of the *Jersey*, which blew up early in the afternoon. Of about fifty-five vessels in the neighbourhood of Conquêt, Captain Pickard destroyed or took upwards of forty, including a large ship laden with ordnance stores.

the attack made upon St. Malo, by Benbow, in 1693. They had little influence upon the course of the war, and, in all probability, they were more disastrous to non-combatants than to combatants. Nor, perhaps, can they be justified, save upon the plea that the French themselves, by their action at Genoa, had already set the example of bombarding coast towns without any other object than the mere annoyance of the enemy.

These attacks were entrusted to a large squadron, which, under the command of Admiral John Lord Berkeley of Stratton (B.),[1] had parted company from the main fleet ere the latter had sailed for the Mediterranean. The first attempt of the series was also the most ambitious. It was directed against Brest, which it was intended not only to bombard, but also, if possible, to seize; and, with this end in view, a strong body of troops, under Lieutenant-General Tollemache, was embarked on board the squadron, which consisted of thirty-six ships of the line, English and Dutch,[2] five frigates, thirteen fireships, and about a dozen small craft of various descriptions, besides transports. It should be said at once that this particular attempt failed mainly in consequence of the treachery of certain highly-placed individuals in England, and that the French, having been elaborately warned of what was intended, were only too well prepared for what occurred. Chief among the traitors was Marlborough, upon whose head lies most of the blood that was uselessly shed on the occasion. His sole motive seems to have been the selfish desire to keep upon good terms with James, so that, in the event of the restoration of the latter, John Churchill might not suffer in place or pocket.

On June 6th, the squadron made Ushant, and, on the 7th, stood into the mouth of Camaret Bay, the French firing at it from five separate batteries. In the early morning of the 8th, there was a thick fog, but, as soon as it cleared, the French fire recommenced, doing, however, no damage. That day a division of nine[3] men-of-war, under the Marquis of Carmarthen,[4] in the *Monck*, was sent in to

---

[1] With his flag in the *Queen*, 100.

[2] The Dutch were under Lieut.-Admiral van Almonde.

[3] The English official account mentions only seven, but the Dutch account adds the *Damiaten*; and, upon the evidence, it appears that eight in all were employed.

[4] He seems to have had an anomalous and purely temporary appointment as a flag-officer; for in 1700–1702 he commanded the *Peregrine*, galley, as a private captain; and only after that was he made a rear-admiral, etc., in the regular course. He was a captain of January 2nd, 1691. Thomas Warren, captain of the *Monck*, was a captain of May 28th, 1689, and was therefore senior to the Marquis.

the head of Camaret Bay, so that later, under cover of its fire, a landing force might be disembarked there. This division was thus composed :—

Ships.	Guns.	Commanders.	Ships.	Guns.	Commanders.
Monck . .	60	Thomas Warren.	*Shoreham* .	32	John Constable.
Greenwich[1] .	54	Frederick Weighman.	*Drakesteijn* .	44	{Jan Erasmus Reining.
Charles, galley	32	Edward Chant.			
Damiaten .	50	— Steijn.	*Wesp* . . .	32	— Watercamp.
			Wolf . . .	36	{Leijden van Leeuwen.

[1] There is some doubt whether she actually entered the Bay.

At 7 A.M. on the 8th, the troops were put into boats and small craft, while the covering squadron, advancing, began to cannonade a fort

THE COAST NEAR BREST.

and two open and two masked batteries on shore. About noon, the boats, with Tollemache on board, also advanced, and under a very terrible fire a few hundred men were landed. But they were soon obliged to retire in much confusion ; and, as there was a difficulty, owing to its being low tide, in getting the boats off again, great loss of life resulted. Of all who had set foot ashore, only about a hundred returned to the squadron. The rest[1] were either killed or

[1] Probably about five hundred in number.

taken. Tollemache himself was wounded in the thigh, and died
subsequently at Plymouth. The defence was conducted by the
celebrated Vauban. In the covering division, upwards of a hundred
people were killed and wounded. All the ships, however, succeeded in withdrawing except the *Wesp*, which ran aground, and
which, having lost her captain, her lieutenant, and many of her
men, and having five feet of water in her hold, was forced to
surrender. The unfortunate action lasted for a little more than
three hours.[1]

A council of war decided that any further attempt upon Brest
was out of the question. The squadron, therefore, proceeded to
St. Helens, the troops were landed, and such ships as had suffered
from the fire of the enemy were refitted. At St. Helens, it was
further decided, after orders had been received from the Queen, to
bombard Dieppe, and to do what other damage might be possible
along the coast of France. The squadron sailed again, made prize
in the Channel of a number of neutrals bound to France with corn
and naval stores, and would have proceeded, but was driven back by
foul weather. On July 5th, however, it finally quitted the English
coast, and on the morning of the 9th, arrived off Dieppe. There,
more bad weather was encountered, and the bombardment was not
begun until the 12th. In the course of that day and the following
night, about eleven hundred bombs and carcasses were thrown into
the place, which was set on fire in several spots. The French fired
about fifteen hundred shot and shell in return, but did little damage,
and killed and wounded only four or five people. On the night of
the 12th, the *Nicholas*, machine,[2] was sent in, and exploded against

---

[1] The English official account is in ' Biog. Nav.' ii. 123. *See also* Disps. of
Lt.-Adm. van Almonde and V.-Adm. C. van de Putte in the Rijks Archief; and *Europ.
Mercur.*, June, 1694, 286–297.

[2] The "machine" was a modification of an invention which had been utilised by
Giambelli in 1585 in the Schelde. The modification was introduced in 1693 by
Willem Meesters, a Dutch engineer, and was first employed against St. Malo. Soon
afterwards numerous "machines" were prepared for the English Navy. They may be
best described as fireships specially arranged so as to explode very destructively. They
were not very efficacious and were soon disused; yet at first, so much was thought of
them that, in 1694–1695, no fewer than about thirty vessels of the kind were built or
fitted. The *Nicholas*, above-mentioned, was the first of these to be commissioned,
Captain Dunbar assuming command of her on April 30th, 1694. No new type of
fighting weapon had a shorter vogue; for the last of the machines, the *Mayflower*, No. 2,
was paid off by Captain John Kendall on September 17th, 1695, by which date the
invention was completely and for ever discredited. The machines were also called
" infernals."

the pier-head, but, not being close enough, did no great harm. Her captain, however, Robert Dunbar, did his best, and behaved with great intrepidity, returning on board, after the fuse had gone out, in order to relight it. When the squadron departed, on the afternoon of the 14th, few houses that remained standing in the town had escaped the flames.

Le Hâvre was similarly bombarded on the 16th, Captain John Benbow being entrusted with the conduct of the bomb-vessels and machines. The town burnt that night and all the following day ; and on the 18th, when the flames showed signs of diminishing, more bombs were thrown in. Less damage, however, was done than at Dieppe ; and on the 19th, the weather being bad and the bomb-vessels being nearly all much shaken, or put altogether out of action, the squadron returned to St. Helens. One bomb-vessel, the *Granado*, Captain Thomas Willshaw, was on this occasion blown to pieces by a shell that fell into her from a battery on shore. Most of her people, however, were saved. On the way home, Berkeley alarmed La Hougue and Cherbourg.

After the three-decked ships of the squadron had been laid up for the winter, and Lord Berkeley had hauled down his flag for that year, the ships remaining in commission were left under the command of Sir Clowdisley Shovell, who was empowered, in conjunction with Captain Benbow and Mr. Meesters, to make an attack upon Dunquerque. There was much delay, owing to the dilatoriness of Meesters ; and the squadron, consisting of thirteen English and six Dutch men-of-war, two bomb-vessels, seventeen machines, and various small craft, did not arrive off Dunquerque until September 11th. Dutch pilots had been engaged, but they proved ignorant, cowardly, and insubordinate ; and Benbow had himself to sound the channels and passes ere anything could be attempted. The French, in the meantime, displayed much uneasiness ; and not only the forts but also a twenty-gun ship that lay in the road, fired smartly on the boats that were sounding before the town. On the 12th the *Charles*, galley, the two bomb-vessels, and several small craft were sent in to annoy the place, and, in the afternoon, two machines, the *William and Mary*, Captain Thomas Robinson, and the *Abram's Offering*, Captain Edward Cole, were dispatched against the piers. One of them was fired—probably by the French guns—while she was still much too far off to do any damage ; and, as she could not be moved, she was suffered to burn herself out and explode innocuously. The other nearly reached the mole-head, but at the last moment was drawn away by the tide, and exploded at a cable's length from her goal, so that she also did no harm. Whether, indeed, she could have actually got alongside the pier is doubtful, for the French, always in those days well informed of English preparations and intentions, are said to have driven in piles and sunk old vessels so as to prevent any close approach.

From Dunquerque, part of the squadron, with Meesters and his machines, went to Calais, arriving off that town on September 16th. The weather was bad, yet the place was bombarded on the 17th, and some houses were destroyed, until, the gale increasing, Sir Clowdisley drew off his whole force to the Downs, and thence sent his machines and small craft into the Thames.

Such other actions as were fought near home in 1694 may be briefly summarised, one or two only of them meriting more than the shortest chronicle.

Early in January the *Sheerness*, 32, Captain James Lance, on the Irish station, discovered off the Kenmare River two French privateers, one of thirty-two and the other of twenty-four guns. They had just made prizes of two merchantmen, one of which was a very valuable vessel, from Barbados. Captain Lance engaged the privateers for five hours, but, when night came on, was unable to prevent them from escaping. During the action the prizes separated from their captors, the result being that they were soon afterwards retaken by other cruisers.

On the 14th of the same month Robert Stapylton, master of a small trader carrying eight guns and twenty men, and named the *Conquest*, was attacked off the mouth of the Tagus, while on his voyage home from Seville, by a French ship of war mounting twenty-six guns, and having on board one hundred and eighty men. Most merchant skippers in like circumstances would have surrendered at once. Not so Stapylton. Having some spare ports, he transferred three of his guns, so as to present on one side a broadside of seven ; and most pluckily he fought his big antagonist from 1 P.M. to 7 P.M., when he had but four cartridges left, and eight of his people killed. Firing a last broadside, he accidentally set his own ship on fire. The *Conquest* fell on board the Frenchman ; and in the confusion Stapylton and his surviving crew slipped into a boat and got away in safety to Lisbon. For this piece of bravery

Stapylton was, on 26th September, 1694, made commander of
H.M.S. *Drake*, 16.[1]

On February 24th, the *Centurion*, 48, Captain John Price, in
the North Sea, fought a stubborn action with four Dunquerque
privateers, of which he took the largest one. As the privateers,
together, disposed of fully six hundred men, while Price had only
two hundred and thirty, the merit of the exploit needs no dwelling
upon. In April, on the Irish station, the *Ruby*, 48, Captain
Robert Fairfax, behaved with scarcely less credit, capturing, after
a hot action, the Brest privateer *Entreprenant*, 46. In May,
the *Foresight*, 48, Captain Isaac Townsend, accompanied by an
armed ship and four privateers, took or destroyed in the Channel
ten or eleven vessels laden with corn, in spite of the fact that they
were under the escort of seven French men-of-war, one of which
mounted forty guns.

At that time Du Guay Trouin, in the *Diligente*,[2] 36, was
cruising in the chops of the Channel. On May 3rd he was
chased by the hired man-of-war *Prince of Orange*, 50, Captain
Samuel Vincent. Although Trouin had hoisted English colours he
did not scruple, while they were still flying, to fire at Vincent.
The *Diligente* got away easily, but on May 12th fell in with a
squadron of six English ships,[3] and, being driven among the Scilly
Islands, and a good deal mauled, was taken. Trouin, charged by
Captain Vincent with the offence of, while flying English colours,
firing on an English ship, was put under close arrest at Plymouth;
but escaped with four companions and made his way in a small
boat to the coast of Brittany.[4]

When the *Dunkirk*, 60, Captain Thomas Dilkes, put to sea
again, she cruised in the Channel with the *Weymouth*, 48, Captain
William Jumper; and, on June 17th, the two ships took the
Invincible, 54, after an action which lasted from 2 A.M. to 8 P.M.,
and the brunt of which was borne by the *Weymouth*. Captain
Jumper, one of the first cruiser captains of his day, cruised alone
during most of the rest of the year. On June 31st, after a long

---

[1] She went to the Irish station, and was unfortunately lost with all hands on
December 20th, 1694.

[2] A king's ship, fitted out on terms of partnership by a mercantile house.

[3] *Monck*, 60, Captain Thomas Warren; *Mary*, 62, Captain John Jennings;
Dunkirk, 60, Captain Thomas Dilkes; *Ruby*, 48, Captain Robert Fairfax; *Dragon*, 46,
Captain William Vickars; and *Adventure*, 44, Captain Charles Cornwall.

[4] 'Studs. in Nav. Hist.' 295–300.

chase, he took a 24-gun privateer; on August 31st he took a
privateer of twenty-eight guns, which did not surrender until she had
lost fifty-five killed and wounded; and on September 23rd, although
he had carried away his foretop-gallant-mast and foretop-mast in the
preliminary chase, and had thus crippled himself, he so roughly
treated the St. Malo privateer, *Comte de Toulouse*, 44, that she was
thankful to be able to put herself beyond his reach.

The capture, in June, by the *Montagu*, 60, Captain William
Kiggens, of a large 28-gun ship, laden with corn, was useful rather
than brilliant. Such captures were not, however, always easy. On
June 11th, Captain John Clements (2),[1] of the *Portsmouth*, 32, was
killed while capturing a 36-gun merchantman bound with a rich
cargo from St. Malo to Marseilles, although, as the *Canterbury*, 60,
was also in company, resistance was practically useless. Yet resistance, even in the face of great odds, was no unusual thing on either
side. On July 18th, the *Scarborough*, 32, a cruiser in the Irish
Channel, defended herself most gallantly against two privateers, one
of forty and the other of twenty-six guns, and did not surrender
until she had lost her captain, Thomas Killingworth, and thirty men
killed, besides many wounded.

On July 23rd, the *Soldadoes Prize*, 32, Captain William Allin,
cruising off La Hougue in company with the *Hind*, pink, sighted
a French 26-gun ship, with three privateers and two merchant
ships, which took refuge in a bay. One of the merchantmen got
away, and was subsequently taken by Guernsey privateers. Allin
engaged the rest for six or seven hours; and at the end of that
time they were all aground and deserted by their crews. On the
24th, in spite of a heavy fire from the shore, he burnt the remaining
merchantmen; but the other vessels, having been got off again
and remanned, escaped by superior sailing. In September, Captain
James Lance, then of the *Reserve*, 48, in company with the *Foresight*, 48, took, at the mouth of the Channel, a 28-gun privateer,
hailing from St. Malo. In October, the *Anglesey*, 48, Captain
William Prower, took the privateer *St. Louis*, 38, after an hour's
action; and in the course of the same month the hired man-of-war
Africa, 46, Captain John Knapp, bound with a convoy to New

---

[1] Son of Captain John Clements (1), a captain of 1667, whose last ship was the
St. Andrew, which he quitted on December 3rd, 1693, and who had fought at Beachy
Head. John Clements (2), was a captain of 1693, and had never commanded any ship
save the *Portsmouth*.

England, sustained a very brilliant engagement for three hours with three large French privateers, one of fifty, one of thirty, and one of twenty-four guns, all of which finally sheered off.

Two small actions were fought in 1694 in the West Indies. In April, the *Chester*, 42, Captain William Julius, while cruising off Dominica, drove ashore a French 18-gun privateer, which, taking fire, blew up. In September, the *Advice*, 42, Captain William Harman, with the *Hampshire*, 46, and *Experiment*, 32, was dispatched by the Governor of Jamaica to annoy the coast of Hispaniola (now San Domingo). In a desultory attack upon the town of Léogane, Harman was mortally wounded. He died on October 6th, 1694.

In 1695 the attacks upon French Channel ports were resumed by divisions of the fleet commanded by Admiral Lord Berkeley, who, in the summer, hoisted his flag in the *Shrewsbury*, 80. A Dutch contingent, under Lieutenant-Admiral van Almonde, joined at Spithead on June 16th; and on the 29th the whole force sailed for France.

St. Malo[1] was the first place attempted. The fleet anchored before it on July 4th, and the small craft went in and bombarded the town and batteries on that day and the following. By nightfall on the 5th, the bomb vessels having expended all their ammunition, were withdrawn. The damage done does not appear to have been very serious. On the other hand, the attack cost the squadron a loss of about sixty officers and men killed and wounded; and the *Dreadful*, bomb, Captain John Carleton, was so badly mauled by the enemy's shot that it was deemed advisable to burn her rather than endeavour to carry her off. The *Carcase* and *Thunder*, bombs, were also much knocked about; nor did the covering division escape unscathed. Captain Benbow,[2] who on this as on other similar occasions commanded the in-shore force, was ordered on the 6th to attack Granville, and proceeded thither with five English and three Dutch bombs, besides a few larger craft. He anchored before the town on the morning of the 8th, and bombarded the place all

---

[1] The anxiety of the Allies to harm St. Malo is easily explicable. Between 1688 and 1697 privateers sailing from that port are said by French historians to have taken 3384 English and Dutch merchantmen, besides 162 men-of-war escorting them. Guérin, iv. 42.

[2] Benbow had reconnoitred St. Malo in the previous April; and, in the course of a cruise on the French coast, had taken, driven ashore, or destroyed a number of vessels. He had also seized and dismantled one or two small forts.

that day, leaving it in flames. Granville possessed few, if any, regular defences, but returned the fire of the ships from three guns and two mortars in improvised batteries, doing, however, no harm. On the 9th the detached command rejoined Lord Berkeley off Guernsey.

Lord Berkeley cruised along the French coast to the north-eastward, and on August 1st attacked Dunquerque. The French there were well prepared; and, although the bomb-vessels fired with some small effect and sank three of the enemy's galleys, the machines were unable to approach the works closely enough to make themselves dangerous. The *Gazette*[1] makes no mention of any of these craft having been expended; but other sources of information make it clear that no fewer than four of them were employed without avail. These were the *Ephraim*, Captain John Carleton, the *William and Elizabeth*, Captain William Carleton, the *Mayflower*, No. 1, Captain John Dixon, and the *Happy Return*, Captain Robert Isaac. Moreover, the Dutch ship, *Batavier*, 26, Captain Tuijll van Serooskerke, grounded under the batteries and was burnt by the French, her captain being taken prisoner. So that, upon the whole, this attempt was a very costly one.[2] It was, indeed, a complete failure.

Calais was bombarded with better results on August 17th, the town being much knocked about, the batteries silenced, and many houses burnt. The loss of the allies was small, nor does it seem that any English or Dutch vessels were sacrificed. But Captain Robert Osborne, of the *Aldborough*, ketch, was killed by a shot from the French galleys.[3] It was subsequently decided that the season was too far advanced to warrant the making of any further attacks of the kind; and the fleet returned to the Downs on August 20th. Berkeley, upon reaching Dover on the 18th, had gone ashore, leaving the command to Sir Clowdisley Shovell.

Of the other actions fought in home waters[4] in 1695, the earliest,

---

[1] No. 3102.

[2] Faulconnier; 'Hist. de Dunquerque,' ii. 104–103; Disp. of Van Almonde of Aug. 3/13; 'Europ. Mercur.' (which gives English, French, and Dutch official accounts); 'Vie de Jean Bart,' 164–173; Sylvius; 'Saken van Staat,' 1695, 87; Account by Sir C. Shovell in 'Biog. Nav.' ii. 21.

[3] *Gazette*, No. 3107.

[4] The action of an East Indiaman, the *Henry*, 34, may be mentioned here. She was attacked off the Irish coast by the privateer *Marin*, 36, commanded by a renegade Irishman named Nagle; but she twice repelled the French boarders, and, when boarded a third time, blew up her own round house in self defence. Thereupon the privateer sheered off, leaving a number of her men prisoners in the *Henry*, which, being on fire, had to be run ashore. Most of her cargo and people were saved.

and one of the most important, took place in January. Towards
the end of 1694, the *Nonsuch*, 48, Captain Thomas Taylor, started
on her way home from New England with a convoy of five vessels
laden chiefly with timber, and especially with masts. When about
seventy leagues to the westward of Scilly, the ships were dispersed
by a heavy gale; but on the morning of January 3rd, 1695, they
all rejoined, except one, the *Firtree*, which had been captured on the
previous day by a French cruiser, the *François*, 48, commanded by
Du Guay Trouin, who, after his escape from Plymouth, had lost no
time in putting to sea again. At noon on the 3rd, the *François* got
up with the reassembled convoy and attacked it, first engaging one
of the merchantmen, the *Falcon*, which Du Guay Trouin asserts to
have mounted thirty-eight guns. The *Falcon* was soon crippled, and
the Frenchman then ranged alongside the *Nonsuch*, and twice tried
to grapple and board her, but on each occasion was driven off by the
accidental circumstance of the English ship catching fire. Nightfall
found the *Nonsuch* and *Falcon* lying to for the repair of damages,
the rest of the convoy in flight, and the *François* awaiting a fresh
opportunity to renew the fight. On the morning of the 4th,
Du Guay Trouin brought down the fore and main-masts of the
Nonsuch, thus completely crippling her, took possession of the
Falcon, and, returning to the man-of-war, which by that time had
lost her mizzen-mast also, reduced her without any further fighting.
Captain Taylor, after making a brave defence, had already fallen.
The *Falcon* was subsequently recaptured off Ushant by some Dutch
privateers, but the *Nonsuch* was carried to France, though not
without difficulty. Her name was gallicised into *Sans Pareil*, her
armament was reduced to forty-two guns, and, in the following year,
Trouin himself commissioned her. The court-martial which inquired
into the loss of the vessel, while not impugning Captain Taylor's
courage, came to the conclusion that he had not made the necessary
preparations for action, and had hazarded his convoy.

It is perhaps well, before passing to other events, to follow the
fortunes of Du Guay Trouin. After his very creditable success he
was ordered to refit his ship as soon as possible and to join the
squadron of the Marquis de Nesmond at La Rochelle. This he did;
and the squadron, which consisted of four ships of from fifty to
sixty-two guns, besides the *François*, put to sea for a cruise early
in April, 1695. In the meantime, five English ships had quitted
the Nore in charge of a large convoy bound for the Mediterranean.

On April 14th, owing to the carelessness of an officer of the watch,[1] the convoy and two of the men-of-war parted company from the rest; and thus it was that on April 16th, in the chops of the Channel, five French ships, mounting from forty-eight to sixty-two guns apiece, met the *Hope*, 70, Captain Henry Robinson, the *Anglesey*, 48, Captain William Prower, and the *Roebuck*, fireship, 6, Captain Edward Owen. The *Anglesey*, after having engaged and driven off a French ship of fifty-six guns, made good her escape. The *Roebuck* also got away. But the *Hope*, whose captain was ill, whose ship's company was raw and untrained, and two out of three of whose lieutenants[2] had been left on shore, was taken after a seven hours' conflict, which left her mastless and with seven feet of water in her hold. The French returned to Brest; and Trouin, still in the *François*, afterwards cruised in company with the *Fortune*, 56, round the British Islands. Off the Blaskets he was so lucky as to fall in with and capture three armed East Indiamen, which are said to have been worth together a million sterling.

These were not the only English misfortunes. On February 4th, the *Dartmouth*, 40, Captain Roger Vaughan, while cruising alone in the Channel, met two French vessels, each of force equal to her own, and was taken after a six hours' action, in the course of which she was reduced to a wreck, and her captain was killed. And there were but small compensating successes. In March a small squadron under Captain Edward Littleton, of the *Montagu*, 60, captured, or contributed to the capture of, the greater part of a fleet of about thirty sail of French merchantmen in the Channel; and the *Queenborough*, 24, Captain Theophilus Hodgson,[3] took a Calais privateer called the *Espérance*. In April, the *Assistance*, 48, Captain Thomas Robinson, being with the *St. Paul*, fireship, on convoy duty to the Elbe, took four valuable merchantmen. In May, Captain William Jumper, who was still in the *Weymouth*, picked up two privateers, one of fourteen and the other of sixteen guns; and on July 19th,

---

[1] The sentence on this officer, the senior mate of the *Hope*, is curious. It was ordered " that he be carried with a halter about his neck from ship to ship, to all the ships at Chatham and Gillingham, and his crime be read by beat of drum by each ship's side; that all the pay due to him in his Majesty's service be forfeited to the Chest at Chatham; and that he be rendered incapable for ever of serving his Majesty in any capacity for the future as an officer." 'Studies in Nav. Hist.,' 305.

[2] The only lieutenant on board, Henry Fowlis, was, for his gallantry in the action, made captain of a sixth-rate, the *Deal Castle*, as soon as he was released from captivity.

[3] The *Queenborough*, with all hands, was lost on May 6th, 1695.

the same distinguished officer fought and captured the St. Malo privateer, *Comte de Revelle*, 36. In November, he took a twenty-four-gun ship which belonged to the French navy, but which, like many other vessels, had been fitted out as a privateer. And in the same month the *Charles*, galley, 32, Captain Stephen Elliot,[1] discovered a convoy of about fifty small craft, protected by five men-of-war, off Le Hâvre, and managed to capture two, and to drive ashore many others. Unhappily, however, there were no English performances near home brilliant enough to outshine the achievements of Du Guay Trouin.

In the Mediterranean, matters were more encouraging. In January, 1695, the *Plymouth*, 60, Captain James Killigrew, was detached from the Mediterranean fleet, in company with the *Carlisle*, 60, Captain John Norris, the *Adventure*, 44, Captain Charles Cornwall, the *Falmouth*, 42, Captain Caleb Grantham, the *Newcastle*, 54, Captain Charles Wager, and the *Southampton*, 48, Captain Richard Kirkby, to look for some French men-of-war which were believed to be cruising in the neighbourhood of Malta. Killigrew, who was senior officer, was cruising between Sicily and Cape Bon, when, on January 7th, off Pantellaria, he fell in with the French ships *Content*, 60, Captain du Chalart, and *Trident*, 50, Captain d'Aulnai. He hoisted French colours with a view to deceiving them until his friends should come up. The French, on their part, hoisted English colours with a view to inducing the single ship to allow them to approach. The *Plymouth* engaged both ships for a time ; but when the other English vessels appeared, the enemy began a running fight which lasted during the night and part of the next day. In the course of it Killigrew was killed, and about fifty of his people were killed and wounded. Superiority of force, however, ultimately told, and, after a gallant defence, both French ships struck. They were added to the Navy as the *Trident Prize* and *Content Prize*, the latter as a 70-gun ship.[2]

On the other side of the Atlantic, lack of proper co-operation, or perhaps even jealousy, between the naval and the military leaders

---

[1] Stephen Elliot was originally master of a small trader in the West Indies. He had been given his commission as captain of the *Maidstone* in January, 1696, as a reward for having escaped from a French prison in San Domingo with valuable information respecting a projected attack on Jamaica in 1694. He consequently never served as a lieutenant.

[2] In the following year the *Content Prize*, then commanded by Captain John Norris, one of her captors, took the French *Foudroyant*, 32.

continued to produce prejudicial results. Captain Robert Wilmot was sent to the West Indies as senior officer, with four ships of the line, one "frigate" and two fireships, and with twelve transports full of troops and stores, the troops being under Colonel Lillingston. Having safely reached St. Christopher, Wilmot sailed thence on March 28th, 1695, in order to join the Spaniards, who were meditating the reduction of the French settlements in San Domingo. Cape François was attacked; and, although the Allies were not directly successful, the French found it prudent to abandon and destroy their positions there. Port de Paix was next attempted; and, the French garrison being defeated in a nocturnal sally, the place soon fell. Great booty was taken, and it would appear that the division of the plunder was primarily responsible for the hostility with which Colonel Lillingston ever afterwards regarded the Commodore. Lillingston, backed by the Spanish general, thought fit to oppose Wilmot when the latter proposed a descent upon Petit Guavas and Léogane; and Wilmot, finding it impossible to undertake anything else of moment, refitted at Jamaica and sailed thence for England on September 3rd, leaving behind him four vessels to protect the island and to convoy some merchantmen which were loading for Europe.

The squadron met with dreadful weather, and was very sickly; and among the victims to disease was Captain Wilmot, who died at·sea on September 15th. So terrible were the ravages of scurvy, that only with the greatest difficulty were the ships brought into port. Nor did all ever get there. The *Winchester*, 60, separated by a storm from her consorts, was lost off Cape Florida on September 24th; and her captain, John Soule, suffered so severely from the hardship, fatigue and anxiety, inseparable from the disaster, that he survived only until October 1st.

One more misfortune of the year remains to be chronicled. During the summer a small squadron, under Peregrine, Marquis of Carmarthen,[1] cruised at the mouth of the Channel to protect trade. The Marquis, mistaking a fleet of homeward-bound merchantmen for the French Brest fleet, retired up the Irish Channel; and, while he was thus absent from his station, a number of vessels from Barbados and the East Indies fell into the hands of the enemy. Burnet blames him for the catastrophe. Charnock seeks to defend him. It would appear that, whether Carmarthen was blameworthy

---

[1] Later, second Duke of Leeds. He then held temporary rank as Rear-Admiral.

or not, he was far too inexperienced and young an officer for the position which had been given him; and there is little doubt that his mistake was one of several causes which led, at about the beginning of the eighteenth century, to the final abandonment of the vicious old practice of putting raw officers into commands of great responsibility merely because they happened to be influential noblemen.

Early in 1696 there were apprehensions of an intended French invasion. A great flotilla of transports was reported to be collected along the French shores of the Channel; and squadrons under De Nesmond and Jean Bart were said to be in readiness to escort it. A vigorous effort, therefore, was made to effectively blockade the coast from Dunquerque to Boulogne, pending the adoption of measures for the destruction of the French vessels while they still lay in harbour. In March, divisions under Captain Simon Foulks and Captain Francis Wyvill were dispatched to observe the enemy's motions in Dunquerque and Calais; and a third division, under Captain John Johnson, co-operated with a Dutch contingent in the business of shutting up the French cruisers. On April 2nd, Sir Clowdisley Shovell quitted the Downs with a squadron destined for the bombardment of Calais, before which town he arrived on the morning of the 3rd; whereupon Captain Benbow, with the bomb-vessels and a small covering squadron, went in, and at about noon opened fire. Several conflagrations soon broke out in the place and in the harbour; but little serious damage was done; and towards 8 P.M. the attacking force was drawn off, after having suffered considerably in its spars and rigging. Benbow was wounded in the leg, and about fifteen other people on the English side were killed and wounded.

In the meantime it was rumoured that a large French force lay in Camaret Bay. Proposals were made for an attack upon it, but the project was officially decided to be impracticable. When Captain Basil Beaumont, with a small detachment, looked into the Bay in May, he found only four or five insignificant vessels, which he destroyed.

In the course of the same month, Rear-Admiral John Benbow,[1] with his flag in the *Suffolk*, 70, undertook the blockade of Dunquerque, where lay Jean Bart with nine ships ready to sail on a cruise. Benbow seized an early opportunity for making a

---

[1] Assisted by a Dutch division under Rear-Admiral van der Goes.

personal reconnaissance of the harbour, and came to the conclusion that the French were about to slip out by the northern of the two entrances. But during the following night Bart escaped through the other passage. As soon as he had definite news of his enemy, Benbow would have begun a close pursuit, but that his colleague, Van der Goes, considered himself bound by his instructions to remain off Dunquerque. Jean Bart was in consequence left for a short time free to prey upon commerce in the North Sea; and he utilised his liberty by capturing about half of a large Dutch convoy. But Benbow presently followed the rover, and eventually pressed him so closely that he interrupted him at the moment when he was upon the point of taking toll from another convoy. Jean Bart was then glad to return to Dunquerque to lay up for the winter.

The main part of the combined Channel fleet, under Lord Berkeley of Stratton,[1] did not put to sea until June. There were to be no more attacks upon the French Channel ports. It was thought that the enemy might be more injured by enterprises directed against some of the islands in the Bay of Biscay. As the fleet passed down the coast it sighted the Marquis de Nesmond coming out of Camaret Bay with a squadron convoying a number of merchantmen. The Marquis at once returned to his anchorage, content to await a more favourable opportunity for sailing. Proceeding, Berkeley, on July 3rd, detached a squadron against the island of Groix, and on July 6th, sent off another squadron against the island of Rhé. In the interval he himself, with the main body, anchored off Belleisle, and landed detachments which ravaged the little islands of Hoat and Hoëdic, and brought off much cattle from each. The Groix squadron, under Captain Richard Fitzpatrick (afterwards Lord Gowran), of the *Burford*, 70, destroyed numerous villages, and also secured about 1300 head of cattle. The Rhé squadron, under Captain George Mees, of the *Sandwich*, 90, bombarded the town of St. Martin, and thence sailed to Olonne, on the mainland, into which it threw a great number of bombs and carcases.[2] The chief sufferers must have been non-combatants; yet this inhuman method

---

[1] John Lord Berkeley of Stratton. Captain, 1686. Acting Rear-Admiral under Lord Dartmouth, 1688. Vice-Admiral, 1693. Admiral, 1693. Conducted numerous attacks on French seaports. Admiral of the Fleet, 1696, when Sir George Rooke went to the Admiralty. Died on February 27th, 1697.

[2] While thus detached, Captain Mees took three privateers, one of 38, one of 36, and one of 14 guns.

of warfare would probably have been continued during the remainder
of the summer, had not a large Dutch division been recalled, and had
not the rest of the fleet run short of provisions. Lord Berkeley,
therefore, returned to Torbay on July 20th; and, after awaiting
instructions, anchored at Spithead on August 31st. The fleet
did not again put to sea ere the bigger ships were laid up for
the winter.

The minor actions of the year in home waters were neither very
numerous nor very noteworthy. In January, the *Lichfield*, 42,
Captain Lord Archibald Hamilton, made prize in the Channel of a
St. Malo privateer, the *Tigre*, 24; and, in the following April, she
captured five, and drove ashore several other sail of a fleet of about
sixty French merchantmen off Cherbourg.

Captain William Jumper, of the *Weymouth*, was as active as he
had been in previous years. In February, among several prizes
which he took, was a privateer of twenty guns. In December, in
company with Captain William Cross, of the *Dover*, 48, he engaged
and captured the *Fougueux*, 48,[1] which, unfortunately, having struck
on a rock during the action, foundered soon afterwards. Later in
the same month, being about thirty-five leagues south of Cape Clear,
he fought a French 50-gun ship; and he would probably have taken
her, had not some cartridges in the *Weymouth* accidentally blown
up, disabling a number of men on the quarter-deck, and had not the
Weymouth, when subsequently in close action with her enemy, been
fallen foul of by the latter, and so deprived of her bowsprit, and,
consequently, of all her masts, one after another.

Captain Thomas Robinson, of the *Assistance*, 48, was another
cruiser captain who distinguished himself. While he was convoying
some merchantmen to Hamburg, his charges were attacked on
May 25th by eight French privateers, four of which mounted from
twenty to thirty guns apiece. After a two hours' engagement the
enemy was driven off; but in the afternoon he attacked a second
time. Robinson again repulsed the privateers; which thereupon
relinquished their designs upon the convoy, and gave chase to
some colliers which were close in under the Essex shore. The
Assistance, however, still pursuing, firing, and letting fly her top-
gallant sheets,[2] so effectually alarmed the colliers for their safety
that they had time to place themselves beyond the reach of danger.

---

[1] She was pierced, however, for 60 guns.
[2] As if signalling the presence of the enemy to consorts in the offing.

In the following November, while in charge of another Hamburg convoy, Captain Robinson took a very valuable prize.

In August, Captain Thomas Lyell, of the *Milford*, 32, by well-executed strategy, rid the seas of one of the fastest and most dangerous of the French privateers. He knew perfectly well that he could not catch his fleet enemy. He therefore equipped and manned a small fishing boat, in which he went in search of the Frenchman. The latter, deceived by appearances, suffered the harmless-looking craft to approach, and was then quickly carried by boarding.

A colonial expedition, which might have brought about important results, left England in the spring of 1696, under the command of Captain John Norris of the *Content Prize*, 70. It consisted of four fourth-rates, four "frigates," two bomb-ketches, and two fireships, besides the senior officer's ship; and it was dispatched to attempt the recovery of certain English settlements in Hudson's Bay which had been captured by the French since the beginning of the war.

Putting into the harbour of St. John's, Newfoundland, Norris learnt, on July 23rd, that five French ships of war had been seen in Conception Bay, hard by. Concluding that these ships formed a squadron which was supposed to have been sent from France, under the Marquis de Nesmond, with the special object of destroying the expedition, a council of war somewhat hastily decided to put the harbour of St. John's into a defensible condition, and there to await the expected attack of the enemy. Captain Norris and seven more of the thirteen naval commanders on the spot were opposed to this extraordinary view of the duties of an English naval force when in presence of a foe of no commanding superiority of strength; but they were overborne by the opinion of the military officers with the squadron. Norris would not, however, carry out the decision of the majority until he had first taken measures to assure himself that the premises were correct, and that the ships which had been seen were really fresh from France; and it was presently discovered that De Nesmond had not arrived, and that the vessels which were the cause of the alarm were an inferior force which was returning to Europe laden with the plunder of some of the Spanish West India Islands.

The Commander-in-Chief put this intelligence before the council of war; but in vain. The over-prudent majority declined to credit it; and Norris, much against his will, had to prepare to receive a foe who was particularly anxious to avoid him. Later, however, when the Marquis de Nesmond, with sixteen ships of war, ten of which were of sixty guns or upwards, arrived from France, the fortifications of St. John's proved useful enough. The French officer shrank from attacking a squadron so well protected; and thus it happened that a policy, based on false premises, and entirely opposed to the best naval opinion on the spot, was instrumental in preserving Newfoundland.

At the same time, it prevented the carrying out of some of the original objects of the expedition; and when, in October, Captain Norris returned to England, there was much popular indignation. Yet Hudson's Bay had not been entirely neglected. The *Bonadventure*, 48, Captain William Allin, and the *Seaford*, 20, Captain John Grange, had recovered York Fort, and other settlements, from the French. The *Bonadventure*, when on her way home, fell in near the mouth of the Channel on October 24th, with the vessel which, as the *Mary Rose*, had been captured by the French in 1691, and which, under her new masters, mounted fifty guns. In the action which ensued, Captain Allin, who behaved with great gallantry, unfortunately lost his life, and the *Bonadventure* received so much damage aloft that she had to relinquish the engagement.

In the Mediterranean, the *Romney*, 50, Captain Edmund Loades, while cruising independently in March, 1696, took the French privateer *Phénix*, 30; and, in July, being in company with the *Canterbury*, a Marseilles merchantman mounting eighteen guns. While on his return to England in August, Captain Loades also engaged a Bayonnais privateer carrying fifty-four guns; and he would probably have captured her, had she not, after a two hours' fight, and a loss of upwards of ninety men killed and wounded, taken refuge under the guns of a Portuguese fort. The *Romney*, in this action, lost only seven killed and eight or nine wounded. Another Mediterranean cruiser, the *Rochester*, 48, Captain Robert Kirton, made prize in August of a valuable Marseilles merchantman of twenty guns.

During the summer, Captain James Davidson, of the hired ship *Bonadventure*, 50, was stationed off Iceland for the protection of the whale fishery there, and captured four French armed vessels, which had gone thither in hopes of being able to combine the profits of privateering with those of fishing.

In the autumn of 1696, Vice-Admiral John Neville had been appointed Commander-in-Chief in the Mediterranean; and on November 3rd he had sailed from England for his station with fifteen English and Dutch men-of-war and a large convoy. Not long after his departure, it became known that the French Government intended to attempt some bold stroke in the Spanish West Indies, and that, with that object in view, M. de Pointis was to be sent [1] from Europe to co-operate with M. Ducasse, who was already on the station. Secret instructions were accordingly sent after Neville, who was by them directed to proceed to Madeira. In the meantime, an additional force, under Captain George Mees, [2] was got ready, and also dispatched thither. Both Neville and Mees met with bad weather. The former received his new instructions at Cadiz, where he arrived on December 9th. At Madeira, only portions of the two squadrons joined; but, a further rendezvous having been arranged for Barbados, nearly all the force assembled there on April 17th, 1697.

At a council of war held at Antigua early in May, it was determined to proceed to Puerto Rico, there to pick up the Spanish treasure galleons which were about to sail for Europe; but, almost immediately afterwards, news was received to the effect that a French force of twenty-six men-of-war under De Pointis had already sailed from San Domingo; and, as Jamaica appeared to be threatened, [3] Vice-Admiral Neville steered for that island. Before he he reached it, he learnt that the French squadron had attacked Cartagena. He was not able, however, to leave Jamaica until May 25th, and, making for Cartagena, he heard that the galleons [4] had by that time quitted Puerto Rico, and were on their way to Jamaica for provisions.

Neville, with true instinct, decided that his first duty was to seek his enemy. He therefore sent word to the galleons that he was looking for De Pointis in the direction of Cartagena, and that he would return to Jamaica later. He was about half-way to his

---

[1] With government ships, but at the charges of the merchants.

[2] Captain Mees was privileged to wear a blue flag at the mizzen while in the West Indies, but was never a regular flag-officer.

[3] Burchett seems to think that Neville, after learning, as he did on May 15th, that the French were at Cartagena, should have gone thither at once without halting at Jamaica; and it is certainly somewhat remarkable that we have no explanation of his apparent lack of promptness.

[4] They seem, nevertheless, not to have touched at Jamaica, but have gone to Havana, where the Vice-Admiral ultimately found them.

destination when, on May 27th, he sighted De Pointis,[1] who was laden with Spanish plunder. The Vice-Admiral chased for five successive days. On one occasion, the *Warwick*, 50, Captain Anthony Tollet, got near enough to distantly engage the rearmost ship of the enemy ; on another, it looked so much as if he must be overhauled and forced to fight, that De Pointis formed his line of battle, and fired some shot at the *Bristol*, 42, Captain Stephen Elliot; and on yet another, the *Princess Ann*, hired ship, Captain William Wakelin, and the *Hollandia*, 72, Captain Hoogenhoeck, cut off from the French a Spanish prize which was laden with plate, powder, and negroes. The *Warwick* also captured a fly-boat. But in the chase several of the ships of the Allies sprang their topmasts and otherwise damaged themselves ; and at last the pursuit had to be relinquished. Cartagena had been given to the squadron as the rendezvous. Neville, therefore, went thither, and arrived to find that, after the departure of the French, the buccaneers had harassed the place, and that the Spaniards were in great distress.

Neville sailed again with very little delay, sending one of his smaller vessels to Havana to apprise the Spanish governor there of what had happened. He tried to make Cape Tiburon[2] at the western end of Haiti ; but, failing that, he went on to San Domingo ; off which town he anchored on June 19th. On the way thither he destroyed a number of privateers, and took one buccaneer of twenty-four guns.

From San Domingo, Captain Mees, with nine ships, was detached to destroy the settlement of Petit Guavas. Having made his dispositions, he landed about a mile to the eastward of the place on the morning of June 23rd, and marched towards the town. He had ordered two small craft and a number of boats full of men to move parallel with his line of advance ; and, although these did not keep up with him, he nevertheless seized the place by a *coup de main*. Unfortunately his people, in spite of all that their officers could do to prevent them, began to loot; and within a couple of hours most of them were so drunk as to be utterly incapable. In these circumstances, Captain Mees judged it best to collect the few men who remained sober, and, after firing the town, to withdraw with as much semblance of good order as was possible. The enemy did not pursue ; and a few days later the

---

[1] With ten men-of-war and two fly-boats.
[2] Believing, probably, that he could there learn further news of the galleons.

detached force rejoined Vice-Admiral Neville, who had proceeded to sea in search of it. The squadron then headed for Jamaica, and thence steered for Havana, before which city it arrived on July 22nd. On the 20th, Captain Mees had died of fever on board his ship, the *Breda*.

At Havana, Neville found the galleons. The men of the squadron were sickly, and various supplies were needed; yet the governor declined either to admit the English ships into his harbour, or to relieve the necessities of the Allies. Nor was the distrustfulness of the Spaniards manifested in this way only. When the Vice-Admiral informed the general of the galleons that the squadron had come to escort him to Europe, the general politely replied that he had no instructions to warrant him in accepting such protection. This being so, Neville could only retire. He steered for Virginia, soon after reaching which he died, a victim, like Mees and many another gallant officer who served in those days on the West India station, to fever. Captain Thomas Dilkes,[1] as senior officer, brought the squadron home.

Monsieur de Pointis made the best of his way home to France. On August 14th, being then about two hundred and fifty miles S.W. of Scilly, he was sighted by a detached squadron [2] which was cruising off the mouth of the Channel under Captain Thomas Harlow. The squadrons engaged on that day for about three hours, at the expiration of which the French drew off. They were chased, but lost. On the 15th, they were re-sighted and again chased. On the 16th, the chase was continued; but on that day De Pointis shook out his reefs, set his top-gallant sails and, with a fresh gale, left his pursuers far behind him. On the day following, he entered Brest. In the action the English squadron had lost eighteen killed and forty-seven wounded.

After Captain Mees and his squadron had sailed to join Vice-Admiral Neville, and to proceed with him to the West Indies, a further reinforcement was got ready at Portsmouth to follow him,

---

[1] In the *Breda*. While in the West Indies he took a 40-gun ship, the *Cerf Volant*, with a cargo of specie worth nearly £100,000. Thomas Dilkes. Captain, 1689. Served at Cadiz and Vigo. Rear-Admiral, 1703. Knighted, 1704, for his behaviour at Malaga. Concerned in the destruction of the squadron of De Pointis off Gibraltar. Died, it was supposed by poison, on December 12th, 1707, after a public dinner which had been given in his honour at Leghorn, where he lies buried.

[2] Consisting of the *Torbay*, 80, *Devonshire*, 80, *Restoration*, 70, *Defiance*, 64, and the hired vessel *Betty*. De Pointis, according to the official English account, then had with him one ship of about 90 guns, two 70's, one 60, and one 50.

and to convoy the out-going trade.   This consisted of the *Norwich*, 50,
Captain George Symonds (senior officer) ; *Chatham*, 48, Captain
Samuel Whitaker; *Sheerness*, 32, Captain Valentine Bowles ; *Seaford*, 20, Captain George Walton; and *Blaze*, fireship, Captain
John Wooden.   It sailed at the end of April, 1697, and on May 5th,
about sixty-eight leagues from Scilly, encountered four French
men-of-war, one of seventy, one of fifty, one of thirty-six, and one
of twenty-six guns.   The *Seaford*[1] and *Blaze* were taken, after the
former had lost her mainmast.   The enemy kept company for three
days with the other English ships, and then, after a further
engagement, stood away in chase of the merchantmen, which had
separated.   In the course of the fighting the *Norwich* and *Chatham*
each lost about forty men killed and wounded, and received much
damage ; but Captain Symond's conduct of his command was held
to be so unsatisfactory that he was sentenced by court-martial of
February 14th, 1698, to be dismissed the service.[2]

In the course of 1697, Captain d'Iberville, a Canadian by birth,
greatly distinguished himself in the waters of Newfoundland and
Hudson's Bay; and in his ship, the *Pelican*, 50, rendered very
considerable services to the French cause.   English interests were,
unfortunately, ill-protected there, the chief vessel on the station
being no bigger craft than the *Hampshire*, 46, Captain John
Fletcher (2).[3]   D'Iberville, with several armed ships in his company, fell in, on August 26th, with the *Hampshire* and some
merchantmen under her convoy, and, after a hot action, sank the
man-of-war, whose captain perished with her ; and took or destroyed
all her consorts.   D'Iberville subsequently captured Fort Nelson.
On other foreign stations few events of the slightest interest
happened.   Off the coast of Iceland, Captain James Davidson, in
the *Assistance*, 42, protected the fishing, and took a large privateer,
similar in character to the vessels which he had captured in the
previous year when in command of the hired ship, *Bonadventure.*

Nearer home, the most successful cruising officers were Captains

---

[1] The French burnt the *Seaford*.

[2] The *Etna*, fireship, was also taken this year, on April 18th, and her captain,
Kenneth Anderson, fell ere she surrendered ; but the circumstances of her capture are
obscure.

[3] There were at the time two Captains John Fletcher in the Navy.   John
Fletcher (1), a commander of 1690 and a captain of 1692, commanded the *Britannia* at
La Hougue, and the *Royal Sovereign* at Cadiz, and, being later re-appointed to that
ship, died in command of her on January 23rd, 1705.   John Fletcher (2) was a
captain of 1693, when he was appointed to the *St. Paul*, fireship.

John Jennings and William Jumper. Jennings, in the *Plymouth*, 60, on January 27th, took, after a long chase, the St. Malo privateer *Concorde*, 14. On February 5th, in company with the *Rye*, 32, Captain Richard Haddock, he captured the *Nouveau Cherbourg*, 36, and the *Dauphin*, 28, after a very hot three hours'. action, in which the latter lost thirty-three killed and wounded. And on February 25th, in company with the *Rye* and the *Severn*, 50, Captain Richard White, he took, or assisted in the taking of, six merchantmen and an 8-gun man-of-war which, with another ship, was convoying them. Captain Jumper, who still commanded the *Weymouth*, 48, took a Granville privateer of eighteen guns in April ; and on July 19th, off Olonne, by a fine display of strategy, seamanship, and bravery, took the French man-of-war *Aurore*, 24, in presence of a large squadron of merchantmen powerfully convoyed.

Captain William Cleveland, in the *Medway*, 60, who cruised on the Irish station, fell in on April 30th with the French privateer *Pontchartrain*, of fifty guns and ten patereroes, and with about four hundred men on board. The enemy tried to grapple and board, but was repulsed ; and the action, continued within musket shot for about three hours, and then, developing into a chase, ended, after a four hours' fight, in the Frenchman's surrender. She had lost nearly one hundred killed and wounded. The *Medway*, which had been admirably handled, had lost only five killed and about a dozen wounded.

On August 22nd, the *Expedition*, 70, Captain James Stewart, when twenty-four leagues S.S.W. of Scilly, hailed two vessels which carried English colours and declared themselves to be the *Lenox* and the *Weymouth*. They kept company with her all night, and, at 6 A.M. on the 23rd, bore down on her port side and, hoisting French colours, began to engage very warmly. One mounted 60 and the other 50 guns. Stewart obliged them to sheer off, whereupon they made for the *Society*, hospital ship, Captain John Chapman, which was with the *Expedition*. Their broadsides killed Chapman and wounded seven of his people ; but they did not wait to press the attack, and, an hour after the beginning of the action, stood away. The *Expedition's* loss in this creditable affair was thirteen killed and thirty-nine wounded.

Nearly the last gun of the war was fired by the *Rochester*, 48, Captain Robert Kirton, which, cruising in the Soundings, in September, took a French 24-gun ship. But the sacrifices attributable to the war did not end even when peace had been concluded. The *Hastings*, 34, Captain John Draper, had been employed for some time off the coast of Ireland, and was about to come home to be paid off, when, on December 10th, 1697, she was lost with all hands on the shores of Waterford.

As soon as the strain upon the naval resources of the country had been somewhat relieved, the government again turned its attention

MATTHEW, LORD AYLMER, ADMIRAL OF THE FLEET.

(After the portrait by Sir P. Lely, by permission of H. C. Norris, Esq.)

to the repression of piracy. Vice-Admiral Matthew Aylmer (R.) was appointed to the chief command in the Mediterranean, with his flag in the *Boyne*, 80, and with instructions to confirm the treaties with Tunis, Tripoli, and Algier. In 1698-9, he visited each of those places, and, when he returned home, the Moors were more peaceable and tractable than they had been for many years previously. In his negotiations he was greatly assisted by Captain George Delavall, of the *Coventry*, 42, and by Captain John Munden, of the *Winchester*, 60, who cruised with a small force against the Salletines.

The Moors, however, were not the only pirates of the time. There were worse outlaws of the same trade in the West Indies and in the Indian Ocean ; and some of them, it was notorious, sailed out of English colonial ports, and even out of New York. The last-mentioned consideration had appealed during the later years of the war with peculiar force to the Earl of Bellamònt, who had been appointed Governor of several of the North American colonies ; and the Earl had made a strong effort to root out the malefactors. Mr. Robert Livingston, of New York, had advised him to send a vessel of force against the rovers, and had introduced one, William Kidd, as a man competent to command such a vessel, both because of his knowledge of seamanship, and because of his familiarity with the habits and resorts of the pirates. But the war was still in progress, and regular men-of-war could not be spared for the service. The upshot had been that Bellamont and Livingston, in conjunction with other noblemen and gentlemen, and with the sanction of the King, had procured and fitted out a vessel called the *Adventure Galley*, and had engaged Kidd to command her. Kidd sailed from Plymouth for New England in April, 1696.

Whether Kidd was at first sincere in his offers of service against the pirates is doubtful. He may have been ; but it is certain that he had not been very long master of a well-armed ship ere he became himself a pirate. He went eastward of the Cape of Good Hope, and he is said to have ravaged the seas from Madagascar to Malabar. After about three years he returned to American waters. The extent of his depredations has probably been exaggerated, and it cannot now be determined. In 1699, he was so indiscreet as to appear on shore at Boston. Governor Lord Bellamont seized him. A considerable amount of booty which he had secreted in Gardiner's Bay, Long Island, was recovered ; and Kidd was sent prisoner to England, on board the *Advice*, 42, Captain Robert Wynn. He arrived early in 1700 ;[1] but there was much delay ere he was tried and sentenced, and he was not hanged until May, 1701.

In the meantime, Kidd's excesses had had a share in influencing the dispatch of two separate expeditions from England, one under

---

[1] In 1700 seven pirates were executed at Charleston, South Carolina ; and in March or April, on the coast of Virginia, the *Shoreham*, 32, after a ten hours' fight, took a pirate of twenty guns, and retook from her two merchantmen.

Rear-Admiral John Benbow, who sailed from Portsmouth on November 29th, 1698, for the West Indies and the coast of America; the other under Captain Thomas Warren, who sailed for the waters of Madagascar. Benbow, who reached Carlisle Bay, Jamaica, on January 7th, 1699, saw nothing of Kidd, but rendered some useful quasi-diplomatic services; though, as his instructions did not permit him to use force against the Spaniards of Puerto Bello, and the Danes of St. Thomas, both of whom had outraged the English flag, he was not so successful as he might have been, had not his hands been fettered. Warren also did more by tact than by force. By promises of pardon he detached from their leaders many of the common people who had been led astray by Kidd, and by freebooters in league with him. But he unfortunately died in Madagascar on November 12th, 1699, ere he had completed his mission. It was taken up and continued by Captain James Littleton, who, before he exhausted the resources of negotiation and promise, destroyed a number of pirate vessels and their haunts, and practically put an end to the evil trade for some years. He returned in 1701.

One of the ships sent to the West Indies in 1698 for the ordinary service of the station was the *Speedwell*, 32, Captain Christopher Coulsea. This officer had previously commanded the *Spy*, brigantine, and the *Vulcan*, fireship, in the capacity of Master and Commander, but his post-rank dated only from the end of 1697.[1] While the vessel was on her passage to Barbados, one Jonathan Bear, a midshipman, and some others, formed a project to seize her, murder her principal officers, and run away with her. The plot was fortunately discovered in time, and, the ringleaders, being seized, were sent to England for trial. Mutiny of so uncompromising a sort has always been rare in the Navy, and the episode is mentioned here chiefly because of its unusual character. It may be that the piratical atmosphere of the West Indies of those days was dangerous even to the loyalty of English seamen. Certain it is that, in nearly every other respect, the station was singularly fatal to the efficiency of the fleet. The deaths of Captain Mees and Vice-Admiral Neville have been already chronicled. It may be added that, of the numerous captains who went out with them from England, or who were out there when they arrived, few besides Captain Dilkes[2] lived

---

[1] He died at Barbados, still in command of the *Speedwell*, on September 21st, 1698.

[2] Lediard, 720, incorrectly says that Dilkes was "the only surviving captain of the whole fleet." Yet the mortality was frightful. Captain James Studley, of the

to return home. In Benbow's squadron the mortality was almost equally terrible ; and, owing to the difficulties of navigation, and the frequent violence of the weather, the loss of material was nearly as serious as the loss of *personnel.* Many examples of this have been already chronicled. In 1699, the *Southsea Castle,* 32, Captain Henry Stepney, and the *Biddeford,* 20, Captain Henry Searle, were added to the number of ships lost on the station. Both of them were wrecked on November 12th, Captain Searle perishing with his ship. At home, the *Mermaid,* 28, with Captain Thomas Pindar, and all hands, was lost off Plymouth, on January 5th, 1699. In the following year, the *Carlisle,* 60, Captain Francis Dove, was accidentally blown up in the Downs on September 19th ; and all who were on board at the time were lost. Captain Dove chanced to be on shore. The only other loss previous to the recommencement of war seems to have been that of Dampier's ship, the *Roebuck,* 12, which sank at her anchors, off Ascension, on February 4th, 1701.[1]

The only important minor expedition of the first year of the war of the Spanish succession was that of Sir John Munden. In April, 1702, it became known in London that it was intended to dispatch from Corunna a squadron of French ships to convoy to the West Indies and Mexico the Duke of Albuquerque and a number of troops ; and it was decided, if possible, to intercept the expedition. Rear-Admiral Sir John Munden (R.) was pitched upon for the service, and was given command of eight third-rates, a fourth-rate, and three small craft. All haste was used in getting ready the squadron, which sailed on May 10th. On May 15th, it made the coast of Galicia, and the *Salisbury* and *Dolphin* were sent ahead to procure intelligence, while the other ships stood on and off. A second effort to gain news resulted in the receipt of a report that thirteen French men-of-war were then (on May 25th) expected at Corunna from La Rochelle. Sir John thereupon worked to windward in order to be in a position to intercept them ; and on May 28th he sighted fourteen sail of the enemy under the shore near Cape Ortegal. But, although he chased, they were too fast for him, and they got into Corunna before he could get near them. At a council of war, in view of the

---

Pembroke, died on May 28th; Captain Nicholas Dyer, of the *Lincoln,* on June 4th ; Captain Robert Holmes, of the *Ruby,* on July 12th ; Captain John Litcott, of the *Pembroke,* on July 23rd ; and Captain Roger Bellwood, of the *Sunderland,* on August 11th, 1697; and these are but some of the captains who perished by disease.

[1] See next chapter.

facts, or supposed facts, that there had already been other ships in Corunna, that the harbour could not be entered, and that the English ships were falling short of water, and had suffered somewhat from the weather, it was decided on June 20th to return to port.

The squadron had done nothing but capture two richly-laden merchantmen from Martinique, and there was great public clamour; but a court-martial, held in the *Queen*, at Spithead, on July 13th, with Sir Clowdesley Shovell as president, acquitted Sir John upon all counts against him; and he re-hoisted his flag in the *Victory* on the 21st. In his defence, he wrote, very justly—

"It is an easy matter for any standers-by to say, after a design has miscarried, that, if you had been on this place instead of that, you had infallibly succeeded. . . . But if it be considered that the sea is a wide place, and that we did not miss the enemy above an hour and a half's time, 1 hope my enemies will be persuaded to have another opinion of me."

A sacrifice was, however, demanded; and, in spite of the verdict of acquittal, the *Gazette*, No. 3835, contained the following extraordinary notice :—

"The Queen, having required the proceedings upon the trial of Sir John Munden, Rear-Admiral of the Red Squadron, to be laid before her, and having considered all the circumstances relating to the expedition against Corunna, Her Majesty, finding that Sir John Munden had not done his duty, pursuant to his instructions, does not think fit to continue him in her service, and has therefore declared her pleasure that His Royal Highness, the Lord High Admiral, should immediately discharge him from his post and command in the Royal Navy; and His Royal Highness has given the necessary orders for it."

Poor Munden, who had fought gallantly at La Hougue, and whose reputation had, to that moment, been unsullied, was thus driven into a retirement, in which he died in 1718.

Another minor expedition of 1702 was one to Newfoundland, under Captain John Leake, who sailed from Plymouth, on July 23rd, with a small squadron, and arrived in the Bay of Bulls (St. John's) on August 27th. Hearing that there were two French men-of-war at Placentia, and that French vessels were resorting thither for convoy, Leake cruised off the mouth of Placentia Bay, and made a number of small prizes. He also destroyed many boats, drying stages, etc. Before the end of October he took twenty-nine sail, burnt two, and demolished St. Peter's Fort.

In the course of the summer, a small squadron of observation, under Captain Basil Beaumont, cruised off Dunquerque; and, after its

return, another, under Captain Thomas Foulis, reconnoitred Calais,
Gravelines, and Dunquerque; but the French remained in port; nor
were there, during 1702, many signs of French activity in the
Narrow Seas. Captain James Littleton, in the *Medway*, 60, picked
up a few small prizes in the Channel; Captain Thomas Butler, of
the *Worcester*, 50, did likewise; and Captain Robert Bokenham, of
the *Chatham*, 50, won some trifling successes of the same kind. On
the other hand, the *Otter*, sloop, Captain Isaac Andrews, was
captured by two French ships on July 28th. But there were no
single ship actions of any interest.

It has been mentioned in the last chapter that, after the death of
Benbow, Captain William Whetstone, with the local rank of rear-
admiral, succeeded as senior officer in the West Indies. After the
battle of Vigo, Sir George Rooke detached to that station a substantial reinforcement, under Captain Hovenden Walker, in the
Burford, 70; and in January, 1703, when the news of Benbow's
death became known in England, Vice-Admiral John Graydon (W.) [1]
was appointed, as regular Commander-in-Chief, to take his place.
His instructions were to proceed, with certain ships, and with transports carrying troops, to pick up the ships already upon the station;
to concentrate the whole force at Jamaica; to make provision for
the sending home of prisoners, and for the protection of the English
islands and of the trade; and then to sail to Newfoundland, and to do
as much damage as possible to the French on those coasts. Graydon
sailed on March 13th in the *Resolution*, 70, Captain Thomas Lyell,
with the *Blackwall*, 50, Captain Thomas Day, and with the
Montagu, 60, Captain William Cleveland, and the *Nonsuch*, 50,
Captain Robert Thompson, which last had been ordered to see him a
hundred and fifty leagues upon his voyage. On March 18th, in
lat. 47° 30′, he met four ships of the little squadron [2] with which
Ducasse had engaged Benbow in the previous August. The
Montagu, which led the English line, bore down to engage the
rearmost and smallest of the French vessels, but was presently called
off by signal from the Vice-Admiral, who conceived that his orders
obliged him to make the best of his way to his destination, and
prevented him from engaging, unless in self-defence. Thus the
enemy got safely into Brest.

In the meantime, Whetstone, cruising off San Domingo,

---

[1] He was, during his absence, advanced to be Vice-Admiral of the Red.
[2] *See* p. 369, *ante*.

destroyed a number of privateers there,[1] and Hovenden Walker made descents upon St. Christopher and Guadaloupe. Graydon arrived at Jamaica on June 4th, and, having made the necessary dispositions, sailed thence to Bluefields, on June 21st, for water, and so to Newfoundland, which he sighted on August 2nd. Immediately afterward the squadron was dispersed by a fog, nor did it completely reassemble until September 3rd, when, a council of war being held, it was unanimously decided that, owing to the sickliness of the ships, the nature of the enemy's defences, the scarcity of provisions, the lateness of the season, and the rigour of the climate, nothing could be attempted against Placentia, which was then the chief French settlement on the island. Graydon and Whetstone therefore returned ingloriously to England.

On March 17th, 1704, a Committee of the House of Lords resolved "that Vice-Admiral Graydon, with a squadron of Her Majesty's ships of war under his convoy, meeting with four French ships in his passage to the West Indies, and letting them escape without attacking them, according to his duty, from the pretence of his instructions, has been a prejudice to the Queen's service, and a great dishonour to the nation." On the following day the Committee further censured Graydon, and petitioned that he might be no more employed. He was no more employed; his pension was discontinued in 1705; and he died in 1726 without having been ever restored to his place on the active list.

Burnet characterises him as "a man brutal in his way." Charnock[2] opines that he was, however, able and spirited, and, in proof of that theory, alleges that, when Graydon was offered the West Indies command, he accepted it, declaring "that it was his duty to go wherever the Queen thought proper to command him, and that he knew no difference of climate when he was to obey her orders." It is to be feared that the attribution of this very proper sentiment to Graydon is as unwarrantable as the attribution to the Duke of Wellington of a certain appeal to the Guards at Waterloo. Nay, Charnock[3] himself makes the sentiment do duty twice. He avers that Benbow, before going to the West Indies, said that "he knew no difference of climates. For his part, he thought no officer had a right to choose his station, and he himself should be, at all times, ready to go to any part of the world His Majesty thought proper

---

[1] Especially at Petit Guavas and Léogane.   *Gazette*, No. 3926.
[2] 'Biog. Nav.' ii. 163.   [3] *Ib.* 231.

to send him [to]." That Graydon was rough, overbearing and truculent, rests on better evidence. That he was an incompetent officer seems certain ; and that he thoroughly deserved his fate is altogether very probable.

Jean Bart had died at the very beginning of the new war ; but he left behind him a not unworthy successor in the Chevalier de Saint-Pol, who, in 1703, cruised from Dunquerque, and made many prizes, especially from the Dutch. In April, May and June, a small squadron, under Rear-Admiral Basil Beaumont, scoured the North Sea in search of him, but in vain. Beaumont then turned his attention to blockading Dunquerque, and convoying merchantmen, and was still busied with these duties when, in November, he perished in the great storm.[1]

Saint-Pol's chief success against English cruisers was won early in April, and was the immediate occasion of Beaumont's being sent in search of him. The *Salisbury*, 52, Captain Richard Cotten, *Adventure*, 40, Captain John Balchen, and *Muscovia Merchant*, hired armed ship, Commander Daniel Parsons, with the trade and some yachts, were on their way from Goeree, in the Netherlands, when, on April 10th, they were attacked by Saint-Pol with the *Adroit*, 40, *Ludlow*, 32, and *Milford*, 30, besides a Spanish man-of-war and three small privateers. The *Muscovia Merchant*, though a ship of some force, struck immediately ; the *Adventure*, which was astern, stood away to save herself ; and the *Salisbury* was left to bear the brunt of the action. She fought gallantly for two hours, until, being quite disabled, and having seventeen killed and thirty-four wounded, including both her lieutenants, she struck.[2] Saint-Pol got into port with his prizes, and subsequently added the *Salisbury* to the squadron with which he resumed his cruise.

Elsewhere, in home waters, the French were less fortunate. In January, 1703, the *Dover*, 50, Captain Nicholas Trevanion, while cruising off Scilly, captured the large privateer *Comte de Toulouse*, which had on board three hundred French troops, and which did not surrender until she had fought for six hours and suffered a loss of upwards of fifty killed. The *Dover* also retook a valuable prize which the Frenchman had seized on the previous day. And in July, Rear-Admiral Thomas Dilkes (W.), who had hoisted his flag in the *Kent*, 70, set out on a little cruise, which was one of the most brilliant

---

[1] *See* p. 388.

[2] Four ships of the convoy were also taken.

of the early part of the war. His chief object was the destruction of
a fleet of merchantmen, which lay with their convoy in Cancale Bay.
He sailed from Spithead on July 22nd ; and, on his way, learnt
that on the 15th a fleet of forty sail had been seen endeavouring to get
into Granville. At daybreak, on the 26th, the enemy was discovered
at anchor about a league to the westward of that town. At the
approach of the English, the French slipped, and ran inshore, chased
by Dilkes, who, in spite of the anxiety of his pilot, would not bring
up until he had under him barely four feet more water than the *Kent*
drew. Under the shore were seen forty-five merchantmen, convoyed
by three small men-of-war, the *Joyeuse*, the *Victoire*, and another.
The Rear-Admiral manned and armed all his boats, and, by noon, had
taken and brought off fifteen sail, burnt six, sunk three, and driven
the rest so far up towards Avranches that they could not at once be
followed. But on the 28th, again utilising his boats, and supporting
them with the ships of least draught of water, he, and all his
captains, went in, caused the destruction of two of the men-of-war,
brought off the third, and burnt or destroyed seventeen more of the
merchantmen, so that, of the whole flotilla, only four escaped. This
service was rendered with small loss of men, and with the expenditure of but one small vessel mounting six guns ; and it was so
well thought of that the Queen ordered gold medals to be struck and
presented to Dilkes and his principal officers.

Among the other events of 1703 should be mentioned the
capture by Captain John Norris, of the *Orford*, 70, of the privateer
Philippeaux, 36, which lost fifty men ere she surrendered ; and of
a 16-gun privateer. Both these were taken while the *Orford* was
on her way to the Mediterranean, where she served under Shovell.
When the fleet was returning into the Channel in November the
Orford, with the *Warspite*, 70, Captain Edmund Loades, and the
Lichfield, 50, Captain James, Lord Dursley, being ahead, took the
Hasard, 52, which resisted in the most determined way for six
hours, and struck only after she had been reduced to a perfect
wreck. Among the catastrophes of the year were the foundering
of the *Lincoln*, 50, Captain Henry Middleton, with the captain
and nearly all the crew, on January 29th ; and the loss of the
Firedrake, bomb, Captain Edward Raney, with all hands, on
October 12th.

One of the earliest single ship actions of 1704 was fought off
the Deadman on January 15th, by the *Lyme*, 32, Captain Edward

Letchmore, with a French privateer mounting forty-six guns. The *Lyme* carried on the action for three hours, at the expiration of which her opponent had had enough of it; but the English ship was too much disabled to pursue. She lost thirty-six people killed and wounded; and the gallant Letchmore was so severely injured that he survived only until the following day.

On March 12th, being with the fleet off Lisbon, and having been ordered by Sir George Rooke to chase to the south-west, Rear-Admiral Thomas Dilkes, with the *Kent*, 70, Captain Jonas Hanway, *Bedford*, 70, Captain Sir Thomas Hardy, Kt., and *Antelope*, 50, Captain Thomas Legge, overhauled, and, after some resistance, captured the Philippist Spanish ships *Porta Cœli*, 60, and *Santa Teresa*, 60, and the merchantman *San Nicolas*, 24, all laden with ordnance and other military stores. In June, Captain Salmon Morris, in the *Advice*, 50, took a French 18-gun man-of-war, which was subsequently added to the Royal Navy as the *Advice Prize*.

On July 24th, the *Coventry*, 50, Captain Henry Lawrence, was taken by the enemy in circumstances which led to her captain being dismissed the service and mulcted of all his pay.[1]

On August 4th, the *Revenge*, 60, Captain William Kerr, and the *Falmouth*, 48, Captain Thomas Kenny, fell in with the little squadron of Du Guay Trouin. Kerr was adjudged by a court-martial, which subsequently inquired into the circumstances, to have behaved very meritoriously in the consequent action. As for Kenney he fell gallantly fighting his ship. But, in spite of the *Falmouth's* vigorous defence, and the assistance rendered to her by her consort, she was at length obliged to strike.

In the course of the same month the *Dreadnought*, 60, Captain John Evans, *Falkland*,[2] 50, Captain John Underdown, and *Fowey*, 32, Captain Richard Browne, while returning from Virginia, captured a French fifty-four, which, in consideration of the leading part taken by the *Falkland* in the affair, was added to the Navy as the *Falkland Prize*. In the latter part of the year Du Guay Trouin, in the *Jason*, 54, still cruised in the Soundings in company with the *Auguste*, 54, and *Valeur*, 26; and on November 12th he met and brought to action the *Elizabeth*, 70, Captain William

---

[1] C. M. January 5th, 1705. The *Coventry* was taken by Du Guay Trouin. Guérin, iv. 116.

[2] The *Falkland* is noteworthy as having been the first regular man-of-war ever built in North America. She was launched at Piscataqua in 1690. Cooper, 'Hist. of the Navy of the U.S.A.' i. 28.

Cross, and the *Chatham*, 48, Captain Robert Bokenham. The *Auguste* devoted her attention to the *Chatham*, which finally got away; but the *Elizabeth*, closely attacked by the *Jason*, struck after a feeble and disgraceful defence. Cross, excusing himself at his trial,[1] alleged that he was not well manned, that his surgeon was sick, that several of his crew went under hatches and would not fight, and that others got drunk. He had a long and honourable record of service, yet it was plain that he had grossly misbehaved himself, and he was sentenced to be cashiered, to forfeit his arrears of pay, and to be imprisoned for life. The last part of the sentence was mercifully remitted, and Cross appears to have spent his old age as an ordinary pensioner in Greenwich Hospital, where he died in 1746.

Beyond the captures above-mentioned, the only one of the slightest importance that was made by English detached cruisers in 1704 was a 22-gun vessel, which was taken by the *Lichfield*, 50, Captain Rupert Billingsley, and added to the Navy as the *Sun Prize*. England seems in those days to have had remarkably few cruiser captains of exceptionable ability or dash. The best of them all, Captain William Jumper, had quitted his famous fourth-rate, the *Weymouth*, at the end of 1697, and always afterwards commanded a third-rate, generally, of course, with a fleet. The French, on the other hand, had more brilliant cruiser captains than at any other period in their history. Du Guay Trouin, the Chevalier de Saint-Pol, Coëtlogon, Forbin, d'Iberville, and Cassard, were all fighting for her; and seldom has any country disposed at one time of a more gallant band of adventurous seamen. It is not astonishing that the honours of the *guerre de course*, to which France was beginning to confine herself, lay almost exclusively with her.

It was therefore a subject of much rejoicing when, early in 1705, one of Trouin's ships was taken. The *Jason* and *Auguste* were in January again cruising near the mouth of the Channel, when, on the 13th, they sighted and chased their old opponent the *Chatham*, 48, Captain Robert Bokenham, which belonged at the time to Sir George Byng's fleet, but which had temporarily lost sight of it. The *Chatham* fled.[2] The *Jason* and *Auguste* chased; and presently they found themselves within uncomfortable distance of

---

[1] C. M., August 25th, 1705.

[2] After she had lost her pursuers on the 14th, she met, fought, and took a 30-gun privateer called the *Connétable*, from St. Malo.

Sir George Byng's command. The French ships separated. The *Auguste*, harried by several of her enemies, made a good fight of it, but ultimately struck, and was taken possession of. She was added to the Navy as the *August*. The *Jason*, with Trouin himself on board, was overtaken and engaged by the *Worcester*, 50, Captain Richard Canning, in a very determined manner, until other vessels came up. But the English, believing the *Jason* to have been more seriously mauled than was really the case, ceased their attacks upon her during the night; and, a breeze arising, she got away, chased to the last, however, by the *Worcester*. The *August* is, curiously enough, not mentioned in a list, published by authority, of prizes made by Byng's fleet during the early part of this cruise. The list, however, includes one man-of-war, the *Thétis*, 44, and twelve privateers, the *Desmaria*, 36, *Philippe*, 32, *Connétable*, 30, *Valeur*, 28, *Royal*, 26, *Beringhen*,[1] 24, *Sans Pareil*, 20,[1] *Minerve*, 16, *Merveilleux*. 14, *Postillon*, 10, *Bonaventure*, 10 and *Admirable*, 12.[2]

In the West Indies, whither Rear-Admiral William Whetstone, who was knighted in February, went as Commander-in-Chief in March, several small prizes were made; and on June 18th, 1705, after a smart chase, a French 46-gun ship was taken. The *Bristol*, 50, Captain John Anderson, and the *Folkestone*, 32, Captain Henry Gore, also took several vessels of a French convoy, in search of which they had been detached. A sad accident happened in the autumn to the Rear-Admiral's flagship, the *Suffolk* 70. The after powder-room blew up owing to some carelessness, killing thirty people, and wounding or burning seventy more, most of whom died.

In European waters there were, upon the whole, more disasters

---

[1] St. Malo privateers taken by the *Triton*, 50, Captain Joseph Taylor.

[2] *Gazette*, 4116. But for the very excellent paper on Trouin in Laughton's ' Studies in Naval History,' I should have missed a letter of Captain Bokenham's which certainly seems to show that the *Auguste* must have been taken in the middle or end of January, 1705. Yet, even so, the date remains in some doubt. The *Auguste* was first commissioned under her new flag by Captain Robert Bokenham on September 11th, 1705. A notice in *Gazette*, No. 4148, states that on the Friday before August 12th, 1705, the *Chatham*, Captain Bokenham, brought the *Auguste* into Plymouth, and that the *Chatham* had taken her with a loss of one killed and fourteen wounded. This seems to imply that the capture was then quite a recent one. Moreover, the fact that the *Auguste* does not figure among the prizes made during the early part of the cruise is, to me, most significant. I therefore only accept Professor Laughton's date (in January) on the assurance of so high an authority that " there is no doubt whatever " about it. Personally, I incline to the beginning of August as the date, and to the idea that the *Chatham*, after losing the *Auguste* in January, met her again in the summer. But the *Chatham's* log is non-existent.

than successes. The *Rochester*, 50, Captain Edward Owen, picked up a small new "frigate," which was afterwards taken into the Navy as the *Rochester Prize;* retook a valuable Jamaica merchant called the *Richard and Sarah;* and captured a Dutch-built French privateer of twenty-four guns. And in November, in the Mediterranean, the *Antelope*, Captain Philip Cavendish, most pluckily sustained for two hours a hot combat with a French seventy, and finally drove her off, losing twelve killed and seventeen wounded. On the other hand, St. Pol, who cruised with four men-of-war and five armed ships of the merchants, fell in, on October 20th, with a home-coming Baltic convoy escorted by three English men-of-war, and captured, not only the whole convoy of twelve ships, but also the *Pendennis*, 50, Captain John Foljambe, the *Sorlings*, 32, Captain William Coney, and the *Blackwall*, 50, Captain Samuel Martin. Captains Foljambe and Martin bravely defended their ships with their lives. The triumph was a considerable one for the French; but it was costly, for the Chevalier de Saint-Pol also fell. To add to the tale of English misfortunes for the year, the *Plymouth*, 60, Captain Hercules Mitchell, foundered at sea with all hands on August 11th.

In 1706, Captain William Kerr, as Commodore, was appointed to proceed with a small squadron to the West Indies in succession to Rear-Admiral Sir William Whetstone. Kerr joined Whetstone at Jamaica in July, and with him went on a short cruise. Whetstone then returned to England, and Kerr sailed on an expedition against San Domingo. An attempt upon Petit Guavas failed; disease became so rampant as to disable the squadron; and Kerr, perhaps disappointed in his ambition to make money honourably, so far forgot his position and responsibilities as to descend to take bribes for permitting and protecting contraband trade, and for sparing the property of the enemy. He returned in 1707; and in 1708, an inquiry having been held, the House of Lords petitioned the Queen to dismiss him the service. He was accordingly dismissed. During the latter part of the time when he was present on the station Rear-Admiral Sir John Jennings (B.) commanded in chief there; but he was able to effect nothing, the Spaniards in the West Indies being for the most part close adherents of King Philip.

In April, 1706, Vice-Admiral Sir Stafford Fairborne (R.) was given command of a small squadron which was intended for the destruction of French shipping in and near the mouth of the river Charente, and especially of any vessels that might be fitting out at Rochefort. He sailed on May 6th, but was much hampered, first by bad weather, and then by the nature of his instructions; and he was only able to destroy a few traders, and to take six small prizes. He returned to Plymouth on May 17th and was soon afterwards ordered to Ostend to co-operate with the allied army in the siege of that town. He took part in a combined bombardment and assault by sea and land, with the result that the place capitulated on June 25th, three days only after the trenches had been opened. The ships in harbour[1] were not included in the terms of capitulation, and fell into the hands of the victors.

On the Irish station, in June, the *Speedwell*, 20, Captain George Cammock, and the *Shoreham*, 20, Captain George Saunders, fell in with a small flotilla of ten sail of French merchantmen bound to the West Indies, and took five of the vessels; and in the North Sea, in July, the *Adventure*, 40, Captain Edmund Hicks, and the *Tartar*, 32, Captain Richard Leake, while returning from Hamburg, whither they had convoyed the trade, took a 24-gun ship, which was added to the Navy as the *Child's Play*.

In the Mediterranean, the *Romney*, 50, Captain William Coney, distinguished herself on December 15th by entering Malaga Bay under French colours, anchoring within pistol-shot of a French 16-gun privateer, which was laden with guns from the wreck of the French ship *Magnanime*,[2] hoisting her own colours, and capturing and bringing out the vessel from under the fire of about fifty guns in the fortifications. The *Romney* in this affair did not lose a single man.[3] The *Milford*, 32, Captain Philip Stanhope, and the *Fowey*, 32, Captain Richard Lestock, junior, seem to have been present on the occasion, but to have remained outside the harbour. A few weeks later these vessels, or some of them, appear to have been instrumental in the driving ashore and burning of the *Content*, 60, under Cape de Gata, and in the capture of the *Mercure*, 42, a French man-of-war fitted out by the merchants upon terms of partnership with the government.[4] The chief material loss of the year 1706 was that of

---

[1] The ships taken were: *Santa Maria*, 70, *Flandria*, 50, *Reina de España*, 40, *Nettuno*, 24, *Maria*, 22, *Catarina*, 16, *Doña de Clara*, 14, *Re de España*, 14, one vessel of ten guns, and upwards of forty merchantmen.

[2] Late flagship of De Pointis. She had been driven ashore by Leake's squadron. *See* p. 406.

[3] *Gazette*, No. 4298.   [4] *Gazette*, No. 4304.

the *Winchelsea*, 32, which was taken by the enemy after a gallant defence. Her captain, John Castle, fell in the action, which was fought on June 6th.

The year 1707 was withal the most active one of the whole campaign. In 1706, Forbin had fitted out in Dunquerque a squadron of eight men-of-war, half of which were prizes taken from the English Navy, and had begun a series of cruises, which, continued in company with Du Guay Trouin, raised the reputation of the French *corsaires* to the highest pitch. In June, 1706, Forbin had taken part of an English convoy off Ostend, and had played havoc with the Dutch merchantmen; but his great exploits were performed in 1707.[1]

In the spring of 1707, Forbin cruised in the North Sea with the *Mars*, 54, his own flagship *Blackwall*, 54, *Salisbury*, 52, *Protée*, 48, *Jersey*, 46, *Griffon*, 44, *Dauphine*, 44, *Fidèle*, 44, and another man-of-war, besides four corvettes or "barques longues," and several small privateers. On May 1st, the *Royal Oak*, 76, Captain Baron Wyld, *Hampton Court*, 70, Captain George Clements, and *Grafton*, 70, Captain Edward Acton, left the Downs with a convoy of about forty[2] merchantmen bound to the westward. On the same day, off Brighthelmstone, Forbin, who had doubtless had his eye for some time upon the convoy, came up with and attacked it. Says the official English account :—

"the *Grafton* was boarded by three men-of-war of fifty-six guns, who carried her after a warm dispute of half an hour. The *Hampton Court* was attacked by one of the men-of-war, and afterwards boarded by two others; from which, with great difficulty, she disengaged herself; but, as she was bearing away, fell in with two fresh ships which shot away her mainmast and foretop-mast. The *Royal Oak*, Captain Baron Wyld, commander, came up to her assistance, but, finding her ensign struck, made the best of her way to save herself, having eleven feet water in the hold, and being very much shattered. In the engagement he had received several shots under water from two French men-of-war, of fifty and fifty-six guns, that were on board him above half a quarter of an hour; but he plied them so warmly that they were forced to sheer off, not without being much disabled." [3]

The *Royal Oak* made her way back as far as Dungeness, where she beached herself. She was ultimately saved; but both the *Hampton Court* and the *Grafton* were carried into Dunquerque. Captain Clements, mortally wounded by a shot in the belly, had

---

[1] He was then a *chef d'escadre*.

[2] Forty is the lowest estimate. Many English historians say there were fifty-five merchantmen, and Forbin says there were eighty.

[3] 'Biog. Nav.' ii. 115.

continued to fight his ship until he had fallen senseless on her
deck, and until she had lost two hundred of her people killed and
wounded.   Soon after the vessel was taken possession of, a young
midshipman,

" taking an opportunity of the confusion which prevailed at that time, and the greater
attention of the enemy to the plunder than the care of their prisoners, caused his poor
dying commander to be conveyed through a porthole into the longboat, which
happened to be astern. He himself followed with seven others of the crew.   They
concealed themselves under the thwarts as well as they could, till the *Hampton Court*
and the enemy's squadron had drifted so far with the flood as to render it safe for
them to take to their oars, when, by a very happy but almost incredible exertion, they
reached Rye on the 3rd of May." [1]

Captain Clements died in the boat.   Captain Acton also perished,
fighting with the utmost gallantry.   According to Forbin, the
privateers took twenty-two of the merchantmen.   The French
losses were very heavy, and among the dead was Captain de Vezins,
of the *Salisbury*.

This affair caused great excitement in England, it being generally
assumed that the disaster might have been avoided if the Admiralty
had caused itself to be properly informed of the movements of the
enemy, and if it had provided adequate convoy.   But Captain Wyld
was not blamed ; and he was, indeed, as soon as his ship had been
refitted, again employed on similar service.

Forbin, in the meantime, continued his cruise ; and on July 11th,
off the Lofoten Islands, he took fifteen merchantmen belonging to
a Russia convoy under charge of Captain Richard Haddock, in
the *Swallow*, 50.   The adventurous Frenchmen then returned to
France by way of the west coast of Scotland and Ireland.   He
and Du Guay Trouin, a few months later, dealt an even worse
blow at the commerce and prestige of Great Britain.

On October 9th, 1707, a fleet of about one hundred and thirty
sail, bound for Lisbon with merchandise, warlike stores, and horses,
sailed from Plymouth under convoy of the *Cumberland*, 80, Commodore Richard Edwards, *Devonshire*, 80, Captain John Watkins,
Royal Oak, 76, Captain Baron Wyld, *Chester*, 50, Captain John
Balchen, and *Ruby*, 50, Captain the Hon. Peregrine Bertie.   By
that time Du Guay Trouin, who had been cruising against the
Portuguese in the Atlantic, and had also captured several British
vessels, had returned to Brest with his six ships.   There Forbin,
returning from his northern expedition, had joined him ; and the

[1] ' Biog. Nav.,' ii. 66.

two commanders had received orders to put to sea together against the Portugal convoy. Forbin's division still consisted of eight of the nine men-of-war which had been engaged in the affair of May 1st; Du Guay Trouin's was made up of the *Lys*, 72, his own ship, *Achille*, 64, *Jason*, 54, *Maure*, 50, *Amazone*, 40, and *Gloire*, 38. The French had thus fourteen[1] men-of-war to pit against the British five; and about six hundred guns to pit against the British three hundred and thirty-six.

The French fell in with the convoy off the Lizard on October 10th; and the British captains, in order to give time for the merchantmen to save themselves, engaged the enemy with great stubbornness, and studiously intercepted him. In point of fact very few of the merchantmen were taken;[2] but in other respects the result of the action was most serious. The *Cumberland* struck to the *Lys*, the *Chester* to the *Jason*, and the *Ruby* to the *Amazone*.[3] The *Devonshire*, after making a running fight with five vessels until the evening, blew up; and, of all on board, only two men were saved. As for the *Royal Oak*, she was run foul of by the *Achille*, each ship losing her bowsprit by the shock; and, having repulsed an attempt to board, she got away with a loss of but twelve men killed and twenty-seven wounded. Picking up a few straggling merchantmen, she reached Kingsale in safety with them.

Captain Edwards, after his release from captivity, was brought before a court-martial, which honourably acquitted him; Captain Watkins perished with nearly nine hundred of his men; Captain Wyld, who was deemed to have misbehaved himself, especially in breaking the line, was sentenced to dismissal from the service; but was subsequently, and perhaps deservedly, restored to it. Captain Balchen returned to England, and was absolved by a court-martial[4] from all blame for the loss of his ship. Captain Bertie did not live to return, but died while still a prisoner in France.

There seems to have been lack of good feeling and loyal co-operation between Du Guay Trouin and Forbin; and there is much reason to believe that, had they worked together better than they did, not a single ship, either of the escort or of the convoy would have escaped them.

[1] Forbin says "fourteen"; but Du Guay Trouin's account says only twelve.
[2] In spite of the French claim to have captured sixty.
[3] But Forbin claimed that the *Ruby* and *Chester* fell to his division; and some accounts say that the *Ruby* struck to the *Maure*.
[4] C. M., October 27th, 1708.

The two convoys above-mentioned were not, unfortunately, the only ones which, with more or less success, were attacked by the French during the year 1707. In February, fourteen merchantmen bound for Lisbon in charge of the *Swiftsure*, 70, Captain Richard Griffith, and the *Warspite*, 70, Captain Thomas Butler, were attacked by a squadron of French cruisers on the way from Brest to the West Indies, and several of them were taken. And on August 25th, the *Nightingale*, 24, Captain Seth Jermy, being with a convoy off Harwich, was fallen in with by six French galleys. Jermy made one of the most spirited and protracted defences on record, and afforded time for his charges to escape, but was himself taken. The *Nightingale* was carried into Dunquerque. There was at that time in France a renegade, Thomas Smith,[1] who, in 1703, had been dismissed the English service and fined six months' pay for malpractices committed when in the command of the *Bonetta*, sloop. Smith commissioned the *Nightingale* as a privateer, and, towards the end of the year, cruised in her in company with the *Squirrel*, 24, another English prize. On December 30th these two cruisers were encountered in the North Sea by the *Ludlow Castle*, 40, Captain Nicholas Haddock. After several hours' chase, the *Nightingale* was brought to action and was forced to strike; but while she was being secured, the *Squirrel* got away. Smith was tried for his traitorous conduct, and was very deservedly hanged on June 18th, 1708.

The other events of the year on the home station were not numerous. On February 10th, the *Hastings*, 32, Captain Francis Vaughan, while putting back into Yarmouth, after having endeavoured, in face of bad weather, to leave with a convoy for Holland, ran upon the sands and capsized, her captain and most of her crew perishing. In May, the *Bridgwater*, 32, Captain Thomas Lawrence, cruising in Irish waters and learning of the presence of some French privateers off the coast, put to sea from Kingsale in search of them ; and at about midnight on the 16th fell in with three vessels, which proved to be the *Affaire*, 24, the *Cocarde*, 12, and their prize. Lawrence engaged the two privateers for two hours and a half, at the expiration of which they crowded all sail and made off, leaving

---

[1] Charnock, 'Biog. Nav.' ii. 192, 193, confuses this Thomas Smith with one or more others. This particular man was a captain of 1696, when he was appointed to the *Germoon Prize*. His only other English command was the *Bonetta*. *See Gazette*, No. 4398.

their prize to be taken possession of. And in the course of the winter, the *Dover*, 48, Captain Thomas Mathews,[1] took the French man-of-war, *Bien Aimé*, 26.[2]

On the other side of the Atlantic, Captain John Underdown, of the *Falkland*, 50, acting as commodore on the Newfoundland station, destroyed a number of French vessels, settlements, and stages. In this he was assisted by Captain John Carleton, of the *Nonsuch*, 48, and Captain Thomas Hughes, of the *Medway's Prize*.[3] In the West Indies, a terrible hurricane which burst over St. Christopher on August 30th, caused the loss of the *Child's Play*, 24, Captain George Doyley, and all, or very nearly all hands. The *Swan*, 24, with Commander Charles Howard, was lost on the 17th of the same month ; but upon what station does not appear.

In the Mediterranean several creditable actions were performed. On March 13th, the Earl of Peterborough, who was for the moment devoting himself to the military rather than to the naval aspects of the campaign, took passage from Barcelona in the *Resolution*, 70, commanded by his son, the Hon. Henry Mordaunt, with the intention of proceeding to Italy to consult with the Duke of Savoy. The *Resolution* was accompanied by the *Enterprise*, 20, Captain William Davenport, and the *Milford*, 32, Captain Philip Stanhope. On the 19th, about fifteen leagues from Genoa, the little convoy fell in with a French squadron consisting of two 80's, two 70's, one 68, and one 58, which chased. The Earl went on board the *Enterprise*, and, in her, made for Leghorn, which he reached in safety. The *Milford* also got away to that port. But early in the morning of the 20th, the enemy began to creep up within gunshot of the *Resolution* ; and from about 7 A.M. to 3.30 P.M. a brisk action was maintained. Seeing then no prospect of saving his ship, which was badly damaged, Mordaunt ran her ashore ; but he continued to defend her, and resolutely beat off the boats which were sent to burn her. On

---

[1] Thomas Mathews. Born. 1676. Captain, 1703. Commanded the *Chester* in the action with the *Glorieux*, 1709. Commanded the *Kent* off Cape Passaro. Commander-in-Chief in the Mediterranean, 1742. Fought a partial action off Toulon in 1744, but was improperly supported. Was condemned by a court-martial and dismissed the service. Died, 1751.

[2] In this year, also, the *Worcester*, 48, Captain Richard Canning, while employed as a Channel cruiser, appears to have taken the *Valeur*, 24.

[3] *Gazette*, No. 4378.

the following morning he burnt her himself, landing all his company and most of the ship's valuables.[1]

In June, the *Lancaster*, 80, Captain James Moody, being at the time detached from the main body of the Mediterranean Fleet, and in company with the *Warspite*, 70, Captain Thomas Butler, and *Triton*, 48, Captain Joseph Taylor, rendered most valuable service to the cause of King Charles of Spain by succouring the town of Denia, which would otherwise have surrendered to the Philippists. He landed guns, four hundred men, and supplies, and was of so much assistance that the enemy, two days' later, raised the siege. And in August, at the time of the operations against Toulon, Captain James, Lord Dursley, of the *St. George*, 96, riding off the isles of Hyères, landed, surprised a fort there, and afterwards obtained the surrender of two other works.

Early in 1708 it became known in England that France, taking advantage of the dispatch of the British main fleet under Sir John Leake to the Mediterranean, meditated an expedition to Scotland from Dunquerque on behalf of the Pretender, and that the conduct of the adventure was to be entrusted to Forbin. Forbin's force[2] consisted of eight ships of the line, twenty-four smaller men-of-war, and no fewer than seventy " barques longues." Admiral Sir George Byng (B.)[3] was given command of a squadron of twenty-three British and three Dutch ships of war, with which to intercept this attempt; and with his flag in the *Swallow*, 60, Captain Jordan Sandys, he sailed from the Downs on February 27th. After watching Gravelines and Dunquerque, he was driven from his station by a gale of wind on March 2nd, whereupon the French hastily embarked and sailed on the 6th.

Byng, by that time reinforced, had forty-two men-of-war under his orders, and quitted the Downs a second time on the same day, but did not learn until the 9th that Forbin had put to sea. He detached Rear-Admiral John Baker (W.) to Ostend for troops, which were to be carried thence to strengthen the forces in North Britain;

---

[1] Captain Mordaunt was wounded in the thigh by a cannon shot. *Gazette*, No. 4324. This wound prevented him from ever going to sea again. He died at Bath on February 24th, 1710.

[2] On board were about ten thousand soldiers, with the Pretender himself at their head.

[3] The second in command was Vice-Admiral Lord Dursley (B.), who, on January 26th, had been promoted to that rank over the heads of scores of old officers, and who was only twenty-seven years of age. *See* note, p. 518.

and he himself proceeded in chase. On the 13th, he sighted the enemy in the Firth of Forth; but Forbin had been long enough there to satisfy himself that there were no signs of a rising on shore, and was already on his way out again. By a display of seamanship and judgment he evaded Byng, whose movements were hampered by a land breeze; and, steering to the northward, he made for Moray Firth. Byng chased, and his van soon got within gunshot of Forbin's rear ; but the only result of the partial action was the cutting off of the *Salisbury*, 52, Captain de Nangis, which, after three years' service under the French flag, thus reverted to her original owners.[1] She was first engaged by two other vessels, but was ultimately taken by the *Leopard*, 50, Captain Thomas Gordon.

MEDAL COMMEMORATIVE OF THE FAILURE OF THE FRENCH ATTEMPT AGAINST SCOTLAND, 1708.

(From an original kindly lent by H.S.H. Captain Prince Louis of Battenberg, R.N.)

Byng did not pursue further than Buchan Ness ; and Forbin, giving up all hope of effecting a landing, and indeed disbelieving, it would seem, in the Pretender's popularity in Scotland, returned home.[2]

The British Admiral's management of his command gave rise to many popular murmurs ; but these were taken no notice of by the administration, and presently died down. Looking to the great superiority of the British force, and to the fact that Byng caught Forbin in a *cul-de-sac*, the public lost sight of such important factors as the foulness of the British ships, and the value of the

---

[1] She was commissioned as the *Salisbury Prize* by Captain Edward St. Loe on March 15th, 1708.

[2] On his voyage he lost, in addition to the *Salisbury*, the *Blackwall*, 50, *Deal Castle*, 24, and *Squirrel*, 24, all prizes taken from the British. They either foundered at sea or were wrecked on the Dutch coast.

land breeze to the French at the critical moment. Upon the whole it is probable that Byng, who was by no means a brilliant strategist, did the best that lay in him.

After Byng's return to the Downs, it was determined to alarm the French coasts with a prospect of invasion; and a strong squadron put to sea from Spithead on July 27th, with a considerable body of troops on board under General Erle. On August 1st, the force anchored before Boulogne; and on the following day preparations were made as if for landing troops. Similar demonstrations were subsequently made off other places; and it is possible that they had the desired effect of inducing the French to withdraw some of their troops from Flanders for the defence of their own territory; but no actual attack was anywhere made. In the autumn, Lord Dursley,[1] with part of the fleet, cruised in the Soundings, but took only six or seven small prizes. It was, upon the whole, an inactive year, so far as minor operations are concerned.

The work of Wager in the West Indies, up to the time of his return to Port Royal in July, 1708, has been described in the previous chapter. Several ships of his squadron returned home in September. Others cruised with good success among the islands. The *Dunkirk's Prize*, 24, Captain George Purvis, after making several captures, unfortunately ran herself ashore off the coast of San Domingo on October 18th, while in pursuit of a Frenchman, and became a wreck. Captain Purvis, however, took his opponent, which carried fourteen guns, and returned in her to Jamaica.

Early in 1709, Rear-Admiral Wager's cruisers [2] continued to make numerous prizes in the West Indies. But the only exploit performed on the station during the year, and calling for special mention here, was the gallant action which resulted in the recapture of the *Coventry*,[3] 50. Captain Stephen Hutchins, of the *Portland*, 50, while convoying trading vessels, found himself off the Bastimentos, near Puerto Bello, and there, on April 15th, learnt that four large ships were at anchor in the port. He reconnoitred them; but as

---

[1] James, Lord Dursley, grandson of George, first Earl of Berkeley. Born, 1680. Captain, 1701. Commanded the *Boyne* at Malaga, 1704, and the *St. George* at the siege of Toulon. Vice-Admiral, 1708. First Lord of the Admiralty, 1717. Admiral and Commander-in-Chief of the Fleet, and Vice-Admiral of England, 1719. Died, 1736. He had succeeded to the Earldom of Berkeley in 1710.

[2] One of these, the *Adventure*, 40, Captain Robert Clark, was taken by the enemy, and her captain killed, on March 1st, 1709.

[3] Taken by the French on July 24th, 1704.

they appeared to be much too strong to be properly attacked with the force at his disposal, he stood away, hoping to induce the enemy to separate. On the 22nd, he was informed by a canoe which he had left to observe the foe, that two of the vessels had sailed, and that the two remaining were the *Coventry*, 50, and the *Mignon*, 40, both of which had recently arrived from Guinea. Hutchins thereupon returned to the Bastimentos. On May 1st, he received intelligence that the *Coventry* and *Mignon* had sailed on the previous evening; and he at once weighed and went in chase of them.

At 8 A.M. on May 3rd, he sighted them from the masthead; and on the afternoon of the same day the French, which were to windward, bore down upon him, and opened fire at extreme range. They apparently desired to provoke him to attack them, while they kept their wind; but they did not approach him closely. He, for his part, did what he could to get to windward, and took care not to lose sight of them during the night. At 7.30 A.M. on the 4th, he had worked up to within half pistol-shot of the *Mignon*, and, satisfying himself that if he engaged from windward he would be unable to use his lower-deck guns, he opened fire from leeward without manœuvring any further for the weather-gauge. After he had been for some time occupied with the *Mignon*, the *Coventry* placed herself on his lee bow, and began to aim at his spars, but at first without much effect. Captain Hutchins declined to allow his attention to be diverted, and steadily hammered away at the *Mignon* until he was temporarily crippled by the loss of his main-topsail-yard. This disaster enabled the French ships to get ahead of him; but he did his best to keep up with them, while splicing his rigging, bending on new sails, and repairing damages.

At 3 A.M. on May 5th, and for many hours afterwards, boats were seen passing and repassing between the *Mignon* and *Coventry*, as if engaged in removing goods from the former to the latter.[1] All day calms and baffling winds prevented the *Portland* from approaching; and not until 7 A.M. on the 6th could Hutchins renew the action. This time he devoted himself more especially to the *Coventry*. The *Mignon* lay off at some distance, firing occasionally, but doing little harm. At noon the *Coventry's* mainmast went by the board; and a little later the ship struck. While the *Portland* was securing her, the *Mignon* made off. The two French ships lost

---

[1] During that time, all the *Mignon's* people, except those absolutely necessary for the carrying of the ship into port, were transferred to the *Coventry*.

between them about seventy killed and wounded. The *Portland's* success cost her only nine killed and twelve wounded, out of two hundred and thirty-two on board at the beginning of the action. In the prize about twenty thousand pieces of eight were taken. Rear-Admiral Wager returned to England, reaching St. Helens on November 20th, 1709, and leaving as senior officer on the West Indies station, Captain Tudor Trevor, of the *Kingston*, 60.

At home, Lord Dursley, who had been promoted to be Vice-Admiral of the White, cruised with a squadron in the Channel. Du Guay Trouin also cruised there, having quitted Brest at the end of February with the *Achille*, 64, his own flagship, *Gloire*, 38, *Amazone*, 40, and *Astrée*, 22.[1] At about the same time Captain Anthony Tollet, of the *Assurance*, 70, with the *Sunderland*, 60, *Hampshire*, 50, *Anglesey*, 50, and *Assistance*, 50, left Cork with a convoy of merchant ships[2] for England. What followed may best be told in the words of a letter,[3] dated from the *Assurance*, in Hamoaze, on March 3rd, and worded as follows :—

"On Sunday last, sailing from Ireland, the *Anglesey* and *Sunderland* lost company with us, and went away with some part of our fleet. Yesterday morning, about five o'clock, we saw four sail standing after us, we steering away E. by N., the Lizard then bearing about N.N.E., distant, by estimation, about eight leagues. About seven they came within random shot, and then brought to. We then made a signal for the *Hampshire*[4] and *Assistance*[5] to draw into a line, and another for the merchant-ships to bear away, which they took no notice of. About eight they bore down to us, having made the signal for a line; and, when they came within musket-shot, hoisted French colours. The commodore, who was in a ship mounting seventy guns or upwards, came ranging along our larboard side, and fell on board us, so that we engaged yard-arm and yard-arm for almost the space of half an hour ; during which he plied us so warmly with small shot that he cut off most of our Marines and seamen quartered upon deck. He after that put off, and fell soon after on board again on our lee side ; first ranging on our bow, and then on our quarter. We fired upon him, with the utmost vigour, our upper-deck, and part of our lower-deck guns, so that we obliged him to quit us once more, standing away ahead of us towards the merchant-ships. Then the three other ships, of forty and fifty guns each, came ranging along our side, firing several broadsides into us ; and, after that, bore away as the former. The damage we received was very great, we having our ship's side in a great many places shot through and through, our shrouds and back-stays cut to pieces, as also our main and false-stay,[6] which, if not timely seen, had occasioned the loss of our mast. Our fore-sail and fore-topsail were torn to pieces, the best bower cut away by their shot, one of the flukes of the spare anchor shot off, and the small bower, by the enemy's

---

[1] The force of these ships has been generally exaggerated by British historians, and was even exaggerated by the dispatch writers at the time.

[2] The French accounts say sixty sail.

[3] 'Biog. Nav.' iii. 114.   [4] Captain Henry Maynard.

[5] Captain Abraham Tudor.   [6] "False-stay," *i.e.*, "preventer-stay."

boarding,[1] driven through our bow. We endeavoured, with what despatch we could, to fix our rigging, which took up some time, and bent a new fore-sail and fore-topsail. After that, we all bore down to secure what merchant-ships we could, expecting likewise to engage the enemy again ; which they declined, standing away to cut off part of our convoy ; which might, if they had regarded our signal, have got in shore and been secure. Some we brought in here, and, when engaged, saw others bear away for Falmouth, so that we are not certain how many they took. The dispute lasted about two hours, in the beginning of which our captain [2] was wounded upon deck, whither he was carried in a chair, having, for almost four months, been so ill as to be unable to go out of his cabin. Our first lieutenant was shot in the leg ; which he got dressed ; and returned to his charge on the deck. Our second was killed, as were also several of the French (refugee) officers that we brought with us from Ireland, and some of them wounded." . . . " Captain Tudor, who commanded the *Assistance*, is dead of his wounds. This ship (the *Assurance*) had 25 men killed and 53 wounded, four of them mortally. In the *Hampshire* were 2 killed and 11 wounded ; in the *Assistance*, 8 killed and 21 wounded."

The French, on this occasion, seem to have taken only five of the merchantmen, and, even of these, two were lost before they could be carried into port. Having regard to the fact that Du Guay Trouin's was not superior to Tollet's force, and that all the merchant-men of those days were armed, it is almost astonishing that the French succeeded in taking any. That much may be said, and the enterprise and gallantry of the French commander's action may be admitted, without, however, in any way depreciating the manner in which the British officers defended their ships and their charges. They, and Tollet especially, behaved admirably.

The news of this exploit naturally spurred Lord Dursley and his captains [3] to increased activity and vigilance. A division of observation was sent off Brest for intelligence, and careful provision was made for the safe convoy of the Lisbon fleet. Yet, on April 24th, within a few miles of the main body of the fleet, Du Guay Trouin, with the *Achille*, 64, and *Gloire*, 38, fought and took the *Bristol*, 50, Captain Henry Gore. But the great corsair had become too daring. Before he could refit his prize he was sighted by the headmost ships of Lord Dursley's command. These chased, and Trouin had to abandon the *Bristol* without even taking off the crew which he had put on board her. She was overhauled and retaken as a matter of course ;[4] and, although Du Guay Trouin, in the *Achille*, himself escaped, he lost the *Gloire*, which struck, after a short conflict, to

---

[1] *I.e.,* " falling on board of us."   [2] Anthony Tollet.

[3] In March, the *Salisbury*, Captain Francis Hosier, took a large and valuable French Indiaman, and the *Romney*, Captain Thomas Scott, a Frenchman of 20 guns.

[4] The *Bristol*, which had received a shot in her breadroom, foundered almost immediately after her recapture.

the *Chester*, 50, Captain Thomas Mathews, who, in the chase, had far outsailed all his brother captains.

The *Achille* went into Brest to repair damages, and, issuing thence again in October, captured, on the 26th of that month, the *Gloucester*, 60, Captain John Balchen,[1] who thus, for a second time within little more than two years, saw the inside of a French prison. Balchen surrendered only after his ship had been reduced to the condition of a shambles. He was carried into Rochefort.

Dursley continued to cruise in the Channel or the North Sea until after the conclusion of the year, taking numerous small prizes, yet being quite unable to altogether repress the privateers of the enemy. Never was there a better illustration of the truth that a Power, possessed of practically unchallenged command of the sea, may, nevertheless, suffer very severely by the enemy's prosecution of a determined *guerre de course*.

On December 25th, the *Solebay*, 20, Captain George Stidson, while in charge of a convoy bound to Lynn, Norfolk, was lost on Boston Knock with nearly all hands.[2]

One or two of the actions fought in home waters by detached vessels were particularly creditable. Captain George Cammock, in the *Speedwell*, 32, off Bantry Bay, retook, in May, a very valuable West Indiaman, the *Ruth*, of London, and took one of the two privateers which had captured her. In the same month,[3] the *Falmouth*, 50, Captain Walter Riddell, returning from New England with a convoy, was attacked, about twenty-four leagues from Scilly, by a French man-of-war of sixty guns. Riddell handled his ship with great ability, laying her athwart the enemy's hawse, raking the Frenchman fore and aft for a full hour and a half, and repulsing several attempts to board. The Frenchman, after hacking away all the laniards of the *Falmouth's* fore and mizzen shrouds, with a view to crippling her, got free at last, and stood after the convoy; but Riddell, rapidly repairing damages, followed her so closely, that he saved all his charges and carried them safely into Plymouth. Captain Riddell received several injuries, and had thirteen men killed and fifty-six wounded in the course of this gallant encounter.

In September, the *Plymouth*, 60, Captain Jonas Hanway, being

---

[1] The *Gloucester*, with the *Hampshire*, which escaped in a shattered condition, was in charge of a convoy, off the Irish coast.

[2] The convoy, consisting of eight sail, was also lost.

[3] On May 18th.

on her way to Plymouth from the main fleet to repair defects occasioned by a severe gale of wind, fell in, on the 20th, off the Deadman, with the French man-of-war *Adriade*, mounting forty guns, but pierced for forty-eight. The *Plymouth* was scarcely fit for action; yet she gave chase to the enemy, overhauled him, and, after an hour's fight, obliged him to strike. The *Adriade* lost fifteen killed and about sixty wounded; the *Plymouth*, seven killed and sixteen wounded. On the other hand, the *Sweepstake*, 32, Captain Samuel Meade, was taken, on April 16th, by two privateers, in circumstances so unsatisfactory, that a court-martial subsequently condemned Meade to be dismissed the service. He was afterwards restored, but not until he had spent four years in retirement.

In the Mediterranean, though the command of the sea was, as much as elsewhere, in the hands of the British, the French cruisers also succeeded.[1] Towards the end of the year 1709, the *Pembroke*, 64, Captain Edward Rumsey, and the *Falcon*, 32, Captain Charles Constable, were detached from the fleet to cruise between Toulon and Corsica. On December 29th they sighted three ships, which they took to be part of Sir Edward Whitaker's squadron, but which presently proved to be French,[2] under the command of the corsair Cassard, of Nantes. The British vessels made all possible sail away from the enemy, but were come up with and taken, after a smart action, in which Captain Rumsey was killed, and Captain Constable was dangerously wounded. The *Pembroke* did not strike until she was completely disabled and had lost one hundred and forty killed and wounded. The *Falcon* made, if possible, an even more determined defence, if it be true, as is alleged in contemporary accounts, that, when she surrendered, only sixteen of her people remained unwounded. Besides these misfortunes, the loss of the *Arrogant*, 60, Captain George Nichols, must be chronicled. She foundered on January 5th, 1709, while on her way to Port Mahon, laden with naval stores.

As a precautionary measure, a squadron under Vice-Admiral Sir John Norris (R.) was sent to the Baltic early in 1709, but the expedition was merely a peaceful demonstration, and it returned without having had occasion to fire a shot in anger.

---

[1] In the "latter end of June," the *Fowey*, 32, was captured in the Mediterranean, Campbell (1817) iv. 86. But she was not in commission after April 4th.

[2] One of 70, one of 60, and one of 50 guns, according to British accounts.

The year 1710 witnessed a decline, if not in the activity, at least in the success, of the French cruisers. In the Channel, Lord Dursley cruised as before, until May, when he struck his flag. Several small privateers were taken by his captains, but no action deserving of special mention was performed. Under the command of Admiral of the Fleet Matthew Aylmer, who succeeded him, a small French convoy, bound for Martinique and Newfoundland, was fallen in with by the fleet off the Lizard. The *Kent*, 70, *Assurance*, 70, and *York*, 60, were ordered in chase. The weather was, however, hazy, and although the *Kent*, Captain Robert Johnson, was so fortunate as to secure the *Superbe*, 56,[1] the larger of the two men-of-war with the convoy, the other man-of-war, the *Concorde*, 30, and all the merchantmen, except one, succeeded in getting away. This action occurred on July 30th. Several other prizes of less value were taken on the Irish station by the *Hastings*, 40, Captain John Paul.[2]

An action is said by several historians[3] to have been fought in the Mediterranean on November 8th, 1710, by the *Centurion*, 50, Captain James Mighels, and the *Defiance*, 64, Captain John Evans. These vessels are alleged to have met two French men-of-war, of force about equal to their own, between Almeria and Malaga, and to have fought them from 8 A.M. until noon, when the enemy drew off, the *Centurion* having lost upwards of sixty, the *Defiance*, ninety, and the Frenchman, upwards of one hundred killed and wounded. Such an action may have taken place, but it certainly was not fought in the conditions specified. Captain James Mighels commanded the *Hampton Court* from August 26th, 1709, to February 13th, 1713, and never commanded the *Centurion ;* and although Captain John Evans did command the *Defiance*, it was from August 18th, 1708, to August 28th, 1710, and not in November, 1710. But as Captain John Mihill commanded the *Centurion* from October 18th, 1708,

---

[1] She struck, after an hour's warm action, and being added to the Royal Navy under her French name, was first commissioned, on September 23rd, 1710, by Captain William Elford.

[2] Charnock, iii. 133, in his notice of Francis Hosier, says that that officer, cruising on the Irish station in the *Salisbury* with the *St. Albans* in company, in March, 1710, captured a French 60-gun ship, which was taken into the service as the *Salisbury Prize*. He also marvels that no notice is taken of the capture by any historian. The fact is that there was, during the reign of Anne, but one *Salisbury Prize* in the Navy, and that she entered it, as described on p. 517, in March, 1708. She was thenceforward continuously in commission until December, 9th, 1714, when Captain John Clifton paid her off. MS. List of Commissions in Author's coll.

[3] *See e.g.* 'Biog. Nav.' ii. 391 ; iii. 76.

to July 26th, 1710, it is probable that Evans and Mihill were the heroes of the adventure, and that it happened in November, 1708 or 1709. The matter is scarcely, however, sufficiently important to warrant further inquiry.

But, in 1710, there were several notable little Mediterranean actions concerning which there is much less obscurity. On May 2nd, Vice-Admiral Baker, being off Messina with his division, gave chase to four ships and as many settees. The *Suffolk*, 70, Captain William Cleveland, and the *Fame Prize*,[1] Captain Streynsham Master, were among the best sailers in the division; and on the following morning the *Suffolk* captured the French man-of-war *Gaillard*, 56 (only thirty-eight mounted), and the *Fame Prize* took a smaller vessel.

In July, when Sir John Norris, after having shown himself off Marseilles and Toulon, stood into Hyères Road, he found there, newly arrived from Scanderoon, a French ship of fifty guns, which lay under the shelter of three forts. The duty of dealing with her was entrusted to several British and Dutch light craft, under the orders of Captain Thomas Stepney, of the *Bedford*, 70, who quickly drove the defenders out of the vessel, and out of one of the forts commanding her. Boats then advanced to take possession of the prize; but no sooner were the seamen on board her than she blew up, killing or wounding thirty-five of them. It was alleged by the captors that the French, before quitting their ship, had lighted a slow match communicating with the magazine. This they were, of course, quite entitled to do, provided that they had not first struck their flag in token of submission. Yet, contemporary accounts are written as if the enemy had been guilty of the wickedest treachery.

On December 13th, the *Warspite*, 70, Captain Josias Crow, and the *Breda*, 70, Captain Thomas Long, being detached by Sir John Norris, sighted and chased the *Maure*, 60. The *Breda* first got up with the enemy; and there resulted a smart, but brief, action, in the course of which Captain Long was killed. The *Warspite* then took up a position on the Frenchman's quarter, and made ready to board, whereupon the *Maure* at once struck. She was added to the Navy as the *Moor*.[2]

In the West Indies, Captain Tudor Trevor was succeeded, as senior officer, by Captain Jonathan Spann, who, in turn, was

---

[1] A 6th-rate.

[2] And first commissioned on May 8th, 1711, by Captain Michael Sansom.

succeeded by Commodore James Littleton.[1] This officer sailed from
St. Helens on August 24th, and reached Jamaica on November 2nd,
1710; but little of importance happened during the year upon the
station.[2] Very different was the case on the coast of North
America.

The presence in London of some Indian chiefs had interested the
Government and the nation in the affairs of Newfoundland and Nova
Scotia; and in the early part of the year an expedition was fitted out
at Portsmouth to proceed against Port Royal, now called Annapolis,
on the Bay of Fundy. The expeditionary force ultimately consisted
of the following ships :—

Ships.	Guns.	Commanders.
Dragon	50	Captain George Martin.
Falmouth	50	„ Walter Riddell.
Chester	50	„ Thomas Mathews.
Feversham	36	„ Robert Paston.
Lowestoft	32	„ George Gordon.
Star, bomb	..	Commander Thomas Rochfort.

The *Dragon*, *Falmouth* and *Star*, sailed from Spithead [3] on May 8th,
and reached Boston, Massachusetts, on July 15th. The *Feversham*
and *Lowestoft* proceeded with a convoy to New York, and thence
joined Captain Martin in September. The *Chester* was already on
the coast. Colonel Francis Nicholson went out with Captain Martin
in command of the troops, and, upon arriving in New England, he
conveyed to the various governors the Queen's orders for them to
further in every way the objects of the expedition. Five provincial
regiments were, in consequence, raised; and numerous small craft
were provided by the colonies. The whole force [4] left Nantasket
Road on September 18th. On September 24th, the squadron
anchored off the harbour; on the 25th, the army landed in two
divisions; on the 26th, Colonel Nicholson advanced; and at night
the works were bombarded. On the following days bad weather

---

[1] With a captain under him.

[2] The *Scarborough*, 34, Captain Edward Holland, was taken by the enemy on
November 1st, 1710.

[3] With a convoy, and transports having on board a regiment of Marines.

[4] Except the *Chester*, which sailed a few days in advance to endeavour to intercept
any supplies that might be intended for Port Royal.

interfered somewhat with the operations of the ships; yet, on October 2nd, the French governor was glad to capitulate, and on the 5th, Colonel Nicholson took possession of the place, to which he gave the new name of Annapolis Royal. Captain Martin sailed again on the 19th, leaving Colonel Vetch in command of the town; and, on the 26th, he reached Boston, whence he returned to England. The expedition, unlike most of the combined expeditions of the time, was well planned, and smoothly carried out, Martin and Nicholson co-operating in the most loyal and generous manner. It is also specially notable on account of the considerable share borne in it by the young colonies.

In the meantime, the *Rochester*, 50, Captain John Aldred, *Severn*, 50, Captain Humphrey Pudner, *Portland*, 50, Captain George Purvis, and *Valeur*, 18, Captain John Hare, were exceedingly active on the coast of Newfoundland, destroying nearly all the French settlements there, and burning or taking numerous vessels.[1] In the course of the operations, the *Valeur* was surprised by a French party while lying at anchor, and was taken, but was quickly retaken.

These North American successes encouraged the fitting out of a more ambitious expedition in 1711. The project originated in New England, and it would appear that the home Ministry, suspecting that British public sentiment would regard it with apprehension and disfavour, prepared it with a haste, a lack of forethought, and a secrecy which materially contributed to its ultimate failure. The naval command of it was entrusted to Rear-Admiral Sir Hovenden Walker (W.), and the military, to General Hill. A large force was collected for the adventure; and, in addition to the men-of-war concerned, thirty-one transports, carrying 5303 troops, one hospital ship, eight storeships, and one tender, were employed. Such of the ships as were not already in North America sailed from St. Helens on April 29th, and reached Nantasket Road, near Boston, on June 24th.[2] It had been determined to essay a blow at the very heart of the French dominions in America, and to attack Quebec.

It is not necessary here to describe the various dispositions which

---

[1] Among the large ships taken were the *François de la Paix*, 30, *Marquis de Braie*, 28, *Comtesse d'Evreux*, 16, *François Marie*, 18, and *Aigle Noire*, 12.

[2] At Boston Sir Hovenden found the *Windsor*, 60, Captain George Paddon, which had come in with a prize, the French man-of-war *Thétis*, 42. The *Windsor* was retained; the prize was sent to the West Indies.

were made by Sir Hovenden,[1] or to specify what ships were detached by him for purposes germane to the objects of the expedition. It will suffice to say that, after having experienced some difficulty in obtaining in New England such provisions as he needed, he sailed on July 30th, and, on August 18th, anchored in Gaspé Bay, near the mouth of the St. Lawrence, with the following formidable force, besides transports, etc. :—[2]

Ships.	Guns.	Commanders.
Edgar	70	Rear-Admiral Sir H. Walker. / Captain George Paddon.
Swiftsure	70	„ Joseph Soanes.
Monmouth . . .	70	„ John Mitchell
Sunderland . .	60	„ John Cockburn.
Kingston	60	„ Joseph Winder.
Montagu	60	„ George Walton.
Windsor . . .	60	„ Robert Arris.
Dunkirk	60	„ Henry Gore.
Leopard . .	50	„ Isaac Cook.
Enterpris' . . .	40	„ Nicholas Smith.
Sapphire . . .	40	„ Augustine Rouse.
Lowestoft . . .	32	„ George Gordon.
Triton Prize . .	30	Commander Richard Burlington.
Basilisk, bomb . .	..	„ Robert Harward.
Granado, bomb . .	..	„ James Grainger.

Detached, besides the *Feversham*, 36, there were the *Torbay*, 80, Captain James Moody, *Devonshire*, 80, Captain John Cooper, *Humber*, 80, Captain Richard Culliford, *Chester*, 50, Captain Thomas Mathews, *Diamond*, 40, Captain Tobias Lisle, *Bedford Galley*, Captain Andrew Lay, and *Experiment*, 40, Captain Matthew Elford.[3]

On August 20th, the wind being fair, the fleet weighed, and left the Bay, and on the following day it turned into the river St. Lawrence. There it met with thick weather, and with currents which, at that time, were little known to British seamen ; nor were such pilots as had been obtained competent to navigate large ships

[1] It should, however, be said that for chasing without orders on May 28th, Captain Soanes, then of the *Edgar*, was fined, and Captain Thomas Butler, then of the *Dunkirk*, was dismissed, the latter by sentence of a court-martial held on June 27th.

[2] The *Feversham*, 36, Captain Robert Paston, was to have joined from Virginia with stores, but was delayed, and on October 7th, foundered off Cape Breton with the captain and nearly all hands, and with three transports which were under her convoy.

[3] The names of the Captains are given from an Admiralty MS. register in the Author's collection, and are those of the officers actually commanding on August 18th. A few weeks previously there had been extensive changes, far more than those which are noted in Walker's dispatch of August 14th, written off Bird Islands.

in such waters.   On the night of the 22nd, the flagship narrowly
escaped running aground ; and, on the 22nd and 23rd, eight transports were wrecked, and eight hundred and eighty-four men, out of
less than fourteen hundred on board them, perished.

The Rear-Admiral thereupon called a council of war on board
the *Windsor*.   The pilots who attended expressed their unwillingness to risk the attempt to carry up the fleet to Quebec, and the
Captains, as well as the military officers, came to the conclusion that
the prosecution of the undertaking was impracticable.   A suggestion
that Placentia should be attacked was negatived on the plea of the
advanced season of the year, and the condition of the remaining
stock of provisions ; and at length, after certain ships and troops had
been dispatched to stations where it was supposed they would be
useful, the fleet sailed on September 16th from Spanish River Bay,
and, October 9th, arrived at St. Helens.   On October 15th, as if to
seal the misfortunes of this ill-considered undertaking, the *Edgar*
accidentally blew up at Spithead.   Both Sir Hovenden and Captain
Paddon were on shore at the time ; but the disaster cost the lives of
several hundred people, and, moreover, involved the destruction of
valuable papers which were afterwards sorely needed when the Rear-
Admiral and his flag-captain were called upon to defend their conduct
while in North America.[1]

In the West Indies, Commodore James Littleton spent the early
part of the year in providing for the safety of the trade, and in
endeavouring to ascertain the whereabouts of a French squadron
which, under Ducasse, was supposed to be on the station.   As
before, also, efforts were made to ensure that the homeward-bound
Spanish galleons should never reach the Philippists.   On May 23rd,
the capture by the *Jersey*, 60, Captain Edward Vernon, of a Brest-
bound trader, provided Littleton with intelligence that Ducasse had
gone to Cartagena, and that the French force there was intended to
escort to Havana, and thence to Cadiz, the galleons in question.

Cartagena was reconnoitred ; and it was found, on June 28th, that
twelve ships and five small sloops lay there.   Upon hearing this,

---

[1] No inquiry was instituted at the time; but, after the accession of George I., the
administration took up the question, and Walker was struck off the flag-list and
deprived of his half-pay.   Paddon also was dismissed the service, and afterwards
entered that of Peter the Great.   Apart from the intrinsic merits of their case, it seems
hard that the two officers should have been thus dealt with when their conduct had
been condoned, if not tacitly approved, by the fact of their appointment to fresh
commands after the return of the Quebec expedition.

Commodore Littleton sailed from Jamaica on July 15th, with five two-decked ships and a sloop; and arrived off the coast of the main-land on the 26th. That day he chased five large vessels, but they ran under Bocca Chica, at the entrance to Cartagena harbour. The British squadron stood off for the night; and on the following morning, while stretching in again, sighted four other ships and chased them. One of these proved to be the vice-admiral of the long-looked-for galleons. She mistook Littleton for Ducasse, and therefore lay to so long that the leaders of the squadron, the *Salisbury*, 50, Captain Francis Hosier, and the *Salisbury Prize*, 50, Captain Robert Harland, were able to get up with and engage her. She held out until the Commodore got within pistol-shot of her, and then she struck. She carried sixty brass guns, but was a much less less valuable prize than had been anticipated. The little action, however, cost the British only one man killed and six wounded. The *Jersey*, 60, Captain Vernon, captured another of the ships in company, but the rest escaped. In the autumn the Commo-dore was temporarily called away from his observation of Cartagena by a report, which turned out to be baseless, that a large French force had reached Martinique, and was preparing to attack the British West India Islands. In his absence, Ducasse and the galleons made their way in safety to Havana, whence the latter ultimately reached Europe.

During the continuance of Commodore Littleton's command, numerous small services were performed by the cruisers which he detached from time to time for various purposes. On June 10th, for example, the *Newcastle*, 50, Captain Sampson Bourne, engaged off Martinique a French flotilla consisting of a 36-gun ship, a 24-gun hag-boat, nine privateer sloops, and two other vessels, and drove them, in a very shattered condition, into the harbour of St. Pierre, thus putting an end to a filibustering expedition which had been designed against Antigua. He subsequently foiled a similar design against Montserrat. The *Jersey*, 60, Captain Edward Vernon, and *Weymouth*, 50, Captain Richard Lestock, were among the other vessels which particularly distinguished themselves by their activity. The *Anglesey*, 50, Captain Thomas Legge, and the *Fowey*, 40, Captain Robert Chadwick, retook the *Scarborough*, 34, which, under Captain Edward Holland, had been taken by the French on November 1st, 1710.

In the Mediterranean the chief occurrences of 1711, other than

those chronicled in the foregoing chapter, were the wreck of the
Resolution, 70, Captain Richard Haddock, near Barcelona, on
January 10th, and the wreck of the *Restoration*, 70, Captain John
Hartnoll, on November 9th, near Leghorn. But two small actions
deserving of mention were fought there. On March 22nd, when
Sir John Norris was lying in Vado Bay, his look-out cruisers, the
Severn, 48, Captain Humphrey Pudner, *Lion*, 60, Captain Galfridus
Walpole, and *Lyme*, 32, Captain James Gunman, signalled that
four enemy's ships were in sight; whereupon the *Nassau*, 70,
Captain Charles Strickland, and *Exeter*, 60, Captain Baymond
Raymond, were ordered to slip and to chase with the cruisers.[1]
The strangers appear to have been the French *Phénix*, 40,
Pembroke, 60, *Rubis*, 56, and *Trident*, 56, under the orders of
M. de l'Aigle. The cruisers overhauled the enemy, and brought on
an action which lasted for about two hours. The French then
made sail to get away, the British ships, except the *Severn*, which
was too much disabled, pursuing until nightfall. Towards the end
of the engagement the *Exeter* also got up and, for two hours, fought
the *Pembroke*. But all the French vessels, though heavily mauled,
finally escaped. The *Severn* had twenty-three people killed and
wounded ; the *Lion*, whose captain lost his right arm, forty. The
Lyme suffered far less and had but six hurt. Towards the end
of the year, as the *Hampton Court*, 70, Captain James Mighel,
with the *Stirling Castle, Nottingham, Charles Galley*, and *Lynn*,
was returning to Port Mahon after a cruise on the Catalonian
coast, she sighted the two French men-of-war *Toulouse*, 62, and
Trident, 56. The *Hampton Court* brought the former to action,
and, when the *Stirling Castle* also drew up, took her.[2] The
Hampton Court's masts were so badly wounded that, on the
following day, when the wind freshened, they all went by the board,
and the ship had to be towed into Port Mahon.

On the home station Rear-Admiral Sir Thomas Hardy (B.), with
a small squadron, blockaded Dunquerque, chiefly in order to intercept the numerous corsairs belonging to that port ;[3] but he was
driven off the coast by a S.S.W. gale and forced into Yarmouth,

---

[1] The *Dartmouth* and *Winchelsea* were sent after them later, but did not get up
with the foe.

[2] The "second captain" of the *Toulouse* was one Edward Rigby, who, in 1698,
when captain of the *Dragon*, 40, had been convicted of a detestable crime, and had fled
the country. At Port Mahon he again escaped.

[3] His ships made several small prizes.

whence he was sent with a convoy to the northward. Returning, he was ordered in search of Ducasse, who was expected home, but who was not sighted. During this long absence of Hardy from before Dunquerque, a privateer named Saus slipped out and captured sixteen out of twenty-two sail homeward bound from Virginia. Either Saus's squadron, or another[1] from Dunquerque, had, in the meantime, fallen in with the *Advice*, 46, Captain Kenneth, Lord Duffus, off Yarmouth, reduced her to a wreck, and taken her on June 27th. Lord Duffus, who was wounded in five places, and who had behaved himself most gallantly, was, in the following year, appointed to a new ship bearing the same name as that which he had so creditably commanded in the action.

In 1712, Sir Thomas Hardy left Plymouth early in the year with his squadron and cruised for a considerable time off Cape Finisterre.[2] He took no prizes of note until August, when he fell in with a squadron of six French vessels and a tartan. The enemy made an effort to form a line, supposing, as was afterwards admitted, that the strange ships were four Flushing privateers and two prizes; and, when he found his mistake, he hauled his wind and crowded sail to escape. The British squadron took the *Griffon*, 44,[3] the *Aventure*, 12, the *Incomparable*, 16, and the *Rubis;* and one vessel, the *St. Esprit*, 36, blew up while in action with the *Windsor*. All these craft were richly laden; but one, the *Aventure*, producing the Queen's pass, had to be permitted to proceed on her voyage; and the captors found it impossible to obtain the condemnation of the other prizes, the Ministry of the day having, so Charnock suggests, a kindness for the late enemy, and a willingness to believe that the French had had no hostile intention.[4]

On the Irish station the *Monck*, 60, Captain George Cammock, took a privateer, the *Salamandre*, 16, on April 28th, and on the day following retook a valuable trader belonging to Cork. Hearing that several privateers were off the south coast, Cammock hastily, but effectively, fortified Crookhaven as a refuge for the merchantmen in the neighbourhood, and, putting to sea, discovered the *Comte de*

---

[1] Consisting of eight ships.

[2] Chiefly with a view to intercept Ducasse and Du Guay Trouin, who, however, were not seen.

[3] A ship of the French Royal Navy, fitted out by the merchants.

[4] A suspension of hostilities was concluded on August 19th. Hardy seems to have assumed that the French effort to form line argued a hostile object, and to have known nothing of the progress of negotiations.

Giraldin, 40, of St. Malo, one of the most daring of the corsairs. He took her after a two hours' engagement, in which the Frenchman lost thirty killed and ten wounded, and in which the *Monck* had not so much as one man dangerously hit. Indeed the British Navy in 1712 had almost unchallenged control of the Narrow Seas. Its only serious loss there, that of the *Dragon*, 50, Captain George Martin, which was wrecked on the Gaskets on March 16th, was not occasioned even indirectly by the operations of the enemy.

In the Mediterranean, Vice-Admiral John Baker was detached by Sir John Jennings, the Commander-in-Chief, to cruise on the coast of Portugal; and there he drove ashore a Spanish ship of sixty-guns on February 16th, and took a valuable French vessel bound for Martinique. Several detached ships of Baker's division, notably the *Lynn*, 40, Captain Henry Blinstone, *Ludlow Castle*, 40, Captain Arthur Field, *Royal Anne*, galley, Captain Robert Trevor, and *Port Mahon*, Captain William Haddock, also did most useful service.

Elsewhere, little that is worth mentioning happened. A gallant engagement fought off the coast of Guinea on March 11th, 1712, by the *Falmouth*, 50, Captain Walter Riddell, and the *Mary Galley*, 26, Captain William Mabbott, with two French men-of-war of superior force, terminated, unfortunately, without decisive result. In the West Indies, Sir Hovenden Walker, who sailed from St. Helens on April 28th to relieve Commodore Littleton, did nothing of moment prior to the proclamation at Jamaica of the suspension of hostilities; and soon afterwards he was recalled. He arrived off Dover on May 26th, 1713, about two months after the conclusion of the Peace of Utrecht.[1]

---

[1] The ships of the French Royal Navy taken or destroyed by the action of the English during the war of the Spanish Succession seem to have been as follows :—

Class.	Number.	Total guns.
80 to 100 guns . . .	6	528
70 to 80 guns	7	516
60 to 70 guns	15	942
50 to 60 guns	12	642
40 to 50 guns	10	438
Total ships of two decks	50	3066

besides about eighty-five vessels of inferior rate. In addition, upwards of fifty sail of French men-of-war were lost by accident during the continuance of hostilities. These

Between the day of the Peace and that of the death of Queen Anne, the only operations during which any ships of the Navy were called upon to fire a shot in anger were some, undertaken under the direction of Captain George Paddon, then of the *Ruby*, for the purpose of once more reminding the Moorish pirates that Great Britain was not inclined to allow them unchecked freedom. Captain Paddon ordered reprisals for the seizure of a small English craft at Oran, and then, after negotiating with Marocco, obtained not only a satisfactory renewal of the old truce with England, but also the liberation of sixty British captives.

---

figures may be taken to be as exact as any which, after so great a lapse of time, can be compiled; yet they differ greatly from those given by Burchett and copied by Lediard. According to those historians, the entire French loss, by capture and destruction, as well as by accident, during the war, was but fifty-two sail, mounting 3094 guns. Burchett should have been better qualified to speak of the total British loss. He places this at thirty-eight ships (of which sixteen were of the line), mounting 1596 guns. Yet I am convinced that Burchett under-rates the British as gravely as he does the French loss. Indeed, he includes in his list no British vessel mounting less than twenty-two guns. Still, it is probably safe to conclude that the British loss, no matter what the exact figures may have been, did not much exceed one-half the loss of the French. A tentative list of British men-of-war taken, destroyed, or lost in the period 1688–1714 will be found in the Appendix which follows this chapter.

APPENDIX TO CHAPTER XXIV.

LOSSES OF H.M. SHIPS FROM THE REVOLUTION TO 1714.

NOTE.—This list is merely a tentative one. There do not appear to be now in existence materials for compiling one which could be pronounced to be absolutely complete. Yet it is believed that the long catalogue below, which has been prepared almost entirely from contemporary MS. authorities, will be found much more nearly perfect than anything of the kind that has been previously attempted.

Year.	Date.	H.M. Ship.	Guns.	Commander. [* Lost his life on the occasion.]	Remarks.
1688	Nov. 17	*Heldenberg*	32	Capt. Albion Howell.	Wrecked off the Isle of Wight.
1689	Jan. 2	*Sedgemoor*	48	,, David Lloyd.	Lost in St. Margaret's Bay.
	Mar. 14	*Samson*, f.s.	12	,, John Harris.	
	May 11	*Elizabeth and Sarah*, f.s.	6	,, Edward Dover.	
	June 21	*Alexander*, f.s.	..	,, Thomas Jennings.	
	Aug. 9	*Portsmouth*	46	,, George St. Loe.	Taken by the French.
	,, 26	*Deptford*, ketch . . .	10	,, Thomas Berry.*	Wrecked off Virginia.
	Oct. 4	*Lively Prize*	30	,, William Tichborne.	Retaken by the French.
	,, 26	*Pendennis*	70	,, George Churchill.	Wrecked on the Kentish Knock.
	Nov. 29	*Charles and Henry*, f.s.	6	,, William Stone.	
	Dec. 25	*Henrietta*.	62	,, John Neville.	Wrecked near Plymouth.
	,, 25	*Centurion*	48	,, Basil Beaumont.	Wrecked near Plymouth.
1690	Jan. 12	*Dragon*, sloop	..	,, Frederick Weighman	
	,, 12	*Supply*, hir d	..	,, William Harding.	
	,, 13	*John of Dublin*, f.s. . .	..	,, Thomas Warren.	
	Mar. 18	*Mary*, hired	..	,, Abraham Wise.*	Wrecked.
	,, 23	*Kingfisher*, ketch . .	4	,, Robert Audley.	
	July 6	*Anne*	70	,, John Tyrrell.	Burnt after the Battle of Beachy Head.
	Oct. 9	*Dartmouth*	32	,, Edward Pottinger.*	Wrecked on the Isle of Mull : nearly all lost.
	,, 12	*Breda*	70	,, Matthew Tennant.*	{Accidentally blown up at Cork ; nearly all lost.
	,, 16	*Dreadnought* . . .	62	,, Robert Willmot.	Foundered off the North Foreland.
1691	June 6	*Dumbarton* . . .	20	,, Simon Roe.	
	July 12	*Constant Warwick* . .	42	,, James Moody.	Taken by the French.
	,, 12	*Mary Rose*	48	,, John Bounty.	Taken by the French.
	,, 12	*Talbot*, ketch . . .	15	,, Charles Staggins.*	Taken by the French.
	Sept. 3	*Coronation*	90	,, Charles Skelton.*	Foundered off Ram Head ; 300 lost.
	,, 3	*Harwich*	70	,, Henry Robinson.	Wrecked near Plymouth.
	,, 12	*Exeter*	70	,, George Mees.	Accidentally blown up at Plymouth.
	Oct. 13	*Enquiry*, sloop, hired .	..	,, Peter Knight.*	Taken by the French.
	Nov. 4	*Happy Return* . . .	54	,, Peter Pickard.	Taken by the French.
	Dec. 18	*Jersey*.	48	,, John Bomstead.	Taken by the French.
1692	Feb. 9	*Crown Prize*	..	,, William Tichborne.*	Wrecked near Dartmouth ; 20 lost.
	Apr. 12	*Phœnix*	42	,, Jacob Banks.	Burnt to save her from capture.
	May 19	*Cadiz Merchant*, f.s. .	12	,, Robert Wynn.	Expended at the Battle of Barfleur.
	,, 19	*Fox*, f.s.	..	,, Thos. Killingworth.	Expended at the Battle of Barfleur.
	,, 19	*Phaeton*, f.s..	..	,, Robert Hancock.	Expended at the Battle of Barfleur.
	,, 19	*Hopewell*, f.s.	..	,, William Jumper.	Expended at the Battle of Barfleur.
	,, 19	*Extravagant*, f.s . . .	..	,, Fleetwood Emes.	Expended at the Battle of Barfleur.
	,, 22	*Blaze*, f.s.	..	,, Thomas Heath.	Expended in Cherbourg Bay.
	,, 22	*Wolf*, f.s..	..	,, James Greenaway.	Expended in Cherbourg Bay.
	,, 22	*Hound*, f.s.	..	,, Thomas Foulis.	Expended in Cherbourg Bay.
	,, 24	*Half Moon*, f.s. . . .	8	,, John Knapp.	Expended in La Hougue Bay.
	,, 24	{*Thomas and Elizabeth*, f.s. . . . . . .}	10	,, Edward Littleton.	Expended in La Hougue Bay.
	June 9	*Hart*, ketch	..	,, David Condon.*	Taken by the French.
	Oct. 6	*Norwich*	48	,, Richard Pugh.*	Wrecked in the West Indies ; all lost.
1693	Jan. 3	*Nonsuch*	42	,, Richard Short.	Taken by the French.
	,, 12	*Scarborough*, ketch. . .	..	,, Thomas Taylor.	Taken by the French ; retaken by the York.
	June 17	*Sun Prize*	..	,, Francis Manly.*	Taken by the French.
	Sept. 20	*Diamond*	48	,, Henry Wickham.	Taken by the French.
	,, 20	*Cygnet*, f.s.	6	,, John Perry.	Taken by the French.
	Nov. 21	*Mordaunt*	46	,, Francis Maynard.*	Wrecked off Cuba ; all lost.
	Dec. 1	*Milford*	32	,, Roger Vaughan.	Taken by the French.

Year.	Date.	H.M. Ship.	Guns.	Commander. [* Lost his life on the occasion.]	Remarks.
1693	Dec. 9	*St. Albans*	50	Capt. Thomas Gillam.*	Wrecked near Kingsale; nearly all lost.
	,, 22	*Lucas*, galley, hired	..	,, John Hardham.*	Foundered or wrecked.
1694	Feb. 19	*Sussex*	80	{Rear.-Adm. Sir Francis Wheler (R.).* Capt. Charles Hawkins.* }	Foundered off Gibraltar; all lost save two.
	,, 19	*Serpent*, bomb . . .	18	Com. Abraham Colfe.	Wrecked off Gibraltar; 15 lost.
	,, 19	*William*, ketch . . .	10	Lieut.	Wrecked off Gibraltar; 15 lost.
	,, 19	*Mary*, ketch	10	,,	Wrecked off Gibraltar; 16 lost.
	,, 19	*Cambridge*	70	Capt. John Ward.	Foundered off Gibraltar; 100 lost.
	,, 19	*Lumley Castle*, hired	56	,, George Meester.	Wrecked off Gibraltar; 130 lost.
	May 1	*Falcon*	36	,, Thomas Bigant.*	Taken by the French.
	July 12	*Nicholas*, mach.. . .	..	,, Robert Dunbar.	Expended at Dieppe.
	,, 16	*Granado*, bomb . . .	..	,, Thomas Willshaw.	Blown up before Le Hâvre.
	,, 18	*Scarborough*	30	,, Thos. Killingworth.*	Taken by the French.
	Sept. 12	{*William and Mary,* mach. . . . . }	..	,, Thomas Robinson.	Expended at Dunquerque.
	,, 12	*Abram's Offering*, mach.	..	,, Edward Cole	Expended at Dunquerque.
	Dec. 20	*Drake*.	16	,, John Stapylton.*	Wrecked off Ireland; all lost.
1695	Jan. 4	*Nonsuch*	40	,, Thomas Taylor.*	Taken by the French.
	Feb. 4	*Dartmouth*	52	,, Roger Vaughan.*	Taken by the French.
	Apr. 16	*Hope*	70	,, Henry Robinson.	Taken by the French.
	July 5	*Dreadful*, bomb . . .	..	,, John Carleton.	
	Aug. 1	*Ephraim*, mach. . . .	..	,, John Carleton.	Expended at Dunquerque.
	,, 1	{*William and Elizabeth,* mach. . . . . }	..	,, William Carleton.	Expended at Dunquerque.
	,, 1	*Mayflower I.*, mach. .	..	,, John Dixon.	Expended at Dunquerque.
	,, 1	*Happy Return*, mach. .	..	,, Robert Isaac.	Expended at Dunquerque.
	,, 8	*Terrible*, bomb . . .	..	,, Thomas Kenny.	
	,, 14	*Betty*, hired	..	,, John Papwell.*	Taken by the French.
	,, 17	*Aldborough*, ketch.. .	..	,, Robert Osbourne.*	Destroyed by the French.
	,, 22	*Fly*, advice boat . . .	..	,, Cornelius Willmore.*	Wrecked.
	Sept. 24	*Winchester*	50	,, John Soule.	Lost off Florida Cape.
	Oct. 25	*Berkeley Castle*	..	,, William Beaves.*	Taken by the French.
1696	Jan. 29	*Royal Sovereign* . .	100	(Not in commission).	Accidentally burnt in the Medway.
	Apr. 5	*Thunder*, bomb . . .	4	Com. Nathaniel Symonds.	Taken by the French.
	May 31	*Lizard*	24	Capt. Joseph Welby.*	Wrecked off Toulon; all lost.
	July 5	*Newport*	24	,, Wentworth Paxon.	Taken by the French.
1697	Apr. 18	*Etna*, f.s..	..	,, Kenneth Anderson.*	Taken by the French.
	,, 30	*Looe*	40	,, Richard Paul.	Wrecked near Baltimore, Ireland.
	May 5	*Seaford*	20	,, George Walton.	Taken by the French off Scilly.
	,, 5	*Blaze*, f.s.	..	,, John Wooden.	Taken by the French off Scilly.
	Aug. 21	*Flame*, f.s.	..	,, Henry Searle.	Foundered in the Atlantic.
	,, 23	*Society*, hosp. s.. . .	..	,, John Chapman.*	Taken by the French.
	,, 26	*Hampshire*	40	,, John Fletcher.*	Sunk in action by the French.
	Dec. 10	*Hastings*	34	,, John Draper.*	Wrecked off Waterford; all lost.
1699	Jan. 5	*Mermaid*	28	,, Thomas Pindar.*	Wrecked off Plymouth; all lost.
	Nov. 12	*Southsea Castle* . . .	32	,, Thomas Stepney.	Wrecked on Point Bague.
	,, 12	*Biddeford*	20	,, Henry Searle.	Wrecked on Point Bague.
1700	Sept. 19	*Carlisle*	60	,, Francis Dove.	Accidentally blown up in the Downs.
1701	Feb. 24	*Roebuck*	12	,, William Dampier.	Sank off Ascension.
1702	May 30	*Post Boy*, brigantine .	8	Com. Gilbert Frankland.	Taken by the French.
	July 28	*Otter*, sloop	..	Capt. Isaac Andrews.	Taken by the French.
	Aug. 14	*Prohibition*, sloop . .	6	Com. John Barter.	Taken by the French.
	,, 18	*Swift*, sloop	10	,, John Brokus.*	Taken by the French.
	,, 29	*Martin*, ketch . . .	10	,, Thomas Warren.	Taken by the French.
1702	Jan. 16	*Ludlow*	32	Capt. William Cock.	Taken by the French.
	,, 29	*Lincoln*	50	,, Henry Middleton.*	Foundered; nearly all lost.
	Mar. 29	*Shark*, sloop . . .	6	Com. George Fisher.	Taken by the French.
	,, 31	*Swallow*, sloop . . .	6	,, Peter Chamberlain.	Taken by the French.
	Apr. 10	*Salisbury*	50	Capt. Richard Cotten.	Taken by the enemy.
	,, 10	*Muscovia Merchant*. .	..	Com. Daniel Parsons, jun.	Taken by the French.
	Sept. 21	*Squirrel*	24	,, Gilbert Talbot.	Taken by the French.
	Oct. 12	*Firedrake*, bomb . . .	..	Capt. Edward Raney.*	Foundered; all lost.
	,, 15	*Serpent*, bomb . . .	..	Com. John Williams.	Taken by the French.
	Nov. 24	*York*	60	Capt. John Smith.	Wrecked off Harwich; four lost.
	,, 27	*Vanguard*	90	(Not in commission).	Sank in the Medway.
	,, 27	*Restoration*	70	Capt. Fleetwood Emes.*	Wrecked on the Goodwin; all lost.
	,, 27	*Stirling Castle* . . .	70	,, John Johnson.*	Wrecked on the Goodwin; 206 lost.
	,, 27	*Resolution*	70	,, Thomas Lyell.	Wrecked off Sussex.
	,, 27	*Northumberland* . .	70	,, James Greenaway.*	Wrecked on the Goodwin; all lost.
	,, 27	*Mary*	60	{R.-Ad. Basil Beaumont.* Capt. Edward Hopsonn. }	Wrecked on the Goodwin; 269 lost.
	,, 27	*Newcastle*	50	,, William Carter.*	Wrecked at Spithead; 193 lost.
	,, 27	*Reserve*	50	,, John Anderson.	Wrecked off Yarmouth; 175 lost.
	,, 27	*Vigo Prize*	50	,, Thomas Long.	Wrecked off Hellvoetsluis.
	,, 27	*Eagle*, advice boat . .	18	Com. Nathaniel Bostock.	Wrecked off Sussex.
	,, 27	*Canterbury*, st. s. . .	6	Capt. Thos. Blake.*	Wrecked at Bristol.
	,, 27	*Portsmouth*, bomb . .	..	Com. George Hawes.*	Wrecked.
	Dec. 2	*Mortar*, bomb . . .	..	Capt. Baymond Raymond.	Wrecked on the Goodwin; nearly all lost.
	,, 19	*Vesuvius*, f.s. . . .	..	Com. George Paddon.	Wrecked at Spithead; all saved.
1704	Jan. 16	*Colchester*	50	Capt. David Wavell.*	Foundered; nearly all lost.

Year.	Date.		H.M. Ship.	Guns.	Commander. [* Lost his life on the occasion.]	Remarks.
1704	June	24	*Wolf*	6	Com. Wagdolen Baker.*	Taken by the French.
	July	24	*Coventry*	50	Capt. Henry Lawrence.	Taken by the French ; retaken 1709.
	Aug.	1	*Fowey*.	32	,, Richard Browne.	Taken by the French.
	,,	4	*Falmouth*	50	,, Thomas Kenny.*	Taken by the French.
	Oct.	17	*Terror,* bomb	..	Com. Isaac Cook.	Taken and destroyed by the French.
	Nov.	12	*Elizabeth*.	70	Capt. William Cross.	Taken by the French.
1705	Aug.	11	*Plymouth*	60	,, Hercules Mitchell.*	Foundered ; all lost.
	Oct.	10	*Flamborough* . . .	24	Com. Joseph Winder.	Taken by the French.
	,,	20	*Pendennis*	50	Capt. John Foljambe.*	Taken by the French.
	,,	20	*Blackwall*	50	,, Samuel Martin.*	Taken by the French.
	,,	20	*Sorlings*	32	,, William Coney.	Taken by the French.
	Nov.	24	*Lightning,* f.s.	..	Com. Archibald Hamilton.	Taken by the French.
1706	May	25	*Ferret,* sloop	10	,, Nicholas Smith.*	Taken by the French.
	June	6	*Winchelsea*	32	Capt. John Castle.*	Taken by the French.
	July	3	*Deal Castle*	24	Com. Chaloner Ogle.	Taken by the French.
	,,	7	*Squirrel*	24	,, Daniel Butler.*	Taken by the French.
	,,	28	*Gosport*	32	Capt. Edward St. Loe.	Taken by the French.
	Oct.	10	*Comet,* bomb	..	Com. Francis Gregory.	Taken by the French.
1707	Feb.	9	*Hastings*	32	Capt. Francis Vaughan.*	Capsized off Yarmouth ; nearly all lost.
	Mar.	21	*Resolution*	70	,, Hon. Hen. Mordaunt.	Burnt to save her from capture.
	May	1	*Grafton*	70	,, Edward Acton.*	Taken by the French.
	,,	1	*Hampton Court* . . .	70	,, George Clements.*	Taken by the French.
	Aug.	17	*Swan*	24	Com. Charles Howard.*	Foundered.
	,,	25	*Nightingale*	24	,, Seth Jermy.	Taken by the French.
	,,	30	*Child's Play*	24	,, George Doyley.*	Foundered off St. Kitt's.
	Oct.	10	*Cumberland*	80	Capt. Richard Edwards.	Taken by the French.
	,,	10	*Devonshire*	80	,, John Watkins.*	Blew up in action ; two saved.
	,,	10	*Ruby*	50	,, Hon.Peregrine Bertie.	Taken by the French.
	,,	10	*Chester*	50	,, John Balchen.	Taken by the French.
	,,	22	*Association*	90	{Ad. Sir Clowdisley Shovell.* Capt. Edward Loades (1st).* ,, Samuel Whitaker (2nd).*	}Wrecked off Scilly ; all lost.
	,,	22	*Eagle*	70	,, Robert Hancock.*	Wrecked off Scilly ; all lost.
	,,	22	*Romney*	50	,, William Coney.*	Wrecked off Scilly ; all lost.
	,,	22	*Firebrand,* f.s.	..	Com. Francis Piercy.	Wrecked off Scilly ; 25 saved.
1708	Oct.	18	*Dunkirk Prize* . . .	24	Capt. George Purvis.	Lost near Cape François.
1709	Jan.	5	*Arrogant*	60	,, George Nichols.*	Foundered ; all lost.
	Mar.	1	*Adventure*	40	,, Robert Clark.*	Taken by the French.
	Apr.	4	*Fowey*.	32	Capt. Richard Lestock, jr.	Taken by the French.
	,,	16	*Sweepstake*	32	,, Samuel Meade.	Taken by the French.
	,,	24	*Bristol*	50	,, Henry Gore.	Taken ; later retaken, and sank.
	Oct.	26	*Gloucester*	50	,, John Balchen.	Taken by the French.
	Dec.	25	*Solebay*	20	,, George Stidson.	Wrecked near Boston.
	,,	29	*Pembroke*	64	,, Edward Rumsey.*	Taken by the French ; retaken later.
	,,	29	*Falcon*	32	,, Charles Constable.	Taken by the French.
1710	Sept.	6	*Valeur*	18	Com. John Hare.	Taken by the French.
	Nov.	1	*Scarborough*	34	Capt. Edward Holland.	Taken by the French ; retaken 1711.
1711	Jan.	10	*Resolution*	70	,, Richard Haddock.	Wrecked near Barcelona.
	May	11	*Dragon*	50	,, George Martin.	Wrecked on the Gaskets.
	June	27	*Advice*	46	,, Lord Duffus.	Taken by the French.
	Oct.	7	*Feversham*	36	,, Robert Paston.*	Foundered off Cape Breton.
	,,	9	*Edgar*.	70	,, George Paddon.	Accidentally blown up at Spithead.
	Nov.	9	*Restoration*	70	,, John Hartnoll.	Wrecked off Leghorn.
1712	May	29	*Star,* bomb	8	Com. Thomas Smart.	Wrecked in the West Indies.

In addition, a *Guernsey* and a *Firedrake,* bomb, were said by Charnock to have been lost between 1689 and 1697 ; but particulars have not been found.

CHAPTER XXV.

VOYAGES AND DISCOVERIES, 1660–1714.

SIR CLEMENTS MARKHAM, K.C.B., F.R.S.

Narbrough to the Pacific—John Wood in search of a north-east passage—The
Buccaneers — Sharp — Coxon—Richard Sawkins—John Watling—John Cook—
Edward Davis—William Dampier—The voyage of the *Welfare*—Halley and the
variation of the Needle—Dampier in the Royal Navy—Voyage of the *St. George*
and the *Cinque Ports*—Woodes Rogers—Alexander Selkirk—Dampier's work.

AFTER the days of Fox and James, almost a
generation passed away before England again
began to renew her exploring efforts. At length
Captain Narbrough received his commission to
command H.M.S. *Sweepstake*, of 300 tons, with
36 guns and a crew of eighty men and boys, victualled for fourteen
months. The *Bachelor*, a pink of 70 tons, commanded by Captain
Humphrey Fleming, was to accompany her. The object of the
voyage was the discovery of Chile by way of Magellan's Strait, and
the opening up of commercial relations with that distant and, to
Englishmen, almost unknown Spanish settlement. If possible,
Narbrough was to return by discovering a northern route between
Tartary and America. His most prominent officers were Lieutenant
Nathaniel Pecket, and a master's mate named John Wood. Nar-
brough was accompanied by a man who was supposed to be well
acquainted with the South American colonies, and who, named
Carlos Enriquez Clerq, was known on board as Don Carlos.

Sailing from the Downs on September 26th, 1669, the *Sweepstake* touched at Port Desire on the coast of Patagonia, and entered
the Strait of Magellan on the 22nd of October, 1670. Narbrough
made a careful survey of the Strait, and his journal contains sailing
directions and observations on the natives, and on the vegetation
of the shores. He gave names, some of which have survived,
to several islands, bays, and capes. Passing Cape Pilar on the
19th of November, the *Sweepstake* was steered for Valdivia, the

most southern settlement of Chile. On the 14th of December, Don Carlos was sent on shore to communicate with the Spaniards, dressed in his best clothes, with a bag full of looking-glasses, Jew's-harps, and bells. He was detained, and was executed at Lima in 1682, on a charge of corresponding with the English in Jamaica. On the 15th, a boat was sent to the fort, and several Spanish officers came on board, and told Captain Narbrough about their incessant war with the Araucanian Indians, and some details respecting the trade along the west coast of South America. The *Sweepstake* was then anchored in the river of Valdivia. But on the 18th two English officers and two men, who had landed, were seized and detained by order of the Captain-General of Chile. This put Narbrough on his guard. He had been invited to come higher up the river, and there was a treacherous intention to seize the ship. The prisoners were not released, and nothing more was seen of Don Carlos. Lieutenant Armiger, one of the prisoners, was forced to live at Valdivia for sixteen years, when he was accused of treason and executed. No step was ever taken by the British government to obtain his release. The fate of the others is unknown. The captain hoped that they would eventually find their way home in Spanish ships. On the 22nd he left Valdivia, returning to the Strait. The expedition arrived in England in June, 1671.

No new discoveries were made, but Narbrough was a keen observer; he made a careful survey, and his journal was a useful directory for the navigation of the coast of Patagonia and Magellan's Strait. This was the commencement of those purely naval expeditions which have formed so important a feature in the subsequent history of our country, as the best training-ground for officers and men. To Narbrough's expedition is due the education of the famous admiral Sir Clowdisley Shovell, of John Wood, the Arctic navigator, and of Greenville Collins, whose excellent surveys of our coasts, published in the ' Coasting Pilot,' were for more than a century the only guides to our seamen.

In 1676 John Wood, the master's mate of the *Sweepstake*, submitted a plan for discovering the passage to the Indies by the north-east. He had studied the subject with some care, and his arguments commended themselves to Mr. Samuel Pepys, the Secretary of the Admiralty, who gave him command of the *Speed-well*, "frigate," with a pink called the *Prosperous* as a tender. Wood's old shipmate, Greenville Collins, accompanied him as master, and the expedition sailed from England on the 28th of May, 1676. On the 22nd of June they sighted the edge of the ice in 76° N. on a meridian midway between the North Cape and Novaya Zemlya. Wood then stood along the ice to the eastward, but could find no opening. He came in sight of Novaya Zemlya on the 26th, and in the night of the 29th the *Speedwell* ran on a reef of rocks and became a wreck. Wood, with his crew, went on board the *Prosperous*, pink, and returned home in August. He reported his conviction that there was no passage between Spitsbergen and Novaya Zemlya. It was more than sixty years before this country resumed her work in connection with Arctic exploration.

We must now turn to some of those buccaneers who harassed the Spanish trade and settlements in the Western Indies. With their piratical doings in the Spanish main we have no concern ; but when some of these daring seamen crossed the isthmus and commenced an adventurous career in the South Sea, their proceedings come within the scope of our history. Although they did not make any discoveries of consequence, many of the places they visited were discoveries so far as English seamen were concerned ; and it is the progress of English discovery with which we have to do.

After the plundering of Puerto Bello in 1680, the English buccaneers separated from their French associates and assembled off the most eastern of the Samballas, or San Blas Isles, on the coast of Darien. There were seven armed vessels, commanded by Captains Coxon, Harris, Sawkins, Sharp, Cook, Alleston, and Macket. William Dampier, who had been ten years at sea and was then aged twenty-six, and Lionel Wafer, who afterwards wrote such an excellent account of Darien, were in this lawless squadron. The Mosquito Indians, a most ingenious and intelligent people, who were devoted to the English, and had voluntarily declared themselves to be subjects of the King of Great Britain, formed part of the crew of a buccaneer's ship. Living on the shores of the Gulf of Honduras, they were specially useful for their expertness in the use of the harpoon and in taking turtle, besides being thoroughly reliable and loyal.

The English buccaneers resolved to cross the isthmus of Darien, and to visit a Spanish town called Santa Maria, situated on a river flowing into the Pacific. Captains Alleston and Macket were left in charge of the ships, and on the 5th of April, 1680, a force of three hundred and thirty-one men landed, well armed, and each carrying four dough-boys as provisions. Captain Sharp and his men took the lead, the rest being marshalled in divisions under their respective commanders. It was an expedition similar in design to that of the ill-fated John Oxenham. A large body of Darien Indians accompanied the buccaneers, who were nearly all English; and supplied them with fruit and venison. Forcing their way through dense forest, on the eighth day they reached a river flowing to the Pacific, and the whole force embarked in canoes. On the 15th of April the stockaded fort of Santa Maria was captured, but the buccaneers were disappointed in their hopes of plunder; so they resolved to embark on the Pacific ocean in canoes, and to capture prizes. The Darien Indians returned to their homes, except the chief Andreas and his son "Golden Cap," who continued with the buccaneers. Captain Coxon was elected to be leader of the expedition, which descended the river of Santa Maria to the Gulf of San Miguel. On the 18th it put to sea.

A Spanish vessel of thirty tons was captured in the Bay of Panama, and next day another small bark was taken. On the 23rd three armed Spanish ships came out of Panama to attack them. A fight ensued, in which eighteen buccaneers, including Captain Harris, were killed, but two of the Spanish ships were carried by boarding, and the third made all sail and escaped. This victory is said to have been mainly due to the valour of Captain Sawkins, who led the boarders. The buccaneers then captured some other vessels at anchor, including the *Trinidad*, of four hundred tons, with a cargo of provisions and money. They were thus supplied with a small but effective fleet, with which they blockaded the city of Panama. Captain Coxon and seventy men parted company, having resolved to return across the isthmus. Richard Sawkins was then elected general of the fleet; and during his stay off Panama he captured vessels with specie amounting to about $60,000. After a short stay off the delightful island of Tobago, Sawkins attacked a town on the mainland called Pueblo Nuevo, where he was killed while advancing against a breastwork. Captain Sharp, who succeeded to the command, resolved upon a retreat. He anchored off Quibo Island, while about seventy men, who did not like him as their commander, and the rest of the Darien Indians, returned across the isthmus. Sharp was left with one hundred and forty-six men, in two ships. He sailed from Quibo for the coast of Peru, where one ship was abandoned, and all embarked on board the *Trinidad*.

After taking some prizes and plundering the town of Coquimbo in Chile, the buccaneers anchored in the south bay of Juan Fernandez on Christmas Day. There Sharp was deposed from the command, and an old pirate named John Watling was elected in his place. In the hurry of quitting the island, a Mosquito Indian named William was accidentally left on shore. He was away in the woods hunting goats, and did not hear the recall.

On the 30th of January, 1681, Captain Watling captured the town of Arica; but he, with a number of his men, was killed in assaulting the fort, and the rest retreated to their boats. Sharp was then reinstated in his command, but many men were opposed to him. The majority kept to the ship with Sharp as their leader: the rest went in boats to the gulf of San Miguel, and returned across the isthmus. This company consisted of forty-four Englishmen, including William Dampier and Lionel Wafer. Sharp took some more prizes on the coast of Peru, and returned to the West Indies by way of Cape Horn. He landed at Nevis, and took a passage to England, where he was tried for piracy, but escaped conviction owing to the absence of evidence.

Among those who left Sharp and returned across the isthmus was an experienced sailor named John Cook. He succeeded in capturing a vessel of eighteen guns, which was named the *Revenge;* and in August, 1683, he sailed for the Pacific with a crew of seventy buccaneers, including Ambrose Cowley, William Dampier, Lionel Wafer, and Edward Davis. Leaving a port in Virginia on the 23rd of August, 1683, they visited the Cape Verde Islands and the coast of Guinea. There they captured a fine Danish ship of thirty-six guns, which they exchanged for the *Revenge* and named the *Bachelor's Delight*. Making a southerly course, and rounding Cape Horn, they were steering for the island of Juan Fernandez when they fell in with an English ship named the *Nicholas*, commanded by Captain John Eaton. The crews, being engaged on the same errand, resolved to keep company together. On March 22nd, 1684, the *Bachelor's Delight* and *Nicholas* arrived at Juan Fernandez. A boat was sent on shore, and in it were Dampier and a Mosquito Indian named Robin. They saw William, who had been left behind, standing on the beach ready to receive them. Robin jumped on shore and threw himself at William's feet, who raised him, and threw himself at the feet of Robin. Dampier says: " We stood with pleasure to behold the surprise, tenderness, and solemnity of this interview, which was exceedingly affectionate on both sides." William had lived in solitude on Juan Fernandez for three years, concealing himself from the Spaniards when they landed, clothing himself in goat skins, and making harpoons and fish-hooks out of his gun-barrel by heating the iron and hammering it into the shapes he wanted with stones. He made fishing-lines with thongs from seal skins.

Leaving Juan Fernandez in April, they captured some prizes and took them to the Galapagos Islands. There a survey of the islands was made, and a chart was drawn which saw the light in Cowley's narrative of the voyage, where there is also an account of this interesting group. Thence they shaped a course for the coast of Mexico; and, early in July, Captain Cook died. He was succeeded by Edward Davis; and in September the *Bachelor's Delight* fell in with the *Cygnet*, commanded by Captain Swan, a vessel which had come out from London for the purpose of trade. Meanwhile Eaton's ship, the *Nicholas*, had sailed for the East Indies; and eventually she reached England in safety.

Captain Davis continued to harass the towns on the coasts of Peru and Mexico, capturing prizes, and receiving reinforcements of buccaneers across the isthmus. In August, 1685, the pirates sacked and burnt the town of Leon in Nicaragua, and in May, 1686, they fought a long engagement with a Spanish squadron, outside the Bay of Guayaquil, with no result. Davis visited the Galapagos Islands three times, and found a careening place at Santa Maria de la Aguada. In 1687 he sailed southward from the Galapagos, and distinctly felt the shock of an earthquake when far out at sea. In 27° 20′ S. Davis fell in with an island which may have been the Easter Island claimed to have been discovered by Roggewein in 1722.[1] In fact Roggewein found it by following the directions given by Davis and Wafer. Returning by Cape Horn, Davis reached the West Indies in the spring of 1688, and, availing himself of a proclamation offering pardon to all buccaneers who should quit that way of life, he went to England. He was an excellent commander, prudent and courageous, and he restrained the excesses of his men. All seamen had implicit confidence in his leadership and willingly obeyed him. He did good service to geography by his detailed examination of the Galapagos group, and by his discovery of Easter Island. Dampier always speaks of him with respect.

---

[1] Captain Carteret thinks that Davis sighted S. Felix and S. Ambrose Isles.

William Dampier had joined Captain Swan on board the *Cygnet*, which parted company with Davis and proceeded to the coast of Mexico, visiting Guatulco and Mazatlan. In March, 1686, the *Cygnet* sailed from the American coast and eventually reached Mindanao. From thence she proceeded to the Bashee Islands, which Dampier surveyed and named, one after the Duke of Grafton, for the reason that Dampier had married his wife out of the Duchess's household and left her at Arlington House [1] when he went abroad. Another was named the Duke of Monmouth's Island, and a third Orange Island. The whole group received the name of Bashee, from a liquor so called, made plentifully by the natives from the juice of the sugar cane. The *Cygnet* went thence to the northwest coast of New Holland, and afterwards to the Nicobar Islands, where Dampier left her. Being old and rotten, she was finally abandoned by her crew in St. Augustine's Bay, in Madagascar, where she sank at her anchors.

In 1689 some English merchants fitted out a ship called the *Welfare* to trade with the Spanish settlements in the Pacific during the war with France. She was a well-armed vessel, with a cargo of merchandise and a crew of ninety men, commanded by Captain John Strong. He reached Davis's Southern Islands in January, 1690, and entered a deep sound to which he gave the name of Falkland. By some misapprehension the whole group has since been called the Falkland Islands. Strong was about three months passing through the Strait of Magellan. In August he was on the coast of Peru. He succeeded in disposing of some of his merchandise at the mouth of the river Tumbez, and visited Juan Fernandez, returning to England in June, 1691. The voyage of the *Welfare* caused a loss of £12,000 to the owners; but the Falkland Islands received their present name.

A purely scientific expedition opened the history of discovery in the eighteenth century. Dr. Edmund Halley, the Astronomer Royal, received the temporary rank of a Captain in the Navy, and was given command of the pink *Paramour* [2] in order to make his attempt to discover the laws by which the variation of the magnetic needle is

---

[1] Arlington House, on the site of Buckingham Palace, was inherited by the Duchess of Grafton from her father, the Earl of Arlington.

[2] He commanded her from August 19th, 1698 to July 20th, 1699; again from August 24th, 1699, to September, 18th, 1700; and, yet again, from April 30th, 1701, to October 16th, 1701. His name appears in an MS. Navy List of 1698 as Edmund Hawley—a form which indicates its pronunciation.—W. L. C.

governed, by investigations in the South Atlantic. He sailed in November, 1698; but he soon found that the officers resented being placed under the orders of a civilian, and were inclined to be insubordinate. Halley, therefore, wisely returned to England and got his officers changed. In September, 1699, he again sailed, crossing the line on November 16th. He took many observations for longitude, and fixed the position of the rock of Trinidad; but

CAPTAIN WILLIAM DAMPIER, R.N.

(From C. Sherwin's engraving after a portrait formerly in the British Museum.)

his principal work consisted in observations for variation in the South Atlantic. Dr. Halley returned to England on September 6th, 1700, and in 1701 he published his map of magnetic variations.

William Dampier also received command of a naval expedition at this time, but it has been seen that he had had a long training in another school. The son of a farmer at East Coker in Somersetshire, young William Dampier was a very observant, intelligent boy. Having lost both his parents he was sent to sea at the age of sixteen, in 1668. After his first three voyages he came home and found welcome and rest in his native village. In 1674 he sailed for the West Indies, and soon afterwards entered upon the hazardous and unhealthy life of a logwood cutter in the Bay of Campeachy. There he made the acquaintance of the Mosquito Indians, and obtained much knowledge, especially respecting the uses of plants and the habits of animals. Nothing seemed to escape his observation, and he acquired the excellent habit of regularly writing a journal. In 1678 he was at home again and married a young person in the household of Lady Isabel Bennet, the great heiress who afterwards became Duchess of Grafton. Returning to the West Indies in 1679, he joined, as has been seen, the English buccaneers, passed over the Darien Isthmus, and served under several captains in the Pacific, until he crossed that ocean in the *Cygnet*, and left her at the Nicobar Islands.

In May, 1688, Dampier made a most perilous voyage from the Nicobar Islands to a port in Sumatra, near Acheen, in a small canoe. Taking a passage in an East Indiaman, he arrived in the Downs on September 16th, 1691, having been absent more than twelve years. His wife and all his near relations appear to have died in the interval, and he was quite alone in the world. He possessed, however, many years' experience as a sailor, had acquired skill in surveying and chart drawing, and, above all, had kept a journal. When he published his ' New Voyage Round the World ' in 1697, it was read with avidity and established his fame. He was thenceforth looked upon as a scientific seaman of great experience. He dedicated his work to the President of the Royal Society and showed a deep interest in Halley's magnetic voyage.

In the year 1698 the government of William III. ordered that an expedition should be fitted out for the discovery of the unknown parts of New Holland and New Guinea. The First Lord of the Admiralty, who was then the Earl of Pembroke, selected Dampier for the command, with the rank of a Captain in the Navy. An old vessel called the *Roebuck* [1] was commissioned, with a crew of fifty men and boys, and the ship sailed from the Downs on January 14th, 1699. Dampier, who was anxious to assist the investigations of Dr. Halley, was diligent in taking magnetic observations, and in recording in his journal everything of interest.

[1] Dampier commanded the *Roebuck* from August 11th, 1698 to February 24th, 1701.—W. L. C.

The *Roebuck* was a very unseaworthy craft, but her skilful commander reached the western coast of Australia, sailed along the northern shore of New Guinea, and discovered, between that island and New Britain, the strait which is still called Dampier's Passage. The *Roebuck* sank at her anchors off Ascension in February, 1701; but her people returned safely, and Captain Dampier published a well-written account of the voyage.

In 1703 some merchants offered Dampier the command of two vessels, the *St. George* and the *Cinque Ports*, intended to cruise in the Pacific. This he accepted. His own vessel, the *St. George*, was old and rotten. He had with him a mate named John Clipperton, and a steward, William Funnel. The name of the captain of the *Cinque Ports* was Stradling, and the mate was Alexander Selkirk. Rounding Cape Horn, the two ships arrived at Juan Fernandez in February, 1704. Thence they made a cruise along the west coast of South America, eventually parting company in the Bay of Panama. The *Cinque Ports* returned to Juan Fernandez, where Stradling quarrelled with his mate. Alexander Selkirk, a young Scotsman of twenty-six, declared that he wished to sail no longer with so tyrannical a commander. He was landed with a gun and ammunition, his chest, and a few necessaries. But, when the boat had shoved off, he repented and called out to be taken on board again. Stradling refused and sailed away, finally stranding the *Cinque Ports* and giving himself up to the Spaniards. Dampier was very unfortunate. He took no prizes of value, and his mate Clipperton deserted with twenty-two men. In December, 1704, the steward Funnel also deserted with thirty-four men, returned home, and published a false account of the voyage. The *St. George* was so unseaworthy that Dampier was obliged to abandon her at the island of Lobos de la Mar, off the coast of Peru; and, crossing the Pacific in a prize brigantine with the remnant of his crew, he reached Java. He was a ruined man when at length he arrived in England.

The Bristol merchants fitted out two ships in 1708—the *Duke*, of 320 tons, with thirty guns and one hundred and eighty-three men, under the command of Captain Woodes Rogers, and the *Duchess*, of 260 tons, with Stephen Courtney as her captain. They were to make war with the French and Spaniards in the Pacific. Dampier was glad to obtain the appointment of pilot on board the *Duke*. Edward Cooke and Simon Hatley were mates, and Thomas

Dover, the inventor of the well-known Dover's powders,[1] was surgeon. Sailing from Bristol in August, 1708, they rounded Cape Horn, and reached Juan Fernandez on the 1st of February, 1709. As the boat, with Dr. Dover steering, approached the shore, a man was seen waving a flag. It was Alexander Selkirk, clothed in goat skins. He had lived there in complete solitude for four years and four months. During that time he had killed five hundred goats, and had caught as many more by running them down. These he had marked on the ear and let go. If a man had to live in a wild solitude there can be no more charming abode than Juan Fernandez. Dampier gave to Captain Woodes Rogers an excellent character of Alexander Selkirk, who was made second mate of the *Duke*. The cruise of the two Bristol ships was very successful. Many rich prizes were taken, and they returned by the Cape of Good Hope, arriving in the Thames on October 14th, 1711.

This was William Dampier's last voyage. He was in his sixtieth year. Admiral Burney said of him very truly: " It is not easy to name another voyager or traveller who has given more useful information to the world, or to whom the merchant or the mariner is more indebted." He set an example which every young sailor ought to follow. He regularly kept a journal, and was most careful to preserve his books from injury, keeping them in cases made water-tight with wax. He was a good seaman, a scientific observer, and an attentive meteorologist; but it is more especially as a journal writer that William Dampier should be remembered and imitated.

[1] A sudorific mixture of opium, ipecacuanha, etc.—W. L. C.

PUBLISHER'S NOTE

In the original edition the nineteen photogravure plates and the full-page illustrations faced the text pages as listed on page XI. In this edition these illustrations are collected on the following pages in the order in which they appeared in the first edition. The original position indicators have been retained.

[To face page 2.

H.M.S. *ROYAL PRINCE*, 55. BUILT IN 1610.

(*After Charnock's drawing, from a contemporary picture.*)

H.M.S. ROYAL SOVEREIGN, 100. BUILT IN 1637. CUT DOWN IN 1652.

(*After the picture by W. van de Velde*)

[*To face page 6.*

Robert Blake

Admiral and General at Sea

From J. Mallison's engraving after the picture in the possession
of the Warden and Fellows of Wadham College, Oxford.

THE ACTION OF NOVEMBER 30TH, 1652.

(*From P. Velijn's engraving, after the picture by K. Vettewinkel.*)

[To face page 172.

ENGLISH SECOND-RATE OF THE SMALLER CLASS: ABOUT 1670.

Possibly H.M.S. *Victory*, 82. Built 1665.

(*From a drawing by W. van de Velde.*)

[*To face page* 222.]

DUTCH SECOND-RATE: ABOUT 1670.

(From a drawing by W. van de Velde.)

[*To face page* 242.

A FRENCH SECOND-RATE OF 1670.

(*After W. van de Velde.*)

[*To face page* 248

                                                    Printed in Paris

Michiel Adriaanszoon De Ruijter
Admiral
After the engraving by A. Blotelingh

Sampson Low Marston and Company Ltd. London

[To face page 274.

THE THIRD DAY OF "THE FOUR DAYS' FIGHT," JUNE 3RD, 1666.

(From Nieuwhoff's engraving after W. van de Velde's drawing in the Rijks Museum at Amsterdam.)

[To face page 292.

VIEW OF ROCHESTER, CHATHAM, AND THE MEDWAY ON THE OCCASION OF THE DESCENT OF THE DUTCH
UNDER DE RUIJTER IN 1667.

(From a contemporary Dutch engraving by Stoopendal.)

[*To face page* 310.

H.M.S. *ROYAL CHARLES.* BUILT IN 1673.

Prince Rupert's Flagship in the Battles off Schooneveld.

(*From a drawing by W. van de Velde.*)

A CHART of the ENGLISH CHANNEL with the adjacent Coasts of ENGLAND and FRANCE By Thos. Kitchin Geogr.

MODEL (IN FRAME) OF AN ENGLISH FIRST-RATE.

Supposed to be the *Britannia*, 100, which was built at Chatham in 1682, from designs by Sir Phineas Pett, and which was Russell's Flagship at La Hougue.

(Photographed, by permission, from the original in Trinity House.)

[*To face page* 350.

THE WEST INDIES AND PART OF THE SPANISH MAIN.

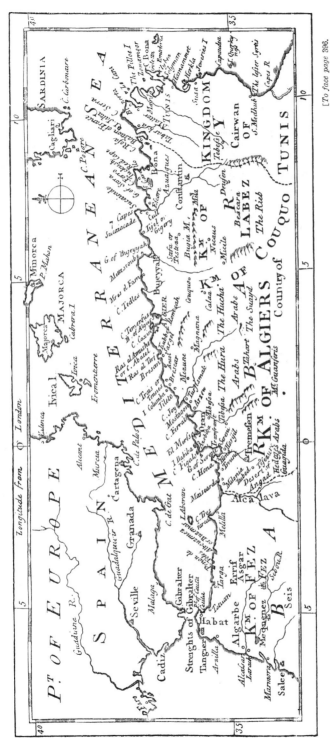

THE WESTERN MEDITERRANEAN.

(*From an Eighteenth Century Map in the "London Magazine."*)

[*To face page* 396.]

Edward, Lord Hawke, K.B.
Admiral of the Fleet
From H.T. Ryall's engraving after the portrait by F. Cotes R.A.

Lemerciergravure   Printed in Paris

THE *MARY ROSE*, 48, CAPTAIN JOHN KEMPTHORNE, R.N., AND SEVEN ALGERINES, 1669.

(From F. Kirkhall's mezzotint engraving, after the picture ascribed to W. van de Velae, at Greenwich.)

[*To face page* 438.

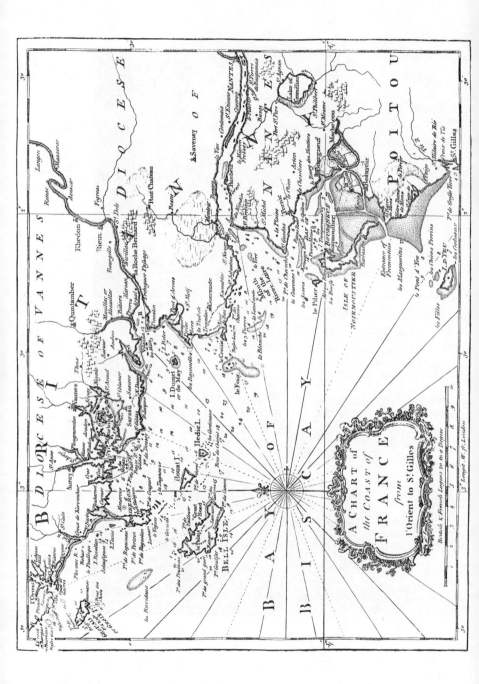

A CHART of the COAST of FRANCE from l'Orient to St. Gilles

Admiral the Hon. Edward Boscawen

From Mc Ardell's mezzotint, after the portrait
by Sir J. Reynolds.

Sampson Low, Marston and Cᵒ Lᵗᵈ London.

INDEX.

VOLUME II.